THE ECONOMICS OF
INTERCOLLEGIATE SPRTS

Second Edition

THE ECONOMICS OF
INTERCOLLEGIATE SPRTS

Second Edition

Randy R Grant (Linfield College, USA)
John C Leadley (Western Oregon University, USA)
Zenon X Zygmont (Western Oregon University, USA)

 **World Scientific**

NEW JERSEY · LONDON · SINGAPORE · BEIJING · SHANGHAI · HONG KONG · TAIPEI · CHENNAI

Published by

World Scientific Publishing Co. Pte. Ltd.

5 Toh Tuck Link, Singapore 596224

USA office: 27 Warren Street, Suite 401-402, Hackensack, NJ 07601

UK office: 57 Shelton Street, Covent Garden, London WC2H 9HE

Library of Congress Cataloging-in-Publication Data
Grant, Randy R.
    The economics of intercollegiate sports / by Randy R Grant, Linfield College, USA, John C
Leadley, Western Oregon University, USA, Zenon X Zygmont, Western Oregon University, USA.
-- Second edition.
        pages cm
    ISBN 978-9814583367 (hardcover) -- ISBN 978-9814583374 (softcover)
    1. College sports--Economic aspects--United States. 2. College sports--Organization and adminis-
tration--United States. I. Leadley, John. II. Zygmont, Zenon X. III. Title.
    GV350.G73 2014
    796.04'30973--dc23
                                                                    2014001981

British Library Cataloguing-in-Publication Data
A catalogue record for this book is available from the British Library.

In-house Editors: Sutha Surenddar/Philly Lim

Typeset by Stallion Press
Email: enquiries@stallionpress.com

Printed in Singapore by B & Jo Enterprise Pte Ltd

Contents

Introduction

On January 7, 2013, an estimated 27.3 million television viewers watched the University of Alabama football team defeat Notre Dame in the Discover BCS Championship Game in Miami, Florida. The Crimson Tide and Irish earned a combined US$30 million, a handsome payoff for a single game. ESPN paid US$500 million for the rights to televise the championship bowl game from 2011 to 2014, as well as the Fiesta, Orange and Sugar Bowls. In 2012, ESPN agreed to a $600 million contract to broadcast the other major bowl game, the Rose Bowl, from 2015 to 2026.

The NCAA men's basketball championship, better known as "March Madness," is also extremely successful. In 2011, CBS and Turner Broadcasting began payments that will total US$10.8 billion to broadcast the tournament through 2025. More than 23 million viewers watched the April 7, 2013 showdown between Louisville and Michigan, and large numbers of fans watched games in the earlier rounds of the competition (especially those hoping to win their office pool!). In fact, the value of the broadcast contract for the college tournament is eclipsed only by the National Football League. Clearly, college sports are big business, and is an industry in and unto itself. *Or is it?*

Florida, Ohio State, and over one thousand other colleges and universities belong to the National Collegiate Athletic Association, or NCAA for short. Established in 1906, the primary mission of the NCAA is "to maintain intercollegiate athletics as an integral part of the educational program and the athlete as an integral part of the student body and, by doing so, retain a clear line of demarcation between intercollegiate athletics and professional sports." Over the past one hundred years, the NCAA has evolved from an obscure organization to a trusted brand name, an organization whose rules govern every facet of college sports in the United States.

The NCAA is proud of its educational mission. The term "student-athlete" was created by the NCAA to emphasize that the more than 450,000 men and women now playing college sports are also getting an education. You may have heard about the NCAA's recent policies to increase the graduation rate of student-athletes and ensure that the athletes are preparing for their future, a future in which, as the athletes featured in NCAA television commercials say, "most of us will turn pro in something other than sports." As Myles Brand, the former president of the NCAA, has said, "The fundamental purpose of intercollegiate athletics is the education of student-athletes in both the classroom and on the field or court." *Or is it?*

The NCAA ensures that member schools comply with the myriad rules included in its by-laws. Every year hundreds of rules infractions occur; some are fairly minor — like a college football coach contacting a potential high school recruit more times than the rules allow. Others are more serious, such as a star basketball player getting tens of thousands of dollars in illegal payments. To give you an idea of the magnitude of NCAA violations, try typing the phrase "NCAA violation" into an Internet search engine like Google and see how many results you get. Clearly, the fact that so many violations are uncovered every year must mean that the NCAA is doing a good job of policing college sports. *Or is it?*

In this book, you will learn about the activities of the NCAA from the perspective of economics. Many of these activities, as you will see, appear to be consistent with the NCAA's mission statements. This can lead people, including you and me, to conclude that the NCAA is an organization acting solely in the best interests of student-athletes, its member universities, and the general public. *Or is it?*

Henry Hazlitt's *Economics in One Lesson* is one of the best books ever written on the importance of "thinking like an economist." To Hazlitt, *"The art of economics consists in looking not merely at the immediate but at the longer effects of any act or policy; it consists in tracing the consequences of that policy not merely for one group but for all groups [italics in original]."*[1] In this book, we examine not only the readily visible activities of the NCAA and the college sports industry, but the impact of those actions which are not always immediately obvious. By analyzing college sports using the tools of economics, we not only better understand the college sports industry but we also learn that there is an altogether different perspective on the NCAA than the public interest. We invite you to join us in exploring this "hidden world" of college sports.

As you read this book you will notice several "themes" that appear and reappear. These themes represent the core ideas of the book, the ideas that we believe are most important in understanding the world of college sports. We list those themes now, so that you will be prepared when you come across them as you read the book.

1. The NCAA is a cartel. Cartels cause economic harm.
2. The primary economic harm is borne by the student-athletes, although other individuals are harmed as well.
3. Like most cartels, the NCAA generates significant monopolistic profits that are shared among the cartel members (the colleges and universities). And like most cartels, there is also a significant temptation to cheat.
4. Unlike most cartels, the NCAA has a very large number of members. This both increases the amount of cheating and leads to the creation of "cartels within the cartel."
5. The NCAA implements more rules to discourage cheating over time; nevertheless, member institutions are always discovering new ways to cheat on the cartel. We call this the "little Dutch boy" phenomenon.
6. Because members of the NCAA cartel cannot engage in competition based on price, they rely instead on non-price competition. This results in an "arms race" among member institutions, especially in the form of new facilities construction.

---

[1] Hazlitt, H. (1946). *Economics in One Lesson.* New York: Harper & Brothers Publishers.

7. Because of the arms race, the athletic departments at most NCAA member institutions lose money, although a handful of schools do generate substantial profits.
8. The media has played an integral role in the operation and growth of revenue-generating sports, and the financial fortunes of the media and university athletic departments are strongly intertwined.
9. As in many American institutions, discrimination on the basis of race and gender persists, but has improved through a combination of market forces and legislation.
10. *Plus ça change, plus c'est la même chose* (or, the more things change, the more they stay the same). Many past reforms have been mere "window dressing" that do little to change the underlying problems in college sports. The NCAA is on a "treadmill of reform" — taking steps but not moving forward.

We are hopeful that you will enjoy and become better educated about the college sports industry in the United States as you read our book. We also encourage you to explore, and learn even more, by choosing among the many excellent readings included in the selected bibliography.

Preface

As economics professors we often tell our students that if there is an unmet want with the potential to generate economic profits, someone will attempt to fulfill that want. That is what we're attempting to do with this book, though not so much for the economic profits, but to satisfy our own desire for a textbook covering the economics of intercollegiate sports. Existing textbooks emphasize the economics of professional sports, and do well at that task, but the economic structure of college sports is uniquely different and deserving of a separate, detailed treatment. Whether you are reading this book as a professor preparing a class in sports economics, a student taking a course in the economics of sports, or someone just seeking to learn more about the economics of intercollegiate sports, we hope that this book will provide you with new information and insights.

Intended Audience

When we first started writing this book, we were looking to augment our own sports economics classes with detailed coverage of intercollegiate sports. In keeping with our usual audience, we have aimed the book primarily at undergraduates who have completed economics at least through the introductory level. We see this work being suitable for a stand-alone course in the economics of intercollegiate sports, or as a text representing the collegiate portion of a broader sports economics class. As with many applied textbooks, however, this work may prove useful to other areas and levels of study. Programs in sports management or sports marketing, at the graduate or undergraduate level, may also find this text useful.

Features

This book has a number of features designed to facilitate the study of college sports economics:

1. *The first of its kind?* While there are many great books on the economics of intercollegiate sports, this text is constructed specifically with the classroom in mind. Combining central ideas of the discipline with numerous real world examples, this text covers the major economic issues in college sports, balancing theoretical economics with practical application.
2. *Casual, yet straightforward.* While we take the subject matter seriously, we try not to take ourselves too seriously. We have attempted to write a book that not only conveys important information in an easily understood manner, but that is also as much fun to read as it was for us to write.
3. *Boxes* and *Fast facts.* These sections provide specific illustrations of the general concepts, sometimes affirming the conventional wisdom, occasionally providing a unique counterexample.
4. *Review, Discussion,* and *Internet Questions.* These questions help reinforce the main ideas of each chapter. Review questions assess the ability to recall and explain key information. Discussion questions focus more on application and extension — putting pieces together. Internet questions require trips to websites to gather data to test (informally) hypotheses presented in the text, or to update cases that may have changed since the book went to press.
5. *Selected Bibliography and Internet Sites.* In the process of writing this book, we have studied extensively the works of others and compiled lists of valuable readings and websites we have encountered. These are not exhaustive lists, but rather a good place to start for those interested in learning more about the economics of intercollegiate sports. We note, however, that website links do change, but all listed were accurate when the book went to press.
6. *Chapter Appendices.* Chapters 3, 5 and 8 contain appendices that add a layer of complexity to the discussion for those who want

it. These generally involve a more rigorous theoretical presentation, and can be easily skipped without losing the main ideas.

A Disclaimer

Reflecting the accumulated evidence and existing literature on the subject, this text does not always put higher education, particularly at Division I institutions, in the most flattering light. While we stand by our analysis and conclusions, we recognize that there are exceptions to these generalizations. We applaud our colleagues at DI institutions who provide quality undergraduate teaching, often in the face of pressure to focus instead on research or graduate teaching. We also recognize that there are some quality teaching assistants out there who are well on their way to distinguished undergraduate teaching careers. Finally, we acknowledge that while the discussion focuses on problems at DI schools, Division II and III colleges and universities are not immune from these issues. They just tend to see less of them, mainly because the stakes are smaller.

Acknowledgments

Like head coaches and quarterbacks, we authors get more credit than we deserve for the success of the book. On a project like this, there are many people behind the scenes who deserve thanks for helping our labors come to fruition. Among them are Linfield College students, past and present, including Ben Pappas, Mark Kessler, Heather Correia, Casey Stepan, and the many in Randy's "Economics of College Sports" classes who provided invaluable insights into what parts of the first edition worked and which didn't. There are many to thank at Western Oregon University as well, including Hamid Bahari-Kashani, Dianna Hewett, and David Ashby, all from the Division of Business and Economics; the staff of Hamersly Library; and Zenon's "Economics of Intercollegiate Sports" classes. Outside of our own institutions we would like to thank Daniel Rascher, Professor of Sports Management at the University of San Francisco; Stephen Shmanske, author of

Golfonomics and Professor of Economics at Cal State East Bay; and Chuck McAllister, who spent many hours proofreading the first edition, finding everything from the smallest typos to the most egregious errors in fact or analysis. Finally, we would like to thank Juliet Lee Ley Chin and the rest of the staff at World Scientific that helped bring this book to press. Coaches and quarterbacks generally receive too much blame if things go wrong, but we won't. Any errors, be they of omission or commission, are our own.

Preface to Second Edition

Six years ago the first edition of this book was published. To our surprise, the sales of the book were apparently sufficient to justify a new and improved edition. In this second edition, we do the standard updating and editing you should expect, like fixing typos, checking to see if references and URLs are current, adding and deleting end-of-chapter questions, and revising the list of recommended readings. But we do more as well. The last few years of college sports has seen a flurry of activity, including significant conference realignment; increasing income disparities between the financially well off athletic programs and their poorer counterparts; the implementation of a playoff for the Football Bowl Subdivision (what used to be called Division I-A); extensive discussion about paying athletes; frequent criticism of college sports by the media; punishment of schools that fail to meet the NCAA's new academic requirements; NCAA sanctions on several high profile institutions because of violations of the association's bylaws (e.g., USC [the Reggie Bush case], Auburn [the Cam Newton affair], Ohio State [the Jim Tressel/football players "tats" scandal]); and, in a category by itself, the disturbing events at Penn State. Consequently, all nine chapters have been revised, some more than others, and one chapter has been added. A new section on competitive balance is added in Chapter 2, a brief overview of regression analysis is included as an appendix to Chapter 5, and a new Chapter 10 summarizes four recent case studies, including Penn State. We also added a glossary of key terms at the end of the book. Instructors interested in getting a set of PowerPoint slides should contact us (leadley@wou.edu); we intend to have a complete set of slides ready by the end of 2014. We can also provide sample syllabi (contact: rgrant@linfield.edu or zygmonz@wou.edu). We hope you find this second edition useful and interesting; we are thankful to all the individuals that demonstrated a willingness to pay for, or adopted this book. As always, comments, criticisms, and questions are welcome; please contact us at the email accounts listed above.

Chapter 1

The History of Intercollegiate Athletics and the NCAA

I will not permit thirty men to travel four hundred miles merely to agitate a bag of wind.

— Andrew D. White, Cornell University President, 1873

There is no more gratifying scene to me than a crowd of youngsters playing football. I always feel that the community in which they live will be stronger and more useful as a direct consequence of it.

— Edgar Allen Poe, 1890

Yet, when all is said, the attention to athletics by the general public is surprising and is excessive.

— Frank Taussig, Harvard University
Professor of Economics, 1905

1.1 Introduction

Before you can study the economics of college sports and the **National Collegiate Athletic Association** (NCAA), you need a basic understanding of how they operate. While you may consider yourself to be a knowledgeable fan, there are aspects of big-time athletics that would surprise many people. This chapter begins with a look back at the history of American higher education and the early years of intercollegiate sports. Coverage of the modern era focuses on the evolution of college football and basketball, including postseason championships and bowl games, and the role of

1

television coverage. The organizational structure of college sports is also examined, including conferences, divisions, and the administrative and legislative workings of the NCAA. The topics presented here will be analyzed in greater detail, and with more emphasis on economic theory, later in the book.

You — and perhaps your professor — may be tempted to downplay or even ignore the history of the NCAA. After all, time is scarce; why rehash events of the 19th and 20th centuries and instead just skip to the events of the present day? Well … it might surprise you that few controversies in college sports are brand new — players being paid under the table, concern about excessive coaching salaries and expenses on athletics facilities, violations of rules on recruiting, and academic improprieties existed from the earliest days of college sports. As you read this book, you will find numerous examples of history repeating itself. For example, consider illegal payments to athletes (referred to today by the NCAA as an *extra or impermissible benefit*). A recent example involved University of Southern California running back, and 2005 Heisman Trophy winner, Reggie Bush. In 2010, after a lengthy investigation, the NCAA substantiated allegations that Bush accepted "impermissible benefits in the form of cash, merchandise, an automobile, housing, hotel lodging and transportation" from two sports agents hoping to represent Bush when he began his NFL career.[1] The value of the benefits Bush received in 2004 and 2005 was estimated at US$290,000.

Yet, how different is the Bush case from the following historical examples? When James Hogan was team captain of the Yale football team, not only was his tuition and room and board paid for, he was given a 10-day vacation in Cuba, and received a percentage of sales for programs sold at Yale baseball games as well as a commission on cigarettes sold in New Haven (Riess, 1995, 127). This occurred in 1904.

Tom "Shorty" McWilliams played halfback for Mississippi State in 1946–1948. He transferred from Army to Mississippi State after the 1945 season because the latter institution offered him "a

---

[1] *University of Southern California Public Infractions Report*, June 10, 2010, §A, Introduction.

particularly lucrative financial offer": a car, a US$300 per month job, a job offer after graduation and, if that was not enough inducement, US$15,000 in cash (Sperber, 1998, p. 169; the equivalent value of the job today is US$3,800 per month and the bonus US$192,000).

Finally, in one of the most notorious scandals in college football history, after a series of rules infractions and punishments, the NCAA decided to pull the plug on the Southern Methodist University (SMU) football program in 1987, shutting it down for two years. This drastic measure, known as the **death penalty**, was triggered by an extensive system of illegal payments to SMU football players from alumni and boosters dating back to the 1970s, payments made with the knowledge of the coaches, athletic directors, university administrators (including a former and future Governor of Texas) and the president.[2]

All three of these cases were, and remain, explicit violations of *amateurism* — the core tenet in college sports. Yet such violations continue to occur, even after decades of oversight and regulation by the NCAA. What does that tell us? Does it mean that such problems are endemic to college sports and can never be eliminated? Does it mean that the NCAA, an institution with scarce resources, should tolerate some amount of cheating, and only prosecute those cases where the perceived benefits exceed the perceived costs? Does it mean that the NCAA needs to devote more resources to catch cheaters and/or write additional rules making clear what is prohibited? These are just a sample of the myriad questions we can ask about college sports in the United States in the 21st century. We will return to many of these questions in the forthcoming chapters and it will be up to you to think about the relative importance of these questions and the appropriate answers.

1.2   A Brief History of Higher Education

Harvard College, founded in 1636, was the first institution of higher education in the American colonies. The college admitted

---

[2]Watterson (2000a, pp. 353–374). The NCAA shut down SMU's entire 1987 season and all its home games in 1988. The university then cancelled all 1988 away games.

young men from prominent families, typically between the ages of 12 and 15, and prepared them to serve as ministers for Puritan congregations in New England. Its approach to education was based on the classic course of study at English universities, with an emphasis on Greek, Latin, mathematics, and philosophy.

By the time of the American Revolution, nine colonial colleges had been formed. All but one was affiliated with a particular religious denomination. These schools were quite small, even when compared to current liberal arts colleges. In the middle of the 18th century, Harvard's enrollment averaged only 150 students. By 1776, there were just 3,000 college graduates in the Colonies, out of a total population of 2,500,000.

The number of colleges increased steadily after the war, particularly in the expanding western territories (back when Illinois was considered the West). Most of the new schools did not survive for long, but by 1860, there were more than 200 active colleges. The majority of them were still private and church affiliated, but state and municipal colleges were increasingly common.

With this growth came opportunities for a broader cross section of the population, including children from the emerging middle class, and to a lesser extent, women and Blacks. The purpose of higher education also was evolving. During the 1820s and 1830s, in an effort to adjust to the "spirits and wants of the age," colleges broadened their curricula to include the study of history, literature, geography, modern languages, and the sciences. Businessmen began to supplant members of the clergy on college governing boards. To educate more members of the working class and meet the need for workers with technical skills, Congress passed the **Morrill Acts of 1862 and 1890**, creating the federal land grant system. Lands owned by the federal government were offered to the states to finance schools to teach agriculture, military tactics and engineering in addition to the traditional curriculum. The first new land-grant university was Kansas State Agricultural College, now Kansas State University, established in 1863.

American colleges were quite different from the preeminent European research universities, particularly those in Germany.

Prior to 1880, Yale was the only U.S. school to offer degrees beyond the Bachelor of Arts. In America, the focus was on teaching people to think and appreciate intellectual pursuits, rather than promote academic scholarship and research in narrow disciplines. However, in the face of the demand for advanced study and professional programs, many established East Coast colleges chose to pursue the comprehensive university model. They did so by adding a graduate school on top of the existing undergraduate program, offering doctoral degrees in science, literature, law and medicine. The new colleges in the fast-growing Midwest followed this trend in the 1890s.

To support these new graduate programs, universities needed to grow. The ability to offer courses in many different disciplines and specialties required a large faculty. Individual academic departments were formed, with each demanding their share of revenue. As they expanded, universities were able to exploit significant **economies of scale**.[3] However, with schools growing in both size and number, there was increasing competition to fill them with students. One way to increase a school's visibility and prestige was through sports programs. Success on the field was as widely reported by the newspapers of the day as it is today.

In the 20th century, a major cause of growth at US colleges and universities was passage of the G.I. Bill near the end of World War II. The federal government offered to pay the entire cost of college education for these veterans, and they took advantage of the opportunity in huge numbers. From 1940 to 1950, college enrollment increased from 1.5 million to 2.7 million, nearly doubling in just 10 years. Federal financial aid programs for

---

[3]Economies of scale occur in the long run, when the cost per unit decreases as output increases. You may remember this from microeconomics as the downward-sloping portion of the Long Run Average Cost curve. One explanation is that some inputs, such as the most efficient machinery, are not available in smaller sizes. Only a large firm can afford this capital, giving them a cost advantage. For higher education, a comprehensive library is one such asset. It is difficult to have a small library and still offer all of the resources needed for students and faculty. A large university can offer more services at a lower cost per student.

non-veterans began during the 1960s, continuing the expansion in college education, with enrollment at two and four year institutions reaching 20 million by 2009. The typical student body has become more socially and economically diverse, with increased representation from minorities and women (the latter are now a majority of college students).

To absorb all of these new students, universities expanded in size and new campuses were established. For example, since the end of World War II, the California State University system expanded from 9 to 23 campuses, while the University of California expanded from 3 to 10. The two university systems have approximately 427,000 and 220,000 students respectively.

From its modest beginnings, nearly 400 years ago, U.S. higher education has been transformed from small colleges educating the upper classes in the classics into universities with tens of thousands of diverse students in many different disciplines. In many cities, the local university has become one of the largest employers. By any measure, higher education is now big business. We now examine how the role of college sports has been altered as the schools themselves have evolved.

1.3   The Beginnings of College Athletics

In the early years of American higher education, the faculty actively discouraged physical activity, deeming it unseemly for the offspring of the country's elite. Rough and tumble games were fine for the ignorant working classes, but not for boys destined for the ministry. However, by the 1820s, despite faculty's disapproval, a form of soccer was being played as a loosely organized intramural sport. At the Ivy League colleges such as Harvard, Yale, and Princeton, the games served as a way of bonding new students with upperclassmen. At Harvard, the game played on the first Monday of the fall term became known as "Bloody Monday." A similar game was played at other colleges:

> Yale also started an annual freshman-sophomore "rush" in the 1840s, a kind of mass hazing ritual that soon grew into an event

of great formality, with exploits commemorated in songs and poetry. Yale students had to abandon the rushes in 1858, however, when the city of New Haven refused to let them use the town green. When they tried to move the game elsewhere, the faculty, which had long taken a dim view of all this foolishness, banned it outright. Harvard outlawed Bloody Monday in 1860, while the Brown faculty halted its annual freshman-sophomore game two years later, only to reinstate it in 1866. (Bernstein, 2001, p. 4)

Rowing, with its association with prestigious English schools and high society, was more acceptable to the faculty than soccer. In England, 20,000 spectators watched the Oxford–Cambridge regatta of 1829, and it had become an important event in the social calendar. Amateur boating clubs were formed in the United States in the 1830s, and the first collegiate boat club was organized at Yale in 1843.

Rowing was the first intercollegiate sport, that is, the first to have contests between students at different colleges. As Bernstein (2001, p. 5) notes:

> Many of the rivalries that today characterize the Ivy League, not to mention many of the ills that still plague intercollegiate athletics in general, had their origins on the water rather than the gridiron. In the 1840s, while football players were still slugging each other on campus greens, both Harvard and Yale organized their first crews. When the two met on New Hampshire's Lake Winnipesaukee in 1852, in the nation's first intercollegiate athletic contest, their expenses were paid as part of a railroad promotion to lure tourists to the White Mountains. Intercollegiate match races proved so popular with spectators (including gamblers) that they were moved to Saratoga, the fashionable New York summer resort and horse racing capital that was something like the Las Vegas of its day. Within a few years, Brown, Columbia, Dartmouth, and Princeton crews were also competing in what came to be known as the Rowing Association of American Colleges. Unable to dominate the sport any longer, Harvard and Yale withdrew from the association in 1875, vowing henceforth to row only against each other. Others tried unsuccessfully to continue the regattas, but learned an early lesson in how important affiliation with the Big Two could be.

Baseball was another popular sport of that period. Amateur teams in New York played a version of the game as early as 1823. The first team to play by modern rules was the New York Knickerbockers, a social club for wealthy New Yorkers. In 1867, there were over 400 amateur clubs in the United States. By 1871, when the first professional baseball game was held between the Cleveland Forest Citys and the Fort Wayne Kekiongas, newspapers were already referring to it as the "national pastime."

Baseball clubs were formed at many colleges, and it was popular among the less affluent students that were starting to appear on campuses. Unlike rowing, the cost of outfitting a baseball team was negligible. In addition, many of the veterans returning from the Civil War had played the game while in the army. The first intercollegiate baseball game was played between Amherst and Williams in 1859. Harvard won the first Championship of American Colleges in 1868, defeating Yale by a score of 25 to 17. Student clubs also played against amateur clubs and professional teams.

In 1879, students from Amherst, Brown, Dartmouth, Harvard, Princeton, and Yale founded the American College Baseball Association. The group voted to prohibit professional players from their teams, although many of their best players spent their summers on professional teams, making this rule open to interpretation. They also began a championship, with Princeton the winner of the first pennant.

The fact that baseball's organizing body was run by students was typical of college sports of that era. Intramural and intercollegiate sports were organized by the students and were financially independent from the college. The students formed clubs, with the costs covered by subscription fees paid by the members, alumni contributions, and later, gate receipts. An alumni committee, not the university, purchased the land for Harvard's baseball field, Jarvis Field. Students set the rules and arranged for contests with other schools. This approach persisted at most colleges until the early 1900s.

When did today's most popular college sports, basketball and football, appear on campuses? The game of basketball was developed by James Naismith in 1891 as a physical activity during the winter months for students at the Young Men's Christian Association (YMCA) International Training School. The school's graduates quickly spread the game to YMCAs all over the country. The first intercollegiate basketball game was between student clubs from the Minnesota State School of Agriculture (now University of Minnesota, St. Paul) and Hamline College, which the Minnesota students won by the score of 9–3. Midwestern schools played an important role in the development of the sport. The first game played using five-player teams was held in 1896, when the University of Chicago defeated the University of Iowa 15–12. The Big Ten Conference sponsored its first basketball championship in 1906.

The evolution of football is a bit more convoluted. The first intercollegiate game was played in 1869, between students from Princeton and Rutgers, with about 100 fans in attendance. The style of play was similar to English soccer, with players unable to run with the ball in hand. Each team had 25 players on the field. A second Princeton–Rutgers game was played the following week, but the alarmed faculty at both schools cancelled a scheduled third game. Games between other New England schools were played during 1870, but no intercollegiate games took place in 1871. In 1872, students at Yale and Princeton attempted to organize a game, but faculty at both schools refused to excuse them for long enough to travel to the other campus. Instead, Yale invited students from nearby Columbia, and Princeton hosted Rutgers. The Princeton organizers charged admission (25¢) and attracted more than 400 fans.

At this time, the rules of the game were mainly *ad hoc*, the competing teams would negotiate and agree on the applicable rules before each game. The rules also varied significantly from school to school and changed over time, sometimes making it difficult to organize contests between colleges. A group of students from Yale, Princeton, and Rutgers met in 1873, to develop a common set of rules. Students from Harvard did not attend, preferring to play a game similar to English rugby, which allowed players to run with the ball. In 1875, they challenged students from their archrival Yale.

The rugby-style game proved such a success that the other colleges abandoned the soccer style and adopted Harvard rules. Student delegates from Harvard, Columbia, Yale, and Princeton met in 1876 and founded the **Intercollegiate Football Association** (IFA). The IFA Rules Committee was the authority for college football for the next 18 years. When Harvard and Columbia withdrew from the IFA in 1894, a new Intercollegiate Rules Committee was formed by students from Harvard, Yale, Princeton and the University of Pennsylvania.

In 1880, Walter Camp, a Yale alum and their first full-time coach, championed rule changes that created the uniquely American game of football. The scrum that follows the tackle of the ball carrier in rugby was replaced by the scrimmage, with a short break to allow each team to set up again. There were now two squads of 11 players, one for offense and the other for defense. In 1882, Camp proposed allowing each team just three tries (downs) to gain at least five yards, so one team could not just sit on the ball and run out the clock. To determine yardage, a series of lines were drawn on the field, the now familiar gridiron. Another difference between rugby and American football was that in rugby players could not protect the ball carrier by blocking opposing players (interference was not allowed).[4]

From its inception, football was a tough physical sport. In 1885, the Athletic Committee at Harvard, a football powerhouse of that era, recommended a ban on the sport, noting that it had degenerated into "modified mayhem." Harvard's president, Charles W. Eliot, was a frequent and outspoken critic of college football. Nevertheless, the ban lasted just one season, with Harvard resuming play in 1886 after the introduction of rules designed to address their concerns.[5] The Harvard team went on to win one game by 156–0 and score a total of 765 points for the season, a record that has yet to be surpassed.

---

[4]Riesman and Denney (1951) provide a good synopsis of the rules changes in the early years of college football.

[5]Miller (2011, p. 108) blames pressure by the alumni, an increasingly powerful voice on campus affairs, as a factor in the ban being rescinded.

The reduction in violence was short-lived. In 1888, Walter Camp championed a rule change to allow tackles below the waist. This proved to be such an advantage for the defense that teams had to develop new methods for protecting the ball carrier. The V-wedge was introduced in 1889, with the offensive players interlocking their arms and moving at a slow run straight into the defenders. When they had pierced the defensive line, the ball carrier would run through the opening. In 1892, Harvard deployed the flying wedge, in which the players would run in from the sidelines, gain momentum, and then focus their attack on one side of the opposing line. The halfback was effectively screened from the defenders by a wall of moving bodies. This description by Gall (1929) of Notre Dame football in the 1890s captures the spirit of the day:

> Back in the "good old days," the flying wedge was the most popular form of assault. It was a cross between a steam roller and a 42-centimeter shell. The center was under no obligation to pass the ball. Whenever he felt moved by a spirit he would tear through the line himself with the whole team concentrating its weight in the small of his back, while the opposition concentrated their weight in the pit of his stomach. Skill was never permitted to enter into the limelight along with weight, blood-thirstiness and the desire to trample the opposition into the sod. … [T]he atmosphere was rent by the dull crunch of breaking bones and the occasional thud of a luckless player exploding between the impact of two tons of beef. (¶ 14)

While the Rules Committee outlawed the flying wedge in 1894, other mass momentum plays continued to be used. The 1894 Harvard–Yale game was so brutal that the two schools stopped all contact, not just athletic competition, for two years. The Army–Navy game was also cancelled from 1894–1898 by order of President Grover Cleveland. In 1896, new rules briefly reduced the rate of serious injury, in part by allowing only one player to be in motion at the snap of the ball. The problem was that violence worked, giving the teams an incentive to find ways around any new rules. And despite the mayhem on the field, or perhaps because of it, football was growing in popularity.

In 1876, the Intercollegiate Football Association organized a championship game for Thanksgiving Day in Hoboken, New Jersey. After it was moved to New York City in 1880, attendance increased steadily:

> Within a decade, it was the premier athletic event in the nation. Princeton and Yale played each other almost every year in this game, and by the 1890s they were drawing crowds of 40,000. Players, students, and fans wore their school colors, while banners flew from carriages, hotels, and the business establishments of New York City. Thanksgiving Day church services were ended early to accommodate the fans, and the game became the event that kicked off the season for New York's social elite.
>
> By the mid-1890s, 120,000 athletes from colleges, clubs, and high schools took part in 5,000 Thanksgiving Day football games across the nation. Gate receipts from the Yale–Princeton Thanksgiving Day game of 1893 earned $13,000 for each school [*equivalent to $407,000 at 2012 prices*] and immediately became the primary source of revenue for their athletic programs. (Crepeau, 2001, ¶ 4–7)

The increasing popularity of college football — especially among middle class fans who were neither students nor alums — was due in large part to the mythology created around the athlete as a hero, on and off the field. Walter Camp, in particular, influenced the public's perception of college football through books and numerous newspaper and magazine articles. The ideal of gentlemanly play was also extolled in popular fiction, such as the "Frank Merriwell at Yale" series of dime novels by Burt Standish (pen name of Gilbert Patten). These books had sales of more than two million copies *per week* in the 1890s. Merriwell was able to accomplish amazing feats on the football field by relying on his traits of honesty, bravery and self-sacrifice.[6]

---

[6]Miller (2011) argues that the British novel *Tom Brown's Schooldays*, written by Thomas Hughes and published in 1857, also influenced the development of college sports in the United States, especially in the inculcation of characteristics like manliness, sportsmanship, and fitness.

Publishers wanted to create heroes to sell books and magazines, and what better than young men playing for nothing more than the love of the game? These fictional students excelled in academics and athletics, with no mention of eligibility scandals or deaths due to excessively violent play. The era of hero-worship of college athletes had begun, with benefits to the press and to the colleges that saw the popularity of their football teams soar.

Newspapers also went along for the ride. The entrepreneurial publishers Joseph Pulitzer and William Randolph Hearst realized that weekend games meant material for their papers when business and political news was scarce (Oriard, 1993). Pulitzer introduced a separate weekend sports section and the era of the sportswriter was born.

With their huge circulations, daily newspapers were largely responsible for the growing interest in college football beyond students and alumni. Fans could follow their favorite team even if they were unable to attend games in person. In turn, sports reporting helped sell more newspapers, with roughly one quarter of subscribers indicating that their main interest was reading the sports page. (Evenson, 1993)

As college football became more popular, money became increasingly important. Having a successful program meant more revenue, but it also meant spending more. Facilities had to be expanded to accommodate more paying fans. The old wooden bleachers had limited capacity and were prone to fire. Harvard Field, the first permanent collegiate stadium, was constructed in 1903, at a cost of US$310,000 (US$9 million in 2012 prices). Able to accommodate nearly 31,000 fans, it was the first massive reinforced concrete stadium in the world. It was funded by past and projected future ticket sales and a gift of US$100,000 by alumni from the Class of 1879. Permanent stadiums built on other campuses were more modest in size, usually seating less than 10,000, although they could accommodate more fans using temporary bleachers.

Such a costly facility could not have been built without a dependable stream of revenue. Fortunately, growing popularity meant money from ticket sales and alumni donations to the football club, at least if the team was winning games. At Yale, revenue in 1893 was US$31,000 (nearly US$1 million in current dollars), rising to more than US$100,000 in 1903. Unfortunately, the combination of financial resources and the pressure to win led to various abuses at many schools, including the hiring of professional players and paying inducements to recruit the most talented students. Columbia was reported to have only three undergraduates on its 1900 squad.

Competition for the best coaches drove up their salaries. At Harvard, football coach Bill Reid was paid more in 1905 than any faculty member, and just less than the president of the University.[7] This probably contributed to the growing belief by many of the faculty, and even university presidents, that football had become a distraction from the real purpose of the institution — education.

Always eager for a scandal to sell more newspapers, the press periodically reported on the various ills of the game, including payments from gamblers to players, deaths and serious injuries from violent play, payments to recruit students, and the use of professional athletes. However, little was done to reform the sport. While editorial writers decried these abuses, sports writers continued to focus on the excitement of the game. The image of the athlete as hero was already deeply engrained in the American psyche, and at least for now, fans were willing to overlook the occasional scandal. The abuses continued in part because they did not seem to significantly damage the popularity of the sport.

The lack of reform in football programs was also due to the fact that the faculty and administrators were not really in charge. Students managed the clubs, hired a coach for the season, and organized the contests, but who watched and guided them? At many schools, it was not members of the faculty, who were either disinterested or openly hostile. They had abdicated their responsibility, and efforts to reclaim it were mostly unsuccessful. It was not

---

[7]Reid's annual salary at this time was roughly US$7,000, about US$200,000 in today's dollars.

the administrators, who often shared the faculty viewpoint but could do little to oversee student clubs that were independent financially. It was largely the alumni that stepped into this role, donating their time, experience, and money. Some had been athletes during their own college days and wanted to help out the latest generation; others were attracted by the chance to be part of the excitement.

A report by the Carnegie Foundation for the Advancement of Teaching (Bentley, McGovern, Savage and Smiley, 1929) traced many of the problems in college sports of the 1920s to the growing influence of alumni in the late 1800s:

> Training was intensified and elaborated, and trainers were employed. Coaching began to be a progressively technical task, and paid coaches grew to be the rule rather than the exception. Equipment ashore and afloat grew in amount, in complexity, and, above all, in cost. All of these factors were reflected in rapidly rising expenditures for athletics, which called for increased funds for their support, whether from subscriptions or from gate receipts or from both. Special financial support began to be solicited from alumni. One result was that alumni who made generous contributions to college athletics received, openly or covertly, in return, a generous share in their control; and alumni who became active in that control gained or retained their power and prestige by their own contributions of money and by subscriptions which they solicited from other alumni and from friends of the college. The reciprocity that underlay this situation was generally regarded as a fair exchange. (pp. 22–23)

If the faculty lacked meaningful control at their own institution, one way to regain some influence was for them to form an association of universities to oversee all intercollegiate athletics. Faculty had an almost schizophrenic perspective on college football. As Riess (1995, p. 116) notes "[p]rofessors believed athletics kept students busy, taught proper social habits, developed manly traits and character, and advanced American civilization." On the other hand, they "… complained that commercialization of sport fostered nonexistent or weak eligibility standards, the recruitment of tramp athletes, and unsportsmanlike conduct" (1995, p. 129).[8] It was only a matter of time before the tug-of-war between students, faculty and administrators over governance of college football would be decided. In 1895, the presidents of seven Midwestern universities met to discuss the regulation of college athletics. They agreed to limit eligibility to full-time students in good standing, and to send faculty delegates to a second meeting to form a permanent organization.[9] The Intercollegiate Conference of Faculty Representatives, also known as the Western Conference, was founded in 1896. The charter members were Chicago, Illinois, Michigan, Minnesota, Northwestern, Purdue, and Wisconsin. With the addition of Indiana and Iowa in 1899, it was referred to as the Big Nine, and later the Big Ten (a name it did not officially adopt until 1987). The Southern Intercollegiate Athletic Association was formed by six schools (Alabama, Auburn, Georgia, Georgia Tech, North Carolina, and Vanderbilt) in 1895. Six more universities joined them the following year (Clemson, Kentucky, Louisiana State, Mississippi State, Tennessee, and Tulane). Other regional conferences were established in the early 1900s, including the Pacific Coast and Southwestern.

These conferences established rules for athletic eligibility and organized championships. The first official Western Conference championship event, for outdoor track, was held in 1906. Imposing limits on athletic programs, however, met resistance at some member institutions. In 1906, the organization responded to concerns over athletic eligibility and student financial mismanagement. They adopted rules to make freshmen and graduate students ineligible and require transfers to complete one year of residence.

---

[8] Leave it to an economist to express an even more dismal opinion about intercollegiate athletics. According to Thorstein Veblen, University of Chicago Professor of Economics (1899, p. 256), "[t]he addiction to sports ... marks an arrested development of the man's moral nature."

[9] Rudolph (1962, pp. 374–375) mentions an incident in 1890s in which the University of Oregon football team found itself playing against the *same* player three games in a row even though they played against three *different* teams.

Separate dining ("training tables") and residence facilities for athletes were outlawed, and coaches were required to have regular faculty appointments at "modest" salaries. When the faculty representatives from the University of Michigan returned to campus, they were met by protest from outraged alumni, students, and administrators. The faculty committee on campus that had advocated for these changes was abolished and the University refused to comply with the new rules. As a result, Michigan was expelled from the conference (or quit, it is not clear) and it remained independent until returning in 1916. Clearly, winning at football had become important to many people, and they resisted anything that threatened continued success. Alumni were particularly vocal in their opposition to meaningful reforms, in part because they would lose their influence over student-run programs.

1.4   A Crisis in Football

Meanwhile, little had been done to correct the problem of excessive violence. During the period 1890 to 1905, a total of 330 students died as a result of injuries sustained on the football field (at all levels of football: high school, college, and recreational), and many more were seriously injured (Zimbalist, 1999, p. 8). During the 1905 season, 3 college players were killed and 88 were seriously injured. In addition to these deaths at the college level, 15 other players also died that year as a result of football injuries.

While the 1905 season was not much worse than others during the previous 15 years (or the next eleven for that matter — see Table 1.1), news coverage and editorials finally caught the public's attention, threatening to derail the sport's continued popularity (not to mention the lives of the players). President Theodore Roosevelt invited representatives from three of the football powerhouses, Harvard, Yale (including Walter Camp), and Princeton, to a meeting at the White House on October 9th. These schools, along with Pennsylvania, were the members of the Intercollegiate Rules Committee. Roosevelt, claiming that football was "on trial," convinced them of the urgent need for reform and elicited a promise to

Table 1.1.   Football deaths and serious injuries, 1905–1916.

	Deaths		Serious injuries	
	All levels	College	All levels	College
1905	18	3	159	88
1906	11	3	104	54
1907	11	2	98	51
1908	13	6	84	33
1909	26	10	69	38
1910	14	5	40	17
1911	14	3	56	36
1912	11	1	26	17
1913	14	3	56	36
1914	12	2	NA	NA
1915	NA	NA	NA	NA
1916	<u>16</u>	<u>3</u>	NA	NA
	160	41	692	370

NA = not available.
Source: Watterson (2000a, p. 401) and Watterson (2000b, p. 294).

change the rules after the end of the 1905 season.[10] With the addition of Chicago, Cornell, and the US Naval Academy, a new American Football Rules Committee was formed, and it met in December 1905.

Roosevelt's actions, and his use of the "bully pulpit," reflected the political spirit of the times. You may recall from American history the Progressive Era, the late 19th and early 20th century, political and social reforms that brought about "trust-busting, railroad regulation, the passage of food and drug laws, restrictions on child labor, the prohibition of alcohol, and the implementation of a federal income tax" (Miller, 2011, p. 14).[11] Also, it is important to stress

---

[10] Miller (2011, p. 187).
[11] Ingrassia (2011) provides a summary of efforts to reform football in the context of the Progressive Era. He mentions "[r]eformers wanted to regulate intercollegiate football because they saw it as a venue in which the pursuit of money, fame and pleasure held the power to corrupt" (2011, p. 63).

that Roosevelt — himself a Harvard grad — was not an anti-football advocate and "did not object to [football] because it was rough" (Rudolph, 1962, p. 377). Roosevelt was primarily concerned about amateurism and good sportsmanship. Even the Carnegie Report, which appears over 20 years later, focused on abuses concerning subsidies and recruiting, not football injuries.[12]

At their first meeting, the new committee adopted rules against kneeing and slugging, created stronger penalties for rough play, and added an umpire. To many, these changes fell far short of what was needed. This is not very surprising, given that these schools were the dominant powers in football and had the most to lose from anything that changed the nature of the game. One rejected proposal was to allow forward passes, which would move the action away from the line of scrimmage. The forward pass would allow teams with smaller, faster players to outmaneuver the existing powerhouse teams with their large players. The perennial winners had grown accustomed to the financial rewards and public exposure from their football programs and did not want to risk losing them.

But what if Roosevelt was correct that the public outcry against violence and corruption in college football threatened the very existence of the sport? His meeting with the big three schools took place at the beginning of the season and yet the violence continued unabated. Why were the teams unable or unwilling to promptly change their tactics to reduce the chance of serious injuries when the alternative was to do nothing and risk the end of the sport? Why did they have to wait for a change in the rules? Economists have an explanation for this behavior, based on the theory of **externalities** and **public goods**.

Externalities occur when the production of a good or service has a positive or negative impact on someone other than the producer or consumer, that is, there is an effect that is external to the

---

[12]Watterson (2000a, p. 171) argues the report should have placed more emphasis on football violence. However, college sports historians debate whether the media — chiefly newspapers — sensationalized gridiron mayhem to increase sales (e.g., Oriard, 2012, p. 6).

market transaction. A frequent example in economic textbooks of a negative externality is the damage caused by industrial pollution. A company that makes paper may release chemical byproducts into a river and harm people and other businesses located downstream. The river is a common resource, that is, it is not owned by any individual but is available for everyone to use or misuse. The producers of paper do not have to pay for the damage they cause. If they were required to compensate the people who are harmed, the producers would have to raise their prices to cover the increased cost. With higher prices, consumers would buy less paper. The decrease in paper production will mean less pollution. For society, the gain from less pollution would more than compensate for the loss in paper production, but as long as firms can pollute for free, they will continue to produce too much pollution and too much paper.

How does the theory of externalities apply to college football? The public's perception of the sport is the common resource, like the river. The violence that damages football's popularity is the negative externality, like pollution. One of the differences is that the colleges also live along the river they pollute, that is, they are causing damage to themselves. If the public loses interest in the sport, all schools will be hurt, even those that choose to limit the mayhem on the field.

Public goods are defined as those that are consumed collectively rather than individually. A candy bar is a private good; if I eat it, you cannot also eat it. Heating a classroom in the winter is a public good because you and I can both enjoy the benefits. The fact that you are also warm and cozy does not make me less warm — you do not "use up" the heat. Economists refer to this condition as **non-rival** consumption. Pure public goods are also **non-excludable**, which means that a consumer cannot be excluded from getting the benefits. It would be very difficult to heat just part of a classroom so that only some students would be warm and the rest cold.

Economic theory predicts that markets will produce less than the socially optimal quantity of public goods. This is because of the phenomenon of **free-riding**. When you are listening to your local public radio station and they ask for people to call in and pledge their financial support, what do you do? If you are like 95% of the listeners, you do nothing. You know that the quality of service will not improve if you give them US$100 and that you will be able to listen to their programs even if you pay them nothing. Why not let other people pay so you can get it for free? The economic problem with free-riding is that if we all do it, the producer gets no money and nothing is produced, even if this is something that everyone values.

Returning to the pollution example, what would you do if you were one of the people harmed by the paper mill's pollution? You might decide to lobby the government to impose limits on pollution. This will be a costly effort, both in time and money, well beyond the benefits you will personally receive from a reduction in pollution (increased value of your riverfront property, for example). Recognizing that other people will also benefit, you might ask your neighbors for financial contributions. How will they respond, or at least, how would an economist expect them to respond? If there are only a few people, each person might recognize that unless they all contribute nothing will get done. With a larger number of neighbors, however, each person will probably try to be a free rider and get the benefits of less pollution without paying.

How does the theory of public goods apply to college football? The public good is continued popularity of the sport, and each school can contribute by adopting a less violent style of play. If enough contribute, the number of injuries should decrease significantly, which will benefit all schools with a football program.

What would be the cost to your school of contributing to the public good? Quite simply, it is winning fewer games than if you had continued your violent ways. If other teams change their tactics, then you can win more games by being a bit more physical than they are. If the other teams do not reduce their use of violent tactics, then you will lose more games if you play a less physical style. Either way, the cost to your school of trying to do the right thing is fewer wins, giving you a strong temptation to be a free rider. This is an example of the classic prisoners' dilemma, which we illustrate in Chapter 2.

A complicating factor is that the cost of losing is higher for some schools, particularly those with perennial winning records. Yale would have more to lose from a decline in its on-field performance than a school without a strong tradition (and expectation) of winning. It may prefer the status quo, even with a decline in the overall popularity of the sport, to changes in the rules that might level the playing field.

While this discussion has focused on the problem of violence, it applies with equal force to the other threat to the popularity of the game, the use of professionals and payments to students. The only difference is that in 1905 it was harder for the public to ignore students dying on the field than secret payments to star players. Something had to be done quickly about the level of violence, and it looked as if the existing powers were unable to do so.

How does our society deal with other public good problems? If the problem is that nobody sacrifices voluntarily, someone has to step in with the authority to mandate that everyone contribute to the solution. We all know that having a fire department is a good thing, but how many of us would contribute to a fund to pay for one? The solution is that the government *tells* us to pay — it does not ask if we *want* to. We are not allowed to become free riders.

For football, the eventual solution began with the death of yet another young man during the 1905 season. Harold Moore, a player for Union College, collapsed on the field after running head first into the New York University offensive line. He died at a hospital a few hours later. The Chancellor of NYU, Henry McCracken, witnessed the tragedy and resolved to put an end to the brutality. He invited representatives from other universities to meet to discuss ending or reforming the sport. Although McCracken favored abolishing football, the 13 delegates attending that initial meeting chose the path of reform, voting 8–5 to pass a resolution to meet again to form a rules committee.

The second meeting was attended by delegates from 68 schools, most of whom were faculty from schools with less prominent football programs. They voted to form a new association, the

Intercollegiate Athletic Association of the United States (IAAUS), and established their own rules committee. The following month, the new IAAUS rules committee met with members of the existing rules committee, Walter Camp's IFC. They agreed to cooperate to introduce a more open style of play, with fewer clashes between massed groups of players. The rule changes for the 1906 season included the introduction of the forward pass, the creation of a neutral zone around the line of scrimmage, and the requirement that at least 6 offensive players be on the line rather than in the backfield. Without the ability to stand back from the line of scrimmage, the entire offense could not take a running start at the defensive line.

These changes may not have occurred without the strong support of Harvard's coach, Bill Reid, and its president, Charles Eliot. Reid explained to the other committee members that if the new rules were not adopted, then Harvard would drop its football program. Columbia, MIT, Northwestern, Trinity, Duke, Stanford, California and others had already announced their intentions to drop football. If Harvard had ended its program, even more schools would likely have followed suit. In a last ditch effort to minimize the effect on established teams, Yale's Walter Camp proposed simply widening the field by 40 feet rather than allow the forward pass. Unfortunately for Camp, the new Harvard Field was too narrow and his proposal was rejected. Facing the end of the sport or accepting the new rules, they were adopted. The two committees agreed to continue to work together on further refining the rules.

With a solution to one problem in hand, the IAAUS turned to other concerns, namely the lack of faculty oversight over athletic programs and the resulting mismanagement by students and their alumni backers. As mentioned earlier, the Intercollegiate Conference of Faculty Representatives (Western Conference) had taken some steps to address this issue in 1906. In that same year, the University of Pennsylvania circulated a letter to the presidents of all colleges and universities in the United States outlining three simple rules, including a requirement that all members of athletic teams be genuine students of the college which they represent and a prohibition on using social or monetary inducements to procure good players from other colleges. They suggested that the rules be adopted by a "gentleman's agreement" without the need for any enforcement mechanism. Given the simple fact that each school had an incentive to violate the agreement if it meant getting better players and winning more games, a more formal system was needed, with all colleges and universities following the same rules. With the formation of the new IAAUS, that process was begun.

1.5   The Early Years of the NCAA

At their inaugural meeting in 1905, the members of the newly formed IAAUS resolved to reform all of intercollegiate athletics, not just football. An Executive Committee was formed and charged with writing a constitution for the association. Led by Captain Palmer Pierce of West Point, the group completed its draft by the end of March 1906. The second article of the new constitution stated that the purpose of the organizations was "the regulation and supervision of college athletics throughout the United States, in order that the athletic activities in the colleges and universities of the United States may be maintained on an ethical plane in keeping with the dignity and purpose of education."

By the time of the 1906 Convention, only 39 schools had ratified the constitution (see Table 1.2), and just 28 attended the meeting. Harvard, Columbia, and Yale did not join. The University of Pennsylvania was the only Ivy League school and the only member of the Football Rules Committee to do so. Minnesota was the lone member from the powerful Western Conference, and Vanderbilt and North Carolina were the only representatives from the Southeast. The schools that did join were typically smaller and not affiliated with a major conference. While the University of Chicago, another member of the influential Football Rules Committee, did not join immediately, its legendary coach and Athletic Director,

Table 1.2.   Charter members of the IAAUS.

Allegheny College	Oberlin College
Amherst College	Ohio Wesleyan University
Bucknell University	University of Pennsylvania
Colgate University	University of Rochester
University of Colorado	Rutgers College
Dartmouth College	Seton Hall College
Denison University	Swarthmore College
Dickinson College	Syracuse University
Franklin & Marshall College	Tufts College
George Washington University	Union College
Grove City College	United States Military Academy
Haverford College	Vanderbilt University
Lehigh University	Washington and Jefferson College
Miami University (Ohio)	Wesleyan University (Connecticut)
University of Minnesota	Western University (Pennsylvania)
University of Missouri	Westminster College (Pennsylvania)
University of Nebraska	Williams College
New York University	Wittenberg University
Niagara University	University of Wooster
University of North Carolina	

Amos Alonzo Stagg, attended the convention and voiced his strong support.

Many universities, particularly those with successful athletic programs, were naturally skeptical of an organization with a stated purpose of regulating all college athletic activities. Would it attempt to impose its rules on everyone, and who would decide what those rules would be? To alleviate these fears, the constitution stated that "the acceptance of a definite statement of eligibility rules" would not be a membership requirement. Members were free to choose their own methods for preventing violations of the organization's principles. In short, there was no enforcement mechanism. This individual autonomy was referred to as **home rule** (see Smith, 1988, p. 207 and Oriard, 2012, p. 7).

The bylaws adopted at the first convention focused on the issue of amateurism. Among the most significant elements were:

1. A ban on payments to students based on their athletic abilities by the university or individual alumni.
2. A ban on recruiting of prospective athletes from preparatory (high) schools.
3. Declaring students as ineligible if they had ever received any payment for competing in a sporting event.
4. Limiting eligibility to four years and requiring successful completion of at least two-thirds of the previous college year.
5. Requiring freshmen and transfer students to complete one year of college before being eligible.
6. Declaring students as ineligible if they were not enrolled full-time.

The Executive Committee was given the authority to propose changes to the constitution and bylaws. These would be submitted to the delegates at the annual conference, with each member having one vote. After just one year, the delegates amended their Constitution to state that the member institutions were bound by its regulations unless they filed an appeal of a specific rule to the Executive Committee. The era of central control was already beginning.

The IAAUS continued to grow, and in 1910, it changed its name to the National Collegiate Athletic Association (NCAA). By 1911, it had expanded from the original 39 members to 95, including Chicago and Harvard. By 1915, both Yale and Princeton had joined.

The attraction of an organization with overall authority over college sports was based on many factors. Faculty had been unsuccessful at taking control from students and alumni on their own campuses, and the NCAA gave them a chance to do so at a higher level. Many resented the emphasis on sports as a distraction from the real purpose of higher education, and the high salaries paid to coaches did not help matters. They also pointed to common abuses and the moral obligation of the college to correct them.

Colleges had long been expected to act in the best interest of students, taking on the role of a parent. In this regard, they are acting *in loco parentis* — which, contrary to what you might believe — does not mean "you must be crazy to have children" but rather "in place of the parent."

There is also the economic justification for such an organization based on the theory of public goods discussed earlier. It can take actions that no individual would be willing to do alone, but that benefit all members when enough participate. I am happy to pay my taxes, not because I want to have less money, but because I know that everyone else is required to do so and that the government will use the money to provide services such as education and public safety. I support this system because it is better than the alternative of a government that cannot afford to provide the services that we want. After going to the effort to create an organization to deal with one problem (violence in football), the members immediately began to focus on other issues of mutual concern, such as amateurism.

In an article chronicling the first 25 years of the NCAA, Carter (2006) identifies six key internal debates that occurred during that period:

1. Amateurs and amateur programs;
2. Preserving academic integrity standards;
3. Controlling the rising cost of athletics;
4. Securing the status of coaches as full time teachers;
5. Safety and the future of football;
6. Scheduling, postseason games, and travel.

There were also two external conflicts, pitting the NCAA against professional sports and the news media. Carter's discussion of these debates is summarized in Section 1.5.1.

1.5.1 *Amateurism*

As noted above, amateurism was addressed in the bylaws adopted at the first annual convention in 1906. Interestingly, those rules were not concerned with colleges profiting from athletics, only with the students doing so. Some of the delegates had wanted to go further and minimize intercollegiate athletics in favor of intramural activities, that is, to remove colleges from the business of sports. They argued that intercollegiate sports have limited participation, while intramurals can benefit the entire student body. Travel to other colleges and practice sessions, also takes time away from academic pursuits. Another suggestion was for universities to fund athletic programs rather than keeping them dependent on gate receipts and alumni donations. Without this direct support, athletics were under pressure to win to keep the interest of paying fans and donors. A few delegates even argued that schools should stop collecting gate receipts at sporting events. Needless to say, they lost these debates.

The sport with the most significant problems related to the use of non-amateur players was baseball. Professional leagues were already well established and many college players had the opportunity for employment during the summer. Rather than declare the majority of their baseball team ineligible, most colleges chose to look the other way and disregard the NCAA bylaws. In 1908, there was support for an explicit summer baseball exemption, but no action was taken.

By 1925, dissatisfaction by the proponents of amateurism with the growing importance of intercollegiate sports and ongoing abuses led the NCAA to call for a study by the aforementioned Carnegie Foundation for the Advancement of Teaching. The Carnegie Report was issued in 1929 and drew nation-wide attention. It documented widespread subsidies to athletes and improper recruiting. Out of 112 universities examined, payments to athletes occurred at 81, and at 61 of those, multiple agencies (administration, alumni, and athletic association) were involved. Clearly, the majority of colleges were not following NCAA guidelines. The Commission recommended that university presidents and faculties take charge, not just in name but also in deed. Unfortunately, little was done, and a follow-up by the *New York Times* found that the majority of schools identified by the Carnegie Report were continuing to violate the rules.

1.5.2 *Academic standards*

To field a team of the best possible athletes, schools are tempted to admit students who do not meet their admission standards, and to keep students who are not making satisfactory progress in their studies. Faculty might be pressured to give passing grades to athletes, and special courses may be offered with minimal academic requirements. The NCAA's bylaws reduced the incentive to admit unprepared students by banning freshmen from varsity athletics. If students were not expected to survive the first year, they were not worth recruiting. However, this was not a perfect solution, and some schools simply chose to disregard this rule. Many schools took steps to maintain academic standards, but such efforts were not universal. Issues related to academic integrity continue to plague college sports today, and they are addressed in much greater detail in Chapter 4.

1.5.3 *Rising costs of facilities*

Football continued to grow in popularity, with the most obvious evidence being the building boom for stadiums. Harvard Field was eclipsed in 1914 by the Yale Bowl and Princeton's Palmer Stadium, accommodating 70,000 and 41,000 fans, respectively. Midwestern universities were not far behind, with Illinois, Iowa, Ohio, Michigan, and Notre Dame all completing stadiums in the 1920s with capacities of at least 50,000. With construction costs in the tens of millions in today's dollars, they put a substantial burden on athletic programs and their universities to keep gate receipts and alumni donations coming in.

Some argued against building such large facilities, as their counterparts continue to argue today. As we will see in Chapter 6, they noted that those dollars could be used to construct facilities more directly connected to the students' education, such as a new chemistry building. There is also risk to building sports facilities based on projected future revenue. What if the popularity of football diminished? In economic terms, a stadium represents a **sunk cost**, with no opportunity to recover the money if conditions change. It is also a

Table 1.3.   Stadiums built 1903–1930 that belong to current FBS and FCS institutions.

Institution	Year built	Institution	Year built
Alabama State	1922	Michigan	1927
Alabama	1929	Mississippi	1914
Alabama-Birmingham	1926	Mississippi	1915
Arizona	1928	Missouri	1927
Army	1924	Nebraska	1923
Brown	1925	North Carolina	1927
Bucknell	1924	Northwestern	1926
Butler	1928	Notre Dame	1930
California-Berkeley	1923	Ohio State	1922
Cincinnati	1924	Ohio	1929
Colorado	1924	Oklahoma State	1920
Cornell	1915	Oklahoma	1925
Dartmouth	1923	Portland State	1926
Davidson	1923	Purdue	1924
Drake	1925	Rhode Island	1928
Duke	1929	Southeast Missouri	1930
Florida	1930	Southern	1928
Fordham	1930	Stanford	1921
Georgia Tech	1913	Tennessee	1921
Georgia	1929	Texas A&M	1904
Hampton	1928	Texas Christian	1929
Harvard	1903	Texas	1924
Holy Cross	1924	Tulsa	1930
Illinois	1923	UCLA	1923
Indiana State	1925	Valparaiso	1919
Iowa	1929	Vanderbilt	1922
Kansas	1921	Villanova	1927
Lafayette	1926	Washington	1920
Louisiana State	1924	Wisconsin	1917
Michigan State	1923	Yale	1914

http://en.wikipedia.org/wiki/List_of_NCAA_Division_I_FBS_football_stadiums.

large **fixed cost** with a **marginal cost** (the cost of admitting one more customer) close to zero, requiring a high level of output (attendance) to break even. With fans anxious to buy tickets and alumni eager to make donations for such a tangible outcome, arguments for construction won out. Proponents pointed out that connecting with alumni by bringing them back to campus increased the chance that they would donate for other purposes, including that new chemistry building. It also served to advertise the university to the public, leading to increased enrollments and greater tuition dollars.

1.5.4 *Status of coaches*

The annual budgets of athletic departments were also rising due to higher salaries for head coaches and expanding coaching staffs. By the early 1900s, the coach's salary at some schools surpassed even that of the university president. There was also the issue of their professional status on campus. Football coaches were usually hired for just one season, with very little job security. While some faculty objected to what they saw as a high salary for just a few months' work, their opportunities for off-season work were limited.

One way to gain some control over hiring coaches and their salaries is to make them part of the regular teaching staff. However, this puts them on the same professional level as the faculty, something many were unwilling to do. Nevertheless, the NCAA adopted a resolution at its 1910 meeting that coaches should be regular members of the teaching staff and employed for a full academic year. It also recommended that athletics become a department with equal standing to all other departments. With faculty egos and the distribution of financial resources at stake, it took many years for athletics to be accepted as a part of the curriculum. The current state of coaching salaries and athletic department budgets and will be discussed in Chapters 5 and 6 respectively.

1.5.5 *Safety of football*

Public concern over violence returned in 1909, with 26 football-related deaths. While disputing these numbers, the joint Football Rules Committee made additional changes to the rules. Offensive players were not allowed to link arms or push the ball carrier forward. On the defensive side, diving tackles and interference with pass receivers were penalized. Recognizing the link between player exhaustion and injuries, the length of each half was reduced and a break introduced between the quarters. A player could also leave the game and reenter at the start of the next quarter. The NCAA also required an internal investigation of any football deaths.

1.5.6 *Scheduling games*

A major concern for faculty was that intercollegiate sports took time away from academic pursuits, a concern that many of us share today. It is then ironic that when faculty and administrators took

---

Box 1.1.   Player safety.

Player safety in professional and amateur sports continues to attract attention. As an example, in 2011 former National Football League (NFL) safety Dave Duerson committed suicide, shooting himself in the chest and requesting that his brain be examined. Duerson was only 50 years old. In 2012, NFL veterans Junior Seau (age 43) and Ray Easterling (age 63) also killed themselves. Prior to their deaths, all three exhibited signs of depression, loss of memory and dementia, all signs of a type of traumatic brain injury known as chronic traumatic encephalopathy (CTE) believed to be caused by repeated concussions. At the time this book was revised, over 2000 current and former NFL players were part of a class action lawsuit against NFL for neglecting to adequately warn and protect players from the detrimental effects of blows to the head. While denying any liability, the NFL has responded with rules changes, notably moving kickoffs up five yards (from the 30 to the 35 yard line) and increased use of penalties and fines for helmet-to-helmet contact. Economists LeBron and Angus boldly predict that CTE will lead to the demise of professional and collegiate football in the United States within the next 20 years. (Cowen and Grier, 2012)

---

control from students, the number of games played during the regular season in most sports increased. Games between schools in different conferences, which involve even more travel time, also became more frequent. These intersectional games were early versions of today's bowl games, and they were promoted by local business interests as a way to attract large numbers of visitors. When the NCAA attempted to limit the number of games played during the regular season, these games were simply moved to the preseason or postseason, further extending the time away from school and studies.[13] Also, with games starting earlier in the academic year and ending later, the first practices had to be pushed back, often beginning before the start of classes. Spring practice for football was also added, meaning an even greater time commitment for the student-athletes.

A different type of intersectional game was played during the preseason between a team from a large school in a major conference and one from a smaller school. The attraction for the small school was their share of the gate receipts from a game at a school with a big stadium and a large fan base. For the larger university, they got the chance to sharpen their skills with little chance of a loss. For them, it was a warm-up game before the start of the real season. However, the schools were often far apart, involving even more travel time for the smaller school's players.

Why was the faculty unable to curb these trends? The short answer was money. As long as large numbers of fans bought tickets for each game, more games meant more money. Because it took increasingly large amounts of money to maintain a winning program, this was treated as a necessity, not a choice. The loss of a winning program could also impact all areas of campus, not just the

---

[13]When an authority tries to fix a problem by imposing restrictions rather than changing the underlying incentives, they often make the problem worse. By adopting a rule limiting the regular season, the NCAA clearly intended to reduce the impact on student-athletes. However, because schools had a monetary incentive to schedule as many games as possible, they found a way around the limit that actually led to even more time demands for students. This is an example of the **Law of Unintended Consequences**.

athletic program. This could damage the reputation of the university, leading to lower enrollments. The connection between alumni and the university could suffer, leading to a drop in donations. The voices of those arguing for amateurism for the university, not just amateurism for the students, were drowned out.

1.5.7   *Professional sports*

Colleges saw the emergence of professional football after World War I as a major threat. Professional teams could lure away the best players, and more importantly, the paying fans. They also publicly professed concern for the student-athletes, who would be morally corrupted by playing football not for the pure love of the game, but with the goal of eventually signing a lucrative contract. The NCAA passed a number of resolutions, including one that would revoke the varsity letter of any former student who played professional sports after graduation. Most of the major conferences refused to hire coaches or officials that played, coached or officiated for professional teams. The College Football Coaches Association, formed in 1921, and open only to coaches at NCAA institutions, advocated similar steps to thwart professional football. In 1926, the NCAA recommended that schools fire anyone who had been employed in any capacity by a professional team.

In the face of these actions, the owners of the professional teams looked for a compromise with the NCAA. The league, which changed its name to the National Football League in 1922, agreed to not draft any player until his class had graduated, even if the player did not attend college. A high school football player could not bypass college and go directly to the pros. This was enough to placate the NCAA and a truce was called. College football became a willing supplier of trained talent to the NFL, essentially serving as an unpaid minor league. Concerns voiced over the moral status of college players disappeared.

1.5.8   *Media*

The other conflict of that era was with the media. Press coverage was not always favorable. Stories on excessive violence, payments to students and gambling scandals sold papers, and some editors and columnists were willing to expose the hypocrisy of the NCAA's focus on student amateurism while colleges reaped huge financial rewards. Even the entertainment industry got involved, with movies such as the Marx Brothers' *Horse Feathers* lampooning colleges and college football. The NCAA needed to rework its message.

Box 1.2.   Horse feathers.

In this scene from the 1932 Marx Brothers film *Horse Feathers* Groucho Marx, portraying President Wagstaff of fictional Huxley College, is speaking to two of the university's professors:

Wagstaff: And I say to you gentlemen, this college is a failure. The trouble is, we're neglecting football for education.

Both professors: Exactly. The professor is right.

Wagstaff: Oh, I'm right am I? Well, I'm not right. I'm wrong. I just said that to test you … What I meant to say was that there's too much football and not enough education.

Both professors: That's what I think.

Wagstaff: Oh, you do, do you? Well you're wrong again! … Where would this college be without football? Have we got a stadium?

Professor One: Yes.

Wagstaff: Have we got a college?

Professor One: Yes.

Wagstaff: Well, we can't support both. Tomorrow we start tearing down the college.

Both professors: But professor! Where will the students sleep?

Wagstaff: Where they always sleep. In the classroom.

Source: http://www.marxbrothers.org/whyaduck/info/movies/scenes/wagstaff.htm.

While newspapers had been an early contributor to the popularity of the college sports, and football in particular, radio broadcasts of games were seen as direct competition. If fans could listen to the game for free, fewer might buy tickets to attend. It was also viewed by supporters of amateurism as a corrupting influence, with too much media attention paid to star athletes and coaches. However, it was soon apparent that wider exposure created more fans and increased the demand for tickets. When radio stations started selling advertising time during games, colleges were quick to negotiate payments for broadcast rights. With no financial harm, concerns related to amateurism and professionalizing the sport were swept away.

1.6   College Sports in the Modern Era

The modern era for higher education and college sports began in the 1940s, after the end of World War II. Rapidly increasing enrollments combined with expanding television coverage to make sporting events more popular than ever. College athletics was transformed into a billion dollar business, and with more money at stake came more temptation to break the NCAA's rules. In the face of widespread reports of payments to athletes, sham college courses, influence by gamblers, and recruiting violations, the NCAA was finally given the authority by its members to enforce the rules.

1.6.1   *Amateurism: payments and scholarships*

Perhaps, the most visible role for the NCAA is to protect the amateur status of college athletes. In 1922, the members unanimously adopted a Ten Point Code of Eligibility, which forbade any payments to students for their participation in sports, including athletic scholarships. This principle was reiterated in a code of "fair practices" in 1934. However, in regions where competition between schools was particularly active, the temptation to offer financial aid (and even secret payments) was too strong to resist. In 1935, the

Southeastern Conference was the first to allow athletic scholarships. At the time, the major conferences had more influence over colleges than the toothless NCAA, and when one conference starts allowing payments to athletes, even if limited to the cost of education, the others will have to follow.

By 1948, there was sufficient support within the NCAA for a return to pure amateurism to ban athletic scholarships, and to give the NCAA the authority to enforce the new rules (students could still receive financial aid based on need and academic performance). The legislation was initially called the "Purity Code," but it was promptly changed to the "**Sanity Code**" after the name was ridiculed in the press. Surprisingly, the proposal originated, not from the smaller colleges where amateurism was firmly entrenched, but from a group of the "win at all costs" major conferences. A cynic might conclude that the financial cost to schools of competing for athletes was getting uncomfortably high, and they needed the NCAA to make sure that everyone cooperated. To enforce the rules, two new NCAA committees were formed, one to investigate suspected violations and the other to hear cases. The only penalty specified in the legislation was expulsion from the NCAA.

You may be familiar with the slogan "If guns are outlawed, only outlaws will have guns." Many schools refused to give up their guns and became outlaws. If they could no longer offer payments to athletes out in the open, they would do so in secret. Some coaches and athletic directors replaced scholarships with more creative ways of getting money to students, such as well-paid jobs that involved minimal time and effort. These phantom or sham jobs proved an effective inducement, and they continued even after athletic scholarships were reinstated by the NCAA. This led to even more NCAA rules, including a cap on the combined amount of scholarships and income from on-campus employment.

Economists understand that people respond to incentives, and when you block one path they will find another. Like the proverbial **little Dutch boy** plugging the leaking dike with his fingers, as each hole is plugged with a new NCAA rule, other leaks appear and even more rules will be needed.

In 1950, seven schools were judged to have violated the Code and the sanctions committee recommended their expulsion, the only action available to the NCAA. Their recommendation, however, failed to get the required two-thirds majority of delegates at the annual convention. For most members, the punishment was too extreme. In 1951, a critical section of the Sanity Code was repealed by the membership, and the Code was rendered unenforceable.

To avoid the impression that the NCAA had lost control over college sports, it adopted an aggressive new public relations campaign and instituted more changes to its constitution. By 1957, students could be awarded grants-in-aid (scholarships based on their athletic ability), but the funds had to be administered by the financial aid office, not the athletic department. The amount was limited to tuition and fees, and payments from sources outside the university (e.g., alumni boosters) were banned. Payments to student athletes were now officially sanctioned, but under stricter control by the institution and with NCAA oversight. Off-campus recruiting of high school students was also allowed, but with limits. Not all conferences allowed athletic scholarships. The Ivy League adopted a formal ban on football scholarships the following year, and the Big Ten Conference did not vote to allow full scholarships until 1961.

To enforce the growing number of rules and to reassure the public that the NCAA was taking violations seriously, in 1953, the NCAA Council was finally given the enforcement powers it needed to be effective. *First*, it could impose sanctions without the approval of a majority of delegates. *Second*, the sanctions included a wide range of options, not just expulsion. The Council could ban a school from postseason play (including bowl games), limit television appearances, limit regular season contests to schools in their own conference, restrict the number of allowable recruiting visits, and reduce the number of students offered scholarships. Still short of expulsion, they can also impose the death penalty, which requires a school to drop the offending sport for a specified number of seasons. Starting in 1993, schools were also required to undergo a certification process every 10 years, showing that they had structures in place on campus to oversee athletics. The enforcement process is discussed in greater detail in Chapter 2.

The NCAA rules at that time did not limit the number of scholarships, although some conferences imposed their own limits. This led to concerns about **competitive balance**, particularly in football. A school that could afford a large number of scholarships could attract more of the best athletes and have multiple reserves for each

---

Box 1.3.   The death penalty.

The NCAA punishment that forces an athletic program to cease operations for one or more seasons, officially came into effect in 1985, in response to the SMU scandal discussed on page 3 of this chapter. Yet it is generally acknowledged that the cancellation of the University of Kentucky (UK) 1952–1953 basketball season was the first application of the death penalty, however unofficial. This punishment was imposed as a result of gambling by UK players, specifically point shaving. Point shaving occurs when a team does not try to change the outcome of the contest by "throwing" the game; rather, it allows the opposing team to score more points, thus narrowing the spread between the two teams' points. This action impacts betting markets and the point spreads established by odds makers and essentially allows gamblers to cheat in an attempt to get a high payoff. As a result of an investigation by the New York City District Attorney (some of Kentucky's games were played in New York at the 1949 NIT tournament), UK players were arrested for taking bribes from gamblers. The suspension of Kentucky basketball, along with the establishment of the Television Plan (discussed in Section 1.6.7), are considered the watershed events that transformed the NCAA from an advisory to a regulatory body. The age of home rule was no more.

position. They might even offer scholarships to some players simply to keep them away from their opponents. This could lead to a situation where the same schools dominate the sport year after year, resulting in a loss in fan interest. If schools compete with each other by offering larger numbers of scholarships, this could also raise costs to a point that threatens the existence of many football programs.

To address these concerns, the NCAA voted in 1973 to limit the number of scholarships in varsity sports, with football restricted to a total of 105. Surprisingly, Sutter and Winkler (2003) discovered that the schools with the strongest football programs were more likely to have voted in favor of this rule. Given that the top programs are unlikely to support a change that will promote parity with other teams, the motive of keeping costs down may have been the deciding factor. Beginning in 1992, the total number of football scholarships was reduced to 85. We return to competitive balance in Chapter 2.

Having a large football team is less important if you are unable to substitute players during games. Starting in 1906, substitutions were only allowed for injured players, and if they were able to return to the game they had to wait for the start of the next quarter. The same "platoon" of players was on the field for both offense and defense. In 1941, the NCAA changed the rules to allow two platoons, one for offense and one for defense, but the squads were still unable to substitute freely. Unlimited substitution was allowed in 1947, but one-platoon rules were reinstated in 1953. The modern system of two platoons with unlimited substitutions did not begin until 1965.

While the ability to substitute and allowing players to specialize in offense or defense is an interesting historical tale, it also has an impact on the economics of college football. Single platoon football with limited substitutions promoted parity by taking away some of the advantages otherwise enjoyed by large schools. Why have 85 players on full scholarship if only a handful will get to play? Schools that could only afford to offer a small number of scholarships might actually be able to compete in the big time.

Think of modern college basketball, where recruiting a few talented players might just be enough to become the next Cinderella team at the national tournament. The end of one-platoon football in 1965 made it more difficult for schools with limited budgets to stay competitive. In addition, with more incentive to offer a full complement of football scholarships, fewer scholarships could be offered in other sports.

Starting in 1982, the NCAA created two different kinds of limits on scholarships. Sports in the **head count** category, including football, have the number of scholarships limited.[14] A student that is awarded even a US$100 scholarship counts against the allowed number. This creates an incentive to offer only full scholarships in that sport. For an **equivalency** sport, the amount of a full scholarship can be divided among any number of athletes. If the women's soccer team is allowed 12 scholarships at US$5,000 each, they can choose to divide the total amount of money among a full roster of 26 students.

What if a student is injured and no longer able to play? Will she lose her athletic scholarship and possibly be forced to drop out of college? What if she decides that sports are taking too much time away from her studies and quits the team? Until 1967, a scholarship was best viewed as a gift from the institution to the student, and once given, it could not be taken back. In that year, the NCAA adopted a rule allowing schools to revoke the scholarship of athletes that voluntarily withdraw from sports, making scholarships more clearly a payment for services rendered. However, an athlete forced to withdraw due to injury was allowed to keep her scholarship. She had not violated the terms of the contract and could continue her studies.

Another significant change occurred in 1973, when the NCAA required schools to offer only one-year athletic scholarships, with the option to renew the offer each year. This meant that a student who was injured, or just not as talented as initially thought, might not have her scholarship renewed for the following year.

---

[14]The head count sports are football, men's and women's basketball, and women's gymnastics, tennis and volleyball.

A particularly talented athlete could be kept on scholarship while recovering from an injury, in the hopes that she could return in subsequent years. The decision to renew is made by a university — wide committee, but with significant participation by the coaching staff.

1.6.2 *Eligibility*

Three issues related to eligibility are (1) freshmen participation on varsity teams, (2) admission requirements for athletes, and (3) satisfactory academic progress. The first year of college is challenging enough without the added demands of athletics, and for many years freshmen were generally not eligible for intercollegiate competition. The Big Ten conference banned freshmen from varsity sports in 1906, and the NCAA's 1922 Code included a similar provision. The NCAA lacked the power to fully enforce this rule until the 1950s, but starting in 1939, it refused to allow freshmen to participate in its national championships. In 1968, the NCAA reversed its position and allowed freshmen to participate in all sports other than football and basketball. Freshmen were allowed to play football and basketball in 1972.

To ensure that schools only admit bonafide students who are adequately prepared to balance the demands of sports and academics, the NCAA began imposing minimum entrance requirements for athletes in 1965. The initial standards were quite lax, in part because at that time freshmen were still not eligible to play. **Rule 1.6** required students to have a sufficient high school GPA and test scores to predict that they would earn at least a 1.6 GPA during their first year of college. The requirement was not raised after freshmen were allowed to play in the "non-revenue" sports, because in those sports there is less pressure to admit an academically-challenged promising athlete. In 1973, after freshmen were granted eligibility in football and basketball, the rule was changed to a 2.0 overall high school GPA.

For high school athletes hoping for a college scholarship, this created an incentive to avoid difficult courses like mathematics and science in favor of easy electives. Faced with news stories of college athletes who never learned to read in high school, the NCAA passed **Proposition 48** in 1983, at the urging of the American Council on Education, an organization representing college presidents. When it was implemented in 1986, for students to qualify for athletic scholarships and to play intercollegiate sports they had to be a high school graduate, earn a high school GPA of 2.0 in 11 core courses, and score a total of at least 15 on the ACT or 700 on the SAT. A student who failed to meet the ACT/SAT minimum but met the first two requirements was a "partial qualifier" and could be awarded an athletic scholarship but could not play for the first year. The freshmen year for partial qualifiers also counted against their four years of athletic eligibility. **Proposition 42**, adopted in 1989, banned scholarships completely for partial qualifiers.

There was widespread public concern about the disproportionate impact of Propositions 48 and 42 on minority athletes, particularly the ban on scholarships for partial qualifiers. A compromise was reached in 1990 that allowed partial qualifiers to receive financial aid based on need but not on athletic ability. The source of funds for these scholarships could not be the athletic department. The rules were modified again in 1992, with passage of **Proposition 16**, and in 1997, with **Proposal 68**. Proposition 16 restored athletic scholarships to partial qualifiers but expanded the number of core high school courses to 13 and required higher minimum ACT/SAT scores for students with low grade point averages. Proposal 68 gave back the year of lost eligibility to partial qualifiers. In 2002, the NCAA Division I Board of Directors voted to eliminate the partial qualifier category, effective August 1, 2005.

To maintain their eligibility after they are admitted, athletes must demonstrate satisfactory academic progress toward graduation. This does not mean just accumulating credits with passing grades, but fulfilling requirements for a baccalaureate degree, including their choice of a major. The decision on a specific degree program must be made by the beginning of the third year of collegiate enrollment. In 2003, the "**40/60/80 Rule**" specified by Bylaw 14.4.3.2 requires a student entering his third year to have completed

40% of the course requirements in his chosen program. Students entering their fourth and fifth years must have completed 60 and 80% of those requirements, respectively. Beyond the fifth year, students are no longer eligible for intercollegiate athletics, with some exceptions (service in the armed forces or the Peace Corps, a church mission, pregnancy, or serious injury or illness).

1.6.3 *Divisions*

The NCAA was originally organized with seven regional districts and an Executive Committee consisting of the national officers and one representative from each district. The districts were required to issue an annual report on the state of college athletics in their region. By 1916, reorganization and the addition of more schools on the Pacific coast led to the current nine districts. All schools had equal representation in the national organization, based on the principle of one member–one vote.

There is a common saying that over time "the rich get richer and the poor get poorer." The same can be said about college athletics in the modern era. Major universities grew dramatically in size, and revenue from television broadcasts allowed their athletic budgets to keep pace. Smaller universities and liberal arts colleges had neither the desire nor the budget to put as much emphasis on intercollegiate sports. To allow schools to compete at levels appropriate to their resources, the Collegiate and University Divisions were created for championship tournaments in 1956. For most sports, the existing tournament became the University Division championship and new championships were created for the College Division. The first College Division championship in basketball took place in 1957, and regional championships in football began in 1964.

Schools were not officially members of a division; they simply decided which championship would be more appropriate for each of their teams. By 1968, with College Division championships in place for nearly all sports, member institutions were required to pick a division. Two hundred thirty three chose the University Division and 386 the College Division.

Within a few years, it became apparent that there were still significant differences among schools within the College Division. In addition, the schools in the University Division resented that smaller schools could vote on policies that primarily affected the larger institutions. A policy of asking schools to voluntarily abstain from voting on issues that did not affect them was not entirely effective. A member of the University Division could lobby schools in the College Division to vote at the national convention on the issues it cared about in exchange for voting for issues they favored, a practice known as **logrolling**. For example, a group of schools from Texas traded their votes for ice hockey legislation for support by schools from the northeast on adding an eleventh game to the football season. (Mott, 1996, p. 11)

In 1973, a special convention of the NCAA created three divisions for legislative as well as competitive purposes. The University Division was renamed Division I, and the College Division was divided into Divisions II and III. While each division had its own steering committee, the NCAA Council retained its overall authority and all NCAA members voted on changes in policy. A majority of the positions on the Council were reserved for representatives from Division I institutions, even though they comprised a minority of the total membership.

Division I was intended for universities with enough resources to support competition at the highest level, while schools in Division III are barred from offering any athletic scholarships. Compared to Division I, schools in Division II typically have fewer students, fewer varsity sports, and athletes are less reliant on athletic scholarships. Coaches in Division II usually perform other duties at their school, including teaching, while coaching at Division I schools is a full-time activity. More than half of current Division II schools have total undergraduate enrollment of less than 2,500, and less than 10% have more than 7,500. In contrast, only 12% of Division I schools have fewer than 2,500 undergraduates, and more than 15% exceed 15,000.

The requirements for membership in a particular division are based on the number of varsity sports, the number of scholarships funded, and ability to schedule games against opponents in that division. For 2011–2012, an institution can qualify for Division I membership by (1) providing at least 50% of the maximum allowable financial aid in 14 sports, at least 7 of which must be women's sports, (2) sponsor at least one sport in each season, and (3) play the minimum acceptable number of games in each sport (e.g., 27 in baseball and 11 in soccer) against Division I opponents.

A handful of schools have been allowed to have memberships in more than one division. This allows smaller schools that have historically played at a high level in a particular sport to continue to do so. For example, St. Lawrence University, with an enrollment of 2,300, has traditionally competed in hockey against much larger D-I universities. In all other sports, it competes in Division III. Membership in Division I is important because it allows the University to offer scholarships to hockey players. The NCAA bylaws were revised in 2004, to formalize this arrangement. One men's team and one women's team can be classified at a higher level, with the exception of football and basketball.

There were still large differences within Division I when it came to the most expensive sport, football. In 1978, Division I was subdivided into I-A and I-AA for football only. As a result, the number of schools in I-A fell from 180 to 105. To be eligible for I-A, a school had to sponsor at least 16 sports, play at least 60% of its games against other I-A teams, average at least 15,000 in paid attendance at home games, and provide at least 90% of the allowable number of football scholarships. The term I-AAA was adopted later for Division I schools that do not have a football program. In 2006, the NCAA approved a change in the labels to "**Football Bowl Subdivision**" for I-A and "**NCAA Football Championship Subdivision**" for I-AA. The bowls and championship tournaments for football are discussed later in this chapter (and in greater detail in Chapters 2 and 7) at which point the rationale for the new titles will be clearer.

In 2012, there were 340 institutions in Division I, 120 in the Football Bowl Subdivision (formerly known as I-A), 122 in the

Football Championship Subdivision (I-AA), and 98 with no football (I-AAA). There were 290 schools in Division II and 436 in Division III.

1.6.4 *Conferences*

With few exceptions such as Notre Dame football, colleges and universities are also members of athletic conferences. The basic function of a conference is to coordinate competition during the regular season and organize postseason championships among that group of schools. In the modern era, they also negotiate television contracts and distribute the proceeds and any other revenue they agree to share, such as payments for bowl appearances. The formation of conferences and the selection of members are not controlled by the NCAA.

Because conferences do not schedule championships in all possible sports, schools are often members of more than one conference. The University of Wisconsin-Madison is located in the frigid north between two lakes. Not surprisingly, it fields varsity teams in both hockey and rowing, but the Big Ten Conference does not sponsor either sport. The school is a member of the Western Collegiate Hockey Association for hockey and the Eastern College Athletic Conference for rowing.

> **Fast fact.** *The Eastern College Athletic Conference is remarkable for two things. First, instead of the usual 8 to 16 schools, it has 317 member institutions. Second, it combines schools from NCAA Divisions I, II, and III. It sponsors competition in a wide variety of sports, including field hockey, synchronized swimming, and water polo.*

As discussed earlier, several major conferences predate the NCAA, and for many years they had significantly more power over colleges and universities than did the NCAA. The Big Ten was particularly influential in early attempts to promote the amateur status of student athletes. The Pacific Coast Conference had a history of being very strict with regards to its standards. It had a paid commissioner, an elaborate constitution, a formal code of conduct, and a system for reporting student-athlete eligibility. Unfortunately, this was not enough to eliminate rampant recruiting violations. Other conferences took a more hands-off approach, imposing few limits on their members. The Southeastern Conference was long known for looking the other way if it helped their football teams.

Every school wants to be in a conference that will enhance its status and media exposure. What characteristics would you look for? Playing schools in your part of the country will make travel easier and exploit existing regional rivalries. Your opponents should be roughly equivalent in resources, resulting in rough parity on the field. At the same time, you want to join with other schools that are playing at the highest level, resulting in more national interest and coverage.

The rise and fall of athletic programs over time result in the need to realign conference membership. Schools that have de-emphasized athletics, perhaps unable to devote the resources it takes to compete with their current conference rivals, will either decide on their own to move to another conference or be asked to leave. Meanwhile, other schools will be looking to move up in the world, perhaps hoping that more media attention will enhance their ability to attract students and alumni donations. They will be in a position to take the place of the declining school. It is important for conferences to maintain enough schools for scheduling purposes, and the NCAA requires a minimum number of members to recognize a conference championship for invitation to bowls or the NCAA tournaments.

What is the optimal size of a conference? A large number of members increases the chance that it will produce a team capable of earning an invitation to a major bowl game, with a big payday to share with the entire conference. However, this also means more schools to share with, decreasing the payoff per school. A larger conference also increases travel distances, increasing travel costs and time away from school. As will be discussed in Chapter 2, a large number of members makes it more difficult to avoid a costly "arms race," with schools investing in state-of-the-art training and playing facilities to help recruit the most talented athletes.

The number of regular season games allowed by the NCAA also plays a key role. The limit of 11 football games per season imposed on all Division I teams was raised to 12 for those in I-A for the 2006 season. Consider a conference with 6 members. During an 11 game season, they could play each other twice per season plus one game against an opponent outside the conference, or once per season plus 6 outside opponents. If the fans prefer both games against a variety of opponents and those against conference rivals, neither option is attractive. On the other hand, a conference of 12 schools can play each other once every season.

By comparing revenue and costs for conferences with varying numbers of members, Depken (n.d.) attempted to answer the question of optimal conference size empirically. He found that as the size of a conference increases, revenue per attendee (revenue divided by attendance) rises and then declines, with a maximum reached for a conference with 10 members. The cost per attendee declines and then rises, with a minimum average cost at 14 members. Profits are maximized (marginal revenue = marginal cost) where the number of members equals 11.76, which rounds to 12 members. Of course, which 12 teams maximizes conference profits is another question.

For the FBS, the last few years was a period of significant realignment.[15] When there is inter-conference movement there are often ripple effects, as conferences that lose membership scramble to find enough new schools to remain viable. A similar type of behavior can be seen in the business world, when one or two mergers take place in an industry. The rest of the firms often start

---

[15]The FBS conferences are: Atlantic Coast (ACC), Big 12, Big East, Big Ten, Pacific-12, Southeastern (SEC), Conference USA (C-USA), Mid-American (MAC), Mountain West (MWC), Sun Belt, Western Athletic (WAC), and the Independents (Army, BYU, Notre Dame).

looking to merge to avoid being left without a suitable partner (and the same might apply to marriage!). As you will see from the following example, one of those conferences that is feeling jilted is the Western Athletic Conference (WAC) which at present, is scheduled to have only two football programs in its conference when the 2013 season begins (Idaho State and New Mexico State).

In the past, a significant number of schools chose to remain independent of a conference for some sports, particularly football. Notre Dame is probably the best-known example. Given its national reputation, it was able to schedule football games with

---

Box 1.4.   The conference merry-go-rounds.

In 2010–2013, Nebraska left the Big 12 to join the Big Ten as its 12th member. The Pac-10 also increased membership to 12 teams by adding Colorado (formerly Big 12) and Utah (which left the Mountain West Conference — MWC). Texas Christian bolted from the MWC for the Big East then decided it had a better offer from the Big 12, which it joined along with West Virginia (which also left the Big East). New to the Atlantic Coast Conference are Pitt and Syracuse (from the Big East). The Big East added Boise State and San Diego State (both MWC), Navy (Independent), Central Florida, Houston, and Southern Methodist (all three from Conference USA), and allowed Temple to rejoin. Fresno State, Hawaii, Nevada-Reno, San Jose State, and Utah State (all WAC) moved to the MWC. Texas State and Texas-Arlington left the WAC for the Sun Belt. Missouri and Texas A&M (both Big 12) joined the Southeastern Conference. North Carolina-Charlotte (Atlantic 10, in the FCS), Florida International (Sun Belt), Louisiana Tech (another WAC refugee), North Texas (Sun Belt), Old Dominion (Colonial Athletic Association, also FCS), and UT-San Antonio will join Conference USA. Georgia State (Colonial Athletic Association) joins the Sun Belt.

other independents as well as members of major conferences. A game against Notre Dame was guaranteed to bring media attention and increase ticket sales. The number of independents has dwindled, with just Army, BYU, and Notre Dame remaining as of 2012.

Fast fact. *For 2013–2014, a total of 49 Division I schools changed their conference affiliation. Most were responses to earlier realignments to the ACC, Big 12, Big Ten, Pac-12 and SEC. The Big East was divided into the American Athletic Conference for football and the new Big East for non-football schools. The Great West Conference was officially dissolved. ("49 NCAA schools," 2013)*

1.6.5 *NCAA governance*

The NCAA's system of governance was significantly revised in 1997. The current federated system is illustrated in Figure 1.1. Each of the three NCAA divisions has its own governing body that sets the overall direction of policy (a Board of Directors for Division I and the Presidents Councils for Division II and III) and a Management Council that makes recommendations to the Board/Council and handles responsibilities assigned to it by the governing body. The Board and the two Councils are composed entirely of presidents or chancellors of member schools. Positions on the Management Councils are filled by athletic directors, faculty, and in the case of Division III, student-athletes and college presidents. The Management Council for Division I has 49 members, with a majority of positions dedicated to representatives from I-A conferences.

Above these boards and councils is the NCAA Executive Committee, which is comprised of 12 university presidents from the Division I Board of Directors and two presidents each from the Presidents Councils. They are joined by the NCAA President and the chairs of the three Management Councils as *ex officio* (non-voting) members. The Executive Committee has the authority to approve

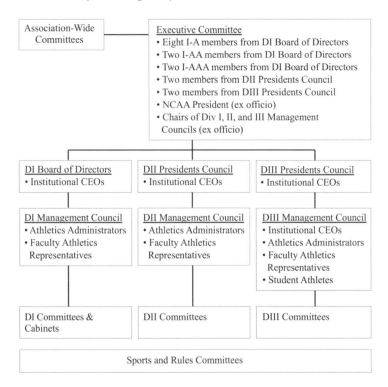

Figure 1.1.   NCAA organizational chart.

the budget, create special committees, call for votes on constitutional changes, refer any action by a division that it deems contrary to basic principles to the entire membership, and resolve issues related to actions taken by the Association.

Much of the work of the NCAA is conducted by various cabinets, committees and subcommittees. As of 2012, there were 125 committees overall, including 15 that reported directly to the Executive Committee, including the Committee on Sportsmanship and Ethical Conduct, the Olympic Sports Liaison Committee, the Committee on Women's Athletics, and the rule-making committees for various sports. The Division I Management Council had nine subcommittees, including Budget, Governance, Membership, and Strategic Planning. It also has two cabinets, for Academics/Eligibility/Compliance, and for Championships/Competition.

Prior to 1997, the entire membership of the NCAA voted on all legislation. After the restructuring, each division manages its own affairs, and only Divisions II and III retained the one member–one vote policy for approving legislation. In Division I, a vote by all members only occurs when there is a call to override a decision by the Board of Directors. Otherwise, the Management Council acts much like an elected legislature, such as the U.S. House of Representatives.

In Division I, legislation can be referred to the Management Council by a conference, a cabinet or committee, the Board of Directors, or any constituent group. The Council conducts an initial formal consideration and either forwards it as approved to the Board of Directors, votes to not approve it, or establishes a 60-day comment period for the membership and then has a second consideration. If it reaches the Board for their consideration, they can approve it with or without significant modification, vote to not approve, or take no action at all. If there is significant modification, it goes back to the start of the process. If the Board approves or rejects it, there is a 60-day period for the membership to request an override. If there is no call for an override, the Board takes a Final Action. An override request must have the support of at least 30 division members. In that case, the Board reconsiders, and if they decline to reverse their decision, it is put to a vote by the membership at the annual convention each January. It requires a 5/8ths majority to override the Board, and the results of the vote are final.

1.6.6 *Other amateur sports organizations*

While the NCAA is the organization we associate with college sports, it had competitors for that role in the past. The **Amateur Athletic Union** (AAU) was founded in 1888 to promote amateur sports, particularly track and field, in an era when many people did not go to college. It trained athletes and organized teams to participate in the Olympic Games and represented the United States in international sports federations. It also promoted sports for women nearly a century before the NCAA became involved.

In 1899, the AAU gave up its claim of authority over most college sports, but it continued its efforts to control all amateur lacrosse, basketball, and most importantly, track and field.

A critical dispute between the two organizations was whether athletes would be eligible for the Olympics if they participated in an event not sanctioned by the AAU or accepted financial payments from colleges (i.e., scholarships). When the NCAA began its own championships in track and field in 1921, the battle escalated. General Douglas MacArthur, who was elected President of the American Olympic Committee in 1927, persuaded the parties to put aside their differences for the sake of the 1928 Olympics. In 1930, the Olympic Committee was reorganized to reduce the overwhelming influence of the AAU, and the AAU agreed to modify its stance on eligibility. In 1946, the Alliance Agreement between the AAU and NCAA was signed.

By the late 1950s, the battle heated up again. The AAU was unwilling to give up its majority on the Olympic Committee or its position as the country's representative at international sports federations. The NCAA ended the Alliance in 1960, and two years later, it organized a meeting of amateur athletic organizations. This led to the formation of separate federations for baseball, basketball, gymnastics, and track and field, with NCAA officials in control. Neither Attorney General Robert Kennedy nor his brother, President John F. Kennedy, were able to settle this dispute. It was only resolved with passage of the Amateur Sports Act of 1978, which created the United States Olympic Association and stripped the AAU of its power.

The AAU refocused on promoting grass-roots sports at all levels. It sponsors national championships in 36 sports, including baseball, football, karate, and surfing. They currently have 500,000 participants and 50,000 volunteers. It plays a significant role in the development of promising high school basketball players. After the regular high school season is over, the players can join AAU teams, some of which are sponsored by the shoe companies Nike and Adidas. The teams have paid coaches and they offer students the chance to test their skills against other talented players.

Of course, they also offer companies like Nike a way to establish a relationship with these players, which will hopefully lead to endorsement contracts with the best of them when they reach the NBA. The AAU coordinates its player-development leagues and camps with the NCAA, NBA, and others.

A different competing organization, the **National Association of Intercollegiate Athletics** (NAIA), has its roots in small college basketball. In 1937, James Naismith, the creator of basketball, helped organize a tournament for teams from small colleges. Based on the success of that tournament, a group of small colleges met in 1940, to form the National Association of Intercollegiate Basketball. When the organization broadened its scope in 1952, the name was changed to the NAIA. Championships in other sports were added and membership increased.

With the NCAA focused on the major colleges and universities, there was a market niche for the NAIA. By the 1970s, membership reached 561. However, when the NCAA split its College division in 1973 and created Division III for small schools without athletic scholarships, membership in the NAIA began to decline. The NCAA had more resources, and Division III is governed by its own Board and committees, keeping small colleges at arm's length from the pressures and scandals of big-time programs. By 2012, the NAIA had dropped to 257 schools, less than half of its peak. Most of the defections have occurred since 1985, with membership falling by 212.

While there is concern that the NAIA may collapse, it has two key selling points. *First*, it is positioned between NCAA Division II and III. A small university may not have the resources to compete in Division II but Division III would be a step downward. *Second*, it offers less oversight and fewer rules than the NCAA. At 276 pages, the NCAA Division III 2011–2012 Manual is slimmer than its Division I counterpart by a hundred pages or so, but it is still a hefty tome. The cost of compliance with NCAA regulations is not insignificant, particularly for a small athletic department.

Another niche not addressed by the NCAA was intercollegiate sports for women. Opportunities for women to compete were very limited until the late 1950s and 1960s. The NCAA was not interested in devoting any resources to something it viewed as entirely secondary to the real business of men's sports. In 1964, the Executive Committee inserted a line into its regulations that read "[T]he games committee shall limit participation to eligible male athletes." To fill this vacuum, the **Association of Intercollegiate Athletics for Women** (AIAW) was founded in 1971, with 280 charter members. Not surprisingly, they banned many of the hallmarks of men's sports under NCAA leadership, including off-campus recruiting, athletic scholarships, and restrictions on transfer between colleges. By 1981, they had more than 900 members with national championships in 19 sports.

Even with passage of **Title IX of the Education Amendments of 1972**, the NCAA continued to largely ignore women's sports. Title IX prohibits gender discrimination at institutions that receive federal funds. It was assumed by some athletic directors that because sports did not directly receive any money from the federal government, they would not be affected. This was not the case, and schools were soon obligated to bring women's intercollegiate sports closer to parity with programs for men.

By 1980, spending on women's sports was 16% of the average athletic department budget, up from less than 1% ten years earlier. The AIAW had demonstrated that women's sports could be successful, and the NCAA took notice of rising attendance, corporate sponsorship, and a million dollar television contract with NBC. They began to offer their own women's championships, first in Division II and III, and by 1981, in Division I. By scheduling its own tournaments at the same time as the AIAW events, they forced schools to make a choice. Given the superior resources of the NCAA, including their offer to pay all transportation costs to participating members, schools chose NCAA championships. In addition, at many schools the athletic directors had initially wanted nothing do with women's sports, allowing them to operate independently. By 1981, the growth of women's athletics had led to their merger with the men's programs and the athletic directors (almost exclusively male) were more comfortable dealing with the NCAA. The AIAW ceased operations in 1983, after an unsuccessful lawsuit against the NCAA. They had lost the battle, but were a large part of winning the war for gender equality. Chapter 8 will examine the details and impact of Title IX.

1.6.7 *Radio and television coverage*

The first commercial radio stations were established in 1920. Broadcasts of sporting events were very popular, particularly professional boxing, professional baseball, and college football. The first college games to be covered were regional rivalries, such as the "Backyard Brawl" between the University of Pittsburgh and West Virginia University in 1921 (Covil, n.d., ¶ 10). Starting with the broadcast of the 1922 Princeton–Chicago game, "radio had made itself part of the nationalization of football, by making interregional competition immediately available to masses through the airwaves" (Smith, 2001, p. 17). Using a series of stations connected by phone lines, NBC's coverage of the 1927 Rose Bowl game was the country's first coast-to-coast radio broadcast. (Covil, n.d., ¶ 12)

In the early years, radio stations aired college football games without advertising. The broadcasts were free public exposure for the college, and radio stations used them to build up an audience of loyal listeners. As radio stations began to line up advertisers, some colleges rebelled at the growing commercialization and imposed restrictions. For example, the Southeastern Conference banned broadcasts of intersectional games.

Colleges experienced declining attendance at football games in the early 1930s, due to the Great Depression. Reasoning that radio broadcasts were partly responsible, many conferences reacted by imposing further restrictions. However, selling the broadcast rights proved attractive to make up for some of the lost ticket sales. In addition, if more people became fans because of the broadcasts, then ticket sales might rebound. By 1935, all the conference-wide bans were rescinded.

The University of Pennsylvania hosted the first television broadcast of a college football game in 1938. By 1950, Penn was able to sell the season's broadcast rights to ABC for US$150,000 (about US$1.4 million today). Several other schools signed television contracts in 1949. Some involved straightforward payments, including Wisconsin's deal for US$10,000, Tulane's for US$7,500, and USC and UCLA's for US$34,500 each. Others were structured to protect against attendance loss, such as Michigan's deal for US$2,000 per year plus reimbursement for reduced attendance.

Some members of the NCAA were skeptical about television coverage, concerned that it would reduce attendance and gate receipts. The NCAA commissioned two market research studies, which found some indication of a drop in attendance for televised games. However, the evidence of a decline was far from definitive, and the possible replacement of gate receipts with television revenue was not considered.[16] Nevertheless, the delegates at the 1951 Convention voted for a ban on broadcasts for the upcoming football season. Pennsylvania refused to comply with the ban, and it signed a new US$200,000 contract with ABC (about US$1.8 million in today's dollars). When the NCAA threatened it with expulsion, which would require other NCAA members to cancel their games with Penn, the university was forced to back down.

Facing a public outcry and the threat of antitrust hearings, the NCAA allowed the broadcast of a limited number of sold-out games in 1951. The following year they implemented the **Television Plan** devised by its Football Television committee. The TV Plan restricted network television broadcasts to one game per week, with no school appearing more than twice each year. The NCAA negotiated the contract and divided the revenue between its members. In 1955, under pressure from the Big Ten, regional broadcasts of games that had not been chosen by the network as the national Game of the Week were allowed during five selected weekends. The dollar value of the NCAA television contract increased

---

[16] Factors other than television may have contributed to a decline in football attendance. As examples, the large postwar enrollment cohort of veterans would have graduated by the early 1950s. And universities located in urban areas were experiencing demographic changes as households began migrating toward newly developed suburban communities.

steadily, surpassing US$60 million in 1983. The NCAA distributed most of the proceeds to the schools that appeared on television, with a small percentage going to the rest of the members and to the NCAA itself to finance its operations.

By 1976, the schools with the most popular teams were sufficiently dissatisfied with the television agreement to form a new organization, the **College Football Association** (CFA), to advocate for their interests. The CFA represented seven major football conferences and the independents Notre Dame and Penn State. They argued against the limited number of televised appearances and for a larger share of the money. The split of Division I into I-A and I-AA was partly in response to pressure from the CFA for greater autonomy for its members. The maximum number of televised games per year for each team was also increased from two to three. While lobbying for change within the NCAA, the CFA also approached the television networks for their own contract. In 1981, NBC offered the 62 members of the CFA a US$180 million four-year deal (equivalent to about US$500 million currently). The NCAA responded by threatening to expel the members of the CFA. The CFA backed down, in part because expulsion would exclude them from the other lucrative televised event, the men's basketball tournament. They did not give up the fight, however, and a lawsuit was filed against the NCAA.

On behalf of the CFA, the University of Oklahoma and the University of Georgia sued the NCAA for violating the **Sherman Act of 1890**, the primary antitrust law in the United States. They alleged that the NCAA's television contract was a *restraint of trade*. In 1982, the U.S. District Court agreed that the NCAA was acting as a *cartel* to restrict output and raise prices. While the case was under appeal, the NCAA negotiated a new set of contracts for the 1984 season with ABC, CBS, and ESPN, with a total value of US$73.6 million. Before the start of the 1984 season, the Supreme Court upheld the lower court's decision. This gave individual schools and conferences the rights to negotiate their own television contracts. The NCAA retained the right to ban a school from appearing on television as a disciplinary action for violating other rules. But the fact remained that the Court labeled the NCAA a cartel, an outcome with a strong basis in economic logic.

In a dissenting opinion, two Supreme Court justices argued that the NCAA's limit on the number of TV appearances decreased the importance of winning. If more games were televised as a result of eliminating the existing Television Plan, and the networks paid large amounts to schools with winning programs, then the incentive to develop a powerful team would increase. The dissenting justices feared that this could lead to less emphasis on academics and more recruiting violations.

> **Fast fact.** *One of the dissenting justices was Byron "Whizzer" White, who served on the Supreme Court from 1962 to 1993. Whizzer was an All-American football player for the University of Colorado Buffaloes in the 1930s. He went on to play three seasons in the NFL, leading the league in rushing yards in 1938 and 1940. He did not play professional football in 1939, instead studying at Oxford University in England as a Rhodes Scholar. An honors graduate of Yale Law School, he was renowned for his humble manner and sharp legal mind. A true scholar-athlete, he was in a unique position to judge the likely impact of an ever-larger financial emphasis on college football.*

The CFA negotiated a new broadcast contract on behalf of its members, but it was unable to persuade the Pac-10 and Big Ten to join with the other elite conferences. Rather than a new cartel consisting of all the top football programs, there were now two major competitors, the CFA and the Big Ten/Pac-10 coalition. Because each competitor dominated a geographical region, they were each able to exert a degree of monopoly power, but less than if there had been a unified cartel. A significant difference between the CFA contract and the earlier NCAA deal was that the rights for games not selected by the network for broadcast reverted back to the schools, allowing them to sell those rights on the open market, as long as they were not shown in the network's time slot.

The CFA was unified until 1991, when Notre Dame signed its own contract with NBC for US$38 million, twice what it was getting from the CFA (Sandomir, 1991). In 1995, the FOX network outbid CBS for the NFL contract, leaving CBS without any football games to broadcast. To fill this gap, CBS lured the popular Southeastern Conference (SEC) away from the rest of the CFA with an US$85 million, five-year contract. Facing further defections, the CFA was dissolved in 1997, and the schools and conferences went their own way.

Compared to the era of one contract with a single network for all Division I-A football, today's television coverage is a complex arrangement with conferences having contracts with multiple networks.

1.6.8 *Postseason bowls and tournaments*

The NCAA organizes postseason championship tournaments for all sports. The men's Division I basketball tournament is notable for the huge profits it generates for the NCAA and its members. While the NCAA organizes championships in football for FCS, DII and DIII, there is no such tournament for schools in the FBS. Instead, a lucrative system of postseason football bowl games has evolved over time, with its origins predating the NCAA itself.

The first bowl game was the Rose Bowl, played on New Year's Day in 1902 as part of the annual Tournament of Roses in Pasadena. The Tournament, which began in 1890, refers to the contest between displays of flowers on floats, not the football game. The event was intended to showcase the community's warm climate to residents of other parts of the country. Michigan's 49–0 blowout of Stanford in that first game was not well received by the California fans and organizers, and football did not return until 1916. The format of pitting the conference champions from the Pac 10 and Big Ten against each other was adopted in 1947. To accommodate the growing crowds, the city of Pasadena constructed the Rose Bowl stadium in 1923. With a capacity exceeding 95,000, it has sold out for every Rose Bowl game since 1947.

In the 1930s, other sun-belt cities arranged contests on New Year's Day to stimulate their flagging Depression-era economies, including the Orange Bowl in Miami, the Sugar Bowl in New Orleans, the Sun Bowl in El Paso, and the Cotton Bowl in Dallas. During the 1950s, the NCAA stepped in to create a more orderly system, reducing the number of events from 50 to just 9, and requiring their approval for any new bowl games. For the 2011–2012 bowl season, there were 35 sanctioned bowl games, and only members of the FBS are eligible to be invited. The NCAA collects only a modest annual licensing fee of US$12,000 for these events.

With the advent of television, the bowl games moved beyond a way to bring in tourist dollars. Television created the American tradition of sitting down to watch football on New Years Day, and with large audiences comes big money. A single 30-second commercial was priced at US$500,000, during the 2005 Rose Bowl. While this is significantly less than the US$2.4 million for the 2005 Super Bowl, the total cost of an ad run during the four major bowl games was US$1.35 million. Another source of revenue for the bowl organizers is corporate sponsorship. We now have such official names as the Tostitos Fiesta Bowl and the Federal Express Orange Bowl.

With organizers receiving significant revenue from television networks and corporate sponsors, they are able to offer large payments to the participating schools. For appearing in the 2006 Fiesta Bowl, Notre Dame received US$14.87 million. Its opponent, Ohio State, received slightly more, although it had to share with the other schools in the Big Ten Conference. An appearance at even a minor bowl can earn a school in excess of US$1 million, although it may spend most of that on travel and other costs. While the NCAA does not manage these events or collect any of the revenue, these large payouts do give the NCAA some leverage. It can ban a school from participating in postseason play, including bowl games, giving it an effective tool to punish schools that break its rules.

In 1992, the Bowl Coalition was formed by five major football conferences (ACC, Big 8, Big East, SEC, and Southwest), the independent Notre Dame, and the organizing committees for the

Cotton, Fiesta, Orange, and Sugar Bowls. The members agreed to have the top two teams from those conferences meet in a self-declared national championship at one of the bowls on a rotating basis. This further differentiated both the four bowl games and the six conferences from their rivals. By acting together, this also gave the organizing committees a more powerful position when negotiating with the networks for the broadcast rights. However, the system for selecting teams for the championship game was far from perfect. *First*, the Big Ten and the Rose Bowl, which hosted the top teams from the Big Ten and the Pac-10, were not members of the Coalition. *Second*, three of the bowls were hosted by a conference champion (SEC for the Sugar Bowl, Southwest for the Cotton Bowl, and Big Eight for the Orange Bowl), and they were not allowed to play in the assigned championship bowl even if ranked first or second (unless their bowl happened to host the championship that year). *Third*, as Mondello (2008, p. 169) notes, the Coalition failed to solve a persistent problem in college football, during the period 1945–1991, the top two ranked teams faced each other in a postseason bowl only eight times.

The Bowl Coalition was replaced in 1995 by the Bowl Alliance, which was replaced by the **Bowl Championship Series** (BCS) in 1998. The Cotton Bowl and Southwest Conference were dropped from the group, the Big Ten joined, and the Rose Bowl Management Committee reached an agreement to release the Big Ten and Pac-10 champions if they were ranked one or two. Although there is no contractual relationship between the Rose Bowl and the BCS organizers, it is part of the rotation to host the national championship game and is commonly referred to as a BCS bowl. The Rose Bowl has its own network contract, separate from the BCS contract.

With a total of four bowl games and six conferences, there were openings for two schools from other conferences or independents (with Notre Dame automatically displacing other contenders if it met certain criteria) to play in the national championship or one of the other BCS bowls. The system for selecting the two at-large slots has been controversial, with only two teams outside of the six member conferences appearing in a BCS bowl during the first 10 years (Utah in 2004 and Boise State in 2007). The system was further modified for the 2006–2007 season. *First*, the champion from one of the five non-BCS conferences will automatically qualify for a BCS bowl if it is ranked in the top 12 or in the top 16 and higher than a BCS conference champion. *Second*, a new national championship game was created, to be hosted by one of the four BCS sites but one week after the other four bowls.

Appearing in one of the BCS bowls is important for the status, television exposure, and money it brings the participants. In 2003, ABC paid US$100 million to broadcast the BCS bowls, while the television rights for the other 24 bowl games sold for less than US$20 million. The eight teams appearing in the BCS bowls were paid more than US$117 million in 2003. The distribution of revenue for these bowls will be examined in more detail in Chapter 2, which focuses on cartels in college sports, and again in Chapter 7, which examines the role of the media. The BCS changed yet again in 2012, adopting a four team playoff beginning in 2014, culminating in the national championship game. More detail about the new playoff system is covered in Chapters 2, 7, and 9.

What about the teams relegated to one of the minor bowl games? While these schools might receive US$1 million or more, the expenses can be nearly as large. They are usually required to buy a large block of tickets, and if they are unable to resell them to their fans they must cover the expense. A bowl invitation is usually viewed as a way to reward those who have supported the team, and a large number of individuals expect to get a free trip to somewhere warm, including the band, cheerleaders, administrators, and boosters. The cost of transporting, housing and feeding upwards of 500 people is significant.

In basketball, the first college championship was the 1938 National Invitation Tournament (NIT) in New York City. Originally organized by the Metropolitan Basketball Writers Association, management was handed over to the Metropolitan Intercollegiate Basketball Association (MIBA), a group of five NYC colleges, in 1940. The first NCAA championship tournament was played in 1939.

There were just eight teams, which were the winners of their conference championships. The University of Oregon from the Pacific Conference defeated Ohio State of the Big Ten to win the title.

In the early years, the NIT was able to consistently attract some of the best teams in the country. In the days before national television coverage, the media exposure surrounding an event in New York City was a powerful lure for the colleges and talented players hoping for a professional career. Also, the independent colleges were not eligible for the NCAA Tournament.

To establish its dominance as the premier college basketball tournament, the NCAA expanded its field and extended invitations to nationally ranked teams that did not happen to be conference champions, including the independents. They also forbade any team that was invited to its tournament to play in the NIT instead. With the NIT relegated to a tournament for teams that could not qualify for the real thing, the MIBA sued the NCAA for restraint of trade under federal antitrust laws. With the trial underway, the NCAA purchased the rights to the NIT in 2005 for US$56.5 million, putting a quick end to the litigation.

Television has made the NCAA Tournament, known by the registered trademark March Madness, an immense success. The championship game was televised locally for the first time in New York City, with an estimated viewing audience of 500,000. The first national TV broadcast of the NCAA championship game was in 1954, and the first network broadcast was on NBC in 1969. NBC also broadcast first and second round games on stations in local markets. In 1980, the new ESPN signed its first contract with the NCAA to show regional games. CBS took over the broadcast of all games in 1991, and in 1999, it signed a US$6 billion contract to continue through 2013. CBS, now in partnership with Turner Broadcasting, continues to hold the broadcasting rights. In 2010, it signed a 14-year contract for US$10.8 billion. As we indicate below, the basketball broadcasting rights constitute the single largest source of revenue for the NCAA. The NCAA collects additional revenue from corporate sponsors, including a US$500 million 11-year marketing deal with Coca-Cola. Finally, there is strong demand for tickets. In 1993, total paid attendance exceeded 700,000 for the first time, with the Final Four played in the spacious New Orleans Superdome. The 2012 tourney, with the championship again at the Superdome, drew a similarly large turnout.

1.6.9   *NCAA finances*

It is fitting to end this chapter with a look at the finances of the NCAA. For 2011–2012, total revenue was US$872 million, total expenses were US$801 million, and US$71 million was added to the association's reserves (retained earnings).[17] The relative sizes of revenue sources and the expenditure categories for the 2011–2012 are shown in Figures 1.2 and 1.3.

On the revenue side, the sale of television and marketing rights, primarily for the men's basketball tournament, generated US$706.3 million, or 81% of the total. Ticket sales for championships, also including men's basketball, brought in another US$95.9 million, or 11% of the total. The combination of television/ marketing rights and ticket sales for championships accounted for 92% of revenue. The remainder came from investment income (US$34.9 million), the NIT tournament and operations of Limited Liability Corporations (US$17.4 million), sales and services (US$8.7 million), and all other (US$8.7 million).

---

[17] You may be wondering: a NCAA budget of more than US$800 million does not sound like a lot of money, especially in comparison to the earnings generated by the high profile schools. For example, Ohio State's Athletic department had a proposed budget of US$126 million for 2011–2012 and Texas has revenues of US$150 million in 2011. For colleges and universities, especially in DI, disbursements from the NCAA are not trivial but are generally outweighed by myriad other revenue resources available to athletic departments. The NCAA itself says that "[t]he most recent estimate from the NCAA research staff is that college athletics programs annually generate about US$6.1 billion from ticket sales, radio and television receipts, alumni contributions, guarantees, royalties and NCAA distributions. Another US$5.3 billion is considered allocated revenue, which comes from student fees allocated to athletics, direct and indirect institutional support, and direct government support." (NCAA, n.d., 'Frequently asked questions'). Athletic department finances are examined in detail in Chapter 6.

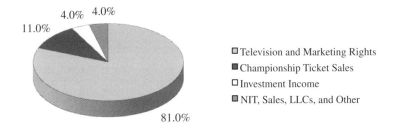

Figure 1.2. NCAA revenue for 2011–2012.

Source: NCAA (http://www.ncaa.org/wps/wcm/connect/public/NCAA/Finances/index.html).

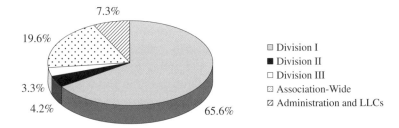

Figure 1.3. NCAA distributions and expenses for 2011–2012.

Source: NCAA (http://www.ncaa.org/wps/wcm/connect/public/NCAA/Finances/index.html).

The NCAA's expenses consist primarily of payments to its members, both schools and conferences. The colleges and universities in Division I received a total of US$504 million in 2011–2012. A total of US$202 million was distributed based on each school's performance in the men's basketball tournament over the previous six years. Another US$202 million was awarded based on the number of full-time equivalent grants-in-aid each school provided to student-athletes (US$134.7 million) and the number of sports it sponsors (US$67.3 million). The schools also received a total of US$24.6 million to enhance academic-support programs, such as tutorial services.

Besides payments directly to the schools, the Division I conferences received a total of US$42.9 million. Conferences that sponsor men's or women's basketball were given US$8.3 million in grants to expand opportunities for women and minorities, improve officiating, and develop educational programs on drug use and gambling. They collected US$15.1 million for the Special Assistance Fund for Student-Athletes and US$51 million for the Student-Athlete Opportunity Fund. The Special Assistance Fund is intended to meet emergency or other essential needs when other financial assistance is not available. According to the NCAA (n.d., Section 6) the purpose of the Opportunity Fund is to:

> assist student-athletes in meeting financial needs that arise in conjunction with participation in intercollegiate athletics, enrollment in an academic curriculum or that recognize academic achievement. Accordingly, receipt of Student-Athlete Opportunity Fund monies shall not be included in determining the permissible amount of financial aid that a member institution may award to a student-athlete. Further, inasmuch as the fund is design to provide direct benefits to student-athletes, the fund is not intended to be used to replace existing budget items.

The final amount allocated to Division I was US$80 million to cover the costs of the championship tournaments, including travel expenses for the teams and officials. The grand total was US$584 million, or 63% of all NCAA expenses. Division II schools, conferences, and championships received a total of US$32 million, and US$24 million was paid to Division III conferences and championships. These represent 4% and 3% of the NCAA's budget, respectively.

A total of US$56 million, or 13% of expenses, was for programs considered to be association-wide rather than for a particular division. These include legal services, public relations, student-athlete insurance, governance, enforcement, and general administration. The remaining 7% of expenses were for administration and operation of the LLCs, including the eligibility clearinghouse.

1.7 Chapter Summary

Early American colleges did not encourage athletics, leaving students to organize their own competitions with little faculty oversight.

As colleges became universities and grew in size, they discovered that intercollegiate athletics were an effective way to promote the institution and attract additional students. As higher education became big business, so did college sports.

At the beginning of the 20th century, the popularity of football was threatened by increasing violence on the field. It took the creation of a new organization, which would later become the NCAA, to force changes in the rules. The NCAA went on to focus on other issues related to intercollegiate athletics, including amateurism, academic standards, the rising cost of sports facilities, the status of coaches, scheduling of games during the academic year, the effect of professional leagues on college sports, and the effect of adverse media coverage.

With the explosive growth of higher education after World War II, the gap in size between large and small institutions increased. Some schools had significantly more resources to devote to athletics than others, making competition between them unrealistic. The NCAA divided its membership into two divisions in 1968, and then three divisions in 1973. For competition in football, the top division was further split into two subdivisions in 1978. Schools are also organized into conferences, such as the Big Ten, Pac 10, and SEC.

The revenue generated each year by television coverage (currently in the hundreds of millions of dollars) has had a profound impact on college sports. The NCAA was initially able to limit the number of football games broadcast each week, resulting in higher prices and substantial profits. As the revenue increased, so did the competition for the largest share. With the help of a favorable antitrust decision by the Supreme Court in 1984, the strongest competitors were able to break free and negotiate their own contracts. Television revenue has also fueled the men's basketball tournament and the football bowl games. The current BCS system bestows tens of millions of dollars each year on schools in the elite conferences.

You now have a good grasp on the origin and evolution of the NCAA. While this chapter has introduced some economic concepts like fixed, marginal, and sunk costs, it has not yet provided you with an economic perspective of the NCAA as an *organization*. As we move forward, you will learn how economic theory helps explain the NCAA as the entity that sanctions college sports, establishes championships, and defines and enforces the rules. Theory also sheds light on the NCAA's relationship to the hundreds of schools that make up its membership. The next chapter explores the economics of the organization, offering a perspective on college sports that is not widely understood.

1.8 Key Terms

40/60/80 Rule	Little Dutch boy
AAU	Logrolling
AIAW	Marginal cost
BCS	Morrill Act
CFA	NAIA
Competitive balance	NCAA
Death penalty	Non-excludable
Economies of scale	Non-rival
Equivalency sport	Proposition 16
Externality	Proposition 42
Fixed cost	Proposition 48
FBS	Proposition 68
FCS	Public good
Free riding	Rule 1.6
Head count sport	Sanity Code
Home rule	Sherman Act
IAAUS	Sunk cost
IFA	Television plan
Law of unintended consequences	Title IX

1.9 Review Questions

1. What are four ways that institutions of higher education have changed since 1800?
2. Why were alumni influential in the early days of college sports?

3. How did the media add to the popularity of college football? How did it benefit from that popularity?

4. Why was the Intercollegiate Conference of Faculty Representatives formed? What is it known as today?

5. What are the two conditions that define a public good? Can you list three non-athletics examples of a public good? Why are many public goods provided by the government rather than voluntary markets?

6. What is an externality? What are the two kinds of externalities? In what sense does it result in a market failure?

7. Burlette Carter mentions six debates that prevailed in the first 25 years of the NCAA's history. What were those debates?

8. What was the Sanity Code?

9. What was the 1.6 rule? What is the 40/60/80 rule?

10. Why was the NCAA separated into divisions?

11. Explain the differences between the three subdivisions in Division I.

12. Who were the members of the CFA? Why did they oppose the NCAA's television plan?

13. Does the NCAA control postseason competition in all sports? If not, who does?

14. What are the primary sources of revenue for the NCAA? What are their primary uses for that revenue?

1.10 Discussion Questions

1. Why was violence in college football a good example of "free-riding"?

2. What are some of the explicit economic costs associated with new facilities construction? What is the primary implicit cost?

3. What are some of the problems associated with scheduling games and practices?

4. Do you think any of those debates mentioned by Burlette Carter are still relevant in today's college sports world?

5. After 1973, schools offered scholarships year-to-year instead of a full four years. What are the pros and cons of this change

from the perspective of a student-athlete, a head coach, the Athletic Director, and the president of the university?

6. How might a student-athlete's education be negatively impacted by the 40/60/80 rule?

7. Is your institution a member of the NCAA? What conference does it belong to? Does it play all sports in the same conference?

8. What is the mission statement for your college or university (look in the catalog or web site)? Does it reference athletics? Assuming that you can find the institution's budget, does the amount spent on athletics reflect the mission statement?

9. Why do you think Boston College, the University of Miami, and Virginia Tech wanted to leave the Big East Conference to join the ACC? Why would the other ACC schools allow them to join?

10. Why did Oklahoma and Georgia challenge the television plan? Does the 1984 ruling by the Supreme Court make sense to you from the perspective of economic analysis? Explain using basic economic theory.

11. What is the purpose of collegiate sports in the United States (why do universities have intercollegiate sports programs)?

12. The first universities were modeled along the lines of institutions of higher education in Europe, especially universities in England and Germany. But those universities never included intercollegiate sports as part of the curriculum. This remains true even in the present day. Moreover, with the exception of schools in Canada, no university outside of North America considers competitive sports to be part of the mission of post-secondary education. Can you think of some reasons why the United States and Canada are unique? In other words, what factors contributed to the rise of college sports as part of university life and why missing from schools around the world?

13. Can you think of an economic argument why the NCAA had different scholarship rules for head count and equivalency sports?

1.11 Assignments/Internet Questions

1. Search for the NCAA Injury Surveillance System. Compare the number of injuries by sport and how rates have changed in recent years. Can you find any evidence of catastrophic injuries?
2. Visit the web sites for four Division I-A conferences and determine whether membership has changed in the last five years.
3. Visit the NCAA web site (www.ncaa.org) and search for information on the most recent NCAA convention. Examine the *Proceedings* and summarize one of the proposals that was voted on.
4. Visit the NCAA web site (www.ncaa.org) and locate the page on Finances under About Us. Examine the budget for the most recent year and compare it to the information in this text. How much has the total amount changed? Have the percentages for expenses and revenue changed substantially?
5. In the state where your school is located, how many D-I FBS institutions are there? List them. How many D-I FCS? List them. D-II? D-III?

1.12 References

49 NCAA Schools Have New Addresses (2013, July 2). *The Seattle Times*, p. C6.

Bentley, H. W., J. T. McGovern, H. J. Savage and D. F. Smiley (1929). *American College Athletics*. New York: Carnegie Foundation for the Advancement of Teaching.

Bernstein, M. F. (2001). *Football: The Ivy League Origins of an American Obsession*. Philadelphia: University of Pennsylvania Press.

Carter, W. B. (2006). The age of innocence: The first 25 years of the National Collegiate Athletic Association, 1906–1931. *Vanderbilt Journal of Entertainment and Technology Law, 8*, 211–291.

Covil, E. C. (n.d.). Radio and its impact on the sports world. *American Sportscasters Online*. Retrieved from http://www.americansportscastersonline.com/radiohistory.html on July 25, 2012.

Cowen, T. and K. B. Grier (2012). What Would The End of Football Look Like? *Grantland.com*. Retrieved from http://www.grantland.com/story/_/id/7559458/cte-concussion-crisis-economic-look-end-football on July 24, 2012.

Crepeau, R. (2001, August 24). Thanksgiving & Football: They Go Way Back. *SportsJones.com*. Retrieved from http://www.sportsjones.com/sj/199.shtml on September 20, 2006.

Depken, C. A. (n.d.). Realignment and Profitability in Division IA College Football. Manuscript submitted for publication. Retrieved from http://belkcollegeofbusiness.uncc.edu/cdepken/P/confsize.pdf on July 25, 2012.

Evenson, B. J. (1993). Jazz age journalism's battle over professionalism, circulation, and the sports page. *Journal of Sport History*, 20, 229–246.

Gall, A. E. (1929, November). Cartier Field — The old and the new. *The Notre Dame Scholastic*.

Ingrassia, B. M. (2011). Public influence inside the college walls: Progressive Era universities, social scientists, and intercollegiate football reform. *The Journal of the Gilded Age and Progressive Era*, 10(1), 59–88.

Miller, J. J. (2011). *The big scrum: How Teddy Roosevelt Saved Football*. New York, NY: HarperCollins Publishers.

Mondello, M. (2008). The college football postseason mess: Economic perspectives. In B. R. Humphreys and D. R. Howard (eds.), *The Business of Sports, Volume 3, Bridging Research and Practice* (pp. 168–189). Westport, CT: Praeger.

Mott, R. (1996, January 8). Association's Structure a Work in Progress. *The NCAA News Convention Supplement*, pp. 10–12.

National Collegiate Athletic Association (n.d.). *Finances*. Retrieved from http://www.ncaa.org/wps/wcm/connect/public/ncaa/finances/index.html on July 25, 2012.

Oriard, M. (1993). *Reading Football: How The Popular Press Created an American Spectacle*. Chapel Hill, NC: The University of North Carolina Press.

Oriard, M. (2012). NCAA academic reform: History, context and challenges. *Journal of Intercollegiate Sport*, 5(1), 4–18.

Riesman, D. and R. Denney (1951). Football in America: A study in cultural diffusion. *American Quarterly*, 3(4), 309–325.

Riess, S. A. (1995). *Sport in Industrial America: 1950–1920*. Wheeling, IL: Harlan Davidson, Inc.

Rudolph, F. (1962). *The American College and University: A History.* New York: Alfed A. Knopf.

Sandomir, R. (1991, August 25). Notre Dame Scored a $38 Million Touchdown on its TV Deal. *New York Times*, s 8 p 9.

Smith, R. A. (1988). *Sports and Freedom: The Rise of Big-time College Athletics.* New York: Oxford University Press.

Smith, R. A. (2001). *Play-by-play: Radio, Television, and Big Time College Sport.* Baltimore: Johns Hopkins University Press.

Sperber, M. (1988). *Onward to Victory: The Crises that Shaped College Sports.* New York: Henry Holt.

Sutter, D. and S. Winkler (2003). NCAA scholarships limits and competitive balance in college football, *Journal of Sports Economics*, 4(1), 3–18.

University of Southern California Public Infractions Report (2010, June 10). §A, Introduction. NCAA Major Infraction Database. Retrieved from https://web1.ncaa.org/LSDBi/exec/miSearch on July 18, 2012 (registration and login required).

Veblen, T. B. (1899). *The Theory of the Leisure Class.* New York: The Modern Library (1934).

Watterson, J. S. (2000a). *College Football: History, Spectacle, Controversy.* Baltimore, MD: The Johns Hopkins University Press.

Watterson, J. S. (2000b). The gridiron crisis of 1905: Was it really a crisis? *Journal of Sport History*, 27(2), 291–298.

Zimbalist, A. (1999). *Unpaid Professionals: Commercialism and Conflict in Big-Time College Sports.* Princeton, NJ: Princeton University Press.

Chapter 2

Cartels in College Sports

The NCAA is the clear choice for best monopoly in America.

— Robert Barro, Harvard economist

If it walks like a duck and talks like a duck, it is a duck.

— Robert Tollison, Clemson University economist,
on the NCAA cartel

2.1 Introduction

The statement above would probably surprise many college students, parents, alumni, fans, and legislators. Most people do not think of college sports as a business, and even if they did, with hundreds of colleges and universities competing against each other, how can the market for college sports be a **monopoly**? Monopolies act only to increase their profits at the expense of customers and suppliers. Does this model really describe the behavior of US institutions of higher learning? The NCAA's stated purpose is "to maintain intercollegiate athletics as an integral part of the educational program" (Article 1.3.1 of the NCAA constitution), not to promote anti-competitive behavior.[1]

A monopoly can occur in a market with multiple firms when they cooperate to limit the total quantity produced and thereby raise the price, a practice known as **collusion**, or in its most organized form, a **cartel**. While the conferences and the NCAA do facilitate the cooperation of their member institutions on rules of play, scheduling, recruiting, broadcasting, tournaments, and the amateur

---

[1]The NCAA's constitution, operating bylaws, and administrative bylaws appear in the Division I Manual (ncaapublications.com).

status of athletes, does this qualify them to be a monopoly? Professor Barro is hardly unique among economists in describing the market for college sports as a cartel, particularly for the big-time sports of football and men's basketball. For example, see Koch (1971), Becker (1987), Barro (2002), and Kahn (2007) among many others. For a good recent summary, see Tollison (2012).

Does this mean that colleges and universities are greedy profit-maximizers that reduce the benefits of college sports to the athletes and fans, or do their actions create a greater good? The enforcement of rules against paying college athletes can be seen as exploitation (keeping the price of labor low to increase profits) or as protection of a feature valued by fans, namely the amateur status of the players. In support of the latter, Vrooman (2009) argues that professional sports leagues are examples of natural cartels. Unlike the automobile industry, where a customer purchases either a Ford or a Toyota, the product of any sport is a game between two competing teams. One team cannot produce a game by itself. Would you buy a ticket to watch the New York Yankees play a baseball game against themselves? The appeal of the product also depends on the quality of both teams. Would you pay to see the Yankees play a local semi-pro team? As he notes, "[T]he natural duality of sports leagues implies that any team is only as strong as its weakest opponent" (Vrooman, 2009, p. 5). Rules that limit the ability of a few teams to dominate the sport will improve competitive balance and its popularity, and while college sports has inherent differences from professional sports, they share this basic feature. Cartels can create good outcomes, even if the reason for their behavior is to increase profits (cooperation = good entertainment = lots of fans = high profits).

This chapter begins with an overview of the economic theory of collusion, including the inherent internal struggles and how they can be overcome. The theory is then used to identify and analyze examples of collusive behavior in big-time college sports. The results will be valuable both for understanding the actions of colleges and universities and suggesting possible reforms to benefit the student-athletes, the fans, and the institutions of higher education.

2.2 Collusion and Cartels

Collusion occurs when the firms in a market cooperate rather than compete with each other. In its simplest form, the firms agree to raise their prices. This is commonly known as **price-fixing**, and it is strictly illegal in the United States. It can also be surprisingly difficult to accomplish. While they all want to charge a higher price, the result will be less total quantity demanded by consumers, which means total output will also have to decrease. A higher price with a lower quantity is good, but a higher price with the same or higher quantity is even better. If one of the firms chooses not to reduce its output, it will be unable to sell it all if it charges the same high price as the others. It may lower its price slightly to attract customers away from the other firms. With their sales falling even more than they expected, the other firms will probably retaliate and the agreement will fall apart. The renegade firm may also resort to other methods to attract additional customers, such as advertising and product innovation. The cost of such non-price competition can quickly dissipate the gains from raising prices.

In some cases, market conditions favor successful collusion. Beginning in the 1950s, the Ivy League colleges agreed to limit the amount of need-based financial aid they offered to prospective students. The schools, known collectively as the Overlap Group, met each year to set the size of a standard aid package. By reducing financial aid, this practice effectively raised the price paid by students (and their parents). The system worked well because the Ivy League reputation allowed them to be highly selective, that is, accept only a fraction of those that applied for admission. Even with a higher price, there was still enough demand to allow each school to fill its entering class. They were not tempted to offer slightly higher financial aid to lure students away from the other schools.[2]

---

[2] The government began an investigation of this practice and filed an antitrust lawsuit in 1991. The schools agreed to stop colluding, but Congress passed legislation that allowed limited agreements between colleges on financial aid.

In many other cases, the urge to compete and the lack of trust among firms are too strong, and a simple agreement to raise prices is not sustainable. An alternative is a cartel. a more structured type of collusion, with formal agreements on how much each firm will produce and sell, and limits on other forms of competition, such as advertising. For example, the Organization of Petroleum Exporting Countries (OPEC) meets regularly to decide how much crude oil each member country should produce. By limiting their total output, the market price of oil increases. For decades, DeBeers has successfully controlled the world price of diamonds by arranging with the major producers, including the former Soviet Union, to sell all diamonds through a single location in London. The DeBeers cartel strictly controls the number of diamonds released to the market, leading to much higher prices and higher profits for its members.

A cartel can control the price charged for the output (e.g., tickets to a baseball game) or the price paid for an input (baseball players). In the past, Major League Baseball owners agreed to limit the ability of players to switch teams, which enabled them to keep salaries low. This practice was known as the Reserve Clause. The owners could decide to trade a player to another team, but the player could not try to get a higher salary by having teams compete for his talents. A player's only leverage to negotiate for a higher salary from his current team was the threat of leaving professional baseball completely. When the owners' collusive conduct was declared to be illegal, and players were able to become free agents, salaries increased dramatically.

So are college sports a cartel? To answer this question, we must explore cartel behavior in more detail, review the history of college sports and the NCAA, and then determine whether it fits the pattern of a cartel.

2.3 The Three Challenges

For any form of collusion to be successful, the conspirators must overcome three inherent problems: reaching **agreement** on the appropriate actions by all members of the group, preventing **cheating** by some members, and dealing with **entry** into the market by producers attracted by the high profits. We will discuss each of these challenges in order.

2.3.1 *Agreement*

In theory, a cartel should make decisions as if it were a monopoly, with the members behaving like the divisions of one large firm. But there is a big difference between a single large firm and a group of smaller ones acting together. For a monopoly, if one of its factories is old and inefficient, production would be shifted to one that operates at a lower cost per unit, resulting in higher overall profits for the firm. In a cartel, while such a decision would increase total profits, it would reduce profits for one producer and increase them for another.[3] In the absence of some form of profit sharing between the members, the losing firm would not agree to a lower output target while others are producing more, preferring an equal output for each producer.

Figure 2.1 illustrates the situation of two firms, with firm #2 having a higher **marginal cost** curve than for firm #1. Suppose that the firms agree to share the market, so that each firm's demand curve is one half of the total (represented by 1/2D in the figure). Notice that the profit-maximizing price (the price that corresponds to the quantity where **marginal revenue** equals marginal cost) is higher for firm #2 than for firm #1, while its profit-maximizing quantity is slightly lower. The problem is that if firm #1 charges a lower price than firm #2, it will capture more than half of the market, resulting in less demand (and thus less profit) for firm #2. To keep its share of the market, firm #2 would have to match #1's lower price, which also reduces its profits. If the firms were acting as a monopolist to maximize joint profits, with a combined marginal cost curve (MC1 + MC2) and the entire market demand

---

[3] The increase in profits for one firm would be larger than the decrease in profits for the other firm, so total profits increase.

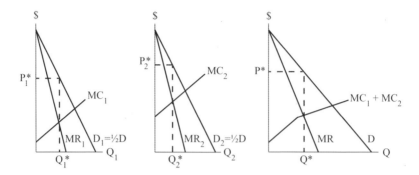

Figure 2.1. Collusion with cost differences.

curve, the optimal price (P*) would be between the values for each firm. Just reaching an agreement on output targets can become quite complicated!

A difference in costs is not the only possible cause of disagreements. Suppose that the products sold by the members of the cartel are not identical, and that consumers consider some to be better than others. If you were the producer of the less popular good, would you agree to charge the same price as the other producers? If you did, you would not be able to sell your entire output. Having different objectives can also create problems. Some firms may be focused on increasing profits in the short term, while others would prefer to sacrifice some current profits to increase market share and long-term profits.

Have you ever been required to do a group project for a class? One of the first problems is getting everyone to agree on a time to meet. While some people will get exactly the time they wanted, others will end up making sacrifices (rearranging a work schedule, paying for an extra hour of childcare, missing a favorite TV show). These people may resent the rest of the group and not work as hard as they might have, hurting everyone's grade. They may also decide to join a rival group. In the world of cartels, if an agreement favors some producers over others, it may be sowing the seeds of discontent and eventual collapse.

2.3.2 *Cheating*

If you were a member of a cartel, reaping above normal profits, would you be tempted to violate the agreement, and if so, how? Even in a cartel, each firm will act in its own self-interest, not for the good of the other firms. If its self-interest is served by cooperating with the others, it will do so. But if there is a way to increase profits even more, it will do that instead.

Each firm does not agree to reduce its output unilaterally because it will benefit directly. If it reduces its output, the market price will not rise appreciably and its market share and profits would fall. However, if *all* the firms reduce their output at the same time, the market price will rise, market shares will remain constant, and everyone's profits will increase. Each firm only reduces its output because all of the others agree to do the same. If it did not believe that the others would abide by the agreement, neither would it.

Unfortunately, if a firm believes that the others will *decrease* their output, the resulting rise in market price creates an incentive to *increase* its own output, causing its profits to increase even more dramatically. If the other firms do something that increases the profit per unit, why reduce your output? Every extra unit you sell will bring in a significant profit. You may be tempted to exploit the willingness of others to reduce their output to make even higher profits for yourself.

Economists use **game theory**, a model of behavior developed by mathematicians such as John Nash, to explain cheating and the unstable nature of cartels. A common illustration of game theory is the **Prisoners' Dilemma**. Suppose that two criminals, Bob and Sue, have been arrested for a theft at a jewelry store. The police find some of the stolen goods in their apartments, but they cannot prove that Bob and Sue were the ones to actually rob the store. As they are being taken to jail, Bob and Sue agree to not confess to the robbery. They know that without a confession from one of them, they can only be convicted of possession of stolen property. However, the detectives are clever. They put the two criminals in different rooms and make each one the same one-time offer. In return for confessing to the robbery and agreeing to testify against their partner, the district attorney will ask for a light sentence, perhaps even probation. However, if one of them does not confess, and their partner does, then they will be sentenced to a long stretch in the slammer. Each one is told that their partner is being given the same offer, and that they must make their choice now. Anyone who has watched crime shows on television is probably familiar with this gambit. The possible outcomes are summarized in the payoff matrix in Figure 2.2.

Given this situation, what should Sue do? If she believes that Bob is a standup guy and will not confess, she can either not confess and serve two years, or confess and serve just one year. If she believes that Bill is a ratfink and will confess, she can choose to not confess and serve ten years, or confess and serve five years. Whether Bill confesses or not, it turns out that she gets the shortest sentence by confessing. This is known as a **dominant strategy**. Faced with the same situation, Bill will also confess to the crime, and both will be sentenced to five years in prison.

What would have been the optimal outcome for the criminals? It is for neither one to confess and to both serve two years for possession of stolen property. However, each person acts to either exploit their partner (to get a 1 year sentence) or out of fear that their partner will attempt to exploit them (to avoid a 10 year sentence). They will both end up spending five years in jail.

Why do criminals not always betray each other in the real world? Because the actual payoff matrix is more complicated. If Bob testifies against his partner, expecting to serve a short time, he

		Sue	
		Confess	Not confess
Bob	Confess	Sue: 5 years Bob: 5 years	10 years 1 year
	Not confess	1 year 10 years	2 years 2 years

Figure 2.2.   The payoff matrix for a prisoners' dilemma game.

may serve a short but very unpleasant sentence. Prison is not a friendly place for squealers. Sue could also make a very clear threat while they are in the police car riding to jail. "Testify against me and I will kill you when I get out." If he makes the same threat, and they believe each other, then no offer of a shortened sentence will induce either one to confess.

If Bob and Sue are habitual criminals and are likely to be arrested again in the future, Sue can threaten to retaliate to Bob's confession today by testifying against him the next time the 'game' is played. For such a **repeated game**, one possible outcome is for each player to adopt a **"tit-for-tat" strategy**. Each person states that they will do tomorrow what the other person does today. If Bob does not confess this time, then Sue will not confess next time. If he tries to exploit her and confess this time, then she will confess next time. He might gain this once (serve one year rather than two), but he will be hurting himself in the long run by eliminating the possibility of a shorter sentence for both (when neither one confesses) in the future.

So how does game theory apply to the incentive for firms in a cartel to cheat? First, in many situations firms do not compete with each other just once, so the model of repeated games is more appropriate than the simple Prisoners' Dilemma. A firm may be tempted to increase its output or lower its price to get a higher short-term profit, but it knows that this may destroy the cartel and reduce profits in the long run. This increases the chance that collusion can be sustained.

Second, the firms can change the payoff matrix to reduce the incentive to cheat. If the colluding firms discover that one of their members is violating the agreement, they can impose a penalty. For example, the non-cheating firms can offer the cheater's regular customers a heavily discounted price and reduce its sales for a period of time. Once it is clear that cheating will be punished, the incentive to do so can evaporate. Of course, if the punishment is too severe, such as forcing the offender out of business, it is unlikely to ever be used. If it is too lenient, it may not have the desired effect.

Third, even if firms are able to suppress the incentive to compete with each other on price, other forms of competition may take over. The non-repeated Prisoners' Dilemma is more applicable to non-price competition, such as advertising and product innovation. The decision to launch a new advertising campaign or develop a new product will have lasting consequences. There are often advantages to acting first, making it difficult for the others to fully respond. With uncertainty about how rivals will respond and the fact that it will probably take them some time to do so, the temptation to try and steal their customers is stronger for non-price methods than it is for price cuts. Just because firms are able to cooperate to raise prices does not mean that they feel all warm and fuzzy about each other. If they can find a way to stab their rivals in the back and be safe from retaliation, at least for now, they will be tempted. In addition, the high price both increases the incentive to steal customers and gives firms the resources to spend on research & development and advertising. Each firm engages in such non-price competition both because it hopes to gain an advantage over its rivals and because it knows that its rivals will be attempting to do the same thing to it. The economic rents achieved by cooperating on price are competed away in the ensuing non-price arms race.

2.3.3 *Entry*

The more successful a cartel is at increasing the profits of its members, the more it encourages other firms to enter that market. The entrants can either join the cartel or act independently. If they join, then the existing firms must give up some of their market share to keep total output from rising and the price from falling. This will reduce profits per firm. If the entrants do not join the cartel, then the added output will depress the price, reducing total profits.

When OPEC reduced their output of oil and caused world oil prices to increase, oil exploration in other countries increased. Oil fields in areas such as Alaska and the North Sea were developed.

Before the rise in oil prices, this would not have been economically feasible, but they became profitable at the higher price. The result was an increase in world production capacity. The members of OPEC faced the choice of further reducing their own output to maintain the higher price or letting the price fall. The high price also encouraged energy conservation and the production of alternative energy sources. The long-term result was a decline in oil prices (after adjusting for inflation) and a decrease in OPEC's global market share.

2.4 The Keys to Success

Given these challenges, when is a cartel most likely to be successful? In general, when the rewards from cooperation are high and the costs are low. If collusion can increase profits substantially, the conspirators will find a way to solve any problems that arise. For an output cartel, a partial list of specific conditions includes inelastic demand, growing demand, a small number of competitors, no firms on the edge of bankruptcy, similar firms (products, cost structures and goals), and tolerant government policy. For a cartel that controls the market for an input, the conditions would include inelastic supply and growing supply. We will examine how each of these conditions affects the rewards and/or costs to collusion.

An output cartel operates by reducing the quantity produced and thereby increasing the market price of the product. If the **elasticity of demand** by consumers is low, then a relatively small decrease in total output will result in a large increase in market price and profits. This will occur if consumers consider the product to be a necessity and there are few close substitutes. A cartel consisting of the producers of purple paper clips is unlikely to be successful because any attempt to raise the price would cause consumers to buy blue, red or even plain paper clips (or staples, or binder clips, or…) instead. With highly elastic demand, the rewards from cooperation would be very low. Even if some consumers prefer purple paper clips, it would take a huge reduction in output to increase the price by even a small amount.

Similarly, for an input cartel a low **elasticity of supply** will result in a large decrease in the price paid for that input with only a small reduction in the quantity used. The reward to cooperation, namely a lower cost of producing goods that use that input, will be substantial. This will occur if the owners of the input have few alternative uses, so they will continue to supply it even when the price they are paid decreases. If the input is labor, economists refer to the wage that is high enough to convince them to forgo the alternatives (such as working in another occupation or staying home to take care of children) as the **reservation wage**. If many of the workers have low reservation wages, then they will continue to work even if the wage rate falls. Only those few workers with better alternatives to this occupation will leave the market, resulting in an inelastic (unresponsive) supply.

If demand is stagnant or contracting, it will be more difficult to assign enough of the reduced output to each firm to allow it to operate efficiently. Most producers prefer to operate in the region of 80–90% of capacity. This is because cost per unit generally falls until output approaches capacity, where it begins to increase (remember those U-shaped cost curves from microeconomics). If demand is growing, all firms can experience higher output and rising sales without resorting to cheating.

A cartel with a small number of members is more likely to be successful. Just from everyday life, it is obvious that trying to get fifty people to agree on something is much more difficult than for just two or three. The effect on cheating is a bit more complex. *First*, with a large number of conspirators, each one may think that they can get away with just a little bit of cheating. After all, the impact on any other member of the cartel will be quite small. Suppose that there are fifty firms, each selling 100 units. If a cheater can lure away just one customer from each of the others, its sales would increase from 100 to 149 units. The other firms might not notice the drop from 100 to 99. Even if they did, would it be worth retaliating against the cheater? This lowers the expected cost of cheating. *Second*, it is more difficult for a cartel to monitor fifty members than just a handful. Unless the cartel is willing to devote significant resources to monitoring each other, the chance of catching cheaters is lower. If the cartel does spend a large amount on monitoring, then the net gains from collusion are reduced. Every dollar spent is one less dollar of profit to act as an incentive to keep the cartel together. If a firm gains little from being part of the cartel, it will be less concerned about taking actions that might lead to its demise.

If there are any producers that are on the edge of failure, even with the cartel raising the price, then they have little to lose by cheating. If they do not cheat, then they will probably fail. If they do cheat, then there is at least a chance that they will succeed and survive. Even if the other producers detect the cheating, they may be persuaded to forgive and forget rather than risk a complete breakdown in the cartel. In recent years, it has been particularly difficult for airlines to raise fares because so many have been in bankruptcy or close to it. If the other airlines raise fares, the weak ones will be tempted to raise theirs by less and hope to increase their number of passengers. This just forces all airlines to revoke their fare increases, leaving everyone with lower profits.

As noted earlier, it will be easier for the firms to agree on output quotas and/or a price structure if the firms have similar products, costs and objectives. Having products of different perceived quality will require a more complex system with some prices lower than others. If not, the producers of the less desirable goods would lose too many customers to make collusion worthwhile. If some producers have substantially higher costs due to aging factories or small size, then they will want a higher price structure to make a profit. Firms with large factories and low costs would favor a somewhat lower price and greater sales. If some firms were more interested in increasing profits in the long run, they would also favor a lower price to increase demand for the product.

One of the most important issues related to the success of collusion is its legality. Overcoming the problems of agreement and cheating is much easier if the firms can meet to work out their differences. When collusion is against the law, having regular meetings only increases the chances of getting caught. By enforcing antitrust laws, not only does the government create a penalty that may dissuade some firms from colluding in the first place, it also makes collusion more difficult to manage. By agreeing to go easy on firms that turn themselves in, it also encourages firms that have been taken advantage of by other members of a cartel to get back at them.

In the United States, there are a number of statutory exemptions from antitrust laws. For example, the Sports Broadcasting Act of 1961 allows teams in professional sports leagues to cooperate to jointly sell broadcast rights.[4] Some activities by labor unions are also exempt, as is Major League Baseball (how could a senator vote against a law to protect the financial stability of "America's Pastime?"). There are also judicial exemptions. The courts have been willing to allow collusion if it results in some greater social good. After an impasse was declared in labor negotiations in the NFL in 1996, the owners collectively imposed a salary of US$1,000 per week for substitute players on development squads. The Supreme Court allowed this joint action by the team owners, arguing that such behavior as part of the collective bargaining process is important to the industrial relations system.

2.5   The Market for College Sports

The remainder of this chapter will examine whether the theory of cartel behavior applies to the market for college sports. An important first step in analyzing any industry is to carefully define the relevant market. For example, if you were studying the footwear industry, would you include dress shoes and running shoes in the same market? What about men's and women's dress shoes? Your

---

[4]The league is considered as a single entity, rather than a collection of individual teams. Antitrust laws outlaw conspiracy among a group of firms, but if there is just one big firm then there cannot be a conspiracy.

answers will determine whether Nike and the Italian designer Manolo Blahnik will be treated as competitors. In the case of college sports, is women's lacrosse at Harvard in the same market as men's basketball at Duke? Are men's basketball at Duke University and Carleton College, the latter a small liberal arts college in Minnesota, in the same market?

Economists resolve this type of issue by asking two questions. *First*, will customers switch from one product to another when their relative prices change?[5] In other words, do consumers treat the two as substitutes? Do men begin buying women's shoes if the price of men's shoes rises? Probably not, suggesting that they do not belong in the same market. *Second*, can the firms switch their production from one to the other in response to price changes? Could Nike easily begin selling expensive designer women's shoes if the price of sneakers falls? Nike may lack the design expertise, production facilities and distribution channels to give it a significant share of that market. Again, this means that the two products should be put in separate markets.

Is there evidence that consumers view various college sports as poor substitutes for each other? CBS and its advertisers certainly believe so. If not, why pay hundreds of millions to broadcast March Madness, the men's basketball tournament, and not even televise the field hockey championship? The only other college sport that can command such lucrative broadcast fees is football, both regular season and the bowl games. Many of the same companies advertise during both football and basketball broadcasts. If advertising fees for one increased significantly, no doubt they would reallocate their spending between the two. On this basis, we can put these two sports in one market and the rest of college sports in a different market.

---

[5] The change in demand for a product when the price of a different product changes is measured by the **cross-price elasticity** of demand. For substitute products, an increase in the price of one will cause demand for the other to increase, resulting in a positive cross elasticity. The cross-price elasticity is negative for complementary products, and it is zero if the products are unrelated (so the price of one has no effect on the demand for the other).

If there is another product to put in the same market with big-time college sports, it is professional sports. Colleges have always viewed professional teams as competitors for fan interest. As mentioned in Chapter 1, they once even tried to restrict their graduates from playing professionally. To increase the separation between college and professional football, an understanding was reached, with colleges playing on Saturday and the pros on Sunday. In basketball, both college and professional games are now played throughout the week, making them closer substitutes. Still, for many fans the excitement of a college game is not matched by the business-like attitude of highly paid professional athletes. The NCAA certainly goes to great lengths to remind the public that its players are students, not professionals. There is also the devotion by alumni of a particular school that a professional franchise cannot match. While not as clear cut as the difference between football and field hockey, we can discuss college sports as a distinct market as long as we keep the shrinking gap between college and professional in mind.

In the future, it is possible that the popularity of other college sports may increase enough that they will need to be put in the same big-money market as football and men's basketball. ESPNU, the new sports cable network, signed an agreement with the NCAA in 2005 to televise all or part of tournaments in 10 sports, including baseball, softball, ice hockey, lacrosse and wrestling. Parts of some of these Division I tournaments were already televised on ESPN or ESPN2, such as the semi-finals and finals for men's ice hockey (the Frozen Four), but this expanded coverage to include earlier rounds and switch some games from regional to national coverage. This expanded coverage was due in part to the willingness of the NCAA to cover production costs. The NCAA has subsidized telecasts of some Division I tournament games, such as early rounds of men's ice hockey, and in 2005, it decided to allocate funding for selected Division II championships. The objective is to make the public aware of these events and increase their popularity with viewers to the point that subsidies will no longer be needed. A new agreement with ESPN was signed in 2011 to cover 24 NCAA championships through the 2023–2024 season, with a total value of US$500 million.

Just as many viewers treat other college sports as a poor substitute for football and basketball, Division I-FBS is significantly different from the other NCAA divisions, and strong differences exist even between I-FBS conferences. Attendance at football games in Division I-FBS averages more than 45,000, with the elite programs limited only by the capacity of their stadiums. As of 2011, the University of Michigan had played 238 consecutive home games with attendance of at least 100,000. Tickets for individual games, when available, can sell for US$300 or more. Average attendance for Division I-FCS is less than 10,000; nearly five times lower than for DI-FBS. In Division III, attendance per game averages less than 2,000 and ticket prices are much lower, if not free. At Western Michigan University, a Division I-FBS school that is not a member of one of the big-time conferences, a sideline ticket sells for just US$20. Clearly, the fans treat football at the top DI-FBS programs as a unique product.

Television contracts tell a similar story. In 2008, the Southeastern Conference signed fifteen year broadcast deals in with CBS and ESPN worth roughly US$55 million and US$150 million per year, respectively. In 2013 they announced an extension to the ESPN contract, creating the SEC Network with an undisclosed increase in the dollar value (Sandomir, 2013). In contrast, the Mountain West Conference will be paid just US$18 million per year by ESPN starting in 2013 for the rights to football and basketball (Lyell, 2013), and its games are mostly relegated to late night and early morning broadcast times.

Even merchandise sales make the distinction clear. When Ohio State won the national football title in 2003, its royalties from merchandise sales doubled to US$5 million. This amount is bigger than the entire athletics budget of most Division II programs!

2.6 How Schools Benefit from Sports

The last step before examining cartel behavior in the market for football and men's basketball is to ask what the individual colleges and universities hope to gain from those programs. For most cartels, the members are profit-maximizing companies. Their objective is simple — maximize financial returns to their owners. Colleges and universities, many of which are public institutions, may have different desired outcomes that can complicate the analysis.

One possible objective is to generate profits that can be used to fund other programs on campus. To the extent that the revenue generated directly by the football and basketball programs (ticket sales, broadcast contracts, bowl games, the NCAA basketball tournament, merchandise sales and donations by boosters), exceeds the costs, the athletic department will have additional funds to pay for other sports programs, such as men's lacrosse or women's swimming. If an athletic department reports only a small surplus, or even a deficit, this may only mean that they spent the money on other sports rather than turn it over to the university's general fund. The university could also choose to devote the profits to academic pursuits instead, such as higher salaries to attract the best possible faculty.

With literally thousands of colleges and universities in the United States, there is considerable competition for student enrollment. Increasing enrollment brings more tuition revenue, and for public institutions, greater government subsidies. The marginal cost of educating these additional students can be quite low, with excess capacity existing in many classes (although many faculty will argue that adding ten more students to a class of twenty can affect teaching and learning adversely). Marketing campaigns directed at prospective students have been increasing steadily, including direct mail and media advertising. What better way to advertise than have millions of viewers tune in to watch a game or read reports in the sport pages? If the television network will pay you for the broadcast rights, even better!

An athletics program can also enhance loyalty on the part of alumni and other supporters of the institution. These people often show their support by making donations to the university. The donors may stipulate that funds go to a specific program, including athletics or academics. The money may be directed to athletic scholarships, a new stadium, faculty salaries, or a library.

What does it take to achieve these desired outcomes? In one word, winning. In the words of the late Vince Lombardi, legendary coach of the Green Bay Packers, "Winning isn't everything, it's the only thing." Few fans will attend games if there is little or no chance that their team will win. Teams that have poor regular seasons will not be invited to compete in the lucrative NCAA basketball tournament or the top-tier football bowl games. If the team is a perennial loser, that image can even be associated with the entire institution, hurting efforts to attract students. After all, if the school cannot field a winning football team, why would its academic programs and campus life be any different? Boosters will be unwilling to make generous contributions if there is little to show for their efforts. Losing can even become self-perpetuating, with the best athletes choosing to attend a school with a better record. Their path to the pros is not through a losing program. The relationship between spending on athletics, winning, and returns to the university will explored in greater detail in Chapter 6.

2.7 Evidence of Cartels

If there is an effective cartel operating in college football and basketball, we should be able to find evidence of high profits. We can also look for more direct evidence of cartel behavior, such as higher prices charged for their output or lower prices paid for their inputs.

2.7.1 *High profits?*

We saw in Chapter 1 that the amount of revenue flowing to athletic programs at the top-tier schools is substantial. How many of these programs are operating in the black, that is, with revenue greater than costs? Unfortunately, there is little consensus on profitability at Division I-FBS schools, in part because there is little incentive for athletic departments to report profits accurately. As we will examine in more detail in Chapter 6, the Athletic

Director (AD) may be reluctant to report a substantial profit to the university administration, which would probably appropriate it for other uses on campus. One solution is to use creative accounting to hide revenue or overstate costs. The AD can also allocate the profits from the football and basketball programs to subsidize other sports, resulting in a balanced budget for the entire department. If the profits from these sports are to be spent by someone on campus, the AD would probably prefer to be the one to do the spending.

Another way that high profits can be disguised is by paying artificially high salaries to coaches and other staff. Sharing **economic rents** with employees is common in cartels. For example, when the government prohibited price competition between airlines, the pilots were able to bargain for very high wages. This reduced the profits reported by the airlines and paid to their stockholders, but it really meant that the stockholders had to share some of their profits with the pilots. When airlines were deregulated and forced to compete on price, the result was lower airfares and eventually lower salaries for pilots. As we will see in Chapter 5, the salary of an elite college coach exceeds US$5 million per year. If college sports were unprofitable, do you think that they would be able to command such high salaries?

As discussed earlier, the lack of price competition in a cartel may lead to greater non-price competition. When airlines could not lure customers from their competitors by lowering fares, they began offering more frequent flights, more legroom, decent food and hired only single, attractive flight attendants. Flying between Detroit and Memphis four times per day with planes that are only half full is very costly compared to two full flights, but if customers are unable to choose an airline based on low fares they will use other criteria, such as the frequency of flights. Fares were high, but costs rose to match them. In college sports, if schools are unable to get the best athletes by paying them more, they will be compelled to spend money on the other things that the athletes look for, like luxurious locker rooms, state-of-the-art training facilities, and stays in five star hotels on road trips. College sports may be a successful cartel when it comes to price, but their inability to control other forms of competition can mean that they end up with little in the way of profits.

2.7.2   *Low input prices?*

One objective of a cartel is to lower the price paid for its inputs, with only a small reduction in the quantity offered by the suppliers of the inputs. In this case, the suppliers are the high school and junior college athletes who wish to play at the college level. The NCAA restricts the amount that colleges and universities can pay their players, and to make sure that each school has a chance to get a fair share of the talented athletes, they have rules about recruiting, limits on the number of student-athletes on the payroll (i.e., on scholarship), and rules to make it more difficult for students to transfer to a college that makes a better offer.

Economists measure the increased revenue generated by one more unit of an input as the **marginal revenue product**, or MRP. As will be discussed in greater detail in Chapter 3, according to economic theory the wage rate (w) should equal the MRP in a competitive labor market. However, if the college sports cartel is successful, then w will be less than MRP. Is there any evidence that $w <$ MRP in football and mens basketball?

To answer this question, we must first measure the wage rate for college athletes. As discussed in Chapter 1, NCAA rules place an upper limit on grants-in-aid equal to the dollar value of tuition and room and board for regular students. All other payments by the school or a booster are prohibited, whether in the form of cash or the use of an apartment or car. For Stanford University, a private school, the equivalency value exceeded US$40,000 in 2006. The dollar amount is usually smaller at public universities, which receive financial support from state governments and charge less for tuition. However, the tuition for students that are not residents of a state is often close to the amount at private schools. An out-of-state student attending the University of California would pay more than US$35,000 for tuition and fees in 2013.

Measuring the marginal revenue product is much more complex. How does an athletic team contribute to the revenue earned by the university? How does a particular athlete affect the contribution made by his or her team? As discussed above, a winning program can increase revenue to the school in a number of ways, including payments for bowl games, donations by boosters and more favorable media exposure for the university. Each player contributes by increasing the team's winning percentage. Putting a dollar value on that contribution is difficult.

The *San Jose Mercury News* (Wilner, 2006) estimated the MRP for Marshawn Lynch, the star tailback at the University of California-Berkeley. The newspaper collected data on the athletic department's revenue from ticket sales, donations, television contracts, corporate sponsorships and Pac-10 revenue sharing (but they omitted indirect benefits to the university, such as greater interest by prospective students). Total revenue for the football program in 2006–2007 was estimated to be US$25 million. To assign a value to each player on the football team, they used a formula based on the split of revenue in an actual market, namely professional football. In the NFL, the players get nearly 60% of team revenue. Adjusting for the fact that college coaches take a much larger share of revenue for their salary than do NFL coaches, this study estimated that California's players would receive 40% of the US$25 million if the school had to compete for their services. With the top running backs in the NFL paid 8% of total team payroll, they estimated Lynch's free-market value to be 8% of 40% of the US$25 million, or US$800,000. In return, the school provided him with an athletic scholarship worth US$16,800, plus the cost of books. In his case, w was certainly less than MRP!

Before considering this as proof of cartel behavior, you might be asking yourself about the rest of the players on the team. The MRP for second and third string players is probably much lower, perhaps even lower than their w. If their MRP is close to w, then the evidence for a cartel would appear to be much less compelling. However, unlike star athletes like Marshawn Lynch, these players were probably not heavily recruited out of high school. They were not expected to be "franchise" players that can make the difference between winning and losing big games. Just as football at UCLA is in a different market than Harvey Mudd's team, the elite athletes coming out of high school are in a different market than even the average DI-bound player. The evidence above suggests that in the market for the most talented recruits, the NCAA is apparently acting as a highly successful cartel. The members of the cartel simply choose to share some of the resulting profits with the less talented players (the difference between Lynch's estimated MRP and his w will cover the full scholarships of 47 other players).

You may also be thinking about highly recruited high school players that end up making only minor contributions to winning (and revenue). Some heavily recruited athletes end up as bench-warmers, not stars. This suggests that we should compare w to the *expected* MRP, not the MRP for the players like Marshawn that turn out to be as good, or better, than anticipated when they were recruited. Suppose that out of every ten highly recruited high school athletes, one goes on to be a star player and the rest contribute absolutely zero to revenue. In that case, the expected MRP would be one-tenth of US$800,000, or US$80,000. That is still far greater than w = US$16,800, and those assumptions are rather extreme. The case for an input cartel is hard to ignore. More evidence of the disparity between w and MRP will be examined in Chapter 3, The Labor Market for College Athletes.

> **Fast fact.** *On January 2, 2007, Marshawn Lynch announced that he would skip his senior year at California and enter the NFL draft. After just three seasons, he was already the schools second-leading rusher, with 3,230 yards. In his final game for the Golden Bears, he led his team to a 45-10 victory over Texas A&M in the Holiday Bowl.*

2.7.3 *High output prices?*

It is difficult to determine the extent to which the NCAA has been able to influence the price of the outputs, primarily television broadcasts of regular season games and postseason tournaments and bowl games. There is no doubt that prices are high, as was shown in Chapter 1, but what would they be without the cartel? One potential piece of evidence comes from the period after the NCAA lost its control over the broadcast of regular season football in 1984. Individual conferences were able to negotiate their own television contracts with the networks, resulting in more games on television. As shown in Table 2.1, when the number of televised games increased the price per game fell sharply. Comparing 1983 to 1985, the price paid by the networks decreased by almost 74% when the number of games increase by nearly 60%, causing total revenue to decrease significantly. The contract originally negotiated by the NCAA for the 1984 season, which was cancelled due to the court's decision, would have brought in US$134 million (in 2004 dollars). This suggests that the NCAA had been successfully increasing revenue by restricting the quantity supplied. However, the steep drop in prices after 1983 may have been due in part to a lack of experience in contract negotiations by the conferences, which the networks were able to exploit, rather than the increase in the quantity of games

Table 2.1.   Television broadcast contracts before and after the 1984 court decision (in millions of 2004 US$).

Year	Number of games	Total revenue	Price per game
1980	24	US$70.46	US$2.94
1981	24	68.00	2.83
1982	28	114.52	4.09
1983	28	120.35	4.30
1984	36	39.66	1.10
1985	42	47.00	1.12
1986	42	49.56	1.18
1987	42	46.17	1.10
1988	43	44.13	1.03

Sources: Fort (2011) and Kahn (2006).

available for broadcast. As demand has grown and the conferences have become more sophisticated in their dealings with the networks, the size of television contracts has increased dramatically.

As we saw in Chapter 1, and will revisit later in this chapter, the prices of broadcast rights for the postseason have skyrocketed. The most popular events are the NCAA men's basketball tournament and the BCS bowl games. The former generates hundreds of millions for schools in Division I, while the latter yields more than US$180 million each year for schools in the BCS conferences.

Is there significant evidence of a cartel in college sports? For most economists, the answer is a clear yes. We turn next to a more detailed analysis of how big-time college sports has dealt successfully (or not) with the challenges of agreement, cheating, and entry.

2.8 Cartel Agreements in College Sports

The agreements between schools cover both inputs and outputs. As discussed above, for the athletes this appears to be relatively straightforward — have the NCAA enforce a rule to pay them no more than the cost of tuition, room and board, textbooks and some fees.[6] The schools also agree to avoid non-scholarship inducements to prospective athletes, such as use of an automobile, a round of golf, or even popcorn and a soda at a baseball game. This covers the school and anyone associated with it, including alumni and other boosters. A booster who allows a student to use a cell phone for a long distance call, even if they have free nationwide calling, has caused a violation of the agreement.

Until 2012–2013, the NCAA also prohibited multiyear scholarships. Without such a ban, schools competing for the best prospects would be tempted to offer these students four-year scholarships. If the school cannot compete on the basis of the amount of the scholarship, at least they could compete by offering

---

[6]The rules are designed to avoid opportunities for the student to profit in any way other than attaining an education. For example, any textbooks purchased from the scholarship award are the property of the athletic department and must be returned upon completion of the degree program.

to cover the student's costs for all four (or five) years it takes to graduate. This could potentially increase costs for athletic departments that are stuck paying for scholarships for players that are not able to contribute as expected. For the athletic department it makes sense to cut their losses and offer the money to another prospect, even if the student cannot afford to remain in college. The members of the NCAA voted in 1967 to allow coaches to revoke multiyear scholarships for students who voluntarily withdraw from a sport, and in 1973 they limited the guaranteed length of a scholarship to just one year. The institution could choose to renew that offer each year, but an athlete who is injured or underperforms may not be renewed.

In October of 2011, the NCAA Division I Board of Directors approved a proposal to allow multiyear scholarship. More than the required number of 75 schools asked for an override and the Board elected to allow all 350 Division I members to vote on the issue. The attempt to override the Board's decision fell just two votes short of the required five-eighths majority. For some schools, the reason for opposing the change was about more than money. With a high turnover rate among head coaches, an athlete granted a five-year scholarship by one coach could end playing much of that time for a coach with a style of play where the athlete's skills are not a good fit. However, most of the opposition came from schools with smaller budgets for athletics, fearing that they could not afford to compete against richer programs. While a majority of the top programs did not oppose the plan, four of the ten schools with the wealthiest athletic departments voted for the override, as did the national champion in football, the University of Alabama.

At the end of the 2012–2013 recruiting season, a majority of schools in the major FBS conferences had offered multiyear scholarships to at least some prospective student-athletes. However, multiyear awards were less than one-tenth of all awards at those schools. The University of Illinois had the largest number at 192. Among the schools choosing to stay with one-year scholarships were Texas, Georgia Tech, and Oregon. (Wolverton and Newman, 2013)

The members of the cartel agreed in 1977 to limit the number of scholarships, which further reduced competition for players. For football, the maximum is 85 in Division I-FBS and 63 in I-FCS, while Division II is capped at just 36. By comparison, an NFL team is limited to a roster of 46 for each game plus seven reserves. Basketball teams in Division I are limited to 13 scholarships, and similar rules are in place for all other men's and women's sports. There are no limits on the number of players on the roster, and some sports have a significant number of athletes who do not receive any financial compensation.[7] The average Division I-FBS football team has 32 "walk-ons," players who were not recruited or awarded a scholarship. Many basketball teams have a few walk-ons.

By keeping the amount paid to athletes low compared to their financial value to the institution, the cartel creates an incentive to recruit the most talented players by whatever means necessary. In a free market, they would offer slightly more money than their rivals, but the agreement keeps that from happening. To avoid excessive spending on recruiting, a vast array of rules has been put in place over time. The number and timing of visits by a coach or other representative is restricted, as is the nature of visits by prospective students to campus. When the University of Oregon picked up prospects in private jets and drove them from the Eugene airport in Hummers, the NCAA quickly imposed rules forbidding their use. The NCAA is forced to keep up with colleges looking for new ways to stand out from the crowd.

For a period of time, the cartel members were also able to restrict the amount paid to another labor input, assistant coaches. In 1992, the NCAA implemented a rule that capped the salary of the least senior member of the coaching staff at US$12,000. It also limited their employment to five years. While the stated rationale was that this benefited those same assistant coaches by creating

---

[7]Football rosters are limited to 105 before the start of the academic year. In most sports there is no maximum size of the team, but a limited number can suit up for each game.

more entry-level positions, the number of coaches allowed by the NCAA was actually reduced from five to four. This practice only ended after a successful lawsuit by a group of assistant coaches (*Law v. National Collegiate Athletic Association*, 10th Cir. 1998). In fact, when the rule was overturned, a number of smaller schools expressed concern that schools with larger budgets would steal the best assistant coaches, not that the coaches would suffer from fewer openings. While the NCAA argues that low salaries are good for assistant coaches, there has never been an agreement to restrict payments to head coaches. In recent years, salaries for coaches at the top-tier programs have exceeded US$5 million. The economic reasons for such high salaries will be discussed in Chapter 5.

Perhaps the most difficult agreement to reach concerns building and upgrading facilities such as stadiums, arenas, practice fields, weight rooms and locker rooms. With no easy way to take into account different needs, existing facilities, use of facilities by other groups, it should be no surprise that there have not been any attempts to reign in this expensive form of competition between schools. Even a school like Baylor, which has not had a winning season in nine years, was compelled to spend more than US$2 million on a new locker room for its football team as a way to compete for players. Myles Brand, the former president of the NCAA, repeatedly called for discussions to end the spiral of escalating costs, but no action was or has been taken. He has also suggested that universities consider paying for these costs with funds from the general operating budget (see Box 2.1).

The lack of rules on spending for facilities demonstrates the existence of a cartel within the NCAA cartel. The elite schools, with revenue from loyal donors, ticket sales, and the proceeds from postseason bowls and tournaments, are able to perpetuate their advantage in recruiting the best high school athletes. As in many aspects of modern life, the gap between the haves and have-nots is only increasing.

The other major agreements concern the output market, namely the rights to televise regular and postseason football and

Box 2.1. Excerpt from the speech "Academics First: Progress Report" by NCAA President Myles Brand at the National Press Club, March 4, 2003.

There is another element to the reform movement, which is exceptionally difficult to know how to resolve. It is the rapidly increasing costs for a competitive program, especially in Division I-A. This problem has been labeled in the media and other quarters as "the arms race."

No single university can unilaterally withdraw from the arms race without putting its athletics program in an uncompetitive position. Like everyone else, salary and earning guarantees matter to coaches, and facilities do play a role in student-athlete recruiting.

It has been suggested that universities band together and agree to salary limitations and facility construction. Conferences are likely not a large enough group to be effective; it would take several conferences or, likely, all of the Division I-A schools organized through the NCAA to make a difference.

This approach, however, suffers from being illegal. Antitrust laws prohibit institutions from engaging in constraint of trade. When the NCAA tried to restrict the earnings of assistant basketball coaches several years ago, it was sued and lost the case, resulting in a US$55 million settlement.

The question before us soon may be whether the ingrained presumption that athletics departments should be self-sustaining is justified.

There is a truth about universities that is rarely spoken about in public. Namely, internal budgeting involves massive cross-subsidization. Research and graduate education is subsidized through undergraduate tuition. Federal indirect costs for research fall short of the actual expenses. Some academic programs are subsidized by others; for example, service courses in

(Continued)

Box 2.1.   (Continued)

English, math and psychology help support music and classics departments. This is perfectly acceptable, since a university must offer a wide range of subjects to be viable as an educational and research institution.

Is the next logical step to openly cross-subsidize athletics programs within the larger university budget? If we believe these programs have educational and developmental value in ways similar to a number of academic programs — and I certainly do — should they enjoy the same type of financial security as other academic programs? Of course, not every university's athletics program needs to be subsidized; some, in fact, can provide funds for academic programs.

---

basketball games. For the regular season, there are three issues that complicate the ability for cartel members to agree. First, if the number of games that will be sold to the networks is reduced to create a shortage and raise the price, which teams will participate in the televised games? For example, if the networks broadcast just two football games each weekend, then only 48 of the 120 I-FBS teams can make an appearance on national television that year. With some regional broadcast allowed the total could double, but that is still short of allowing all teams to appear. If the objective is to collect as much money as possible from the networks, the games that will attract the largest expected audience should be selected. Fans are more likely to watch games between highly ranked teams that are evenly matched (watching a blowout is much less exciting).

If this strategy maximizes the dollar value of the television contract, as long as each school's share is more than it could make selling its own broadcast rights in a competitive market, why is there a problem? One of the benefits to the college or university of a sports program is exposure. Prospective students and their parents, donors, legislators, high school teachers and high school athletes get a chance to see the school on television. Television coverage is also important to the athletic department itself. Many high school athletes have dreams of playing professionally, and it is important to get national recognition while in college to increase the chance of getting a lucrative pro contract. All else equal, a student will likely choose a school where he can count on playing in front of a national television audience. If only the best teams are televised, and that allows them to attract the best athletes, the lower-tier schools are caught in a Catch-22. They need top athletes to play at a level that national audiences will want to see on TV, but without that kind of exposure they will not be able to attract those top athletes.

A second issue is how to distribute the proceeds of the television contract. The conferences with the most popular teams will argue for a larger share, based on the fact that it was their teams that were responsible for generating the revenue. Within each conference, the teams that appear on television most often will want more money. This can create a widening gap between the haves and the have-nots. If the teams with the best records are selected more often for the Game of the Week on Saturday afternoon, and thereby get more revenue from the contract, they will have the resources to continue to support a winning program.

Chapter 1 detailed how the NCAA was able to overcome most of these issues and negotiate a single contract for all college football in 1952. It helped that the agreement did not have to be unanimous, only a voting majority. As long as a large block of schools did not break away, the NCAA could deal with lone dissenters. When the University of Pennsylvania negotiated its own contract, the NCAA simply banned other member schools from playing it. Without any opponents, Penn was forced to back down. The number of broadcasts was strictly limited, and only the most popular match-ups were televised. No school was allowed to play on television more than twice each year. The NCAA paid 90% of the proceeds to the schools that appeared on television, with the remaining amount distributed to the other colleges and universities.

By the 1970s, with the rising popularity of college football broadcasts, and therefore more money at stake, nearly everyone was unhappy with this arrangement. The conferences most responsible for generating the revenue were dissatisfied with the restrictions on the number of appearances. The smaller schools that did not appear on television wanted a larger percentage of the money. After all, by agreeing to appear on television infrequently, if ever, they were doing their part to limit output and maximize revenue. Why should they be denied a significant share of the proceeds? Remember, cartels work best when the members have similar products and costs, which was not the case here.

As discussed in Chapter 1, the College Football Association was formed in 1976 by members of the major football conferences. The purpose was to either get the changes they wanted within the NCAA or negotiate their own television contract. One favorable result for them was the NCAA's decision to split Division I into I-A and I-AA for football, with only the top 105 programs assigned to I-A. Some of the CFA members were dissatisfied with this and other concessions, and they filed an antitrust lawsuit against the NCAA. In 1984, the Supreme Court agreed that the NCAA was guilty of price-fixing, and the member institutions were free to negotiate their own TV contracts. Rather than each university negotiating on its own, the I-FBS schools attempted to form their own cartel within the NCAA cartel, with the CFA in charge. By limiting membership to schools with large programs, which have similar goals, costs, and products, they would have an easier time reaching an agreement. However, the CFA was unable to convince a coalition of the Big Ten and Pac-10 to join their new cartel, and the NCAA monopoly was replaced by a duopoly (two large producers, the CFA and the Big Ten/Pac-10). The number of televised games increased, with a predictable effect on prices. There were still enough differences within the CFA that some independents (particularly Notre Dame) and conferences decided after a time that they could make more profits on their own. The CFA ceased operation in 1997, and individual conferences now negotiate their own broadcast contracts.

The other major product for college sports is postseason games, including championship tournaments and bowl games. The basic issues are the same as for the regular season; which teams will participate and who will get the revenue? In the case of men's basketball, the NCAA retains control over the choice of teams and the distribution of the revenue (nearly US$11 billion over the life of the current 14 year contract). As noted in Chapter 1, most of the money goes to the members of Division I. Approximately half of that allocation is based on each school's performance in the men's basketball tournament over the last six years, so having a winning team is important financially. The evolution of the tournament will be covered in more detail in Chapter 7.

For football, there was no NCAA championship tournament until the 2014 season. Instead, another cartel formed within the NCAA. As seen in Chapter 1, the Bowl Championship Series (BCS) is an agreement between the major football conferences, the organizers of the major bowl games, and Notre Dame (the only remaining major independent). It effectively limited the appearances in those lucrative bowls to teams from the automatic-qualifying BCS conferences. The BCS bowls have been an immense financial success for the schools in those conferences and have a continued role in the new College Football Playoff.

The total revenue for the 2010–2011 BCS games was US$182 million. A small portion of that amount, less than US$3 million, was paid to the DI-FCS conferences. The lion's share is paid to the six BCS automatic qualifying conferences, based on the number of teams they send to these bowls and the national championship. The revenue sources (from the BCS's media contracts/sponsorships and the individual bowl organizing committees) and distributions (to each conference) for the period 2008–2011 are shown in Table 2.2.

There are other postseason bowl games, but none that come close to the BCS bowls. The number of secondary bowls sanctioned by the NCAA is growing, from 13 in the early 1990s, to 18 in 1999, 24 in 2006, and 30 in 2012. This expansion can dilute the value of any individual game. Average attendance for all 35 bowls in

Table 2.2.   Revenue and conference distributions for BCS bowl games (in US$).

	2008–2009	2009–2010	2010–2011
Television/Title Sponsorships	90,200,000	96,400,000	120,000,000
Revenue from:			
Fiesta Bowl	6,000,000	6,000,000	6,000,000
Sugar Bowl	6,000,000	6,000,000	6,000,000
Orange Bowl	6,000,000	6,000,000	6,000,000
National Championship	6,000,000	6,711,698	8,000,000
Subtotal	24,000,000	24,711,698	26,000,000
Rose Bowl Payout	33,964,228	34,058,912	35,912,310
Total BCS Revenue	148,164,228	155,170,610	181,912,310
Big Ten	23,172,725	16,295,461	28,515,095
Southeastern	23,172,725	16,247,847	28,515,095
Big 12	23,172,725	20,795,460	22,515,095
Pac-12	18,672,743	19,787,058	28,515,095
Atlantic Coast	18,672,725	16,247,847	16,594,444
Big East	18,672,725	16,247,847	16,594,444
Mountain West	9,788,800	9,878,710	12,734,033
Western Athletic	3,224,000	7,798,925	4,033,917
Conference USA	2,659,200	2,719,140	3,333,800
Mid-American	2,094,400	2,139,355	2,633,683
Sun Belt	1,529,600	15,595,700	1,933,567
Notre Dame	1,331,860	1,352,565	1,702,742
Big Sky	225,000	225,000	250,000
Atlantic 10	225,000	225,000	250,000
Mid-Eastern	225,000	225,000	250,000
Missouri Valley	225,000	225,000	250,000
Ohio Valley	225,000	225,000	250,000

(*Continued*)

Table 2.2. (*Continued*)

Southwestern Athletic	225,000	225,000	250,000
Southland	225,000	225,000	250,000
Southern	225,000	225,000	250,000
Big South			250,000
U.S. Military Academy	100,000	100,000	100,000
U.S. Naval Academy	100,000	100,000	100,000
Total BCS Distribution	148,164,228	155,170,610	181,912,310

Source: NCAA (http://www.ncaa.org/wps/wcm/connect/public/NCAA/Championship+Bids/Postseason+Football/Financial+Reporting).

2011–2012 dropped below 51,000 for the first time since 1979 (Solomon, 2012). An invitation to one of the minor bowls is based in large part on the school's ability to get its fans to travel to other parts of the country and spend freely once they are there. The schools are often required to buy a large number of tickets, which they can try to resell or give to faithful supporters. They often spend nearly as much transporting, feeding, and housing a large contingent of players, administrators, band members, cheerleaders, and boosters as they are paid by the bowl organizers. Zimbalist (1999, p. 123) describes the situation of Michigan State, which spent US$150,000 more than it earned for appearing in the 1998 Aloha Bowl, including US$300,000 for a chartered flight to Hawaii.

The bowl system illustrates an effective solution to the problem of reaching an agreement among a disparate group — simply exclude the weaker ones. A group of just the strongest producers will have more in common and find agreement much easier to reach and sustain. This method also serves to increase the gains to the members of the cartel, since they are not sharing any profits with the excluded producers. Andrew Zimbalist likens this to a caste system, with the 65 teams from the top conferences in the privileged group (Woolsey, 2006). The six elite conferences are the Atlantic Coast (ACC), Big 12, Big East (renamed the American Athletic Conference in 2013), Big Ten, Pac-12, and Southeastern

Table 2.3.   2011–2012 revenue and expenses for all bowl games, by conference (amounts of US$).

Conference	Bowl revenue	Participating institutions' expenses	Excess of revenue over expenses
ACC	42,533,800	13,364,046	29,169,754
Big East	29,617,134	8,103,773	21,513,361
Big Ten	46,744,601	18,316,518	28,428,083
Big 12	40,867,131	14,175,304	26,691,827
Conference USA	7,976,796	3,372,512	4,604,284
Mid-American	4,492,085	2,783,799	1,708,286
Mountain West	6,338,615	5,272,425	1,066,190
Independent	5,963,629	2,601,862	2,461,767
Pac-12	38,840,263	11,311,887	27,528,376
SEC	47,182,963	16,356,936	30,826,027
Sun Belt	3,895,880	2,029,539	1866,341
WAC	2,800,850	1,218,683	1,582,167
Other	2,450,000		2,450,000
2011–2012 Totals	278,803,747	98,907,284	179,896,463
2010–2011 Totals	281,045,775	90,944,650	190,101,125
2009–2010 Totals	237,445,071	80,172,786	157,272,285
2008–2009 Totals	228,164,307	80,000,281	148,870,332

Source: NCAA   (http://www.ncaa.org/wps/wcm/connect/public/NCAA/ Championship+Bids/Postseason+Football/Financial+Reporting).

(SEC). The have-nots are the schools in the five other Division I-FBS conferences (Conference USA, Mid-American, Mountain West, Sun Belt, and Western Athletic), and all of those in DI-FCS.[8] Table 2.3 shows the 2011–2012 total bowl revenue paid to each

---

[8]Due to changes in conference membership, the Western Athletic Association dropped football as a sponsored sport starting in 2013–2014.

conference, the expenses for the teams participating in the bowls games, and the net revenue for the conference.

This system also creates an effective barrier for schools trying to move their way up to the elite ranks. If a school does not have a top caliber football program, it cannot have the kind of winning season that would even give it a shot at the revenue from one of the top five bowls. Without the revenue from a BCS appearance, it is difficult to upgrade a program to compete at the highest level. Even if a team from outside of the six automatic qualifying BCS conferences has an undefeated season, it must still be rated in the top 12 of the BCS standings (or in the top 16 and higher than one of the automatic qualifiers). The BCS standings are based in part on the strength of opponents, so a team that does not play, and get a chance to beat, teams from the "power" conferences may receive a lower rating. As of 2013, just six non-automatic qualifying BCS schools had been invited to play in one of the major bowls.

Besides near-exclusivity for the BCS bowls, membership in the elite six conferences also gives these schools greater access to the more lucrative minor bowls. In addition to the Rose Bowl, the Pac-12 has contracts with five other bowl committees (Emerald, Hawaii, Holiday, Las Vegas, and Sun). In 2012–2013, eight of the twelve Pac-12 teams played in bowl games. While Oregon State's 9-4 record in 2012 placed it third in the Pac-12, it was still invited to Brut Sun Bowl, for which it received more than US$3 million.

So what about the teams in the major conferences that do not make it to bowl games? Do they lose out on the big money and start a downward spiral? Without a dependable flow of revenue, do they have a chance of making it back into contention? It turns out that the schools in these conferences look out for each other by sharing the proceeds from the bowls and television contracts. This keeps games competitive and more exciting for fans, which benefits all teams in the conference. A typical arrangement is for the schools that participate in bowls to hand over the payments from the bowl committees to the conference office. Each bowl participant is given an allowance for bowl-related expenses, and the rest

Table 2.4.   Bowl appearances and payouts for Pac-12 teams in 2012–2013.

Bowl	Team	Record	Payout (US$)
Rose	Stanford	12-2	17,000,000
Tostitos Fiesta	Oregon	12-1	17,000,000
Bridgeport Education Holiday	UCLA	9-5	4,075,000
Valero Alamo	Oregon State	9-4	3,175,000
Hyundai Sun	USC	7-6	2,000,000
MAACO Las Vegas	Washington	7-6	1,100,000
Kraft Fight Hunger	Arizona State	8-5	837,500
Gildan New Mexico	Arizona	8-5	456,250

Source: NCAA Football (http://www.ncaafootball.com/Bowls.aspx).

of the money is split among all conference members. In 2012, the SEC was paid US$47 million for member schools' participation in bowl games, with US$34 million of that distributed to all members of the conference. An additional US$207 million from other sources, primarily television contracts, was paid out to the 12 SEC members, for an average of US$20 million ("2011–2012 SEC revenue distribution," 2012). While this is below the amount earned by each Big 10 school, the new SEC Network and other changes are predicted to increase the payout per SEC member 50% by 2014. ("SEC revenue set to jump," 2013)

In addition to access to revenue from bowl games and big TV contracts, members of the elite conferences also benefit from hosting well-known opponents at their home games, increasing their ability to sell out their stadiums. An additional 10,000 fans for 6 home games at US$50 per ticket equals US$3 million in additional revenue. The result is that even the perennial conference doormat can end up with more revenue from its football program than a school that dominates one of the non-major conferences. The total bowl income in 2011 for the top four non-major conferences (Conference USA, Mid-American Conference, Mountain West Conference, Western Athletic Conference) was US$37.5 million, compared to US$50 million for the SEC. The average revenue distribution of US$1.67 million per school in these four conferences was US$19 million less than the amount earned by Kentucky in the SEC, which went 2–10 that year. As extolled by advertising campaigns for American Express, "Membership Has Its Privileges." The danger for a doormat team is that the other members of the conference may eventually decide that another school would add more value to the group, and tell the perpetual loser to find another conference to join.

The alternative to a collection of bowl games is a national championship tournament, like the NFL's playoffs, which culminates in the hugely popular Super Bowl. A playoff system has been used for Division I-FCS schools since 1973. If a significant part of the revenue from a DI-FBS tournament was distributed to a larger number of teams, and more schools outside the automatic-qualifying BCS conferences were eligible to participate, this could help to equalize funding and opportunities. It would also give the NCAA further influence over college sports in general, since they would then control the postseason for the two big money sports, men's basketball and football.

In the first edition of this book we asked why this has not happened. Our answer was that it is opposed by the bowl committees and the schools that benefit from the current system, namely those in the privileged conferences.[9] Some educators argue against a tournament because it would extend the football season even later. The NFL may also prefer not to have competition for football viewers during the playoffs leading up to the Super Bowl.

In 2012, the commissioners of the BCS announced that a four-team playoff system would debut at the end of the 2014–2015 season. With just four teams and the semifinal games hosted by existing BCS bowls (with the addition of the Cotton and Chick-fil-A), this is very different from the 24-team playoff used in Division I-FCS. The revenue from the US$7 billion 12-year

---

[9]Many coaches at BCS schools have expressed support for a football championship tournament, but university presidents were mainly united in their opposition.

contract with ESPN will be distributed to the existing five automatic-qualifying BCS conferences (71.5%), the other five FBS conferences (27%), and the FBS independents (1.5%). When combined with revenue from its contract with the Rose Bowl, the Big Ten could receive US$90 million each year. ("College football playoff revenue distribution set," 2012)

2.9   Competitive Balance

One potential rationale for NCAA rules forbidding compensation of athletes (beyond a free education) is to allow all schools to compete equally for talented athletes and thus have a chance for a winning sports program. Without such rules, the best players would attend the colleges and universities that could afford to pay the most. This could lead to a vicious circle of the schools with winning programs generating more revenue and using that money to attract the best athletes to continue to be winners. The rest would have poor to mediocre teams and lower revenue. Except for games between equally talented teams, many would be blowouts. Not only would paying players be costly for the schools, reducing the profits generated by athletic departments, but the resulting imbalance could have a negative effect on the popularity of individual games and even college sports in general.

A significant amount of research on **competitive balance** has appeared in the sports economics literature, including how to measure it and how it affects attendance. While most of the literature has focused on professional sports, the results may apply to college sports as well. One way of framing the issue is by focusing on the probability that the home team will win. If fans only care about the success of their team, then the probability that will maximize home attendance is 1.00. If fans only want to experience a close game where either team can win, then the optimal probability is 0.50.

A study by Daniel Rascher and John Paul G. Solmes (2007) examined attendance at National Basketball Association games for the 2001-02 season. They found that the home team winning probability that maximized attendance was 0.67, so the home team is twice as likely to win as the visitor. This compares to an estimated value of 0.70 for Major League Baseball. Apparently, fans want their team to be favored to win but still want the excitement of not knowing who will win, that is, they want some competitive balance. The home team can be favored even with perfectly balanced teams due to the emotional and vocal support from home fans, familiarity with the idiosyncrasies of their facility, more rest without the burden of travel, and possible bias by the local officials. In sports like baseball, the home facility can be fine-tuned to suit the talents of the team, such as longer or shorter distances to the fences. Rascher and Solmes also noted that the optimal home probability depends on the importance of an individual game outcome for reaching the postseason. In baseball a single loss will have little impact, while one additional loss in football can be a deciding factor. For sports with fewer games per season the optimal home winning probability is likely to be higher. [10]

One way to achieve greater balance is to group teams by the amount of resources they have, so good teams play good teams and the rest play each other. This was the intention of the system of divisions within the NCAA. Big universities are generally in Division I while smaller schools populate Divisions II and III. This was also a major motive for conferences to form and for membership in conferences to be adjusted over time. A team that is the perpetual doormat of the division is likely to be asked to find a different division to join. In response to a recent increase in the pace of conference realignment, researchers have begun examining whether it affects competitive balance within those conferences. Studies of changes in membership of the Big 12 and Conference USA find that competitive balance in football improved (Perline *et al.*, 2013). An earlier study of realignment in the Western Athletic Conference and the Mountain West Conference

---

[10]For 2012–2013 the median home winning percentage in the Pac-12 for games against conference opponents was 0.67 for men's basketball and 0.60 for football.

found an increase in competitive balance in football but no impact in basketball. (Rhoads, 2004)

Another solution is to impose rules to limit the resources that can be used to recruit the top athletes. Professional sports leagues impose salary caps, luxury taxes (for teams that exceed the payroll cap), and revenue sharing. College sports impose a type of salary cap by paying nothing above the cost of an education. The NCAA also limits the resources that athletic departments can devote to recruiting, such as the number of coaching staff visits to players. When the University of Oregon used a private jet to pick up recruits, the NCAA outlawed the practice.

Have NCAA rules had an effect on competitive balance? Daniel Sutter and Stephen Winkler (2003) found that competitive balance in college football has not increased in the post-World War II era, when many of the rules were adopted. They examined the effect of reducing the number of scholarships and found mixed evidence for a change in competitive balance. However, a study of Division I football from 1953 to 2003 by Craig Depken II and Dennis Wilson (2006) concluded that enforcement of NCAA rules has improved competitive balance. Unfortunately, the NCAA is not able to control other ways that schools can spend money to attract top-rated prospects, such as hiring the best coaches and building state of the art facilities. Even the opportunity for a world-class education at an Ivy League university can be an inducement for some student-athletes.

Research by Eckard (2013) found that the formation of the Bowl Championship Series and its predecessors led to a decrease in competitive balance among all DI-FBS schools but an increase in parity among the automatic-qualifying conferences. The huge payouts to schools in the elite conferences gives them the resources to compete in ways not restricted by NCAA rules. He concludes that this supports the cartel within a cartel view of the BCS and should be of concern to the NCAA. Whether the new College Football Playoff system will open more opportunities for those outside the current elite or will solidify the position of the top conferences remains to be seen.

2.10 Cheating in College Sports

Until 2013, the NCAA divided violations of its rules into **major and secondary violations**. A secondary violation was "isolated or inadvertent in nature, provides or is intended to provide only a minimal recruiting, competitive or other advantage and does not include any significant recruiting inducement or extra benefit" (2011–2012 NCAA Bylaw 19.02.2.1). All other infractions were considered major violations, "specifically including those that provide an extensive recruiting or competitive advantage" (Bylaw 19.02.2.2). Secondary violations were further divided into Level I and Level II based on a list of specific bylaws. For example, inappropriate donations to the university from a professional sports organization (Bylaw 12.6.1) is a Level II violation, while student representation by an agent (Bylaw 12.3.1) is Level I. Multiple secondary violations may collectively be considered a major violation.

In 2012, the Division I Board of Directors adopted a system with four levels of violations, to be implemented in October 2013. The new definitions are described in Box 2.2. The NCAA's intention is to enable the investigators and the Committee on Infractions to focus on the most serious violations (the new Levels I and II).

The incentive for athletic programs to cheat is a function of the expected gains, the probability of getting caught, and the costs of any punishment. The optimal amount of cheating will occur where the marginal benefit (the gains associated with an increase in winning percentage) just equals the marginal cost (the increase in the probability of getting caught times the penalty).

For each school, the benefits from cheating depend on whether rival teams also cheat. If the rivals cheat, they will have greater success in recruiting the most talented athletes in that region and will win more games. A school that is not currently cheating will be tempted to do so, since it will help them avoid a losing season that could cost the coach and athletic director their jobs. If the rivals are not cheating, then the incentive to cheat is based on increasing the probability of a winning season. This can lead to more job security and higher pay for the coach and AD. An important issue is whether the two situations are symmetric. Is the possible damage

Box 2.2.   Revised NCAA Division I violation structure.

Level I Violation: Severe breach of conduct

Violations that seriously undermine or threaten the integrity of the NCAA collegiate model as set forth in the Constitution and bylaws, including any violation that provides or is intended to provide a substantial or extensive recruiting, competitive or other advantage, or a substantial or extensive impermissible benefit.

Level II Violation: Significant breach of conduct

Violations that provide or are intended to provide more than a minimal but less than a substantial or extensive recruiting, competitive or other advantage; includes more than a minimal but less than a substantial or extensive impermissible benefit; or involves conduct that may compromise the integrity of the NCAA collegiate model as set forth in the Constitution and by laws.

Level III Violation: Breach of conduct

Violations that are isolated or limited in nature; provide no more than a minimal recruiting, competitive or other advantage; and do not include more than a minimal impermissible benefit. Multiple Level IV violations may collectively be considered a breach of conduct.

Level IV Violation: Incidental issues

Minor infractions that are inadvertent and isolated, technical in nature and result in a negligible, if any, competitive advantage. Level IV infractions generally will not affect eligibility for intercollegiate athletics. (This level may be revised or even eliminated pending outcomes from the Rules Working Group's efforts to streamline the Division I Manual.)

Source: Brown (2012).

from a losing season equal in magnitude to the possible gains from a winning season? If not, and the coach is more concerned about avoiding a really bad season than having a really good one, the marginal benefit from cheating will be higher if other schools are also cheating.

What about the cost of cheating? As the amount of cheating increases, the likelihood of getting caught by the NCAA increases and the penalties increase in severity. Other schools are more likely to turn in what they see as flagrant violators, and the NCAA may be alerted by sudden dramatic changes in team performance. Violations which have a significant impact on recruiting success are punished more severely than secondary violations.

How can the NCAA reduce the amount of cheating by its members, particularly major infractions? It can either reduce the benefits that schools generate when they cheat or increase the expected costs from getting caught. It can accomplish the first by imposing still more regulations, such as the requirement that athletes who transfer to another college or university sit out their first year. A cheater may still try to lure good athletes away from their current school, but if those players are ineligible for an entire year the benefit to the cheater will be diminished. The second method, increasing the expected costs, requires an effective way to catch cheaters and impose significant penalties.

How can the NCAA detect cheating? They could assume that most violations are caused by rogue individuals, such as boosters and misguided staff members, and that the university will discover and report such activity on its own. In 1993, the NCAA initiated a certification process that requires all Division I members to undergo a comprehensive peer-reviewed self-study of its athletic program every ten years. The NCAA (2006, p. 6) identifies three benefits to the institutions. *First*, it can educate the university community about the purpose of the athletics program and the challenges it faces. *Second*, it can identify aspects of the program that are worthy of praise. *Third*, it can identify weaknesses in the institution's control of the athletics program. With an adequate system of internal scrutiny, the isolated actions of a lone assistant coach or booster should be discovered and reported to the NCAA. The administration has an incentive to self-report such activities, since failure to do so can result in additional penalties when the NCAA eventually uncovers the infractions. If the school's administration chooses not to report violations, concerned individuals may contact the NCAA Enforcement Office directly.

So do schools actually report violations voluntarily? "It is not unusual to report 50-60 violations in a given year — depending on the number of sports, coaches and administrators. Provided the violations are not major in nature, are not committed willfully and do not constitute a pattern of violations by a specific person or program or in a specific area of the rules, this is acceptable. In fact, the NCAA may become as concerned about those schools that report very few violations each year (e.g., 10) as they are about those who report a very high number of violations" ("Violations," n.d., ¶ 5). From 1997 to 2003, the number of self-reported violations in Division I increased by 40%, which probably indicates an increase in the willingness to disclose minor infractions rather than an increase in the number of actual violations.

Does a significant number of self-reported infractions each year prove that the system is working? Not necessarily. If you are expected to report your illegal activities to the police, and you know that they will start asking questions if you have nothing to report, what would you do? I would tell them about the times I drove 34 mph in a 30 zone, crossed the street before the light changed to WALK, and failed to tell the IRS about the US$20 I got for looking after my neighbor's cats. I would not report the US$50,000 I embezzled from the Girl Scout cookie sale. A school may decide to report that a student intern placed the name of a high school recruit on a locker, but will it be as willing to disclose that a booster paid US$5,000 to that same prospect? The current system allows the NCAA to burnish its image as the protector of the noble ideals of amateur athletics, while allowing schools to keep the NCAA at a comfortable distance.

If the NCAA suspects that schools are not reporting all violations, particularly serious ones, it can still conduct its own investigations. One method is to look for indirect evidence of recruiting violations. They may view as suspicious any significant change in team performance. After all, if a school has not been successful in the past, what else besides cheating could explain a large improvement from one season to the next? Economists Trey Fleisher, Brian Goff and Robert Tollison (1992, pp. 111–112) examined NCAA enforcement actions over a 30-year period and verified that a change in performance is more likely to result in an investigation, while consistently high performance does not. They offer two possible explanations. *First*, the schools with perennially strong teams have shaped the enforcement system to keep other programs from becoming more competitive. The former may be just as likely as the up and coming programs to commit violations but they are less likely to be caught because the NCAA's attention is focused on the latter. *Second*, the most successful programs do not need to commit violations to remain highly competitive. Their winning traditions, combined with the facilities their greater revenue stream can pay for, allow them to recruit the premier athletes without resorting to illegal inducements. In this case, the lesser degree of scrutiny by the NCAA is justified.

If you were the athletic director at a major university, would you be anxious to report suspicious activities at other schools? After all, your opponents could be weakened by NCAA sanctions, such as a loss in scholarships. The danger in doing so is that the other schools will now be much more likely to report your violations. Unless your program has no skeletons to hide, the last thing you want is to start opening closets. However, if a school starts getting too many of the best recruits and wins significantly more games, it risks retaliation, particularly from schools that have little to hide. Even the other violators may see a need to put them in their place. After all, there is honor even among thieves.

How many violations of NCAA rules actually occur, and how many of those are investigated? Zimbalist (1999) supplies answers to both questions:

> David Berst, the NCAA's chief of enforcement from 1988 to 1998, estimates that every day at least ten of the biggest universities are

involved in a serious violation of NCAA rules. … When all is said and done, Berst's office conducts 20–25 investigations a year — not many if Berst is correct that there are 10 major infractions per day, just among the big schools. (p. 174)

The number of major investigations has not increased in the intervening 15 years, with the NCAA reporting in 2011 that its enforcement department processes approximately 25 major cases each year ("NCAA enforcement restructures," 2011). Even prior to several high-profile staff departures in 2013, there was concern that the staff was spread too thin trying to catch sophisticated cheaters (Wolken, 2013). In mid-2013, there were just two investigators with experience in major football and basketball cases. (Thamel, 2013)

With only 23 investigators for 340 institutions in Division I (plus 312 in DII and 444 in DIII), the NCAA largely relies on the schools to investigate themselves. Many schools choose to hire an outside investigator, hoping to increase the credibility of their report to the NCAA Committee on Infractions.

Suppose you were charged with robbing a store, and the court asked you to submit a report on your alleged illegal activities. You could simply investigate yourself and claim that there was no evidence of wrongdoing. The court may suspect that you were biased in your own favor and convict you anyway. It would be better to hire someone the court trusted. Who would you hire? Someone with a track record of thorough investigations that resulted in convictions and lengthy prison terms? Not if you actually robbed the store. How about someone that used to work as a court investigator, is still close friends with the judge, and has a history of issuing reports that contain evidence of only minor crimes that result in probation? I would pick the latter, even if he charged very high fees, particularly if the judge recommended him to me. According to Zimbalist (1999, p. 174), colleges and universities make this same choice. From 1986 to 1988, one third of all "independent" investigations were made by one particular consultant. This attorney had worked for the NCAA for seven years and was still a golfing buddy of the NCAA chief of enforcement.

The possible lack of impartial investigations is further complicated by the high rate of turnover among members of the NCAA enforcement staff, who often take jobs with colleges and universities after they leave. Four investigators who departed in 2013, including the managing director of enforcement for development and investigations, all took jobs in compliance offices at DI-FBS institutions. Julie Roe Lach, the former head of enforcement, was forced out after it was discovered that evidence for the University of Miami investigation was improperly collected; she is now a consultant with universities and conferences (Wolken, 2013). Given their professional expertise in NCAA rules and regulations, it makes sense for former investigators to find a job that utilizes that experience. This creates two potential problems. *First*, while at the NCAA they may be reluctant to be aggressive with schools where they may later apply for a job. *Second*, once at a university they may be able to influence their former colleagues at the NCAA. In this sense, the investigators may be "captured" by those that they are supposed to investigate.[11]

For an effective deterrent against cheating, violations must be punished once they are discovered. Schools are typically placed on probation, with additional penalties including a reduction in the number of scholarships allowed, a reduction in recruiting visits, fines, and a ban on television appearances or postseason tournaments. Coaches are also subject to suspension, including a head coach who fails to promote an atmosphere of compliance. Suspensions can range from 10% of a season to an entire season. If a school is placed on probation, it risks more severe penalties if subsequent transgressions are discovered.

Zimbalist (1999, p. 179) notes that while the length of probations has increased from the 1970s to the 1990s, the length of actual penalties such as prohibitions on postseason play and TV appearances has diminished. During the twenty years prior to 2006, there was also a remarkable decrease in the number of significant sanctions. As shown in Table 2.5, bowl appearance bans were the only penalties still imposed in the latter period (the scholarship reduction was self-imposed in an attempt to avoid more serious sanctions), and they were used at a rate three times lower than in the earlier period.

---

[11]Nobel laureate George Stigler was one of main developers of capture theory, or the economic theory of regulation. See Stigler (1971).

Table 2.5.   Sanctions against DI-FBS football programs, 1987–2013.

Sanction	1987–1995	1996–2006	2008–2013
Bowl appearance bans	16	5	1
TV broadcast bans	10	0	0
Scholarship reductions of 20 or more	5	1	1

Sources: NCAA infractions database; research by ESPN.com (Farrey, 2001) for 1987–2001, the authors for 2002–2006, Jude (2013) for 2008–2013.

Depken and Wilson (2004) examined the impact of sanctions placed on NCAA Division I football programs during the period 1996–2000, and estimated that the cost of probation is close to zero, while any financial impact of scholarship reductions and postseason bans is shifted to women's basketball and men's and women's non-revenue sports. The offending program is basically held harmless, at least from a financial standpoint.

One reason for the apparent reluctance by the NCAA to impose its most powerful sanctions is that the cost of these penalties has increased significantly, to the point where the membership is unwilling to support their common use. As a member of society, I support fines for speeding, knowing full well that I might be ticketed. However, if the standard fine for driving less than 10 miles per hour over the limit increased from US$100 to US$1,000, I would vote to stop the courts from fining drivers unless they exceeded the limit by a larger margin. In the case of college sports, when the stakes were smaller the NCAA may have been more willing to impose significant penalties.

Consider one of the primary tools available to the NCAA — a ban on postseason bowls and tournaments. The creation of the Bowl Championship Series, a cartel in itself, has increased the stakes to schools in those conferences. Remember that a school can receive more than US$10 million for a BCS appearance, and the television exposure is invaluable for recruiting the best prospective athletes. Is it a coincidence that the number of bowl bans decreased at the same time that the size of the payouts was increasing?

The most severe sanction is the **death penalty**, which bans a school from participating in intercollegiate athletics in that sport for up to two years. Also known as the repeat-violator rule, it was passed in 1985 by a 427-6 vote of the member institutions. A sport can be suspended if a major infraction occurs within five years of another major violation. This has been used just once in Division I, when the football program at Southern Methodist University was shut down for the 1987–88 season (see Box 2.3 for a description of

---

Box 2.3.   Violations at Southern Methodist University.

In August 1985, the NCAA determined that the coaching staff at Southern Methodist University had been aware of flagrant violations by boosters during the period 1981–1984, including payments to potential recruits and student-athletes. Nine boosters were banned from any contact with athletes, and an assistant coach was prohibited from participating in the recruiting process. The university was prohibited from offering any athletic scholarships in football for 1986–87 and just 15 scholarships for 1987–1988. It was banned from postseason competition in 1986 and 1987 and appearances on live television in 1986. SMU was also placed on probation for three years. This was the fourth instance of NCAA actions against SMU in 11 years, with documented violations in 11 of the previous 14 years.

The following November, a former player disclosed in a television interview that he had been paid US$750 per month by the university's recruiting director. Two days later, a current student revealed that he had been living rent-free in an apartment owned by one of the banned boosters. The NCAA Committee on Infractions eventually determined that 13 football players had been paid a total of nearly US$47,000 during the 1985–1986 season and another US$14,000 during the last four months of 1986. These violations occurred after the university had been placed on probation in 1985.

the violations in that case). All home games for 1988–1989 were canceled, but away games were allowed to minimize the impact on opposing teams. However, SMU chose to cancel all games for 1988–1989. After compiling a 52-19-1 record during the seven years prior to the penalty, the SMU football program had a difficult time recovering. During the next 17 years, the team's record was 47-119-3, with only one winning season and just two victories over nationally ranked teams. The penalty also contributed to the demise of the Southwest Conference in 1996 and the move by SMU to the non-BCS Western Athletic Conference.

Fast fact. *Sports at two other schools have been subject to the death penalty. In 2003, the Division II Morehouse College soccer program was canceled for two years. In 2004, the Division III MacMurray College tennis team was also given a two-year suspension. It probably did not help that the tennis coach, a professor of mathematics, was criticized by the DIII Committee on Infractions for calling the rules a "joke". (Timanus, 2005)*

During the next 15 years, 10 other college football programs have been judged to be similar repeat offenders, but none have been given the death penalty, and some have received only probation. John Lombardi, who was president of the University of Florida when it went before the NCAA Infractions Committee for major violations, was quoted as saying that "SMU taught the committee that the death penalty is too much like the nuclear bomb. It's like what happened when we dropped the (atom) bomb in World War II. The results were so catastrophic that now we'll do anything to avoid dropping another one" (Farrey, 2001, ¶ 15). This appeared in an article that was part of a series at ESPN.com on the lack of effective punishment in Division I-A football. The series was aptly subtitled "The Death of the Penalty," reflecting the fact that the actual use of the Death Penalty may have led to its effective demise. The 2010 penalties imposed on USC are viewed as the stiffest since

SMU, including a two-year postseason ban and the loss of 30 football scholarships over a three-year period. (Jude, 2013)

How can we determine the **optimal amount of policing** for a cartel like the NCAA? As usual, economists compare the benefits from more policing (marginal benefit) with the costs (marginal cost). The quantity that maximizes the difference between the total benefits and total costs occurs where MB = MC. To use this approach, we must identify the benefits and costs of policing to the members of the NCAA.

The benefit from additional policing efforts is a reduction in the level of cheating. Cheating hurts the members of the NCAA in two ways. *First*, it increases costs. A bidding war for the most talented athletes could lead to wages close to their marginal revenue product, which can be considerable. *Second*, it damages the carefully guarded reputation of college athletics as a bastion of amateurism. If fans knew that college athletes were being paid, particularly when such payments are against the rules, would they lose interest? The athletes would not just be professionals, they would be cheaters too. Fans may be willing to overlook minor infractions, and even the occasional major one, but a widespread pattern of abuse is likely to change the public's perception of the game. Presuming that even a minimal amount of policing will deter many of the most flagrant major violations, and that increases in policing will deter progressively minor infractions, the MB curve will be downward-sloping.

The marginal cost of policing is based in part on the expense of the NCAA's enforcement division and the compliance efforts by individual campuses. As noted earlier, the NCAA's enforcement staff is relatively small. A typical compliance office at a major university employs a director, associate director, assistant director, and support staff. Multiply this by hundreds of NCAA institutions. The cost of detecting the flagrant major violations should be fairly low, but unearthing additional more subtle violations will be more difficult, resulting in the familiar upward-sloping MC curve.

Effective policing also requires punishments that will deter violations, and these punishments create their own costs. Stricter punishments will result in fewer violations, which is the desired outcome, but at a higher cost. The collective cost of mild sanctions should be quite small. If the football team loses five scholarships for four years, which prospective athletes will the school choose to not recruit? Certainly not the most talented ones. Even if the result is that the team loses an extra game or two each season, other teams in the conference will win more games.[12] With stricter sanctions come more substantial costs. If the NCAA bans a school from postseason play, then it may have to forgo a football bowl game or a berth in the men's basketball tournament, both of which are very lucrative. If the offender loses a significant number of scholarships, the competitiveness of its program may suffer serious damage. This can even harm the reputation of the entire conference. If a school from the Pac-12 is crushed by its Big Ten opponent on national television, fans may start to believe that the Pac-12 is losing its ability to produce winning programs. Many people put much of the blame for the demise of the Southwest Conference on the inability of SMU to regain national prominence after its two year Death Penalty in football. The implication is that because policing to deter more and more cheating will require stiffer penalties, and those penalties will cause greater harm, the marginal cost curve for policing is upward-sloping.

The optimal amount of policing effort is shown in Figure 2.3 where MB and MC intersect at Q^*. Much like Goldilocks, who did not want her porridge too hot or too cold, the members of the NCAA do not want to conduct more or less policing than Q^*. For their mutual benefit, they want to deter a certain amount of cheating, but to stop at the point where the cost of further deterrence becomes too great.

How might the value of Q^* be affected by the growing popularity of college basketball and football? Unfortunately, there is no clear answer to this question. On the one hand, if the economic impact of sports for each school increases, then the damage caused

---

[12] This is what economists refer to as a zero-sum game. When one person loses, somebody else wins an equal amount. As a result, the cost to the group is zero.

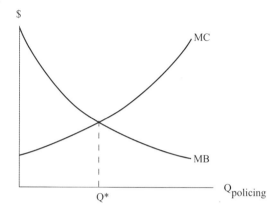

Figure 2.3. Costs and benefits from policing.

by media reports of widespread cheating is greater. Policing, which prevents that damage, is increasingly valuable. This shifts the MB curve upward, resulting in a higher Q^*. On the other hand, if part of the rise in popularity and commercialization of college sports has been an increased acceptance of cheating (at least by the school you are loyal to), and thus less benefit from deterrence of cheating, the MB curve shifts downward and Q^* decreases. On yet another hand, the potential damage to schools and conferences from more severe sanctions also increases, which shifts the MC curve upward and reduces Q^*.[13]

If Q^* is relatively low, that is, it is optimal for the NCAA to do little in the way of investigation and punishment, why does the organization have so many rules and regulations? One explanation is that it is trying to create the perception that it is in control. If the public's confidence is bolstered by a proliferation of rules that cover all the details of recruiting and eligibility, then many of the benefits of actual policing can be had without the costs. A sustained public relations campaign, complete with

---

[13] A frustrated President Harry Truman is reputed to have once said, "Give me a one-handed economist!" Economists are infamous for believing that there is always more than one answer to a question.

Box 2.4.   What constitutes cheating in the college sports cartel?

Explicit cheating is doing something that violates the rules of the cartel, such as paying the best student-athletes to get them attend a particular university. If some schools start paying athletes, then the other schools will have to do the same thing or risk losing the top recruits. This will increase costs and decrease net revenue for all members of the cartel.

Implicit cheating is doing something that is not against the rules, but is still against the *mutual* interest of the members of the cartel. This includes anything that a particular university or group of universities might do to gain an advantage, but by forcing other schools to do the same thing results in an eventual loss to all members of the cartel.

Are any of the following an example of implicit cheating? If it redistributes net revenue from one school to another but does not affect the total amount, is it still cheating?

1. Increase spending on facilities and coaching staff to appeal to the best recruits.
2. Negotiate a television contract on behalf of an individual conference or school.
3. Create a postseason system that effectively excludes some schools from a chance to participate and thereby earn a significant payout.
4. Realign membership in a conference to exclude those that are not contributing to its national reputation and popularity.

---

examples of such serious violations as a free ham sandwich given to a recruit while visiting a campus, can create the **illusion of control**. We use the term **ham sandwich violation** to represent inadvertent and trivial benefits given to student athletes that have been treated as violations by the NCAA. If the NCAA is going after even this kind of incident, they must really have a handle on the major ones, right?

2.11 Entry in College Sports

Thus far, we have examined how the college sports cartel has dealt with the challenges of reaching an agreement and minimizing cheating. The remaining challenge is to prevent **entry** by schools lured by the promise of substantial benefits to their institutions. Before examining the cartel's strategy for dealing with this threat, a few clarifications are needed. *First,* the focus of the cartel is on the revenue sports, primarily the football and men's basketball programs at major universities. If UCLA adds a lacrosse team, or tiny Harvey Mudd (enrollment of 700) starts a football program, the profitability of nearby USC's athletic department is not in jeopardy.

Second, entry is most likely to take place within the NCAA itself. The greatest threat is from current NCAA members trying to move up to the elite ranks (DI in basketball and DI-FBS in football). *Third,* the damage from entry is the additional supply of games for broadcast, which would decrease the market price, and the additional demand for athletes, which would lead to an escalation of the arms race, including more temptation to offer illegal payments. *Fourth,* college sports is inherently different from other markets. Unlike most goods, which can be sold without any cooperation from other producers, athletic teams need to play other teams. Any new program that cannot schedule a full season of games will not be viable.

Imagine yourself as the president of a state university that is currently competing in Division I-FCS football. Attendance at home games averages only about 5,000 and donations from the booster club are meager. In your daydreams, the school is playing against FBS opponents, ticket sales are way up, booster excitement (and contributions) have increased, the team is able to attract better athletes, and the school is getting increased media exposure. If your team is really good, you might even get invited to one of the top bowl games, which can mean millions in revenue. Median revenue for FBS schools is US$40.6 million, compared to just US$3.8 million in FCS. So how to make the switch? One option is to operate as an FBS independent and try to schedule a season of games against other independents and teams in FBS conferences. Even better, you could convince a major FBS conference to let you join. This would guarantee a full schedule and a share of the bowl revenue paid to other conference members. If the conferences are not interested, you could contact other FCS schools to find out if they interested in forming a new FBS conference.

To implement your vision, you create a campus committee to write a report on the feasibility of the different options. Perhaps unwisely, you put the university's Nobel Prize-winning sports economist in charge of the committee. After a six-month wait, the report arrives, and it is not what you expected. First, it notes that the NCAA rules impose a number of costly requirements for acceptance into Division I-FBS, including more varsity sports, more scholarships, and a stadium large enough for at least 15,000 fans. There is also a two-year waiting period, during which you will no longer be eligible for the FCS championship. Second, your plan to be an independent, in the tradition of Notre Dame, is hampered by NCAA limits on the number of games a school can play each season. While FBS schools in your region might otherwise be interested in scheduling a game with your team, they are already at the maximum of twelve.[14] With most conferences having eleven to twelve members, just playing each of the other members uses up all but one or two of the slots unless they split into two divisions.[15] Many schools use one of those to play a

---

[14] A total of 13 games can be played under specific circumstances. For example, an extra game can be scheduled in Alaska, Hawaii, or Puerto Rico against an active member located in one of those areas. For a complete list of exemptions, see Bylaw 17.11.5.2.

[15] For basketball, the limit is 29 games per season. For a conference with 12 members, if each school plays one home game and one away game against each opponent, then there are 7 open slots per season.

warm-up game against a FCS team before the start of the regular season. They also try to schedule a game against a top-ranked team to get national television exposure, stimulate fan interest, and bolster their chance for a bowl bid if they win the game. With the number of other independent schools dwindling to just three (Army, BYU, and Notre Dame), you cannot rely on them for a full season of competition.[16]

Third, it will be difficult to join an existing DI-FBS conference. The committee cites a study that estimates that the optimal size of a conference is twelve, and most conferences are already at that number. They do not want to grow and it will be hard to convince them to dump another school and admit you. After all, you are only an FCS program with aspirations but no long-term record of competing at the elite level. Even if they have a particularly weak member, there is a strong tradition of competition that still brings in the fans. The report also notes that the school should be careful about which FBS conference to join. The really big money is in the automatic-qualifying BCS conferences. Remember that even the lowliest members of these conferences have greater annual revenue than some entire FBS conferences, in large part because of revenue-sharing agreements for television contracts and bowl appearances. Unfortunately, as the old adage goes, you may not want to join a club that would have you as a member, and the clubs you want to join do not want you.

As for the final option, creating a new conference, the report again notes a number of roadblocks. To qualify for DI-FBS status, the NCAA requires that a conference must have at least eight full FBS members, so forming a new conference with a few other schools in your area is out of the question. While there may be

---

[16]BYU became an independent in 2011 following its departure from the Mountain West Conference. After many years as an independent, Navy announced in 2012 that it would join the American Athletic Conference, the renamed Big East, in 2015. New Mexico State and Idaho were independents for just one year between the decision by the Western Athletic Conference to drop football and joining the Sun Belt Conference as football-only members.

seven other FCS institutions contemplating a move to FBS, they are spread out all over the country. Your travel budget will be enormous, and students will spend even more time away from school just getting to and from games. Without regional rivals, fan interest may also be low.

Even if you could find enough schools for a new conference, the networks are unlikely to pay large amounts to broadcast games between relatively unknown former DI-FCS schools. The bowl committees are looking for schools that will draw a large television audience, making it difficult to negotiate agreements like the Pac-12 has that guarantee invitations to even fourth and fifth place finishers. If you were hoping to win your conference's basketball tournament and earn an automatic berth in the national tournament, NCAA rules require that a conference have at least seven core institutions that have been Division I members for at least eight years, and at least six of those members must have competed together for a minimum of five years. There are no exceptions to the five-year waiting period.

At this point, you may decide that sports economists have spent too much time in the ivory tower, that just about *everyone* knows that DI-FBS is the place to be, and that you need to appoint a new committee to write the report you wanted in the first place. You will make sure they do not read the NCAA study which found that for most of the 19 teams that moved up from 1978 to 2010, expenses increased by more than revenue while subsidies increased by US$1–2 million per year and winning percentage decreased. The report also concluded that "FCS institutions provide more sports and more opportunities for student-athletes, providing a well rounded collegiate experience" (McNeely, 2013). After all, this will be the legacy that you leave to the university. People will remember you and what you did for the institution, not that idiot economist who reads too much.

Hopefully, instead of moving ahead you stop and think of why there are obstacles to joining the elite ranks of college sports.

Put simply, the schools already at the top have no reason to dilute their share of the profits by letting you in. Over the years, they have passed the NCAA rules mentioned in the report. Of course, creating barriers to entry was not the rationale used publicly at the time. When the number of games per season was limited, it was argued that this would keep the student-athletes from spending too much time away from classes. It just happens that this also makes it harder for new programs to find opponents. If you were the president of a university in one of the BCS conferences, you would also be trying to lock the gate behind you. The more that schools like yours want to get into the top ranks, the more rules that will appear to keep them out. While you are already part of the NCAA cartel, there is an even more powerful cartel at the top that wants things to stay just as they are. Listen to your economist!

2.12 Chapter Summary

A cartel benefits its members in part by restricting the total quantity produced, thus increasing the market price (or reducing the quantity of an input purchased and thereby decreasing the price paid). In some cases, cooperation between members can also increase the value of, and thus the demand for, the product. We saw that a cartel faces three inherent challenges: agreement, cheating, and entry. The conditions that make cartels more likely to succeed include inelastic demand for the product (or supply of the input), a small number of firms, and similar products, production costs, and objectives.

After defining the relevant market as the revenue sports of football and men's basketball at the elite universities, we examined how a successful athletics program can benefit its institution. A winning team can generate significant revenue from ticket sales, donations from alumni and other boosters, contracts for television and radio broadcasts, and payments for appearances in postseason bowl games and tournaments. Institutions can also benefit from higher attendance and the ability to be more selective in admitting new students.

On the basis of high prices for outputs and low prices for inputs, it appears that cartel behavior does exist in college sports. However, the NCAA has not been completely successful. On the output side, the growing disparity between the elite programs and the rest of the members eventually led to a revolt against the regular season football television plan. The NCAA does control the lucrative postseason tournament for basketball, but the regular season for basketball and the post season for football have eluded them. The major football bowls are controlled by the automatic qualifying BCS conferences, a cartel within the cartel, and this is unlikely to change under the new College Football Playoff. On the input side, cheating in the form of recruiting violations continues, due in part to the relatively small amount of resources devoted to policing by the NCAA. The proliferation of self-reported minor violations can create the illusion that the NCAA is in control. The NCAA has no authority over coaching salaries and spending for state-of-the-art facilities, the major elements of the current arms race. The existing structure of conferences and NCAA divisions is an effective barrier to entry for schools that attempt to move up to the elite ranks. It is particularly difficult for teams to enter the ranks of the top DI-FBS football programs.

A cartel creates benefits to its members at the expense of its customers (who pay more and get less) and its input suppliers (who get paid less and sell less). If you do not watch sports on television (customer) or are a college athlete (supplier), why should you care? To an economist, the answer is simple: The benefits to the winners are less than the harm to the losers, resulting in a net loss to society. In economic terms, this is known as a **deadweight loss**. We will examine this loss in the market for college athletes in the following chapter.

2.13 Key Terms

Agreement
Cartel
Cheating
Collusion
Competitive balance
Deadweight loss
Death penalty
Dominant strategy
Economic rent
Elasticity of demand
Elasticity of supply
Entry
Game theory
Ham sandwich violation
Illusion of control
Level I violation

Level II violation
Level III violation
Level IV violation
Major violation
Marginal cost
Marginal revenue
Marginal revenue product
Monopoly
Optimal policing
Price fixing
Prisoners' dilemma
Repeated game
Reservation wage
Secondary violation
Tit-for-tat

2.14 Review Questions

1. In collusion, for firms to be able to raise their prices, what else must they agree to do?
2. What are the three challenges for any form of collusion?
3. In the Prisoners' Dilemma, why does each person confess?
4. What are some of the conditions that make collusion more likely to succeed? How does the price elasticity of demand influence the success of a cartel?
5. What are economic rents? How can they by dissipated in a cartel?
6. What two questions do economists ask to decide if two products belong in the same market?
7. Why did the NCAA need to impose rules on recruiting after it limited payments to athletes to a full scholarship?

8. As the agent for a cartel, why does the NCAA put a limit on the number of scholarships that can be awarded in each sport?
9. What is an example of a "cartel within a cartel" in college sports?
10. Why is competitive balance important for sports leagues? How do the NCAA and conferences promote balance? Have they succeeded?
11. What was the difference between major and secondary violations? What are the differences between Levels I–IV?
12. How does the NCAA learn about most violations? Who investigates those violations once they are reported?
13. For each school, what are the benefits and costs of cheating?
14. For the NCAA, what are the benefits and costs of policing?
15. What are examples of NCAA rules that make it more difficult to enter the elite ranks of college sports?

2.15 Discussion Questions

1. How might a drug-smuggling cartel change its payoff matrix to reduce the incentive for members to cheat on the agreement?
2. Should beer and wine be considered as part of the same market or as different markets?
3. A professor announces the following grading system for the final exam. If all the exams are blank, everyone gets a zero, but since this is the average score they all get a C. If some students leave it blank and others write even one correct answer, the former will get an F and the latter an A. She leaves the room for a few minutes to let the class discuss what to do, and everyone agrees to turn in a blank exam. What do you think will actually happen? What could the group do to reduce the incentive to cheat?
4. Does the market for big-time college sports meet each of the six conditions for successful collusion?
5. Would cigarette companies have been in favor of the government ban on cigarette advertising on television and radio? What do you think happened to profits in the cigarette industry immediately after the government implemented this ban? What do you think eventually happened to profits?

6. If there is extensive cheating in a cartel, the cartel will probably fall apart. In the NCAA there are so many rules violations each year yet the cartel remains in place. How is this possible?
7. If the NCAA hired another 50 investigators, what would happen to the optimal amount of cheating?
8. Should DI-FBS split into two divisions, with one for just the schools?

2.16 Assignments

1. Visit the web sites for three schools in your state, with one from each NCAA division. Find and compare information on football ticket prices and availability.
2. Choose a sport and DI conference and search the Internet for the standings for both home and away games (e.g., www.si.com/college-football/standings or www.si.com/college-basketball/standings). Calculate the home winning percentage and find the median value. How does this compare to the estimated value that maximizes attendance in professional sports?
3. Visit the NCAA web site (http://www.ncaa.org) and locate the Major Infractions Database (at press time, accessed via the Resources tab; the name may also change based on the new violation structure adopted for 2013). Search the database for violations in Division I-FBS football programs within the last year. Did any result in penalties other than probation?

2.17 References

2011–2012 SEC Revenue Distribution (2012, June 1). Retrieved from http://www.secdigitalnetwork.com/NEWS/tabid/473/Article/235147/2011-12-sec-revenue-distribution.aspx on June 18, 2013.

Barro, R. (2002, December 9). The Best Little Monopoly In America. *Business Week*, p. 22.

Becker, G. (1987, September 14). The NCAA: A Cartel in Sheepskin Clothing. *Business Week*, p. 24.

Brown, G. (2012, October). Board Adopts Tougher, More Efficient Enforcement Program. *NCAA.org*. Retrieved from http://www.ncaa.org/wps/wcm/connect/public/NCAA/Resources/Latest+News/2012/October/Board+adopts+tougher+more+efficient+enforcement+program on June 29, 2013.

College Football Playoff Revenue Distribution Set (2012, December 11). *USAToday.com*. Retrieved from http://www.usatoday.com/story/sports/ncaaf/bowls/2012/12/11/college-football-bcs-playoff-revenue-money-distribution-payouts/1762709/ on June 1, 2013.

Depken, C. and D. Wilson (2004). What is the cost of probation? Evidence from Division IA college football. Working paper. Retrieved from http://www.uta.edu/depken/P/probationcost.pdf on September 28, 2006.

Depken, C. and D. Wilson (2006). NCAA enforcement and competitive balance in college football. *Southern Economic Journal, 72*(4), 826–845.

Eckard, E. W. (2013). Is the bowl championship series a cartel? Some evidence. *Journal of Sports Economics, 14*(1), 3–22.

Farrey, D. (2001, November 30). NCAA's Once Rabid Watchdog Loses Its Bite. *ESPN.com*. Retrieved from http://espn.go.com/ncf/s/2001/1126/1284940.html on November 6, 2006.

Fleisher, A. A., III, B. L. Goff and R. D. Tollison (1992). *The National Collegiate Athletic Association: A Study In Cartel Behavior*. Chicago: University of Chicago Press.

Fort, R. D. (2011). *Sports Economics* (3rd ed.). Upper Saddle River, NJ: Prentice Hall.

Jude, A. (2013, June 10). As Oregon Ducks await their NCAA fate, a look at major violations at FBS schools since 2008. *The Oregonian*, p. D1.

Kahn, L. (2006). The economics of college sports: cartel behavior vs. amateurism, IZA Discussion Paper No. 2186. Retrieved from http://ssrn.com/abstract=918743 on December 6, 2006.

Kahn, L. (2007). Cartel behavior and amateurism in college sports. *Journal of Economic Perspectives, 7*(1), 209–226.

Koch, J. (1971). The economics of "big-time" intercollegiate athletics. *Social Science Quarterly, 52*, 248–260.

Lyell, K. (2013, March 20). Mountain West Conference Reaches Secondary TV deal with ESPN. *Coloradoan.com*. Retrieved from http://www.coloradoan.com/article/20130320/SPORTS/303200035/Mountain-West-Conference-reaches-secondary-TV-deal-ESP on June 6, 2013.

McNeely, T. (2013, May 20). *NCAA Update to National Association of College and University Business Officers* (PDF slides). Retrieved from http://www.

nacubo.org/Documents/EventsandPrograms/2013HEAF/NCAA_ Update.pdf on July 14, 2013.

National Collegiate Athletic Association. (2006). *2006–2007 NCAA Division I Athletics Certification Handbook*. Indianapolis, IN: Author.

NCAA Enforcement Restructures (2011, June 30). *NCAA.org*. Retrieved from http://www.ncaa.com/news/ncaa/2011-06-30/ncaa-enforcement-restructures on June 23, 2013.

Perline, M., G. Stoldt and M. Vermillion (2013). Competitive balance in conference USA football: The effects of membership churning. *The Sports Journal* Retrieved from http://www.thesportjournal.org/article/competitive-balance-conference-usa-football-effects-membership-churning on June 30, 2013.

Rascher, D. and J. Solmes (2007). Do fans want close contests? A test of the uncertainty of outcome hypothesis in the National Basketball Association. *International Journal of Sport Finance*, 2(3), 130–141.

Rhoads, T. (2004). Competitive Balance and Conference Realignment in the NCAA: The Case of the Western Athletic and Mountain West Conferences. Unpublished Paper. Retrieved from http://pages.towson.edu/trhoads/Rhoads%20SEA%20NCAA%20Conference%20 Alignment.pdf on June 20, 2013.

Sandomir, R. (2013, May 3). SEC Will Start TV Network in 2014. The *New York Times*. p. B16.

SEC Revenue Set to Jump 50% with Playoff, New TV Deals (2013, January 16). *AL.com*. Retrieved from http://www.al.com/sports/index.ssf/2012/12/how_many_bowl_games_are_too_ma.html on June 18, 2013.

Solomon, J. (2012, December 14). How many bowl games are too many? College football's devalued position. *AL.com*. Retrieved from http://www.al.com/sports/index.ssf/2012/12/how_many_bowl_games_are_too_ma.html on June 20, 2013.

Stigler, G. (1971). The Theory of Economic Regulation. Bell Journal of Economics and Management Science, 3, 3–18.

Sutter, D. and S. Winkler (2003). NCAA scholarship limits and competitive balance in college football. *Journal of Sports Economics*, 4(1), 3–18.

Thamel, P. (2013, June 13). Under Emmert, NCAA enforcement division has gone from bad to worse. *SI.com*. Retrieved from http://sports-illustrated.cnn.com/college-football/news/miami-ncaa on June 23, 2013.

Timanus, E. (2005, May 4). MacMurray tennis gest fir 'death penalty' in Div. III. *USAToday.com*. Retrieved from http://usatoday30.usatoday.

com/sports/college/other/2005-05-04-macmurray-tennis-death-penalty_x.htm?csp=34 on July 2, 2013.

Tollison, R. (2012). To be or not to be: The NCAA as a cartel. In L. Kahane and S. Shmanske (Eds.), *The Oxford Handbook of Sports Economics: The Economics of Sports Volume 1* (pp. 339–347). Oxford, UK: Oxford University Press.

Violations (n.d.). Retrieved from www.lincolnu.edu/pages/1034.asp on December 20, 2006.

Vrooman, J. (2009). Theory of the perfect game: Competitive balance in monopoly sports leagues. *Review of Industrial Organization, 34,* 5–44.

Wilner, J. (2006, August 27). Is the system fair? *San Jose Mercury News,* p. 1D.

Wolverton, B. and J. Newman (2013, April 19). Few athletes benefit from move to multiyear scholarships. The Chronicle of Higher Education. Retrieved from http://chronicle.com/article/Few-Athletes-Benefit-From-Move/138643/ on June 30, 2013.

Wolken, D. (2013, June 13). Departures sap strength of NCAA enforcement. *USAToday.com.* Retrieved from http://www.usatoday.com/story/sports/college/2013/06/13/ncaa-enforcement-infractions-mark-emmert/2421317/ on 23 June 2013.

Woolsey, M. (2006, December 5). It can pay to lose in college football. *Forbes.com.* Retrieved from http://www.forbes.com/2006/12/04/college-football-profits-biz-cx_mw_1205football.html on December 8, 2006.

Zimbalist, A. (1999). *Unpaid Professionals: Commercialism and Conflict in Big-Time College Sports.* Princeton, NJ: Princeton University Press.

Chapter 3

The Labor Market for College Athletes

Athletes should be able to pursue a professional career in football or basketball without having to pretend they are also students.

— Andrew Zimbalist, sports economist

My concern is a giant chunk of a fairly large culture is drunk with a risky obsession of one pursuit. See, the ripple effect is a killer when the rock skips through the wrong pond. The local newspaper and [ESPN's] SportsCenter can't chronicle all the dudes who bail on everything else, including reading and writing, by the age of 16 because their mammas and their cousins, most of whom have their hands out, tell them they can make the NBA. It's worse than playing the lottery.

— Michael Wilbon, sports columnist

Look at the money we make off predominantly poor black kids. We're the whoremasters.

— Dale Brown, former LSU Basketball Coach

... nearly a third of present and former professional football players ... said they had accepted illicit payments while in college, and more than half said they saw nothing wrong with the practice.

— The Knight Foundation

3.1 Introduction

In Chapters 1 and 2, you learned that the NCAA is a governance structure that provides public goods to its members. Its initial purpose was to deal with the problem of violence in football, something that each school was unwilling to do on its own. Each school had an incentive to free ride on other schools that adopted less violent tactics, since playing a more violent style than your opponent increased the chance of winning. It took a third party to impose new rules on all the schools, and all schools benefited from renewed fan interest. The NCAA later adopted limits on payments to athletes and was granted the authority by its members to enforce those rules. While we acknowledge that the NCAA benefits its members, we also know that the NCAA is a cartel and that cartels cause economic harm to society as a whole. Now we come to a crossroads; if the NCAA produces both benefits and costs, what is the net result? In the previous chapter, we suggested that it is accurate to identify the NCAA as a natural cartel. But even if we choose to do so we must still ask: do the benefits outweigh the costs, or is it the opposite? To help you decide for yourself, we need to delve deeper into the kind of harm the NCAA creates, not only for consumers of college athletics but for the athletes themselves.

In Chapters 3 and 4 we will focus on two ways that the NCAA cartel harms college athletes. *First*, in some sports — notably football and men's basketball — the revenue the athletes generate for colleges and universities is significantly greater than any compensation they receive. College sports are unlike other industries because its primary labor inputs — the athletes — are not paid a salary. *Second*, the education provided to them can be of poor quality and some college athletes never graduate. In some circumstances, this is because the student-athlete is not prepared for the rigors of an undergraduate education. But often these students fail in their pursuit of an undergraduate education because the athletic department considers athletic performance to be the first priority, with academics a distant second. For many students, the combination of these two factors creates a situation in which they earn little in the way of compensation for their athletic performance, never graduate (or graduate with a degree of little value), and are not talented enough to play professional sports. What future is in store for them?

We begin this chapter by studying different types of labor markets in order to understand how the NCAA and its member institutions are able to take economic advantage of student-athletes. We compare four possible labor markets: a competitive market with many buyers and sellers, a market with a single seller, a market with a single buyer, and a market with one buyer and one seller. We provide real-world examples of each type of labor market and see which one best describes the market for college athletes. In the next chapter we consider ways in which student-athletes are short-changed in terms of their education as opposed to salary.

3.2 Labor Markets

A **competitive labor market** consists of many buyers and sellers. Potential buyers are the employers and sellers potential employees. How much employers are willing to pay, and how much employees are willing to accept, determines the prevailing wage or salary as well as the number of people employed. Because there are many college athletes and many colleges and universities, our first impression of the college sports labor market is that it is competitive (see Figure 3.1). Every year, thousands of high school seniors and junior college students offer their athletic skills to a university in return for some financial assistance (tuition, room and board, books) and the promise of an education. Naturally, each athlete prefers more compensation to less. The universities, acting as buyers, want to attract the best athletes possible. Since there are many schools, each competes against the others and the compensation offered to the best athletes will be higher than that for the lower-quality players. Because there are many schools, a high school or junior college athlete — let us call her Jennifer — will often be recruited by several schools and she must decide which school — USC or Notre Dame, for example — offers her the greatest reward for her services. If Jennifer is already playing collegiate sports at USC she may decide to remain there or transfer to an institution like Notre Dame if it offers her a better deal.

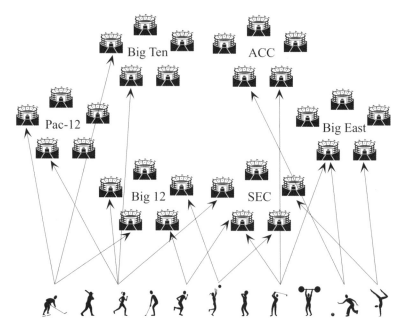

Figure 3.1.   A competitive labor market for college athletes.

Source: Adapted from illustration by Daniel Rascher.

Unfortunately, our first impression is incorrect. Even though there are many schools competing for athletes, there is an overall limit to the amount a student can receive, a full **grant-in-aid** (more commonly known as a "full ride" scholarship) that covers tuition, books, and a stipend for housing, meals and other living expenses. The NCAA limits the "maximum institutional financial aid" an athlete may receive during the academic year (Bylaw 15.01.6). This maximum amount differs from institution to institution and varies by sport.

The NCAA's limitation on the amount of financial aid a student can receive is **price fixing**. Because colleges and universities cannot freely compete on the price they offer to prospective athletes, individuals like Jennifer must take into consideration other factors; for example, the reputation of the school's athletic program, the quality of the athletics facilities, the academic reputation of the school, the variety of majors the school offers, how far away the school is from her home town, the quantity and quality of the amenities offered in the college community, and climate. In other words, while price competition is restricted there is extensive **non-price competition.**

If USC offers, or Jennifer accepts, any monetary or non-monetary compensation above and beyond the approved scholarship amount, the university and she are in violation of NCAA rules and may be punished (Bylaw 15.01.2 states, "A student-athlete shall not be eligible to participate in intercollegiate athletics if he or she receives financial aid that exceeds the value of a full grant in aid ..."). Because NCAA regulations prohibit universities from competing on price, the labor market for athletes is much different than the market for, say, accountants (where there are no limits on how much they can be paid). An accountant who earns income above and beyond her primary job, is awarded a bonus, or works part-time at another job, will not be penalized. The accountant can golf with clients and associates, go to dinner with them, and accept gifts and discounts on goods and services from businesses she patron-izes. A student-athlete can do virtually none of these things. Furthermore, if an accountant decides to quit her job at Microsoft to accept a position at Procter & Gamble, she is free to do so.[1] But if Jennifer decides to transfer from USC to Notre Dame she will be penalized by losing a year of eligibility. But we are getting ahead of ourselves. Before we explore the environment surrounding student-athletes like Jennifer, we need to establish an appropriate basis of comparison as our starting point: a competitive labor market in which employers are free to bid for employees and employ-ees are not restricted from offering their services to the highest bidder.

---

[1] In some occupations, it is common for companies to require their employees to sign do-not-compete agreements. When an employee leaves the company, they are unable to work for a competitor for a proscribed period of time. The rationale is that the employee has acquired valuable inside information that the company does not want to be used against it. Does this rationale apply to college athletes?

Fast fact. *On August 17, 2004, the NCAA ruled against Jeremy Bloom's request that he be allowed to accept endorsement money. Bloom, a wide receiver on the University of Colorado's football team, is a world champion freestyle skier who competed in the 2006 Winter Olympics in Turin, Italy. While Bloom receives some financial support from the U.S. Ski Team, he claimed that it was not sufficient to allow him to train adequately. Bloom accepted endorsement money from the apparel company Under Armour and from Bollé Sunglasses to support his skiing, a sport in which he does not compete at Colorado. The NCAA nevertheless argued that in accepting such endorsements Bloom was no longer eligible to play football for the Buffaloes. Bloom was selected by the Philadelphia Eagles in the fifth round of the 2006 NFL draft. He was later signed by Pittsburgh. His NFL career never panned out, but he co-founded an internet marketing firm, Integrate.com and works as a television analyst for college football games.*

3.2.1   *A competitive labor market*

As previously indicated, one attribute of a competitive labor market is the presence of many buyers and sellers. A good example of such a market is the market for restaurant chefs; in most cities there are quite a few restaurants as well as numerous trained chefs. Each restaurant (acting as a buyer) will hire a chef only if the value of what the chef produces — once all other input costs are taken into consideration — is greater than the cost of hiring the chef (the wage or salary). For example, Chef Suzy can make US$800 of cheesecakes and other desserts each week for the Cheesecake factory, and the cost of the ingredients is US$300. Her employer should be willing to pay her up to US$500 in wages per week. The restaurant would prefer to pay her less of course, but it must take into consideration the fact that other restaurants are competing for Suzy's services. If the Olive Garden offers Suzy a higher wage than she receives at the Cheesecake Factory, she will switch jobs. Similarly,

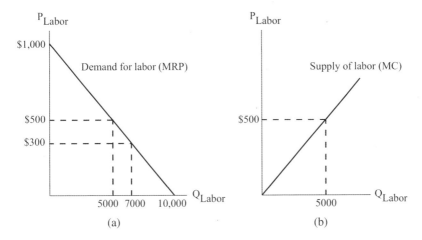

Figure 3.2. Labor demand and supply curves.

while Suzy prefers to earn the highest possible wage, she realizes there are many other chefs in the market. If she demands a wage of US$1000 from restaurants she may find herself unemployed if other chefs are willing to work for a lower wage.

The process just described can be illustrated using the concepts of **demand** and **supply**. Figure 3.2 shows the demand and supply for chefs.[2] The price for chefs (the wage or salary) is measured on the vertical (Y) axis, with the quantity of chefs measured on the horizontal (X) axis. The demand line represents the value of chefs to their potential employers, the restaurants. This value, or willingness to pay, is based on the expected monetary benefit to the restaurant from hiring a chef — what economists refer to as **marginal revenue product** (MRP). If the desserts that Suzy can produce each week would sell for US$500 more than the cost of the ingredients that amount represents her MRP to the Cheesecake factory.

It should not surprise you that the demand line for chefs is downward sloping. What happens if the price for chefs, the wage, falls from US$500 to US$300? Intuition suggests that **quantity**

---

[2] The mathematical equations for our hypothetical demand and supply schedules are included in Appendix 3.1.

demanded will increase as price falls (in Figure 3.2a, from 5,000 to 7,000). If the price of gasoline or bananas falls, people will choose to buy more gas or more bananas. Labor is no different; if the wage for chefs falls, restaurants will hire more chefs (there is an increase in quantity demanded). As indicated in the preceding paragraphs, MRP determines the maximum amount a restaurant will be willing to pay an employee; because of this, the demand line for labor can be interpreted as representing the MRP of each chef hired.

Since we know the demand line has a negative slope, as more chefs are hired (as quantity demanded increases) MRP decreases. For reasons of **diminishing marginal productivity** not every chef hired is equally productive. The first chef hired might be able to produce US$500 worth of desserts each week, while the second is only able to produce US$400, and the third US$300. Why is second chef less productive? Suzy is already making the favorite desserts, so the new chef will have to make something less popular and profitable. Suzy is already using the ovens, so the new chef will get less cooking time. The demand line not only shows us the MRP for each of the chefs in the market but it tell us that MRP differs from chef to chef.

Now let us turn to the supply side of the labor market. We know that there are many people who are willing and able to work as chefs. But we also know that not every person is identical (we have different **opportunity costs**); some people are willing to work for lower wages while others require higher wages to induce them to provide their services. For example, Suzy and Pierre might both be trained chefs but Suzy might have other more highly valued alternative uses of her time than Pierre does; as a result, it will take a higher wage to induce Suzy to work as a chef than Pierre. In the context of labor supply, we refer to a person's opportunity cost as their **reservation wage**, the minimum amount someone must be paid to get them to work. People with a higher opportunity cost will have a higher reservation wage, and people with lower costs will have a lower reservation wage. In our example, Pierre may be willing to work for US$300 per week while Suzy will only work if she gets at least US$500.

Suppose there are 10 chefs offering their services. Chef #1's reservation wage is US$100, Chef #2's is US$200, Pierre's is US$300, Chef #4 is US$400, Suzy is US$500 ... Chef #10, US$1,000. Let us graph this information from the lowest reservation wage to the highest. Figure 3.2b shows the result — an upward sloping supply line for chefs. What else does the supply line tell us? In order to convince more chefs to provide their labor services the market wage must increase. From now on, we will refer to this cost of attracting additional chefs away from their next most highly valued job as the **marginal cost** (MC).

The interaction between many buyers and sellers (demand and supply) determines the prevailing (**equilibrium**) wage and quantity of chefs hired. Our hypothetical example in Figure 3.3a shows that the equilibrium wage (w^*) for chefs is US$500 per week and the equilibrium quantity is 5,000 chefs employed (Q^*). Since we interpret the demand line as MRP and the supply line as MC, at the point of their intersection (Point A) MRP and MC are equal. Point A is where the additional revenue generated by one more chef is equal to the additional cost required to induce the chef work. No more chefs will be hired; if one more chef than Q^* was hired, the

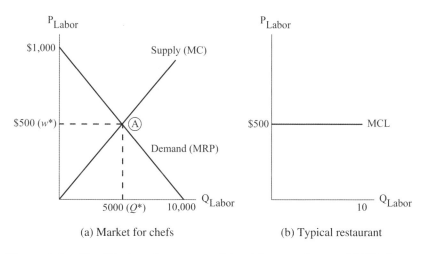

(a) Market for chefs   (b) Typical restaurant

Figure 3.3.   Equilibrium in a competitive labor market and MCL for an individual employer.

cost of hiring that person would exceed that person's contribution in terms of meals produced. Why would restaurants hire a person for a wage of w^* when the value of that chef's output is less than w^*? If the number of chefs hired is less than Q^*, it makes sense to add chefs as long as the additional benefit is greater than the added cost.

Because there are many restaurants and many chefs, each restaurant may hire as many chefs as it wants at the prevailing equilibrium wage without causing the wage to rise. This is because each restaurant is such a small part of the market; if an individual Olive Garden decides to add chefs it can do so without creating a bidding frenzy among all its competitors. In the language of economics, we say that the supply of labor to each restaurant is **perfectly elastic** at the equilibrium wage. Figure 3.3b shows this situation in which each individual restaurant is a price taker, meaning it has no influence over the equilibrium wage. Note that the scale used on the Q axis is different for the typical restaurant (0 to 10 chefs) than for the entire market (0 to 10,000). If we used the same scale, you would need a strong magnifier to see the graph for an individual restaurant.

As you may remember from introductory economics, the equilibrium price or quantity (or both) will change if the market demand or supply lines (or both) shift to the left (decrease) or to the right (increase). Table 3.1 summarizes how the equilibrium price and quantity change when there are shifts in demand and/or supply.

How can we describe the overall benefits to buyers and sellers in the labor market for chefs? What is the gain to chefs from selling their services to restaurants? What is the gain to restaurants from hiring chefs? The gain to restaurants is the difference between the amount they would be willing to pay chefs (MRP) and the amount they actually pay (w^*). If a restaurant was willing to pay Suzy US$700 per week but she is paid the prevailing market wage of US$500, the restaurant gets a gain of US$200 per week when it employs Suzy. This difference is called **consumer surplus** (recall that it is the restaurants who are the consumers of labor). Similarly,

Table 3.1. Changes in equilibrium from shifts in supply and/or demand.

Shifts		Change in equilibrium	
Demand	Supply	Price	Quantity
Increase	—	Increase	Increase
Decrease	—	Decrease	Decrease
—	Increase	Decrease	Increase
—	Decrease	Increase	Decrease
Increase	Increase	Uncertain	Increase
Decrease	Decrease	Uncertain	Decrease
Increase	Decrease	Increase	Uncertain
Decrease	Increase	Decrease	Uncertain

if Suzy is willing to work for US$400 but is paid US$500, she is better off by US$100 every week she works. We call her gain **producer surplus** (because she is the producer of her own labor). Producer and consumer surplus are extremely important economic concepts; if neither sellers nor buyers benefited from trading with one another, if consumer and producer surplus did not exist, there would be less motivation for trade among individuals.

Consumer and producer surplus are represented in Figure 3.4. Consumer surplus is the upper shaded triangle, area CAB; for every chef hired from 0 to Q^*, the restaurants' **willingness to pay** (MRP) exceeds the equilibrium wage, w^*. Producer surplus is the lower shaded triangle, BAE, because every chef from 0 to Q^* gets paid a wage, w^*, which exceeds their reservation wage (MC). Calculating the total surplus for both groups is easy if you remember your high school geometry. In this example, CS and PS both equal US$1,250,000 (see if you can verify this). We refer to consumer and producer surplus added together (area CAE) as the total **gains to trade** in the marketplace. In our example, the gains to trade equal US$2,500,000. In a competitive market with no restrictions on price or quantity, gains to trade will be maximized.

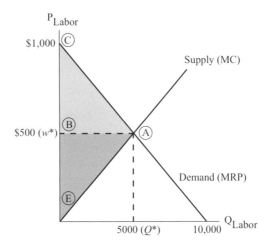

Figure 3.4.   Consumer and producer surplus in a competitive labor market.

Fast fact. Something akin to a free market in college athletes existed prior to and immediately following WWII. The best players attracted bids from schools and — like any supplier of a productive resource — they went where the wage was highest. These wage offers were made not on the basis of need or academic merit but solely on athletic skill. One example was the running back Buddy Young, who returned from the Navy to find that 25 different schools were competing for his services (he ended up at Illinois). Part of the reason for such vigorous competition was due to demographics. The number of colleges with football teams grew rapidly from 220 in 1945 to 650 in 1946 because of the influx of veterans returning from the war. (Sperber, 1998, p. 169)

3.2.2   A labor market with one seller

What happens if there is only a single seller, a **monopolist** supplier, in the labor market? Labor markets typically become monopolized when a **labor union** is formed. There are many labor markets in which unions exist; for example, teachers, airline pilots, actors and songwriters, firefighters, and steelworkers. Labor unions, like the United Steelworkers of America, exist to accomplish two broad objectives for their members: better working conditions and greater monetary compensation. Our discussion focuses on the second objective.

Imagine that you are the only manufacturer and seller of LeBron James Miami Heat replica basketball jerseys. What is the easiest way for you to make the most money possible producing these jerseys? Limit their availability, the supply. Suppose the demand line in Figure 3.2a is for basketball jerseys and not chefs. What happens if only a few jerseys are made available? As we know from elementary economics, greater *scarcity* of any good or service — whether it is chefs, jerseys, bananas, Super Bowl tickets, or gasoline — will result in higher prices.

But what about the market for chefs? If you are the only chef in a city you can demand a very high wage from restaurants since there are no other chefs with whom you must compete. In most circumstances this is an unlikely scenario; chances are there are many chefs in any given city and the equilibrium wage will be close to w^*. But what if you form a labor union with the other chefs and threaten to withhold all labor services unless restaurants increase wages? Restaurants may then have no choice but to hire chefs from the union at wages greater than w^*. In order for your union to be successful, it must restrict the supply of labor *and* ensure that restaurants do not hire a chef unless she belongs to the union. If your union is successful, the wage will rise above w^* and the quantity of chefs supplied will fall below Q^*.

Let us assume that the union is able to establish a new equilibrium, with a wage of w' and Q' chefs supplied (as shown in Figure 3.5). From this graph, we see three obvious differences between a monopolized labor market and a competitive one: wages increase from w^* (US\$500) to w' (US\$666.7), there is a reduction in chefs employed from Q^* to Q' (from 5,000 to 3,333), and the gains to trade decrease. New producer surplus is area HGFE (US\$1,666,666.7) and new consumer surplus is CGH (US\$555,444.5).

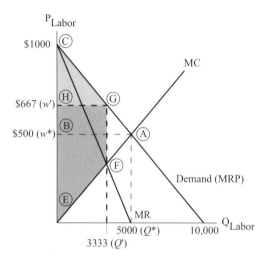

Figure 3.5.   Monopoly labor market.

Table 3.2.   Effect of labor market structure on consumers and producers (in US$).

Labor market structure	Consumer Surplus (CS)	Producer Surplus (PS)	Gains to Trade (GTT = CS+PS)	Deadweight Loss (DWL)
Competitive	1,250,000	1,250,000	2,500,000	0
Monopoly	555,444	1,666,667	2,222,111	277,889
Monopsony	1,666,667	555,444	2,222,111	277,889
Bilateral Monopoly	555,444 to 1,666,667	555,44 to 1,666,667	2,222,111	277,889

Note that the total gains to trade are smaller than they were in a competitive market. This reduction — which economists refer to as the **deadweight loss** — corresponds to area GAF (US$277,888.9). The presence of a labor union means that restaurants are worse off than before, chefs who are still employed are better off, and those chefs who are no longer employed (1,667 chefs) are clearly worse off. To express this slightly differently, if you refer to Table 3.2 you see that while consumer surplus has fallen by US$694,555.5 (from US$1,250,000 to US$555,444.5), producer surplus has only risen by

US$416,666.7 (from US$1,250,000 to US$1,666,666.7). This is the usual result of a monopoly, the amount the beneficiaries (in this case, the chefs who remain employed) gain is less than the amount lost by others (restaurants and unemployed chefs).

Fast fact. Some student-athletes at UCLA have formed a player's union, the Collegiate Athletes Coalition that has since become the National College Players Association. For more information about this organization and its activities visit their web site (http://www. ncpanow.org).

3.2.3   *A labor market with one buyer*

A third type of labor market is when there is only one buyer. This is known as a **monopsony**. Examples include "company towns" in mining regions of the Ohio River Valley and the Australian outback where there is just one employer, or markets in which the government is the only buyer (e.g., for national defense). To understand how a monopsony operates, let's assume all the restaurants join forces to pay chefs a wage lower than w^*.

The fact that the supply line of labor is upward sloping implies that if the monopsony decides to hire more chefs, it must increase wages. Because the restaurants are acting as a *single buyer*, there is an interesting cost implication, one best understood by referring to Table 3.3. Columns A & B describes the supply line by showing how many chefs offer their services depending on the wage. A higher wage results in an increase in quantity hired. Total labor cost is the product of the wage rate and the number of chefs supplied (this is listed in Column C). To determine the right number of chefs to hire, the important cost information for the monopsony is not total cost *but the marginal (additional) cost of hiring chefs*. This **marginal cost of hiring labor**, or MCL for short, is simply the change in total costs when one more chef is hired (MCL information is listed in Column D). For example, when the restaurant

Table 3.3. Revenue and costs for a monopsonist employer (amounts in US dollars).

A Q_{supply}	B wage	C TC	D MCL	E MRP
999	99.90	99,800.10	199.70	900.10
1,000	100.00	100,000.00	199.90	900.00
1,001	100.10	100,200.10	200.10	899.90
1,999	199.90	399,600.10	399.70	800.10
2,000	200.00	400,000.00	399.90	800.00
2,001	200.10	400,400.10	00.10	799.90
2,999	299.90	899,400.10	599.70	700.10
3,000	300.00	900,000.00	599.90	700.00
3,001	300.10	900,600.10	600.10	699.90
3,333	333.30	1,110,888.90	666.50	666.70
3,334	333.40	1,111,555.60	666.70	666.60
3,335	333.50	1,112,222.50	666.90	666.50
3,999	399.90	1,599,200.10	799.70	600.10
4,000	400.00	1,600,000.00	799.90	600.00
4,001	400.10	1,600,800.10	800.10	599.90
4,999	499.90	2,499,000.10	999.70	500.10
5,000	500.00	2,500,000.00	999.90	500.00
5,001	500.10	2,501,000.10	1,000.10	499.90

monopsony employs a total of 1000 chefs and then hires one more (the 1001st), its total costs rise by US$200.10 (from US$100,000 to US$100,200.10) — US$200.10 is the marginal cost to the restaurant monopsony of chef 1001. To determine the most profitable number of chefs to hire, the monopsony compares the value of what the chefs produce to the cost of hiring chefs. The monopsony will hire chefs until the cost of the last chef hired is equal to MRP. The MRP data is provided in Column E of Table 3.3.

The monopsony outcome is depicted in Figure 3.6. To make it easier to compare the monopsony outcome to the competitive labor

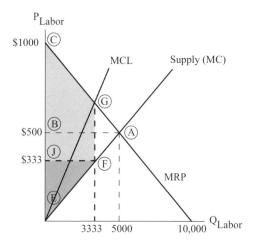

Figure 3.6. Monopsony labor market.

market and the labor union examples, we assume MRP and the supply lines are unchanged. New information, the marginal cost of labor (MCL), is included and we will assume that the MCL line intersects the MRP line at Point G. The monopsony will hire 3,333 chefs because that is where MRP = MCL. Note that while MRP equals US$666.7, the wage paid (Column B) to chefs will only be US$333.3. Compared to the competitive labor market outcome, 1,667 fewer chefs are hired and the wage is lower. This result bears repeating. While the MRP for the last chef hired equals US$666.7, the monopsony is only required to pay the wage based on the supply line (the reservation wage). This difference (US$666.7–333.3), called **monopsonistic rent**, benefits restaurants at the expense of chefs. Put yourself in the shoes of Chef Suzy when the restaurants have formed a monopsony. She will find herself in one of two situations: either she loses her job (she is one of the 1,667 unemployed chefs) or she is employed at a wage of US$333.3 per week, US$166.7 less than what she received when the labor market was competitive. Does either possibility seem fair to you?

Using consumer and producer surplus, we can see how the restaurant monopsony benefits to the detriment of chefs like Suzy. Consumer surplus is area CGFJ (US$1,666,666.7), producer surplus is JFE (US$555,444.5), and deadweight loss is GAF (US$277,888.9).

Unlike the monopoly outcome, restaurants are now better off at a cost to chefs (there is still a reduction in gains to trade). Again, to express this in a slightly different manner, if you refer to Table 3.2 you see that while consumer surplus has increased by US$416,666.7 (from US$1,250,000 to US$1,666,666.7), producer surplus has fallen by US$694,555.5 (from US$1,250,000 to US$555,444.5). The amount the beneficiaries (in this case, the restaurants) gain is less than the amount lost by others (the chefs).

Take a moment to review Table 3.2, which lists consumer and producer surplus, the gains to trade, and deadweight loss for each of the three labor market models we just covered. Does it make sense who benefits and who does not when the labor market is not competitive?

3.2.4   A labor market with one buyer and one seller

The final type of labor market is called a **bilateral monopoly** and it consists of a single buyer and a single seller. Professional sports leagues like the National Football League are good examples of bilateral monopolies. The team owners act like a monopsonist while the players' union (the NFL Players Association) functions as a monopolist. A similar situation would exist if college athletes formed a union to negotiate with the NCAA (see Figure 3.7).

If there is a bilateral monopoly in the market for chefs, the number of chefs employed will be lower than in a competitive market because that is in the individual best interests of both the monopsonist and the monopolist. Referring to our example in Figure 3.8, we observe the optimal quantity for both the monopolist and the monopsonist is 3,333 chefs, so this will be the level of employment.[3] However, we cannot predict what the prevailing wage rate and quantity hired will be. The restaurants will try to drive wages down to US$333.3 while the chefs' union will bargain

---

[3]An identical quantity of labor for a monopolist and a monopsonist will not always occur. In this case, it happens because the slopes of the supply and demand curves are the same (but of opposite signs). However, both quantities will always be less than the competitive equilibrium quantity.

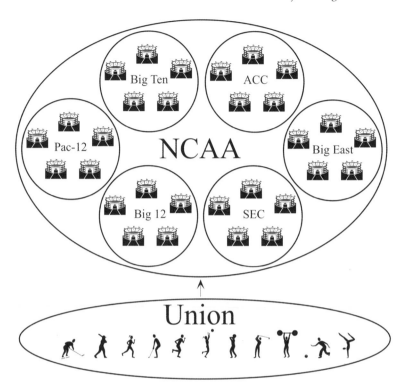

Figure 3.7. A bilateral monopoly labor market for college athletes.
Source: Adapted from illustration by Daniel Rascher.

for a wage of US$666.7. The actual wage rate established will be the result of negotiations between the monopsonist and the union. If one party is either more powerful or a better negotiator, then the wage tends to be closer to their preferred outcome. One interesting possibility is that the two groups agree to "split the difference" and set a wage of US$500, which is the competitive wage rate (but not the competitive quantity, Q^*)! Because there are many possible equilibrium wage rates in a bilateral monopoly, we cannot determine consumer and producer surplus until we know what wage and quantity were agreed to. However, we do know the total amount and that the deadweight loss of GAF (US$278,222.2) will persist (Table 3.2).

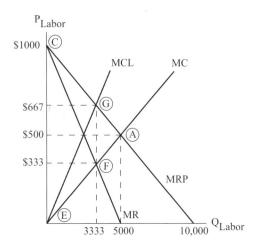

Figure 3.8.   Bilateral monopoly labor market.

Now that we understand each of the four types of labor markets, let us ask *which market best represents intercollegiate sports?* The market for college athletes resembles that of a monopsony (see Figure 3.9). Despite the fact that there are hundreds of colleges and universities competing with one another to attract athletes, the restrictions placed on them by the NCAA are designed to ensure that the institutions do not compete on price.[4] Consequently, the economic contribution of a college athlete (her MRP) to a school is commonly well in excess of her compensation. This difference is captured by the NCAA and its member institutions in the form of a kind of profit called monopsonistic rent. Just imagine if you and your fellow restaurant owners were able to pay chefs a wage far below their economic value to you — imagine all the extra profits you would have!

If Jennifer learns that USC values her soccer skills at US$100,000 each year, but is providing her with a scholarship worth only US$25,000 per year, what are her options? She can remain at USC, transfer to another school like Notre Dame, or stop playing sports

---

[4] Economists have long considered the college athlete labor market a monopsony. See, for example, Koch (1971).

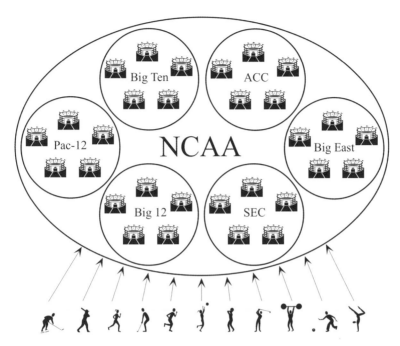

Figure 3.9.   A monopsony labor market for college athletes.
Source: Adapted from illustration by Daniel Rascher.

entirely. Because of NCAA rules, if she transfers to Notre Dame her scholarship will still remain capped well below her economic contribution (her MRP of US$100,000). And, to make matters worse, her transfer will cost her a year of eligibility. Her remaining option — stop playing collegiate sports entirely — is the equivalent of becoming unemployed.

The question of the fairness of monopsonistic exploitation requires us to ask: from whose perspective? While we will continue to use Jennifer as one of our examples of a hypothetical student-athlete, we must clarify that the labor market monopsony model best describes the NCAA's revenue-generating sports — primarily men's basketball and football. While other student-athletes may potentially be exploited by the NCAA and its member institutions, at present it is basketball and football players who are the main victims.

Clearly, some athletes are beneficiaries of the NCAA cartel. We should recognize that scholarship athletes in low revenue sports such as men's wrestling and women's lacrosse are, in all likelihood, receiving compensation close to their MRP or above it. We doubt these athletes are the ones who have an incentive to complain about NCAA practices since they are being subsidized, in whole or in part, by the monopsonistic rents generated by basketball and football but captured and redistributed by the NCAA and the Athletic Departments of its member institutions.

By using the monopsony model, we are also able to explain other outcomes, like why there are limitations on roster size for different sports. As we just observed, in a monopsony the number of persons employed is lower than in a competitive labor market ($Q < Q^*$). Absent the cartel powers of the NCAA, each college or university would both expand its team rosters and increase compensation. Not only would more students be athletes but they would be paid more as well.

3.3   Paying College Athletes

Some people argue that a comparison of chef Suzy to student-athlete Jennifer is misleading because Jennifer receives a benefit that Suzy does not — an education. Research suggests that a person earning an undergraduate degree will, on average, earn approximately one million dollars more in lifetime earnings than a person with only a high school diploma (Burnsed, 2011). In 2011, the median weekly earnings for a person with a bachelor's degree was US$1,551 vs. US$638 for a high school graduate. And the unemployment rate for the more educated person was 4.9% compared to 9.4% (U.S. Bureau of Labor Statistics, 2012). Jennifer's degree will make her better off in the long-run than a person without a degree. In addition, Jennifer may be able to leave college debt-free, unlike the hundreds of thousands of students who finish their undergraduate degree each year owing an average of US$25,250 in loans (Project on Student Debt, n.d.). Her athletic scholarship may also allow Jennifer to avoid having to work during the academic year;

how many of her peers can afford to do the same? Finally, although the probability is low, her athletic scholarship may open the door to the Olympics and subsequent commercial endorsements, or a rewarding career playing professional sports.

Because the issue of paying athletes is controversial, we will approach this question from two perspectives, the positive and the normative. The positive question of whether athletes *can* be paid must be addressed before we consider the normative question of whether they *should* be paid. When we ask the question "can someone be paid" we need to have some idea of how much revenue they generate for their employer. Someone who has a low MRP is unlikely to be paid a high wage or salary while someone who generates a large MRP will earn greater compensation.

What do we mean by the "economic contribution of a college athlete?" The revenue athletes generate for their schools comes from many sources, including television and radio broadcasting contracts, ticket sales, concessions, souvenirs, advertising, alumni and booster clubs contributions, revenues associated with postseason championship games, and possibly increased enrollments. A player such as Emeka Okafor, who played on the University of Connecticut's NCAA DI championship team in 2004, helped UConn attract a share of revenues from television networks such as ESPN (which broadcasts regular season games) and from CBS (which holds exclusive rights to "March Madness"). Why did television viewers choose to watch Okafor and his UConn teammates play during the regular season and the championship tournament — was it the coach, the cheerleaders, the color of the uniforms, the antics of the mascot, or the skills of the UConn players that drew viewers' interest? Whose contribution to the team's success in 2004 was the greatest — the cheerleaders, the equipment manager, the assistant coaches, or the players?

Okafor's skills, combined with those of his teammates, attracted an average of 13,549 fans to Gampel Pavillion for games during the 2003–2004 season. Not only did these fans buy tickets but also concessions and souvenirs. Local merchants and businesses, as well as major corporations, bought advertising in programs, media guides,

---

Box 3.1.   The Flutie effect.

The idea that athletic success and admissions are positively correlated is known as the Flutie effect. Doug Flutie gained national attention as the quarterback for Boston College in the mid-1980s when it won a huge last-minute upset against Miami on a nationally broadcast game. Admissions applications soared at Boston College the next year and university presidents around the country started asking themselves if they could boost enrollments by plowing more resources into their sports program. We discuss the Flutie effect at greater length in Chapters 6 and 7.

---

other team publications, and "signage" in the arena.[5] In the final game of the tournament, UConn defeated Georgia Tech decisively in front of 44,468 spectators in San Antonio and approximately 12% of the nation's television viewers.[6] After the game, replicas of Okafor's jersey went on sale at the UConn bookstore for US$60. Husky fans could also buy items such as a championship hat for US$19.99, a long-sleeved t-shirt for US$26.99, or a DVD for US$21.95. Finally, if the **Flutie effect** holds true (see Box 3.1), Okafor's contribution to UConn's budget may continue even after he leaves school.

How much revenue does a college athlete generate for her institution each year? In Chapter 2, we saw that one particular football player, Marshawn Lynch, contributed an estimated US$800,000 in

---

[5] Connecticut's Athletic Department receives extensive financial support from the business community. A partial list of corporate sponsors as of 2012 on the UConn website (http://www.uconnhuskies.com/sponsorship/corporate-partners.html) includes Allstate, AT&T, Coca-Cola, Dunkin' Donuts, ING Bank, State Farm Insurance, and Toyota.

[6] The Nielsen rating was 11.0. One Nielsen point represents 1% of the nation's households with televisions. The 2004 ratings were the lowest in five years, in part because the game was a lopsided victory for UConn (Martzke, 2004).

revenue to his school. Economists Robert Brown and Todd Jewell have calculated that a star player on the football team or men's basketball team at a Division-I institution generates *US$406,914* and *US$1,194,469* respectively in MRP per season (Brown and Jewell, 2004). Their research also estimates that a star female basketball player generates *US$250,000* (Brown and Jewell, 2006). Providence College economics professor Leo Kahane (2012) conducted a similar study of Division I men's hockey players; he estimated the MRP of the best players to be in the range of *US$131,000–165,000*.[7] Of course, not every player is a star (in the Brown and Jewell studies a star is defined as a player who is drafted by the NFL or NBA). Nevertheless, it seems safe to say that in his three years as a Husky, Mr. Okafor generated revenues for his institution well in excess of his grant-in-aid.[8] To add another example, Baird (2004, p. 221) mentions that in 2001 the *average* revenue created by the 100 players on the Ohio State football team was US$203,000 per player.

> *Fast fact.* During the four years, Patrick Ewing attended Georgetown University (1981–1985), the Hoyas qualified for the NCAA basketball tournament three times and won the 1984 championship. Ewing's MRP during this period was estimated at US$12 million. (Fleisher, Goff and Tollison, 1992, pp. 92–93)

Few intercollegiate sports make money. Recent information provided by the NCAA (Table 3.4) indicates that of the men's

---

[7] Huma and Staurowsky (2012) estimate the average "fair market value" of FBS football and DI basketball players to be US$137,357 and US$289,031. This is estimated by applying the current revenue sharing guidelines used by the NFL and NBA in the collective bargaining agreements with the players' union, to the annual football and basketball revenue generated at each institution.

[8] For academic year 2003–2004, Connecticut's website (http://www.bursar.uconn.edu/forms/Tuition_FeesFY04_Undergrad.html) listed estimated total tuition, fees and room and board at US$13,710 and US$24,494 for in and out-of-state students respectively. Okafor plays for the Washington Wizards in the NBA.

Table 3.4.   Generated revenues and expenses by selected sports in Division I FBS in fiscal year 2010 (median values; amounts in thousands of US$).

Sport	Men's programs			Women's programs		
	Revenues	Expenses	Net revenues	Revenues	Expenses	Net revenues
Baseball	338	1,292	(588)	N/A	N/A	N/A
Basketball	4,776	4,003	788	277	2,168	(1,168)
Crew	N/A	N/A	N/A	105	1,104	(860)
Equestrian	N/A	N/A	N/A	79	910	(854)
Fencing	30	175	(80)	45	244	(96)
Field Hockey	N/A	N/A	N/A	68	817	(714)
Football	16,210	12,367	3,148	N/A	N/A	N/A
Golf	68	382	(228)	48	427	(274)
Gymnastics	61	573	(290)	70	824	(547)
Ice Hockey	919	2,155	(333)	120	1,174	(1,016)
Lacrosse	548	1,161	(460)	157	814	(390)
Rifle	0	28	(28)	31	41	(9)
Skiing	43	379	(190)	43	311	(173)
Soccer	132	811	(501)	67	873	(529)
Softball	N/A	N/A	N/A	66	819	(582)
Swimming	58	625	(448)	47	742	(463)
Tennis	45	448	(290)	27	479	(337)
Track & Field/ X-Country	70	798	(485)	52	941	(596)
Volleyball	162	628	(350)	78	927	(595)
Water Polo	168	539	(335)	35	611	(485)
Wrestling	140	719	(373)	N/A	N/A	N/A
Others	231	365	(273)	14	121	(74)

Note: Generated revenues consist "only of those revenues earned by activities of the athletics program" (Fulks, 2011, p. 7) such as ticket sales, NCAA distributions, appearance guarantees, alumni and booster contributions, broadcasting rights, concessions, souvenirs, advertising and sponsorships, endowment income, and other miscellaneous sources. Revenues allocated through direct and indirect institutional support, students fees, direct government support (in other words, any subsidies to the athletics program), and third party support ("payments to athletics coaches and other personnel from outside parties," Fulks, 2011, p. 107) are **not included**. *Allocated revenue* (not listed in Table 3.4) consists of generated revenues plus all these other revenue sources. The *net revenue* figures listed in Table 3.4 are the difference between *allocated revenues* and *expenses*.

sports in Division I-FBS, only basketball and football typically earn revenues in excess of expenses (Fulks, 2011, p. 36). Revenues for DII and DIII sports are substantially lower. As yet, no women's sport is profitable. This means that payments to athletes based on their MRP would result in an inequality because it would depend on the skills of athlete and the popularity, and revenue-generating ability, of their sport. But do not forget that inequality is already present in collegiate sports; the value of an athlete's grant-in-aid is not constant across sports and gender. Even though the star athletes get a full ride, a benchwarmer on the basketball team or a member of the swimming team might be ecstatic if they each receive a partial scholarship and eat meals at the training table. Furthermore, differences in wages and salaries are a part of everyday life; not every chef or accountant is equally productive, hence they do not earn the same pay. Should college athletes be any different?

What conclusion, if any, should we draw at this point? Could *all* college athletes, regardless of gender and sport, be paid their MRP? Certainly! But many — the majority — of student-athletes would get nothing because their MRP is zero. In the cases of low revenue-earning sports like swimming, the value of an athlete's grant-in-aid exceeds his or her MRP, and these athletes would be harmed by changing the system of compensation from one based on grants-in-aid to payment based on productivity. Before such a change is considered a host of questions must be addressed. Should college sports be financially self-supporting? Should higher revenue sports (men's basketball and football) subsidize sports that generate little or no revenue?[9] The answers depend on whether

---

[9] Here is a contrarian position on the desirability of using football and basketball to subsidize other sports, "the NCAA takes money from financially poor African–American athletes — Division I football and men's basketball players, who generate millions of dollars for the parent cartel and member institutions every year — and redistributes it to middle and upper-income white students (who have grants-in-aid to play on non-revenue sports teams, which are funded largely by football and basketball receipts and are overwhelmingly non-black in composition)". Sanderson (2004)

you believe intercollegiate athletics are an integral part of undergraduate education that should be operated without concern for profitability. The answers to these questions are difficult and will likely be much different for the high profile athletic programs in DI institutions and the less revenue-driven programs in DII and DIII. These questions notwithstanding, many DI schools — *if they choose to do so* — are in the position of being able to pay their football and basketball players a wage that is closer to their MRP. However, unless substantive reforms are enacted in intercollegiate sports, institutions will not share cartel profits — the monopsonistic rents — with their athletes.

As we will see in forthcoming chapters, the monopsonistic rents being captured by universities at the expense of student-athletes are spent in a variety of ways: On Athletic Department personnel salaries, recruiting, supplies, new construction of facilities and maintenance of existing facilities. Paying athletes will not decrease the size of the Athletic Department's expenditures, it will only redistribute it.[10] Instead of paying coaches million dollar salaries, entertaining potential recruits with steak and lobster dinners, and outfitting Athletic Department facilities with leather chairs and sofas, wood paneling, plasma televisions and PlayStations, refrigerators full of Gatorade, and plush carpeting, athletes will earn something like a competitive wage for their athletic prowess. Just like Shorty McWilliams (remember him from Chapter 1?), if an athlete like Jennifer is dissatisfied with her compensation from USC, she will be free to transfer to a school like Notre Dame that is willing to pay her something closer to her MRP. Again, compare Jennifer's situation with that of an accountant or chef. If you were Chef Suzy, would you prefer living in a world where restaurants freely compete for your services or one in which all the restaurants collude to keep your wage as low as possible?

---

[10] However, this raises an interesting question: does the introduction of payments to student-athletes shift the demand schedule for collegiate sports to the right or left (does the popularity of college sports among the population increase or decrease)?

3.4 Early Entry

Early entry is a situation in which a player still has remaining years of eligibility but chooses to opt out of collegiate sports in the hopes of establishing a professional career. Most of the high profile cases of early entry — like Carmelo Anthony leaving Syracuse in 2003 and Kevin Love departing UCLA in 2008 — occur in men's basketball. More recently, an increasing number of football players have been leaving early as well, including the controversial Ohio State running back Maurice Clarett, whom we discuss below.[11] Current NCAA regulations allow a basketball player to leave if more than one year has elapsed since the player completed high school (in football the rule is three years).

Critics of early entry are correct when they point out that the odds of success are stacked against a player who chooses to leave college early. According to the NCAA, the probability of a male high school student playing college basketball (across all NCAA divisions) is about 3.2% and around 6.1% for football. Playing college basketball or footballresult in a probability of 1.2% and 1.7% of making it to the NBA and NFL, respectively. Overall, the probability of a high school student making it to the pros is 0.03% and 0.08% for basketball and football. The chances of a NCAA athlete playing at least one game professionally in baseball is 11.6%. (NCAA, n.d.)

The odds of making it to the pros also depend on the institution you attended. Players like NFL receiver Randy Moss, who attended a DI school in West Virginia (Marshall University) may be overlooked by recruiters, compared to players at better-known schools like Notre Dame and Florida State. Also, keep in mind that playing professionally is not the same thing as making it all the way to the NBA, NFL, or MLB. Many professional careers end in the minor leagues (and playing a single game at the pro level is far different from enjoying a long career). Playing abroad is an option — former

---

[11] In 2004, 35 players entered the NFL draft early. Only two, Clarett and USC's Mike Williams had been in college less than the three year minimum required by the NCAA.

UCLA basketball player Ed O'Bannon's brief NBA career was followed by seven years mostly in Europe with teams in Italy, Spain, Greece, Argentina, and Poland — but many athletes struggle with language and cultural differences and living far from home. For most college athletes that turn pro (whether they leave early or not), a common scenario is: get drafted, get cut during training camp, game over (and the end of their dreams). For every success story, there are many washouts who cannot resume their collegiate athletics career (because of NCAA rules) and returning to university is not an option because of financial considerations.

> **Fast fact.** *Randy Moss was originally recruited by Notre Dame but the school rescinded his scholarship when he was convicted of battery as a result of a fight in high school. Moss transferred to Florida State but was kicked off the team for smoking marijuana while he was still on probation for battery. He served 30 days in jail before he transferred to Marshall.*

The NCAA argues that limitations on leaving early are in the best interests of the student. The NCAA's position is that restrictions on early entry are designed to protect student-athletes, especially those from disadvantaged households, from falling victim to unscrupulous agents, their own unrealistic expectations, or the greed of the player's friends and family.[12] The NCAA encourages players interested in a pro career to either finish their degree first, or complete enough coursework so that the degree can easily be finished later. That ensures that when their pro career ends they have a degree to fall back on or be very close to its completion.

You probably will not be surprised to know that economists view early entry a little differently than the critics and the NCAA. To begin with, while there is an opportunity cost *of not* completing an undergraduate degree, there is also the cost *of* finishing it.

---

[12] For evidence on unscrupulous sports agents, see Luchs and Dale (2012).

Remember that your opportunity cost is the highest valued alternative you give up when you engage in an action. Every hour you spend in college is an hour you cannot spend doing something else (working, watching television, sleeping, eating Chalupas®, or washing your dog). For many of us, if we were not pursuing an undergraduate education we would be working full time. Thus, every hour, week, or month spent at school represents lost earnings. But since we are young, dumb, and unskilled, it probably makes more sense to invest in our education now rather than working at a local restaurant because the future payoff to us, if we finish, will greatly exceed today's earnings.[13]

This economic perspective explains why both Carmelo Anthony left Syracuse and Kevin Love left UCLA after their freshman years to play in the NBA. The opportunity cost to them of remaining at school was too great. For Anthony and Love, every additional year at Syracuse or UCLA meant giving up a year's salary in the NBA (Anthony's salary in 2003–2004 was US$3.2 million, while Love earned US$3.1 million with the Minnesota Timberwolves in 2008–2009). As we have stated elsewhere, a player like Love did not need a Nobel Prize in economics to figure out that his NBA wages would dwarf the value of his athletic scholarship.[14] At the time both players entered the draft they believed they were sufficiently prepared for the rigors of NBA games — any additional time at Syracuse or UCLA was unlikely to improve their skill level and draft selection. Also, if they chose to remain in college there was always a chance of injury that could jeopardize their professional career. The offers they anticipated getting were too lucrative to pass up (NBA contracts for first round draft picks are guaranteed, that is, they get paid even if injured or spend the season sitting on the bench). Plus, the sooner a player enters the NBA, the sooner he becomes a free agent and is able to negotiate potentially even larger contracts. We have every confidence that, if they choose to do so, Messrs. Anthony and Love should be able to afford to return to Syracuse and UCLA and complete their degrees once their professional

---

[13] For a detailed presentation of the early entry decision see Appendices 3.2 and 3.3.
[14] Zygmont (2008).

careers come to an end (if not before; the "Big Aristotle," Shaquille O'Neal, finished his LSU degree during off-seasons while he played for the Los Angeles Lakers).

Another question that an athlete must consider is whether to attend college at all. Why bother with classes, homework, exams, study hall, etc., when your objective is to turn pro? Former NBA guard Stephon Marbury played only one season at Georgia Tech because, as he candidly observed, it was "just a way to position myself for the ... draft" (Zimbalist, 1999, p. 39). Until the rules were changed in 2006, it was becoming more common for players to bypass college entirely and enter the NBA draft right out of high school (notable examples are Kobe Bryant, LeBron James, and Sebastian Telfair). Retired NBA player Jamal Mashburn said "[c]ollege might be necessary for some but not necessary for others. It should be left up to the individual to decide their future — not an age limit delaying their progress."[15]

If the NCAA is concerned about players leaving college early, perhaps it should consider allowing them to renew their collegiate career if they fail as professionals, or pay them a salary closer to their MRP so they can afford to return to school if they wash out of the NBA or NFL. In the meantime, you should expect to see more "one and done" players like Anthony or Love. Some might even follow the route pioneered by Brandon Jennings, who avoided the one and done rule by playing abroad in the Italian League for one season before entering the NBA draft.

> **Fast fact.** *While Kobe Bryant and LeBron James are the highest pro-file players to have gone directly from high school to the NBA, they owe a big debt of gratitude to Spencer Haywood. In 1971, Haywood challenged the NBA's restrictions on high school entry. This resulted in the legal case Haywood v. NBA. On March 1, 1971, the U.S. Supreme Court ruled in Haywood's favor and opened the door for later players like Kobe and LeBron. (Zuhri, 2011)*

---

[15] *Sporting News* (2009, October 27, p. 35).

We must consider the possibility that athletic directors, the institutions they work for, and the NCAA may not have the best interests of the student-athletes in mind when they attempt to restrict early entry. The case of Maurice Clarett, a talented tailback for the Ohio State Buckeyes, is instructive in this regard. As a freshman in 2002, Clarett ran for over 1200 yards and was a key contributor to the Buckeyes' 14-0 record. OSU defeated arch-rival Michigan in the last game of the season to win the Big Ten Championship, and beat the University of Miami 31-24 in an exciting double overtime game at the 2003 Fiesta Bowl. As a result of its outstanding season, Ohio State was unanimously selected national champion by the Associated Press, ESPN and BCS polls. In 2003, allegations concerning the value of items reported by Clarett as stolen after a break-in of his automobile, compounded by allegations of improper payments, led OSU to suspend him for his sophomore season. Clarett and his attorneys, unsuccessful at gaining reinstatement, challenged the NCAA's rules concerning early entry, and petitioned that Clarett be allowed to enter the April 2004 NFL draft. A United States District Court ruled in Clarett's favor in February, 2004 but a higher court, the Circuit Court of Appeals, delayed the lawsuit. To ensure Clarett would be available for the April NFL draft, his attorneys filed an emergency appeal asking the U.S. Supreme Court to immediately consider the case. One day prior to the draft the Supreme Court rejected the request. Since Clarett retained an agent to help him prepare for the 2004 NFL draft, he lost all remaining years of eligibility and was in limbo until the 2005 NFL draft, when he was picked by the Denver Broncos. The Broncos cut him later in the year. In early 2006, he was arrested for armed robbery in Columbus, Ohio. He was found guilty and served three years at a gated community in Toledo, Ohio. After being released, he joined the Omaha Nighthawks of the United Football League. He was not listed on the team roster for the 2012 season. Another player who requested early entry, receiver Mike Williams of USC, was also turned down by the NCAA. Williams was selected by the Detroit Lions in the 2005 draft and played for the Lions, Raiders, Titans, and Seahawks. He was released by Seattle in July 2012.

Had the Supreme Court found in favor of Clarett and Williams an important precedent would have been established, a precedent that the NCAA (and the NFL) hoped to avoid at all costs.[16]

3.5   Should Student-Athletes be Paid?

We have established that it would be feasible to pay athletes a competitive wage. We have also concluded that NCAA limits on compensation increase the opportunity cost of remaining in college until graduation, leading to early entry to professional sports. Let us turn now to the question of whether student-athletes *should* be paid. We believe the answer to this question is yes, but we acknowledge that a movement away from the current NCAA-driven monopsonistic labor market to something more akin to a free market would profoundly change the landscape of collegiate sports. Instead of discussing those implications now, we postpone them until Chapter 9, where we consider the issue of reform. Until then, our reasoning is summarized in Box 3.2.

As we saw in the prior chapters, college sports at the DI level is big business. As we discuss in more detail in Chapter 6, many athletics departments are multi-million dollar enterprises yet, as we know now, their primary producers — the athletes — receive very little of the revenue flow. Knowing that 80% or more of the NCAA's revenue comes from television broadcasting contracts reminds us of a point we raised earlier, when you and I attend a college game, or watch one on television, we want to watch talented athletes playing to the best of their ability in an entertaining and competitive contest. Let's be honest: Do you tune in to watch the announcers, the referees, the coach, or the band? Are you concerned with an athlete's GPA, her major, her year in school, or whether she will graduate? Or do you simply want to be entertained by watching good athletes

---

[16]College football programs like Ohio State's function as minor league franchises for the NFL. Unlike Major League Baseball and the National Hockey League, the NFL makes no financial contribution to college athletics program. The same is true for the NBA. The NFL is free-riding, and has no interest in jeopardizing the status quo. The NFL Player's Association is also against early entry because it increases competition for roster spots.

Box 3.2. The pros and cons of paying college athletes.

The Pros:

- The reduction of economic exploitation. Players' compensation will approach MRP.
- Greater compensation to players will put them in a more advantageous economic position if they do not graduate.
- Allowing universities to freely compete for athletes based on a wage will reduce the incentive to cheat.
- The reduction of cheating will reduce the administrative costs of recruiting, reduce the arms race in athletics facilities, and monitoring and enforcement by the NCAA
- Paying athletes will result in a significant restructuring in college sports (we discuss this in greater detail in Chapter 9). Some universities will be unable to use sports as a means to attract students.
- Colleges and universities will be more likely to pursue working relationships with professional sports leagues (e.g., the NFL and NBA) in which the leagues bear some of the player development costs.
- Discourages early entry.

The Cons:

- Paying athletes will lead to a decreased interest in college sports. Attendance at sporting events and television viewing will erode.
- Decreased interest in college sports may lead to declining enrollments and financial difficulties by some colleges and universities.
- Great inequities in compensation will occur (many athletes will get US$0).
- Paying athletes may require non-revenue producing sports to be eliminated.

(Continued)

Box 3.2.   (Continued)

- Less emphasis will be placed on academics than before and graduation rates will decline further.
- Paying athletes will create an "us vs. them" environment on campus (students vs. athletes).
- There may be increased involvement by professional sports leagues and corporations leading to increased commercialization of college sports.

---

compete against each other? If so, why shouldn't these people — whom an associate athletic director once candidly called "the entertainment product" (Yost, 2009, p. 13) — earn a competitive wage?

The question whether to pay players is the proverbial elephant in the room. Not only is the elephant there, it is growing in size. Influential print media such as *The New York Times* (Nocera, 2011), *The Atlantic* (Branch, 2011), and *Sports Illustrated*, as well as broadcast journalism ("*Money and March Madness*") have recently published lengthy reports about the college sports industry and the question of pay for play. Consider, for example, this recent quote from *Sports Illustrated* writer George Dohrmann (2011):

> The movement among athletes to gain an economic stake is stronger than ever: Last month more than 300 current football and men's basketball players sent a petition to the NCAA demanding a cut of the millions in annual TV revenue from those sports. At the same time, the NCAA and its members assert that mandating such payments is not fiscally possible. The NCAA approved a measure last week to allow conferences to give schools the option to boost scholarships by US$2,000 to cover the full cost of attendance. However, several schools said that they either could not afford such stipends or that they would face a backlash from their faculty if they awarded them.[17]

---

[17]See also Nocera (2011) and Branch (2011).

The athletes themselves are aware that the value of their scholarship pales in comparison to the revenue they generate for the institution. This often leads them to accept "illegal" payments to supplement their scholarship or to engage in academic dishonesty to maintain eligibility (we will elaborate on these academic issues in a moment). Paying the entertainment product a competitive wage, something closer to their MRP, will reduce the incentive to cheat as well as eliminate the sanctimony of the NCAA and its member institutions claiming that college sports is not about money while they keep millions and millions of dollars each year. To argue that no precedent exists for paying athletes ignores history. As you recall, prior to 1952, athletes could essentially sell their services to the highest bidder; a quasi-free market in labor existed, just like the market for chefs or accountants or myriad other professions today.

We recognize that if you counted all the student-athletes who are exploited by the NCAA out of the roughly 166,000 who participate

---

Box 3.3. A better way?

In 2011, *Sports Illustrated* (Dohrmann, 2011) engaged in an important and ambitious attempt to develop a financial model that would allow student-athletes to be paid. *SI* used publically available financial information from four institutions — Louisville, Mississippi, Oregon, and San Jose State — to illustrate possible outcomes from the model. Like all models there are assumptions, these are: The amount paid to athletes (a stipend) would be equal across all sports, men's and women's; the stipend would be in addition to any athletic scholarship; football scholarships would be cut from 85 to 63; and the requirement that each institution offer a minimum number of sports would be dropped. The amount of the stipend would be US$1,000 per month. More detail about this proposal is in Chapter 9.

Box 3.4. What do the players think?

In 2009, *The Sporting News* asked several former college basketball players whether some of the revenue generated from the broadcasting contract for the men's basketball tournament should be shared with the players. Rony Seikaly (Syracuse) said "[i]t would take the purity of college games away." Jeff Fryer (Loyola Marymount) added "[t]he players earn scholarships, I think that is enough." Ken McFadden (Cleveland State) responded "[i]t is a disgrace to every athlete who participates in such an event … and can't get paid."

---

in DI sports (or the 444,000 who play at any NCAA institution) the number is quite small. One might similarly argue that if Chef Suzy and her kitchen colleagues were only exploited by a monopsony in a few selected cities around the United States, then why should we worry, the problem seems trivial. If this were the case, Chef Suzy could move to a city in which the labor market for chefs was competitive. College athletes, in contrast, are trapped by the cartel; they have no other market in which to sell their services. Either you play by the NCAA's rules or you do not play at all. Does the NCAA's statement that "student-athletes should be protected from exploitation by professional and commercial enterprises" (NCAA Constitution, Article 2.9) seem hypocritical when it is the NCAA that is the exploiter? And, to make matters worse, the NCAA's claim that its mission is to ensure that student-athletes receive a solid education is, as we will see in the next chapter, open to dispute. It is not just the star athletes who are affected by the NCAA's lack of concern for student's academic performance — it is all of them.

3.6   Common NCAA Violations

Even with NCAA rules against payments in excess of aid offered to other students, schools are under economic pressure to lure the best athletes with whatever means they can, including violating NCAA rules. In Chapter 2 we discussed why NCAA rules violations are so common and why the NCAA has adopted a policy of selective and limited enforcement. Of the numerous NCAA infractions documented each year, the two most common are **extra/ impermissible benefits** — when a student-athlete receives something of value which is unavailable to other students — and academic impropriety. We defer discussion of academic violations until the next chapter.

NCAA Bylaw 16.01.1 states that "[a] student-athlete shall not receive any extra benefit." The NCAA considers any payment of cash or in-kind transfer above and beyond the athletic scholarship to be an extra benefit and a rules violation unless that benefit is freely available to other students not participating in athletics (Bylaw 16.02.3). Many of the violations involving extra benefits are inadvertent and trivial. In official NCAA language, such a violation is considered *minor* and the punishment usually involves a slap on the hand. The offending student-athlete is typically required to pay an amount equivalent to the benefit and the athletic department must change or clarify its procedures so that similar offenses do not occur again. In Chapter 2, we referred to these kinds of contraventions of the rules as **ham sandwich violations**. The name comes from an actual case involving Nebraska quarterback, Eric Crouch. In May 2000, Crouch accepted a plane ride from a friend and ate a ham sandwich during the trip. An anonymous tip led the NCAA to investigate and Crouch was required to pay US$22.77 in restitution for his travel and meal, which he donated to charity.[18] As we mentioned in Chapter 2, these violations can be interpreted in two very different ways. Either they represent the NCAA's attempt to play "bad cop" by cracking down on all violations, even those that appear trivial, *or* they are examples of the **illusion of control** — a propaganda effort by the NCAA to convince the public that it is

---

[18] http://sportsillustrated.cnn.com/football/college/news/2000/06/07/crouch_sandwich_ap/.

vigilant when, in truth, even more serious violations are occurring regularly.

The often substantial gap between an athlete's MRP and the value of her scholarship explains why universities and the student-athletes have an incentive to break the rules regarding improper benefits and why students-athletes often leave college to enter the professional draft in their sport. By offering talented players unauthorized payments or in-kind transfers, a university may be able to attract and retain better players, players whose contribution on the field will help the team win. And players, especially those from low-income households, may find it difficult to refuse such payments.

In his book *Unpaid Professionals*, economist Andrew Zimbalist (1999, pp. 17–18) described the life of Duke point guard Kenny Blakeney. Even though Blakeney was receiving a full grant-in-aid, and was probably in a more advantageous situation than his counterparts at other schools (see sidebar), he was hardly living a life of luxury. Zimbalist estimated that once rent, utilities, meals outside training table, and incidental expenses were deducted from his monthly scholarship, he was broke at the end of every month (like

---

Fast fact. *In his book* Keeping Score: The Economics of Big-Time Sports, *Richard G. Sheehan (1996) calculated the implicit wage earned by basketball and football players at different US colleges and universities. The implicit wage was calculated by estimating the value of an athlete's grant-in-aid divided by the number of hours the typical athlete spends practicing, playing, watching film, lifting weights, etc. He listed the schools with the highest and lowest implicit wages as well as graduation rates. He found a positive correlation between implicit wages and graduation rates (does this result surprise you?). If Sheehan's approach is applied to the estimates of Brown and Jewell, a star football player generates approximately US$400 per hour in revenue for his institution while a basketball player generates US$1,100 per hour.*

college students since time immemorial). Yet during Blakeney's career at Duke, the Blue Devils qualified for the NCAA tournament three times and won the championship twice, generating hundreds of thousands of dollars for Duke University and its Athletic Department.[19]

The violations that led the NCAA to suspend the football program at Southern Methodist University were examples of *major* violations. In such cases, it is highly likely that the participants were aware that they were breaking NCAA rules. The cause of these violations rests with incentives; schools have an incentive to offer extra benefits and student-athletes have an incentive to accept them. If you are the Athletic Director at USC trying to recruit an 18 year-old prep quarterback who has numerous offers from other schools, and who may play a key role in USC winning the Pac-12 and vying for the national championship, do you have an incentive to offer something "under the table?" Absolutely! If you were the quarterback, would you be able to resist enticements like a US$1 per year lease on a sport utility vehicle, unlimited complimentary major brand shoes and apparel, or an envelope full of US$100 bills? We suspect most would find it difficult.

One of the most publicized major violations involving extra benefits occurred at the University of Michigan. The men's basketball team, known as the "Fab Five" (Chris Webber, Juwan Howard, Jalen Rose, Jimmy King, and Ray Jackson) appeared in the NCAA basketball championship game in 1992 and 1993, but lost both times, first to Duke and then to North Carolina. Webber accepted money — allegedly a total of US$280,000 (the equivalent of US$462,000 in 2012 dollars) — from booster Ed Martin on numerous occasions during his time in Ann Arbor, and then lied about it in court in 2002 when Martin was under investigation for running an illegal gambling operation. In return for Webber's cooperation in indicting Martin, the charges of perjury were dropped. However, Martin's involvement with Webber, and several other Wolverines,

---

[19] Blakeney graduated from Duke in 1995 with a degree in history. He was an assistant coach at the University of Delaware and later, Harvard.

resulted in the NCAA levying harsh punishments on Michigan, including forfeiture of 113 basketball victories and "erasing" all references to the 1992 and 1993 tournament appearances (Shepardson, 2003). While there is no doubt that Webber's actions violated NCAA rules, sportswriter Mitch Albom's book *Fab Five* contains a passage that may help explain Webber's actions. Webber and a friend went to a fast food restaurant for lunch. After placing his order at the counter, he realized he did not have enough money to pay for the meal so he reduced the size of his order. He commented to his friend "I can't believe this **** man. I gotta put back food." Then he pointed to an adjoining store where a replica of his basketball jersey was on display at a price of US$75 and said, "how is that fair?". (Albom, 1993, pp. 214–215)[20]

Fast fact. Bachman (2006) indicates that several universities, including the University of Southern California, Oregon, and Kansas are auctioning "game-worn" player jerseys. While the sales are currently resulting in a few thousand dollars, it is another indication of the aggressiveness athletic departments are demonstrating in identifying revenue sources (a point we elaborate in Chapter 6). It also raises questions about whether such sales are further evidence of the economic exploitation of athletes. If an athlete were to sell his used game equipment he would be in violation of NCAA rules. (see Jung, 2005)

Webber's inability to cash in on the sales of Michigan team gear and other souvenirs bearing his name and/or his likeness is a problem faced by all student-athletes. Each year, prior to beginning

---

[20] Michigan was selling replica basketball jerseys for US$75 and shorts for US$75. The uniform frequently sold out. There were also Wolverine basketball trading cards which sold for US$5.95 per pack. At least 30,000 packs were sold (Albom, 1993, p. 259). Albom also mentions that when Webber was being recruited someone telephoned his father to offer him several hundred thousand dollars if he could convince his son to enroll at Mississippi State (1993, Chapter 8).

competition, Jennifer and all athletes are required to sign a *Student-Athlete Statement*. Completion of this seven page document is a requirement of Bylaw 14.1.3.1 which states, in part, that Jennifer must submit "information related to eligibility, recruitment, financial aid, amateur status, previous positive-drug tests … [and] involvement in organized gambling activities …" On the face of it, the document (NCAA Form 10-3a) appears innocuous; Jennifer is just certifying that she understands the rules and has not violated them. There are seven parts to the form. Part IV authorizes the NCAA to "use your name or picture in accordance with Bylaw 12.5 … [to promote NCAA events]". Bylaw 12.5.1.1(h), in turn, says essentially that the NCAA retains all rights to sell "commercial items with names, likenesses or pictures" of student-athletes like Jennifer. While the phrase "in perpetuity" is not expressly stated in the Bylaw, the NCAA's position is that it, not the student-athlete, holds those commercial rights forever. Take a moment to think through the implications of this. It means that Chris Webber cannot profit from sales of his Michigan jersey (or other commercial items that use his name or image) while he is a student-athlete, and he can *never* profit from those sales, even after his career at Michigan, and even his NBA career, are long finished.

Have you ever played the video games *NCAA Basketball 10* or *NCAA Football 13* on your Xbox 360 or PlayStation? Both games are designed and manufactured by Electronic Arts (EA), one of the biggest sellers of video games in the United States. EA licenses the right to use player images in those games from the NCAA through the Collegiate Licensing Company (CLC) a business that "oversees all licensing, marketing, and distribution of royalties for the NCAA" (Holthaus, 2010 p. 372).[21] CLC, in turn, is owned by the International Management Group (IMG), a prominent global sports and media business. In May 2009, former Arizona State and Nebraska quarterback Sam Keller filed a lawsuit against EA, CLC and the NCAA for using the likeness of college players in video

---

[21] For a list of CLC's clients see http://www.clc.com/clcweb/publishing.nsf/Content/institutions.html.

games without compensation (Holthaus, 2010). Separate, but similar, cases were filed by Ryan Hart (ex-Rutgers QB) and Ed O'Bannon (who played basketball at UCLA). All three claims have been merged into one overarching lawsuit entitled *In re: NCAA Student-Athlete Name & Likeness Licensing Litigation*. Many other athletes have been added to the list of plaintiffs including NBA basketball legends Oscar Robertson and Bill Russell.

For the plaintiffs, the gist of the case is the NCAA has "conspired to artificially depress payments to former student-athletes for the use and sale of their likenesses to zero" (Holthaus, 2010, p. 376). Such an action is alleged to be a violation of the Sherman Antitrust Act. The NCAA denies any violation of the Sherman Act and requested that the case be dismissed. That request was denied and the case is slowly wending its way through the courts. As of December 2012, the case was not yet resolved. To get some idea of the amount of money at stake, consider that in 2008 EA agreed to pay the NFL Players Union between US$30–40 million *per year* for the right to use players' likenesses in video games like *Madden*. When the newest version of *NCAA Football 13* debuted in July 2012, 229,851 Xbox and 184,709 PlayStation units were sold in the first week.[22] At a retail sales price of US$59.99 per unit, that amounts to over US$24 million in revenues in just one week.[23] The stakes are high. Since it is an antitrust suit, treble damages apply. It also raises the question, if former college players can be compensated, why not current college players?[24]

3.7   Chapter Summary

What have you learned from reading this chapter? Our hope is that you discovered a new perspective on the activities of the NCAA and its member institutions. We realize that you might not be entirely convinced by this perspective but our intent is not to tell

---

[22] http://www.vgchartz.com/weekly/41105/Global/.
[23] http://store.origin.com/store/ea/cat/ps3-games/categoryID.8832300.
[24] More discussion about the case can be found in Branch (2011) and Money and March Madness (2011).

you what to think — only to make you aware of a different way to interpret the actions of the NCAA. Whether you ultimately believe the NCAA is a beneficial or harmful institution — or a combination of both — is a conclusion you must reach on your own. If you are interested in exploring the economic perspective at greater length in the future, please refer to the readings listed in the References Section and Selected Bibliography at the end of the book. Now, we move on to Chapter 4 in which we explore the relationship between college athletics and academics.

3.8 Key Terms

Bilateral monopoly	Labor union
Competitive labor market	Marginal cost
Consumer surplus	Marginal cost of labor
Deadweight loss	Marginal revenue product
Demand	Monopolist
Diminishing marginal productivity	Monopsonistic rent
Early entry	Monopsony
Equilibrium	Non-price competition
Explicit costs (appendix)	Opportunity cost
Extra benefits	Perfectly elastic
Flutie effect	Price fixing
Gains to trade	Producer surplus
Grant-in-aid	Public goods
Ham sandwich violation	Quantity demanded
Human capital (appendix)	Reservation wage
Illusion of control	Supply
Implicit costs (appendix)	Willingness to pay

3.9 Review Questions

1. In what two ways does the NCAA harm student-athletes? Can you describe three specific examples of each kind of harm?
2. Why does the NCAA's limit on compensation to a full ride grant-in-aid act like a price control?

3. In a competitive labor market, how is the demand schedule determined?

4. What is marginal revenue product?

5. In a competitive labor market, how is the supply schedule determined?

6. How is a union able to set the wage rate above the equilibrium wage?

7. In a monopsony, how is the wage rate determined? Why is it less than MRP?

8. Why is the equilibrium wage indeterminate in a bilateral monopoly?

9. Which labor market best describes college sports? On what basis did you reach this conclusion?

10. The argument that student-athletes should not be paid because they are already compensated in the form of an education is based on what important assumption?

11. What is early entry? Why are the rules about early entry different for basketball and football than other sports?

12. Why is it that some observers of sports refer to elite high school and college athletes as "lottery tickets" for their friends and families?

3.10   Applied & Discussion Questions

1. What is the purpose of collegiate sports in the United States (why do universities have intercollegiate sports programs)?

2. Contrast the four labor markets in terms of their respective outcomes. In which market is the quantity of labor hired greatest? Smallest? Wage? Consumer Surplus? Producer surplus? Deadweight loss?

3. (Appendix 3.1) Assume the labor market for accountants is competitive. The inverse demand function is $P = 500 - Q$ and the inverse supply function is $P = 140 + Q$. Solve for the equilibrium wage and quantity of accountants hired. Calculate the consumer surplus, producer surplus and gains to trade. Show on a graph.

4. (Appendix 3.1) Assume that the accountants in Question #3 form a labor union and restrict the number of accountants available to work to 120. Assume the demand schedule is unchanged. Calculate the wage, consumer surplus, producer surplus, gains to trade, and deadweight loss. Illustrate with a graph.

5. (Appendix 3.1) Suppose there was no labor union for accountants but there was only one firm hiring accountants. Can you determine the mathematical expression for the marginal cost of labor schedule?[25] How many accountants will be hired and what wage will they receive? At the quantity hired by the monopolist, how much would the monopolist be willing to pay? Calculate consumer surplus, producer surplus, gains to trade, and deadweight loss. Use a graph.

6. (Appendix 3.1) Assume the labor market for accountants is a bilateral monopoly, using the equations from Question #3 draw a graph of the labor market. How many accountants are hired? What is the highest wage possible? What is the lowest wage possible? What is the deadweight loss?

7. Is trade still possible if there is no consumer surplus or consumer surplus?

3.11   Assignments/Internet Questions

1. Using a search engine like Google, type in "NCAA violations" and record how many results are reported. Do the same for "NCAA major infractions" and "NCAA minor infractions."

2. Use Google, or another search engine and the following web site (http://www.ncaa.org/enforcement?division=d1) to identify a major infraction at a university of your choice. The answer the following questions:

   a. At which university did the violation occur?
   b. When did the violation occur?
   c. What is the alleged violation?

---

[25] It is: MCL = 140 + 2Q.

  d. Who committed the violation (e.g., players, coaches)? List the names of all parties involved, their sport, position, year in school, and remaining years of eligibility.

  e. Which NCAA bylaw(s) were violated? The Division I manual, which contains all bylaws, is available at www.ncaa.org under Legislation & Governance.

  f. How were the violation(s) discovered? Who reported them?

  g. What punishment(s) were imposed?

 3. Can you find two or three good examples of minor infractions that might be described as "ham sandwich violations"?

3.12　References

Albom, M. (1993). *Fab Five: Basketball, Trash Talk, the American Dream.* New York: Warner Books.

Bachman, R. (2006, July 22). Colleges ride stars' shirttails to the bank. *The Oregonian,* p. A01.

Baird, K. (2004). Dominance in college football and the role of scholarship restrictions. *Journal of Sport Management, 18,* 217–235.

Becker, G. (1964). *Human Capital.* New York: Columbia University Press for the National Bureau of Economics Research.

Branch, T. (2011, October). The shame of college sports. *The Atlantic.* Retrieved from http://www.theatlantic.com/magazine/archive/2011/10/the-shame-of-college-sports/8643/ on August 1, 2012.

Brown, R. and T. Jewell (2004). Measuring marginal revenue product in college athletics: updated estimates. In J. Fizel and R. Fort (Eds.), *Economics of college sports* (pp. 153–162). Westport, CT: Praeger.

Brown, R. and T. Jewell (2006). The marginal revenue product of a women's college basketball player. *Industrial Relations, 45*(1), 96–101.

Burnsed, B. (2011). How higher education affects lifetime salary. Retrieved from http://www.usnews.com/education/best-colleges/articles/2011/08/05/how-higher-education-affects-lifetime-salary on July 31, 2012.

Dohrmann, G. (2011, November 7). Pay for play. *Sports Illustrated.* Retrieved from http://sportsillustrated.cnn.com/vault/article/magazine/MAG1191778/index.htm on August 1, 2012.

Fleisher, A. A., III, Goff, B. L., and R. D. Tollison (1992). *The National Collegiate Athletic Association: A Study in Cartel Behavior.* Chicago: University of Chicago Press.

Fulks, D. L. (2011). *2004–2010 NCAA Revenues and Expenses of Division I Intercollegiate Athletics Programs Report.* Indianapolis, IN: National Collegiate Athletic Association.

Holthaus, W. D. Jr. (2010). Ed O'Bannon v. NCAA: Do former NCAA athletes have a case against the NCAA for its use of their likeness? *Saint Louis University Law Journal 55*, pp. 369–393.

Huma, R. and E. J. Staurowsky (2012). *The $6 Billion Heist: Robbing College Athletes under the Guise of Amateurism.* A report collaboratively produced by the National College Players Assocation and Drexel University Sport Management. Retrieved from http://www.ncpanow. org on June 19, 2013.

Jung, H. (2005, May 23). Shoe postings pique monitors. *The Oregonian*, p. C01.

Kahane, L. H. (2012). The estimated rents of a top-flight men's college hockey player. *International Journal of Sport Finance 7*, pp. 19–29.

Koch, J. V. (1971). The economics of "big-time" intercollegiate athletics. *Social Science Quarterly 52*(1–2), pp. 248–260.

Luchs, J. and J. Dale (2012). *Illegal Procedure: A Sports Agent Comes Clean on the Dirty Business of College Football.* New York: Bloomsbury.

Martzke, R. (2004, April 7). CBS says NCAAs a 'success' despite ratings dive for final. *USA Today.* Retrieved from www.usatoday.com/sports/columnist/martzke/2004-04-07-martzke-ncaa_x.htm on August 6, 2012.

Money and March Madness (2011, March 29). *Frontline* (PBS). Retrieved from http://www.pbs.org/wgbh/pages/frontline/money-and-march-madness/ncaa-lawsuit/ on August 6, 2012.

National Collegiate Athletic Assocation (n.d.). Estimated probability of competing in athletics beyond the high school interscholastic level. Retrieved from http://www.ncaa.org/wps/wcm/connect/public/Test/Issues/Recruiting/Probability+of+Going+Pro?pageDesign=print+template on August 1, 2012.

Nocera, J. (2011, December 30). Let's start paying college athletes. *New York Times.* Retrieved from http://www.nytimes.com/2012/01/01/magazine/lets-start-paying-college-athletes.html?pagewanted=all on August 1, 2012.

Project on Student Debt (n.d.). Retrieved from http://projectonstudent-debt.org/state_by_state-data.php on July 31, 2012.

Sanderson, A. R. (2004). The puzzling economics of sports. Library of Economics and Liberty. Retrieved from http://www.econlib.org/library/Columns/y2004/Sandersonsports.html on June 19, 2013.

Sheehan, R. G. (1996). *Keeping Score: The Economics of Big-time Sports.* South Bend, IN: Diamond Communications.

Shepardson, D. (2003, July 14). Webber plea to scuttle federal trial. Retrieved from http://usatoday30.usatoday.com/sports/basketball/nba/kings/2003-07-14-webber-plea_x.htm on June 20, 2006.

Sperber, M. (1998). *Onward to Victory: The Creation of Modern College Sports.* New York: Henry Holt.

Sporting News (2009, March 16). Survey says .... *The Sporting News*, p. 7.

U.S. Bureau of Labor Statistics (2012). Education pays. Retrieved from http://data.bls.gov/cgi-bin/print.pl/emp/ep_chart_001.htm on July 31, 2012.

Yost, M. (2009). *Varsity Green: A Behind the Scenes Look at Culture and Corruption in College Athletics.* Stanford Economics and Finance.

Zimbalist, A. (1999). *Unpaid Professionals: Commercialism and Conflict in Big-time College Sports.* Princeton, NJ: Princeton University Press.

Zuhri, C. (2011, April 22). *Today in African American History.* Retrieved from http://todayinafricanamericanhistory.com/african-american-history/april-22nd-in-african-american-history-spencer-haywood/ on August 6, 2012.

Zygmont, Z. X. (2008). Wouldn't it be nice if ... we didn't have to wait so long? *Salem Statesman Journal*, June 24, 2008.

Appendix 3.1 The Mathematics of the Labor Market

The mathematical formulas for the labor supply and demand functions used in this chapter are $Q = 10P$, and $Q = 10{,}000 - 10P$, respectively. The supply function is based on the marginal cost of providing the labor (the workers' opportunity cost of their time, or MC), while demand is based on labor productivity (marginal revenue product, or MRP).

Competitive labor market

The equilibrium in a competitive labor market occurs when the quantity supplied equals the quantity demanded. To find the equilibrium price, simply set the supply and demand functions equal to each other:

$$10P = 10{,}000 - 10P$$
$$20P = 10{,}000$$
$$P = 10{,}000/20 = 500$$

To find the equilibrium quantity, substitute 500 for P in either the supply or demand equation:

$$Q = 10P = 10(500) = 5{,}000$$
$$Q = 10{,}000 - 10P = 10{,}000 - 10(500) = 10{,}000 - 5{,}000 = 5{,}000$$

The competitive equilibrium is $Q = 5{,}000$ and $P = US\$500$.

Monopoly labor market

A labor union is an example of a monopoly. A monopoly maximizes its profits at the quantity where MR = MC. It will take a bit of work to find the MR and MC functions. Given the supply curve, which solves for quantity based on dollars, we can find the MC curve by inverting it, that is, finding dollars based on quantity. For the supply function $Q = 10P$, the inverse function is $P = Q/10$. Because workers supply their labor until the price just equals their marginal cost, we know that MC = $Q/10$.

Deriving the MR function requires some calculus. The demand function must also be inverted to get the price as a function of the quantity. The price is then multiplied by the quantity to get total revenue (TR). The derivative of the TR function measures the change in revenue from an extra unit, or MR. If $Q = 10,000 - 10\ P$, then $P = 1,000 - Q/10$. TR $= PQ = (1,000 - Q/10)\ Q = 1,000Q - Q^2/10$. The derivative of this function is TR$' =$ MR $= 1,000 - 2Q/10 = 1,000 - Q/5$.

The next step is to set MR = MC and solve for Q:

$1,000 - Q/5 = Q/10$
$1,000 = Q/10 + Q/5 = 3\ Q/10$
$Q = 10/3(1,000) = 10,000/3$, which can be rounded to 3,333.

To find the price, substitute the quantity chosen by the labor union into the employers' demand function:

$3,333 = 10,000 - 10P$
$10P = 6,667$
$P = 6,667/10 = 666.7$.

A monopoly results in $Q = 3,333$ and $P =$ US\$666.7, which has a lower quantity and higher price than the competitive equilibrium.

Monopsony labor market

A monopsonist employer maximizes its profits at the quantity where MCL = MRP. Again, it will take a bit of work to find these functions. Given the demand curve, which solves for quantity based on dollars, we can find the MRP curve by inverting it. For the demand function $Q = 10,000 - 10P$, the inverse function is $P = 1,000 - Q/10$. Because firms hire workers until the marginal revenue product just equals the price paid, we can conclude that MRP $= 1,000 - Q/10$.

Finding the MCL curve will require the use of calculus again. The total cost of labor is the price per worker times the quantity of workers employed. Using the inverse supply function $P = Q/10$, we multiply P times Q. TC $= PQ = (Q/10)Q = Q^2/10$. The derivative of this function is TC$' =$ MC $= 2Q/10 = Q/5$.

The next step is to set MRP = MCL and solve for Q:

$1,000 - Q/10 = Q/5$
$1,000 = 3Q/10$
$Q = 10,000/3$, which can be rounded to 3,333.

To find the price, substitute the quantity chosen by the employers into the workers' supply function:

$3,333 = 10P$
$P = 3,333/10 = 333.3$

A monopsony results in $Q = 3,333$ and $P = $ US\$333.3, which has a lower quantity and lower price than the competitive equilibrium.

Appendix 3.2   The Early Entry Decision[26]

What factors influence a student-athlete's decision to turn pro before her collegiate eligibility ends? To answer this question, let's start with Appendix Figure 3.1. From an economic perspective, any student, athlete or not, will continue to acquire years of education as long as the additional benefits of education exceeds the marginal costs of getting an education. If the marginal costs exceed the marginal benefits, the student is making a mistake — why give up more than you get from it? Not surprisingly, the optimal number of years of education is when the marginal costs and marginal benefits are approximately equal (when MB = MC). Looking at Appendix Figure 3.1a, it is easy to see where marginal cost and marginal benefit are equal (at x^* years of education, where the marginal cost and marginal benefit of one more year of education both equal y^*). Appendix Figure 3.1b shows the areas of total benefit and total cost at x^*. The net gain is the difference between the two,

---

[26]This section is based on a presentation by economist Craig Depken at the University of Texas–Arlington. Access via: http://www.uta.edu/depken/ugrad/ sports/section6.pdf.

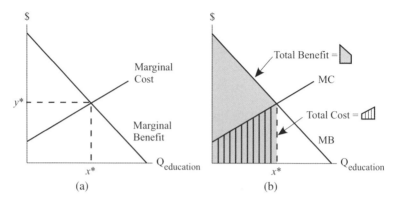

Appendix Figure 3.1.   Costs and benefits of education.

which appears as the triangular shaded area without the pattern of vertical lines.

The marginal cost curve in Appendix Figure 3.1a is upward-sloping, which reflects the fact that the opportunity cost of a year of education is increasing. Each year you stay in college, the higher your annual salary would have been if you had been working instead (assuming that you would get regular raises as your value to an employer increases). The first year out of high school you might earn only US$20,000, but after four years of work you might be earning US$30,000.

On the other hand, the marginal benefit of each year of education is decreasing. While your lifetime earnings do increase with more years of education, the earnings difference between someone with a high school degree ($x = 12$) and someone with an Associate of Arts ($x = 14$), or AA, degree is likely larger than the difference between a person with an AA and a Bachelor of Arts ($x = 16$), or BA, degree. Similarly, the difference between going from an AA to a BA is probably larger than going from a BA to a Masters degree ($x = 18$). Therefore, when we draw the marginal benefit line, we give it a downward slope.

Using Jennifer as our example, let's say that x^* equals 16 years of education. Her plan is to attend USC on a soccer scholarship and earn a bachelor's degree in Electrical Engineering. What might convince Jennifer to leave college before her senior year?

One possibility is that during her sophomore year the women's professional soccer league is reestablished in the United States.[27] This will shift her MC curve upward and to the left, causing x^* to decrease. If she thinks she will earn US$100,000 year playing soccer professionally, it make sense for to leave school early. Even if she only plays a couple of seasons she is better off (and she can then complete her education if she chooses to do so).

Why might Jennifer choose to remain at USC and complete her degree even after a professional women's league is established? The answer has to do with her perceived benefits. Suppose USC hires a new coach for the women's' team. Jennifer enjoys playing for the new coach and she thinks his coaching will help her and her teammates to qualify for the NCAA playoffs and possibly win the championship. The chance of winning the championship might be enough to convince Jennifer to stay at USC longer before she turns pro. Graphically, we demonstrate this situation by shifting her marginal benefit line up and to the right, causing x^* to increase. If the shift in the MB curve equals the prior shift in MC, x^* will return to 16. What would happen if MB and MC shifted by different amounts? Go back to Table 3.1 and see if you can use it to predict the variety of outcomes that can occur in Jennifer's cost-benefit decision-making.

Appendix 3.3   Early Entry as a Human Capital Investment Decision

In economist Gary Becker's *Human Capital* (1964), he sets up a model for evaluating whether one should invest in their **human capital** — acquired skills and knowledge — by attending college. The same model can help us understand the early entry decision by college athletes.

---

[27] The Women's Professional Soccer (WPS) league was founded in 2007, but folded in 2012. The National Women's Soccer League (NWSL) began in 2013 with eight teams.

In Becker's model, the typical college-qualified student faces two choices: Enter the workforce immediately and begin earning income, or attend college. Completion of a college degree provides one main benefit that is weighed against two costs. The benefit is higher earnings with a college degree than would be attainable with a high school diploma (about a million dollars of lifetime earnings). The costs come in two forms. **Explicit costs** are expenses for tuition, room and board, books, etc. that must be paid by the student (ignoring financial aid for the moment). **Implicit costs** are the forgone earnings — what the student could earn in a full-time job if not attending school full-time.

How do the benefits and costs compare for a typical student? While the costs of attending college can be significant, they are generally only incurred for a short period (4–5 years). The excess earnings from having a college degree, however, can extend for many years. A person entering the workforce with a college degree at the age of 22 might well work until retirement around age 67. For most who chose to complete their college degree, those excess earnings far outweigh the costs of attending school.

Consider the example of Kara, who is 18 years old. If she enters the labor market now she will earn an average of US$40,000 per year over 50 years. If she attends college instead, completing her degree in five years, she will face explicit costs of US$10,000 per year (she gets some financial aid), implicit costs of US$20,000 per year in forgone earnings (she wouldn't start out of high school at US$40,000/year), and earn an average of US$60,000 per year over 45 years of work. If lifetime earnings are her only consideration, should Kara attend college or enter the workforce immediately? If Kara begins work immediately, her lifetime earnings will be US$2 million (US$40,000 per year × 50 years). If she attends college first, her lifetime earnings, less the cost of attending college, will be US$2.55 million (US$2.7 million in earnings less US$150,000 in explicit and implicit costs). Based on this, Kara should complete her college degree.

One complication to this calculation is that US$1 today is worth more than US$1 in the future. You may already be familiar with the present value of future dollars from an economics, accounting, or finance course. We use this concept in Chapter 7, so feel free to skip ahead now if you want more information. If Kara places a much higher value on dollars today than on future dollars, she is more likely to skip college to start earning US$20,000 right away.

How does the decision differ for the student-athlete with professional sports aspirations and abilities? On the cost side, we would expect the explicit costs to be much lower — high caliber student-athletes are likely to receive full-ride scholarships. Implicit costs, however, may be much higher. If the student-athlete has professional-level ability before completing their degree, the potential earnings they sacrifice may be substantial. Kobe Bryant and Lebron James, for example, would likely have forgone millions of dollars in salary and endorsement earnings had they chosen to attend college before entering the NBA. They may also be present-oriented due to pressure from family members, agents and others to start earning the big money right away.

On the revenue side, earnings in pro sports don't depend on completion of a college degree, and it is unclear whether there is any premium gained by waiting to enter. In professional sports where there are rookie salary caps and salary scales based on years in the league, delaying entry can mean delaying access to the bigger payoffs that come from free agency (pro sports teams also have monopsonistic power over athletes, though not as much as at the college level). On the other hand, some who enter early find that they're not quite ready for the pro game. If they are still fortunate enough to join a team, they may earn the minimum salary, sit at the end of the bench, and have their development into a top-caliber athlete delayed from a lack of playing time.

Let's assume for the moment that there is an earnings boost from playing at the college level, even if they only attend for a couple of years. If the player has a full career they may last, say, 10 years in the league (a few last much longer, but the average careers are shorter for most pro sports — often less than five years), the earnings premium would have to be substantial to overcome the forgone earnings of delaying entry into the pros. As explained above, college is worth it for most of us because we have so many years to make up the costs of our education. For professional athletes, and some non-athletes like Bill Gates, the implicit cost of completing a college education is too high to make it worthwhile. For Kara, our hypothetical student, if she only had a few years to make up those costs (if for example she is 50 rather than 18 at the point of considering college), it might not be worth it.

Clearly not every athlete reaches professional-level ability at the same age or point in school. Some, like Kobe and Lebron, don't need the experience of the college game to prepare them for the pros. Others are ready after two years, and some only reach professional caliber after four years of college ball.

The early entry decision (and any associated calculation) for athletes is complicated further by the risk of injury. For many of us in the workforce, especially professors, our biggest threat is an infected paper cut. While they are painful, they're generally not career-ending. When an athlete weighs their earning prospects, they also have to factor in the risk that an injury could end their playing career without notice. That risk prompts some to take the "sure thing" of that first professional contract.

Many decry the early entry of athletes and the education they are forgoing, but when viewed as a human capital investment decision, it is hard to find fault with the reasoning.

Fast fact. *NFL quarterback Matt Leinart (Cardinals, Texans, and Raiders), played college football at USC and won the Heisman Trophy his junior year. Leinart had the option, and was encouraged by some, to enter the NFL draft early and exploit his potential earning power. Leinart opted to play his senior year at USC, and took out an insurance policy to protect himself financially against a career-ending injury. Leinart completed his senior season with USC, but although he was a high draft pick, the consensus is that he would have been drafted higher (and therefore had higher earning potential) had he left USC after his junior year.*

Chapter 4

Athletics and Academics

You know what those idiots in Admissions have done? They have refused to admit two of the best basketball players in the country!

— Don Canham, former Michigan Athletic Director

They hired me ... to win. I'd never heard anybody ask me anything about my graduation rates.

— Nolan Richardson, former Arkansas Basketball Coach

I would rather my son be a football player than a Phi Beta Kappa.

— Clarence Munn, former Michigan State Football Coach

College isn't for everyone, and anyone who tells you otherwise is just trying to use you. Do something else with your life ...

— Bobby Knight, former College Basketball Coach

Our bottom line is educating students, whereas the bottom line for the pros is making profits. Athletics contributes to [a] well-rounded education.

— Myles Brand, former NCAA President

4.1 Introduction

In Chapters 2 and 3, you learned that in some sports the revenue athletes generate for their university — their **marginal revenue product** — is significantly greater than the value of the scholarship. We referred to this difference as **monopsonistic rent**, a form of profit that is collected by the university and the athletic department. It is the result of cartel behavior by the members of the NCAA. Because monopsonistic rent is a form of economic exploitation, economists and others suggest that players be paid a wage. This idea is controversial.

One argument against paying college athletes is that they already get compensation in the form of a college education. The quality of that education will vary from school to school and from individual to individual; some athletes at the University of Southern California may take full advantage of the educational resources of that institution and graduate with degrees that enable them to embark on successful careers. Other, less motivated, students at USC may try to skate by with minimum effort. In this regard athletes behave like other students; some work harder than others. In addition, some USC athletes — perhaps those from disadvantaged backgrounds in South Central Los Angeles or other poor urban environments — may be poorly prepared for college; but we could say the same thing about non-athletes as well. Nevertheless, the question remains: how similar are the educational experiences of athletes compared to their non-athlete peers? In other words, any argument that athletes should not be paid

Fast fact. *Dexter Manley is a former defensive lineman who played for the Washington Redskins from 1981–1989, and then briefly for Phoenix, Tampa Bay, and Ottawa (in the Canadian Football League). Manley's career was marred by drug addiction and his surprising admission that he was illiterate. Manley attended Oklahoma State for three years before turning pro without anyone knowing, or caring, that he could not read. He served two years in prison for cocaine possession. A similar story involves basketball player Kevin Ross. Between 1978 and 1982, Ross played for Creighton University in Omaha. Ross was functionally illiterate when he was admitted to Creighton. After four years his eligibility was finished and he left without a degree and still illiterate. He subsequently enrolled in the fourth grade classes at West Side Prep Elementary School in Chicago and eventually learned to read. He was later employed as a janitor in Kansas City.*

because they are receiving a benefit in the form of an education *assumes* that athletes graduate at roughly the same rate as other students *and* the quality of the education they receive is comparable. How much emphasis does the NCAA and its members place on the "student" part of "student-athlete?"

4.2 How Committed is the NCAA to Academics?

Before we examine the specific academic issues of admissions, eligibility, and graduation rates, let us again briefly mention two NCAA policies that seem to contradict the Association's commitment to the education of student-athletes.

In 1972, the NCAA ruled that freshmen were allowed to play football and basketball (four years previously a similar ruling allowed freshmen eligibility in all other sports). Prior to 1968, the NCAA banned freshmen participation in all sports, but they were only able to enforce that ban in championship events. That left freshmen eligibility to the discretion of the universities. Ivy League schools tended to restrict freshmen, the Big Ten Conference limited freshmen participation to students making adequate academic progress, but other schools and conferences were more lenient.

Arguments against freshmen eligibility were based on the belief that incoming student-athletes needed a year to adapt to the rigors of college, and learn to balance the demands between class, study, and practice time before allowing them to suit up and to travel. Think about your own experience. Was your transition from high school to college smooth and painless or difficult and scary? Did you ever consider dropping out during your first year? Would the additional burden of playing a sport — daily practices and team meetings, weight training, scrimmages, and travel — have made that transition easier or harder? If the NCAA is serious about ensuring that student-athletes succeed in the classroom, why not prohibit or limit their athletics participation in their first year to give them a chance to adapt to college? Or is it possible that most NCAA member institutions deem freshmen too valuable (in terms of the revenues they produce) to keep them off the football field or the basketball court?

In 1973, the NCAA decided to allow member institutions to offer athletes one-year renewable scholarships. Prior to that, universities typically granted students financial aid for the entire duration of their eligibility. For a student-athlete, a running back on the football team for example, such a scholarship was especially valuable because it meant that even if he suffered a severe injury and was unable to play, his scholarship would not be revoked and he could complete his degree. After the 1973 decision was enacted (Bylaw 15.3.3), this player's academic future was less certain because the university could choose to not renew the scholarship if it believed that he could no longer play football. But without financial support from the scholarship he might not finish his degree. It is easy to understand why the NCAA would make such a decision on behalf of its member institutions if the primary concern was *money* — why offer financial aid to a player unable to perform? But how can we reconcile such an action with the best interests of injured student-athletes' *education*?[1]

In the remainder of this chapter, we consider evidence that suggests that the NCAA and its member institutions are not fully committed to ensuring a quality education for student-athletes. The reason for this is simple: every hour spent in the library, the classroom or the computer lab is one less hour spent on athletics practice and training. How will the football team or the basketball team win enough games to qualify for a berth in a bowl game or postseason tournament if the players spend more time studying than practicing and playing? If you are a coach or the Athletic Director, will you and your school receive greater financial rewards and publicity, if the graduation rate and GPAs of your athletes increase, or if you win the big game against your archrival and qualify for postseason competition?

---

[1] But, as economists are fond of saying, *on the other hand*, there is an issue of **moral hazard**. As our students, especially student-athletes, often point out, coaches use one year scholarships to motivate better performance. If a student-athlete is guaranteed a four year grant-in-aid, will she have an incentive to shirk?

4.3 Admissions

Suppose that Jennifer, our hypothetical high school athlete, is recruited by the University of Southern California. As we first saw in Chapter 1, NCAA rules stipulate that to play at USC, she must meet the initial **eligibility requirements** (Article 14.3 of the Bylaws). As of August 2008, she is required to complete 16 "core courses" in high school (mainly consisting of English, Mathematics, and Natural and Social Science classes; remedial courses are not counted), earn a core GPA of at least 2.0, and graduate from high school. Ten of the core courses must be completed prior to the senior year and cannot be retaken to improve grades. She must also earn a minimum score of 400 on the SAT (sum of Math and Verbal, each out of 800) or 37 composite score on the ACT (sum of English, Math, Reading, and Science subscores, each out of 36) tests. But there's a twist, the minimum SAT or ACT score depends on her GPA; if she has a lower GPA, she must get a higher test score, if her test score is low, she must earn a higher GPA. Table 4.1 shows different combinations of test scores and GPA that would make her eligible. If Jennifer has, for example, an 800 SAT and a 2.75 GPA she easily meets the eligibility requirement (she is, in NCAA-language, a **qualifier**). The standards were updated effective August 1, 2016 to raise the minimum GPA requirement for qualifier status to 2.30. Students are eligible for athletic aid and practice with GPAs between 2.00 and 2.30, but they cannot compete.[2] As explained in Box 4.1, the NCAA refers to the latter students as "academic redshirts." Keep in mind that the NCAA's initial eligibility requirements represent the minimum standard Jennifer must meet; the school she wants to attend may have more rigorous admissions standards.

What happens if Jennifer is a **non-qualifier** because she does not meet these requirements? According to NCAA bylaws, she can still attend the college or university of her choice, but during her

---

[2]More information is available online at the NCAA Eligibility Center, including a *Quick Reference Guide* (http://fs.ncaa.org/Docs/eligibility_center/Quick_Reference_Sheet.pdf).

Table 4.1.   NCAA freshmen-eligibility standards
(Bylaw 14.3.1.1.2).

Core GPA	SAT (verbal and math)	ACT (Sum of subscores)
≥3.55	400	37
3.50	420	39
3.25	520	46
3.00	620	52
2.75	720	59
2.50	820	68
2.30	900	75
2.00	1,012	86

Box 4.1.   What color is your shirt?

You may be familiar with the term "redshirt." When a player redshirts, it means she is essentially taking five years to complete her four years of athletics eligibility. While there are exceptions, this usually occurs in the student-athlete's first year at the institution. She may be worried that she may get limited, or zero, playing time as a freshman, or perhaps she, or her coach, thinks she needs a year to further develop her skills. If she redshirts, she gets to engage in all activities of the team except participate in intercollegiate competition. She is allowed to accept a grant-in-aid if one is offered to her. Freshmen who had high school core GPAs between 2.0 and 2.3 are considered "academic redshirts" by the NCAA. Another classification is grayshirt. These are usually players who signed a letter of intent to play for a school but learn that not only are their chances of playing immediately doubtful, but there is also no scholarship money for them. If they remain at the institution they may initially enroll as part time students and then, if they choose to remain at that school, begin full-time studies in mid-year (this preserves all of their years of

(Continued)

Box 4.1. (Continued)

eligibility) and hope for a scholarship the following year. A third possibility is to greenshirt. This is when a high school student graduates at the end of fall term and enrolls in college in January. This allows the student to get used to college life and also work out with the team in the spring. While redshirts are widespread across all college sports, gray and green shirts usually refer to football players.

There is some controversy over the use of grayshirts (Karp and Everson, 2011). Grayshirting often occurs because a football coach oversigns too many players, that is, he accepts more letters of intent from high school student-athletes than the number of expected grants-in-aid that are available (the maximum number of letters of intent a coach may accept in FBS is 28 and not more than 25 scholarships may be offered each year). A player may not be made aware of this until he shows up in the fall, at which time not only does he not get any financial aid but he cannot have any involvement with the team. In essence, he gets "stiffed" by the coach (but it is also possible that the coach tells him upfront that he will have to grayshirt). However, a future scholarship may be promised as long as the student agrees to enroll as a part-time student. It is also possible that the player goes from grayshirt to redshirt, meaning that he may be at that institution for a year and half before he gets to play. As a redshirt he may get an athletic scholarship. The Big Ten does not allow oversigning and the Southeastern Conference (SEC) recently imposed conference-wide legislation to reduce oversigning. SEC schools may now sign a maximum of 25 players, a number equal to the maximum possible yearly grants-in-aid.

first year she cannot participate in intercollegiate athletics (practice, play, or travel with the team) or receive athletics-based financial aid. She can still be awarded a scholarship, but it must be based on need and not athletic ability, and the funds cannot come from the athletics department. In addition, she will lose one year of eligibility.[3] She can practice, compete and receive an athletic scholarship after her first year, if she makes satisfactory progress toward her degree requirements.[4]

Unfortunately for Jennifer, she wants to attend USC, which is a member of the Pac-12 Conference. Along with most of the other major DI conferences, the Pac-12 imposes restrictions on non-qualifiers that are stricter than NCAA rules. As a recruited athlete, unless she is able to get a waiver from the NCAA Initial Eligibility Waiver Committee, she will be permanently ineligible for aid, practice, and competition. If she gets a partial waiver, the Pac-12 allows just four per school, with two in men's sports and two in women's, and no more than one in any one sport. Non-qualifying students that transfer from a junior college or a non-conference four-year institution are eligible if they meet NCAA transfer requirements (see following paragraph). The Big 12 Conference goes even further. Students that were non-qualifiers at the time of their initial enrollment (full or part time) at *any* two- or four-year institution are permanently ineligible for practice, competition or financial aid. Even a student that enrolls at a junior college and earns an Associate degree with a 4.0 GPA will never be eligible to play at a Big 12 school. In the SEC, only students with a core high school GPA of at least 2.25 can ever become eligible after enrolling as a non-qualifier. Conferences began imposing these stricter requirements in the mid-1990s to deter member schools from recruiting good athletes–poor students with the promise of "non-athletic" scholarship and a chance to play after a first year filled with easy coursework.

---

[3] A fourth season of eligibility can be granted in her fifth year, if she has completed at least 80% of her designated degree program (NCAA Bylaw 14.3.3.1).

[4] For a complete list of what a non-qualifier is, and is not, eligible to receive from the institution, see Figure 14.1 in the Bylaws.

Students transferring after a year or more at another four-year institution are eligible for practice and aid if they meet their new school's requirements for satisfactory academic progress, although they must wait one year to compete. Eligibility requirements are different for junior college transfers. Students attend junior college for numerous reasons: they may want to remain close to home; they may have a job or family commitments that require them to remain in the area; they may be unsure if college is right for them; they may not yet be academically qualified for a four-year institution; or they may feel their athletics skills still require some "seasoning" before they make the jump to a NCAA institution.[5] Regardless of the reasons, suppose Jennifer would have qualified for admission to USC but chose to first attend her local junior college, El Camino College in Torrance, California. Now, in order to be eligible for competition at USC, she needs to complete at least one term at the junior college with an average of 12 hours per semester and a 2.5 GPA. She would be eligible for an athletic scholarship and practice with the team if her GPA was at least 2.0. If she would have been a non-qualifier to USC directly out of high school, she needs an Associate of Arts degree from El Camino, 48 semester hours (with at least three semesters of residency), and a 2.5 GPA to become eligible. Again, if she fails to meet these requirements she can still choose to transfer as a non-qualifier, forgo an athletic scholarship, sit out one year, and hope to do well enough to qualify the following year. Transfer rules and regulations can be quite confusing (like the case of a "4-2-4" transferee — a student who starts at a four-year institution, transfers to a junior college, and then

---

[5] Sperber (2000, p. 240) has a harsher take on junior college (JUCO) athletes. "JUCO athletes usually belong to the cohort of high school athletes who fail to meet the NCAA's minimal academic requirements for playing intercollegiate athletics as freshmen. As a result, they attend junior college and, after receiving graduation certificates there, move on to an NCAA school. Most important, these athletes are not required to take the SAT/ACT exams or to prove to anyone outside their junior college ... that they can read, write, and count past ten."

transfers back to a four-year school) and even Athletic Directors with years of experience complain about them.[6]

As explained in Chapter 1, the NCAA enacted its first rules on initial eligibility in 1964 with passage of **Rule 1.6**. This was modified by **Rule 2.0** (1971), **Propositions 48** (1986), **42** (1989), and **16** (1992), and Proposal **68** (1997). In general, the requirements for qualifier status have become stricter over time. What is the rationale behind these rules? On one hand, it appears that they are in the best interests of the students. They are designed to prevent schools from admitting a good athlete who has little chance, or no intention, of getting an education. If the coaching staff could squeeze one or two solid seasons out of these athletes before they flunk out, then from the perspective of the Athletic Department, these are blue-chip recruits. On the other hand, even with the current rules, there is substantial evidence of student-athletes being admitted who are not prepared and unlikely to complete a degree.

Some economists and some college coaches argue that these rules are often initiated and promoted by schools like Duke, Northwestern, and Stanford who can easily attract and retain students who are good athletes *and* good scholars. The high school students who apply to these universities — both athletes and non-athletes alike — tend to have excellent grades, high SAT scores, and want to attend an undergraduate institution that is known for its academic exclusivity and intellectual rigor. Increasing admissions requirements from 2.0 to 2.5, or an SAT score from 800 to 1000 will have virtually no effect on a school like Duke because their "pool" of prospective student-athletes have GPAs and test scores

---

[6] The bylaws list many exceptions for transfers. For example, a student-athlete can get a "one-time transfer exception" if she transfers across divisions to play the same sport; moving from DI to DII, or DII to DIII. The exception applies as well to a DI football player moving from FBS to FCS. Inter-divisional transfer is allowed as long as you are not an athlete who plays baseball, basketball, men's ice hockey, or football in the FBS. And there are sometimes special circumstances; for example, in an attempt not to penalize Penn State football players for events beyond their control, the NCAA allowed them to transfer to another FBS program if they chose to do so, without losing any eligibility.

much higher than these thresholds. A school like North Carolina State, on the other hand, may have a substantial number of high school student-athletes hovering around 2.0 and 800. Even a slight increase in the minimum requirements will prevent NC State from admitting these recruits.

Duke has every reason to support an NCAA regulation that is cloaked in the language of good intentions *and* gives it a competitive advantage over rivals like North Carolina State. This line of reasoning makes sense if you remember the fragile dynamics of cartels and the prevalence of **intra-cartel cheating**. Schools like NC State, UNLV, Arkansas State, or Temple have a clear disadvantage when it comes to recruiting good athletes with excellent academic credentials from high school, and schools like Duke, Northwestern and Stanford have every incentive to exploit this disadvantage.[7]

Rules like Prop 48, which was the first to require a minimum score on standardized college entrance exams (700 on the SAT or 15 on the ACT, and a 2.0 GPA for 11 core courses), drew the ire of coaches like John Thompson and John Cheney (former basketball coaches at Georgetown and Temple respectively) as well as college presidents, especially those representing historically Black schools like Grambling State University in Louisiana (Dealy, 1990, 115 ff.). They argued that these requirements disproportionately punish inner-city kids who are good athletes but poor students.[8] Granted, these may be students who have zero interest in academics, but they may also be students who are caught in a crummy school

---

[7] Using past voting records on NCAA rules changes and a regression approach known as a logit model, economists tested the hypothesis that schools like Duke will support more stringent admissions requirements. Their results supported this hypothesis (Fleisher *et al.*, 1992, pp. 123–132).

[8] Cheney was quoted as saying, "The NCAA says it's concerned about the integrity of education. Hell, image is what it's concerned about. If you're a school like Temple, which is not afraid to take a chance on a kid, give him an opportunity to get an education — and that's what I'm all about, opportunity — [the NCAA] begins to look at you with its nose turned up, saying, 'Well, Temple is not as academic as others. They are taking in the sick and the poor.' It is like the Statue of Liberty turning her ass and saying to the sick, the poor, the tired, 'Get the hell out'" (Zimbalist, 1999, p. 30).

system, are from households where education was not encouraged, or grew up in an environment where their parents or guardians were absent, in jail, or dealing drugs (or all of the above). Athletics, regardless of whether they make it to the pros or not, is — rightly or wrongly — seen as a way out of the "hood" or the projects. One may certainly question the motivation of coaches like Cheney and Thompson (are they more concerned with a student's academic progress or his shooting percentage?) but they raised important questions about the rationale underlying minimum academic standards.

Fast fact. *In 1999, in Cureton v. NCAA, four Black high school athletes sued the NCAA alleging that the inclusion of minimum assessment test scores resulted in "unjustified disparate impact on African-American student-athletes" A federal court judge agreed with them but the case was overturned on appeal in higher federal court. However, in 2003, the NCAA modified Prop 16 so that the minimum acceptable SAT score was 400 (combined with a GPA of 3.55). Because students score 400 even if they answer all of the SAT questions incorrectly, the SAT is effectively no longer an admissions requirement for some student-athletes.*

To complicate matters even more, there is an alternative route for a student seeking to gain admission to a university. These students are called **special admits**. Every year, almost every institution of higher education admits a handful of students who do not meet their admissions criteria. The reason for this is often legitimate. As an example, suppose Jennifer is a 17 year old high school dropout from a broken and impoverished home. Her true passion in life is dance and to support herself, she performs freestyle dance at the local train station, bus station, city park, or wherever she thinks passersby will stop to watch her and, hopefully, leave a few coins or bills for her. One day a professor of modern dance at the local university sees Jennifer performing. The professor realizes that Jennifer has the potential to become the next Martha Graham or Gregory Hines, two of America's most talented dancers. When the professor asks Jennifer if she would be willing to train in the university's dance program and earn a bachelor's degree, Jennifer readily accepts the offer. The professor then speaks to the university's Admissions office and requests that Jennifer be allowed to enroll as a special admit, even though she does not have a diploma or a college entrance exam. The school agrees.

One of the strengths of higher education in the United States is its relative openness, especially in comparison to universities in other parts of the world like Japan and Germany. In those nations there are specific exams that high school students must take, and pass, in order to be admitted. Students who do not pass do not get a second chance. They are typically assigned as an apprentice to a trade school or else told to find their own way in the world. Not only is it easier to gain admission to university in the United States, there are plenty of second or third chances available. Students can retake exams like the ACT or SAT, university dropouts can reenroll, and so-called "non-traditionals" (i.e., older students) may begin their studies at age 25 or 55 or 75. Special admits are part of the democratic tradition of higher ed in our country. But the special admit process is open to abuse.

NCAA Bylaw 14.1.7.1.1 states "[a] student athlete may be admitted under a special exception to the institution's normal entrance requirements if the discretionary authority of the president or chancellor (or designated admissions officer or committee) to grant such exceptions is set forth in an official [university] document." Essentially, the NCAA is ok with special admits in athletics as long as the institution is allowing other students, like Jennifer, a similar opportunity (whether the NCAA's position reflects the illusion of control is another question to consider). But research suggests that athletes are for more likely to be special admits than other students. In 2008, an associate athletic director at Oklahoma said that almost 60% of Sooner student-athletes were special admits (Wolverton, 2008). This percentage is not out of the ordinary. At Georgia, the four-year average between 1996 and 1999 was 94.5%

for football players, 75.2% for all student-athletes, and 7.3% for non-athletes. At UC Berkeley the numbers from 2002–2004 were 86.3%, 44.7% and 2%. Some schools, including Virginia and Tennessee do not allow special admits (Scherzagier, 2010). You probably will not be surprised to know that special admits have existed almost since day one in college sports (e.g., Smith, 1988, p. 183).

As it currently stands, since a high school student can score as low as 400 on the SAT, yet still remain eligible for admission to a DI institution, the primary determinant is the student's coursework and GPA.[9] When a higher SAT score was required, it was common to find student-athletes taking the exam multiple times before qualifying, or cheating by having someone else take the exam for them. Since the minimum SAT score is now easy to reach (all a student needs to do to get a 400 is to sign her name on the exam), a student's transcript is the deciding factor. This opens up many questions about the legitimacy of a student-athlete's transcript. A case at University High in Miami, Florida (see Box 4.2) triggered an investigation by the NCAA into so-called "diploma mills," schools that sell a high school degree while requiring little, if any, actual academic accomplishment.

Who determines if a transcript is legitimate or not? In theory the NCAA does. In a student's senior year of high school, she must submit a student release form that authorizes the release of her transcript and test scores to NCAA member institutions. The transcript and scores must be sent directly to the NCAA's Eligibility Center by the student's high school and the College Board (if SAT) or American College Testing, Inc. (if ACT). The Center determines if the student graduated, completed the required 16 core courses, and met the minimum GPA and SAT (ACT) scores. After reviewing this information, the NCAA certifies the student as a qualifier or a non-qualifier and makes this information available to universities. But remember, even if you are a "non-qualifier" you can still be

---

[9] The NCAA defends the use of the sliding scale, arguing that its research indicates that GPA is a better predictor of success in college than test scores (Petr and McArdle, 2012).

Box 4.2.   Diploma mills.

The NCAA has begun cracking down on secondary schools like University High in Miami. The Association claims that these institutions, so-called "diploma mills," are nothing more than correspondence schools. For a fee, reportedly US$399 at University High, a student gets a transcript that "proves" he graduated with a GPA high enough to pass muster with the Eligibility Center. In many cases, these schools have no teachers, classrooms, or textbooks, and exams, if any, are open-book. A recent *New York Times* article points out that part of the problem is the Association's own making. Since 2000, the Center has delegated more responsibility for attesting to the legitimacy of a student high school transcript to the high schools themselves (Thamel and Wilson, 2005). Compounding this is a lack of government regulation of private secondary institutions like University High including requirements like exit exams. This has created a "don't ask, don't tell" mentality among university athletic departments and coaches.

---

admitted to a university (although you cannot be given an athletic scholarship, play or practice during your first year, and you lose a year of eligibility). Additionally, the Center will determine your amateur status, whether you played, or attempted to play, with a professional team, or received any payment or compensation from your athletics participation.[10] If you are not a true amateur you may be ineligible to play college sports.

It makes sense to have the NCAA determine initial eligibility because the alternative, leaving the determination up to the universities, would encourage cheating. Nevertheless, the process is hardly foolproof. You can probably think of a number of ways a student's transcript and test scores could be illegitimate without

---

[10] See the NCAA's *Guide for the College-Bound Student-Athlete* (http://www.ncsasports.org/blog/wp-content/uploads/2011/07/CBSA1.pdf).

the Eligibility Center knowing. And sometimes the Center makes mistakes; as one example, consider the story of Omar Williams, who played basketball at George Washington University in the District of Columbia from 2002–2006. According to an article in the *Washington Post*, "Williams was accepted at George Washington after failing to graduate in five years from his original high school and receiving no grades at three prep schools in the next two years ... [the NCAA] certified his transcript *without any verification*, making him academically qualified for a basketball scholarship" [emphasis added] (Schlabach, 2006b). Not only did the Center fail to carefully scrutinize Williams' academic record, the NCAA bylaws actually create an incentive for students who are not performing well academically in their senior year to flunk out of school, or to drop out, and re-enroll for grade 12 at another institution. If their academic performance improves they can gain initial eligibility and be able to play for four years. However, if instead they enroll in a junior college for one or two years to improve their grades they will lose one or two years of eligibility (Barr, 2004).

We should also mention that some athletes who are admitted to college are less than stellar citizens. In some cases, the schools are well aware that a certain player has already accumulated some crime-related baggage. For example, Miami linebacker Willie Williams or the University of Oregon's Rodney Woods, Williams was admitted to the University of Miami despite pleading no contest to charges on destruction of property and misdemeanor assault in the summer of 2004 (these actions took place in Gainesville, FL while Williams was on a recruiting visit at the University of Florida). Williams was already on probation for burglary and theft and was arrested 11 times while in high school in Miami ("Williams must meet special academic conditions," 2004). Woods, a defensive back, was admitted to Oregon in 2003 despite having participated in the fatal beating of Christopher O'Leary, age 17, at a party in Palmdale, CA in 2000.[11]

---

[11] Woods' felony assault charge was later reduced to a misdemeanor; as a consequence he was able to accept Oregon's offer of a scholarship.

Fast fact. *Willie Williams never became a starting player at Miami so he began shopping for another school. He ended up at West Los Angeles College, a junior college, in August 2006. After one season, he moved on to Louisville where he played in a handful of games before being kicked off the team for possession of marijuana. After that, he popped up at Glenville State, a DII school in West Virginia, but he left after a semester when the NCAA denied his transfer. From there it was on to a Kentucky NAIA school, Union College. He was never drafted by the NFL. He was arrested for burglary in Georgia in 2009 and second degree robbery in Ohio in 2011.*

In other cases, many athletes take advantage of their "big man on campus" status and engage in criminal activity. As an example, consider Marcus Vick of Virginia Tech. Vick, quarterback for the Hokies and brother of "New York Jets" quarterback Michael Vick (himself an ex-felon), was suspended by the university for the 2004 season because of convictions for contributing to the delinquency of a minor, possession of marijuana, and reckless driving. In 2006, he was dismissed from the university because of accumulated driving tickets and an incident involving unsportsmanlike conduct against a University of Louisville player in the Gator Bowl. Vick's checkered college career is summarized in Box 4.3. Vick played one game in the NFL, appearing for the Miami Dolphins in 2006.

In 1999, star wide receiver Peter Warrick of Florida State was prosecuted for misdemeanor petty theft ("Warrick pleads guilty," 1999). With the help of a dishonest employee, Warrick bought US$400 worth of clothes for US$21.40 at a department store in Tallahassee. Warrick's lawyer downplayed his client's actions by saying it was "only a discount" and nothing more. Lawrence Phillips, a former star running back at Nebraska, has a long history of abuse to women ("Phillips arrested," 2005). More recently, between March and May 2012, six University of Arkansas football players were arrested on charges ranging from burglary,

Box 4.3. Marcus Vick's rap sheet.

July 13, 2002   Vick is cited for speeding (60 mph in 45-mph zone) in Newport News, VA.

Oct. 11, 2002   Vick is cited for speeding (49 mph in 25-mph zone) in Montgomery County, VA.

Nov. 1, 2002   Vick is cited for speeding (44 mph in 25-mph zone) Blacksburg, VA.

Sept. 2, 2003   Vick, as a redshirt freshman, is suspended by Coach Frank Beamer one game for violating unspecified team policies.

Jan. 30, 2003   Vick is cited for driving with a suspended license in Newport News, VA.

Feb. 17, 2004   Vick, then 19, and 2 teammates are charged with contributing to the delinquency of a minor, which involved serving alcohol to underage girls in the football players' apartment Jan. 27. All three are convicted but avoid jail and reduce their fines by pleading no contest before a scheduled retrial.

May 2004   Virginia Tech Director of Athletics, Jim Weaver suspends the three players for the first three games of the 2004 season.

July 3, 2004   Vick is stopped for speeding (88 mph in 65-mph zone) and charged with reckless driving and possession of marijuana in New Kent, VA. He later pleads guilty to the first charge and no contest to the latter.

July 6, 2004   Weaver suspends Vick from the team indefinitely.

Aug. 3, 2004   The university suspends Vick for the entire fall season.

(Continued)

Box 4.3. (Continued)

Oct. 1, 2005	After running out of bounds during a game in Morgantown, W.VA., Vick makes an obscene gesture to the crowd and bumps West Virginia assistant coach Tony Gibson's head with his forearm
Dec. 17, 2005	Vick was arrested in Hampton, VA., for speeding (38 mph in 25-mph zone) and is charged with driving on a suspended or revoked license, a misdemeanor.
Jan. 2, 2006	In a Gator Bowl victory over Louisville, Vick stomps on the calf of Cardinals lineman Elvis Dumervil, who had just sacked him. Game officials do not see the incident, which is replayed numerous times on television.
Jan. 6, 2006	Virginia Tech permanently dismisses Vick.
Jan. 9, 2006	Vick brandishes a firearm in Suffolk, VA. He is charges with a misdemeanor.
Dec. 14, 2006	A civil lawsuit is filed against Vick for the sexual molestation of a female minor in Montgomery Co., VA.
June 13, 2006	Vick is charged with DUI in Norfolk, VA.
Oct. 20, 2008	As a result of the DUI, Vick received a suspended jail sentence, pays a fine, is put on probation, and loses his Virginia driver's license for one year.

Source: Schlabach (2006a) and Wikipedia.

drug possession, assault, and use of a stolen debit card.[12] The Benedict–Crosset Study, published in 1995, noted the alarming statistic that "male student-athletes made up 3.3% of the male student population, yet accounted for 19% of the reported perpetrators of sexual assault on college campuses". (Hyde, 2004)

CBS News and *Sports Illustrated* (*SI*) conducted background checks on 2,837 football players who were on the roster of the top 25 teams *SI* ranked in the 2010 preseason. Only two of the ranked schools, Oklahoma and TCU, conduct criminal background checks on their incoming players (and none examine juvenile records even when they are available). Out of the sample, 277 players (7%) had criminal records, including 56 with violent crime felonies. Six schools were in the double digits: Virginia Tech, Penn State, Boise State, Arkansas, Iowa, and Pittsburgh. Pitt led the list with 22 players on its 2010 roster having committed crimes. Of the 25 schools, only TCU had no felons.[13]

While this behavior might seem distasteful to us, and we may question why such people are allowed to remain at our nation's universities, we need to remember that ultimately players like Williams, Woods, Vick, Warrick, and Phillips help their university win games and generate substantial revenues. As long as the team is winning, occasional outbursts of criminal activity are more likely to be tolerated.

But we should also resist the urge to be too judgmental; there is also the possibility that being given a second (or third, or fourth) chance can help someone turn his or her life around. We all make mistakes, and hopefully we learn from them. Consider the case of JamesOn Curry (yes, that's the correct spelling of his first name), who was arrested during his senior year of high school for selling marijuana to an undercover officer. JamesOn had already committed to North Carolina, but the university withdrew their offer after his

---

[12] "Three Arkansas football players charged" (2012). To add insult to injury, Razorbacks head coach Bobby Petrino was fired for lying about a motorcycle accident in which he said he was riding alone. It turns out he had a passenger, his mistress. Not only was the university upset but so was Mrs. Petrino.

[13] See Benedict and Keteyian (2011).

felony conviction (he admitted his guilt and was sentenced to 200 hours of community service and probation). Oklahoma State took a chance on a promising talent (he was the leading scorer in North Carolina high school basketball history), but they ended up with an outstanding citizen too. Having someone else have faith in you can sometimes give you faith in yourself. As of 2012, he was playing in Springfield, MA for a team in the NBA development league. As the *CBS/SI* story aptly put it, "[t]he issue isn't that colleges should never accept a kid who has made a mistake; part of education is second chances. But too many football programs, out of a desire to win more games, either overlook a player's past or don't bother looking into it at all. That's a flaw in the system that has to change."

4.4 Maintaining Eligibility

As discussed in Chapter 1, once a student-athlete like Jennifer is admitted to college she must continue to meet minimum GPA and credit hour requirements in order to maintain her eligibility (the 40/60/80 rule, Bylaw 14.4.3.2). If she is eligible to play but chooses to sit out a year (redshirt), she can use that year of eligibility during her fifth year of college. With only a few exceptions, NCAA rules do not allow students to participate after their fifth year, even if they have not used all four years of eligibility.

To keep student-athletes eligible, universities invest considerable resources in academic support services. Duderstadt (2000, p. 199) noted that at Michigan "the Student Athlete Support Program consists of a director, 6 full-time advisors, 3 assistant advisors, 70 tutors, 10 specialized writing instructors, and 15 proctors for supervised study sessions."[14]

What are some other ways athletic departments keep their athletes eligible? *First*, they encourage students to take easy majors with little or no requirements other than occasionally going to class

---

[14]James Duderstadt, a former president of the University of Michigan, also said that "[w]e bring in people who have no hope of getting a meaningful education, we have them major in eligibility, and we toss them aside when they lose it … " (Price, 2004).

and periodically taking a multiple-choice exam. *Second*, regardless of the student's major, every college campus has its share of professors who are known for having relatively undemanding course requirements or who are predisposed to athletes to begin with. You probably have a class like "Introduction to Gum Chewing" on your campus, or classes taught by a professor who favors athletes.[15] *Third*, athletes may resort to academic dishonesty; for example, they may have another person write a research paper for them.

A classic case involving such activity occurred at the Twin Cities campus of the University of Minnesota. In spring 1999, allegations of academic fraud at the university surfaced in a local newspaper. The NCAA opened an extensive investigation surrounding the Golden Gophers basketball program. Numerous violations of NCAA regulations were found including, among others, academic fraud, unethical conduct, provision of extra benefits, violation of eligibility requirements, and lack of institutional control. The academic fraud involved a department secretary writing an estimated 400 papers for members of the men's basketball team between 1993 and 1998, with the approval of the men's basketball coach. There was also evidence that the athletics department pressured faculty members to change grades. The secretary, an academic counselor, and the coach were dismissed. The NCAA placed the university on probation for four years, reduced the number of scholarships for basketball players, reduced recruiting activity, and required the university to return revenues received from participation in the NCAA tournament in 1994, 1995, and 1997. It also forced the university to erase all references in university publications to its participation in those tournaments as well as the 1996 and 1998 NIT tournaments. Further investigation by the university's administration led to the removal of the athletics director, the assistant athletics director, the

---

[15] Even faculty, who has no desire to favor athletes may be pressured to give "extra consideration." Would you want to be the teacher who kept the star quarterback from playing football by giving him the failing grade that he earned? A meeting with the Athletic Director and your Department Chair to justify your action will be the result. If you are an adjunct or are not tenured, you may be concerned about keeping your job. If other faculty is choosing not to rock the boat, why should you?

director of NCAA compliance, and the vice president of student affairs and athletics. The president of the university was quoted as saying, "the program was corrupt in almost any way you can look at it". (Dohrmann and Borger, 1999)

Fast fact. An article in Sports Illustrated *by Rick Reilly (1998) focused on the story of Ohio State's All-American linebacker Andy Katzenmoyer. In the summer prior to his junior year, Katzenmoyer's academic eligibility was in jeopardy. By fall, he regained eligibility, thanks to summer session classes he completed and a grade change for a course he took in the spring. The summer courses were AIDS Awareness, Golf, and Music, which he passed. He also failed a spring Art class, The Computer and the Visual Arts, but his grade was later changed to a C+. Katzenmoyer, left Ohio State after his junior year to enter the NFL draft.*[16]

4.5 Transfers

The rules for transfer students were introduced in Chapter 1. NCAA Bylaw 14.5.1 states "a student who transfers ... is required to complete one full academic year of residence [at the university] before being eligible." Jennifer may transfer from USC to Notre Dame if she wishes but she will likely lose a year of sports eligibility. In addition, transfer students cannot receive an athletic scholarship during the first year at the new school unless they are given permission to transfer from their original school.

The NCAA discourages transfers because it may impede satisfactory academic progress. The graduation requirements at a new school may be sufficiently different to impede academic progress,

---

[16] Katzenmoyer's former roommate and teammate Damon Moore said "Not everyone comes to college to be in college. I'm that way and [Katzenmoyer] was pretty open about it, too. He was bothered by some people who asked about the grade change. Everybody gets grade changes. I've had some grades changed ... Now were [sic] both headed to the NFL, which is what we came here to do" (Reilly, 1998).

particularly for a student-athlete with additional demands on her time. As discussed in Chapter 2, the rule is also in place to discourage universities from "pirating" student-athletes from other members of the cartel. By imposing costs on the students who transfer, the NCAA makes it more difficult for schools to convince them to switch. Left to themselves, NCAA member institutions would actively recruit students from other institutions and expend resources in the process. Transfer rules are thus yet another example of a deterrent to cheating that reinforces the monopsonistic cartel powers of the NCAA.

Regulating transfers of student-athletes among NCAA institutions raises important questions about fairness. As an example, suppose a student-athlete named Joe Cool is recruited by Oregon State University's Coach Dennis Erickson to play football in 2001. Joe is looking forward to playing for someone with Coach Erickson's experience (he was formerly head coach of the University of Miami and the Seattle Seahawks). At the end of Joe's second year of eligibility, Coach Erickson announces that he is leaving Oregon State to coach the San Francisco 49ers. Joe is disheartened by Erickson's decision and decides to transfer to the University of Utah even though he realizes that he will lose a year of eligibility. Does Coach Erickson suffer a similar penalty? Not at all; he gets a US$2.5 million contract and the opportunity to coach one of the NFL's premier franchises.[17] Does this outcome seem equitable to you? What if Joe was an accounting student, not an athlete, and he decided to transfer from Oregon State to Utah. Would he be required to "sit out" from his accounting classes for a year at Utah? Of course not. Would Chef Suzy be required to sit out a year if she quit the Cheesecake Factory to work for the Olive Garden? Would Derek Jeter have to sit out a season if the New York Yankees traded him to the Boston Red Sox? Why are college athletes treated differently?

---

[17] Erickson coached the Beavers for 4 years (1999–2002) and earned around US$1 million a year. He joined the 49ers in 2003 and his departure stunned members of the Oregon State football community (Maisel, n.d.).

Fast fact. *Where in the world is Dennis Erickson? Erickson may be one of the most traveled football coaches around. He began his college career at Idaho in 1982. In 1986 he was at Wyoming, then Washington State in 1987 and 1988, Miami from 1989 to 1994, Oregon State between 1999 and 2002, then returning to Idaho in 2006. He was head coach at Arizona State from 2007–2011. Erickson also coached in the NFL, spending 1995 through 1998 in Seattle and the 2003 and 2004 seasons in San Francisco.*

4.6 Graduation Rates

One widely used measure of educational performance in the intercollegiate athletics community is the **graduation rate**. While no institution graduates 100% of its eligible students in any academic year, higher rates are preferable to lower ones. Low rates generate criticism that universities are interested only in the athletic achievement of student-athletes and not whether they ever earn a degree.

To measure the graduation rate, you must first define the relevant group of students, or cohort. Until recently, the NCAA typically used one- and four-year cohorts. One advantage of using a four-class cohort is that it is less susceptible to outliers. One particularly good or bad year will be averaged with the three other years. The other benefit has to do with federal privacy laws. If there were only three students in a particular group of interest (e.g., Hispanic female basketball players), data for the group could be used to make inferences about individual students, and thus could not be released. The four-class sample is more likely to have enough students in each group to avoid this problem. The privacy issue will be discussed in more detail below.

Many of those who graduate do so in four years, but given that students may change majors, transfer schools, take a year off to work, or go to school part time, it is reasonable to add a couple more years. The most common measures of graduation rates are based on a six-year period of time. If a longer time period is used, then graduates who take longer than six years will be included, but the report on each cohort cannot be issued while waiting the additional years.

In 1984, when the NCAA first began collecting graduation rate information, the proportion of all students who graduated from college within six years was 53%, while the rate for all athletes was almost identical (52%). For students who entered a Division I college or university in the 1999–2000 academic year, athletes had a slightly higher graduation rate than non-athletes (63% to 61%). Football and male basketball players had graduation rates of 54% and 46% respectively, lower than the rate for all students but up from 47% and 38% for the 1984–1985 academic year.

Data from 2010 shows us that athletes continue to have a slightly higher graduation rate than non-athletes (65% to 63%). Football and male basketball players had graduation rates of 69% and 68%, well above the rates in previous academic years. While these numbers seem encouraging, two important caveats are necessary. First, as we will elaborate in this section, student-athlete graduation rates prior to 1995 cannot be directly compared to rates after 1995. Prior to 1995, the standard statistic used was the **Federal Graduation Rate**. But in 1995 the NCAA began calculating a rate called the Graduation Success Rate, which is not equivalent to the federal rate. Also, a closer review of the data shows problems still exist, especially disparities by race across graduation rates.

Table 4.2 lists graduation rates for Division-I institutions that participated in the 2012 NCAA men's basketball championships. 15 of the 68 schools (22%) had graduation rates above 90% for all of their student-athletes, while only 7% were below 70%. At 10 institutions (15%) Black players had graduation rates greater than 90%. For white players 60% (41 teams) exceeded 90%. Two schools had rates for white players less than 50% and 21 (31%) were below 50% for Black players. Rates for basketball players overall were above 90% at 15 schools and below 50% at 13. According to the Institute for Diversity and Ethics in Sport at the University of Central Florida,

Table 4.2. Six-year graduation rates for 2012 Men's Basketball NCAA Tournament Teams.

School	Overall S-A	Black	White	Overall BB S-A	APR
1. Baylor	79	50	NA	56	972
2. Belmont	91	100	100	100	1,000
3. BYU	76	100	100	100	991
4. Colorado State	83	43	100	64	914
5. Creighton	96	100	100	100	960
6. Davidson	97	100	100	100	995
7. Duke	97	100	100	100	990
8. Florida State	79	57	100	67	926
9. Georgetown	94	67	NA	70	937
10. Gonzaga	94	50	83	73	985
11. Harvard	98	NA	100	100	991
12. Indiana	77	43	100	47	929
13. Iona	83	70	NA	53	955
14. Iowa State	79	29	100	45	936
15. Kansas State	78	38	100	50	937
16. Lamar	68	67	0	65	934
17. Lehigh	86	67	100	85	994
18. Long Beach State	78	44	50	45	950
19. LIU-Brooklyn	83	88	100	91	933
20. Loyola MD	96	83	100	92	966
21. Marquette	92	80	100	91	980
22. Michigan State	83	67	100	82	995
23. Mississippi Valley	42	35	NA	35	884
24. Murray State	72	50	100	56	932
25. New Mexico State	66	23	100	28	906
26. Norfolk State	61	50	NA	43	894
27. NC State	74	83	50	80	985
28. Ohio State	82	50	100	79	952
29. Ohio	82	67	100	79	910
30. Purdue	77	43	67	50	954
31. St. Louis	87	50	100	67	925

(Continued)

Table 4.2.   (*Continued*)

School	Overall S-A	Black	White	Overall BB S-A	APR
32. San Diego State	70	63	100	62	938
33. South Dakota State	80	0	67	50	964
34. St. Bonaventure	88	56	67	65	894
35. St. Mary's CA	94	67	80	82	953
36. Syracuse	86	44	75	54	928
37. Temple	77	36	0	43	954
38. Univ. Alabama	82	60	NA	67	973
39. Univ, Cal-Berkeley	79	14	50	33	948
40. Univ. Cincinnati	81	53	NA	56	992
41. Univ. Colorado	74	42	NA	43	926
42. Univ. Connecticut	81	14	50	25	893
43. Univ. Detroit	92	86	100	89	936
44. Univ. Florida	83	20	100	38	964
45. Univ. Kansas	79	80	100	91	1,000
46. Univ. Kentucky	77	60	100	69	974
47. Univ. Louisville	81	50	100	56	965
48. Univ. Memphis	80	50	NA	55	989
49. Univ. Michigan	82	38	100	45	970
50. Univ. Missouri	81	57	NA	67	974
51. Univ. Montana	74	60	100	75	950
52. UNLV	72	44	100	67	961
53. Univ. New Mexico	75	50	75	57	932
54. UNC Asheville	65	57	50	57	964
55. UNC Chapel Hill	88	86	100	89	985
56. Univ. Notre Dame	99	100	100	100	989
57. Univ. South Florida	74	50	100	44	937
58. Univ. So. Mississippi	81	45	NA	42	910
59. Univ. Texas	74	33	80	67	1,000
60. Univ. Vermont	95	100	100	86	980
61. Univ. Virginia	87	33	100	50	940
62. Univ. Wisconsin	81	29	100	50	970
63. Vanderbilt	92	100	100	93	974

(*Continued*)

Table 4.2. (*Continued*)

School	Overall S-A	Black	White	Overall BB S-A	APR
64. VCU	78	71	NA	67	949
65. West Virginia	80	71	100	83	995
66. Western Kentucky	80	100	100	100	964
67. Wichita State	85	80	100	92	955
68. Xavier	95	92	100	93	980

Source: "Keeping score when it counts" (2012).
Note: Overall S-A is all student-athletes and Overall BB S-A is all basketball players.

the graduation rate for basketball players overall rose from 66% to 67% between 2011 and 2012 but with a significant gap between white players (88%) and Black players (60%). We will discuss the last column of numbers, the Academic Performance Rate, later.

Some institutions, like BYU, Duke, Vermont, and Vanderbilt, appear to be doing an excellent job by being able to qualify for the tournament and graduating all their players. Others appear to be hindering their player's academic success (Iowa State, Mississippi Valley, New Mexico State, Cal, and UConn). Kansas, Kentucky, Louisville, and Ohio State appeared in the final four in 2012. Those schools had overall graduation rates 91%, 69%, 56%, and 57%, respectively.

Table 4.3 shows graduation rates for DI institutions that participated in the 2012 NCAA women's basketball championships. 12 of the 64 schools (19%) had graduation rates above 90% for all of their student-athletes, while 8% (5 schools) were below 70%. At 30 institutions (47%), Black players had graduation rates greater than 90%. For White players, 70% (45 teams) exceeded 90%. No school had a rate for White players less than 50% while only two (3%) were below 50% for Black players. For basketball players overall, graduation rates were above 90% at 38 schools and below 50% at only one. Notre Dame, Baylor, Stanford, and UConn were the final four teams in 2012. Their rates were 100%, 92%, 93%, and 100%. We will discuss the last column of numbers, the Academic Performance Rate, in a few moments.

Table 4.3.   Six-year graduation rates for 2012 Women's Basketball NCAA Tournament Teams.

School	Overall S-A	Black	White	Overall BB S-A	APR
1. Albany	84	100	91	93	967
2. Arkansas	73	78	100	86	974
3. Arkansas-Little Rock	73	60	100	80	932
4. Baylor	79	90	100	92	960
5. BYU	76	100	80	82	975
6. Cal	79	100	100	92	973
7. Connecticut	81	83	100	100	990
8. Creighton	96	100	100	100	994
9. Dayton	95	100	100	100	1,000
10. Delaware	74	67	88	76	972
11. DePaul	93	100	100	100	1,000
12. Duke	97	100	100	100	995
13. Eastern Michigan	72	60	100	86	979
14. Florida-Gulf Coast	78	67	100	85	971
15. Florida	83	100	100	100	981
16. Fresno	66	79	100	86	967
17. Georgetown	94	100	100	100	983
18. Georgia	79	70	100	77	995
19. Georgia Tech	77	75	100	73	957
20. Gonzaga	94	50	100	94	981
21. Green Bay	94	NA	92	92	996
22. Hampton	67	47	NA	47	968
23. Idaho State	86	100	100	100	931
24. Iowa	86	100	100	100	951
25. Iowa State	79	100	100	100	991
26. Kansas	79	50	100	63	988
27. Kansas State	78	100	100	100	995
28. Kentucky	77	100	100	100	976
29. Liberty	70	75	100	93	974
30. Louisiana State	78	100	100	100	971
31. Louisville	81	89	100	93	953
32. Marist	90	100	100	93	986

(Continued)

Table 4.3.   (*Continued*)

School	Overall S-A	Black	White	Overall BB S-A	APR
33. Maryland	82	91	50	81	964
34. McNeese State	70	77	80	78	920
35. Miami FL	89	83	100	94	960
36. Michigan	82	100	63	67	1,000
37. Michigan State	83	67	83	77	996
38. Middle Tennessee	77	82	100	86	976
39. Navy	96	33	100	93	991
40. Nebraska	74	100	100	100	988
41. Notre Dame	99	100	100	100	974
42. Ohio State	82	100	100	100	993
43. Oklahoma	71	100	100	100	1,000
44. Penn State	88	100	100	100	985
45. Prairie View	63	58	NA	62	918
46. Princeton	93	NA	NA	100	1,000
47. Purdue	77	57	80	69	972
48. Rutgers	86	89	100	91	955
49. Sacred Heart	79	100	89	91	990
50. Samford	83	100	89	92	995
51. San Diego State	70	100	75	80	964
52. South Carolina	77	100	100	100	962
53. South Dakota State	80	NA	83	77	996
54. St. Bonaventure	88	75	100	91	990
55. St. John's	91	100	100	100	964
56. Stanford	94	80	100	93	980
57. Tennessee	76	100	100	100	995
58. Tennessee-Martin	69	100	86	93	914
59. Texas	74	75	67	75	964
60. Texas A&M	73	69	83	70	961
61. UC Santa Barbara	84	86	88	89	966
62. UTEP	71	78	0	81	975
63. Vanderbilt	92	100	100	100	995
64. West Virginia	80	69	100	73	972

Source: "Keeping score when it counts" (2012).

Note: Overall S-A is all student-athletes and overall BB S-A is all basketball players.

Many institutions are doing an excellent job in both qualifying for the tournament and graduating all their players. Only one school (Hampton) appears to be truly mediocre and a handful (Kansas, Michigan, Prairie View, and Purdue) are lagging with overall rates for women below 70%. Also, the gap between academic performance by Black and White female athletes is narrower than for the men, and the women clearly outperform the men in terms of graduating. This trend is also true for non-athlete students. According to a 2011 NCAA study ("The racial gap", 2011), for the 2004 cohort of students at DI institutions, the graduation rate for White and Black women was 68% and 46%, while the rate for student-athletes was 74% and 66% respectively. For non-athlete White and Black males the rates were 63% and 38%. Among White and Black athletes, it was 68% and 55%.

As you can see from the data in Tables 4.2 and 4.3, there are several interesting variations across schools and gender. Some institutions reported rates for both the men and women above 90% (among them, BYU, Duke, Notre Dame, and Vanderbilt). At Iowa State, Cal, UConn, Kentucky, and Ohio State, the men's rates are low while the women's are high. The opposite is true at Kansas, and the rates for both genders are low at Michigan and Purdue.

Let us take a quick look at football before we expand on our discussion about graduation rates. The data in Table 4.4 are for teams that appeared in one of the 35 bowl games in 2011–2012. Of the 70 schools listed only two (Northwestern and Notre Dame) had overall football player graduation rates above 90%. Two had rates below 50% (Florida International and Oklahoma). But there is a significant racial gap between Black and White players; the average rate for the former is 60.5% and the latter, 81.4%. At two schools, graduation rates for Black players were above 90% (again Northwestern and Notre Dame) while 18 — over one-fourth of the schools — had rates below 50% (Florida International bringing up the rear). For White players, 15 schools were above 90% and none were below 50%. Comparing football players to other student-athletes, there is very little difference at Boise State, LSU, Notre Dame, and Penn State, with all four schools achieving rates above the overall football

Table 4.4. Six-year Graduation Rates for football teams appearing in FBS bowl games in 2011–2012.

School	APR	Overall FS-A	Black	White	Overall S-A
1. Air Force	978	84	80	85	81
2. *Alabama*	963	69	62	89	82
3. Arizona State	940	64	57	83	79
4. *Arkansas*	937	56	44	80	73
5. Arkansas State	943	73	68	85	77
6. Auburn	940	63	52	95	76
7. Baylor	951	62	62	68	79
8. *Boise State*	981	74	67	78	74
9. BYU	929	57	47	71	76
10. California	949	54	46	56	79
11. Cincinnati	936	79	65	87	81
12. Clemson	977	62	55	100	82
13. Florida	976	76	75	88	83
14. Florida Intl.	936	43	33	53	58
15. Florida State	932	56	44	93	79
16. Georgia	976	65	63	67	79
17. Georgia Tech	966	55	52	68	77
18. Houston	929	57	46	79	69
19. Illinois	949	76	70	84	89
20. Iowa	947	83	72	94	86
21. Iowa State	932	63	40	91	79
22. *Kansas State*	940	62	58	66	78
23. *LSU*	966	77	69	91	78
24. LA Tech	944	75	73	80	72
25. LA-Lafayette	943	56	48	65	65
26. Louisville	908	66	59	80	81
27. Marshall	947	77	69	95	86
28. Michigan	928	71	63	76	82
29. Michigan St.	938	62	52	80	83
30. Mississippi St.	952	62	56	83	79
31. Missouri	967	66	62	78	81
32. NC State	929	56	46	83	74

(*Continued*)

Table 4.4.   (*Continued*)

School	APR	Overall FS-A	Black	White	Overall S-A
33. Nebraska	958	67	58	78	74
34. Nevada	943	70	64	79	78
35. No. Carolina	955	75	68	91	88
36. No. Illinois	987	73	72	84	82
37. Northwestern	993	94	92	96	96
38. Notre Dame	971	97	100	93	99
39. Ohio	950	71	50	96	82
40. Ohio State	985	67	51	84	82
41. Oklahoma	960	48	44	57	71
42. *Oklahoma St.*	942	65	61	72	77
43. *Oregon*	941	63	51	78	80
44. Penn State	972	87	87	89	88
45. Pittsburgh	949	65	56	83	78
46. Purdue	939	59	51	73	77
47. Rutgers	988	89	88	94	86
48. San Diego St.	934	56	58	68	70
49. *So. Carolina*	954	55	45	83	77
50. SMU	939	72	70	73	84
51. So. Miss.	928	78	77	80	81
52. *Stanford*	977	87	75	94	94
53. TCU	972	78	69	91	85
54. Temple	937	60	47	82	77
55. Texas	941	57	47	73	74
56. Texas A&M	940	59	45	92	73
57. Toledo	943	64	58	82	78
58. Tulsa	927	63	49	83	80
59. UCLA	956	59	46	78	83
60. Utah	956	62	52	80	79
61. Utah State	946	77	68	88	84
62. Vanderbilt	977	86	86	88	92
63. Virginia	947	68	60	81	87
64. Virginia Tech	955	79	76	83	91
65. Wake Forest	971	81	78	89	94

(*Continued*)

Table 4.4.   (*Continued*)

School	APR	Overall FS-A	Black	White	Overall S-A
66. Washington	946	76	67	84	83
67. West Virginia	962	75	71	78	80
68. W. Michigan	963	61	43	78	81
69. *Wisconsin*	967	66	50	86	81
70. Wyoming	933	64	47	69	73
Average	951.9	68.2	60.5	81.4	80.4

Source: "Keeping score when it counts" (2011).
Note: Schools listed in italics were in the top ten final BCS standings for the 2011 season.

student-athlete average of 68.2%. However, what is perhaps most revealing is that at only two schools (Louisiana Tech and Rutgers) did football players have rates higher than student-athletes as a whole. Also notable is that of the schools in the top ten final BCS rankings for the 2011 season, only Alabama, Boise State, and Stanford had overall football rates above the average of 68.2%.

What about sports other than basketball and football? Table 4.5 shows average graduation rates by sport for DI institutions. Notice that two rates are listed, the Graduation Success Rate (GSR) and the Federal Graduation Rate (FGR). Also, note that for each sport, the former measurement is larger than the latter. We will discuss the difference between the two momentarily.

You can also look at graduation rates for specific institutions. We chose Texas A&M at College Station (Table 4.6), one of the 346 DI schools. Again, we see a wide variation in graduation rates across sports as well as much higher rates when the GSR is used rather than the FGR. A&M's graduation rate for all its students combined was 79% for the 2004 cohort, and some sports had higher rates than this and some lower.[18]

---

[18] The rate of 79% was reported in A&M's Common Data Set (CDS), an easily accessible document at most institutions of higher education. The CDS can usually be found on an institution's Office of Institutional Research web page.

Table 4.5.   Graduation success rates (in bold) and federal graduation rates (in parentheses) in 2011 for DI men's and women's sports.

Sport	Men	Women
Baseball	**72%** (48%)	NA
Basketball	**66%** (48%)	**84%** (64%)
Bowling	NA	**77%** (56%)
Crew	NA	**92%** (81%)
Cross Country/Track	**76%** (61%)	**85%** (71%)
Fencing	**86%** (77%)	**93%** (81%)
Field Hockey	NA	**94%** (81%)
Football (FBS)	**67%** (56%)	NA
Football (FCS)	**66%** (54%)	NA
Golf	**81%** (65%)	**88%** (72%)
Gymnastics	**88%** (84%)	**92%** (81%)
Ice Hockey	**82%** (62%)	**88%** (75%)
Lacrosse	**88%** (73%)	**94%** (82%)
Rifle	**79%** (66%)	**79%** (NA)
Skiing	**88%** (70%)	**94%** (65%)
Soccer	**79%** (58%)	**89%** (71%)
Softball	NA	**86%** (70%)
Swimming	**85%** (72%)	**91%** (76%)
Tennis	**86%** (65%)	**89%** (70%)
Volleyball	**76%** (66%)	**88%** (70%)
Water Polo	**85%** (72%)	**91%** (75%)
Wrestling	**73%** (56%)	NA

Source: Trends in graduation success rates and federal graduation rates at NCAA Division I Institutions (2011, pp. 8–9; p. 20).

Before we begin our discussion about the differences between the Federal Graduation Rate and the graduation rate as calculated by the NCAA, let's define both using the NCAA's own definitions:

[The] FGR assesses only first-time full-time freshmen in a given cohort and only counts them as academic successes if they graduate

Table 4.6. Graduation rates at Texas A&M, by sport, for 2004 cohort.

Sport	GSR	FGR
Overall	72	63
Baseball	60	41
Men's basketball	69	50
Women's basketball	70	69
Football	59	52
Men's golf	75	67
Women's golf	91	88
Softball	100	89
Women's soccer	100	87
Men's tennis	64	36
Women's tennis	100	100
Men's track	64	58
Women's track	77	67
Women's volleyball	100	90

Source: http://fs.ncaa.org/Docs/new media/public/rates/index.html.

from their institution of initial enrollment within a six-year period. It makes no accommodation for transfers into or out of an institution. The rate is very limited because it ignores the large number of transfer students in higher education, but it is still the only rate that allows a direct comparison between student-athletes and the general student body.

[The] GSR begins with the federal cohort, and adds transfer students, mid-year enrollees, and non-scholarship students (in specified cases) to the sample. Student-athletes who leave an institution while in good academic standing before exhausting athletics eligibility are removed from the cohort of their initial institution. This rate provides a more complete and accurate look at actual student-athlete success by taking into account the full variety of participants in Division I athletics and tracking their academic outcomes.

Source: "Trends in Graduation Success Rates" (2011).

The method used to calculate graduation rates for student-athletes was not developed by the NCAA, but was put in place by the federal government after the passage of the Student Right-to-Know and Campus Security Act in 1990. As a representative example, we duplicate information provided by the Registrar's Office at Texas A&M University below. This is followed by Table 4.7, which displays the latest Federal Graduation Rate data for Texas A&M.

The Student Right to Know Act requires an institution that participates in any student financial assistance program under Title IV of the Higher Education Act of 1965 (as amended) to disclose information about graduation rates to current and prospective students. Institutions that award athletically-related student aid are also required under the Student Right to Know Act to disclose data related to the institution's student population and student-athlete graduation rates to potential student-athletes, their parents, coaches, and counselors.

The Higher Education Act of 1992 mandated that all U.S. institutions receiving Title IV funding complete the IPEDS (Integrated Postsecondary Education Data System) Survey each year to the National Center for Education Statistics. The IPEDS graduation rate survey data is based on a 6-year graduation rate for each cohort of full-time, first-time degree seeking undergraduates. Each April, in conjunction with the Office of Institutional Studies and Planning, the Office of the Registrar prepares and reports on the graduation rates of student-athletes receiving athletically-related financial aid in a specific cohort. Texas A&M University also submits this data (supplemented with information regarding the graduation rates of spring semester freshmen and transfer student-athletes) to the NCAA each year by June 1.

In compliance with the Federal Right to Know and Campus Security Act of 1990, and in accordance with the Higher Education Act of 1965 (as amended), Texas A&M University is pleased to share the following information on the graduation rates of our cohorts of full-time, first-time degree seeking undergraduate and student-athletes that have received athletic financial aid.

While reviewing this information, please keep the following in mind: All graduation rates are based upon 6 years of

Table 4.7.   Federal graduation rates at Texas A&M, college station.

	Men		Women		Total	
	2004–2005	4-Class	2004–2005	4-Class	2004–2005	4-Class
All students	76	75	84	83	80	79
Am. Indian	80	71	89	75	85	73
Asian	72	73	88	84	79	78
Black	60	55	76	71	69	64
Hispanic	69	67	74	75	71	71
Hawaiian/ PI	NA	NA	NA	NA	NA	NA
N-R Alien	88	80	100	89	92	83
Unknown	###	67	###	85	###	74
White	77	76	85	84	80	79

	Men		Women		Total	
	2004–2005	GSR	2004–2005	GSR	2004–2005	GSR
Student-athletes	52	62	91	88	70	73
Am. Indian	###	###	###	###	###	###
Asian	NA	###	NA	###	NA	###
Black	44	46	86	68	57	52
Hispanic	NA	70	NA	80	NA	73
Hawaiian/ PI	NA	NA	NA	NA	NA	NA
N-R Alien	NA	71	NA	75	NA	73
Unknown	###	33	###	67	###	50
White	60	72	93	93	77	82
Basketball	75	69	86	70		
X-country/ Track	60	64	100	77		
Baseball	27	60	NA	NA		
Football	53	59	NA	NA		
Other	80	67	90	94		

Source: NCAA (http://www.ncaa.org/grad_rates/).

attendance which equates to 150% of the normal completion time of our longest program. (For example, the 2001 cohort is comprised of all first-time, full-time degree seeking students who entered Texas A&M University in the fall 2001 semester; and had through the summer 2007 semester to graduate in order to be considered a "completer" for the IPEDS survey.)

Graduation rates do not include students who left school: to serve in the armed forces; on official church missions; with a foreign aid service of the federal government; or students who died or were totally disabled. A pound sign (#) denotes any cohort/ subcohort with three or fewer students. The University is not required to disclose this information.

Source: http://registrar.tamu.edu/general/srtk.aspx

Why does the NCAA use a different rate than the federal government? The NCAA believes that the federal rate methodology is flawed, for several reasons. First, only student-athletes receiving scholarships are included in the calculation. If you play a sport but do not get financial assistance (you are a "walk-on"), you are not included in the sample of athletes. You are also omitted if you are a walk-on who *later got a grant-in-aid*, something that is quite common for athletes competing in equivalency sports like tennis and track and field. At some DI schools, the difference between the total number of athletes who play but are not getting financial aid is considerable. For example, in 2001–2002, at Wisconsin, 44% of the 723 athletes were walk-ons. That meant that Wisconsin's student-athlete graduation rate was determined based on the academic performance of only 56% of its athletes (Ferris *et al.*, 2004). At other institutions, e.g., DI-No Football or DII, the difference may be even larger (in DIII no athletics aid is awarded so the NCAA does not collect graduation rates for these schools). Also, as NCAA researcher, Thomas Paskus (2012, p. 44) mentions, in some sports a considerable number of students may simply drop out of school: "[c]urrent data show that fully 40% of freshmen men's basketball players leave their initial school by the end of their second year at that school. These are not the so-called one-and-done[s]."

Second, the graduation rate may be inaccurate because transfers and early entrants are not included. This is a serious problem; according to recent research, about 20% of all students earn their baccalaureate at a different institution than where they started their education (Burd, 2004). If these excluded students were *more likely* to graduate on schedule than the other athletes, their institution's graduation rate will be biased downwards. If they were *less likely* to graduate than their peers, the rate will be inflated. Whether transfers should or should not be included in graduation rate calculations depends on the purpose for disclosing graduation rate information. If the information is mainly used by high-school students and their families to help them decide where to attend college, then the omission of transfers is irrelevant.

Student-athletes who leave school early but are on track to graduate are also not included which makes the rate look worse than it should. Conversely, a student who leaves early but would not graduate is not counted against the school.[19]

Fast fact. *In 2002, the Oregon State basketball team had a graduation rate of zero (Campbell, 2004). But as Athletic Director Bob De Carolis noted, the rate resulted from having six players transfer (one turned pro). Five of the six transfers were on track to graduate.*

A third problem is that not all graduation data is made public. All student educational records are protected by the **Family Educational Rights and Privacy Act**, known more familiarly as FERPA. Since 1974, FERPA has limited the ability of schools that receive federal educational funding to disclose information about its students to the general public. You have probably experienced situations in which your school was required to get written authorization from you before it released your transcript or similar

---

[19] Many of these calculation problems apply to graduation rates for all students not only athletes. See Burd (2004, A1).

school-related information to a third party such as an employer or graduate school. This is because of FERPA.

FERPA has led to controversy and legal action. For example, when college students first began downloading music from the Internet via campus computers, the recording industry wanted colleges to provide the names of students who were pirating songs without paying for them. These schools tried to use FERPA to prevent such disclosure. Its relevance to college sports is that it allows a school to limit disclosure about athletes' educational progress while they are enrolled (and even after they graduate).

Why does FERPA keep the average graduation data for some groups of students secret? As mentioned above, one issue is the size of the data sample. Schools argue that in situations in which a small number of athletes are provided financial aid, or there are a small number in the sport (especially when you break students out by race), it might be possible to figure out which graduation rates apply to specific students. As an example, it is not illegal to disclose that the graduation rate for all Black women athletes at USC is 69%. But what if the USC women's soccer team has 20 players and only 2 of them — Jennifer and Vanessa — are Black? If the graduation rate for the women's soccer team is broken down by ethnic and/or racial characteristics, it might be easy to figure out if Jennifer and Vanessa graduated or not. If you were in their shoes, would you want that information made public without your prior approval? Fortunately for them, FERPA does not allow this to happen.

But some observers have pointed out that NCAA schools are inconsistent in their interpretation of FERPA. For example, schools are quick to publicize the grade point averages of scholar athletes but reluctant to reveal those in academic difficulty. Is GPA information public or private or is it only public when it suits the purposes of the institution?

Given the complications associated with graduation rates, what can we conclude about them? Nationally, athletes graduate more often than the general student population but graduation rates vary by sport, gender, and race. At some schools, the rates are very low. At others they are quite high. Perhaps unsurprisingly, the

> **Fast fact.** *In 1996, University of Maryland basketball player Duane Simpkins was required to sit out three games by the NCAA because he accepted an illegal payment in the amount of US$2,000 from a former summer league coach. Simpkins reportedly accepted the money to help pay for accumulated parking tickets on Maryland's College Park campus. Simpkins had accumulated 285 tickets and was facing total fines of approximately US$8,000. Yikes! Subsequently, the campus newspaper's request for access to the parking records of other student-athletes was denied by the university because it considered such information to be part of a student's educational record and hence subject to FERPA protection ("Access to Parking Records Denied," 1997). The newspaper then filed a lawsuit against the school and, after several years of legal debate, the Maryland Court of Appeals agreed with the campus newspaper, ruling that parking pickets are not considered to be part of a student's educational record and hence outside the purview of FERPA. ("Athletes Unpaid Parking Tickets," 2000)*

lowest rates are associated with the sports that tend to generate the highest revenues, football and men's basketball. Basketball is perhaps the worst case, especially for minority players. For Black hoops players who began their studies between 1990–1991 and 1994–1995 at 36 selected Division I institutions, not a single student graduated. These schools, while the worst of the bunch, represent roughly 10% of all DI members.[20]

---

[20]The schools are Arkansas, Brigham Young, Cal State-Long Beach, Cal State-Sacramento, Cincinnati, Cleveland State, Colorado, Eastern Washington, Georgia Tech, Georgia Southern, Hawaii-Manoa, Idaho, Jacksonville State, James Madison, Louisiana State, Louisville, McNeese State, Memphis, Minnesota-Twin Cities, Morehead State, Nevada-Las Vegas, Nevada-Reno, Oklahoma, Oregon State, Pacific, Samford, Southwest Missouri State, Texas Tech, Texas-El Paso, Texas-Pan American, Toledo, Wisconsin-Milwaukee, Wyoming, Utah State, Virginia Commonwealth, and Western Illinois.

But we must also keep in mind that the current method of calculating the rate may be misleading. FERPA regulations make it difficult to determine the true value and accuracy of rates. We should also interject the following question: What does a high graduation rate really tell us? Does it suggest that ample resources are made available to help students succeed? Or does it suggest that the academic requirements are so easy that virtually anyone with a pulse and a room temperature IQ can graduate?

Fast fact. Research by Ferris, Finster and McDonald (2004) suggest the importance of taking into consideration the graduation rate of the institution when comparing student-athlete graduation rates to non-athletes. Their findings suggest that at institutions with higher overall graduation rates (e.g., Stanford), the athletes' rate is lower than non-athletes. At institutions with lower overall graduation rates (e.g., Ohio State), the athletes' rate is higher than non-athletes. This raises interesting questions such as "does a lower graduation rate matter for athletes if they are at an institution with higher academic quality"?

The NCAA is taking an aggressive stance in publishing, and publicizing, the graduation rates of its member institutions. In 2004, the NCAA introduced the Academic Performance Program. The NCAA describes the program as "… a system that rewards those institutions and teams that demonstrate commitment toward the academic progress, retention and graduation of student-athletes and penalize those that do not" (Bylaw 23.01.2). The program is centered around two measurements, the Graduation Success Rate (GSR) and the **Academic Progress Rate** (APR). The APR is a measurement of a team's academic performance. It went into effect in fall 2005 and applies to the roughly 6400 teams at the 346 DI institutions. The method used to calculate the APR is described in Box 4.4. The policy establishes a cut-off point at 925 (out of a maximum of 1000); this means that any team that has an APR below 925

Box 4.4. Calculating the academic progress rate.

The APR is determined by two factors: first, whether a student-athlete achieves the minimum GPA and second, if the student stays in school. A student is "awarded" one point if she meets either criterion. Total points (eligibility plus retention points) are calculated for each team and compared to the total points possible for the academic term or year. Let X represent total points achieved and Y total points possible; $(X/Y)1000 = $ *the APR for the team*, the percentage of points earned compared to the amount possible. If the APR (four-year moving average) is less that 925 (92.5%), then the team is subject to penalties (the APR calculation, and cut-off threshold, is slightly different for the handful of DI schools on the quarter term calendar).

Let us use the women's soccer team at the University of Southern California as an example. If there are 20 players on the roster, each semester the team can earn a maximum of 40 points (or 80 points per academic year). This term two players fail to meet the minimum GPA requirement and are academically ineligible to play. However, they remain in school to try to boost their grades and return to the team. This means the team earned 38 out of 40 possible points for an APR of 950 (95%) which exceeds the cutoff of 925. USC will not be penalized. Suppose next semester the same two players again have low grades and decide to leave school (these players are called "0 for 2s"). Now the USC women's soccer team has a score of 36 out of 40, which results in an APR of 900 and falls below the cutoff. Recent NCAA legislation requires teams to have a four-year APR above 930 in order to qualify for postseason participation.

One of the interesting consequences of the APR is that since it uses a percentage, teams with smaller rosters are more likely to be penalized. If the golf team has 10 players and one

(*Continued*)

Box 4.4. (Continued)

player is in academic trouble and leaves school, the team's APR is 900. Compare that to the football team with a roster of 100. It would take 10 players in academic difficulty (and not enrolled) to produce an APR of 900. The NCAA modified the APR in 2007–2008 for teams with less than 30 players to eliminate this problem.

Note that the point system gives schools credit for athletes who have low grades but remain in school. The system also does not penalize students who transfer provided they were academically eligible. It also does not penalize early entry as long as the student was academically eligible. **The 40/60/80 rule** (see Chapter 1) remains in place.

More information about the APR can be found on the NCAA's website (http://www.ncaa.org). Select "Media & Events" then "NCAA Publications" followed by "Research" and "APR."

---

is subject to a variety of penalties. Why is 925 the magic number? According to the Association, an APR of 925 is the equivalent of a 50% graduation rate over a five-year period. This means that another way to interpret the APR is that it wants the graduation rate for all athletes in all sports at all school to be 50% or better.

There are two categories of penalties for the APR, contemporaneous and historical. The **contemporaneous penalties** are determined by, as the NCAA refers to it, "a real-time snapshot of a team's academic performance." For every student-athlete who was on a team with an APR below 925 and who left school before graduation, the team loses that scholarship, usually during the next academic year. Unlike contemporaneous penalties, which are designed to be a kind of "wake-up call" for universities, the second category of penalties, called **historically-based penalties**, are punitive in nature and designed to inflict substantial punishment on teams that are repeat offenders, especially teams that have significantly lower graduation rates than teams at peer institutions, and lower rates for athletes at their own institution than non-athletes.

There is a four-tier penalty system for not meeting the APR threshold. When an institution or team fails to satisfy the requirements of the academic performance program for the first time, it is penalized with a public warning by the NCAA (this is referred to as an "occasion one" penalty). A second failure to comply ("occasion two") results in restrictions on "financial aid, playing and practice seasons and recruiting" (Bylaw 23.2.1.2.2). As an example, following two years of sub-par APR scores, the Portland State University men's basketball team lost two scholarships and four hours of weekly practice time (Beseda *et al.*, 2009). The third time ("occasion three") merits loss of eligibility for postseason competition. Teams with three straight years below a 900 will be restricted from postseason competition for the team, in addition to losing scholarships and practice restrictions. This punishment was recently used in the case of the schools mentioned in the *fast fact* below. If an occasion four, violation occurs, the institution's entire program results in a reclassification of the program to restricted membership status. This means that the school cannot participate in any postseason competition. At the end of one year, if the institution still cannot pass muster with the NCAA's academic requirements, the institution is kicked out of the Association. Box 4.5 lists current APR guidelines.

Fast fact. *In 2012, the NCAA imposed postseason bans on 10 basketball teams and 3 football teams because their APR average for the period 2007–2011 fell below 900. The basketball teams were: Arkansas-Pine Bluff, Cal-State Bakersfield, Connecticut, Jacksonville State, Mississippi Valley State, UC-Riverside, UNC-Wilmington, Texas A&M-Corpus Christi, Toledo and Towson. The football schools were: Hampton, North Carolina A&T, and Texas Southern.*

Box 4.5.   The current APR guidelines.

According to the NCAA, to be eligible for postseason competition in 2012–2013 and 2013–2014, a team must have an average of 900 in the past four years or 930 for the last two years. To be eligible for postseason competition in 2014–2015, a team must have four-year average of 930 or 940 for the last two years. If the team is at a limited-resource institution, the requirement is a four-year average of 910, or 940 for the last two years. To be eligible for postseason competition in 2015–2016, a team must have a four-year average of 930. If the team is at a limited-resource institution, the requirement is a four-year average of 920.

The penalty system has been gradually phased in since the program was introduced in 2004. As of 2011, the NCAA had APR data from 6,365 DI institutions. According to NCAA research, 54 teams (less than 1%) had insufficient scores and were subject to some form of penalty. Of these 54, 43, or 80%, are considered "limited resource institutions." We have been unable to find a precise definition of a limited resource institution but, looking at some of the schools that were recently punished, we estimate these are institutions with athletic department annual budgets of no more than US$10 million. Fifty seven percent (31) are classified as Historically Black Colleges and Universities, and 35 (65%) are FCS institutions; 15 were deemed ineligible for postseason competition ("National and sport-group APR," 2012, pp. 28–29). Unsurprisingly, some critics of the APR allege a bias against predominately Black schools, reminiscent of responses to changes in admission requirements discussed in Section 4.3. The NCAA reacted by slightly reducing the APR thresholds for these institutions, as well as making available supplementary funding. We discuss this in more detail below.

In addition to the APR policy, the NCAA instituted another significant change as part of the 2004 package of academic reforms.

The **Graduation Success Rate** (GSR) is a calculation different from the one used by the federal government. The same penalty system applies to the GSR. The GSR was developed in response to college and university presidents who wanted graduation data that more accurately reflect the mobility among students in today's higher education climate. The NCAA believes the GSR is an improved measure since it accounts for student-athletes who transfer. As indicated earlier, the *omission* of transfers can increase or decrease a school's graduation rate. The same problem can occur when transfers are *included*. For example, Duke University's graduation rate was probably harmed when basketball player Michael Dunleavy Jr. — a good student on track to graduate — turned pro in 2002. But had Dunleavy been an academic liability when he left, his departure would have improved Duke's graduation rate.

What is the relationship between the APR and the GSR? Both are measures of academic performance but from two slightly different perspectives. The APR is designed to capture two things: how well an Athletic Department keeps student-athletes eligible to play sports, and how well it keeps students enrolled. As shown in Box 4.4, the point system gives schools credit for athletes who have low grades but remain in school. Jennifer might not have grades to be eligible to play soccer for USC one season but if she continues to take classes, the soccer team will lose only one point, not two. If her grades improve the following year, she contributes the maximum two points to the team's APR. But the NCAA is concerned about more than keeping Jennifer eligible to play and being enrolled, it also wants her to graduate. That's where the GSR comes in. Ideally, the NCAA would prefer that all schools have high APRs and GSRs.

If you look back at Tables 4.3–4.5 you can see that there is a rough correspondence between the APR and GSR; schools that have a high GSR also tend to have a high APR. But the correspondence is not one-to-one. In the cases where the GSR exceeds the FGR, that is almost always because of the inclusion of transfers and walk-ons who, as indicated earlier, are excluded from the FGR calculation.

There are ways schools can "make up" lost points. For example, if a student-athlete with a GPA of at least 2.6 transfers immediately to a four-year institution, the school will not lose its retention point. There are also situations that are beyond the control of the student-athlete. For example, if Jennifer becomes ill or encounters "family member illness, personal difficulties, natural disaster, family hardship, [her] degree program or sport [is] discontinued, [she has the] opportunity to compete in Olympics or other international competition" (National and Sport-Group APR Averages, Trends and Penalties, 2012, p. 23). In these circumstances, the team's eligibility and/or retention point may be reinstated. Also, if a student-athlete's eligibility expires before they complete their degree, their former team will get an APR point if they return to college and graduate.

The APR and GSR reforms have been praised by some members of the athletics community. For example, University of Washington Athletic Director Todd Turner said "[t]his is the first time that I'm aware of that the NCAA has assigned any kind of competitive penalty to the lack of academic progress or academic success on the part of students. It will change the culture" ("The NCAA Enacts New Academic Standards," 2005). There are already news reports of "success stories" — athletes, coaches, and athletic department staff working together to improve academic performance. Perhaps more important, the graduation rate revision has resulted in a substantial historically-adjusted increase in the rate across almost all sports, a result that the late NCAA President Myles Brand described as "really spectacular." Using the new calculation also raises the ex-post graduation rates for two academically-suspect sports, men's basketball and football. As indicated earlier, 54 teams were penalized in 2011, a significant reduction from the 177 teams punished two years earlier.

The next four tables show evidence to support the NCAA's enthusiasm over the success at Division I institutions of the academic performance program. Table 4.8 compares GSRs in 1995 to 2004 and demonstrates an increase across gender, race, and selected sports. Tables 4.9 and 4.10 provide information about trends in average and median APRs, and APRs for selected sports, between 2004 and 2011. The final table (Table 4.11) shows that the

Table 4.8. Graduation success rates for selected groups of student-athletes, 1995 and 2004.

Student-athlete group	1995 GSR	2004 GSR
Overall	74	82
White	81	87
Black	56	68
White males	76	83
Black males	51	62
White females	89	92
Black females	71	80
Men's basketball	56	68
Men's basketball (White)	76	84
Men's basketball (Black)	46	61
Football (FBS)	63	69
Football (FBS, White)	76	80
Football (FBS, Black)	53	61
Women's basketball	80	86
Women's basketball (White)	87	93
Women's basketball (Black)	70	80

Source: Trends in Graduation Success Rates and Federal Graduation Rates at NCAA Division I Institutions (2011, pp. 12–13).

Table 4.9. Average and median APR by year.

Year	Average APR	Median APR
2004	960.6	971
2005	960.6	971
2006	961.4	971
2007	964.3	974
2008	971.2	981
2009	973.0	983
2010	973.8	984
2011	974.0	983

Source: National and Sport-Group APR Averages, Trends and Penalties (2012, p. 3).
Note: Sample based on 5,828 DI teams.

Table 4.10.   Average APR by sport and year.

Sport	Average APR 2004	Average APR 2011
Baseball	933.2	963.9
Men's Basketball	929.4	950.9
FBS Football	931.0	954.0
FCS Football	929.0	944.0
Women's Basketball	970.8	971.8

Source: National and Sport-Group APR Averages, Trends and Penalties (2012, pp. 6 & 12).
Note: Sample based on 274 baseball, 323 men's basketball, 120 FBS and 110 FCS football, and 321 women's basketball DI teams.

Table 4.11.   Student-athletes leaving school while academically ineligible (0 for 2) by gender and sport (number and % of all student-athletes).

Sport	2004	2011
All men	2,894 (5.1%)	2,091 (3.5%)
All women	917 (1.9%)	688 (1.3%)
Baseball	413 (5.6%)	233 (3.4%)
Men's basketball	319 (7.8%)	182 (4.4%)
Football	1,302 (7.0%)	928 (4.8%)
Women's basketball	135 (3.0%)	99 (2.2%)

Source: National and Sport-Group APR Averages, Trends and Penalties (2012, p. 15).
Note: Sample based on 6,412 DI teams.

percentage of "0 for 2s" — student-athletes who are ineligible to play and do not stay enrolled in college — has decreased across the 2004–2011 time period.

The APR and GSR also have their share of detractors. Studies at the Institute for Diversity and Ethics in Sport suggest that a gap in academic performance still exists between White and Black athletes. As an example, Bachman (*cf.* Canzano, 2005) notes that at Oregon State University the average GPA for Black football players declined from 2.57 to 1.9. Lapchick also mentions that that 23 of the

56 DI-A football teams that went to a 2005 or 2006 bowl game had APR numbers below the cut-off.

Critics point out that student-athletes have access to academic support staff, including tutors, and facilities that non-athletes do not. Their point is not the student-athletes should not have access to such support, only that exclusive access, and access to more support than available to other students, appears to contradict core NCAA rules like extra benefits (recall the NCAA's rule of thumb: if a student-athletes gets something that the typical student does not, or cannot, then a potential violation may exist).[21] Gurney (2011) discussing academic performance standards in general, including initial eligibility, notes that such "measures prompted significant increases in budgets for academic support, as well as pressure on staff members hired to work with marginal athletes — burdens that most institutions can ill afford. The need to employ cadres of academic advisers, learning specialists, and tutors to ensure the eligibility, retention, and graduation of their most high-risk athletes in a massive remediation effort to avoid team and institutional penalties imposed by the NCAA ..."

As noted elsewhere in this book, there is evidence that spending on athletic facilities, including academic support resources, has taken on arms race-like aspects. The steady erosion of eligibility standards (recall that a student-athlete like Jennifer may be eligible even with a 400 score on her SAT) has led to claims that "... it's easier for an athlete to get into college but harder to stay eligible for sports" (Wolverton, 2008). To keep Jennifer and other student-athletes eligible, universities now devote considerable resources in the form of academic support. Here are three examples.

Despite its name, the US$20 million, 40,000 square foot, three story University of Oregon's Jaqua Center for Student Athletes does allow access to all Oregon students, as well as the general public, but only to the first floor, which features a café, auditorium,

---

[21] NCAA Bylaw 16.3 stipulates that while member institutions must provide academic support to student-athletes, such support can come from the department of athletics or the institution's general support services. *It may also provide whatever level of financing it deems necessary for those services.*

and atrium. According to the university "[t]he two floors above are for the exclusive use of Oregon's student-athletes and staff and require secure access. The facility includes a 114-seat auditorium, 35 tutor rooms, 25 faculty/advising offices, conference room, flexible classroom, computer lab with 54 computer stations, graphics lab, 3 teaching labs, library, separate lounges for students, tutors and staff, and 40 study carrels." It is estimated that Duck athletes will have access to 100 tutors and 20 staff members. No wonder that the executive director of the center, Steve Stolp, says "[i]t's literally the Taj Mahal of academic services." (Bachman, 2010)[22]

University of Michigan's Ross Academic Center opened in 2006. It cost US$12 million and the 38,000-square foot building, with 24 staff members and many more tutors, provides services for roughly 700 Wolverine athletes including academic advising, study hall, and labs for help with writing, math and engineering. The campus newspaper ("Ross academic center," 2012) mentioned, "[w]hen University officials opened the center, they spoke of allowing all students to use it. Yet students who are not athletes — but want a quiet place to work — are turned away. The sign posted on the front door reads: "This facility is reserved for student-athletes." All visitors must be accompanied by a student-athlete and sign in at the reception desk. Thank you." The executive associate director of athletics said the center is reserved for student-athletes because there is insufficient space for more than just the student-athletes. There are exceptions, like Ohio State's Younkin Success Center, which is open to all students.

At the University of Georgia, the Rankin M. Smith Center is a US$6.7 million, 31,000-square foot building built in 2002 and "consists of computer labs, multi-media classroom, 20 large and small group tutoring rooms, writing center, counselor's office, and large assembly area with seating for 250." In 2006, it was estimated that the university was spending US$1.3 million to tutor its 600 athletes

---

[22] For images of the Jaqua Academic Center for Student Athletes go to: http://www.goducks.com/ViewArticle.dbml?DB_OEM_ID=500&ATCLID=205015255 and http://www.archdaily.com/137141/university-of-oregon-john-e-jaqua-academic-center-for-student-athletes-zgf-architects/.

and an equivalent amount for the remaining 25,000 undergraduate students. (Thamel, 2006)

Many of these buildings, including the three just mentioned, were funded with private donations. Nike's Phil Knight donated an unspecified amount toward the construction of Oregon's Jaqua Center and former Duck, and NFL, quarterback Joey Harrington chipped in for the first-floor auditorium. Steven Ross, a Michigan alum and New York City real estate mogul, contributed US$5 million to the eponymous building in Ann Arbor. The Rankin M. Smith Sr. family provided US$3.5 million for the facility in Athens. The intention of these donors was to support student-athletes. Nevertheless, *The New York Times* noted, "Few in college athletics doubt the importance of helping student athletes succeed. But while college officials say these programs are necessary because athletes must devote so much time to their sports, few other students whose time is consumed by jobs or activities receive as much assistance. Another issue is oversight: The educational support centers often report to the athletic director, who has an interest in keeping athletes eligible to compete, instead of to the academic leadership". (Thamel, 2006)

There are also arguments that, like many prior NCAA regulatory changes, the APR and GSR are merely "window dressing" (the illusion of control) designed to fool its member institutions, journalists, legislators, and the general public into thinking that it is serious about making substantive changes. Let's look at three specific criticisms of the academic performance program. First, a team can only lose a maximum of 10% of its scholarships regardless of how low its APR is. For example, since the NCAA allows a maximum of 85 scholarships for football and 13 for basketball, the worst academic performers would lose only 9 football scholarships and 2 basketball scholarships respectively. Is that a severe enough penalty to change the incentive structure?[23]

---

[23] Headcount sports lose an entire grant-in-aid while the equivalency sports lose 10% of the maximum grants possible; as an example, baseball has a limit of 11.7 which means the 10% penalty would result in the loss of 1.17 scholarships.

Second, athletic directors and coaches may simply "teach to the test," that is, find ways to meet the new requirements without actually conforming to the intent of the reform. The intent of the APR is to force athletic departments to improve the academic performance of their athletes or face penalties. Imagine that you are Jim Calhoun, head men's basketball coach at UConn (and being paid US$2.7 million annually). Your GSR for the 2004 cohort was 25% and your team will lose scholarships and not play in the 2013 postseason tournament. How can you raise your player's graduation rates quickly and substantially? Also, is it possible to increase the latest 889 team APR to comply with the rules change without improving your athletes' education?[24]

A third argument that challenges the integrity of the APR is based on the enforcement activities conducted by the NCAA. Critics suggest the enforcement of the APR is a manifestation of the "cartel within the cartel" phenomenon and the widening gap between the wealthiest DI programs and the least well off. You may be familiar with an expression economists sometime use, "there is no such thing as a free lunch." Improving the academic performance of student-athletes at an institution requires resources: especially time, facilities and labor. All of these have costs. We have already mentioned the lavish academic support some schools offer. But not all schools have the resources to mimic Oregon, Michigan, or Georgia. Does it seem odd to you that the big-time schools, the schools with the largest budgets and the largest investment in sports are mostly absent from the institutions listed in the fast fact with above Box 4.5? How is a school like Mississippi Valley State (budget of about US$5 million) supposed to conjure up the resources to provide enough academic support to get its teams to the current APR threshold or beyond? Is the APR a "nightstick [or] a measuring rod" (Medcalf, 2012)?

The NCAA's rebuttal is that "[m]ore than US$4.3 million has been provided to about three dozen limited-resource schools

---

[24] Calhoun retired shortly after the NCAA announced that UConn's men's basketball team would not be eligible to participate in the 2013 championship tournament.

annually since 2007, including 21 of the 24 Historically Black Colleges and Universities in Division I. Awards have ranged from

Fast fact. *Sportswriter Michael Wilbon (2002) asks "Do we really want to suggest that the state institutions of Arkansas or Maryland or Ohio have the same educational mission as private schools such as Duke or Vanderbilt or Northwestern? I'd hope not. You know what chance there was that Grant Hill wouldn't graduate from Duke? Zero. It was an open layup he'd graduate. Calvin and Janet Hill guaranteed that with the environment they established for their son, and the example of their own educational achievement. Yale and Wellesley, that's where Grant's father and mother went to school. College wasn't just expected of Grant Hill; it was mandatory, automatic, the minimum required. Compare that with most Division I football and basketball players. Way more often than most folks know, the kids playing in the tournament we've been watching all month are the first members of their family to set foot on a college campus. There's no clue whatsoever about the climb ahead, little preparedness, little in the way of pertinent advice. ... State universities in particular have an obligation, given the constituencies they serve, to do everything possible to help those kids grow and prepare to meet life's challenges. I wonder how far some of those kids who didn't graduate from Arkansas had to go just to get to the starting line. Does a degree adequately measure the value of the college experience in their lives? ... [Schools] can be more creative and vigilant in helping students work toward a degree. No question most of these kids have to be worked with more tenaciously because many weren't adequately prepared in high school. But the last thing I'd want to see is so much emphasis put on graduation rates that kids are processed with little regard to the sheer experience of college. That just allows a school to show off self-serving and flawed statistics, hollow numbers that don't tell us very much at all what some of these kids gain from attending college and what schools and the culture at large gain from trying to educate them."*

US$5,000 to US$50,000 per year and have had a direct academic impact on the school's student-athletes" (Brown, 2012). But is US$50,000 a year enough to provide sufficient resources? This supplementary funding was increased by US$4.8 million for the next three years and a school may qualify for a maximum of US$300,000 each year. Suppose the NCAA awarded all schools US$900,000 for a three year period. That would make the maximum amount of funding available to only five institutions. And what happens when the financial grant expires? Will the NCAA continue to provide subsidies? Finally, is it possible, and does it make sense, that bigger DI institutions, like Oregon, Michigan and Georgia, want to use academic measurements as a way to reduce the competiveness of smaller schools? And is it conceivable that the big dog schools want to pressure smaller institutions to leave DI entirely?[25]

Now we return to one of the central themes of your textbook — how will NCAA member institutions react to these rules changes? Imagine that you are the Athletic Director at a Division I institution. Currently, your graduation rate does not meet the minimum threshold established by the NCAA. What actions will you take to increase graduation? One set of possibilities includes increased monitoring of student performance. You can contact each athlete's professors on a routine basis to make sure the student is attending class regularly and completing all course requirements. You can also enforce study hall and hire tutors. But there is another alternative: encourage students to take easier courses or courses from professors known to play favorites with athletes.

4.7 Degrees Earned

A different way to answer the question "what is the educational quality athletes receive?" is to examine what majors they end up

---

[25] Let's also consider a question before we leave this section of the book. Do you find it odd that the NCAA can penalize a student who transfers (through the loss of a year of eligibility), yet schools can use transfers as a way to improve their graduation rate as calculated by the NCAA?

pursuing. Not all majors require equivalent hours in class and studying, and not all majors will produce a similar flow of earnings in the future. An electrical engineering degree is probably more demanding than a degree in economics, which in turn, is more difficult than education or sociology. Not surprisingly, electrical engineers tend to be paid more than economists who, in turn, earn more than sociologists or teachers. The next time you watch college sports on television, keep an eye out for the occasional student-athlete profiles that list the player's position, year in school, hometown, and major. What are the most common majors for athletes to take? Any guesses?[26]

Does it matter which program of study a student-athlete enrolls in? If the choice of major is entirely up to the student, then the answer is no. If Jennifer is attracted to sociology and is able, through her sociology classes at USC, to challenge herself academically, improve her critical thinking skills, gain perspective on issues such as poverty or discrimination, and prepare herself for the challenges of life ahead of her, then we would be hesitant to second-guess her decision. After all, economists believe the person best suited to making decisions about how we live our lives is us!

But what if Jennifer's choice is not entirely her own? What if her coach or other Athletic Department staff put pressure on her to take sociology rather than a subject she is more strongly attracted to, like electrical engineering? Unfortunately, Jennifer's choice of major is already restricted because any degree program that has afternoon classes or labs is off limits to student-athletes because those classes conflict with practices. As a result, you rarely see student-athletes declared as Art, Architecture, Chemistry, Pre-dentistry or Premed majors. Even if a student is interested in such

---

[26] According to Suggs (2003), the most common majors among DI football players are "business, communication, criminal justice, sociology, and sport management … ." Historian of college sports Ronald Smith (2012, p. 24) asks, "[w]hy do over 8 of 10 members of the University of Michigan's football team major in General Studies? Why do about three-quarters of Georgia Tech's baseball, basketball and football team members major in Management? Why do Stanford players cluster in Sociology?

a course of study, her coaches may try to steer her to something less demanding, something that will not interfere with athletics, even if it is not the student's preferred choice.[27] Another problem is the 40/60/80 rule that we mentioned in Section 4.3. If Jennifer decides to change her major from sociology to electrical engineering she may put her eligibility at risk. Many of the required courses for the sociology major that she has already taken will not apply to the engineering degree requirements. She may be aware that this means an extra year or two in college, but she will no longer meet the NCAA requirement for satisfactory progress in her major.[28]

> **Fast fact.** *The Wall Street Journal conducted a survey in 2010. It reviewed football media guides for BCS schools to determine what majors players were pursuing. Of the 1,104 players in its sample, 155 were declared as Business majors, 134 in Sociology, 108 in Communications and 103 in Liberal Arts. Two players said they were studying Zoology, Architecture or Mathematics. Only one was declared as a Spanish or Philosophy major. Biderman (2010)*

Not only will the Athletic Department "strongly encourage" students to take certain majors and not others, but — as indicated earlier — they will help the student establish a degree plan comprised of as many "gut" or "Mickey Mouse" courses as possible, as

---

[27] Sperber (2000, p. 245) mentions the experience of track athlete Robert Smith who was pressured by the Ohio State coaching staff to not enroll as a premed student. Smith left Ohio State.

[28] The NCAA is concerned about the clustering phenomenon. Paskus (2012, pp. 49–50) mentions, "[r]oughly 80–85% of Division I student-athletes report that they would likely have taken the same classes they did even if they were not student-athletes … [h]owever, nearly half … admitted that practice schedules played a role in their course choices, and a quarter … in the sports of football, baseball, and women's and men's basketball agreed that eligibility concerns played a role in course choice." For evidence that academic advisers sometimes steer student-athletes into "easy" majors, see Brady (2008).

well as courses taught by professors who are known to favor athletes. Some courses are even taught by Athletic Department personnel themselves. A case in point, and one that attracted considerable media attention, was assistant coach Jim Harrick Jr.'s "Coaching Principles and Strategies of Basketball" class at the University of Georgia. His course was notable for the *fiendishly* difficult multiple-choice final exam his students were required to take. How difficult was the exam? Let's see if you can answer *any one* of the following three questions. How many halves are there in a college basketball game? How many points does a field goal count for in a basketball game? How many points does a 3-point shot count for? Did you manage to answer any of the questions correctly? Do your professors ask you hard questions like those on their exams?[29]

Before we conclude this chapter, we should note that more research is needed on what happens to student-athletes after college. The closest relevant example is Adelman's (1990) U.S. Department of Education Report, which summarized a longitudinal study of the labor market careers of college athletes who graduated from high school in 1972. One of the findings (Adelman, 1990, p. vi) was that "… at age 32, ex-varsity football and basketball players had the highest rate of home ownership and the lowest rate of unemployment of all groups [five other subsamples of college students], along with earnings 10% above the mean for all former 4-year college students. Given the fact that a relatively high percentage of these athletes came from low socioeconomic status … backgrounds, these data suggest that a high degree of economic mobility correlates with participation in varsity sports."

4.8 Chapter Summary

Like the previous chapter, you have been introduced to some of the ways in which student-athletes are harmed by the policies of the NCAA and its member institutions. In this chapter, the focus was on academics and different ways in which the college sports industry

---

[29] All of the students in Harrick's class earned a grade of "A."

can compromise the education of some student-athletes. Ultimately, whether you believe any academic harm created or tolerated by the NCAA requires reformation of collegiate sports is something you must decide for yourself. As always, if you are interested in exploring the academic issues raised in this chapter at greater length, please refer to the readings listed in the References Section and the Selected Bibliography at the end of the book. Now let's move on to Chapter 5, in which we explore the labor market for college coaches.

4.9 Key Terms

40/60/80 rule	Monopsonistic rent
Academic Progress Rate	Non-qualifier
Contemporaneous penalty	Partial qualifier
	Proposal 68
Eligibility	Proposition 16
FERPA	Proposition 42
FGR	Proposition 48
Graduation rate	Qualifier
GSR	Rule 1.6
Historically-based penalty	Rule 2.0
Intra-cartel cheating	Special admits
Marginal revenue product	

4.10 Review Questions

1. What are some ways athletic departments keep their athletes eligible?
2. If a high school student-athlete has a 400 SAT score, can she still be admitted to an NCAA school? Under what circumstances could she eventually be allowed to play intercollegiate sports?
3. Why would a NCAA DI institution oppose an increase in eligibility requirements? Which schools would be more inclined to support such an increase? Less inclined?

4. The term "eligibility" has two different interpretations, what are they?
5. In general, are student-athletes more or less likely to gradate than their peers who do not participate in sports?

4.11 Discussion Questions

1. What are some of the flaws in the way graduation rates are calculated?
2. How will NCAA member institutions react to these rules changes? Imagine that you are the Athletic Director at a Division I institution. Currently, your graduation rate does not meet the minimum threshold established by the NCAA. What actions will you take to increase graduation?
3. Discuss the pros and cons of FERPA.
4. Discuss the pros and cons of imposing costs on student-athletes who transfer.
5. If the NCAA imposed stricter academic admission standards, there will be little impact on schools like Duke that typically accept only students with high test scores and good high school GPAs. Schools with much lower admission standards, which in past were able to recruit good athletes that had poor academic qualifications, will be greatly affected. These latter schools might accuse Duke of supporting these changes to gain a competitive advantage. In what sense is, Duke also trying to reduce a competitive disadvantage?
6. In Section 4.4, we discussed a case where the Pac-12 Conference imposed tougher eligibility standards than the NCAA. Why would a conference ever voluntarily choose a higher standard than required by the NCAA?
7. There are many cases where schools have recruited talented athletes with a questionable past. There is a significant chance that these students will continue their anti-social behavior and the school will be forced to expel them or drop them from the team. What is the risk to the school, and why would they do so? Which schools are most likely to recruit such an athlete?

4.12 Internet Questions

1. Go to the NCAA web site (http://www.ncaa.org) and find the link for Graduation Rates on the Research page under About Us. Find the graduation rate information for your school (choose any school if yours is not a member of the NCAA). Compare the results to those reported in Table 4.3.
2. Go to the NCAA site (http://www.ncaa.org) and summarize the current status of APR policy and enforcement.

4.13 References

Access to Parking Records Denied: Department of Ed., NCAA back University of Maryland's stance on FERPA (1997, Fall). *Student Press Law Center Report*, *18*, 11. Retrieved from http://www.splc.org/printpage.asp?id=153&tb=reports&edition=13 on July 18, 2004.

Adelman, C. (1990, December). Light and shadows on college athletes: College transcripts and labor market history. U.S. Department of Education.

Athletes' Unpaid Parking Tickets Recorded in Paper: University no longer able to hide behind FERPA (2000, Spring). *Student Press Law Center Report*, *20*, 17. Retrieved from http://www.splc.org/printpage.asp?id=378&tb=reports&edition=8 on July 18, 2004.

Bachman, R. (2010, January 4). New Oregon academic center, backed by Phil Knight, sets new standards. Retrieved from http://blog.oregonlive.com/behindducksbeat/2010/01/new_oregon_academic_center_bac.html on September 6, 2012.

Barr, J. (2004, July 28). Athletes make the grade sooner by failing first. *Washington Post*, p. A01.

Benedict, J. and A. Keteyian (2011, March 11). College Football and Crime. *SI.com*. Retrieved from http://sportsillustrated.cnn.com/2011/writers/the_bonus/02/27/cfb.crime/index.html on September 8, 2012.

Beseda, J., Hunt, J. and P. Buker (2009, May 7). PSU men's basketball penalized. *The Oregonian*, p. D1.

Biderman, D. (2010, September 16). Why football players don't speak Spanish. *The Wall Street Journal*, p. D7.

Brady, E. (2008). Athlete's Academic Choices Put Advisers in Tough Balancing Act. *USA Today*. Retrieved from http://www.usatoday.com/sports/college/2008-11-20-athletes-advisers-cover_N.htm on September 8, 2012.

Brown, G. (2012, July). Executive Committee funds pilot to help limited-resource schools boost APR. Retrieved from http://www.ncaa.org/wps/wcm/connect/public/NCAA/Resources/Latest+News/2012/July/Executive+Committee+funds+pilot+to+help+limited-resource+schools+boost+APR on September 1, 2012.

Burd, S. (2004, April 2). Graduation rates called a poor measure of colleges. *Chronicle of Higher Education*, p. A1.

Campbell, D. (2004, Winter). Can Athletics and Academics Coexist? Colleges And Universities Wrestle With Big-Time Sports. *National CrossTalk*. Retrieved from http://www.highereducation.org/crosstalk/ct0104/news0104-athletics.shtml on September 2, 2004.

Canzano, J. (2005, October 1). Black Players Struggle to Make Grade at OSU. *The Oregonian*. Retrieved from http://blog.oregonlive.com/johncanzano/2005/10/black_players_struggle_to_make.html on September 14, 2012.

Dealy, F. X., Jr. (1990). *Win at Any Cost: The Sell-out of College Athletics*. New York, NY: Carol Publishing Group.

Dohrmann, G. and J. Y. Borger (1999, March 10). U Comes Clean. *St. Paul Pioneer Press*. Retrieved from http://apse.dallasnews.com/contest1999/writing/all.stpaul10.html on July 20, 2004.

Duderstadt, J. J. (2000). *Intercollegiate Athletics and the American University: A University President's Perspective*. Ann Arbor, MI: University of Michigan Press.

Ferris, E., M. Finster and D. McDonald (2004). Academic fit of student-athletes: An analysis of NCAA Division I-A graduation rates. *Research in Higher Education* 45, 555–575.

Fleisher, A. A., III, B. L. Goff, and R. D. Tollison. (1992). *The National Collegiate Athletic Association: A Study In Cartel Behavior*. Chicago: University of Chicago Press.

Gurney, G. (2011). Stop Lowering The Bar for College Athletes. *The Chronicle of Higher Education*. Retrieved from http://chronicle.com/article/Stop-Lowering-the-Bar-for/127058/ on September 1, 2012.

Hyde, J. (2004, August 30). Rape Allegations Stun BYU: Some Wonder If Athletic Culture Breeds Violence. *Deseret Morning News*. Retrieved from http://deseretnews.com/dn/view/0,1249,595087821,00.html on January 30, 2007.

Karp, H. and D. Everson (2011, March 1). As critics blast the practice, Spurrier, Nutt and Petrino say it's necessary — and helpful. *The Wall Street Journal*, p. D8.

Keeping Score When It Counts: Assessing the 2011–2012 Bowl-bound College Football Teams: Graduation Rates Improve; Racial Gap Persists (2011). University of Central Florida, Institute for Diversity and Ethics in Sport. Retrieved from http://www.tidesport.org/RGRC/2011/2011%20FBS%20Bowl%20Study%28FinalFinal%29.pdf on August 27, 2012.

Keeping Score When It Counts: Academic Progress/Graduation Success Rate Study of 2012 NCAA Division I Women's and Men's Basketball Tournament Teams (2012). University of Central Florida, Institute for Diversity and Ethics in Sport. Retrieved from http://www.tidesport.org/Grad%20Rates/2012%20Women%27s%20Basketball%20Tournament%20Teams%20Study.pdf on August 27, 2012.

Maisel, I. (n.d.). Erickson Didn't Tell School He Was Interviewing. *ESPN.com College Football*. Retrieved from http://espn.go.com/ncf/columns/maisel_ivan/1507364.html on July 20, 2004.

Medcalf, M. (2012, August 9). Poorer Schools Feeling Brunt of APR. *ESPN.com*. Retrieved from http://espn.go.com/college-sports/story/_/id/8250719/poorer-schools-feeling-brunt-apr-men-college-basketball on September 1, 2012.

National Collegiate Athletic Association (2004, March 22). NCAA will collect and publish full grad rate data in response to Dept. of Education decision to suppress rates. Retrieved from www.ncaa.org/releases/miscellaneous/2004/2004032201ms.html July 30, 2004.

National and Sport-Group APR Averages, Trends and Penalties (2012, June). NCAA Research. Retrieved from http://www.ncaa.org/wps/wcm/connect/public/ncaa/pdfs/2012/apr+2012+trends on August 30, 2012.

Paskus, T. (2012). A summary and commentary on the quantitative results of current NCAA academic reforms. *Journal of Intercollegiate Sport* 5(1), 41–53

Petr, T. and J. McArdle (2012). Academic research and reform: A history of the empricial basis for NCAA academic policy. *Journal of Intercollegiate Sport* 51, 27–40

Phillips Arrested; Also Wanted for Domestic Violence (2005, August 22). Retrieved from http://sports.espn.go.com/nfl/news/story?id=2140010 on August 25, 2005.

Price, T. (2004, March). Reforming big-time college sports. *CQ Researcher* 14,11.

Reilly, R. (1998, August 31). Class Struggle at Ohio State. *Sports Illustrated*. Retrieved from http://sportsillustrated.cnn.com/features/1998/weekly/lifeofreilly/0831/index.html on July 20, 2004.

Ross Academic Center Turns Away Non-athletes (2012, September 6). *The Michigan Daily*. Retrieved from http://www.michigandaily.com/content/2009-04-15/ross-academic-center-turns-away-non-athletes on September 6, 2012.

Scherzagier, A. (2010, January 3). Athletes more often get admission exemptions. *The Salem Statesman Journal*, p. 3B.

Schlabach, M. (2006a, January 7). Michael Vick's troubled career. *The Washington Post*, p. E01.

Schlabach, M. (2006b, March 5). A player rises through the cracks. *The Washington Post*, p. A01.

Smith, R. (1988). *Sports and Freedom: The Rise of Big-time College Athletics*. New York: Oxford University Press.

Smith, R. (2012). Reaction to Michael Oriard's "NCAA academic reform: History, Context and Challenges." *Journal of Intercollegiate Sport* 5(11), pp. 22–26.

Sperber, M. (2000). *Beer and Circus: How Big-time College Sports Is Crippling Undergraduate Education*. New York: Henry Holt.

Suggs, W. (2003, January 17). Jock majors: Many colleges allow football players to take the easy way out. *Chronicle of Higher Education*, p. A33.

Thamel, P. and D. Wilson (2005, November 27). Poor grades aside, top athletes get to college on a $399 diploma. *New York Times*, p 1.

Thamel, P. (2006, November 4). Athletes Get New College Pitch: Check Out Tutoring Center. *The New York Times*. Retrieved from http://www.nytimes.com/2006/11/04/sports/ncaafootball/04ncaa.html?pagewanted=all on September 6, 2012.

The NCAA Enacts New Academic Standards For Division I Sports Programs (2005, March 14). PBS Newshour. Retrieved from http://www.pbs.org/newshour/bb/sports/jan-june05/ncaa_3-14.html on September 14, 2012.

The Racial Gap in College Student Graduation Rates (2011, October 29). *The Journal of Blacks in Higher Education*. Retrieved from http://www.jbhe.com/2011/10/the-racial-gap-in-college-student-graduation-rates/ on August 28, 2012.

Three Arkansas Fooball Players Charged (2012, May 13). *Lawrence Journal-World*, p. 2B.

Trends in Graduation Success Rates and Federal Graduation Rates at NCAA Division I Institutions (2011, October). NCAA Research Staff. Accessed August 27, 2012. NCAA.org. Log-in required. Select "Other NCAA resources" then "research reports then "graduation rates."

Warrick Pleads Guilty To Misdemeanor (1999, October 23). Retrieved from http://espn.go.com/ncf/news/1999/1019/122466.html on August 9, 2004.

Wilbon, M. (2002, March 28). Graduation rates deceive. *The Washington Post*, p. D.01.

Williams Must Meet Special Academic Conditions (2004, July 28). Retrieved from http://sports.espn.go.com/ncf/news/story?id=1847322 on August 9, 2004.

Wolverton, B. (2008, September 5). Rise in Fancy Academic Centers for Athletes Raises Questions of Fairness. *The Chronicle of Higher Education*. Retrieved from http://www.google.com/url?sa=t&rct=j&q=&esrc=s &source=web&cd=1&ved=0CCIQFjAA&url=http%3A%2F%2Fchron icle.com%2Farticle%2FRise-in-Fancy-Academic-Centers%2F13493%2 F&ei=3ApJUIqSIoGTiQKB4ICYDA&usg=AFQjCNEsctk6jXwju8Tmq O3PsFTHFjmiDg on September 6, 2012.

Zimbalist, A. (1999). *Unpaid Professionals: Commercialism and Conflict in Big-time College Sports*. Princeton, NJ: Princeton University Press.

Chapter 5

The Labor Market for College Coaches

There is no question we are overpaid.

— Lute Olsen, former University of Arizona Basketball Coach

The hell with gold … I want to buy futures in coaches' contracts.

— Sheldon Steinbach, higher education lawyer

You don't lose your job as a coach because you don't meet educational objectives. You lose your job because you don't win.

— Floyd Keith, Executive Director of the Black
Coaches Association

Fifty thousand people don't come to watch an English class.

— Paul "Bear" Bryant, University of Alabama Football Coach

[T]he determination of a coach's value to a school has fundamentally defied normal business analysis … the bottom line right now is that there is no real way to objectively look at [coach's salaries and compensation].

— Rick Horrow, sports consultant

How much do you think MLB managers would be paid if every major league team was exempt from taxes, was supported by million-dollar operating subsidies from both a university and a state budget and the players' salaries were constrained by law to be no higher than US$40,000 annually …

— Andrew Zimbalist, sports economist

5.1   Introduction

Why do some college coaches earn so much money? In this chapter, we ask two related questions: why is the average salary is so high and why are some salaries much higher than others? You will learn how coaching compensation is determined and what the value of a coach is to a school. As you will soon see, the answer to the question is not so simple. This chapter will not make you an expert on compensation for college coaches, but it will give you some insight into the issue.

Two important and obvious influences are the *market structure* of the NCAA and coaching *productivity* (e.g., winning percentage). As you already know, the NCAA cartel generates significant monopsonistic and monopolistic rents. Some of these rents are captured by the coaches. Also, as in any sport, coaches who win more games usually earn more money than those who do not. But other factors must be considered as well, notably **winner-take-all** labor markets, **risk aversion**, the **winner's curse**, **ratcheting**, and **old boy networks**. Let's explore how all of these elements combine to determine a coach's compensation.

5.2   Trends in Compensation

In January 2004, the Louisiana State University (LSU) Tigers defeated the Oklahoma Sooners in the Sugar Bowl to share a Bowl Championship Series (BCS) national championship with the University of Southern California. LSU's head coach, Nick Saban, was earning US$1.2 million annually but his contract specified that if LSU won a BCS championship he was to be paid US$1 more than the highest paid college coach. Coincidentally, that coach was his Sugar Bowl adversary, Oklahoma coach, Bob Stoops, who was earning US$2.4 million. Shortly after the Sugar Bowl, Saban received a seven-year contract extension valued at US$18.45 million. Despite the substantial pay increase, Saban left LSU to take the head coaching job with the NFL's Miami Dolphins. At the end of the 2006 NFL season, he departed the Dolphins to become head coach at Alabama. The university agreed to make him the highest paid coach in college football at that time, with an 8-year US$30 million-plus contract. Bob Stoops' contract was renegotiated to include a US$3 million bonus, if he remained through the 2008 season. He is still Oklahoma's coach, with yearly compensation of US$4.0 million.

Saban and Stoops are not the only college coaches who earn big salaries. Table 5.1 provides compensation information compiled by *USA Today* for the 15 highest paid DI-FBS football coaches in 2011. Ranked 15th is Jimbo Fisher. Fisher was a rookie head football coach at Florida State (FSU) in 2010. But his team performed well, compiling a 10-4 record and defeating South Carolina in the Chick-Fil-A Bowl. Like many other successful coaches, he got a raise, from US$1.8 to just under US$2.8 million. According to *USA Today*, in 2011, 3 FBS coaches earned more than 4 million, 9 more than 3 million, 32 — Fisher included — more than 2 million, and 64 more than 1 million. Remember that there are 120 FBS schools, so more than half are paying their coach at least 1 million. The average football salary in 2011 was US$1.47 million.

If we rewind to 2006, the average salary in FBS was US$950,000 (which suggests that average salaries rose about 54.7% over a period of 6 years). In 2006, only one coach earned more than 3 million (Bob Stoops), 8 more than 2 million, and 13 more than 1 million. Clearly, the millionaires club in football is growing rapidly. These big compensation packages are not a recent development in college sports. In 1982, Texas A&M offered a salary of US$375,000 (the equivalent of US$890,301 in 2012) to Jackie Sherrill to be the Aggies' football coach (Frank and Cook, 1995, p. 79). Table 5.2 lists compensation for head basketball coaches at selected DI institutions.

Where does the money to pay coaches come from? If you follow college sports with even a modicum of interest, you know that coaching salaries are one of the hot button issues on campuses where tuition is rising faster than inflation (tuition at California's public universities rose almost 100% between 2007 and 2011), the number of classes taught by adjunct or part-time instructors is rising, average student debt is rising (about US$25,000 in 2012), and — for public institutions — subsidies provided by state legislatures are falling.

Table 5.1.   Annual compensation for football coaches at DI-FBS institutions in 2011 (in thousands of US$).

Coach	School	School pay	Other pay	Total pay	Max bonus
Mack Brown	Texas	5,193	1	5,193	850
Nick Saban	Alabama	4,683	150	4,833	700
Bob Stoops	Oklahoma	4,075	0	4,075	82
Les Miles	LSU	3,751	105	3,856	700
Kirk Ferentz	Iowa	3,785	0	3,785	1,750
Bobby Petrino	Arkansas	3,635	3	3,638	650
Gene Chizik	Auburn	3,500	0	3,500	1,200
Brady Hoke	Michigan	3,254	0	3,254	500
Will Muschamp	Florida	3,221	0	3,221	450
Mark Richt	Georgia	2,811	128	2,940	525
Steve Spurrier	South Carolina	2,800	28	2,828	1,000
Chip Kelly	Oregon	2,800	0	2,800	1,035
Bo Pellini	Nebraska	2,775	NA	2,773	1,000
Houston Nutt	Mississippi	2,756	15	2,772	715
Jimbo Fisher	Florida State	2,750	0	2,750	725

Source: Schnaars *et al.* (2011).

Note: Private institutions like Penn State, BYU, and Notre Dame are not required to report financial information, including salaries. *School pay* includes, among other things, "[b]ase salary; income from contract provisions other than base salary that are paid, or guaranteed, by the university or affiliated organizations, such as a foundation. For example, payments in consideration for: shoe and apparel use; television, radio or other media appearances; personal appearances" Schnaars *et al.* (2011). School pay includes both the salary paid by the institution to the coach and pay from third parties. As we mentioned earlier, the latter may be much larger than the former. *Other pay* includes "[i]ncome from sources listed on the coach's most recently available, self-reported athletically related outside income report" Schnaars *et al.* (2011). *Total pay* is school pay + other pay. *Max bonus* is "[t]he greatest amount that can be received if the team meets prescribed onfield performance goals (e.g., win totals, bowl-game appearances, conference and/or national championships, coach of the year awards, etc.), academic and/or player conduct goals" Schnaars *et al.* (2011).

Table 5.2. Annual compensation for basketball coaches at DI institutions in 2011–2012 (estimated, in thousands of US$).

Coach	School	Compensation
John Calipari	Kentucky	5,388
Rick Pitino	Louisville	4,813
Mike Krzyzewski	Duke	4,700
Tom Izzo	Michigan State	3,599
Billy Donovan	Florida	3,640
Bill Self	Kansas	3,634
Thad Matta	Ohio State	2,854
Buzz Williams	Marquette	2,835
Jim Calhoun	Connecticut	2,700
Rick Barnes	Texas	2,400
Matt Painter	Purdue	2,325
Tom Cream	Indiana	2,240
John Beilein	Michigan	2,226
Bo Ryan	Wisconsin	2,175
Bob Huggins	West Virginia	2,015

Source: Schnaars and DeRamus (2012).

Note: *The USA Today* salary database for basketball coaches includes only the 68 coaches whose team appeared in the 2012 NCAA DI basketball tournament, not the entire cohort of DI coaches.

As we will see in Chapter 6, there are many defenders of high pay for coaches, especially university administrators and boosters. It is the contributions from third parties like the latter that make it possible to claim the majority of the compensation a coach gets is not coming out of the university's coffers. For example, at Florida State "football coaches' salaries [are paid] out of funds raised by its booster club" and its President Eric Barron claims "[t]hat's not any different than any other philanthropic contribution, as far as I can tell". (Schnaars *et al.*, 2011)[1]

Perhaps, President Barron considers Coach Fisher a good investment. If you were a college administrator at the University of Texas, would you justify Mack Brown's US$5 million salary on the basis that in 2011 the football team generated US$70 million in revenues for the university? Does US$40 million in football revenues help explain Nick Saban's US$4.7 million compensation package at Alabama? Alabama's President Robert Witt thinks so, he said "Coach Saban's success has justified the investment" (Wieberg, 2010). What about the US$57 million that Sooner football — led by four-million dollar coach Bob Stoops — brought in? An article in *USA Today* (Wieberg, 2011) indicated that "[g]ate receipts for Oklahoma football tripled in Stoops' first seven years. Athletics donation quadrupled. The school's athletics revenue rose from US$26 million in 1998–1999 ... to more than US$93 million" in 2010.

Let us also briefly consider a common claim made by President Barron, and others, that there should be no concern or criticism of coaching salaries because the athletic department is financially self-sufficient, requiring no subsidization from the university. As we will explore in the next chapter, determining whether an athletic department is self-sufficient can be tricky. For the moment, let's look at some data from the NCAA and then *USA Today*.

According to a report published by the NCAA (Fulks, 2011), of the 120 schools belonging to the FBS in 2010, 22 generated athletics revenues in excess of athletics expenses while the remaining 98 spent more than they earned. For the former group, median "profit" was US$7.3 million. Of the latter group, the median "loss" was US$11.6 million (Fulks, 2011, p. 27). Keep in mind, that *generated revenue* does not include any subsidies the athletic department

---

[1] But Schnaars *et al.* (2011) comment: "[e]ven so, taxpayer money is affected at least indirectly. Federal tax subsidies are involved, as are state corporate tax subsidies since the university, athletics department and booster club are exempt from the state's corporate tax structure. (State subsidies for individual returns are not involved as there is no state income tax in Florida)."

Table 5.3.   Top ten schools ranked by athletic
department net gain in, 2011 (in thousands of US$).

School	Athletic department net gain
Oregon	41,853
Alabama	26,600
Penn State	18,573
Michigan	17,507
Oklahoma State	16,961
Iowa	13,771
Texas	13,119
Oklahoma	10,834
Georgia	9,283
Louisiana State	8,704

Source: Schnaars *et al.* (2011).

gets from the institution. Of the 120 schools in total, the median school generated revenues of US$35 million and US$46 million in expenses, a deficit of US$9 million. Once subsidies to the athletics department are omitted, four out of every five FBS universities are *not* self-sufficient. For DI as a whole, median generated revenues as a percentage of total athletics revenues has fallen slightly from 76.2% in 2006 to 74.1% in 2010 (Fulks, 2011, 21). Whether the athletics department should be subsidized or not is a question we consider in the next chapter.

USA Today calculates *Athletic Department Net Gain*. This is similar to the NCAA's estimates, but allows us to identify *specific* schools and determine whether they are self-sufficient or not.[2]

----

[2] According to Schnaars *et al.* (2011), "[t]o calculate whether an athletic department is financially independent, the NCAA uses total revenues minus allocated revenues (university and state funds or student fees), then subtracts department expenses. *USA Today* uses the same methodology from data in the (public) school's annual NCAA report, which assesses whether the athletic department is self-sustaining with generated revenue from ticket sales, licensing and other income. In a few cases, athletics departments also give money back to the university, though that is not included in the NCAA report."

Table 5.4.   Bottom ten schools ranked by athletic department net
gain, 2011 (in thousands of US$).

School	Athletic department net gain
Nevada-Las Vegas	(36,720)
Rutgers**	(26,868)
Air Force	(22,667)
Eastern Michigan	(20,399)
Central Florida*	(19,522)
Florida International	(18,362)
Akron	(17,750)
Ohio	(17,683)
Houston*	(17,420)
San Diego State	(17,014)

Source: Schnaars *et al.* (2011).
Note: Ranking of schools in FBS and FCS with football programs that
reported financial information to *USA Today*. Not all schools reported.
One * means the head coach earns at least one million per year. Two **
indicates two million.

Tables 5.3 and 5.4 list Athletic department net gain for the top 10
and bottom 10 FBS schools. Table 5.5 compares Athletic Department
Net Gain for the institutions employing the coaches listed earlier in
Table 5.1. Florida State is not self-sufficient. Its athletics program
spent 8 million more than it earned in 2011, and football net revenues were US$2.6 million, a little less than Jimbo Fisher's annual
compensation. (Schnaars *et al.*, 2011)

Two clarifications before we continue: Economists recognize
that looking at a person's wage or salary can be misleading if it
excludes other valuable benefits like health and life insurance,
retirement, and vacation pay. Throughout this chapter, unless
otherwise noted, we will use the term *compensation* rather than
salary because compensation includes not just salary but all

Table 5.5. Annual compensation and athletic department net gain for selected DI football coaches in 2011 (in thousands of US$).

Coach	School	Total pay	Athletic department net gain
Mack Brown	Texas	5,193	13,119
Nick Saban	Alabama	4,833	26,600
Bob Stoops	Oklahoma	4,075	10,824
Les Miles	LSU	3,856	8,704
Kirk Ferentz	Iowa	3,785	13,771
Bobby Petrino	Arkansas	3,638	4,575
Gene Chizik	Auburn	3,500	(3,558)
Brady Hoke	Michigan	3,254	17,507
Will Muschamp	Florida	3,221	6,869
Mark Richt	Georgia	2,940	9,283
Steve Spurrier	South Carolina	2,828	(562)
Chip Kelly	Oregon	2,800	418,853
Bo Pellini	Nebraska	2,773	1,745
Houston Nutt	Mississippi	2,772	(3,520)
Jimbo Fisher	Florida State	2,750	(8,076)

Source: Schnaars *et al.* (2011).

benefits, including such perquisites as membership at a private golf club.

Also, it is important to understand that most coaches receive income from more than one source. Typically, a coach receives a base salary from the university and supplementary income. Some of the additional income may come from the university but it is also supplied by third parties outside the university, typically boosters and businesses. This supplementary income is often significantly larger than the base salary. For example, in 1997, Cincinnati basketball coach Bob "Huggy Bear" Huggins' total compensation of US$709,000 included US$571,000 in

Box 5.1. Cash for Cougar's coaches.

The Coaches Circle at Brigham Young University helps "supplement current benefit packages and allow BYU to establish salaries that fairly compensate our outstanding coaches." This organization is the brainchild of Sy Kimball, wealthy owner of a California construction company, who wanted to provide financial support to successful BYU coaches like Bronco Mendenhall and Dave Rose. Joining the club requires a donation of US$25,000 and membership is restricted to 400. About 200 people have joined thus far, putting the endowment at US$5 million, halfway to its goal.

Source: Drew (2011) and http://cougarclub.com/coaches-circle.

payments from non-university sources. When Bob Stoops was paid US$2.4 million annually, US$285,304 was paid by the university (including a base salary of US$200,000). In 2008, Auburn football coach Tommy Tuberville earned more than US$2 million a year, of which just US$235,000 was paid by the university. Roughly 75% of Tuberville's compensation came from a multimedia deal with ISP Sports, now part of sports marketing giant IMG Worldwide.

In terms of supplementary income, it is common for coaches to receive media deals such as television and radio shows, opportunities for speaking engagements and motivational seminars, an expense account for entertainment, use of one or more vehicles, use of private aircraft (Nick Saban gets 25 hours complementary use each year), a clothing allowance, complementary tickets, a percentage of ticket revenues, summer camps (sports skills clinics for kids), performance bonus clauses (e.g., if the team qualifies for postseason championships), as well as discounts at clothing stores, restaurants, and other businesses near campus. The university may also provide the coach with a university-owned residence, assist in the financing of a house, or provide a housing allowance.[3]

Many coaches sign exclusive commercial endorsement contracts with companies like Nike or Adidas or Reebok, from which they receive cash, stock, and apparel. Circa 2005, University of Connecticut basketball coaches Jim Calhoun and Geno Auriemma earned base salaries of US$1.5 million and US$975,000 respectively, but also had endorsement deals worth an estimated US$250,000–500,000 with Nike.[4] Coach K reportedly earns US$1.5 million from Nike and has deals with other companies including American Express and State Farm. Not all endorsement deals are for huge amounts of money with multinational corporations. Louisville basketball coach Rick Pitino (the second highest paid basketball coach), has an endorsement with Rally's, a fast food chain that is home of the Rallyburger® and the Big Buford® burger (for an image go to: http://aht.seriouseats.com/images/20091218-rallys.jpg).

For LSU's Les Miles, US$2.90 million of his US$3.75 million compensation package, or 77%, comes from multimedia contracts, that is, "radio/television/Internet" sources (Gentry and Alexander, 2011). Of course the downside to earning million of dollars every year, and being paid by multiple sources, is that it makes tax

---

[3] See Zimbalist (1999, p. 81). Sperber (1990, 177 ff) reports that during the 1980s, basketball coaches Jerry "The Shark" Tarkanian of UNLV received complementary tickets with a face value of US$40,000, Maryland's Charles "Lefty" Driesell grossed US$231,000 from a summer camp, and John Thompson of Georgetown had a US$200,000 endorsement contract/"shoe deal" with Nike. Football coach Bobby Bowden (Florida State) had a US$25,000 *expense account* (for comparison, the median household income in the United States at that time was about US$40,000). For other examples of compensation packages see Fish (2003).

[4] In February 2005, the Governor of the state of Connecticut, M. Jodi Rell, began an investigation into their endorsement deals. Because UConn is a public institution, Coaches Auriemma and Calhoun are state employees. To avoid improprieties such as conflict of interest, most states have severe restrictions on other sources of compensation that state employees may receive. While there may be an ethical issue that needs resolution, it is not clear that any economic impropriety has occurred (see Sampsell-Jones (2005)).

planning complicated. That's why coaches often set up one or more corporations to reduce their tax liability.

These deals are becoming increasingly important; The *New York Times* (Gentry and Alexander, 2011) noted "[w]here once coaches may have been paid merely an annual salary, now the bulk of their compensation often comes from the portion of their contracts that deals with media appearances and endorsement revenues." And this raises a pivotal question: If half or more of a coach's compensation comes from third party, non-university, source, *for whom does the coach work?* We discuss these commercial ties in more detail in Chapters 6 and 7.

Fast fact. In 2009, one year before Mike Bellotti retired as head football coach and athletic director from the University of Oregon, his total compensation was US$1.45 million. Of that amount about 80% came from third parties like Nike with whom he had an endorsement deal. Since Bellotti worked for a public institution he was entitled to a pension from the state upon retirement. But due to quirks in the state retirement system, the base pay used to calculated his monthly retirement check was not the approximately US$300,000 the university was paying him directly, but his total compensation package. As a result, Bellotti collects a monthly pension of US$41,000 per month, about US$500,000 per year, from the state for the rest of his life. Oregon's taxpayers are displeased.

Source: Sickinger (2011).

Finally, if a coach is fired he may get a **golden parachute** — a generous severance payment. Such payments are increasingly common. The University of Cincinnati paid US$3 million in 2005 to basketball coach Bob Huggins, and the University of Colorado paid a similar amount to Gary Barnett, who resigned in December 2005 from a scandal-ridden football program. University of Tennessee basketball coach Buzz Peterson got US$1.4 million after his team failed to qualify for the 2005 NCAA men's tournament, and Pete

Gillen picked up US$2 million from the University of Virginia for the same reason. If LSU's Les Miles is fired, his current contract stipulates that he will get a US$18.75 million severance payment.

Table 5.6 shows median salaries for coaches in different DI sports; football and men's basketball coaches are clearly at the top

Table 5.6. Median salaries for head coaches by sport at selected DI institutions in 2010 (in US$).

Sport	Men's teams	Women's teams
Baseball	189,000	N/A
Basketball	962,000	348,000
Bowling	N/A	49,000
Cross Country/ Track & Field	76,000	79,000
Equestrian	N/A	97,000
Fencing	50,000	43,000
Field Hockey	N/A	114,000
Football	1,383,000	N/A
Golf	105,000	89,000
Gymnastics	100,000	108,000
Ice Hockey	332,000	152,000
Lacrosse	208,000	110,000
Rifle	28,000	30,000
Skiing	49,000	47,000
Soccer	123,000	112,000
Softball	N/A	115,000
Swimming & Diving	65,000	75,000
Tennis	104,000	83,000
Volleyball	134,000	129,000
Water Polo	137,000	93,000
Wrestling	109,000	N/A
Others	77,000	58,000

Source: Fulks (2011, pp. 37–38).

of the pyramid compared to their peers. As we indicated in Chapter 2, because our focus is on the so-called "revenue sports," our main interest is the compensation received by individuals like Bob Stoops or Jim Calhoun, not the coaches of the "non-revenue" sports. Of course, not every head football and basketball coach is paid the big bucks. Note that these median salaries are based only on pay provided by the institution directly not any compensation received from third parties.

Also, in many sports there are several assistant coaches. Pay for these assistants vary widely across sports as well (Table 5.7 shows the top 10 assistant coaching salaries in football). Assistant coaches at many DI institutions are also well compensated, especially if they are in the football or basketball program. For example, at Kansas in 2002, the nine assistant football coaches earned an average of about US$104,000 a year, almost US$20,000 more than the average full professor received (Mayer, 2002). At the time of the first edition of this book, Georgia paid its nine assistant football coaches an average of US$138,271, a total of US$1.25 million annually.

Table 5.7.　Top 10 assistant coaching salaries in football in 2010 (in US$).

Assistant coach	School	Salary
Will Muschamp	Texas	900,000
Todd Grantham	Georgia	750,000
Kirby Smart	Alabama	750,000
Ellis Johnson	South Carolina	700,000
Nick Holt	Washington	650,000
Norm Chow	UCLA	640,000
John Chavis	LSU	600,000
Justin Wilcox	Tennessee	600,000
Kevin Steele	Clemson	575,000
Gus Malzahn	Auburn	500,000
Tyrone Nix	Mississippi	500,000

Sources: Dienhart (n.d.) and Berkowitz (2010).
Note: Salaries are reported only for public insitutions.

The assistants to Bob Stoops earned between US$170,000 and US$255,000. In 2010, Tennessee distributed US$5.325 million across nine assistant football coaches, an average of US$591,666.

At this point, you might feel a bit bombarded by all this compensation information and find it hard to put it all into perspective. As one of our professors in graduate school used say, sometimes we need to take whatever information we are examining and ask the question "as compared to what?" Let's make some comparisons that might help you establish a perspective on coaching salaries. It is common for a college coach to be the most highly paid employee on campus, earning more than the president, other administrators, and tenured full professors. For example, Jimbo Fisher's almost US$2.8 million in 2011 exceeded Florida State's President Eric Barron by about 5 times. Mack Brown earns 14 times more than the highest paid University of Texas Finance Professor, 18 times more than the highest paid Aerospace/Mechanical Engineering Professor, and 21 times more than the highest paid economist. Former University of Tennessee coach, Phil Fulmer's 2008 US$2.5 million package was estimated to exceed the total salaries for all faculties in the university's History and English departments. The University of Georgia's Mark Richt earns $2.8 million while the average full professor there gets US$107,500.

Table 5.8 shows that of the approximately 4,000 faculty and staff at the University of Arkansas, 6 of the 10 highest paid employees are involved in athletics. Tied for 10th is Don Bobbit, President of the entire University of Arkansas system. Table 5.9 indicates that of all Arkansas state employees, 3 of the top 10 are coaches and the remaining 7 are doctors of medicine. Arkansas Governor Mike Beebe earns about US$87,000. Again, these trends are not recent. In 1985, the University of Wyoming hired Dennis Erickson to coach the football team at a salary of US$80,000, more than Wyoming's governor, attorney general, and state Supreme Court justices (Sperber, 1990, pp. 175–176).[5]

---

[5] These kinds of disparities led William Friday, a former president of the University of North Carolina, to comment "[n]ame me a single company where a CEO works with someone who makes five times more than him" (Drape, 2004).

Table 5.8.   Salaries for top 10 employees at the University of Arkansas-Fayetteville, 2011–2012 (in thousands of US$).

Name	Title	Salary + other compensation
Bobby Petrino	Head Football Coach	2,985,000
Mike Anderson	Head Men's Basketball Coach (UA-F)	2,200,000
Tom Collen	Head Men's Basketball Coach	485,034
Paul Petrino	Football Offensive Coordinator	475,000
Paul Haynes III	Football Defensive Coordinator	475,000
Jeff Long	Athletic Director	475,000
David Van Horn	Head Baseball Coach	413,125
Willy Robinson	Assistant Football Coach	375,000
Brad Coate	University Advancement	338,636
Melvin Watkins	Assistant Basketball Coach	335,000
Don Bobbit	President, UA System	335,000

Source: http://www.arkansasonline.com/right2know/statesalaries/.
Note: Excluding employees of University of Arkansas Medical School.

At many institutions, coaches are considered to be members of the faculty or campus administrators. Why then should they be paid more than the highest paid faculty member or administrator? Is the coach more important than an award winning and world-renowned chemistry professor? Is the coach worth more than the president of the university?

> *Fast fact. In 2007, in how many of the 50 states did the Governor earn more than the highest paid coach at a public university? One. Which state was it? Alaska; Sarah Palin earned US$125,000 while Alaska-Anchorage ice hockey coach David Shyiak got US$112,000 (the school does not have a football program).*

Table 5.9. Salaries for top 10 state employees, Arkansas, 2010–2012.

Name	Title	Salary + other compensation (US$)
Bobby Petrino	Head Football Coach (UA-F)	2,985,000
Mike Anderson	Head Men's Basketball Coach (UA-F)	2,200,000
Gus Malzahn	Head Football Coach (ASU-J)	850,000
John Day	UAMS — Neurosurgery	648,327
Richard Turnage	UAMS — Surgery	630,129
Michiaki Imamura	UAMS — Cardiovascular Surgery	629,838
Daniel Rahn	UAMS — Chancellor	612,000
Stephen Canon	UAMS — Urology	575,000
Thomas Pait	UAMS — Professor	550,000
Richard Nicholas	UAMS — Orthopedics	524,581

Source: http://www.arkansasonline.com/right2know/statesalaries/.
Notes: UA-F — University of Arkansas, Fayetteville campus
      ASU-J — Arkansas State University, Jonesboro campus
      UAMS — University of Arkansas Medical School

5.3   Is a Coach a CEO?

A college coach's compensation is closer to that of a coach in professional sports or a corporate CEO, not a university administrator or faculty member. When signing Nick Saban to his new contract in 2004, the Chancellor of the LSU system, Mark Emmert, justified Saban's new contract by comparing him to a CEO, "it's no different than a corporation … it's a business. You have to make tough calls sometimes." Aside from this rather candid acknowledgement that college sports may be more about the revenues that come from a winning sports program than academics (a theme we revisit in the next chapter), is Chancellor Emmert right? Is a college coach the equivalent of a CEO? And if so, should he or she be paid like a CEO? By the way, Emmert is now President of the NCAA.

Determining the basis for CEO compensation is a complex issue that has been subject to numerous studies by economists and others. The main contribution of this literature is to show which measures of firm performance have the most impact on CEO compensation. Common measures include costs, revenues, profit, market share and stock price. This research stresses **incentive-compatibility**, finding the right combination of rewards that will minimize the potential for moral hazard and maximize the probability that the actions of the CEO are in the best interest of the company's stakeholders in the short and long run. Recent scandals involving executives from Enron, Tyco, and WorldCom — not to mention the financial meltdown in the banking sector, national banks like Washington Mutual and Wall Street firms such as Bear Sterns, Lehman Brothers and MF Global, remind us of the debate about whether it is necessary to pay CEOs millions in annual compensation to get them to perform and how to hold them accountable.

Coaching compensation is also the subject of considerable criticism; but unlike research on CEO pay, there are few studies that answer the question "what determines how much coaches are paid?" Consequently, given the paucity of empirical evidence, our approach in the remainder of the chapter will be *theoretical* rather than *empirical*. This research vacuum is beginning to be filled; your authors recently published a paper concerning head coaching salaries among selected FBS football programs (our research is summarized in Appendix 5.1). As more interest in coaches' salaries and benefits develops, more sports economists and other researchers will take interest and within a few years (perhaps before the next edition of this book), we will gain better understanding of each component that contributes to a coach's overall compensation.

Is the comparison between CEOs and college coaches appropriate? Perhaps not! Most CEOs are employed by for-profit corporations that are subject to a variety of federal rules and regulations. For example, their accounting is subject to the scrutiny of outside auditors and the Internal Revenue Service. They also issue stocks and bonds and publish financial reports in accordance with the Securities and Exchange Commission's requirements and **Generally**

Accepted Accounting Principles (GAAP). If they engage in anti-competitive business practices — like colluding with other firms — they will be prosecuted under federal antitrust laws. The CEOs, and the firms they lead, must compete in labor markets to attract qualified and productive employees, and they must pay the firm's employees a market-based wage or salary or risk losing them. The CEO and her firm face the discipline of the marketplace. If they are not responsive to consumer wants, are slow to adapt to changes in the market, or run the company inefficiently (e.g., by having excessive production costs), the firm may face bankruptcy, a takeover or merger, and the CEO may become unemployed. Even the largest corporations — like General Motors and United Airlines — are not immune from market forces.

In contrast, college coaches are employed by non-profit educational institutions that do not pay taxes. Universities do not issue stock and have considerable discretion in how they choose to publish financial information. In particular, there are no generally accepted accounting practices that athletic departments must follow. A university, and its athletic department, can be prosecuted under federal antitrust law, but this rarely occurs. The government has investigated the NCAA in the past but the NCAA's status as a non-profit educational organization tends to protect it from vigorous scrutiny by the feds. It is true that coaches must compete for athletic talent but remember that they do not pay student-athletes a market-based wage or salary. Since the athletes are not paid, the monopsonistic rents captured by athletic departments can be directed to other expenditures, notably facilities and staff salaries. As we discuss below, coaches are not immune from being fired and some universities face the discipline of the marketplace. However, public universities receive subsidies directly from state legislatures, and both public and private institutions benefit from the subsidies made available to students in the form of government loans and grants. In other words, unlike corporations, athletic departments frequently have **soft budget constraints**; this makes it more likely that they can exceed their budgets without being penalized. Finally, considerable compensation received by coaches is not paid by the university directly but by boosters and businesses.

A second reason why the comparison between CEOs and college coaches may not be appropriate is that while the revenues generated by a DI-FBS athletic department may be in the tens of millions, these revenues pale in comparison to the financial flows in the average corporation. Bob Marcum, the Athletic Director at the University of Massachusetts from 1993–2002, said "[f]or [a CEO to make] US$250,000 in the business world, he'd have to generate US$60 million to US$70 million in sales" (Zimbalist, 1999, p. 74). *Forbes* (DeCarlo, 2012b) listed the 2000 largest public companies in the world. They ranked firms using "an equal weighting of sales, profits, assets and market value to rank companies according to size." The top three were Exxon Mobil, JP Morgan Chase, and General Electric. These companies have sales in the range of US$100–400 *billion* a year and annual profits from US$15–40 *billion*. According to DeCarlo (2012a), the total compensation received by their CEOs in 2011, Rex Tillerson, Jamie Dimon, and Jeffery Immelt, was US$14, US$42, and US$8 million, respectively (or about 0.00034%, 0.022% and 0.00057% of their firms' profits). The highest paid CEO in 2011 was John Hammergren of McKesson, a pharmaceutical company that had revenues of US$109 billion in fiscal year 2010. His total compensation was US$131 million (about 0.1% of revenues). Again, we are neither defending nor criticizing corporate CEO pay, only providing a context in which to think about coaching salaries especially when coaches are compared to CEOs.

According to NCAA financial information for 2010, the median FBS school earned about US$16.2 million in football generated revenue and US$4.8 million from basketball (Fulks, 2011, p. 26). Not only are these numbers well below the US$60–70 million figure mentioned by Marcum, but most DI basketball and football coaches are paid substantially more than US$250,000.

The salaries paid to football coaches comprise a much greater percentage of revenues than do CEO salaries. In 2001, the salaries paid to 22 highest paid football coaches consumed approximately 5.6% of total football revenues (Witosky, 2002). If Jeffrey Immelt of General Electric earned 5.0% of GE's revenues, he would take home US$7.4 *billion* in pay. This percentage will, of course vary from school to school. In 2006, Ohio State coach Jim Tressel's earnings were about 4% of total football revenue, Tommy Tuberville of Auburn earned around 5%, while Kirk Ferentz of Iowa was just shy of 10%. Using data from 2008, the website Coaches Hot Seat estimated the percentage of revenues received for the 25 highest paid coaches to be 3.3% (Georgia's Mark Richt) to 20% (June Jones of Southern Methodist). Mack Brown's five million at Texas is currently about 7% of the US$70 million the football team generated.

Perhaps a better comparison is to NFL coaches. In 2009, *Forbes* estimated that the revenues generated by the Dallas Cowboys were US$420 million. Their coach at that time, Wade Phillips, was earning a salary "in the three million range." If we ballpark his salary at US$3.5 million, his share of total team revenue was less than 1%. Sports economist Dave Berri (2012) found Nick Saban's recent contract similar to New York Giants' coach Tom Coughlin's. Yet, the Giants generated US$292 million in revenue in 2010, compared to Alabama's US$40 million.

5.4   What Determines a Coach's Salary?

Imagine that you are the president of your university or the athletic director, and you are in the process of hiring a head basketball or football coach. What are your expectations for the coach? Do you want a coach with considerable experience, a high lifetime winning percentage, someone who has frequently qualified for postseason championships? Do you want a coach who will increase graduation rates, helps student-athletes increase their GPAs, and will cultivate good sportsmanship and good citizenship among his players? Do you want a coach who has an impeccable record as an ethical and moral person, who has no (or few) NCAA violations? Do you want a coach who will maximize attendance at home games, who will generate increased undergraduate applications and admissions? Do you want a coach who is a good salesman, someone who can schmooze the alumni, the boosters, and the media? Or, perhaps, would you like all of the above?

In the previous paragraph, we asked a normative question: "what *should* coaches be paid to do?" Now, let's turn to a positive question: "what *are* coaches paid to do?" As we saw in Chapter 3, economists believe a main influence on salary is employee *productivity*. If Chef Suzy is more productive than Chef Pierre, and the labor market for chefs is competitive, she should earn a higher salary than he does. The same logic should apply to college coaches. If winning percentage is used as the indicator of productivity, coaches with a greater lifetime winning percentage should earn more. But what about other factors that may contribute to a winning record, such as strength of team schedule and recruiting? Should those factors be included? And what about the other considerations we mentioned like graduation rate, team GPA, television appearances or college applications — where do they fit in?[6]

An economist would translate this series of questions into a mathematical representation:

$$Y_i = f(X_1, X_2, X_3, \ldots X_n).$$ (5.1)

Equation 5.1 simply states that a coach's salary (Y represents the **dependent variable**) is a function of (determined by) a set of independent/**explanatory variables** (the X_s). The variables on the right side of the equation — the explanatory variables — might include winning percentage, strength of schedule, team quality (e.g., how many players were high school All-Americans), number of games televised nationally, attendance, team grade point average, and any other factors believed to determine salary. The data should include recent data (like the winning percentage during the previous season) but also past data reflecting a coach's lifetime experience. Once the data is collected, a statistical technique known as

---

[6] Equal productivity across sports does not result in equal coaching compensation because most college sports do not generate revenues in excess of cost. How closely should a coach's compensation be tied to the revenues generated by the sport? Should a female coach who has a better winning percentage than her male counterpart earn less if her sport produces fewer revenues? We explore gender effects in Chapter 8.

regression analysis can be used to identify which independent variables are most influential in determining coaches' salaries. If you are unfamiliar with regression analysis, or perhaps a bit hazy remembering the details, we provide a quick and simple review in Appendix 5.1.

If we were asked to explain the basis of compensation for coaches in professional sports like the NFL or NBA, our answer would be simple: winning. Professional coaches are paid to win. The easiest way to lose your job in the coaching profession is for your team to have a losing record.

As noted previously, in college sports, there are potentially many more determinants of a coach's compensation besides winning. We suspect that at many schools in Division II and III these other factors play a crucial role in both job retention and compensation. In Divisions II and III, keeping their job may be what coaches value most highly, and things like graduation rates and good team sportsmanship may have greater influences than whether the team had a record of 5-7, or 7-5. After all, nowhere in the NCAA by-laws does it state that winning should be the primary consideration in university athletics!

In Division I, especially FBS, we assume that coaches are rewarded for winning and little else. How can we justify this assumption given that presently available empirical research on coaching compensation is few and far between (an exception is the research discussed in Box 5.2 and Appendix 5.1)? For the moment, we must rely mostly on anecdotes and theory. We assume that college coaches are paid, first and foremost, to win. Why? First, winning percentage is an unambiguous measurement because all sports are a **zero-sum game**. There is a winner, and there is a loser. Measurements of academic performance like GPA and graduation rates are, as we noted in the previous chapter, easily manipulated and subject to considerable interpretation. Winning percentage, on the other hand, is cut and dried.[7]

---

[7]Measurements relevant to CEO compensation are less clear cut because market competition is frequently a **positive-sum game**. Unless a company goes bankrupt, or competition is defined very narrowly (like market share), it remains possible

Box 5.2.   Managerial efficiency and coaching turnover.

One study of NCAA DI basketball coaches (Fizel and D'Itri, 2004) examined the extent to which the probability of coaching turnover (i.e., the likelihood a coach would be fired) is determined by winning percentage and managerial (coaching) efficiency. Managerial efficiency was defined by comparing a coach's winning percentage to that of his peers holding team quality and strength of schedule constant. In other words, two coaches who have teams of the same caliber, and face comparable opponents, should have similar winning percentages. If they do not, the coach with the poorer record is considered to be less efficient. The results of the Fizel and D'Itri study are interesting because they suggest that winning percentage is a much stronger determinant of whether a coach will be retained or fired than his coaching efficiency. For example, suppose the basketball coach at Ball State had a team of average quality which faced many teams of above average quality over the course of a season. Because of the skill of the coach, Ball State posted a winning percentage of 0.600. During the same season the coach of Indiana led his squad to a record of 0.625, clearly a better record than that of Ball State. But suppose the Indiana team was much better than all of the opponents it faced in the course of the season — it was a team of above average quality that played teams of average quality. The coach at Indiana was not as efficient as the coach at Ball State, yet the study suggests the Ball State coach was more likely to be fired than the coach at Indiana.

for all of the firms in an industry to succeed. Not all of Toyota's success necessarily comes at the expense of Ford; Ford and Toyota may both experience increased revenues and profits during the same period of time. In addition, tangible measurements like profit or market share do not apply to universities because they are almost entirely non-profit institutions, many of whom are publicly supported through federal and state taxation, and few of whom ever become insolvent.

Second, when you read about coaches, who have recently been fired, the justification is more often "not enough wins" rather than low graduation rates, player arrests, NCAA infractions, or other issues. Here are a couple examples. As head football coach at Nebraska, Frank Solich compiled a career winning percentage of 0.753 (58-19) from 1998–2003. In 2001, his team won the Big 12 championship and played for the national championship. His 2003 team featured 84 players with a 3.0 GPA or better, and won 9 of 12 games to earn a trip to the Alamo Bowl. After the 2003 season, he was fired and his athletic director described his performance as "mediocre" (Price, 2004). Solich is now coaching at Ohio University.

Tyrone Willingham left the Stanford football program to become head coach at Notre Dame. In 2002, his first season, the Irish went 10-3 and played in the Gator Bowl. The subsequent two seasons were less successful and overall the Irish won 21 games and lost 15 under his leadership, a disappointing record for the Notre Dame faithful. While Willingham had more than his share of critics, others pointed out that three years was insufficient time to recruit athletes and rebuild the program to its earlier glory. He was well-liked by his players and praised by the Athletic Director Kevin White for the academic success of his players and for running a "clean" program. But that was not enough. White said, "[f]rom Sunday through Friday our football program has exceeded all expectations, in every way" ("AD cites," 2004). However, "[w]e have not made the progress on the field that we need to make." Willingham was fired in December 2004.

Third, when you examine coaching contracts it is common to find a variety of performance-based incentive clauses included (e.g., if the team meets or exceeds a specific graduation rate). Ohio's Frank Solich is contractually required to ensure that at least 60% of his players graduate. But academic-based payments are trivial compared to bonuses based on winning. For example, Mike Fish (2003) notes that Bob Stoops' contract with Oklahoma contains 10 performance-related bonus clauses ranging from US$10,000 (if the team has a graduation rate of 70% or better) to US$150,000 (if the team is declared the national champion). Coach Bobby Bowden of Florida State University earns in excess of US$2 million a year and qualifies for a US$16,000 bonus based on graduation rate. How strong is an incentive that rewards him with a payment equal to 0.8% of his total compensation? Even higher bonuses, such as the US$75,000 Iowa's Kirk Ferentz could earn, are a drop in the bucket compared to his total compensation package. The *New York Times* (Gentry and Alexander, 2011) notes that for coaches like Nick Saban and Les Miles, any bonus for academic achievement is substantially less than bonuses for winning and getting into the postseason.

Fourth, as we will argue in more detail in the next chapter, athletic department personnel are not the only people fixated on winning; the university administration, alumni, and boosters are as well. The mantra of college sports is "winning generates revenues, and revenues generate wins." The administration believes a winning sports program will bring in more revenues and publicity for the school, and reinforce the university's "brand" image. They may be right. When you think about the University of Florida, Notre Dame, Alabama, or the University of Oregon what is the first thing that pops into your head?

Fifth, and finally, studies of professional sports franchises suggest that the primary determinant of ticket sales is winning percentage. Teams that win more often sell more tickets than teams with worse won–lost records. It seems highly plausible that the same direct relationship between winning percentage and ticket sales should apply to college sports. One study looked at the decision to renew season tickets for college football and concluded that renewal was more likely if the team had a winning record (Pan and Baker, 2005). As we will see in Chapter 6, the average DI athletic department collects one-quarter of its annual revenue from ticket sales.

Many alums support the expansion of athletics because it increases the prestige of the institution, gives them greater bragging rights, maintains their connection to the university, or reminds them of their carefree days as an undergraduate. It has also been suggested that a successful athletics program increases alumni donations to the university (we examine this claim in Chapter 6). Many boosters, members of the athletics "fan club," are not graduates of the institution and have neither interest nor a stake in the academic side of the university. Their only interest is sports and the continued success of the university's athletics program.

5.5 Is the Labor Market for Coaches Competitive?

Pete Carroll, ex-football coach at the University of Southern California, once suggested the pay received by coaches was merely a matter of "supply and demand" (Drape, 2004). Is the labor market for coaches as competitive as Coach Carroll suggests? Is compensation determined *primarily* by the interaction between reservation wages and marginal revenue products, or are there distortions in the market that influence, and potentially inflate, compensation packages? To better understand this question, we need to consider what kind of labor market best explains compensation patterns for intercollegiate athletics coaches.

At first glance, the market for coaches appears to be competitive because there are many buyers and many sellers. And we know that if the labor market is competitive, then **marginal revenue product** and the employees' **reservation wage** jointly determine the prevailing market wage. Now take a look at the salaries listed in Tables 5.1 and 5.2. If Coach Bob Stoops, or any of his peers, were precluded from coaching football at a FBS school, what do you think their next best alternative would be? Would they be working as investment bankers on Wall Street or as a partner in a prestigious law firm, as a CEO of a Fortune 500 firm, a neurosurgeon, or a professor of economics at prestigious Linfield College? Probably not; in all likelihood they would remain in the coaching profession — possibly for a FCS, DII or DIII football team — but earning less than they are at present. In other words, their current compensation far exceeds their reservation wage. What then accounts for such a wide gap between their compensation and their reservation wage?

To answer this question, you should recall the examples we used in Chapter 3. Why is a typical chef, like Suzy, not paid hundreds of thousands of dollars to work at the Cheesecake Factory? Why is the wage that Suzy receives closer to her reservation wage? As you remember from the analysis of a competitive labor market, the presence of many skilled chefs in the market puts downward pressure on the wage as chefs compete with each other for available positions. This interaction among chefs and restaurants is the process that leads to the establishment of the equilibrium wage in the labor market for chefs.

If Chef Suzy were offered US$500,000 to prepare desserts for a restaurant, she would be ecstatic because this would be well in excess of her reservation wage. She would be earning, in economic terminology, considerable **economic rent**. Since those rents tend to be dissipated in a competitive labor market, the presence of significant economic rent suggests the labor market is not competitive.

How can college coaches earn significant economic rent in a market in which there are many coaches offering their services and many institutions willing to hire them? To answer this question, we first return to the monopsonistic market structure of the NCAA and then consider a series of related issues. As you know, the market structure of college sports is a cartel. Cartels result in monopoly profits for the NCAA and its participating colleges and universities. We should expect in a sports cartel, like any professional sports league, the artificial profits will be divided between the league's administration, the franchise owners, and the employees (the coaches and the players). How the profits are divided is a typically contentious issue, one that lies at the heart of work stoppages and lockouts like those that occurred in the NFL in 1987, in MLB in 1994, in the NBA in 1998 and 2011, and in the NHL in 2004–2005 and 2012–2013. The NCAA differs from the pro sports leagues not because there is a lack of cartel profits, but because the primary source of labor — the athletes — get so little. Since the athletes get essentially no slice of the cartel profit pie, that leaves more for the coach, the athletic department, and the university.

Fast fact. An example of monopsonistic rent: At the time of his resignation in 2011 (because of rules violations), Jim Tressel, former head coach at Ohio State, was earning about US$3.5 million annually. He now earns about US$200,000 in a non-athletics-related administrative position at the University of Akron.

If the NCAA's prohibition on paying athletes was abolished, increased competition for athletes among universities would lead to something closer to a competitive wage or salary. Athletes would get a bigger part of the pie and there would be a reallocation of monopsonistic rents toward the athletes and away from head coaches, and other athletic department expenditures. One consequence of this would be lower *average* and *median* salaries for coaches. This does not mean that every coach would earn lower salaries, only that the redistribution of monopsonistic rents would force a downward compression of average and median salaries; a result that coaches would clearly prefer to avoid.

The current market structure of the NCAA, and the presence of significant economic rent, is the *most important* reason why the salaries of individuals like Bob Stoops and Mike Krzyzewski are so large. But it is not the only reason; let us consider some others.

5.6 Winner-Take-All Labor Markets (The Economics of Superstars)

Universities, especially those attempting to upgrade their athletics program, often compete against one another to hire the "messiah coach," the person who will transform a losing program, or a relatively unknown program, into a high profile program where winning is the rule, not the exception. The "messiah" is typically a person from the coaching community who is perceived to be vastly superior compared to her peers, she is, in other words, a **superstar**. Superstars exist in many professions: athletes, movie stars, novelists, trial attorneys, CEOs, scientists, even economists. The labor market for these stars is intriguing.

Imagine a competitive labor market consisting of many buyers and sellers; a market in which all the potential employees (the sellers) have virtually the same amount of talent or productivity. Microeconomic theory suggests the equilibrium wage or salary paid to each person would be nearly identical (the variance in the wage distribution would be small). But what if it turned out that the distribution of wages was skewed in such a manner that a small percentage of those employed earned a disproportionate amount of the total earnings? For example, suppose Chef Suzy, Chef Pierre, and 98 other chefs make delicious cherry-chocolate cheesecakes. Suzy's dessert is judged by buyers to be slightly superior to those produced by Pierre and the other chefs. If all 100 chefs produce the same number of cheesecakes during a given time period, but Suzy's are slightly better, we expect Suzy's wages to exceed everyone else's by a small amount — say, US$550 per week vs. US$500. But what if it turns out that Suzy is paid US$2,200 per week, not US$550, even though no one would claim that her cheesecakes are four times better than Pierre's or those produced by the other chefs. This concentration of earnings among a few (whom we refer to as the superstars) is one part of what economists refer to as a **winner-take-all** market.[8] The other part is that individuals' earnings are determined by *relative* not *absolute* performance.

Economists define a superstar in this market as "a worker whose compensation level far exceeds those of all of the other workers within the organization even though often his/her skill level is only slightly higher than the next most productive worker; the differential in salary is magnified relative to the differential in productivity" (Benjamin, Gunderson and Riddell, 2002, p. 627). By absolute standards, Suzy produces the same number of cheesecakes as everyone else (the only difference is that each cheesecake she makes is slightly better). But because she competes in a winner-take-all market, "slightly better" allows her to capture the lion's share of the earnings.

We observe winner-take-all markets in many settings, including the film industry. For example, the estimated median earnings

---

[8] The theory of the market for superstars is presented in Rosen (1981). The phrase "winner-take-all is from Frank and Cook (1995).

of salaried actors in 2005 was around US$27,000, yet actors such as Tom Cruise or Leonardo DiCaprio commanded US$20 million for a single film appearance. From your perspective, or that of the average movie viewer, are Cruise and DiCaprio *740 times* better actors than someone earning the median salary? Is it possible that those on the demand side (the buyers) may consider some television and film actors (the sellers) to be of higher quality than they really are, and thus imperfect substitutes for other actors? How these perceptions develop and persist over time is difficult to answer; nevertheless, we will offer one possibility in the next section — risk aversion on the part of buyers. It is also important to note that winner-take-all markets impact not only specific labor markets and professions but also, as economists have recently pointed out, income distribution in the economy as a whole.[9]

Fast fact. *Who won the gold medal in the men's 100 meter sprint at the London Summer Olympics in 2012? If you said Jamaica's Usain Bolt, you are correct. Bolt's 9.63 second dash eclipsed his country-man Yohan Blake and American Justin Gatlin, who ran 9.75 and 9.79, respectively. Like many successful Olympic athletes, Bolt has several endorsement deals with companies, including Gatorade, Hublot, Nissan, and Visa, and is likely to secure a few more deals as a result of his performance in London. But, what about Blake and Gatlin? If Bolt signs a US$963,000 endorsement deal with McDonald's is Blake going to get a similar deal with, for example, Starbucks for US$951,000? Will Gatlin get US$947,000 from Taco Bell? In other words, will their deals reflect the fact that even though Bolt came in first, Blake and Gatlin were only 0.12 and 0.16 seconds behind him? Not hardly. Forbes magazine ranks Bolt only 63rd on the list of the world's highest-paid athletes, "but his income is more than 20 times what other elite sprinters typically make in a year and more than any other athlete in the history of track and field."*

Source: Badenhausen (2012).

---

[9] See, as examples, Cowen (2011) and Frank (2011).

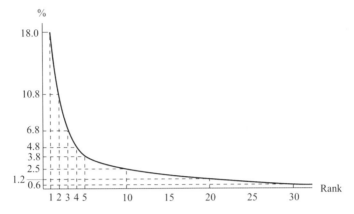

Figure 5.1.   Prize money shares by tournament rank, 2004 PGA
Championship.

Source: http://www.pga.com/pgachampionship/2004/prize_money.html.

Why do winner-take-all markets flourish? One possible answer,
clearly applicable to athletic contests like golf and tennis tournaments, is that the prize structure is purposely skewed to begin
with; economists refer to this as a **rank-order tournament**. Thus,
the woman who finishes 10th at Wimbledon does not receive a
prize 1/10th that of the woman who finished first but rather a prize
perhaps 1/50th in size (Figure 5.1 illustrates this).[10] Suppose a prize
system based on absolute performance was used instead. A person
who finished in nth place would receive $1/n$ of the tournament
winnings that the first place finisher does. Would the quality of the
competition really be any different?[11]

What can we conclude from the economics of superstars and its
application to college coaches? *First,* as in other professions, there

---

[10] In their textbook, Leeds and von Allmen (2005, p. 280) use an example from the
2003 PGA Master's Tournament. The winner, Mike Weir, finished one shot under
Len Mattiace but the former earned US$1,080,00 in prize money and the latter
US$648,000. In addition, "the two players who finished 48th and 49th were also
just one stroke apart, yet they received US$21,000 and US$19,000 … ."

[11] It might. There is evidence that a tournament structured reward system causes
participants to increase their effort. See, Ehrenberg and Bognanno's (1990) analysis of the PGA.

are superstars among the coaching community — Pete Carroll or Mike Krzyzewski — who earn salaries and total compensation packages far beyond those of their peers. *Second*, it suggests that individuals who have similar levels of productivity may receive substantially different salaries from one another, even if they coach in the same sport. We are not suggesting that the productivity of Coaches Carroll and Krzyzewski is identical to all other coaches, only that it may be *perceived* to be far greater than it really is. In practical terms, this means in some cases universities may be paying their coaches far more than necessary to attract a person of comparable experience and talent (keeping in mind that those universities are reaping substantial monopsonistic rents). *Third*, it reinforces the arms race among universities, a topic we introduced in Chapter 2 and one we return to in the next chapter.[12]

5.7 Risk Aversion

Suppose Coach Jimbo Fisher's contract as the head football coach at Florida State University is about to expire. The administrators at the university offer him a new contract at US$4,000,000 per annum. But Coach Fisher, who has a reputation as one of the top coaches in the country, wants to test the waters and see what other schools are willing to offer. South Carolina offers him US$4.5 million and FSU counters with US$4.6 million. Then, the University of Florida offers Fisher US$4.7 million and Oregon responds by tendering US$4.8 million. Next, Notre Dame offered him US$4.9 million and FSU ups its bid to US$5 million, at which point Coach Fisher finally accepts. When does the bidding stop and why does FSU continue to make increasingly higher counter-offers, especially when there are other talented coaches available?

To help answer these questions, imagine that you are the director or producer of a movie like *Master and Commander*, a 2003 film

---

[12] It may also lead to over-crowding in the labor market: too many sellers enter the market in the hope of becoming one of the handful of superstars. As an example, think about the number of men and women waiting tables in Los Angeles who consider themselves to be actors. See Frank and Cook (1995) for a full discussion.

about naval conflict between the British and French during the Napoleonic War, with production costs of US$150 million. As you cast the roles for the film you think to yourself, "is there a large potential audience for a story about the Napoleonic Wars? What if the film is a dud, what happens to *my* reputation? *Will I ever work in Hollywood again?*" Two actors come to mind as you think about who could play the role of Capt. Jack Aubrey, a central figure in the story. The first, Mr. James Purefoy, is a handsome and talented Briton who, at that time, did theater with the Royal Shakespeare Company and had a handful of film and television roles on his resume (since then he did, inter alia, the 2004 film *Vanity Fair*, the excellent 2005 miniseries *Rome*, and the television series *The Philanthropist* and *The Following*). The other actor under consideration is the mercurial Australian, Mr. Russell Crowe. Either candidate would make a convincing Captain Aubrey. If you hire Purefoy his salary is US$200,000. If you choose Crowe, it is US$10 million. Who do you hire? *Remember* — you are worried about the box office — in the back of your mind you are haunted by the question, *what if the movie (which cost US$150 million to make) is a dud*?

You probably pick Crowe. Even though, he is far more expensive, by hiring him you have purchased an insurance policy. If the movie fails you can tell the studio executives, and the people who financed the film, "but Russell Crowe was in it, if Crowe can't make the film a success then no one can. Do not blame me!" But if the movie tanked *and* you hired the less recognized actor, then your future in Hollywood would be jeopardized.[13]

Driving this kind of over-bidding is **risk aversion**, situations in which the decisions we make today are based on the possibility

---

[13] O.J. Simpson paid his attorneys an estimated US$6 million to defend him from charges of double homicide. His defense team, nicknamed "The Dream Team," included legal superstars F. Lee Bailey, Alan Dershowitz, and Robert Shapiro. While Simpson was found not guilty of criminal charges in 1995, it is interesting to speculate whether he could have achieved the same result at a lower cost, *and whether he would have been willing to risk paying less*. We are not certain of the source of this example but we suspect it is George Mason University Economics Professor Tyler Cowen.

that we may face potentially undesirable outcomes in the future. There are many situations in which it is rational to be risk averse and these situations lead us, whenever possible, to try to insure ourselves from those undesirable outcomes. Homeowner's insurance is a good example. Even though the chances of something bad happening to our houses, like damage from a fire, natural gas explosion or tornado, is quite small, the fear of suffering thousands of dollars in property damage convinces most of us to buy insurance for our home.

If you are the president or a top administrator, or the athletic director, and your basketball team finishes the season at 5 wins and 25 losses in its first season under a new head coach, do you want to tell the trustees, the alums, the boosters, the media, and the fans, "hey, we hired superstar Coach Bigbucks and we still lost" or do you want to say "we hired Coach Incognito because he was the cheapest coach we could find?" Which is your choice?[14]

In the next chapter, we examine the arms race going on among universities as they spend more and more money on sports in the belief that a winning athletics program will enhance the status of the university, attract undergraduate students, and generate significant revenues. Part of the arms race is hiring and retaining *the* coach: the big dog coach with the big dog record of winning and postseason appearances. You have to pay the big dog coach big dog money or else the big dog will be hired by another school (or possibly a pro team).

5.8 The Winner's Curse

Have you ever purchased something on eBay only later to regret it because you felt that you paid too much for it? Economists call this the **winner's curse**. Here's an example of the curse: Suppose you fill a one gallon clear glass jar with US$25 worth of assorted flavors

---

[14] Unlike the college sports industry, there is some evidence that Hollywood is questioning the value and wisdom of hiring the expensive "A-list" actors (Dobuzinskis, 2009).

of jellybeans. Then you offer the jar at an auction. Before they bid, each potential buyer will first make an estimate of the value of the contents of the jar. Their estimates will obviously differ from one another's and, if you knew all of these estimates, you would know the distribution of the estimates. Surprisingly, if many people are bidding, the mean (average) of these estimates would probably be very close to the actual value of the jellybeans, even though the winning bid would be in excess of that value.[15] Why does a winning bid above the true value happen? Three factors come to mind. *First*, the bidders have imperfect information. In lieu of a better way to determine the value of the jellybeans (like counting how many are in the jar), they must make a guess. When information is scarce, each individual's estimate is likely to differ from the true value of the good being sold. Roughly half of the bidders will guess less than the actual number and half will guess more. Those who guessed the least will drop out as the bidding progresses. The person who guessed the most will be the high bidder. *Second*, as research in psychology and behavioral economics suggests, most of us tend to be overconfident in our abilities, including the ability to guess the value of a jar full of jellybeans.[16] *Third*, nobody likes to lose, and auctions often lead to us get caught up in the heat of moment and make bids that are too high.[17]

Economists have studied the winner's curse in a variety of contexts, including oil exploration and corporate mergers and takeovers. But what does it have to do with the labor market for college coaches? The competitive process in which a superstar coach is

---

[15] The winner's curse is discussed in Thaler (1988). For a fascinating discussion about why the mean estimate is often accurate, see Surowiecki (2004, Chapter 1).

[16] As an example, suppose you asked 10 of your friends to rate their driving abilities. How many do you think would say they are "worse than average?" This phenomenon in which "everyone is above average" is often referred to as the "Lake Wobegone effect" (from the public radio program Prairie Home Companion). For further discussion, see Belsky and Gilovich (1999, Chapter 6).

[17] Unfortunately, knowing about the winner's curse may not be especially helpful. If you seek to avoid becoming the "cursed" winner you must be willing to offer lower bids, bids that will most often ensure you lose, or else not participate in the auction to begin with.

Box 5.3. Ratings percentage index example.

One of the factors in determining how college basketball teams are seeded in the NCAA tournament is a statistical tool called the Ratings Percentage Index (RPI). The RPI is calculated using a team's winning percentage and its strength of schedule. The latter is weighted more heavily in the RPI, contributing 75% to the RPI number. Since winning percentage is between 0 and 100%, the RPI similarly ranges from 0–100 and the number is usually in the 30–70 range. The *Wall Street Journal* (Futterman, 2009) used the RPI, and the salary of the head basketball coach, to determine, in terms of dollars, who were the most and least valuable coaches. Since an RPI of 50 is, by definition, an average team's record, the *Journal* determined each coach's average RPI between 2006 and 2009 and then divided the coach's salary by the number of RPI points greater than 50. This resulted in an estimate called *value score*. For example, the coach with the worst value score was Georgia Tech's Paul Hewitt. Hewitt's salary of US$1.3 million was divided by 4.5 (the difference between his average RPI of 54.5 and 50). This produced his value score of 288,888. That score says that every RPI point beyond 50 cost Georgia Tech about US$289 thousand. The most valuable (basically the biggest bargain) was Clemson's Oliver Purnell with a value score of 97,087. Hewitt now coaches at George Mason and earns about US$660 thousand. In 2008, Clemson extended Purnell's contract through 2014 and gave him a raise to US$1.3 million, but he left in 2010 to coach at DePaul. He currently earns US$1.8 million. Purnell's success at Clemson may have been an aberration as *Forbes* (Van Riper, 2011) — based on his 0.570 lifetime winning percentage and only six tournament appearances in 23 years — recently called him one of the most overpaid coaches in the college game.

For more on the RPI see, for example: http://en.wikipedia.org/wiki/Ratings_Percentage_Index and http://www.rpi-forecast.com/live-rpi.html.

hired is essentially an auction; numerous bidders (universities) are vying against each other and no one wants to lose. The risk-aversion tendencies we just described contribute to a "win at all costs" mentality that seems to justify higher and higher bids. The process clearly exhibits imperfect information, no single bidder has a crystal ball that will accurately predict the impact the superstar coach will have once he is hired and the additional revenue streams (not to mention publicity) that will flow to the university. Finally, compounding these issues, the college president or administrator who hires the coach is playing with someone else's money, not her own. Would you make a higher or lower offer on the jar of jellybeans if someone else was paying your bid?

5.9 Ratcheting

In Section 5.1, we mentioned that the contract extension Nick Saban received in 2004 was triggered by a clause in his contract that stated, if the LSU Tigers were to win the BCS championship, the contract would be revised so that he received "one dollar more than the highest-paid college coach in the nation." That person was Bob Stoops, the coach of Oklahoma and the team LSU faced in the 2004 Sugar Bowl (Drape, 2004). Because the Tigers defeated the Sooners, Saban's annual compensation rose by 40%, from US$1.6 to US$2.3 million, just above what Stoops was making at the time. More recently, Jimbo Fisher got a raise of almost one million dollars after his first year coaching at Florida State. FSU President, Eric Barron justified this increase by saying that Florida State conducted a market analysis and found Fisher's 2010 pay "was in the middle of the ACC pack and low for the SEC" and that he deserved a raise for coaching the Seminoles to a 10-4 record.

Both of these are excellent examples of a phenomenon known as **ratcheting**. To understand how ratcheting works, let us return to the film industry for a moment. Suppose Julia Roberts, Meryl Streep and Jennifer Lopez each earned US$10 million for their last film and each film was a box office success. This year, Roberts is being considered for a new film — entitled *The Curse of Keynes* — about a former college athlete who overcomes formidable odds to earn her Ph.D. and eventually becomes the second woman to win the Nobel Prize in Economics.[18] Her agent bargains successfully with the film's producers for a salary of US$12 million. Roberts accepts the role and the film is a hit. Around the same time, roles in other films are offered to Lopez and Streep. What salary should be offered to those two stars?

Chances are Lopez and Streep's agents will use Roberts' contract as the basis of comparison. They will argue, "If Julia is worth it, why isn't my client?" Why not indeed? After all, as we saw a few moments ago, the number of superstars is limited (in economics terminology, the market is said to be "thin"). Because there are only a handful of superstars, the number of labor market transactions are few in number and the equilibrium wage is anyone's guess. When the market is populated by only a few buyers (or, as in this case, sellers) there will be few transactions. The net result will be considerable uncertainty regarding the equilibrium wage, a situation in which the last observed trade — regardless how far it may deviate from the equilibrium wage — becomes the *de facto* prevailing wage, the benchmark from which negotiations begin.

When Roberts, Lopez and Streep earn US$12 million a new benchmark is established, a benchmark difficult to break and one that increases over time. Like a ratchet mechanism, once salaries move upward they tend to become locked in place, *even if the movement is triggered by an increase in a single person's salary*. When US$2 million plus salaries are awarded to coaching superstars like Saban and Stoops they set a standard. Similarly successful coaches who are only earning US$1.5 million suddenly say, à la Miss Piggy "hey, what about *moi*?" Are you going to let other schools outbid you? Are you going to risk losing Coach?

Risk aversion and winner-take-all markets contribute to the ratcheting phenomenon. When a coach (or his agent) negotiates

---

[18] Do you know who the first was?

with the university, he will try to convince the administration, he is the messiah and cannot be replaced. But because the outcome of negotiations can be costly for the coach or the university it is increasingly common for contractual provisions to specify that a coach receive a salary comparable to his peers. This has a huge ratcheting impact since all it takes is the salary of one coach to increase to trigger a domino effect across the contracts of dozens of other coaches.

Ratcheting is also compounded by the frequency of coaching turnover. Between the 2004 and 2005 football seasons, 23 out of the 117 DI-A schools had a new head coach. That is a 20% turnover rate in a single year.[19]

5.10   Old Boy Networks

In March 2003, Jim Harrick Sr., head basketball coach at the University of Georgia, was fired because of a scandal involving improper academic and financial benefits ("Lawsuit claims," 2003). As a result, Georgia was forced to drop out of both the Southeast Conference tournament and the subsequent NCAA tournament.[20] Harrick turned out to be a repeat offender. He ran into trouble at UCLA in 1996 because of allegations concerning false expense reports. He left UCLA for the University of Rhode Island, and then went to Georgia in 1999 before accusations regarding sexual harassment, academic improprieties, and improper benefits to players

---

[19]Sperber (1990, p. 158) argues that many coaches change jobs not because they are fired but due to their interest in a higher-paying or more prestigious position (or leaving before any NCAA violations are discovered). And even if they are not fired, universities will offer lucrative bonuses or annuities to try to keep a coach from jumping ship. While Sperber is correct that many coaches leave to move to a higher position on the coaching pyramid, the emphasis on winning percentage is an even more significant contributor to the frequency of coaching turnover.

[20] For a description of the major infractions at Georgia, see: http://www2.ncaa.org/ legislation_and_governance/compliance/major_infractions.html (click "Major Infractions Database" and then enter University of Georgia in the appropriate field).

were made public at Rhode Island. Harrick's coaching record is impressive (470 wins and 235 losses). It includes 16 NCAA tournament appearances and a 1995 NCAA championship at UCLA. And it is the likely reason Rhode Island, and then Georgia, were willing to turn a blind eye to his dirty laundry.

A more recent example is that of Bob "Huggy Bear" Huggins. Huggins was dismissed by University of Cincinnati president Nancy Zimpher in August 2005. Huggins coached the Bearcats for 16 years and compiled a 398-128 record. During that time, the team advanced to the NCAA tournament 14 times. But the program was plagued by low graduation rates, NCAA violations, player arrests, and Huggins' 2004 drunk driving conviction. After accepting a US$3 million buyout, Huggins reappeared in Manhattan, Kansas in 2006 as the new coach at Kansas State. After taking the K-State Wildcats to the NIT tournament, he left after one season for West Virginia in 2007 where he continues to coach and earns two million bucks annually.

Why are coaches with a lot of "baggage" almost always able to find jobs in the college coaching ranks? In other professions, if an employee committed an equivalent violation that man or woman might find it quite difficult to ever regain employment in a comparable job. But in college sports the "coaching door" keeps revolving. Is it solely because of Harrick's record as a winning coach? Or is it also because in the culture of collegiate athletics *who you know* and *who you've worked with* are just as important as your productivity? Is it possible that Harrick and Huggins' lengthy careers as college coaches were due to the tight-knit and insular nature of the coaching community? Before Harrick or Huggins was hired, did the Athletic Director at Georgia or West Virginia think: *I've known Harrick or Huggins for years. He's ok, He's one of us. The NCAA violations at UCLA and Rhode Island? The shenanigans at Cincinnati? Hey, let he who is without past NCAA violations cast the first stone. All of us have dirty laundry and skeletons in the closet. In fact, I'm not sure I'd hire a coach who has never had an infraction because it means he isn't trying hard enough to win.*

> **Fast fact.** *Sometimes, character does matter. In 2003, Alabama foot-ball coach Mike Price was fired by the university for using a uni-versity credit card at a strip club. Price, newly hired, was dismissed before he coached a single game for the Crimson Tide. He was hired in December 2003 by Texas-El Paso.*

The idea of "who you know" is an example of the **old boy net-work**. According to the *American Heritage Dictionary* (2000), an old boy network is "an informal, exclusive system of mutual assistance and friendship through which men [or women] belonging to a par-ticular group, such as the alumni of a school, exchange favors and connections, as in politics or business." Contrary to economic the-ory, it suggests that individuals may be hired because of favoritism and not productivity. Returning to our example of restaurant chefs, suppose Chefs Suzy and Pierre each apply to work at the Cheesecake Factory; Suzy is more productive than Pierre but Pierre is hired because of the old boy network.

For an old boy network to exist, the employer must be willing to bear a cost in the form of lower productivity from the favored employee. In a competitive industry, firms that consistently favor less productive employees may soon find themselves sacrificing profits and revenues and be in jeopardy of going out of business. Therefore, we expect old boy networks to be uncommon in com-petitive markets.

Whether the favored person is truly less productive than the disfavored person is an open question. Economic research suggests that in labor markets where employers are uncertain about the productivity of new hires, they may rely more heavily on informal and subjective information such as "Suzy and Pierre both seem like competent chefs to me. But Pierre and I were fraternity brothers at UCLA and that makes me inclined to prefer him to her." What is interesting about this research is that those persons hired via the old boy network are often better performers and have lower turno-ver than those outside the network (Simon and Warner, 1992). Others (e.g., Sperber, 1990, pp. 171–173) take a harsher view of these networks since they are, by definition, discriminatory and the disfavored, at least in coaching community, tend to be females and Blacks (we examine gender and race-related issues in collegiate sports in Chapter 8).

5.11   Chapter Summary

In this chapter, we asked a fairly simple question: Given the growing number of coaches earning in excess of US$1 million a year, how is coaching compensation determined? We saw that there are several explanations including: the market structure of the NCAA (especially the presence of monopsonistic rents), winner-take-all markets, risk aversion, the winner's curse, ratcheting, and old boy networks. Because of these issues, the labor market for DI-FBS coaches of revenue sports is not competitive — compensation is not determined solely by supply and demand. Coaching productivity (winning percentage) is also significant although until more research becomes available, we cannot tell if other things like graduation rate are also important. We suspect they may be, but are significantly weaker than winning percentage.

What should be done about coaching compensation? University presidents and trustees have some power to rein in salaries and benefits, but recall that the largest portion of income comes from sources like boosters' contributions that may lie outside the control of the administration. Given that university presidents are often advocates for intercollegiate athletics (a theme we develop in the following chapter), it seems doubtful they will take the initiative to address coaching compensation especially if they will face considerable flak from trustees, alums, and boosters. College sports show no signs of losing their popularity, especially among television viewers. As long as these revenues flow to the NCAA and its member institutions, and athletes remain unpaid, coaches — as rational, self-interested individuals — will seek to exploit the financial bonanza available to them.

Some state legislatures, like Iowa's, have attempted — without success — to place limits on coaches' compensation at public institutions.[21] As economists, we are wary of price controls, but we mention such efforts to show the degree of antipathy and frustration among those concerned about spiraling payments to coaches. Ironically, if the NCAA imposed such limits it would certainly find itself under investigation for antitrust violations. We return to reform issues in Chapter 9.

5.12   Key Terms

Autocorrelation (appendix)
Dependent variable
   (appendix)
Generally Accepted
   Accounting Principles
Golden parachute
Heteroskedasticity
   (appendix)
Incentive compatibility
Independent variable
   (appendix)
Old boy networks
Marginal revenue product
Multicollinearity
   (appendix)
Ordinary least squares
   (appendix)
Rank-order tournament

Ratcheting
Regression analysis (appendix)
Reservation wage
Risk aversion
Soft budget constraint
Statistically significant
   (appendix)
Superstar
Winner's curse
Winner-take-all labor market
X-outlier (appendix)
Y-outlier (appendix)
Zero-sum game

---

[21] In an article in *USA Today*, Wieberg (2001) reported that "When Iowa State gave basketball coach Larry Eustachy a US$300,000 raise last year, guaranteeing him US$900,000 annually, state Rep. Ed Fallon took such umbrage that he introduced legislation to cap coaches' salaries at state institutions at US$300,000. Attracting little support, the measure quickly died."

5.13 Review Questions

1. Why is the average head coach's salary so high and why are some salaries much higher than others?
2. Why is market structure a critical determinant of coaching salaries?
3. What are some common kinds of income that coaches receive besides their base salary?
4. What is a "golden parachute?"
5. Is the comparison between CEOs and college coaches appropriate? What are some key difference between a coach and a CEO?
6. How can college coaches earn significant economic rent in a market in which there are many coaches offering their services and many institutions willing to hire them?
7. What two characteristics define a winner-take-all labor market?
8. How does risk aversion contribute to higher coaching salaries?
9. Why are "old boy networks" unlikely to occur in a competitive labor market?

5.14 Discussion Questions

1. If a coach is not successful — e.g., his winning percentage is low — he may be given a severance payment, "golden parachute." If a faculty member is not successful — e.g., her teaching performance is poor — she will not be granted a severance payment. Why do coaches get these payments when faculty members do not?
2. If you were the president of a university what evaluation characteristics would you use to determine, whom to hire as your head football coach? If you were the AD which characteristics would you use?
3. Based on your response to the preceding question, list each characteristic according to its importance. Assign a percentage to each characteristic (make sure the percentages sum to 1.00).
4. How much are coaches paid at your school? A good place to start your search is to see if your school's library has a copy of the annual budget.

5. What are the pros and cons of "old boy networks?"
6. How are "old boy networks," risk aversion, the winner's curse, ratcheting, and winner-take-all markets related?
7. If you were a 19 or 20 year old student-athlete, possibly from a disadvantaged background, and you saw your coach getting a big salary, outside income, a house, a car, a golf club membership and various other perquisites, would that make you *more or less likely* to accept an under-the-table payment from a booster or an agent?
8. (Appendix 5.1) The example discussed in the appendix used compensation of head football coaches at the dependent variable using lifetime winning percentage as one of the independent variables. If you were to conduct an analysis using each coach's winning percentage for a particular season as the dependent variable, what independent variables would you select? Would you use their compensation for that season? Does this suggest the possibility of simultaneous equations?

5.15   Internet Questions

1. Go to the *USA Today* database (http://www.usatoday.com/sports/college/salaries/ncaaf/coach/) and select a head football coach. Divide that coach's salary by football revenue for that school from the Equity in Athletics database (http://ope.ed.gov/athletics/index.aspx). Do the same calculation for a head basketball coach (http://www.usatoday.com/sports/college/salaries/ncaab/coach/).
2. Contracts for basketball and football coaches in Division I are subject to frequent change. Pick one coach each from Tables 5.1 and 5.2 and search for and report on more recent compensation information.
3. Are you aware of a highly-paid coach that is not listed in Table 5.1 or 5.2? Search for and report on recent compensation information.
4. Using the most recent *NCAA Gender Equity Report* (http://www.ncaa.org/about/resources/research/gender-equity-research), update the information in Tables 5.3 and 5.4.

5.16 References

AD Cites Lack of On-Field Progress (2004, December 1). Retrieved from http://sports.espn.go.com/ncf/news/story?id=1935138 on March 8, 2005.

American Heritage dictionary of the English language (4th ed.) (2000). Boston: American Heritage.

Badenhausen, K. (2012, August 4). How Usain Bolt Earns $20 Milllion a Year. *Forbes*. Retrieved from http://www.forbes.com/sites/kurt-badenhausen/2012/08/04/how-usain-bolt-earns-20-million-a-year/ on August 17, 2012.

Belsky, G. and T. Gilovich (1999). *Why Smart People Make Big Money Mistakes*. New York, NY: Simon & Schuster.

Benjamin, D., M. Gunderson and C. Riddell (2002). *Labour Market Economics* (5th ed.). New York, NY: McGraw Hill.

Berkowitz, S. (2010, March 10). Salaries Spike for College Football Assistants. *USA Today*, p. C1.

Berri, D. (2012, April 6). Exploitation in College Sports: It's Not Just Football and Basketball. *Freakonomics.com*. Retrieved from http://www.freakonomics.com/2012/04/06/exploitation-in-college-sports-its-not-just-football-and-basketball/ on August 20, 2012.

Cowen, T. (2011, January–February). The inequality that matters. *The American Interest*, 6(3), 29–38. Retrieved from http://www.the-american-interest.com/article-bd.cfm?piece=907 on August 17, 2012.

DeCarlo, S. (2012a, April 4). Gravity-defying CEO Pay. *Forbes*. Retrieved from http://www.forbes.com/lists/2012/12/ceo-compensation-12_land.html on August 18, 2012.

DeCarlo, S. (2012a, April 18). The World's Biggest Companies. *Forbes*. Retrieved from http://www.forbes.com/global2000/ on August 18, 2012.

Dienhart, T. (n.d.). Top College Assistants Getting Paid Like Pros. *Rivals.com*. Retrieved from http://wap.rivals.com/content.asp?CID=1071601 on August 18, 2012.

Dobuzinskis, A. (2009, November 13). Hollywood Rethinks Use of A-List Actors. *Reuters.com*. Retrieved from http://www.reuters.com/article/2009/11/13/us-alist-idUSTRE5AC5AI20091113 on August 17, 2012.

Drape, J. (2004, January 1). Coaches Receive Both Big Salaries and Big Questions. *New York Times*, p. D1.

Drew, J. (2011, August 5). Perspetions Aside, BYU Coaching Pay Not Lagging. *The Salt Lake Tribune*. Retrieved from http://www.sltrib. com/sltrib/cougars/52199010-88/byu-coaches-pay-average.html. csp on August 20, 2012.

Ehrenberg, R. G. and M. L. Bognanno (1990). Do tournaments have incentive effects? *Journal of Political Economy*, 98, 1307–1324.

Fizel, J. and M. D'Itri (2004). Managerial efficiency, managerial succession, and organization performance. In J. Fizel and R. Fort (Eds.), *Economics of College Sports* (pp. 175–194). Westport, CT: Praeger.

Fish, M. (2003, December 23). Sign of the Times: College Football Coaching Contracts Filled With Lucrative Incentives. *SI.com*. Retrieved from http://sportsillustrated.cnn.com/2003/writers/mike_fish/12/19/coaching.contracts/ on March 12, 2005.

Frank, R. H. and P. J. Cook (1995). *The Winner-Take-All Society*. New York: The Free Press.

Frank, R. H. (2011). How Technology and Winner-Take-All Markets Have Made Income Inequality So Much Worse. *Slate.com*. Retrieved from http://www.slate.com/articles/business/moneybox/2011/12/how_technology_and_winner_take_all_markets_have_made_income_inequality_so_much_worse_.html on August 17, 2012.

Fulks, D. (2011). 2004–2010 *NCAA Revenues and Expenses of Divisions I and II Intercollegiate Athletics Programs Report*. Indianapolis, IN: National Collegiate Athletic Association. Retrieved from http://www.ncaapublications.com/productdownloads/2010RevExp.pdf on August 15, 2012.

Futterman, M. (2009, March 13). College Basketball's Bargains and Busts. *Wall Street Journal*, p. W5.

Gentry, J. and R. Alexander (2011, December 31). From The Sideline To The Bottom Line. *The New York Times*. Retrieved from http://www.nytimes.com/2012/01/01/sports/ncaafootball/contracts-for-top-college-football-coaches-grow-complicated.html?pagewanted=all on August 20, 2012.

Lawsuit Claims Harrick Broke NCAA Rules at URI (2003, March 9). Retrieved from http://espn.go.com/ncb/news/2003/0308/1520390.html on April 20, 2005.

Leeds, M. and P. von Allmen (2005). *The Economics of Sports* (2nd ed.). New York: Pearson Addison Wesley.

Mayer, B. (2002, October 5). College Pay Scale Doesn't Add Up. *Lawrence Journal-World*. Retrieved from http://www2.ljworld.com/news/2002/oct/05/college_pay_scale/ on March 2, 2005.

Pan, D. and J. Baker (2005). Factors, differential market effects, and marketing strategies in the renewal of season tickets for intercollegiate football games. *Journal of Sport Behavior*, 28, 351–377.

Price, T. (2004, March 19). Reforming big-time college sports. *CQ Researcher*, 14, 249–271.

Rosen, S. (1981). The economics of superstars. *American Economic Review*, 71, 845–858.

Schnaars, C. and K. DeRamus (2012). *USA Today*. College Basketball Coaches' Salaries, 2011–2012. Retrieved from http://www.usatoday. com/sports/college/mensbasketball/story/2012-03-28/ncaa-coaches-salary-database/53827374/1 on August 16, 2012.

Schnaars, C, J. Upton and K. DeRamus (2011). *USA Today*. College Football Coach Salary Database, 2006–2011. Retrieved from http://www.usatoday.com/sports/college/football/story/2011-11-17/cover-college-football-coaches-salaries-rise/51242232/1 on August 16, 2012.

Sickinger, T. (2011, December 10). Mike Bellotti: Half-Million Annual PERS Pension of Former UO Football Coach Sweetened by Oregon Sports Network, Nike, Ticket Sales. *The Oregonian*. Retrieved from http://blog.oregonlive.com/politics_impact/print.html?entry=/2011/12/mike_bellotti_former_universit.html on August 20, 2012.

Simon, C. J. and J. T. Warner (1992). Matchmaker, matchmaker: The effect of old boy networks on job match quality, earnings, and tenure. *Journal of Labor Economics*, 10(3), 306–330.

Sperber, M. (1990). *College Sports Inc.: The Athletic Department Vs. The University*. New York: Henry Holt.

Surowiecki, J. (2004). *The Wisdom of Crowds*. New York: Doubleday.

Thaler, R. (1988). The winner's curse. *Journal of Economic Perspectives*, 2(1), 191–202.

Van Riper, T. (2011, March 15). The Most Overpaid College Hoops Coaches. *Forbes*. Retrieved from http://www.forbes.com/2011/03/15/calipari-donovan-self-business-sports-overpaid-college-basketball-coaches.html on August 18, 2012.

Wieberg, S. (2001, August 3). Top college coaches get top dollar. Retrieved from http://www.usatoday.com/sports/college/2001-08-03-coaches-cover.htm on March 22, 2005.

Wieberg, S. (2010, January 4). For Alabama, Nick Saban Has Been Worth Every Penny. *USA Today*. Retrieved from http://www.usatoday.com/sports/college/football/sec/2010-01-03-alabama-nick-saban_N.htm on August 17, 2012.

Wieberg, S. (2011, December 28). College Coaches And Power: How Much Is Too Much? *USA Today*. Retrieved from http://www.usatoday.com/sports/college/football/story/2011-12-22/iconic-college-coaches-paterno-knight-miles-saban/52257024/1 on August 17, 2012.

Witosky, T. (2002, December 6). Bellotti, Erickson Among Highest-Paid Coaches. *Statesman Journal.com*. Retrieved from http://news.statesmanjournal.com/article_print.cfm?i=52918 on December 7, 2002.

Zimbalist, A. (1999). *Unpaid Professionals: Commericalism and Conflict in Big-Time College Sports*. Princeton, NJ: Princeton University Press.

Appendix 5.1 Regression Analysis

Does the number of years someone has been a head coach affect the amount he or she is paid? An economist would answer this question by first collecting data on the years of experience and compensation for a sample of head coaches. This sample might include head coaches at all NCAA member schools, those at Division I institutions, or just head football coaches at the elite BCS schools. Each coach in the sample represents a single observation or case. A mathematical model, such as a linear formula or something more complex, would represent the relationship between experience and compensation. The coefficients for that model, such as the intercept and slope for a linear formula, would then be estimated from the sample data using regression analysis. The goal of this appendix is to familiarize readers with this approach so that they can understand the empirical results from articles in the sports economics literature.[22]

Models and estimation

A typical model will include the variable you are trying to explain, such as compensation for head football coaches in the example above, and the variables that explain it, such as years of experience. The first is called the **dependent variable**, because its value depends on the other variables, and is often represented by the letter Y. The variables that explain it are called the **independent variables**, and may be represented by X. While a researcher may be interested in the effect of just one specific independent variable, it is important to include the other important variables that could affect Y. Regression analysis will determine the effect of each independent variable on the dependent variable while controlling for the other independent variables, that is, holding all other things

---

[22] Our apologies to econometricians for simplifying some important theoretical concepts in the interest of brevity and general conceptual understanding. If you are interested in learning more about regression analysis, take an introductory econometrics class or ask your instructor for additional resources.

constant (you may recall the term *"ceteris paribus"* from your introductory economics course).

Using mathematical notation, the model can be represented by

$$Y = f(X_1, X_2, \ldots, X_n),$$

which translates as "the value of the Y variable is a function of the values of the variables X_1 through X_n (n represents the number of independent variables)." If a linear function is used, the formula would be

$$Y = \beta_0 + \beta_1 X_1 + \beta_2 X_2 + \cdots + \beta_n X_n,$$

where the Greek letter β (beta) is used for the coefficients, including the intercept (β_0) and the slope for each independent variable (β_1 is the slope for the variable X_1). Note that in this specification each independent variable has its own separate effect, that is, they do not interact with each other.

The advantage of a linear formula is that it is simple, but it also assumes that Y will change by the same amount (β) every time X changes by one. In the case of the example above, if the slope for the variable measuring years of experience is 82,675, then earnings will increase by US$82,675 from the third to fourth year of coaching experience and again by US$82,675 from 13th to 14th year, which may not be realistic.

If the financial compensation for head coaches is exactly described by this mathematical formula, each coach would be represented by a point on a line, as in graph on the left in Appendix Figure 5.1. However, some coaches will be above the line, that is, they are paid more than determined by the formula, and others will be paid less and fall below the line, as in graph on the right. This is the part of compensation that the formula cannot explain and it is included in the model as a separate random component, called the error term.

The error component is usually represented by the Greek letter ε (epsilon). This results in the complete formula

$$Y = \beta_0 + \beta_1 X_1 + \beta_2 X_2 + \cdots + \beta_n X_n + \varepsilon.$$

Appendix Figure 5.1.   Observations with and without error component.

The error is assumed to be described by the Normal distribution (the familiar Bell curve) with a mean (center or average) of zero, meaning that about half of the values will be positive and therefore above the line (the other half with negative errors and thus below the line), and most of the errors will be close to zero, so that most of the points will be close to the line.

The most common regression approach is called **Ordinary Least Squares** (OLS), and it will find the formula for the estimated line that is as close as possible to the points. Specifically, it minimizes the sum of squared residuals, where a residual is the distance from a point to the estimated line. All of the residuals are squared and added together, and OLS minimizes this total or sum. One reason for squaring the residuals is to avoid positive values (above the estimated line) canceling the negative values (below the line). The other, and more technical, reason is based on the assumption of a Normal distribution.

Modern statistical analysis software will report the values of the estimated coefficients (the intercept and the slope for each independent variable) and an array of other results. Among the most important are the R-square and the t-statistics. The former measures the percentage of the variation in the dependent variable that is explained by the independent variables. If the value of R-square for the coaching compensation regression is 0.482, then the independent variables, including years of experience, can explain 48.2% of the differences in compensation among the coaches in that particular sample. That leaves 51.8% that is due to the random error or the effect of independent variables that were not included in the regression (referred to as omitted variables).

The value of the *t*-statistic is reported for each of the independent variables and is the difference between the estimated slope (e.g., estimate of β_1) and zero measured in standard deviations (actually, estimated standard deviations, called standard errors). If the slope of a line is zero, the line is flat and a change in the value of the *X* variable will have no effect on the value of the *Y* variable. If the slope of the estimated line for a particular group of coaches is close to zero, then it is likely that years of experience will have no effect on compensation for the general population of coaches. The *t*-statistics enable us to test the hypothesis that the actual slope is zero (so the *X* variable has *does not* have an effect on *Y*, which is the null hypothesis) against the alternative that the actual slope is not zero (so the *X* variable *does* have an effect on *Y*).

The reason for measuring the difference in standard deviations is that the estimated coefficients should be randomly distributed around the actual values based on a *t*-distribution (similar in appearance to a Normal distribution), which allows us to convert distance in standard deviations into probabilities. Appendix Figure 5.2 shows the probability distribution of the estimated coefficient *if* the hypothesis of no effect is true, that is, the actual slope

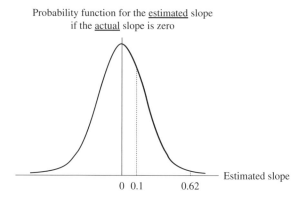

Appendix Figure 5.2.   The t-distribution for the estimated slope.

is zero. For this particular graph one standard error equals 0.2. If the estimated slope turns out to be far away from zero (e.g., 0.62, so 3.1 standard errors from zero), that is, the probability of such a value occurring is low, then we will reject the hypothesis of no effect and conclude that X does have an effect on Y with a high degree of confidence. If the estimated slope is close to zero (e.g., 0.1, or 0.5 standard errors from zero), we cannot reject the hypothesis of no effect.

The criteria for accepting the null hypothesis are expressed in probabilities. If the estimated coefficient is far enough out in the tails of the t-distribution to have a sufficiently low probability, we reject the null hypothesis as highly unlikely to be true and accept the alternative hypothesis that X does have an effect on Y. In that case, the X variable is said to have a **statistically significant** effect on Y.

What do most econometricians consider to be a low probability? A general rule of thumb is 10%, which means that the researcher wants to be at least 90% confident that X has an effect on Y before presenting that conclusion. This generally corresponds to a t-statistic of 1.8 or higher, although the exact value depends on the size of the sample and the number of independent variables. In some cases, a higher level of confidence is more appropriate and cutoffs of 5% or even 1% are used. A common practice is to denote a variable that is statistically significant at the 1% level with three stars (represented by asterisks), while two stars are used for 5% and just one for 10%.

While OLS is well understood and simple to use, it is limited by the assumption that the relationship between X and Y is linear. Fortunately, a bit a mathematical sleight of hand allows us to estimate some specific nonlinear functions. You are probably familiar with the formula for a parabola, $Y = a + bX + cX^2$, which changes the formula for a line, $Y = a + bX$, into one for a curve by adding the squared term. The same can be done in a regression by including both an independent variable and that variable squared. The software will think, it is a new independent variable, but you are smarter than the computer!

Appendix Table 5.1.   Estimating linear and nonlinear functions.

Function	Formula	Estimated	Interpretation of β_1
Linear	$Y = \beta_0 + \beta_1 X_1$	$Y = \beta_0 + \beta_1 X_1$	$\Delta Y / \Delta X$
Exponential	$Y = e^{\beta_0 + \beta_1 X_1}$	$\ln Y = \beta_0 + \beta_1 X_1$	$\%\Delta Y / \Delta X$
Power	$Y = \beta_0 X^{\beta_1}$	$\ln Y = \beta_0 + \beta_1 \ln X_1$	$\%\Delta Y / \%\Delta X$

Two other common nonlinear functions describe an exponential curve and a power curve. [An example of the latter is the familiar Cobb-Douglass production function $Q = AK^{\alpha}L^{\beta}$, where Q is the total quantity produced and K and L are the amounts of capital and labor used.] To estimate these curves using a linear regression program requires replacing one or more of the variables with their natural logarithms. For the exponential curve the natural log of the Y variable (represented in an equation by $\ln Y$) is substituted for the Y variable, while the natural logs of both the Y and X variables are used for the power function. Because these alter the function from a line to a curve, the interpretation of the coefficient is no longer the slope (the slope of a curve changes depending on where you are on the curve). The coefficient is not the *amount* that Y changes (in its units of measurement) when X changes by one *unit* (in its units of measurement), but rather the *percentage amount* that Y changes when X changes either by one unit (in its units of measurement) or by 1%, for the exponential and power functions respectively. This is summarized in Appendix Table 5.1.

Outliers

One problem that can occur is that the estimated line is overly influenced by a single observation in the sample. In Appendix Figure 5.3, the actual relationship is shown as a solid line, while the estimated relationship for this particular sample is shown as a dashed line. In the first graph, the coach with only a few years of experience but a very high salary pulls the left side of the estimated line upward. Remember that OLS will find the line with the

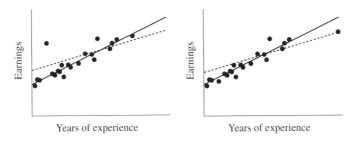

Appendix Figure 5.3.   The impact of outliers on the estimated line.

smallest sum of squared residuals, and the residual for that coach is large enough that when squared it will contribute a VERY large amount to the total (an extra US$100 becomes US$10,000 when squared). By moving the estimated line toward that point the large residual is reduced, significantly reducing the sum of squared residuals (reduce US$100 to US$50 and the squared value drops from US$10,000 to US$2,500). This case is called a **Y-outlier** because the value of the dependent variable is far away from the actual line. As a general rule of thumb, cases that are more than three standard deviations above or below the line are possible Y-outliers and should be examined further. After careful consideration, they may be removed from the sample. If it remains in the sample, the estimated slope will be understated, suggesting that experience has less effect on earnings than it actually does.

In the second graph, there is a coach with many more years of experience than the other coaches. While that coach is paid less than predicted by the actual line, the earnings are not further from the line than for some of the other coaches, so it is not a Y-outlier. However, the estimated line from OLS is likely to be influenced by that case. Essentially, the distance from it to the rest of the cases along the X-axis gives it the leverage to move the estimated line. OLS can reduce the residual to zero for that case by rotating the estimated line slightly. Some software programs will calculate two useful statistics to identify such **X-outliers**. One is the Mahalanobis Distance, which is distance along the X axis from each case to the rest of the cases (complicated by the fact that there are usually multiple X variables). The other is the Cook's Distance, which measures how much the estimated line changes when each case is removed from the sample. Taking out any other case will have little effect on the slope of the estimated line, so this particular coach will have a larger value for the Cook's Distance.

Multicollinearity

Ordinary Least Squares will estimate the effect of each independent variable, holding the other variables constant. It is able to do so even though the variables may be partially related to each other. For example, you might collect data on annual spending, annual income, and wealth of 50 people, with the goal of using income and wealth to explain the amount that people spend each year. Many people with a high income will also have a high wealth, and most with a low income will have a low wealth. This will make it difficult to find the effect of an increase in income on spending holding wealth constant. However, if there are enough people with a higher income and lower wealth or vice versa, then OLS can compare people with high income and high wealth to those with high income and low wealth and estimate the effect of wealth.

Some software programs can diagnose possible **multicollinearity** by calculating the tolerance value for each independent variable (or its inverse, the Variance Inflation Factor), which is the percentage of the variation in that variable that cannot be explained by the other independent variables. It is essentially how different that variable is from the others. In general, a difference of 20% of more is sufficient for OLS to do its job.

If an independent variable is very similar to one or more of the other independent variables, we say that they are highly collinear. While this makes it difficult for OLS to work properly, it will try anyway. Unfortunately the results are likely to be unreliable. If I ask you to separate 5 into 2 other numbers, you might give me 1 and 4, or 2 and 3, but you might also give me 105 and –100. In this case, I may be asking OLS to separate what is essentially one slope into two slopes, and one large positive slope and one large negative slope is a possible result.

Autocorrelated errors

For some studies, the sample is for the same entity observed over time. The dependent variable may be the rate of traffic accidents in Canada for each year from 1990 to 2014. This is called a time series analysis, as opposed to a cross-section analysis like the one for head coaches, which examines the earnings of many different coaches in the same year. An issue particular to time series data is that the value of the random component (the error term) in one year may be affected by the value in previous time periods. If the rate of traffic accidents in Canada has a positive error in 1998 (so it is higher than predicted and lies above the actual line), it may also be positive in 1999. The relationship between the value of the error and its own past values is called **autocorrelation** (correlated with itself), and this violates one of the assumptions OLS makes about the error. This results in misleading conclusions about the statistical significance of the independent variables. Most software programs will calculate the Durbin-Watson statistic, which is one method for testing for autocorrelated errors. The value of this statistic ranges from zero to four, and values close to two suggest that this problem does not occur.

Heteroskedasticity

Another potential problem related to the error term is that the amount of variation changes depending on the value of an independent variable. The term **heteroskedasticity** is a combination of the Greek words for different (hetero) and dispersion (skedasis). An example of positive heteroskedasticity, in which, the amount of variation in the error increases as the value of the X variable increases, is shown in Appendix Figure 5.4. Like autocorrelation, the result is misleading conclusions about the statistical significance of the independent variables.

Appendix Figure 5.4.   Positive heteroskedasticity.

Simultaneous equations

Thus far, we have focused on the possible effect of the independent variables on the dependent variables. However, it is also possible that the dependent variable will affect the independent variables. If true, then the effect of X on Y at the same time as the effect of Y on X means that they are determined jointly or simultaneously. It will take one equation to explain how X causes Y and one equation for Y causing X, hence the term simultaneous equations. Estimation of a system of simultaneous equations requires techniques that are beyond the scope of an appendix, but if you are reading an academic article on sports economics you may see references to structural and reduce form equations, instrumental variables, indirect least squares, two-stage least squares, and three-stage least squares. If you have questions and want to know the answers, see your instructor!

Example: Determinants of FBS head football coach compensation

An example of regression analysis is a study conducted by the authors of this book that was published in 2013.[23] The model attempts to explain total annual compensation for head football

---

[23] See Grant, R., J. Leadley and Z. Zygmont (2013). Just win baby? Determinants of NCAA football bowl subdivision coaching compensation. *International Journal of Sport Finance*, 8(1), 61–74.

coaches at the six BCS conferences for the five years from 2006 to 2010. This is an example of what is called a pooled cross-section time-series analysis, as if compares different coaches and each coach over time.

Our model is expressed mathematically by the equation:

$$W_{ij} = \beta X_i + \gamma Z_j + \eta_{ij},$$

where W_{ij} is the real total compensation of head coach i at institution j, X_i includes personal and professional characteristics of head coach i, Z_j includes academic and financial characteristics of the institution employing the coach, and η_{ij} represents the random error for coach i at institution j. An alternative specification uses the natural log of W. A list of the variables, beginning with the dependent variable W, and the definition of each variable, is in Appendix Table 5.2.

Due to evidence of possible multicollinearity, not all the variables in Appendix Table 5.2 were used in the regression model. Two sets of dummy variables (value of 0 or 1) were also used. One set represented the individual years to capture any changes in the average level of compensation over time. A set of variables representing each institution were used to capture any attributes that are constant over time, such as the school's tradition of football, that were not measured by any of the other variables. Two coaches, Joe Paterno and Bobby Bowden were identified as X-outliers (both had many more years of experience than the other head coaches) and not used for the final results. The results for all but the institutional dummy variables are shown in Appendix Table 5.3.

The value of R square is 0.88 for both specifications, which means that the X independent variables explain 88% of the variation across coaches over the five years 2006–2010. The variables that were statistically significant in both specifications at the 10% level (denoted by at least one *) were the coach's lifetime average BCS rank and lifetime winning percentage, the institution's football revenue, enrollment, and graduation rate, and the dummy variables for 2006, 2007, and 2008. As expected, compensation is estimated to increase for coaches with higher BCS rankings and

Appendix Table 5.2.   Variable definitions.

Total Compensation	Salary plus other income, not including value of perks, standard university benefits, and one-time pay such as signing bonus and other bonuses related to performance goals
Winning % lifetime	Coach's lifetime winning percentage through the previous season
Winning % lagged	Coach's previous season winning percentage
Experience	Coach's total years as head coach
Bowls per year	Coach's lifetime bowl appearances divided by years as a head coach through the previous season
BCS bowls per year	Coach's lifetime BCS bowl appearances divided by years as head coach (from start of BCS system)
BCS rank	Coach's lifetime average points in *USA Today* coaches' postseason poll
APR	Coach's lifetime average NCAA Academic Progress Rate since 2002
Recruiting	Coach's average Scout.com recruiting points for the five previous seasons
Enrollment	Institution's undergraduate enrollment
Applications	Institution's number of undergraduate applications
Admits	Institution's percentage of applications accepted
SAT & ACT	Institution's average SAT and ACT scores for entering freshmen (ACT converted to SAT scale)
Graduation rate	Institution's six-year graduation rate for most recent cohort
Football revenues	Institution's revenue attributable to football program

Appendix Table 5.3.   Regression results.

	Linear	Exponential
APR	−2,873.708	−0.002
	(0.265)	(0.115)
BCS rank	570.415	0.000
	(0.002)***	(0.066)*
Bowls per year	−220,546	−0.122
	(0.260)	(0.282)
Experience	14,357.237	0.005
	(0.117)*	(0.309)
Recruiting	124.370	1.674E−5
	(0.075)*	(0.677)
Winning % lifetime	1,766,346.125	1.568
	(0.002)***	(0.000)***
Winning % lagged	154,475.158	0.057
	(0.441)	(0.626)
Football revenue	0.016	5.189E−9
	(0.003)***	(0.098)*
Enrollment	−92.970	−4.549E−5
	(0.018)**	(0.045)**
Graduation rate	−45,025.612	0.019
	(0.021)**	(0.096)*
2006	−379,333.850	−0.304
	(0.003)***	(0.000)***
2007	−355,251.955	−0.253
	(0.001)***	(0.000)***
2008	−185,870.720	−0.081
	(0.043)**	(0.054)*
2009	−11,382.532	0.010
	(0.881)	(0.823)
R Square	0.882	0.881

Note: The probability of the null hypothesis that the variable has no effect is in parentheses. The notation *** is for variables that are statistically significant at the 1% level, while ** and * are used for 5% and 10%, respectively.

winning percentage (both have positive estimated coefficients) and at institutions with greater revenue generated by their football program. It appears that just winning is not enough. A coach needs to win games at the right times against the right opponents to end the season with a high ranking in the polls.

An unexpected result is that compensation decreases at institutions with higher enrollment (a negative estimated coefficient). The direction of the effect of graduation rates is different for the linear and exponential functions. Compensation is estimated to be lower in each year compared to 2010, which is the base year. The fact that the negative values for years before 2010 decrease each year, suggests that compensation was increasing steadily over time. Recruiting success and years of experience were statistically significant only for the linear model, with both having the expected positive estimated coefficients.

One additional interesting result is that the coach's record for getting students to succeed academically, as measured by the Academic Progress Rate for teams he has coached, has a negative estimated effect on compensation, although it is not statistically significant. This would suggest that those who determine a coach's salary see academic progress as a distraction from the real goal, which is athletic success.

To show how each estimated coefficient is interpreted, look at the values for lifetime winning percentage in each column, or 1,766,346.125 and 1.568, respectively. The first value means that compensation will increase by 1,766,346.12 when winning percentage increases by 1. This sounds like a huge effect, but we need to look at the units used for winning percentage. It was expressed in our dataset in decimal form, so a value of 50% was entered as 0.500. This means that an increase of one for a coach with an average record would go from 0.500 to 1.500, or 50% to 150%. This is clearly not possible, and the huge estimated increase in salary for such a change is no long surprising. So, how do we interpret the number in a more meaningful way? Instead of changing X by 1.0, change by 0.1 by moving the decimal point over one space. This would be equivalent to increase the percentage from 50% to 60%.

The estimated increase in compensation will also change by one decimal point, to 176,634.61, a much more reasonable result. The same can be done for the exponential specification, with the result that compensation will increase by 15.68% (1.568 represents 156.8%, but we move the decimal over one space) when winning percentage increases by 0.10, or 10%. If you are confused about the sudden switch to percentage change for compensation, go back to Appendix Table 5.1.

The interpretation of the estimated coefficient for years of coaching experience is much easier. Just remember that it is measured in years, so five years of experience was entered as 5. Go ahead, give it a try!

Chapter 6

The Athletic Department and the University

Simply put, success in … football is essential for the success of Louisiana State University.

— Mark Emmert, former LSU Chancellor,
now NCAA President

There is an arms race in college sports … the only thing worse than being in an arms race is not being in the arms race.

— Bob Bowlsby, University of Iowa Athletic Director

6.1 Introduction

In his presidential address to the 2005 NCAA convention, Myles Brand referred to the "spending spiral" for athletics programs at DI institutions (see Box 6.1). He voiced concern about the growing trend of athletic departments becoming financially independent from the university and he stressed that athletics "must be fully integrated into the educational mission" of the university. President Brand's comments reflect the main concerns of this chapter: the apparent unrestrained growth in athletic department budgets, the consequences of that growth, and the proper relationship between the athletic department and the university.

6.2 Growth of the Athletic Department

While operating expenditures of athletic departments at DI universities are a small percentage of total university spending (usually in the range of 1–4%), they have grown faster than university

---

Box 6.1.   Excerpt from NCAA President Myles Brand's
2005 address.

… this mounting financial problem threatens the integrity of the university. When the public — both local and en masse — begin to believe that the value of the institution is to be measured by the success of its athletics teams, the core mission of the university is threatened. The central role of the faculty is ignored in favor of winning the big game or recruiting the next young man with athletics star potential. And the ability of the university to successfully educate and push forward the boundaries of knowledge and the creative arts is compromised.

The popular view is that you have to increase spending to increase wins, and you have to increase wins to increase revenues. However, a major NCAA-funded economic study released last year shows no correlation — at least over the medium term, that is, about a decade — that this view is correct. The study found no correlation between increased spending and increased winning or between increased winning and increased revenues.

But these data and results have made little difference. The spending spiral has not abated, and the strong if mistaken belief that spending more than your competitors will lead to increased winning has propelled athletics departments to increase expenditures … no matter the facts. The behavior is irrational in light of the available evidence, but there it is, nonetheless.

From a practical perspective, it doesn't work. About 40 of the approximately 325 Division I institutions claim that they operate athletics in the black. I am skeptical. When all the costs are taken into account, including facilities and physical plant, academic support, grants-in-aid partially absorbed by the general fund, and hidden subsidies, I suspect the numbers that genuinely balance expenses with revenues is not much more than a dozen.

Source: Brand (2005).

expenditures as a whole (Brady and Upton, 2005).[1] From 2005 to 2010, athletic spending at public four-year institutions increased faster than tuition. At Division I Football Bowl Subdivision (DI-FBS) schools, athletic spending has increased by 50% over that time, more than twice the rate of increase for academic spending. (Desrochers, 2013)

Athletics budgets are increasing because athletics directors and coaches are convinced that greater spending results in greater sports success, which then causes an increased flow of revenues to the university. The problem is that if the other schools are doing the same thing, then they will have to increase the budget even further to have the anticipated effect. As universities attempt to outspend one another, an **arms race** occurs.

As noted in Chapter 2, it is not just athletic directors and coaches who advocate bigger sports programs; many university presidents also favor increased investment in athletics. The latter believe that greater investment in sports causes undergraduate enrollment and the academic quality of entering students to increase. In addition, alumni donations are expected to increase with athletic success. Thus, athletics is thought to generate revenues to both the athletic department, through sources such as increased ticket and merchandise sales, and to the university, from increased undergraduate enrollments and donations.

For anecdotal evidence to support this view, consider the football programs at Boise State University and the University of Texas at El Paso (UTEP). Boise State officials claimed that, because of media attention received during their 11-0 record in 2004, applications by out-of-state students rose 20%, donations to the university foundation rose, sales of university merchandise at the bookstore increased 66%, and season ticket sales for football increased

---

[1] According to Orszag and Orszag (2005, p. 2), approximately 3% of a DI-A university budget was spent on athletics in 1997. By 2001, spending on athletics had increased to approximately 4%. It is important to note that their estimates did not include capital (i.e., facilities) spending. Desrochers (2013) reports that athletic spending increased at least twice as fast as academic spending on a per capita basis from 2005 to 2010 in all three Division I subdivisions.

Box 6.2.   The Taj Mahal syndrome.

The race to construct and upgrade facilities to make a school more appealing is not limited to athletics. A new science center may attract aspiring premeds, and future economics majors may be excited about classrooms with smart boards on all four walls to draw and upload graphs. While these facilities can enhance the academic experience, what happens when other schools respond by offering the same thing? And what about facilities that are not directly related to academics? A 2012 article in the *New York Times* noted that "some colleges and universities have also borrowed heavily, spending money on vast expansions and amenities aimed at luring better students: student unions with movie theaters and wine bars; workout facilities with climbing walls and "lazy rivers"; and dormitories with single rooms and private baths. Spending on instruction has grown at a much slower pace, studies have shown. Amid increasingly intense competition for better students and higher rankings, college administrators across the country during the last decade have deployed a relatively simple strategy borrowed from the movies: if you build it, they will come. Construction starts on college campuses were 32.6 million square feet in 2008, the highest in two decades and up from 12.1 million square feet in 1990, according to a 2010 study by McGraw-Hill Construction. Construction declined after the financial crisis but is beginning to recover, McGraw-Hill officials said." (Martin, 2012)

---

roughly 60% (Buker, 2005). According to UTEP, three winning seasons, and a trip to the Houston Bowl in December 2004, helped contribute to a six-year increase in enrollment from 14,695 to 19,264 (Adams, 2005). However, as noted by Dr. Brand and others, the actual benefits to most schools may be less than the amount invested in athletics.

Faculty members, arguing in terms of misplaced priorities and opportunity costs, often criticize the special status granted to sports and the size of athletics budgets relative to other departments. They suggest that an emphasis on sports can compromise the educational mission of the institution, as well as its reputation.[2] They also point out that every dollar from the university's budget that supports the athletic department is one less dollar for academic programs. Expenditures that increase academic quality may have an even greater effect on enrollments and donations than dollars spent on athletics. This opportunity cost argument has become especially powerful at public universities where reduced support from state legislatures has placed schools in a financial bind.[3]

One prominent faculty critic is Murray Sperber, a former Professor of English at Indiana University, now retired. He not only challenges the belief that athletics benefits the university financially, but he levels an even more serious indictment: universities promote athletics in order to distract undergraduates from thinking about the poor education they are receiving (we discuss Sperber's perspective, which he calls **beer and circus**, in Section 6.9).

Advocacy groups such as the Knight Foundation Commission on Intercollegiate Athletics, the Coalition on Intercollegiate Athletics, and the Drake Group — among many others — offer numerous criticisms of the current state of collegiate sports and proposals to reform it (you will learn about the activities of these groups in Chapter 9). Even the broadcast and print media seem to be paying more attention to questions about the wisdom of pumping more and more resources into sports rather than academic programs. (Bolt, 2001)

---

[2] For example, University of Oregon Professor Jim Earl suggests there is a "big clash of values" between the megabucks athletics at Oregon and the core academic mission of the university (Pittman, 2001).

[3] As Brand (2005) noted, "[i]t is critical to note that these budgets have risen at the same time higher education has gone through a series of economic downturns. The financial pressures of maintaining and enhancing large physical plants, competing for, hiring and retaining faculty and staff, and increased technology demands have exacerbated the problem."

One reaction by the athletic department is to insulate itself from, or deflect, these criticisms by attaining financial independence from the university. As an example, consider the University of Oregon. In the 1980s, concerns about the financial health of the University led to speculation that drastic changes would soon be imposed on its athletic department, including a reduction in the number of varsity sports and dropping out of the Pac-10 Conference (Sperber, 2000, pp. 57–59). Not only were these draconian proposals never implemented, the university instead committed to making sports one of its highest priorities. This strategy appears to be paying off; the University of Oregon's athletic department currently has a budget of roughly US$40 million a year, requires no financial support from the university, has significant donations from alumni and non-alumni (one of its biggest contributors is Phil Knight of Nike), and is one of the most envied and recognized sports programs in the nation.

Given numerous concerns across the nation about college sports draining resources away from the university and compromising the academic mission of the school, you might expect Oregon's initiative, and those of other schools, to be applauded by President Brand. Instead, he is critical even though he acknowledges that the philosophy of DI is that each member institution should strive "to finance its athletics programs insofar as possible from revenues generated from the program itself."

6.3   The Athletic Department Budget — Revenues

Table 6.1 illustrates the range in the amount of revenue for athletic departments in the DI-FBS, with the 10 largest and 10 smallest by total revenue. Table 6.2 lists the revenue sources at the average DI-FBS school for fiscal year 2010. The six biggest items (not including the category "miscellaneous") are ticket sales, cash contributions from alumni and others, institutional support, NCAA and conference distributions, radio/television broadcasting, and student activity fees. Rather than discussing each budget item individually, we will instead highlight those sources of revenue we

Table 6.1.   Largest and smallest DI-FBS athletic department revenue for 2008 (in millions of US$).

Institution	Revenue	Institution	Revenue
University of Alabama	123.8	Kent State University	18.1
University of Texas at Austin	120.3	Florida Atlantic University	16.6
Ohio State University	115.7	University of Idaho	15.2
University of Florida	106.6	Louisiana Tech University	14.7
University of Tennessee	101.8	Troy State University	14.3
University of Michigan	99.0	Utah State University	13.5
Oklahoma State University	98.9	University of Louisiana-Lafayette	11.5
University of Wisconsin	95.1	North Texas University	10.2
Texas A&M	92.5	University of Louisiana-Monroe	9.4
Penn State University	91.6	Arkansas State University	8.4

Source: ESPN.com (http://espn.go.com/ncaa/revenue).

believe are most important, the most interesting, or the ones that may be unfamiliar to you.

Ticket sales and contributions, which are the two largest sources of revenue, are relatively straightforward. NCAA and conference distributions, the third largest category, includes payments for direct participation in bowl games and tournaments, including March Madness, and from conference revenue sharing. The latter includes television contracts negotiated by conferences and the revenue generated when any team in the conference participates in a bowl game. If two schools from the Southeastern Conference (SEC) go to major bowls and together earn US$50 million, then the surplus after expenses will be split evenly among conference members. The category of broadcast rights includes payments directly to the individual school, usually for games that are not chosen for broadcast under the conference contract.

Table 6.2.   Revenue sources for DI-FBS institutions in 2010.

Category	% of revenue
Ticket sales	23%
NCAA and conference distributions	16%
Guarantees and options	2%
Cash contributions from alumni and others	21%
Other	
Concessions/Programs/Novelties	2%
Broadcast rights	3%
Royalties/Advertising/Sponsorship	7%
Sports camps	1%
Endowment/Investment income	2%
Miscellaneous	2%
Total generated revenues	**80%**
Direct institutional support	9%
Indirect institutional support	3%
Student fees	6%
Direct government support	1%
Total allocated revenues	**20%**

Source: Fulks (2011, p. 40).

Direct institutional support is the amount provided by the university for routine operations of the athletic department, including unrestricted and Federal Work Study funds. Indirect support includes the value of facilities and services not charged to Athletics, including utilities, depreciation, and maintenance. Student fees are assessed by the institution and restricted for support of intercollegiate athletics. In total, the university administration and student body contribute one-fifth of all revenue.

Because of the significance of television broadcasting rights, and the complexities involved both in the evolution of the relationship between the NCAA and the television networks (and also between the NCAA and the conferences), we defer further discussion about the revenues generated from media broadcasting until the next chapter and turn to ticket sales.

6.3.1 *Ticket sales*

At the premier programs, tickets for football and men's and women's basketball are usually hard to come by. While most schools designate some tickets for students at little or nominal fee, athletics programs increasingly view ticket sales as a vital revenue stream, a flow of revenues that they seek to maximize with little regard for ticket availability to the student body. As other revenue sources have increased, the percentage of total revenue accounted for by ticket sales has decreased (from 59% in 1969 to 23% in 2010), but it is still the largest revenue line item. To maximize this revenue, universities are adopting many ticketing innovations pioneered by professional sports franchises. These innovations include personal seat licenses (PSLs), differential pricing by opponent, club seating and luxury boxes.

A **personal seat license** represents a payment for the option to buy a season ticket. For example, if you want to buy a season ticket for football at the University of Michigan you must first make a donation of between US$75 and US$600, depending on seat location (the US$75 charge for end zone seats was introduced for 2013–2014). After buying the PSL, you must still pay the per-game ticket price of US$75 or US$95 for games designated as premium, such as their rivalry with Michigan State University. Fans at many universities are required to buy a PSL for a minimum number of years, so a US$600 annual fee can mean as much as US$6,000. If the holder of the PSL decides to stop buying season tickets after five of the ten years, they forfeit the PSL with no refund. See Table 6.3 for more examples of prices of PSLs and game tickets. Note that these are for the *least* expensive season tickets at each school.

There are a number of variations on the basic PSL. In some cases, a PSL is required to buy a season ticket anywhere in the stadium or arena, while some schools only require a license for the best seats. For example, 25% of the seats in the Texas Tech basketball arena require a PSL. Season tickets for the rest can be purchased without a PSL, and any seats in the premium section that are not purchased by a PSL holder are sold on the week of the game (and often at a higher per-game price than the PSL holder paid).

Table 6.3. PSL for least expensive football season tickets in 2010 (in US$).

School	Annual PSL cost	Season ticket price
Ohio State	1,500	607
Notre Dame	1,250	490
University of Wisconsin	1,000	294
Auburn University	220	445
University of Nebraska	50	378

Source: Rivals.com (http://collegefootball.rivals.com/content.asp?CID=1094191).

PSLs are an example of price discrimination. You probably recall from principles of microeconomics that price discrimination occurs when the same product is sold to different buyers at different prices. If you take your grandmother and your eight-year old niece to see a movie, the price for your ticket will be higher than those for granny and your niece. This is because the movie theater recognizes that individuals have different **price elasticities of demand**. The group of customers that will not significantly reduce their quantity demanded if the price is increased (inelastic demand) will be charged more, while those that are most sensitive to the price (elastic demand) will be charged less. This strategy increases the theatre's revenue and profits. This example of **third degree price discrimination** is illustrated in Figure 6.1. Your granny and niece are in group #2, while you are in group #1. The prices are set to maximize total profit (the shaded areas), which corresponds to the point on each demand curve where MR = MC. This situation could be applied to ticket sales for college football or basketball games, where the two groups of customers are adults and students. In this scenario, would the adults be in group #1 or #2?[4]

---

[4] A more complete treatment of third degree price discrimination in college sports would include the effect of capacity constraints and the fact that the cost of providing a seat for an additional fan is essentially zero until the point of capacity is reached.

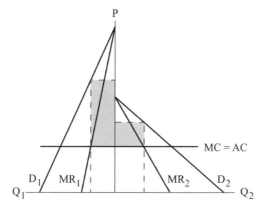

Figure 6.1. Third degree price discrimination.

PSLs represent a two-part tariff, which is a type of **second degree price discrimination**. Suppose that a 10-year PSL costs US$5,000 and the price of a season ticket is US$1,000. If a fan buys season tickets for all 10 years, the total price per season is US$1,500 (or (US$5,000 + US$10,000)/10). However, if the fan only buys tickets for the first five seasons, the price per season is US$2,000 (or (US$5,000 + US$5,000)/5). The more seasons you buy tickets for, the lower the price. This is an example of a quantity discount, which is the defining feature of second degree discrimination. Customers with higher demand will buy a larger quantity, resulting in a lower price than that paid by those with lower demand.

What is the optimal combination of PSL and season ticket prices? A high PSL/low ticket price will lead to a significant decline in the total price per season as the number of seasons increases. This will convince more customers, particularly those that are price sensitive, to buy season tickets for all 10 years. In economic terms, the low price per season ticket increases their quantity demanded (convinces them to attend for more seasons) and increases their consumer surplus. However, the school is able to turn around and extract much of the increased consumer surplus by charging a high price for the PSL. Consumers are better off because of the lower ticket price, but must share all or part of that gain with the school.

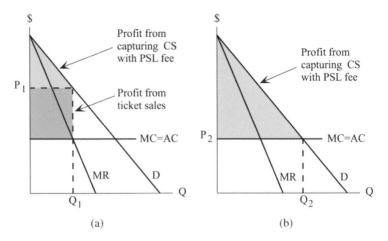

Figure 6.2.   Increase in total profit resulting from marginal cost pricing.

Figure 6.2 above shows that setting the price for season tickets (P_1) at the point where MR=MC and capturing the resulting consumer surplus via a PSL (Figure 6.2a) results in less total profit than setting the price equal to marginal cost (the competitive price) and capturing the much larger consumer surplus (Figure 6.2b). Profits directly from season ticket sales have dropped to zero, but they are more than replaced by the higher PSL fee.

The difficulty for colleges is that all fans do not have the same demand for tickets. Figure 6.3 compares two fans with different demand curves for season tickets. In both graphs, the price has been set equal to marginal cost, so they both pay the same amount for the tickets. If the PSL price is set equal to the first fan's consumer surplus, the second fan will decline to pay it and will not buy any tickets. If the PSL price is set equal to the second fan's consumer surplus, then the first fan will pay less than they would be willing to pay. With a large number of potential buyers, the school will have to strike the right balance between exploiting those who are willing to pay the most and losing sales to fans that are not willing to pay a hefty PSL fee.

Another trend that has spilled over from professional to collegiate sports is the use of **premium seating**, more commonly called

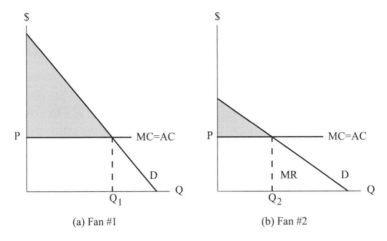

Figure 6.3. PSLs for fans with different demand schedules.

club seating. These are seats that are usually in better viewing locations (e.g., near midfield for football games) and also offer amenities like wider seats, more legroom, cup holders, and a server to bring food and drinks. Club seats are often located adjacent to a concourse, elevator or escalator that is restricted to the use of the occupants of the club seats. In some stadiums and arenas premium seats also include **luxury suites** or skyboxes, private rooms in which spectators may sit on cushy chairs and sofas while dining on catered food and watching the game through large sliding glass windows and on big screen televisions. These seating arrangements are expensive. For example, the 2008 renovation of 109,901 seat Michigan Stadium ("The Big House") added 79 private suites that lease for US$55,000–85,000 per year (Mandina, 2009). The 347 luxury box seats in the "Bull Gator Deck" of the University of Florida's Ben Hill Griffin Stadium bring in roughly US$5 million every season (Twitchell, 2004, p. 114). Because universities are non-profit institutions, wealthy boosters, alums, or corporations can write off 80% of the cost from their income taxes when they purchase club seats and luxury suites.

Another innovation is the use of differential ticket pricing by game. This system of **premium ticket pricing** was first adopted by several Major League Baseball teams, and requires fans to pay different prices depending on the opponent, regardless of seat location. As an example, for the 2013 football season, the University of Oregon posted reserved seat prices of US$34 for Division I-FCS opponent Nicholls State, US$88 for Washington State and Utah, US$93 for Cal and UCLA, and US$99 for instate rival Oregon State.

It is important to note that premium seating and premium ticket pricing are *not* examples of price discrimination. Prices are different, but so is the product that fans are purchasing.

Fast fact. *In September 2006, Nebraska played at USC. Some die-hard Nebraska football fans purchased USC season tickets to guarantee seats to the game. What does this say about their elasticity of demand? Nebraska lost the game, 28-10.*

6.3.2   *Appearance guarantees*

Did you ever wonder why many top-ranked college teams play pushover opponents early in the season? As an example, on November 12, 2011, the Duke University Blue Devils basketball team demolished their non-conference opponent, the Presbyterian College Blue Hose, by a score of 96-55. The purpose of such a mismatched contest is simple: Duke wants to fill in its schedule (preferably with home games), sell more tickets, and give the team an easy opponent early in the season to "fine-tune" the lineup before intra-conference competition begins (Duke belongs to the highly competitive Atlantic Coast Conference). It was also Coach Mike Krzyzewski's 902nd career win, tying him with Bob Knight for the most wins in Division I. What did the Blue Hose get, aside from a sound thrashing? They received a large check, their **appearance guarantee**, from Duke. We do not know the precise amount of that appearance guarantee, but it is common for these to be in the range of US$25,000–300,000 for basketball teams. (Armstrong, 2005)

The rewards in football are even greater. In 2011, Ohio State paid the University of Colorado US$1.4 million, while Kent State received US$1.2 million from Alabama. In 2012, Florida Atlantic was paid US$1 million each by Georgia and Alabama, and Arkansas State got US$1 million for playing at Nebraska ("Nebraska locks up Arkansas State," 2012). If you refer back to Table 6.1, you will note that Arkansas State, Florida Atlantic, and Kent State were all ranked in the bottom 10 of DI-FBS athletic departments for total revenue.

It is not always the weaker teams that collect guarantees. In September 2004, the Oregon State football team visited Baton Rouge to play the then top-ranked Louisiana State University (LSU) Tigers. For Oregon State, this was a strictly win–win situation. The Beavers received an appearance fee of US$1 million and the opportunity to garner some free publicity in a game broadcast nationally by ESPN. Since the Beavers were not expected to win, and this was a non-conference game, even a blowout victory by the Tigers would not have damaged Oregon State's rankings or adversely impacted its standings in the Pac-10 conference. LSU paid OSU with the expectation of a win over a team with a decent reputation. The game also came with no strings attached, that is, OSU did not expect LSU to play a game in Oregon the following year, which would have used up one of LSU's valuable 12 games per season. Fortunately for LSU, OSU lost in overtime 22-21.

For a school in one of the elite conferences, such as Oregon State University or Michigan State University, scheduling one of the scarce preseason non-conference games as an away game has a high opportunity cost. They could play a home game against a weaker opponent and sell enough tickets to fill all or most of a large stadium. For Delaware State University, whose stadium has 7,000 seats, sharing part of the revenue from an away game in the 109,901 seat Michigan stadium is very tempting. Their US$550,000 payment in 2009 was equivalent to more than two years of home games. (Carey, 2009)

Appearance fees are a relatively small fraction for DI-FBS schools. In 2010, the median public FBS school paid US$1.2 million in fees and received US$737,000. In contrast, the median public FCS school earned US$452,000 and paid just US$52,000. However, if a 2013 ban on football games against FCS opponents by the Big Ten is adopted by other FBS conferences, this source of revenue for smaller programs may be threatened. (Belzer, 2013)

6.3.3 *Donations*

Philanthropic donations have always provided a vital source of funding for colleges and universities. These donations are used to provide student scholarships or solicited for specific purposes such as construction of new campus facilities like libraries or to create endowed teaching positions to attract top-notch faculty. Harvard University's endowment in 2012 was the highest in the United States at over US$30 billion dollars.

Donations to athletics departments come from two sources, alumni and non-alumni. These contributions are important and provide an average of 21% of revenues (Table 6.1). Stinson and Howard (n.d., p. 9) indicate that patterns of donations from alumni are determined predominately by their undergraduate experience. If they valued academics more than athletics, they are likely to make donations for academic purposes such as a new library or scholarships for students with financial need. However, if they enjoyed attending athletics event, or were athletes themselves, they might choose to contribute almost exclusively to the athletic department. Some alums exhibit a combined pattern of philanthropy. Phil Knight, former CEO of Nike, donated US$59 million to the University of Oregon when it renovated its football stadium and US$100 million for the new Matthew Knight basketball arena (named in honor of his son, who died in an accident at the age of 34). He has also earmarked tens of millions for academic purposes at UO, and gave US$105 million in 2006 to the Graduate School of Business at Stanford University. Another example is Steve Smith, a former NBA player who attended Michigan State. He has donated a combined total of more than three million dollars for academics and athletics.

One type of donor is of special interest to athletics departments — **boosters** — individuals who restrict their donations to sports. Virtually every college sports program has a booster club. The club usually consists of alums, parents of students, people prominent in the local community, like civic leaders and businessmen, and people who have no obvious ties to the school other than having a strong devotion to the football or basketball team. University athletic departments recognize that the members of these clubs have a pronounced **willingness to pay** for college sports, and the athletic department is eager to exploit this demand (to learn how such organizations operate, see Box 6.3).

Contributions from boosters are substantial. In 2008, Oklahoma State University brought in US$55 million in donations, followed by the University of Florida at US$43 million. The top 42 fundraisers in Division I each collected US$10 million or more. In 2003, the University of Oklahoma completed a fund-raising campaign that collected US$123 million for Sooner sports. This money is used for a variety of purposes including capital expenditures, endowed athletics scholarships, and supplementary income for the coaching staff. Unlike the direct payments from boosters to athletes common in the past, the booster clubs of today usually channel their funds through the university.

Since boosters are mainly interested in sports, they tend to focus on whether the team is winning or losing and have little tolerance for a coach who is not winning enough, regardless of his performance in other areas (e.g., the team's graduation rate). Putting the interest of athletes ahead of winning is unlikely to save a coach's job. As we saw in Chapter 5, boosters' financial contributions supplement coaches' salaries; consequently, they want influence over who gets hired and fired. The former president of the University of Michigan, James Duderstadt (2000, p. 10), mentions that if the team is losing "boosters and alumni are not only likely to call for the firing of the coach, but will go after the athletic director and the president as well."

Individual boosters are often involved in questionable activities concerning the recruiting of student-athletes; in some cases this

---

Box 6.3.   Membership requirements of the Sooner Club.

The Sooner Club at the University of Oklahoma publishes a guide detailing membership requirements and benefits. The 2013 guide described the purpose of the club as follows: "The Sooner Club is the principle [sic] fund-raising arm of OU Athletics. It provides a way for individuals to help talented student-athletes receive a quality education from The University of Oklahoma while ensuring OU's tradition of excellence continues to grow. OU Athletics is entirely self-supporting and receives no state funds. This reality creates a significant need for private contributions."

There are seven levels of membership available to boosters; they may choose to join the Century, Crimson, Coach's, Bronze, Silver, or Golden Circles for a minimum yearly donation of US$100, US$250, US$500, US$1500, US$3000, or US$5000, respectively. The remaining level is the elite Bud Wilkinson Society, which requires a minimum annual investment of US$10,000. Not surprisingly, greater donations translate into greater benefits for booster club members. Century Circle members get, among other things, a window decal, club magazine, and their name in the football game program. Bronze members get the same benefits plus a media guide and reserved parking for basketball games. Higher donations earn invitations to a complimentary tailgate buffet before football games, reserved parking at football events, and access to a members-only lounge located in the football stadium. In 2012, there were 10,660 members of the Sooner Club, second in number in the Big 12 only to the 12,000 members of the University of Texas Longhorn Foundation (where the top level of membership requires a minimum of US$25,000).

(Continued)

Box 6.3. (Continued)

Note however, that not all benefits are guaranteed, and not all Sooner Club members are equal. Tickets to events for which demand exceeds supply, like the big football game vs. Texas, are allocated on the basis of "priority points." These points are similar to other merchandising schemes like frequent flier miles or credit card usage. The guide mentions: "In an effort to more equitably serve Sooner Club members, a system was developed and implemented in 1995 to determine ranking for season ticket placement and acquiring tickets to high-demand events like the annual Red River Rivalry, away games, postseason tournaments and championships, bowl games and other special events. The Priority Point System is also used to allocate Sooner Club benefits like priority parking and requests for seating upgrades." Points are awarded for current donations (3 points per US$100) past donations (1 point per US$100), season tickets purchased (1 point per sport), donations for facilities and scholarships (1 point per US$100), attendance at events for which members have season tickets (4 points for 100% attendance), and membership in the separately-chartered Touchdown Club (2.5 points). For 2012, the 50th ranked member had a total of 5259 points! Donations may be made in monetary or nonmonetary (in-kind) forms. One notable example of the latter is automobiles. Local car dealers are encouraged to share in Sooner Club benefits by providing "reliable transportation" — that is to say, new vehicles — to "OU coaches and administrators." More than 30 car dealers participate.

This system is not unique to Oklahoma, virtually every DI athletics department utilizes a similar scheme.

Source: http://thesoonerclub.com.

is because boosters are naïve or not aware of the NCAA's rules on recruiting. But in other cases their actions suggest they know the rules but choose to ignore them. In one case, University of Alabama football booster Logan Young was sentenced to six months in prison for racketeering. He paid high school football coach Lynn Lang an estimated US$150,000 to convince star defensive lineman Albert Means to enroll at Alabama.[5] Young's actions — major violations of the NCAA bylaws — were also costly for the Crimson Tide; the NCAA cut 15 Alabama football scholarships and prohibited it from playing in any bowl games for two years. Boosters also often provide extra benefits to athletes (like the under the table payments to Chris Webber we described in Chapter 3). Because of potential for violations involving boosters, many schools provide boosters with information telling them what they can and cannot do (see, e.g., Box 6.4).

A contributionis allocated in one of two ways; either it is designated for a dedicated expense (like construction of a new weight room) or it is invested in a financial portfolio (**endowment**) that generates a stream of revenue over time. Income from endowments is becoming increasingly important as a source of revenue; Table 6.4 lists the 10 largest endowments held by athletic departments in the country.

To help you understand the importance endowments can have for an athletic department, let us consider UNC's US$212 million endowment. If the money is invested in a diversified financial portfolio it could generate, on average, a minimum real return of 4% per year, or US$8.5 million. If a "full-ride" athletics scholarship for out-of-state students at UNC costs US$40,000, income from the endowment would fully fund 212 scholarships every year. Given that there were about 437 male and female athletes at UNC in 2008, these investment returns would cover the scholarships of one half

---

[5]See, among others: (Fish, 2005) and ("Alabama banned," 2002). Young was murdered while awaiting sentencing ("Coroner examining," 2006). Means played one season for Alabama and transferred to Memphis where he finished his football career.

Box 6.4. DePaul University information for boosters.

DePaul University provides a detailed list of unacceptable activities:

1. Make in-person contact (on- or off-campus), telephone, e-mail or write a prospect for recruiting purposes.
2. Have communication (e.g., phone call, text message) with a prospect or the prospect's relatives or legal guardians at any time. As well, a booster should not contact a prospect to congratulate him or her on committing to DePaul.
3. Visit a prospect's high school/prep school to pick up film/videotape or transcripts pertaining to the evaluation of the prospect's academic eligibility or athletics ability.
4. Contact a prospect's coach, principal, or counselor in an attempt to evaluate or recruit the prospect.
5. Directly or indirectly make any arrangements for a prospect to receive any financial aid, cash, loans, discounts, or other benefits of any kind.
6. Provide, arrange, or pay for any type of transportation, including an automobile, for a prospect.
7. Make contact with a prospect when he or she is on-campus for an official or unofficial recruiting visit (except for unavoidable, incidental contact).
8. Provide cash to a prospect for entertainment or any other purpose.
9. Provide anything to a prospect without prior approval from the Compliance Office of the DePaul Athletics Department.
10. Contribute funds to finance a scholarship or grant-in-aid for a particular student-athlete.
11. Provide a student-athlete, his or her relatives, or friends with professional services without charge or at a reduced cost.

(Continued)

Box 6.4. (Continued)

---

12. Provide a loan or guarantee a bond for a student-athlete, his or her relatives or friends. Additionally, you may not sign or cosign a note with an outside agency to arrange a loan for a student-athlete, his or her relatives, or friends.
13. Provide an automobile or the use of an automobile to a student-athlete, his or her relatives, or friends.
14. Pay for, arrange for payment of, or provide cost-free transportation for a student-athlete, his or her family, or friends.
15. Provide a student-athlete, or his or her relativesor friends, with a special discount, payment arrangement or credit on purchases (i.e., airline ticket, clothing) or services (i.e., dry cleaning, laundry).

Source: http://www.depaulbluedemons.com/compliance/boosters.

Table 6.4. Athletic department endowments for 2008.

Institution	Endowment (US$)
University of North Carolina	212,000,000
Duke University	150,717,426
Boston College	100,000,000
Georgia Tech	80,058,950
University of Virginia	61,873,981
University of Washington	56,000,000
University of Georgia	51,000,000
Pennsylvania State University	49,390,069
University of Connecticut	48,051,366
Ohio State University	46,139,682

Source: Chronicle of Higher Education (http://chronicle.com/ article/Athletics-Endowments-vs/47396).

of all their athletes. If student-athletes were eligible for instate tuition and fees of US$20,000, it could cover every single athlete in perpetuity!

Athletic departments originally used these endowments only to fund athletics scholarships. But some schools now indicate that they will use endowments to fund all athletic department expenses (including salaries), which increases the likelihood that they will become self-sufficient.

Athletic directors across the country dream of contributions like the US$165 million gift T. Boone Pickens gave his alma mater, Oklahoma State University, in December 2005. His gift ranks 17th on a list of all donations to institutions of higher education since 1967. Of course, universities and their athletic departments will not spurn smaller donations and many now target senior citizens (often alums) and ask them to consider purchasing an annuity or to leave money to the university in their will.

> **Fast fact.** *You can now be buried in a casket in your school colors! Collegiate Memorials, a company in Forsyth, Georgia, manufactures caskets for "die-hard" college sports supporters. The top seller is the Oklahoma University casket which sells for US$4,600 and features the school colors and the school's logo. The university earns a royalty of 8% for each casket sold. (Bailey, 2005)*

6.3.4 *Corporate sponsorships*

Another lucrative source of revenue for athletic departments are **corporate sponsorships**. The next time you attend a college game, or watch one on television, play close attention to the advertising displayed in the arena or stadium and in the game program, the corporate logos on player uniforms and coach's apparel, the advertisements featured during television or radio station breaks, and public announcements during the game. Visit the athletic department website and see if there is a link to "corporate partnerships or sponsorships."

We define sponsorships as monetary and nonmonetary payments made by a company to a university. Monetary payments are a fixed sum of money for a period of time in which a company typically purchases the right to advertise in athletic department facilities (e.g., banners and signs at the football stadium or basketball arena), or on player uniforms (usually in a logo).

Corporations sponsor college athletics mainly as a marketing platform to promote the corporation's products. As we discuss in the next chapter, the growth in the popularity of college sports is due in large part to television broadcasting. Every corporate logo or billboard displayed during a game broadcast on television translates into valuable exposure for that company. Corporations are also buying access to an affluent segment of the population. The University of Michigan says that 65% of "Michigan fans" have household incomes greater than US$75,000 a year and 48% of their fans have incomes greater than US$100,000. ("Michigan fan demographics," n.d.)

Perhaps the best-known business partnerships are with sports apparel companies like Adidas, Nike and Reebok. These firms typically provide uniforms and equipment at no charge or else at minimal cost. In return, the corporate logo is prominently displayed on players' uniforms, warm-ups, equipment bags, coaches' apparel.

Why do athletic departments accept sponsorships? The answer is simple: money. The revenue potential is hard to resist, especially for the top-level programs where financial independence is the goal. In 1994, the University of Michigan struck a seven-year deal with Nike that paid it around US$25 million and also provided apparel, equipment and footwear. A new contract for US$28 million was signed in 2001. In 2008, they negotiated an eight year contract with Adidas for US$60 million.

The list of corporate sponsors go far beyond sports apparel companies. In 2011, UPS signed a deal worth US$100 million over four years with a group of 68 colleges. The contract was negotiated by IMG College, a leading sports marketing firm (Smith, 2011). Other major sponsors include Allstate, AT&T, Coca-Cola, Lowe's, MillerCoors, Pepsi, Pizza Hut, Southwest Airlines, and State Farm.

Sponsorships can also generate controversy. Some people are wary about any relationship between business and academia. This concern extends beyond the athletic department. It is argued that the academic mission of an institution may be compromised by its links to corporations. For example, in Oregon there are claims that corporate support by the timber industry unduly influences academic research at Oregon State University's nationally recognized School of Forestry ("Forestry Dean," 2006). Chemistry departments at U.S. universities are sometimes criticized for accepting financial support from the pharmaceutical industry. But others have argued that for public institutions in particular, decreased financial support from state governments forces universities to seek funding elsewhere or risk having to cut programs and staff.

Some sponsorships attract more criticism than others. Perhaps the most publicized recent example is related to the **sweatshops** issue. Factories in less-developed countries like Pakistan and Vietnam manufacture sports apparel and shoes for corporations like Nike. In November 1997, a confidential report prepared for Nike by the consulting firm Ernst & Young was leaked to the *New York Times*. The report claimed that workers at a Nike facility in Vietnam worked 65 hours a week, received low wages, and were subject to unsafe working conditions. As a consequence, many colleges and universities chose to ally themselves with an organization called the Worker's Right Consortium, a labor organization affiliated with the AFL-CIO and a strident critic of Nike and other multinational corporations.[6]

One university that considered joining the Worker's Right Consortium was the University of Oregon. Oregon has a unique relationship with Nike because Nike's founder and CEO, Phil

---

[6]Information about the WRC is available at: http://www.workersrights.org/.

Knight, is an Oregon alumnus and an individual who had donated millions of dollars to the university and the athletics department. In response to the threat of Oregon's alliance with the Worker's Right Consortium, Knight retracted a US$30 million gift. His donation was later restored after the University agreed to end its support of the Worker's Right Consortium. This generated even more debate.

Suppose a student-athlete is involved in a campus group like the Worker's Right Consortium. Would that student put her athletics scholarship in jeopardy? Will her coaches try to get her to shut up? Will she be cut from the team? It is possible. A Reebok contract with Wisconsin prohibited any university employee or representative from "disparaging Reebok" (Zimbalist, 1999, pp. 144–145). After catching considerable flak, Reebok eliminated the clause but it raised the question of whether accepting a college athletics scholarship requires students and staff to give up their constitutionally guaranteed rights to free speech.

What if a student-athlete refuses to wear corporate provided apparel or footwear, or covers up the corporate logos on her jersey or shoes? In the fall of 2005, Arkansas State basketball player Jerry Nichols refused to wear Adidas sneakers because he hurt his knee while playing in them. He preferred Nikes instead. Because the university had a contract with Adidas, the athletic director told Nichols he had to wear Adidas provided shoes or else he would not play ("Adidas says," 2005). Adidas told Arkansas State to grant Nichols an "exemption." He later tore a ligament in his knee and was finished for the 2005–2006 season.

6.3.5 *Naming rights*

The final source of revenue we discuss, one that overlaps with corporate sponsorships, is **naming rights**, a marketing tool in which the right to name an existing, renovated, or new college sports facility is offered to the highest bidder. Naming rights are another example of athletic departments adopting marketing techniques from professional sports.[7] Until quite recently, most college athletics facilities had a functional, if non-descript, name (e.g., Ohio Stadium at Ohio State University), or else they were named in honor of a former athlete or coach (e.g., Jesse Owens Memorial Stadium or Woody Hayes Athletic Center, also at Ohio State). For a substantial donation an individual or corporation can buy the right to have their name displayed on an athletics facility. As of 2013, only 11 DI-FBS schools had sold the naming rights to their football stadiums. The University of Louisville football stadium is called "Papa John's Cardinal Stadium" after the pizza baron who paid the university US$5 million in 1998. An additional US$10 million paid in 2007 extended the rights until 2040. In 2005, TCF Bank acquired the naming rights for the new University of Minnesota stadium for 25 years with a US$35 million dollar contribution.

An example from 2013 shows that the athletic department's pursuit of revenue from naming rights can be controversial. Florida Atlantic University announced a US$6 million deal to name its new stadium for the GEO Group. The GEO Group operates private prisons in the U.S. and worldwide, including one located less than 10 miles from campus. The Stop Owlcatraz Coalition (the FAU mascot is an owl), an umbrella group of student organizations, organized protests based on the company's history with abuse investigations. Some pundits suggested changing the football uniforms to stripes (Bishop, 2013). Citing the distraction created by this controversy, GEO Group later withdrew its offer.

Examples of naming rights for arenas and other sports facilities are more common. The Jerome Schottenstein Center at Ohio State University, which hosts basketball and ice hockey, is named for the Schottenstein family who contributed US$12.5 million toward its construction. Louisville-based Yum! Brands paid US$13.5 million

---

[7]For a partial list of naming rights for professional and collegiate sports facilities around the world: http://en.wikipedia.org/wiki/List_of_sports_venues_with_sole_naming_rights.

in 2010 for the naming rights to the new University of Louisville basketball and multipurpose arena that was under construction, opening later that year as the KFC Yum! Center.

Fast fact. *The University of Pennsylvania, a member of the Ivy League, ("Campaign for Penn Athletics," 2010) published a brochure with a list of 90 naming opportunities ranging from US$10,000 for a row of lockers in the women's lacrosse locker room to US$500,000 for an entrance gate at the George A. Weiss Pavilion to US$10 million for a renovated building in the Palestra Hutchinson Complex with practice courts, offices, and the rowing center. If every one of these naming rights requests were fulfilled, Penn Athletics would raise US$38 million.*

6.4   The Athletic Department Budget — Expenditures

We now turn to the expenditure side of the budget for a typical DI-FBS institution. Table 6.5 lists median values for the most common expenditure items, ranked by magnitude. As we did with the revenue side of the budget, we will focus on only a couple of the most important line items: grants-in-aid, (athletics scholarships), salaries and benefits, and recruiting. A few words of caution before we begin. *First*, the reported expenditures are only for the 120 DI-FBS institutions, which make up approximately one-third of Division I. *Second*, as we discuss below, the information may be inaccurate. And *third*, the information usually omits many expenses, including fringe benefits for athletic department staff, legal, accounting and computer services, janitorial and maintenance services, and — perhaps most importantly — the costs of construction of new athletics facilities and the renovation of existing facilities.[8]

---

[8] For an extensive list of expenses that are often omitted from athletic department budgets see Lombardi (2003, p. 21).

Table 6.5. Athletic department median operating expenses at DI-FBS universities for 2010.

Category	Expenses (in US$)	Percentage
Salaries and benefits	15,881,000	34
Grants-in-aid	7,244,000	16
Facilities maintenance and rental	4,631,000	10
Team travel	3,192,000	7
Game expenses	1,660,000	4
Guarantees and options	1,258,000	3
Fundraising	1,097,000	2
Equipment/uniforms/supplies	1,096,000	2
Recruiting	721,000	2
Medical	545,000	1
Other	3,505,000	8
Total	46,688,000	100

Source: Fulks (2011, pp. 31–32).

6.4.1 *Salaries and benefits*

We stated at the beginning of this chapter that the operating expenditures of athletic departments at DI universities are a small fraction of total university spending, but are growing more rapidly than university expenditures as a whole. An NCAA report on Division I revenue and expenses shows that the median percentage of a DI-FBS university's budget devoted to athletics increased from 4.6 to 5.5% from 2004 to 2012. In DI-FCS and DI without football, the increases were 5.2 to 6.0% and 4.5 to 5.9%, respectively. After removing the effect of inflation, expenditures on athletics at FBS schools grew at a median annual rate of 9% over that time period. The rates for FCS and DI without football were 5 and 7%, respectively. For 2011–2012, the rate of growth for FBS was almost 11%, more than twice the rate for the other two subdivisions. (Fulks, 2013)

What accounts for this rapid increase in athletic expenditures? According to an earlier study by the *Wall Street Journal* (Adams,

2006), the largest, and fastest growing, line item was salaries and benefits. The NCAA report shows this has continued to be true and that scholarship costs have increased quickly as tuition rates rise (Fulks, 2013). Given the trend in compensation for head coaches we saw in Chapter 5, the increase in salaries and benefits should not be surprising. But it is not just coaches who pull in the big bucks. Nine of the athletic directors at DI-FBS institutions were paid more than US$1 million per year in 2013, with Tom Jurich at Louisville earning US$1.4 million (Upton and Berkozitz, 2013). For comparison, the President of Louisville, James Ramsey, only earns US$600,000. Unfortunately for athletic departments, rising salaries are market driven and outside the control of an individual school, and the NCAA has not attempted to impose any limits as they have for student-athlete compensation.

6.4.2   *Athletics scholarships*

Currently, the average DI school spends about 18% of its budget on scholarships. This percentage is growing but it is not due to an increase in the number of scholarships. Remember that the NCAA limits the number of full grants in aid in both "head count" and "equivalency" sports (e.g., 85 in DI-A football and 13 in DI basketball). Instead, the dollar value of each scholarship is increasing rapidly due to national trends in tuition, on-campus housing and dining, and textbooks.

When the athletic department at the University of Washington says that it spent US$9.9 million on scholarships in 2012, how accurate is that number? How is the "cost" of a scholarship determined? How close is that accounting cost to the economic cost? Why might there be a difference between the accounting and economic costs? Suppose that the value of a full grant-in-aid at Duke University is US$45,000. That figure represents the accounting cost and includes tuition, housing, meals. The price of each of these items is listed in the college catalog and in other university print and electronic documents. The grant-in-aid will also include a stipend for other incidental expenses. But is US$45,000 equal to the true cost—the economic or **marginal cost**—of educating the student-athlete? Maybe.

Imagine that you are sitting in your Economics of College Sports class. It is the first week of the semester and there are 40 students enrolled in class. Each of the 40 students, including you, is paying US$500 in tuition for the class. Suppose another student, Mia Hamm, comes into the room hoping to add the class. The Professor agrees to let Mia add the class provided that she registers and pays the university US$500. Now the crucial question: did the cost of teaching the class rise when student enrollment increased from 40 to 41? If it did, by how much? Is the marginal cost equal to US$500?

The accounting cost is an **average cost** that the university calculates based on an approximation of the total costs of educating a specific number of students. But it is not the same thing as marginal cost. You remember the difference between average and marginal costs; average cost is total cost divided by total output and marginal cost is the *change* in total costs (or variable costs) from producing one more unit of output. As you can see from the short run cost curves in Figure 6.4, marginal costs can be higher, lower or equal to, average costs — depending on the amount of output produced. But usually they are not equal to one another.

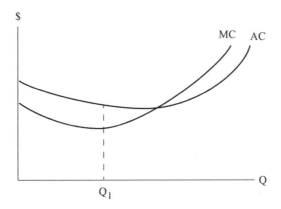

Figure 6.4. Average and marginal cost curves.

Understanding the difference between the two costs is very important. On most college campuses across the country, the cost of educating one more student (marginal cost) is likely to be less than average cost. The main reason for this is **excess capacity** (such as atquantity Q_1 in Figure 6.4). Universities usually have considerable flexibility in determining the maximum number of students that can be taught each semester. Simply put: most universities have room to add more students.

Marginal cost will equal average cost when the university has a strict limit on the number of students who can attend each semester. This usually only occurs at highly selective private institutions like Harvard, Princeton, or Yale. Every year Harvard has more applicants than it has room to admit. Suppose Harvard is considering admitting only one of two students. Student X is not an athlete and Student Y is an athlete. If student X is accepted, the student will pay the list price of US$50,000 per year. If student Y is admitted, the student will receive a full grant-in-aid from the university valued at US$50,000. Student Y will not pay a penny to attend Harvard. If Harvard admits Y instead of X, then the average and marginal costs are the same because Harvard gave up the opportunity to collect US$50,000 from Student X. (What would happen if Student X could only pay US$25,000 and asked for the remaining financial aid from Harvard? The opportunity cost would fall from US$50,000 to US$25,000.)

Let us summarize: At a university with excess capacity, the marginal cost will be less than the average cost, the list price. Only a handful of selective institutions will have no excess capacity. In that case, the marginal cost is determined by the cost of prospective students who are denied entry (displaced) because an athlete was admitted. In some situations, marginal cost may be close to, or equal, the average cost (list price). But in either case, it is the marginal cost that represents the true economic cost of educating a student.

When an athletic department reports the cost of a scholarship it uses average not marginal costs. As Goff (2000, p. 87) notes, this inflates the expenses side of its budget since the marginal cost of educating, housing, and feeding a student-athlete is lower than list price if the university has excess capacity. This raises the question whether the athletic department is distorting its budgetary numbers on purpose or if it is simply following the accounting rules established by the university.

6.4.3 *Recruiting*

Recruiting the best available athletes is one of the coach's most important jobs. Every coach wants to attract as many top caliber athletes as possible. Two things are striking about the recruiting process: the amount of resources that athletic departments are willing to spend, and the innovative recruiting techniques used to attract athletes.

The recruiting process is hyper-competitive. It is not uncommon for a high-school All-American to be coveted by dozens of DI programs. Since there are no NCAA regulations on the amount of money a school can spend on recruiting — only rules on specific forms of recruiting — it should not be surprising that many schools pull out all the stops to convince a talented football player or basketball player to sign their national letter of intent with them.

The situation is analogous to what happens when there is a shortage of a product, such as the latest video game console or must-have toy for Christmas, and sellers are unwilling to raise the price.[9] Consumers will go to great lengths, including camping out in front of the store, to be among the lucky few to buy the product. Some enterprising people will buy as many as possible and immediately put them up for sale on eBay for a quick profit. In the case of athletes, the NCAA does not allow colleges and universities to offer more than a full scholarship. The fact that recruiting is so competitive is an indication that the NCAA is operating as an effective cartel and keeping the price far below the amount that would equate supply and demand.

---

[9] In a free market, a rising price will eliminate any temporary shortage. In the case of the latest hot toy, by not choking off the shortage with a higher price, the manufacturer can actually encourage even greater demand. A gift that required a great deal of effort to buy may mean more to a recipient, who can proudly show off their new toy to their envious friends.

One of the most aggressive institutions has been the University of Oregon. In 2004, the University of Oregon's football recruiting budget was approximately US$600,000. During one weekend in January 2004, Oregon hosted 24 recruits for a visit that cost the athletic department US$140,875 for transportation, lodging, meals, and entertainment. That represented 25% of the entire recruiting budget and was an average of US$5,635 spent on each recruit during a three-day period.

Most of Oregon's prospects came to campus via regularly scheduled commercial flights but a few fortunate athletes flew on a chartered Lear Jet. Once the recruits arrived in Eugene, they were shuttled around campus in the athletic department's vehicles, including a bright green and yellow Hummer. The recruits left with personalized posters, videos, and comic books (Bachman, 2006b). Were these expenses worth it? 12 out of the 24 recruits signed letters of intent with Oregon.

At that time, none of Oregon's recruiting activities violated NCAA rules (Section 13 of the bylaws). However, several of these activities — the use of private jets and the provision of any "personalized recruiting aid" — were subsequently prohibited by the NCAA. This is another example of the **little Dutch boy** story we introduced in Chapter 1; schools use innovative, and sometimes questionable, recruiting techniques. If the NCAA later bans these tactics, the schools simply find other means.

Athletic departments are aggressively adopting technologies that help them gain a recruiting advantage. Before recruits choose the campuses to visit they are bombarded with various publications — often sent by express mail — videos, emails, and phone calls from their suitors. Some of these mailings were produced using specialized software provided by Recruiting Pro, located in Madison, WI, or Scoutware in Aurora, IL. These programs cover every facet of the recruiting process and allow each school to produce customized communications and marketing information to attract recruits.

Sometimes this aggressiveness can backfire. NCAA rules limit the number of contacts that can be made in person and by telephone. Coaches quickly adopted email and text messaging as a way to circumvent the rules and provide a more personalized communication with the prospective athlete. The NCAA Student-Athlete Council complained about the deluge of emails and text messages received by many prospective recruits, particularly because the recipient of the message often has to pay the cost of the communication (Bachman, 2006a). David Berst, Vice President of Division I, noted the case of someone waking up to 52 text messages ("Text-messaging ban," 2007). In April 2007, the NCAA Division I Management Council and the Board of Directors approved a proposal, sponsored by the Ivy Group but opposed by coaches associations and NCAA committees for the major sports, to eliminate text messaging of prospective student-athletes. (Sherman, 2013)

While an attempt to override the ban on text messaging at the 2008 NCAA Convention failed, a proposal to allow unlimited texting (and up to 10 telephone calls per day to each prospect) was passed by the Division I Board of Directors in 2013. Enough Division I members submitted override votes to require a review, and the board subsequently decided to suspend implementation of the new rule. (Sherman, 2013)

6.5 Are Athletic Departments Profitable?

Having examined the major sources of revenue and the primary expenditures for athletic departments, it is time to see how many operate with a profit or a loss. Using publicrecords requests, *USA TODAY* gained access to the financial data reported to the NCAA from 228 public universities in Division I.[10] Private universities are

---

[10] The *Indianapolis Star* collected data on 164 public universities for 2004, and that data is available at http://www2.indystar.com/NCAA_financial_reports/. It reports detailed revenue and expenses for football, men's basketball, women's basketball, all other sports combined, and the total. ESPN requested data from the 120 schools in DI-FBS for 2008. For private universities that declined to release their reports to the NCAA, ESPN was able to collect some of the data from reports submitted to the US Department of Education's Office of Postsecondary Education

Table 6.6.   Net revenue for DI institutions in 2012 (amounts in US$).

Institution	Net revenue
1. Texas A&M	37,910,104
2. Texas	25,025,405
3. Michigan	24,931,000
4. Ohio State	17,623,645
5. Arkansas	17,287,009
6. Alabama	16,695,078
7. Florida	15,669,908
8. LSU	12,798,670
9. Kansas State	12,276,830
10. Oklahoma	10,206,288
219. Missouri-Kansas City	−2,763,991
220. Utah	−2,881,285
221. Washington State	−5,232,707
222. Arizona State	−5,732,395
223. Iowa	−6,755,772
224. North Texas	−7,512,835
225. Kansas	−8,744,528
226. Oklahoma State	−9,512,021
227. West Virginia	−12,904,091
228. Missouri	−16,261,224

Source: USAToday.com (http://www.usatoday.com/sports/college/schools/finances/).

not legally obligated to disclose financial information, and none provided any data. Tables 6.6 and 6.7 shows the 10 most- and least-profitable athletic departments. Table 6.7 includes the profit or loss generated by the athletic department excluding revenue from student fees and institutional support.

(OPE). The ESPN database is available at http://http://espn.go.com/ncaa/revenue.

Table 6.7. Net revenues without institutional subsidy for DI institutions in 2012 (amounts in US$).

Institution	Net revenue w/o subsidy
1. Texas A&M	32,710,104
2. Texas	25,025,405
3. Michigan	24,672,115
4. Ohio State	17,623,645
5. Arkansas	15,337,829
6. LSU	12,798,670
7. Florida	11,313,451
8. Alabama	11,233,878
9. Oklahoma	10,206,288
10. Kansas State	9,540,897
219. Georgia State	−22,672,771
220. Eastern Michigan	−23,034,138
221. Florida International	−23,238,642
222. Delaware	−23,434,793
223. Massachusetts	−24,079,190
224. Old Dominion	−25,152,501
225. Air Force	−26,170,275
226. James Madison	−27,298,448
227. Rutgers	−27,996,056
228. Nevada-Las Vegas	−32,481,998

Source: USAToday.com (http://www.usatoday.com/sports/college/schools/finances/).

While the NCAA does not disclose financial data for individual members, it does report average revenue and costs for all schools in each division. Table 6.8 shows average revenue, costs, and net revenue in DI-FBS for selected years from 1985 to 2010. In 2010, the median revenues and expenses were US$48.3 and US$46.7 million, respectively, leaving an accounting profit of US$1.6 million. This profit, however, is illusory; once institutional support is subtracted, the profit turns into a median loss of US$9.5 million. You can see

Table 6.8.   Reported revenue, expenses, profits, and deficits for Division I-FBS (amounts in thousands of current US$).

	1985	1989	1993	1997	2001	2005	2010
Average revenue	6,900	9,700	13,600	17,700	25,100	32,849	48,298
Average expenses	7,000	9,700	13,000	17,300	23,200	31,128	46,688
Average net	−100	0	700	400	1,900	121	413
Average net w/o Institutional support	N/A	N/A	−200	−800	−600	−5,565	−9,466
% Reporting profit w/o Institutional support	N/A	N/A	51%	43%	35%	15%	18%
Average profit	N/A	N/A	1,700	1,700	5,260	2,613	7,367
% Reporting loss w/o Institutional support	N/A	N/A	49%	57%	65%	85%	82%
Average loss	N/A	N/A	2,100	2,800	3,770	7,167	11,597

Source: Fulks (2011, pp. 23, 27).
Note: Median values are reported for 2005 and 2010 rather than average values.

similar, but less dramatic, results occurring in previous years. The percentage of schools reporting a loss when institutional support is not included has risen from just under 50% in 1993 to 82% in 2010. Would you consider an industry to be profitable if four out of five firms were losing money?

Who covers losses when they occur? Sometimes it is the athletic department itself; a deficit is paid out of a reserve fund from surpluses in previous years. If reserves are not available, the university will have to provide additional unbudgeted support. Recently, Peter Likins, the President of the University of Arizona and the Chairman of an NCAA committee on fiscal responsibility, was quoted as saying "the most rapidly growing revenue stream is the transfer of funds from the parent university." (Brady and Upton, 2005)

As first mentioned in Chapter 2, athletic departments can engage in "creative accounting" to make their profits and losses appear smaller or larger than they really are. Why might an athletic department want to declare smaller profits or larger losses? One possibility is that the athletic department wants to keep all its profits to itself; that is, to avoid losing money via a cross-subsidy to the university's general fund. Alternately, it may inflate its losses in order to increase its subsidy from the university. However, large losses may invite unwanted scrutiny by the administration that might mandate cost-cutting measures to the athletic director. To avoid this scenario, the athletic director may be tempted to deflate its losses to avoid administrative interference and potential negative repercussions from alumni or, in the case of public institutions, taxpayers.[11]

As indicated in Section 6.3.2, how scholarships are accounted for can make a big difference to an athletic department's bottom line. Goff (2000) mentions other "sleight-of-hand" tricks, such as assigning athletics revenues — like the sales of souvenir jerseys and hats — to the university's general fund or charging athletics expenses (for example, janitorial serves at the football stadium) to the general fund rather than the athletic department.[12]

The most common source for university athletics budgetary information is the OPE of the U.S. Department of Education. Postsecondary institutions are required by law to submit a report every year, including the number of undergraduates attending the institution, the name of the athletic director, the NCAA division (if applicable), a list of intercollegiate sports offered to men and women, the total number of athletes by gender, operating expenses per team, revenues for football, men's and women's basketball and

---

[11] Also, publicly supported institutions must broach the issue of the extent to which taxpayers should finance the expansion of athletics departments rather than academic programs or facilities.

[12] Goff (2000) mentions that when more transparent, and theoretically sound, accounting estimates were applied to the athletics budget at Western Kentucky University, a US$1.2 million surplus was reduced to US$300,000. An apparent US$700,000 loss at Utah State was actually a US$366,000 profit.

all other sports combined, the dollar amount of athletics scholarships awarded, and recruiting information.

Given this source, why are we relying on data collected by the staff of a newspaper? The reliability of the information disclosed to the Department of Education (DOE) was called into question. An article in *USA Today* (Upton and Brady, 2005) determined that 41 out of 119 DI-A schools reported inaccurate financial information. While some of these errors were minor, others were significant, including a US$34 million error by the University of Texas. The article noted that the NCAA was aware of the problem but was unwilling to provide the correct figures to the DOE because of "privacy considerations." These kinds of problems with financial information are well recognized (Lombardi, 2003, Appendix 3) and imply that those of us interested in athletic department budgets must exercise caution when using that information.

6.6 Causes of Athletic Department Losses

We do not expect businesses to earn a profit every year, as long as they are profitable over the long term. Losses in one year can be offset by profits in other years. What we observe in college sports is persistent losses for many athletic departments. It is natural to ask how this came to be such a common occurrence and why it is tolerated at those schools. We will consider several possible explanations, including schools trying to enter the big time in college sports, cross subsidization within the athletics department, and the arms race among programs already in the big time.

6.6.1 *Moving up to the big time*

In Section 10 of Chapter 2, we introduced you to the president of a DI-FCS university who was contemplating a move to DI-FBS. His hope was that spending more on athletics would eventually enhance the status of the institution and create enough new revenue to pay for the increase in expenses. The same logic can be used by DII schools that want to move up to DI. The problem is that not

Table 6.9. Portland State University Budget (dollar figures are in thousands).

Category	1996 Amount	Percent (%)	2005 Amount	Percent (%)	1996–2005 % change	2007 (Projected)
Revenue						
Tickets	US$444	13	US$393	5	−11	US$350
Guarantees	136	4	349	5	157	400
Postseason	0	0	0	0	0	15
Donations	209	6	571	7	173	580
Lottery	413	12	358	5	−13	400
Other	382	11	645	8	69	655
Student fees	1,408	41	2,339	30	66	2,710
General fund	904	26	3,056	40	238	2,996
Total	3,881	100	7,711	100	94	8,106
Expenses						
Payroll	US$1,493	38	US$2,969	38	99	US$3,211
Scholarships	743	19	2,483	32	234	2,634
Guarantees	174	4	160	2	−8	50
Travel	477	12	862	11	81	910
Depreciation	0	0	27	0	100	27
Other	1,004	26	1,324	17	32	1,255
Total	3,891	100	7,825	100	101	8,087
Net Income	−US$10		−US$114			US$19

Source: Oregon State Board of Higher Education (2005).

everyone can develop consistently winning programs (for every winner there must be a loser), and many of these efforts will end with less than the expected results.

Consider the case of Portland State University (PSU), a former DII institution that joined DI-FCS in the fall of 1996. Table 6.9 shows PSU's Athletic Department revenues and expenses in 1996 and 2005. Total revenue and expenses doubled in that period, with expenses rising slightly more than revenue. Appearance guarantees, postseason income, and donations all rose substantially. But notice two quirks — ticket revenue fell and subsidies to the athletic department (student fees and institutional support from the university's general fund) rose. In fact, institutional support had the single largest increase. Now look at expenses — payroll doubled and scholarship expenses more than tripled. Given this information, what was the financial justification for PSU moving from DII to DI?

Now look at the last column, which was their projected budget for fiscal year 2007. It suggested that the Athletic Department would be breaking even (earning zero accounting profits). Pay attention to the projected student fees and institutional funds subsidy. What happens to the bottom line if either of those revenue items, or both, are eliminated? Without the subsidies, which provide 70% of revenues, you are left with a US$5.7 million loss. Imagine that you are the president of PSU. How would you explain to students and taxpayers why their contribution is so important for the Athletic Department and the University? Is it possible that PSU's sports program was responsible for the university's growth in enrollment (10,268 in 1996 and 18,891 in 2006)? Is it possible that the sports program enables the school to attract better students and higher quality faculty? Does the PSU sports program enhance the quality of life in the Portland metropolitan area?

Did PSU actually achieve financial independence for athletics, or at least make progress? Based on data from the usatoday.com database, the answer is no, at least as of 2012. Generated revenue fell, with decreases in ticket sales, guarantees, and donations, although media rights and licensing have increased. All expense categories increased, with coaching/staff salaries and scholarships both up by 60%. Student fees and university funds continue to make up the difference, with the subsidy covering an increased 73.4% of expenses. An additional subsidy now comes from the Oregon Legislature, which decided in 2013 that the solution is to spend more on facilities, with US$20 million allocated to renovate the Stott Center.

What gives schools like PSU the hope that more spending will translate into athletic success and eventually profitability? We do not have to look far to see the answer. Just 110 miles down Interstate 5 from Portland is Eugene, home of the University of Oregon. As we noted in Section 6.2, Oregon has reaped significant rewards from its investments in athletics. A report by the American Association of University Professors (Stern, 2003) notes that "… as some smaller institutions have coveted the potential revenues and public notice associated with high-profile sports programs, the temptation for these institutions to promote athletics has been intense and at times irresistible." The example of Longwood University, which became a full member of Division I in 2007, is discussed in Box 6.5. As of 2013, two schools are in transition to full Division I membership, Northern Kentucky University (2015) and University of Nebraska at Omaha (2016). Four other schools have announced that they will begin the process of moving up from Division II. One school, Centenary College of Louisiana, will complete the transition down from DI to DIII in 2014.

6.6.2 *Cross subsidization within the athletic department*

A different explanation will have to be used for one of the biggest money losing institutions, the University of California at Berkeley. It is one of the best-known universities in the world, consistently ranked as a top Tier 1 school by the *US News and World Report* and other surveys. Cal has a reputation for undergraduate and graduate academic excellence and the faculty currently consists of six Nobel Prize winners as well as numerous recipients of other prestigious academic awards. Judged by undergraduate admissions, it is one of the most selective of any institution, public or private. It is a member of the Pac-12 with a winning record over the past 10 years with eight bowl appearances. Why does Cal feel compelled to spend over US$70 million on athletics in 2010 and run a US$7 million deficit (generated revenue minus expenses)? Will Cal's reputation suffer if athletics spending is reduced and the school

Box 6.5.   Longwood University moves from DII to DI.

Longwood, a school of approximately 4,300 located in Farmville, Virginia, had a highly successful athletic program in DII, notably in men's basketball. Nevertheless, the administration decided in 1999 to jump to DI. President Patricia Cormier said "We have made our first successful step to Division I and this is a natural and logical move for Longwood. Our academic profile has been raised over the past few years and we believe that Division I status will enhance both our institutional image and our recruitment efforts." Athletic Director Rick Mazzuto commented "[w]e want people to have heard of Longwood." New DI members are typically required to play as "independents," schools not affiliated with a conference and they must meet extensive compliance requirements over a five-year period. Without being able to share in conference revenues, DI independents must travel extensively and rely heavily on the appearance guarantees we discussed in Section 6.3.2. Between December 26, 2004 and January 11, 2005, the men's basketball team traveled 7,850 miles to play seven games. The team lost all seven and finished the season with a record of 1-30. As of 2012, student fees and institutional support comprised 85.6% of the athletics budget. Their acceptance rate for new freshmen, a measure of selectivity, increased from 62% in 2005 to 76% in 2010, and the percentage of accepted students that enrolled at Longwood decreased from 51% to 37%. What would you conclude about the outcome?

Sources: "NCAA Division I update" (2003), "NCAA Division I reclassification timeline" (2005), USAToday.com database, and Longwood University Factbook 2012–2013.

decides not to try to mimic a football school like Alabama or a basketball school like Arkansas, schools that are consistently ranked far lower than Cal in every academic category possible?

We need to dig a bit deeper into Cal's athletic department budget to find a possible explanation. According to information from the U.S. Department of Education database (http://ope.ed.gov/athletics/), their football and men's basketball programs generated positive net revenues in 2011 of US$6.8 and US$1.6 million, respectively. Investments in these programs were apparently successful. So how did they end up with a deficit? By spending US$15 million more on other sports than those programs generated in revenue. Without the profits from their revenue sports, other programs would have to be reduced or the institutional support increased.

It is common for supporters of men's basketball and football to insist that since those sports subsidize the others, more financial resources must be identified in order to not jeopardize sports like softball and wrestling. In other words, the pursuit of increased revenues by the athletic department is justified on the grounds that not doing so will imperil many sports for both genders. As University of Tennessee Athletic Director Doug Dickey put it, "[t]he biggest fans of our football program are the volleyball coach and the crew coach" (Weiner, 2002). Most athletic departments engage in interdepartmental subsidization across sports, as is readily apparent from the revenue and expense data we saw in Chapter 3. At a typical institution, most college sports — both men's and women's — lose money.[13] While men's programs as a group typically generate an overall profit, it is due almost entirely to football and basketball. In 2010, median generated revenue for men's sports exceeded costs by US$2.5 million, with football and men's basketball accounting for 91% of the revenue and 79% of the costs. (Fulks, 2011)

---

[13] Some exceptions exist. For example, men's and women's ice hockey at Wisconsin-Madison and women's basketball at Connecticut are profitable programs.

However, with many athletic departments operating in the red, it should not be surprising that some subsidized sports programs are in peril. Between 2001 and 2003, the average DI-A school reduced the total number of sports from 19 to 16 and DI-AA and DI-AAA institutions went from 19 to 15, and 16 to 14 (Fulks, 2005, p. 18). It is commonly asserted that these cuts fell predominately on men's sports and were necessary in order to protect women's sports and comply with Title IX legislation. Bill Moos, former Athletic Director at Oregon, cited this concern when arguing for further investments in the revenue sports of football and basketball: "The need to secure additional revenue streams in order to ensure our continued success is important to the future of all our sports programs. In addition, the need to add an additional sport, or perhaps sports, will be necessary in order for us to comply with Title IX requirements. The areas of access, improved amenities, and overall comfort for our fans were also important in the decision process" (Munsey and Suppes, n.d.). A counterargument is that many schools have cut sports even during periods of increased revenues to the athletic department. We return to the issues surrounding Title IX in greater detail in Chapter 8.

6.6.3   *The arms race*

The NCAA cartel has been spectacularly successful at generating huge revenues for its members, primarily through broadcasting rights for bowl games and postseason basketball competitions. The universities have supplemented this windfall with the various marketing innovations discussed in Section 6.2. On the cost side, the NCAA achieves similar success by restricting price competition for athletes. With the possible exception of graduate students in academic departments, no other unit on campus is able to hire employees without paying them a market determined wage. At the same time, the NCAA has been spectacularly unsuccessful in restricting non-price competition and the ability of member institutions to earn durable profits.

As we described in Chapter 2, an inherent problem with any cartel is that by increasing the profit per unit the incentive to steal customers from other members of the cartel increases. A firm may cheat on the cartel by charging a slightly lower price for its product or a slightly higher price for its input, or it may engage in **non-price competition**, such as advertising or improving product quality. Cheating can lead to the collapse of the cartel, and non-price competition can increase costs to the point that cartel members may earn only **normal profits** or, remarkably, a loss.

As discussed earlier, this is exactly what happened to the airline industry during the era of government regulation. Until 1978, the Federal government did not allow the airlines to charge fares lower than those set by the Civil Aeronautics Board (CAB). These fares were higher than levels that would have prevailed in a competitive market. The government was essentially forcing the airline industry to act as a cartel. To get a bigger share of this lucrative market, each airline tried to offer more of the amenities that appealed to customers, such as hot meals and free movies. They also appealed to business travelers by scheduling frequent flights, even if meant that most of their planes were only half full. Because all of the airlines engaged in this type of non-price competition, their costs went up but market shares stayed the same, resulting in lower profits for everyone.

This example provides an important lesson for the NCAA. NCAA schools are prohibited from paying large amounts to the best student-athletes, but they still want to recruit these players in order to maximize their chances of winning. How does the University of Oregon football team convince a high school all-American running back to play for the Ducks rather than some other DI-FBS team? The answer is simple: "shock and awe." As Christine Plonsky, associate athletic director at the University of Texas said, "It's all about recruiting … [w]hat you want is for kids to walk into your place and say, Wow! This is nicer than any other place I've been"(Gaul and Fitzpatrick, 2000).[14]

---

[14]Recruits are not the only ones who are impressed. Mitch Barnhart, Athletic Director at Kentucky, recounts a trip he made while he was working at Oregon State. Barnhart and Bob De Carolis, Oregon State's Athletic Director, went to Eugene, Oregon to look at new athletics facilities on the University of Oregon

When a high school football recruit makes a visit to Oregon's campus in Eugene, Oregon, his tour will include stops at Autzen Stadium, the Moshofsky Center, the Casanova Center, Matthew Knight Arena, and Jaqua Center. Autzen is the university's 54,000 seat football stadium, originally built in 1967 but renovated several times since then. The most recent refurbishment, begun in 1999 and completed in 2002, cost US$90 million and expanded seating by 12,000 (including 3,200 club seats), added 32 luxury boxes (which generate US$1 million in revenues each year) and the 10,000 square foot "Club at Autzen" (access restricted to premium seat ticket holders and boosters), and installed FieldTurf, a state-of-the-art artificial playing surface ("Autzen Stadium," 2006; Munsey and Suppes, n.d.).

The Moshofsky Center, which cost US$15 million to construct, is notable because it was the first indoor practice facility in the Pac-12. It contains a regulation sized synthetic turf football field and a four-lane track, classrooms, a souvenir shop and concession facilities open to the public during games at Autzen Stadium. An adjacent outdoor practice field includes soccer and football fields designed for year round use ("Autzen Stadium & Moshofsky Center," 2006).

The 102,000 square foot, US$12 million Casanova Center houses the football locker room, weight room, a kitchen for training table meals, trainer's room, as well as offices for coaches and athletic department administrators, conference rooms, and media studios ("Casanova Center," n.d.). The US$3.2 million football locker room features a two-story atrium lounge and "includes personalized lockers, Internet hookup, satellite television on 60-inch plasma screens, high-tech stereo equipment, an Xbox game machine, climate controls, calibrated lighting and leather couches" (Vondersmith, 2003). The lavishly appointed weight room cost US$4 million. If that is not enough, a fingerprint scanning system, right out of a *Mission Impossible* movie, controls access to the building.

---

campus. He said they were "amazed" and wondered "[w]hat have we got ourselves into ..." (Beseda, 2006).

The Matthew Knight Arena opened in January 2011 as the most expensive university-owned college arena ever built, and it maintains that status two years later (Bolt, 2011). Amenities for fans include padded seats (except the student section), while players get centralized practice and training facilities, including a pool with an underwater treadmill that can be adjusted to the height of each individual. All of the prospective athletes signing letters of intent that year mentioned it as a factor in their decision. (Clark, 2011)

Facilities are a major component in the arms race and Oregon is not the only university that is actively upgrading its athletics faculties. Here are just two of many examples:

- Penn State built the US$14.7 million football facility — the Lasch Football Building — a "wood-paneled locker room that some say is nicer than any in the NFL, a two-story weight room, a spa, and a 180-seat auditorium for viewing game film" (Gaul and Fitzpatrick, 2000). Penn State's football stadium was renovated at a cost of $85 million. The renovation included the installation of 60 luxury suites that rent for $40,000–65,000 per year.
- The University of Wisconsin opened a US$76 million multipurpose arena, the Kohl Center in 1998. A university publication describes the facility as featuring "39 luxury suites that rent for $35,000 annually … a 2300 square foot sports medicine facility [as well as a] 1600 square foot strength and conditioning room … eight state-of-the-art-locker rooms … designed with the needs of student-athletes in mind including team organizational meetings, an athletes social area, and study carrels. The athletes have a lounge area with sound system, video room, computers available in the study room, and, of course, a spacious dressing and shower area complete with multiple outlets and lighted mirrors". ("The Kohl Center," n.d.)

Facilities expansion as a part of the recruiting strategy is not limited to practice and playing facilities. As an administrator at Michigan State noted, "[t]he athletics arms race has moved to academic support" (Alexander, 2004). For example, the University of North Carolina at Chapel Hill opened the US$70 million Loudermilk Center for Excellence in 2011, including the John W. Pope Student-Athlete Support Center with classrooms for teaching and tutoring, advanced computer technology, a writing lab, reading rooms, and office space ("Alumnus Loudermilk commits," 2011). The University of Oregon's John E. Jaqua Academic Center for Student Athletes opened in 2009 at a cost of US$42 million. A three-story state-of-the-art glass cube, it was made possible by a gift from Phil and Penny Knight ("John E. Jaqua Academic Center," n.d.). Significant resources are then required to staff these facilities.

The fact that institutions spend money on recruiting visits and the construction and renovation of facilities is not conclusive evidence of excessive non-price competition. Periodically, existing facilities need to be refurbished, new buildings need to be erected, and every year athletes need to be recruited. But at what point does a "reasonable and necessary" expenditure by the athletic department become part of excessive spending to attract top athletes? One way to understand this issue is to ask the following question: if universities paid athletes an amount equal to their **marginal revenue product (MRP),** would expenditures on state-of-the-art facilities and campus visits remain the same? It is likely that athletic departments would be guided by the "reasonable and necessary" principle rather than a policy of "spend more than competing DI-FBS institutions."

The arms race continues because most school believe that they have no incentive to stand down unilaterally. The net result is that profits for athletic departments are continually eroded, to the point that some schools may contemplate abandoning their football program or divert funds from other areas of campus. As University of Oregon Professor James Earl (2003), a member of the Coalition on Intercollegiate Athletics, put it, "[a]s in the Cold War version, everyone involved seems to realize its danger … but no one sees a way out. And no school can slow down unless all the others do, too, or risk a disadvantage on the playing field. Antitrust laws even prohibit any agreement to limit spending."

Increased non-price competition is not inherently unprofitable. If the airline industry can attract more total passengers as a result of airlines competing to make the flying experience better (wider seats, frequent flights), then revenues increase along with costs. Unfortunately, this is not the case with the arms race in college football. Schools are competing for a limited number of top athletes, and NCAA rules put a limit on the number at each school. Further, the very nature of athletic competition makes it a **zero sum game**. For every winner there is a loser. To understand this, consider the following example provided by Robert Frank (2004), an economist who has studied **winner-take-all** markets in considerable detail. Suppose that 1,000 universities are considering whether or not to start an intercollegiate athletics program at a cost of US$1 million per year. Each university knows with certainty that every year the universities with the 10 best winning percentages will each collect US$10 million in the form of a payoff. In essence, each university's decision is a gamble and the decision to participate or not is influenced by the **expected value** of the gamble. Suppose further that each university's athletic program is identical in terms of the quality of its athletes, coaches, and

---

Box 6.6. Is there really an arms race in college sports?

Economist Rod Fort (Fort and Winfree, 2013, Chapter 2) questions whether the arms race model is appropriate in explaining and predicting athletic department behavior. He believes a principal–agent model provides better theoretical and explanatory value. At a minimum, Fort's argument suggests that any discussions about arms races in college sports make clear whether the formal game-theoretic assumptions of the arms race are being met, or if the phrase "arms race" is being used merely as a metaphor. In addition, Fort examines how best to evaluate the financial performance of the athletic department.

facilities to every other's. Should a university participate? The answer is "no" because in any given year the expected value is negative US$890,000![15] The only way for the average university to at least break even would be if only 100 schools competed for the 10 prizes of US$10 million. In that case, each university would, on average, collect 10 million once every 10 years, the amount exactly equal to the cost of running the program for that period of time.

6.7   Why Stay in the Game?

If a typical athletic department is losing money, or facing that prospect in the near future as the arms race continues to escalate, why do they stay in the game? Reducing spending on football and men's basketball is not an easy solution, since the school will be unable to recruit good athletes and will end up losing most of their games, but there is always the option to move down to a lower division or even drop those sports.

Put another way, why do schools engage in a gamble with a negative expected value? Frank's explanation is similar to one we encountered in Section 5.8, the tendency for individuals to overrate their chances for success. As Frank (2004, p. 9) mentions, "since it is unpleasant to think of oneself as below average, a ... solution is simply to think of oneself as above average." It should come as no surprise that the kinds of psychological biases we introduced in the previous chapter also apply to university administrators and athletic directors when they are estimating the anticipated revenues and publicity. Consequently, they tend to step into the same trap; as Frank (2004, p. 10) states, "the university administrators who decide whether to launch [or continue to support] big-time athletic programs are like normal human beings ... they are likely to overestimate the odds that their programs will be successful."

Advocates for intercollegiate sports also raise a legitimate question when they ask "if the library, or the registrar's office, or the chemistry or history departments are not required to show a profit,

---

[15] Here's the math: EV = (0.01)(US$10,000,000) + (0.99)(−US$1,000,000) = −US$890,000.

why should the athletic department be treated any differently?" The library does not charge students or faculty for their services, and yet few complain about its large annual "deficit." At the same time, academic departments that attract few students are likely to suffer a reduction in their staffing. The point is that balancing dollars against services provided is far from an exact science.

Few would deny that athletics provide a real benefit to academic institutions. The entertainment and pleasure derived from college sports plays a unique role on campuses across the nation. Consider the following perspective:

> The vast majority of faculty members in a university are intellectual workers, specialists, professionals, whose work is as grubby as that of other workers in society and just as practical ...
>
> Most, indeed, think their work is more important than that of coaches and players. Economically and socially, however, it would be difficult for them to prove that their work does have larger public significance ...
>
> Were I the president of a new state university or private college, or a member of the faculty, I would strongly encourage the development of a high-level athletic program within the realistic means of the school. The costs are great, but so are the returns — the rejoicing of the human spirit, the unifying of many ...
>
> Universities ... that have turned away from intercollegiate sports seem to suffer from a lack of lightness and fun; a kind of stuffiness and arrogance surround them ... There are not many activities that can unite janitors, cafeteria workers, sophomores, and Nobel Prize winners in common pleasure. (Novak, 1994, pp. 290–300)

Our point is not to begin a "which is more important, sports or academics" debate because we know education is far more valuable to society than sports (see Box 6.7). Like it or not, most of us understand that intercollegiate sports is an important part of university life and that many people, not just students, derive considerable **utility** from watching sports, reading about sports, and talking about sports. It is part of our culture. Moreover, sports and

Box 6.7.   The diamond-water paradox applied to college sports.

The diamond-water paradox (also referred to as the paradox of value) was of interest to the classical economists including Adam Smith. In Smith's *The Wealth of Nations* (Book I, Chapter IV, ¶ 13), he wrote that "Nothing is more useful than water; but it will purchase scarce anything; scarce anything can be had in exchange for it. A diamond, on the contrary, has scarce any value in use; but a very great quantity of other goods may frequently be had in exchange for it." The question Smith was asking is simple: why is the price of water so cheap and the price of diamonds so expensive when the value of water to us is far greater than the value of diamonds?

The paradox is easily resolved using the graphs above. The demand curve for water is drawn much farther to the right than the demand for diamonds because the demand for water is greater than for diamonds. The supply curve for water is drawn farther to the right because it is abundant while diamonds are scarce. Based on the configuration of the demand and supply curves, the equilibrium price (P*) of diamonds is greater than that of water. That should make sense: how much would you have to pay for one gallon water? For one carat of diamonds?

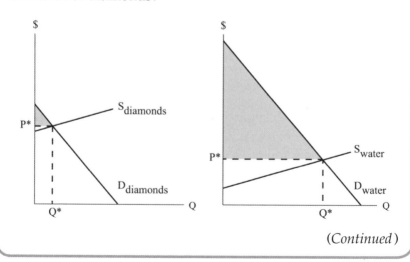

(Continued)

Box 6.7.   (Continued)

The net benefit to consumers from diamonds and water can be shown using the concept of consumer surplus, represented by the shaded area between the horizontal line at the equilibrium price and the demand curve. Notice that the value of consumer surplus for water is much higher than for diamonds.

If you think of college sports as diamonds and undergraduate education as water, then the value of education far exceeds that of college sports.

---

academics are not an "either/or" proposition; men and women can enjoy sports while simultaneously understanding and appreciating the value of higher education. That is the essence of the quotation above.

Finally, even with rising costs due to the arms race, some members of DI are profitable. We saw in Table 6.7 that about 20% of DI-A athletic departments reported a profit in the 2010, even when excluding institutional support. This gives those athletic departments a degree of financial autonomy. While the university administration may favor a move to drop out of the arms race, it is less likely that they could influence an athletic department that is not dependent on financial support. How can the president complain about a US$4 million salary package for a head football coach if the athletic department can claim that it will be entirely funded by revenue generated by the football program, and they will be able to subsidize non-revenue sports as well?

6.8   Can Athletics Be a Good Investment?

Why does a university want to promote its intercollegiate athletics program? The President of the University of Oregon, David

Frohnmayer said that Oregon athletics provide the institution with national exposure, attracts the attention of prospective students and their parents, and generates donations for both sports and academics. Recall at the beginning of the chapter, we told the tale of the University of Oregon. Oregon ran into financial difficulties and there was pressure to drop out of the then Pac-10 and reduce its financial commitment to intercollegiate sports. Oregon's president at that time fought tooth and nail not only to prevent budget cuts to the athletic department but also to increase athletics funding. The president believed that a higher profile athletic department would pay dividends in terms of increased applications and admission. He was right, Oregon athletics is now nationally recognized and the university is larger and better known. Who was Oregon's president at that time? None other than Myles Brand!

It may seem ironic that Brand condemned the arms race — a Pandora's Box he helped to open — but the empirical evidence supports his criticisms. Research suggests that spending more on athletics does not lead to more on-the-field success. During the period 1993 to 2003, Orszag and Orszag (2005, p. 6) indicate, "[w]e continue to conclude that increased operating expenditures on football or basketball are not associated with medium-term increases in winning percentages, and higher winning percentages are not associated with medium-term increase in operating revenue ..." In addition, "[o]ur statistical analyses suggest that between 1993 and 2003, an increase in operating expenditures of US$1 on football or men's basketball in Division I-A was associated with approximately US$1 in additional operating revenue, on average. The implication is that spending an extra US$1 was not associated with any increase or decrease in net revenue ..." (Orszag and Orszag, 2005, p. 5). Humphreys and Mondello (2007) estimated that postseason appearances were associated with a significant increase in restricted donations but no increase in unrestricted donations at public institutions, while only postseason tournament appearances in basketball had an effect on restricted donations to private institutions. More recently, Anderson (2012) estimated that an extra unexpected football victory increases alumni athletic donations by US$134,000, increased student applications by 1%, and improve 25th percentile SAT score by 1.8 points. However, he also notes that a simultaneous increase in spending by all schools will have a smaller effect because not all teams can increase their winning record.

The disappointing returns to investments in athletics describes what is happening at institutions like the University of Buffalo, Portland State University, and many other "wannabe" universities, especially those DI institutions outside the Bowl Championship Series (BCS). Why are schools like Buffalo and Portland State trying to run with big dogs like Alabama or Oregon? While there are many possible explanations, we will finish this chapter by exploring one with troubling implications for the state of higher education.

6.9 Beer and Circus[16]

The films *Ben-Hur*, *Gladiator*, and *Spartacus* depict the citizens of Rome being entertained with gladiatorial combat and chariot races, spectacular and violent entertainment provided by the Roman government. The Roman politicians believed that if the people were well fed, and amused by the brutal spectacles in the Circus Maximus and the Colosseum, they would be disinterested in current events — like the consolidation of political power in the hands of the Emperor and military threats to the Republic. Hence, the phrase "bread and circus" came to symbolize the victuals and entertainment provided to keep attention diverted from more pressing matters.

In his book *Beer and Circus*, Murray Sperber (2000) suggests something similar is happening in American universities. Sperber has long been a critic of the empire building and the arms race mentality demonstrated by the big-time sports programs. Unlike other critics who claim that "out-of-control" athletic departments

---

[16]This section discusses a controversial book by Maury Sperber. Sperber's book is highly critical of college sports and higher education. While the authors of this textbook may not agree with his conclusions, we believe that his viewpoint warrants inclusion.

simply need to be brought under control by university administrators, he believes that university presidents, boards of directors, and other officials actively encourage and collaborate to increase athletics spending to increase the visibility of the athletics program and the university.

Sperber claims that the modern day equivalent to "bread and circus" is "beer and circus." Instead of Roman emperors it is university presidents, and instead of Roman citizens it is undergraduate students and donors to the university. But the goal is the same: keep Romans from noticing the corruption and social decay in Roman society and politics, and keep students and donors from noticing the low quality of education.[17] If everyone is having a good time, why worry that athletic spending per athlete is as much as twelve times greater than academic spending per student, as it is in the SEC? (Desrochers, 2013)

While preparing his book, Sperber did a survey of college students around the nation. One question was "How important a factor in your decision to attend your university was the fame of the school's intercollegiate athletic teams?" One woman responded by saying, "What kind of dumb-ass chooses their college on the basis of its sports teams?" As it turns out, 56% of the male students and 26% of the women surveyed said that the prestige of the university's athletic department was very or moderately important.[18]

---

[17] Sperber (1998) quotes a university official at a school with a "big-time" program: "We certainly can't give our students a quality degree ... but at least we can encourage students to have fun, and identify with our teams while they're here ... Football Saturdays are great here, and so are winter basketball nights. In our Admissions Office literature, we have stopped saying that we provide a good education — our lawyers warned us that we could get sued for misrepresentation" (p. 509).

[18] A study by Lovaglia and Lucas (2005) buttresses Sperber's survey. However, there is evidence to the contrary. A survey of 500 high school seniors in 2000 ("Intercollegiate athletics," 2000) suggested that only 10–15% considered intercollegiate sports to be a significant consideration in their choice of college or university. Of greater weight were job and internship opportunities, student organizations, community service opportunities, and intramural sports. The report also suggested that students who most considered intercollegiate sports to

If you are the president or a member of the administration at Arizona, Florida State, Oregon, or any other DI institution, this can actually be welcome news. How do you get college-bound students to apply to your school? Convince them that they will be happy partying in Tucson, Tallahassee, or Eugene and rallying around the Wildcats, Seminoles, or Ducks.[19] As far as their education ... we will come back to that.

The beer and circus story consists of two assertions: first, greater investment in sports causes undergraduate enrollment, and the academic quality of entering students, to increase; second, donations increase with athletic success. We examine these ideas in turn.

6.9.1 *Beer and Circus — Does athletic success increase enrollment?*

The first assertion is that a successful athletic department increases awareness of the institution by potential students and their families. This is a form of advertising, designed to increase applications, student enrollment, and academic quality (a university can be more selective in admissions). Even if it only attracts a specific kind of student, one who places considerable value on the sports program, more students means more revenue for the university. Athletics gets much more media exposure than academic programs. As noted by Gordon Aubrecht, an Ohio State University physics professor, "It's not, 'Oh, yeah,

---

be an important consideration had "significantly lower SAT/ACT scores and household incomes than those who did not" (p. 3).

[19] In fairness to high school seniors everywhere, they might choose a school based partly on its athletic programs even if they have no intention to party before, during and after big games. A record of winning sports teams may convince the general public that the university's academic programs are of high quality as well. If employers are influenced by a school's reputation as a winner or loser, even subconsciously, then it makes sense for prospective students to take this into account. Sperber's survey did not ask students *why* they valued athletic success.

Ohio State, that wonderful physics department.' It's football". (Pappano, 2012)

The idea that athletic success causes increases in applications is famously expressed as the **Flutie effect**. On November 23, 1984, Boston College upset defending national champion Miami 47–45 in a nationally broadcast football game. This victory was largely the result of the last minute heroics of the quarterback, five-foot nine-inch Doug Flutie (who went on to win the Heisman Trophy). Admissions applications rose 12% at Boston College the following year and university presidents around the country started to ask themselves if they could accomplish the same result by plowing more resources into their sports program (Johnson, 2006a). Similar enrollment increases occurred elsewhere, including Georgetown when the basketball team was dominant in the mid-1980s, and at Northwestern when the football team made a surprising appearance in the 1996 Rose Bowl (Wharton, 2005). Similar effects for Boise State and the UTEP were discussed earlier in Section 6.2.[20]

Does an emphasis on a winning sports program actually increase applications and enrollment, or are these examples just isolated incidents that could have been caused by other factors? In the case of Boston College, applications had increased 12 times in a 13-year period (1970–1983), including a 17% in 1999 following a 4–7 season by the football team. The college claims that aggressive marketing, networking with alumni, and improvements to non-athletics physical capital were mostly responsible for an increase in applications and enrollments. (McDonald, 2003)

A study by Evan Osborne suggests that university administrators may actually be onto something. More spending on athletics is positively correlated (and statistically significant) with

---

[20] Sperber suggests that a beer and circus campus environment may be necessary for the Flutie effect to work. Economist Victor Matheson argues that the Flutie effect may operate in a manner similar to "loss leaders" at retail stores, with schools using athletics to get prospective students "in the door" (see Johnson, 2006b).

the SAT scores of incoming freshmen, suggesting that greater demand allows schools to be more selective. Osborne (2004, p. 61) notes that "universities with more resources ... spend more on athletics, and get better students as a result ... [s]chools spend resources on athletics because it, along with better education, is what students ... want." Pope and Pope (2009) examined the effect of college football rankings and participation in the NCAA men's basketball tournament on the number and quality (SAT scores) of student applications. They estimated an increase in applications of 2% to 8% for schools with football programs in the top 20 and basketball teams that reach the top 16. Anderson (2012) estimated that each *unexpected* victory in football increased student applications by 1%, and improve 25th percentile SAT score by 1.8 points. Winning when you are expected to win is not enough!

Other researchers have found no relationship between expenditures on athletics and quality of applicants. For example, a survey of this research by Frank (2004, p. 25) concluded that "the existing empirical literature suggest that success in big-time athletics has little, if any, systematic effect on the quality of incoming freshmen ... ." Orszag and Orszag (2005, p. 7) indicated that "no relationship exists — either positive or negative" between spending on football and men's basketball and the academic quality of undergraduate applicants.

While individual institutions may benefit from spending when it translates into athletic success, not all schools can benefit simultaneously. *First*, unless more people choose to go to college because of the excitement of college athletics (total market demand increases), each applicant will end up choosing just one school. *Second*, athletic competition is a zero sum game — for every school moving up the standings there must be one moving down. Osborne (2004, pp. 55–56) echoes this concern, "one could infer that the pursuit of athletic success by many schools simultaneously will create many losers for every winner, damaging the vast majority of schools that spend liberally in an attempt to achieve athletic success."

Box 6.8.   The effect of the death penalty at SMU.

As we noted in Section 2.9, the most severe penalty ever inflicted by the NCAA was the "death penalty" applied to Southern Methodist University (SMU) in 1987. While there is some evidence that SMU's athletic department has never fully recovered from that sanction, it remains less clear if the death penalty hurt the institution as a whole. The table below shows undergraduate enrollment trends at SMU from 1987–2006. Also, Goff (2000, p. 100) indicates that the death penalty did not reduce "SMU's ability to attract funds other than those funds that were attracted due to its becoming a national football power."

Year	Enrollment	Year	Enrollment
1987	8,794	1997	9,708
1988	8,944	1998	10,038
1989	8,924	1999	10,361
1990	8,798	2000	10,064
1991	8,746	2001	10,266
1992	8,978	2002	10,961
1993	8,931	2003	11,161
1994	9,014	2004	10,901
1995	9,172	2005	11,152
1996	9,464	2006	10,941

Source: Mr. John Kalb, SMU Office of Institutional Research, Personal communication.

6.9.2   *Beer and Circus — Does athletic success increase donations?*

The second assertion is that a high profile athletic department increases donations to the academic mission of the university. This relationship continues to be vigorously debated by scholars. The suggestion is that athletics donations cause a **positive externality**; even if donors are interested in athletics and not academics, their donations trigger additional donations by others. To put it in plainer economic terminology: donations to athletics and donations to academics are **complements**; not only do they tend to increase in the same direction, contributions to the athletic department increase athletics success and increase the publicity for the institution. This, in turn causes increased contributions for academic purposes as well as for sports, and some statistical evidence supports this assertion.[21] Stinson and Howard (2010) focus on split donors, that is, those that contribute to both academics and athletics. They conclude that these donors give larger average gifts than those making athletics-only gifts and are retained at a higher rate than those making academic-only gifts, giving them a higher lifetime value to the institution.

Other researchers disagree. They argue that athletics endowments are **substitutes** for academics, and that every US$1 donated to the athletic department causes US$1 less to be directed to academics. For example, Zimbalist (1999, p. 168) argues that no studies show a statistically significant relationship between "athletic success and general endowment gifts." Orszag and Orszag (2005, p. 7) find no relationship between increased spending on football and men's basketball and alumni donations. Frank (2004, p. 26) suggests while the "overall net effect of athletic success on alumni giving is positive, it is likely to be small." And Lombardi (2003, p. 12) notes, "[w]hile it appears that highly successful athletic programs can enhance giving to sports, it is not at all clear that sports success contributes to academic fund-raising." As mentioned earlier, Humphreys and Mondello (2007) estimated that postseason appearances were not associated with an increase in unrestricted donations at public or private institutions. More recently, Anderson (2012) estimated that each extra unexpected football victory increases alumni athletic donations by US$134,000 (a 5% increase

---

[21] See, e.g., McCormick and Tinsley (1987), Grimes and Chressanthis (1994), and Baade and Sundberg (1996).

for an average institution). However, he also notes that a simultaneous increase in spending by all schools will have a smaller effect because not all teams can increase their winning record.

Even if donations for academics and athletics are complements, not substitutes, there are other issues to consider. If athletic success does lead to increased contributions then a lack of success could reduce both kinds of contributions. Access to philanthropic donations by academic programs may be jeopardized simply because of a losing season or bad publicity about the athletic department.[22]

6.9.3   *Beer and Circus — How does an emphasis on athletics compromise the quality of education?*

Sperber's argument goes beyond the fact that university administrators think the sport is a good investment. He also states that the fixation on sports is accompanied by a profound lack of interest in undergraduate education.

There are many ways the educational mission of a university can be compromised. It may be unable to attract good faculty or not have enough resources for the library, science labs, language labs, or tutoring centers. Its classes may be too large or crowded, and classes may not be offered or offered often enough. The quality of the education provided in the classroom may be poor. Sperber emphasizes the last possibility. What is the key component in determining the quality of your education? It is probably what

---

[22] Grimes and Chressanthis (1994) found that bad publicity, especially major violations of NCAA rules, causes donations to fall. This literature is summarized in a study by Stinson and Howard (2007). They differentiate between alumni and non-alumni donations to academics and athletics. Their results point to some of the complexities involved in attempting to predict how athletic performance will impact giving. They suggest that variations in athletic success tend to impact alums and non-alums giving about the same, "team success does appear to influence donors to athletics programs more than donors to academic programs." They also conclude that the effect of athletic performance on giving is less at schools with strong academic reputations but that a larger percentage of giving was directed to athletics for all levels of schools.

goes on in class. That raises the question: what is the contribution by the professor?

What does a typical professor at a major research university want out of life? She wants a big salary and fame, and time to pursue her research interests. She wants to travel to academic conferences and take frequent sabbaticals. She wants to experience the satisfaction of pursuing her own interests and the prestige from publishing articles in academic journals and books. She wants promotions, to earn tenure and then eventually become a full professor. With promotions comes higher salary. Her research can open up other sources of revenue like financial support (grants) from foundations and government. Her research activity can become self-reinforcing; grant money can be used to "buy out" from teaching (hire a temporary replacement), which leaves more time for research. More research results in more prestige, more money, and promotion. If she achieves all of these things she will live a pretty good life. Unfortunately, she must also find the time and energy to teach.

Even professors who are not economists understand the concept of **opportunity cost**. They know that every hour in class (or preparing for class) is an hour not spent on research. They know that while helping students succeed can bring great satisfaction, less research = less prestige = less money = less satisfaction = less of everything. Professors are like other homo sapiens, they are rational and self-interested beings who want to maximize their utility. Maximization of utility requires that they respond to the incentive structure of the university.

What is the incentive structure in a modern university like Arizona, Florida State, or Oregon?[23] If you are a professor who publishes often, you will be rewarded with promotions, higher salary, a reduced teaching load, opportunities to travel, and greater prestige. You will be held in great esteem by the administration at your university, even if you are a poor teacher. But suppose you are

---

[23] These schools are among the 108 research universities rated as RU/VH (very high research activity) in the Carnegie Classification of Institutions of Higher Education. Another 99 are rated as RU/H (high research activity).

an excellent teacher but not a very good researcher. What happens? You get no rewards and probably will not get tenure and your contract will not be renewed. Once you get denied tenure you are like the woman in *The Scarlet Letter*. No one in the academic world wants anything to do with you.

What leads to a lack of research by a professor? Sometimes it is sloth, other times incompetence. But it usually comes from insufficient time. We already said that every hour in class (or preparing for class) is an hour not spent on your research. How do you capture time for research? You create it. You work evenings, you work weekends, and you reduce your commitment to your classes. You use the same notes, the same text, the same examples, the same exams, year after year after year. You reduce your office hours. You offer multiple choice exams rather than essays. You assign no writing assignments. Every hour you can "reclaim" is an hour for research, for your future success, for prestige, promotion and higher salary. Every hour in class, or preparing for class, or talking to students outside class, is like digging another foot deeper in your grave. That is the way the system works.

Are all schools like this? Absolutely not. But the schools that are most like this tend to be the same schools with a big-time sports program. And that is Sperber's point. These schools are research universities that reward faculty if they are accomplished scholars, not if they are accomplished teachers. But here is the catch; these schools cannot subsist solely from foundation and government grants, tuition from graduate students, and public subsidies; they need undergraduate tuition to survive even though they have no interest in educating undergraduates. So, how do they keep the undergraduates contented and unaware that the degree they are earning will be of little value? By encouraging them to party until the day they graduate.

Students also face an opportunity cost for their time. More studying means fewer hours to spend working to earn money, sleeping, socializing with friends, or attending the big game on Saturday (to be followed by party to celebrate the win or commiserate over the loss). A study by Lindo *et al.* (2012) examined transcripts for 29,737 University of Oregon students from 1999 to 2007 and compared grades to the football team's record. In years when the team won more games, the GPA for men during the fall term (football season) decreased, while women's grades were not affected. These researchers also conducted a survey of 263 students enrolled in economics courses in 2011. These students also reported studying less, drinking more, and partying more when the football team was successful, although many fewer women reported a decrease in studying.

According to Sperber, with a few exceptions, most students understand that there is a nonaggression pact — a "live and let live" policy — between faculty and undergraduate students.[24] This is also known as the "I pretend to teach if you pretend to learn" phenomenon. I will make this class as easy as possible for you. I will put a copy of my lecture notes on library reserve (the same notes I prepared 10 years ago). I will ask the same exam questions I have been asking for the last 10 years. All exams will be multiple-choice. I will do nothing to deter cheating. We will watch at least one video every week. I will use a very generous curve and most of you, regardless of whether you have learned anything, will get an A or B. If you want to use class time to read a magazine, talk to your friends, pass notes, eat your lunch, check text messages, or listen to your iPod, go ahead. In fact, if you prefer skipping class entirely, I do not grade by attendance. I discourage questions and I will be impossible to find outside of class. Go ask the teaching assistants; that is why they are here. And by the way, I have tenure so you are stuck with me; I cannot get fired. Do not ask me about a

---

[24] Sperber does mention some exceptions; here's one student comment from his survey: "In my four years at Michigan State, I have had exactly four classes under twenty-five students and a real professor in charge. All the rest of my courses have been jumbo lectures with hundreds of students, and a professor miles away, or classes with TAs, or not regular faculty, people who come in off the street and teach a course or two" (Sperber, 2000, p. 78).

letter of recommendation for a job or grad school because I do not know anything about you — you are just one of 499 other students in this class — and that is the way I like it (over 80% of DI-FBS schools have enrollments in excess of 20,000). Hopefully, you can party a lot, watch the Wildcats, Seminoles or Ducks play, and leave with a completely worthless degree. Just be sure to pay your tuition on time. As John Belushi's character in the film *Animal House* said, "seven years of college down the drain."

Is the Beer and Circus story accurate? We will leave that to you to decide. But Sperber is not the only person suggesting that undergraduate education is being compromised by athletics (see, e.g., Twitchell, 2004, pp. 167–191; Gerdy, 2006). What do you think? Do you believe that athletics are overemphasized at your university? Do you have large classes taught mostly by teaching assistants (TAs)? Are your professors hard to find and uninterested in talking to you? Are your fellow students attending the university mainly for booze, parties, sex, and sports? When you are in your Wednesday morning macroeconomics class with Professor Tedious, do you find yourself dreaming about the weekend and the big game and the keggers? Are you getting a good education? Do you care? Does the faculty at your university care? Does anyone?

6.10   Chapter Summary

We began this chapter by introducing you to some common kinds of athletic department revenues and expenses. Then, we presented evidence that suggests that with only a handful of exceptions, the typical DI-FBS athletic department loses money and requires subsidies, usually from student activity fees and the university's general fund. We stressed that subsidization is not inconsistent with university policy. Operational units like academic departments, administration, or the library are not required to show a profit; why should sports? However, unlike other units, athletic departments are engaged in an arms race, a race in which there are more losers than winners.

What should be done about the profligate spending at DI-FBS institutions? We will get to that in Chapter 9. But first, we want you to learn about two more important topics: the role of the media in college sports, and discrimination in intercollegiate athletics.

6.11   Key Terms

Appearance guarantee	Personal seat license
Arms race	Positive externality
Average cost	Premium seating
Beer and circus	Premium ticket pricing
Boosters	Price elasticity of demand
Complements	Second degree price
Corporate sponsorships	discrimination
Endowment	Substitutes
Excess capacity	Sweatshops
Expected value	Third degree price
Flutie effect	discrimination
Marginal cost	Utility
Marginal revenue product	Willingness to pay
Naming rights	Winner-take-all
Non-price competition	Zero sum game
Normal profits	

6.12   Review Questions

1. Other than tickets for college sports games, what other examples of second degree price discrimination can you think of? What other businesses use second degree price discrimination by charging a fixed fee (a license to buy) and a separate usage fee?
2. What are the pros and cons of booster contributions? If you were a university president, what restrictions, if any, would you impose on booster contributions?

3. Apply the diamond-water paradox to a concept covered in Chapter 5.
4. Why is it important to differentiate between average costs and marginal costs when determining the cost of an athletics scholarship?
5. If the NCAA allowed student-athletes to be paid the value of their MRP, what impact would this have on the importance of campus visits for recruiting?
6. Summarize reasons why an athletic department might want to inflate its losses or deflate its profits.
7. Describe how non-price competition can decrease the profitability of an athletic department.
8. Suppose that there are 100 schools competing for the 10 prizes of US$10 million each, and that the cost of competing is US$1 million per year. Calculate the expected value of the gamble.

6.13   Discussion Questions

1. Is your school part of the overall arms race in higher education, that is, has it built or upgraded academic or non-academic facilities to attract more students? Who pays for new facilities on your campus?
2. How much of a subsidy does the athletic department at your school receive from the school's general fund? How much from student fees?
3. Choose any DI school. Go to the athletic department or athletics web page and see if there is a link to a booster club. What sort of benefits do boosters get that are unavailable to the average student at that school?
4. What national sponsorships does your school's athletic department have? What local sponsorships?
5. If you were a university administrator, what rules would you impose on corporate sponsorships of athletics?
6. Should athletes be forced to wear athletics apparel and equipment provided by corporate sponsors? If you were a

student-athlete, can you think of circumstances in which you might be reluctant to support a corporate sponsor of your team?

7. Do naming rights only apply to sports facilities? Can you think of any non-sports facilities or academic programs on your campus that are "named?"

8. Is athletic department independence from the authority of the university desirable? You may remember from your macroeconomics or money and banking classes that the Fed does not rely on Congressional appropriations (unlike, e.g., the Department of the Treasury). The Fed generates its own income from interest earned on government securities and payments for services provided to banks and other financial institutions. The Fed has freedom to act with less political interference. This independence is generally thought to be beneficial for our country because it prevents monetary policy from becoming politicized (for example, it prevents Congress from manipulating the money supply and interest rates to serve its own interests). Is athletic department independence from the authority of the university similarly desirable?

9. Should an athletic department show a profit? Describe reasons why it may be unnecessary or undesirable for the department to earn a profit. Describe reasons why it may be the department should earn a profit?

10. You are the president at a DI-FBS public university like UC-Berkeley. Your athletic department is losing millions of dollars each year. You and the AD must prepare a plan to bring athletics to a point where it is close to breaking even. What actions will you take in the short run to achieve the objective? What actions in the long run?

11. Assume that there are two universities, the University of Boregon and Boregon State University. Use the prisoners' dilemma model from Chapter 2 to show why schools have an incentive to engage in the arms race. Your available strategies are "spend high" and "spend low." For the payoffs use the net

revenue, the athletic department expects to receive depending on the outcome of the game.

12. How would the quality of education change if professors at DI universities were paid to teach rather than do research?
13. At your school, and in your experience, is there any evidence that Sperber's "Beer and Circus" story is true?
14. Can a "Beer and Circus" environment exist without a Greek system and/or a "college town" atmosphere? Can you think of any other factors that contribute to "Beer and Circus?"

6.14   Assignments/Internet Questions

1. Go to the USA Today database (http://www.usatoday.com/sports/college/schools/finances/) and select any DI-FBS institution. Calculate the percentage of revenue for each category and compare to the data in Table 6.2. Do the same for expenses and compare to Table 6.5.
2. Go to the ESPN database for 2008 (http://espn.go.com/ncaa/revenue) and select any DI-FBS institution. Calculate the percentage of revenue for each category and compare to the data in Table 6.2. Do the same for expenses and compare to Table 6.5.
3. Go to the U.S. Department of Education's OPE database (http://www.ope.ed.gov/athletics) and select any DI-FBS institution. Using total revenue and total expenses for each team (by sport and gender), calculate net revenue and identify which teams generated a positive net revenue.
4. Skim the last three issues of the *Sports Business Journal* and see what new marketing innovations are being used by pro sports franchises and by college athletic departments. Are any of the new pro innovations not yet at the college level? If your library does not subscribe, headlines and brief descriptions are also available at http://www.sportsbusinessdaily.com/journal.aspx.
5. Choose any three DI schools. Go the athletic department or athletics web page and see if there is a link to a booster club. Download the information for all three schools and compare and contrast.

6. Go to www.ballparks.com, select football and then present NCAA stadiums. Choose a conference and then a particular stadium. Have there been any major renovations in the past 10 years, including the addition of luxury boxes and other amenities?

6.15   References

Adams, R. (2005, November 12). Why Your School Has Hope. *Wall Street Journal*. Retrieved from http://online.wsj.com/public/article/ SB113174157617795065f9lKtBJ5ZyxlE44iTr6fMNSCsqQ_20061114. html?mod=rss_free on August 6, 2006.

Adams, R. (2006, March 11). College Basketball: Pay For Playoffs. *Wall Street Journal*, p. P1.

Adidas Says It Won't Make Arkansas Player Wear Its Shoes (2005, October 20). *SportsLine.com*. Retrieved from http://www.sportsline. com/collegebasketball/story/8987679 on August 12, 2006.

Alabama Banned From Bowl Games for Two Years (2002, February 1). *ESPN.com*. Retrieved from http://espn.go.com/ncf/news/2002/ 0201/1321198.html on September 8, 2006.

Alexander, C. (2004, September 18). Tutors Serve As a New Recruit Tool: Sports 'Arms Race' Touts Academics. *News & Observer*, p. A1.

Alumnus Loudermilk Commits $7.5 Million To Support Facilities for Student Athletes (2011, April 8). *uncnews.unc.com*. Retrieved from http://uncnews.unc.edu/content/view/4446/68/ on June 20, 2013.

Anderson, M. (2012). The benefits of college athletic success: An application of the propensity score design with instrumental variables, NBER Working Paper No. 18196.

Armstrong, D. (2005, March 14). Winning by losing. *Wall Street Journal*. p. R10.

Autzen Stadium. (2006, August 31). *GoDucks.com*. Retrieved from http:// www.goducks.com/ViewArticle.dbml?SPSID=3802&SPID=252&DB_ OEM_ID=500&ATCLID=22175 on September 5, 2006.

Autzen Stadium & Moshofsky Center (2006, January 14). *GoDucks.com*. Retrieved from http://www.goducks.net/sports/football/autzen. shtml on September 5, 2006.

Baade, R. and J. Sundberg (1996, December). Fourth down and gold to go? Assessing the link between athletics and alumni giving. *Social Science Quarterly*, 77, 789–803.

Bachman, R. (2006a, January 29). E-mails: To measure the interest of prospects, coaches are turning to companies that utilize modern technology. *The Oregonian*, p. C01.

Bachman, R. (2006b, January 29). UO's creative recruiting. *The Oregonian*, p. C07.

Bailey, B. (2005, October 23). Sooner Born, Sooner Dead. *OUDaily.com*. Retrieved from http://www.oudaily.com/vnews/display.v/ART/2005/10/13/434f2a222197a on August 10, 2006.

Belzer, J. (2013, February 19). Elimination of Guarantee Games Increases Likelihood of NCAA Breakup. *Forbes.com*. Retrieved from http://www.forbes.com/sites/jasonbelzer/2013/02/19/elimination-of-guarantee-game-increases-likelihood-of-ncaa-breakup/ on June 24, 2013.

Beseda, J. (2006, July 30). Bob the builder. *The Oregonian*, p. B1.

Bishop, G. (2013, February 19). A Company That Runs Prisons Will Have Its Name On a Stadium. *The NY Times*, p. B11.

Bolt, G. (2001, May 31). Athletic Department Subsidy At University To Be Phased Out. *The Eugene Register-Guard*, p. 1B.

Bolt, G. (2011, January 4). Legacy Fund Gives You a Leg Up On financing, *The Register Guard*, p. E7.

Brady, E. and J. Upton (2005, November 17). NCAA recognizes growing problem with costs. *USA Today*. Retrieved from http://www.usatoday.com/sports/college/2005–11–17-financial-report_x.htm on March 4, 2006.

Brand, M. (2005). NCAA President Calls For Value-based Budgeting for Intercollegiate Athletics Programs. *NCAA.org*. Retrieved from http://www2.ncaa.org/media_and_events/press_room/2005/january/20050108_soa_speech.html on December 6, 2006.

Buker, P. (2005, September 6). Broncos' bid to take it up a notch takes a hit. *The Oregonian*, p. D01.

Campaign for Penn Athletics Naming Opportunities (2010, November 3). Retrieved from http://www.pennathletics.com/pdf8/720690.pdf on July 11, 2013.

Carey, J. (2009, September 3). For Small Schools, There's a Big Payoff to Road Trips. *USAToday.com*. Retrieved from http://usatoday30.usatoday.com/sports/college/football/2009-09-02-smallschool_payoffs_N.html on June 24, 2013.

Casanova Center (n.d.). *GoDucks.com*. Retrieved from http://www.goducks.com/ViewArticle.dbml?SPSID=3802&SPID=252&DB_OEM_ID=500&ATCLID=22183 on September 5, 2006.

Clark, B. (2011, January 4). Amenities Put Men's Team in Hoops Heaven. *The Register Guard*, p. E6.

Coroner Examining Brutal Death of Alabama Booster (2006, April 12). *CSTV.com*. Retrieved from http://www.cstv.com/sports/m-footbl/ stories/041206aao.html on September 10, 2006.

Desrochers, D. (2013). *Academic Spending Versus Athletic Spending: Who Wins?* Washington, DC: American Institutes for Research.

Duderstadt, J. J. (2000). *Intercollegiate Athletics and The American University*. Ann Arbor, MI: University of Michigan Press.

Earl, J. W. (2003, August 10). The athletics arms race. *The Oregonian*, p. F01.

Fish, M. (2005, October 22). The Crimson Hide: How Vols Boosters Dug Up The Dirt That Sent 'Bama's Biggest Braggart To The Big House. *ESPN.com*. Retrieved from http://sports.espn.go.com/espn/eticket/ story?page=crimson on July 18, 2006.

Forestry dean at Oregon State U. draws fire for role in research controversy (2006, May 19). *The Chronicle of Higher Education News Blog*. Retrieved from chronicle.com/news/article/464/forestry-dean-at-oregon-state-u-draws-fire-for-role-in-research-controversy on May 25, 2006.

Fort, R. and J. Winfree (2013). *15 Sports Myths and Why They're Wrong*. Palo Alto: Stanford University Press.

Frank, R. (2004). *Challenging the myth: A review of the links among college athletic success, student quality, and donations*. Knight Foundation Commission on Intercollegiate Athletics. Retrieved from http://www. knightfdn.org/default.asp?story=publications/2004_frankreport/ index.html on May 10, 2005.

Fulks, D. (2005). *2002–2003 NCAA Revenues and Expenses of Divisions I and II Intercollegiate Athletics Programs Report*. Indiana, IN: National Collegiate Athletics Association.

Fulks, D. (2011). *2004–2010 NCAA Revenues and Expenses of Division I Intercollegiate Athletics Programs Report*. Indiana, IN: National Collegiate Athletics Association.

Fulks, D. (2013). *2004–2012 NCAA Revenues and Expenses of Division I Intercollegiate Athletics Programs Report*. Indiana, IN: National Collegiate Athletics Association.

Gaul, G. and F. Fitzpatrick (2000, September 12). On campus, an edifice complex. *Philadelphia Inquirer*, p. A01.

Gerdy, J. (2006). *Air ball: American Education's Failed Experiment With Elite Athletics*. Jackson, MS: University of Mississippi Press.

Goff, B. (2000). Effects of university athletics on the university: A review and extension of empirical assessment. *Journal of Sport Management*, 14, 85–104.

Grimes, P. W. and G. A. Chressanthis (1994). Alumni contributions to academics: The role of intercollegiate sports and NCAA sanctions. *American Journal of Economics and Sociology*, 53(1), 27–40.

Humphreys, B. and M. Mondello (2007). Intercollegiate athletic success and donations at Division I Institutions. *Journal of Sport Management*, 21, 265–280.

John E Jaqua Academic Center for Student Athletes (n.d.). *GoDucks. com*. Retrieved from http://www.goducks.com/ViewArticle.dbml? ATCLID=205015255 on July 12, 2012.

Johnson, G. (2006a, July 31). The Flutie Effect. *NCAA News*, p. 5.

Johnson, G. (2006b, December 22). Football Success Gives Schools Reason to Cheer. *Los Angeles Times*. Retrieved from http://www.latimes. com/sports/college/football/la-sp-bcs22dec22,1,4920072.story? coll=la-headlines-sports on December 24, 2006.

Lindo, J., I. Swensen and G. Waddell (2012). Are big-time sports a threat to student achievement? *American Economic Journal: Applied Economics*, 4(4), 254–274.

Lombardi, J. V. (2003). *The Sports Imperative in America's Research Universities*. Gainsville, FL: University of Florida, The Center. Retrieved from http://mup.asu.edu/TheSportsImperative.pdf on April 10, 2012.

Lovaglia, M. and J. Lucas (2005, Winter). High visibility athletic programs and the prestige of public universities. *The Sport Journal*, 8. Retrieved from http://www.thesportjournal.org/2005Journal/Vol8-No1/ michael_lovaglia.asp on December 17, 2005.

Mandina, C. (2009, August 27). Michigan Big House Suites Cost up to $85K PerYear. *MLive.com*. Retrieved from http://www.mlive.com/ wolverines/football/index.ssf/2009/08/michigan_big_house_ suites_cost.html on June 23, 2013.

Martin, A. (2012, December 14). Building a showcase campus, using an I.O.U. *The New York Times*, p. A1.

McCormick, R. and M. Tinsley (1987). Athletics versus academics? Evidence from SAT scores. *Journal of Political Economy*, 95, 1103–1116.

McDonald, B. (2003, Spring). The "Flutie factor" is Now Received Wisdom. But Is It True? *Boston College Magazine*. Retrieved from http://bcm.bc.edu/issues/spring_2003/ll_phenomenology.html on May 12, 2004.

Michigan Fan Demographics (n.d.). *MGoBlue.com*. Retrieved from http://www.mgoblue.com/document_display.cfm?document_id=10571 on February 20, 2006.

Munsey, P. and C. Suppes (n.d.). Autzen Stadium. *Ballparks*. Retrieved from http://football.ballparks.com/NCAA/Pac10/Oregon/index.htm on December 6, 2006.

NCAA Division I Update for Longwood University (2003). *Longwood University Lancers*. Retrieved from http://www.longwoodlancers.com/Sports/gen/2003/Division%20I%20Update.asp on May 5, 2005.

NCAA Division I Reclassification Timeline (2005). *Longwood University Lancers*. Retrieved from http://www.longwoodlancers.com/Pdfs/gen/2005/11/6/NCAADIReclassification.pdf on August 10, 2006.

Nebraska Locks Up Arkansas State (2012, September 13). *ESPN.com*. Retrieved from http://espn.go.com/college-football/story/_/id/8374015/nebraska-pay-arkansas-state-1-million-guarantee-1-game on June 24, 2013.

Novak, M. (1994). *The Joy Of Sports: Endzones, Bases, Baskets, Balls and the Consecration Of the American Spirit* (Rev. ed.). Lanham, MD: Madison Books.

Oregon State Board of Higher Education (2005, January 6). Fiscal status of intercollegiate athletics as of June 30, 2005.

Orszag, J. M. and P. R. Orszag (2005). *The Empirical Effects of Collegiate Athletics: An Update*. Washington, DC: Competition Policy Associates.

Osborne, E. (2004). Motivating college athletics. In J. Fizel and R. Fort (Eds.), *Economics of College Sports* (pp. 51–62). Westport, CT: Praeger.

Pappano, L. (2012, January 22). How Big-Time Sports Ate College Life. *The New York Times*, p. ED22.

Pittman, A. (2001, June 21). Inflated Ducks. *Eugene Weekly*. Retrieved from http://www2.eugeneweekly.com/2001/06_21_01/coverstory.html on December 6, 2006.

Pope, D. and J. Pope (2009). The impact of college sports success on the quantity and quality of student applications. *Southern Economic Journal*, 75(3), 750–780.

Sherman. M. (2013, May 3). NCAA suspends recruiting proposals. *ESPN.com*. Retrieved from http://espn.go.com/college-sports/recruiting/story/_/is/9237054/ncaa-suspends-rule-change-unlimited-text-messages-recruits on June 28, 2013.

Smith, M. (2011, September 5). IMG's reach creates big college platform for UPS, *Sports Business Journal*. Retrieved from http://m.sports

businessdaily.com/Journal/Issues/2011/09/05/Marketing-and-Sponsorship/IMG-UPS.aspx on June 18, 2013.

Sperber, M. (1998). *Onward To Victory: The Creation of Modern College Sports.* New York: Henry Holt.

Sperber, M. (2000). *Beer and Circus: How Big-Time College Sports is Crippling Undergraduate Education.* New York: Henry Holt.

Stern, C. S. (2003). The faculty role in the reform of intercollegiate athletics: Principles and recommended practices. *Academe,* 89(1), 64–70.

Stinson, J. L. and D. R. Howard (2007). Athletic success and private giving to athletic and academic programs at NCAA institutions. *Journal of Sport Management,* 21(2), 235–264.

Stinson, J. L. and D. R. Howard (2010). Athletic giving and academic giving: exploring the value of SPLIT donors. *Journal of Sport Management,* 24(6), 744–768.

Text-messaging ban to be implemented Aug. 1 (2007, April 26). *ESPN.com.* Retrieved from http://sports.espn.go.com/ncaa/news/story?id=2850555 on June 1, 2013.

The Kohl Center (n.d.). *UWBadgers.com.* Retrieved from http://www.uwbadgers.com/facilities/kohl_center/index_47.html on September 5, 2006.

Twitchell, J. (2004). *Branded Nation: The Marketing Of Megachurch, College Inc., And Museumworld.* New York: Simon and Schuster.

Upton, J. and S. Berkowitz (2013, March 6). Athletic Directory Salary Database. *USA Today.* Retrieved from http://www.usatoday.com/story/sports/college/2013/03/06/athletic-director-salary-database-methodology/1968783/ on July 11, 2013.

Upton, J. and E. Brady (2005, October 18). Errors Mar Equity Reports. *USA Today.* Retrieved from http://www.usatoday.com/sports/college/2005–10–18-equity-reports-cover_x.htm on August 12, 2006.

Vondersmith, J. (2003, November 7). Duck Vets Have Known Good and Bad. *Portland Tribune.* Retrieved from http://www.portlandtribune.com/sports/story.php?story_id=21238 on March 10, 2004.

Weiner, J. (2002, August 18). College Football 2002 Arms Race: Gophers Trail in 'Arms Race.' *Star Tribune.* Retrieved from http://www.highbeam.com/doc/1G1–90510383.html on September 20, 2002.

Wharton, D. (2005, December 30). Success Yields Few Startling Admissions. *The Los Angeles Times,* p. D1.

Zimbalist, A. (1999). *Unpaid Professionals: Commercialism and Conflict in Big-Time College Sports.* Princeton, NJ: Princeton University Press.

Chapter 7

The Media and Intercollegiate Sports

Coaches get put under the pressure of not graduating ... players ... but then you're going to play during the week .... the NCAA wants to talk about ... graduation rates, but they allow — and TV dictates it — that kids go out and miss classes due to games during the week.

— Randy Edsall, UConn Football Coach

The financial stake in television revenues of those colleges and universities with big-time programs has become enormous, ... even those schools with Division III programs share modestly in the revenues generated by the NCAA contract to televise "March madness."

— James Schulman and William Bowen,
authors of *The Book of Life*

7.1 Introduction

As noted in earlier chapters, network contracts provide the National Collegiate Athletic Association (NCAA) and its members with hundreds of millions of dollars in annual revenue. CBS and Turner Sports' deal to broadcast the NCAA basketball tournament games will pay the NCAA US$10.8 billion over a 14-year period. The payments of nearly US$771 million a year represent a 41% increase over the previous 11-year contract. The agreement also locked in expansion of the tournament field to 68 teams, up from 65 (O'Toole, 2010). During the 2013–2014 college football bowl season, 70 teams (over half of the Division I-FBS teams) played in 35 games, splitting over US$286 million in bowl revenue. The largest payouts, US$22 million per team, went to the two participants in the Bowl Championship Series (BCS) National Championship Game, and an additional US$18 million per team went to schools in the elite conferences that have agreements with the organizers of the other four BCS games ("2013–2014 College Football Bowl Game Schedule," n.d.). Entertainment and Sports Programming Network (ESPN) held exclusive rights to broadcast all BCS bowl games through 2014, including the BCS National Championship game. These rights came at a cost of US$155 million a year to ESPN, who outbid previous rights holder FOX Sports. On November 21, 2012, ESPN agreed to pay over US$500 million per year for the rights to broadcast, across multiple media platforms, all six bowl games, plus the national championship game, of the new four-team college football playoff system, starting in January 2015. ("ESPN lands rights," 2012)

In this chapter, we look at the relationship between the media and college sports. We first look at how media coverage has expanded in recent years. Next, we examine the questions of whether and why the media and college sports think they need each other for their economic well-being, and how media coverage has changed college sports. Finally, we look beyond the media and colleges to assess the wider impacts on the economy and society.

7.2   Recent Expansion of Sports Media

For many years college sports fans turned to the major networks (ABC, CBS, and NBC) for coverage of games. One or two games on a Saturday were the most one could hope for, except for special events like the college football bowl games on New Year's Day. The first network devoted to sports programming, ESPN, began broadcasting on September 7, 1979. Fans could now watch sports programming 24 hours a day, 7 days a week, but expansion of the sports media did not stop there. Since 1979, ESPN has added new television networks (including ESPNU, ESPNU HD, ESPN2, ESPNEWS, ESPN Classic, ESPN International, ESPN HD, and ESPN 3D, and Spanish-language ESPN Deportes), digital television channels ESPN Now and ESPN Extra, ESPN Radio, *ESPN The*

Magazine, the website ESPN.com, and multiple sports-based entertainment venues called ESPN Zone. ESPN programming is now available in more than 98 million U.S. homes, which represents 220 million Americans and nearly 86% of all American homes owning a television. ("BCS, ESPN reach deal," 2008)

College Sports TV (CSTV) was the first network devoted exclusively to college sports. CSTV debuted in early 2003, and launched its first full season of programming in August 2003. Its first fall lineup included the usual fare of college football games, preview and highlight shows, but CSTV also provided regular coverage of soccer (men's and women's) and volleyball ("CSTV kicks off," 2003). While the primary focus remains on football and basketball, CSTV, along with its website, CSTV.com, now covers virtually every college sport, from baseball to wrestling, bowling to ultimate Frisbee. Purchased for US$325 million in November 2005, CSTV is now a division of CBS Corporation ("CBS officially acquires CSTV," 2006). Its digital television service reaches more than 21 million households, and its Internet division, CSTV.com, contains a network of about 215 official college athletic websites. ("About us," n.d.[a])

ESPN, wanting its piece of the college-only sports market, launched ESPNU on March 4, 2005. ESPNU programming and content appears not only on television, but across the range of print, internet, radio and mobile media offered by ESPN. FOX College Sports, a third entrant into the college sports broadcast market, is part of the FOX Sports network of stations. FOX College Sports is separated geographically into FCS Pacific, FCS Central, and FCS Atlantic, with its programming coming from the 20 FSN and FSN affiliated regional sports networks. Like CSTV, ESPNU and FOX College Sports cover a wide range of college sports, and all three networks also provide limited coverage of high school sports, mainly to give college sports fans a taste of what is to come.

Sport broadcasting occurs in an **oligopoly**, that is, a market with a relatively small number of producers. Depending on their structure and the number of firms involved, oligopolies can be more or less competitive. As we've just seen, the number of networks has grown over recent years with the additions of FOX, ESPN, and CSTV. While this has worked to make the market appear more competitive, this is deceiving given that ABC owns 80% of ESPN, and CSTV is owned by CBS. Mergers and buyouts of the networks are examples of **horizontal integration**, a strategy of acquiring multiple firms at the same stage of production in an industry that can effectively limit competition, to the benefit of the remaining firms.

New competition in the sports broadcasting market has emerged from the conferences themselves. In summer 2006, the Big Ten conference signed a deal with FOX Cable Networks to create the Big Ten Channel. Debuting in August 2007, the Big Ten Channel features sporting events of the 12 member schools, as well as non-sports programming. Each university is allowed to provide 60 hours of programming each year. In the view of Big Ten Commissioner James Delany, "this will create enormous opportunities for journalism, film, and other academic programs and provide the ability to highlight academic achievement throughout the universities" ("FCN to create the Big Ten Channel," 2007). Other conferences, seeing the success of the Big Ten Channel have launched their own networks. In July 2011, less than four weeks after officially renaming the conference, the Pacific-12 announced the creation of the Pac-12 Network. The ACC, Big East, Big 12, SEC, and many non-BCS conferences have separate conference broadcast arrangements with ABC, CBS, ESPN, and FOX.

An interesting component of the Big Ten Channel is that in keeping with conference branding standards, the channel presents no alcohol or gambling-related advertising ("FCN to create the Big Ten Channel," 2007). Given the prevalence of beer advertisements in sports broadcasts, this will likely affect the marketing strategy of beer producers. Likewise, the Big Ten Channel will likely receive less revenue from advertisers, as demand for advertising slots will be lower than for broadcasts on other networks.

Fast fact. *Offered through major cable companies such as Time Warner, Insight, and WOW, ESPN and ESPN2 are available in more than 98 million U.S. homes. ESPNU, however, is generally only offered through satellite companies like DirecTV or The Dish Network, or through premium cable packages. The result is that ESPNU can only be seen regularly in about 74 million homes. In fall 2006, when only about 22 million households had ESPNU, the Disney Corporation, parent company for both ESPN and ABC, stepped up its efforts to make ESPNU part of standard cable packages. Holding the rights to broadcast Big Ten conference football games, Disney opted to show the October 19 game pitting number-one ranked Ohio State v. Indiana on ESPNU, effectively shutting out hundreds of thousands of angry viewers in Ohio. Earlier in the season, Penn State's season opener was also shown on ESPNU, much to the chagrin of Nittany Lion fans. Disney's strategy was to apply pressure on the cable companies by having disgruntled fans complain to their cable providers and threaten to switch companies. Meanwhile, the Big Ten worked with FOX to create the Big Ten Network, to keep fans happy and avoid being caught in what they see as "Mickey Mouse" negotiating tactics. In 2009, Disney and Comcast announced the inclusion of ESPNU into standard cable packages, raising access from around 9 million homes to the nearly 74 million homes currently served.*

As the list of ESPN "channels" reveals, expansion of the media is not limited to television broadcasts. In 2012, for example, ESPN.com had an average audience of 77,000 per minute, and this does not include the visitors to ESPN's other online sport- and market-specific sites ("ESPN, Inc. fact sheet," n.d.). CSTV.com claims to be the "most-trafficked college sports web site," with over 100 broadband channels devoted to college sports, and nearly 10,000 live events ("About us," n.d.[a]). Access to games, scores, and other sports news is also readily available through mobile web and apps technology.

As the technology allows, media providers adapt the sports broadcast product to reach every potential revenue-generating fan.

Fast fact. In the 1930s, while other schools were selling their radio broadcast rights, the University of Notre Dame gave theirs away to anyone wanting to broadcast Notre Dame Football. Notre Dame claimed it was acting in the spirit of both amateur sports and its religious convictions, but the end result was a huge financial payoff. Notre Dame built a nationwide fan base and is now the only major college football team with its own network contract (with NBC, for 2011–2015 estimated to be worth over US$15 million per year).

Why would Disney, which owns ABC and ESPN, offer so many channels and means of delivering content? Obviously, Disney believes that such expansion will increase profits, but let's look a little deeper to see how that might work. On the surface, one might question the proliferation of channels, given that they are all substitutes for each other. Except perhaps at a sports bar, or using "picture in picture" technology, one can only watch one station at a time. All television channels compete with each other for viewers' attention; they simultaneously compete with other delivery methods such as radio and internet broadcasts. There are a limited number of both potential viewers and advertisers, so to the extent that ESPN broadcasts compete with events on ABC, ESPN2, ESPNU, etc., Disney is fighting with itself over limited potential revenue. In earlier chapters, we introduced the concept of marginal revenue product (MRP). The MRP for additional channels in the sports market is relatively low, but Disney is betting that it is sufficiently positive to cover the costs of providing new channels.

What makes Disney's expansion of channels and media viable is that it can do so at a relatively low cost. In the language of economics, Disney is able to exploit both **economies of scale** and **economies of scope**. Economies of scale exist when a firm is able to lower its per-unit production costs by producing a large amount of the good it sells. Economies of scale extend over a large range of output when there is large and expensive capital used in production, and when firms can achieve extensive labor and managerial specialization, such as in the production of automobiles, software, or pharmaceuticals. In creating the college sports product, production facilities (studios, communication equipment) are large and expensive forms of capital. As long as it does not push past the existing capacity, a network can produce additional programming with those facilities at relatively little cost. The cost of facilities and management gets spread out over a larger quantity of sports content, lowering the average cost of each sporting event produced.

Economies of scale are also facilitated by **simultaneous consumption**, which refers to a product's ability to satisfy multiple users at the same time. Unlike a car or a cup of coffee, a sports broadcast can be enjoyed by millions of viewers simultaneously, and at little or no additional cost to the seller. Like computer software or downloadable music, any given sports broadcast need only be produced once to be available to millions of potential consumers. As the number of consumers increases, per-unit costs fall.

Economies of scope exist when a firm can reduce the cost per unit (and/or expand revenues) by using its resources more efficiently to produce a wider range of products. For example, in filming movies and television shows (sports or otherwise), there are often "out-takes," parts cut out because the performer misspoke a line or couldn't keep a straight face during a serious scene. These out-takes, also referred to as "bloopers," are a by-product of the process of filming. Over the years, studios and networks have learned that this "waste" can have economic value if turned into its own programming. Use of by-products in this way creates economies of scope. Most of the costs have already been incurred; the cost of collecting and editing the out-take footage is relatively small. For the sports product, such by-products include highlight reels, used in end-of-the day sports news shows, or sometimes as a stand-alone show of great plays with additional commentary to provide context or other important information.

Another way for companies like Disney and FOX to achieve economies of scope is through re-broadcasting events, or broadcasting over different media. Once a network has purchased the rights for and produced an event, the cost to re-broadcast or send it in a different form (over the Internet as well as the television) is insignificant. ESPN Classic, for example, shows replays of particularly memorable championship or rivalry games. ESPN and ESPNEWS often replay the day's sports highlight shows multiple times, keeping costs lower and giving viewers numerous opportunities to catch up with news on their favorite teams.

ESPN's new line of networks and platforms is an example of **brand proliferation**. By dramatically expanding its product line, ESPN is attempting to fill as many niches in the market as possible. Economies of scope facilitate this process by expanding, at relatively low cost, the content available for broadcasting. Brand proliferation creates a barrier to entry, as potential entrants into the market will have trouble finding areas of service where they can establish a foothold with consumers. It also helps ESPN exploit economies of scale in production and advertising. Programming and advertisements can be transferred easily among the various channels and media, dropping the per-unit cost of each show or commercial produced. These economies of scale serve as another barrier to entry, as new firms find it difficult to achieve or compete with the lower per-unit production costs enjoyed by established firms.

Economies of scale and economies of scope help media providers maximize profits by getting the most out of their production efforts. There are limits, however, to the economies that can be achieved, and whether or not Disney has extended the ESPN line too far remains to be seen. Clearly their expectation is that this expansion will be profitable, but even if Disney is overproducing, it may be a profitable strategy in the long run. As noted above, these various sports media products are substitutes for each other; if the market becomes saturated it may weaken the profitability of other networks, potentially driving them out of the market and discouraging new firms from entering, all the while boosting Disney's long-run profit potential.

7.3 The NCAA and Media Providers: Symbiotic Relationship or Mutual Addiction?

Mutually beneficial exchange is a cornerstone of market-based economies. Sometimes however, as in the case of the NCAA and the media, these transactions are criticized for their negative impacts on society, or for disrupting the more noble pursuits of the institutions involved. Is the relationship between the NCAA and the media just another series of economic transactions made in an effort to better satisfy wants, or are the two institutions intertwined in a relationship of unhealthy codependence? We explore their interdependence here, on our way to deciding if the relationship is, on balance, beneficial for the participants and society.

7.3.1 *Why does the media need intercollegiate sports?*

For media providers, intercollegiate sports are a vital source of revenue. Advertisers shell out billions of dollars for television, radio, and internet ad slots during college sporting events. From 2000 to 2005, advertisers spent more than US$2.2 billion on the NCAA men's basketball tournament (Jacobson, 2006). In 2012, ad revenue for the tournament exceeded US$1 billion for the first time (Marte and Morgan, 2013). In the three television seasons spanning 2001–2004, ABC had the highest weekly ratings amongst the four major networks (ABC, CBS, FOX, and NBC) only seven times. Three of those weeks saw ABC broadcast BCS bowl games (the other four were the 2003 NFL Super Bowl and three years of Academy Awards shows) (Frank, 2004). More recently, all of the "Big Four" networks (ABC, CBS, FOX, NBC) have lost significant ratings shares, as viewers flock to cable programming and on-demand services such as Netflix. With most of the losses coming from the non-sports programming side, sports programs become that much more valuable to networks.

In addition to direct revenue generated from advertising during the event, media providers use sports broadcasts to promote non-sports programming. During the NCAA Basketball

Tournament, for example, CBS promotes upcoming episodes of primetime shows like *Survivor* and *Big Bang Theory*. By increasing the number of viewers (and thus ratings) for their non-sports programs, television networks charge more for ad time and generate additional revenue. Even if the media provider pays more for the broadcast rights than is earned from advertising during the actual event, the gains from non-sports programming generally result in a net profit.

Sports-based stations like ESPN can benefit by promoting future sports broadcasts, but also from **ancillary programming**. Examples of ancillary programming include the NCAA basketball tournament selection show, ESPN's "College Football Game Day," and pregame and postgame shows for the BCS title game. Ancillary programming that directly precedes or follows a major event is also referred to as **shoulder programming**. Ancillary programming serves two purposes. First, it helps stimulate demand for the main event by educating and exciting fans with everything from player injury reports to analysis of intriguing match-ups (games within the game). For some fans, this ancillary programming is not simply added entertainment, it provides information that might be helpful in winning the office pool or otherwise profit from gambling on the event.

The second purpose of ancillary programming is to generate additional revenue by essentially expanding coverage of the actual sporting event. If a major college sporting event is expected to attract, say, 100 million viewers, even a small percentage watching the hour-long pregame show can provide strong ratings for a sports network. Advertisers will be particularly interested in slots appearing in the minutes approaching the event, as viewers turn on their sets early in preparation for the big game.

7.3.2   *A simple model for TV and other broadcasting contracts*

How does a media provider determine how much to offer the NCAA for the rights to broadcast college football games? Like any firm, it must weigh the cost of buying the rights (the TV contract) and airing the event against the revenue earned from advertisers and selling access to local affiliates. If the revenue earned is projected to exceed the cost, then the media provider should buy the rights. Equation 7.1 below represents a simple model for determining the maximum a media provider should be willing to pay for broadcast rights to an event.

$$MCO = (ER_s + ER_a + ER_n) - (EC + IC). \qquad (7.1)$$

MCO is the **maximum contract offer** the media provider is willing to make; ER_s is the expected revenue generated from advertising shown during the sporting event; ER_a is revenue anticipated from ancillary programming; ER_n is the boost to revenue generated from non-sports programming promoted during the sporting event; EC is the **explicit cost** of putting on the event (camera crews, announcers, etc., not including the contract cost), and IC is the **implicit cost** of airing the event, including forgone profits from the next best programming alternative. The maximum the media provider should be willing to pay is the positive difference between the expected revenues and the expected costs.

For example: Suppose that the CBS contract with the NCAA to broadcast March Madness is up for renewal. If CBS were to continue the relationship, it would expect over the life of the contract to generate US\$2 billion in revenue from sports programming, US\$300 million from ancillary programming, and another US\$200 million in revenue from the boost to non-sports programming shown by the network. CBS estimates that it will have explicit costs of US\$400 million, and implicit costs of US\$1.5 billion from sacrificing their next best alternative. Under these circumstances, the most CBS should be willing to pay the NCAA is US\$600 million [US\$600 million = (US\$2 billion + US\$300 million + US\$200 million) − (US\$400 million + US\$1.5 billion)].

Sometimes in the bidding process for these contracts, networks are so anxious to secure the programming (sometimes to keep competitors from securing the contract) that they will overbid for the broadcast rights. This phenomenon, introduced in Chapter 5 as the **winner's curse**, can occur if networks overestimate the revenue or underestimate the cost of programming. The winning bidder ends up losing money, hence the curse.

Notice in our example that if we exclude the revenue from non-sports programming, the maximum CBS would be willing to pay is US$400 million. If CBS were to pay US$500 million, it might appear to the untrained eye that CBS bid themselves into a winner's curse, but with the additional revenue generated from non-sports programming, CBS would actually realize an economic profit of US$100 million (US$2.5 billion in revenue minus US$2.4 billion in implicit and explicit costs, including the US$500 million contract). The challenge for economists is in determining how much of the revenue generated from non-sports programming is the direct result of following or being promoted by the sports programming.

7.3.3   *The impact of time on the contract value*

Many media contracts, such as the CBS contract to broadcast the NCAA basketball tournament for US$10.8 billion over 14 years, extend for more than one year of the particular sporting event. In these cases, the model presented above becomes a bit more complex, as firms must consider the expected *stream* of payments (revenue and costs) over the life of the contract. Economists measure the **present value** of these anticipated benefits and costs, based on the notion that payments received in the present are worth more than those received in the future.

As a simple example, suppose that you are given the choice whether to receive US$100 now or US$100 one year from now. All else equal, economists would expect you to choose the US$100 now, with the cost of waiting depending on the interest you could have earned over one year. If the interest rate is 10%, you could invest US$100 today and have US$110 after one year (US$100 principal + US$10 interest — 10% × US$100). We would say that US$100 is the present value of US$110 received one year from now. To find the present value of a future payment, we use the following formula:

$$PV = \frac{FV}{(1+i)^t},$$

(7.2)

where PV is the present value, FV is the future value (the amount you receive at some future time), i is the interest rate (determined in the market), and t denotes time ($t = 1$ would represent a payment received at the end of one year).

At an interest rate of 10%, our US$100 payment received one year from now would have a present value of US$90.91 [= US$100/ $(1 + 0.1)^1$]. This means that if you start with US$90.91 today, you would earn enough interest in one year to end up with US$100. If we change the time period, we can see how the present value changes. If $t = 0$ (we receive the US$100 now), Equation 7.2 tells us that the present value is US$100 (no big surprise). If instead we have to wait two years to receive our US$100, the present value of that payment is only US$82.64 [= US$100/$(1 + 0.1)^2$].

Applying the concept of present value to our media contracts, and recognizing that there will be a series of revenue and cost payments, we can re-write the simple model presented in Equation 7.1.

$$MCO = \sum_{t=0}^{n} \frac{(ER_s + ER_a + ER_n) - (EC + IC)}{(1+i)^t}.$$

(7.3)

For example: Big Time Network (BTN) is considering a bid for the rights to broadcast the Humungous Corporation Bowl for three years. BTN estimates that it will receive the earnings and incur the costs identified in Table 7.1.

If the interest rate is 5% and expected to remain at that value over the life of the contract, and if the payment for the rights must be paid at the signing of the contract ($t = 0$), what is the maximum

Table 7.1. Hypothetical expected revenues and costs from broadcasting the humungous corporation bowl (amounts in millions).

	Year 1 (US$)	Year 2 (US$)	Year 3 (US$)
ER_s	200	250	300
ER_a	50	50	50
ER_n	100	110	120
EC	150	180	210
IC	100	120	140

contract offer BTN will be willing to make? Plugging these amounts into Equation 7.3, we get:

$$MCO = [(200 + 50 + 100 - 150 - 100)/1.05] + [(250 + 50 + 110 - 180 - 120)/1.05^2] + [(300 + 50 + 120 - 210 - 140)/1.05^3]$$
$$= US\$298.68 \text{ million.}$$

The present value of the expected revenue minus the expected costs, and the maximum BTN should be willing to bid, is just under US$300 million. For a bit more of a challenge, see if you can calculate the maximum contract offer if the rights will be paid for in three equal installments from $t = 1$ to $t = 3$. The answer appears in the footnote below.[1]

7.4   Media Providers' Dilemma

In Chapter 2, we talked about the Prisoners' Dilemma and the incentive for cartel members to cheat. Here, we apply the concept to scheduling broadcasts of college football bowl games and similar events.

---

[1] BTN would be willing to pay just over US$329 million, roughly US$109.68 million per year. It shouldn't surprise you that BTN would be willing to pay more than the original US$298.68 figure, as the dollars paid at the end of years 1–3 will have a lower present value than dollars paid at the contract signing.

As we observed earlier, networks sell the sports product in an oligopoly market. In your study of microeconomics, you learned that oligopoly markets consist of a few firms whose pricing and output decisions are interdependent. There is often an opportunity for these firms to increase profits by colluding in their pricing or division of the market. For the networks broadcasting college sports (ABC/ESPN, CBS/CSTV, FOX, and NBC), this often comes in the form of scheduling contests. Those that fail to coordinate schedules and instead compete head-to-head may be sacrificing potential profits.

Traditionally New Year's Day was crowded with college football bowl games, many competing for the same viewers. Broadcasters airing the games earned fewer profits than they could have if they were the only networks showing a game at any particular time. In recent years, however, broadcasts of the major bowl games (BCS games primarily) have been staggered to reduce the overlap. Game theory helps us understand and represent the media providers' incentive to cooperate rather than engage in a bowl game arms race.

Suppose that ABC and FOX are both scheduled to broadcast a major bowl game on New Year's Day. Assume that no other networks are broadcasting games, and that there are two good time slots available in which to broadcast bowl games, but one is better than the other (we'll call these "best" and "second best"). Figure 7.1 represents the payoff matrix faced by ABC and FOX given the available choices of the best and second best time slots.

		FOX	
		Best	Second best
ABC	Best	FOX: US$10 ABC: US$10	US$8 US$16
	Second best	US$16 US$8	US$5 US$5

Figure 7.1. The payoff matrix for a bowl scheduling game (amounts in millions).

The payoff matrix tells us that if they both choose the "Best" time slot, each will receive a profit of US$10 million. Likewise, if they go head-to-head in the "Second best" slot, each will profit US$5 million. Alternatively, if they stagger the bowls such that one is broadcasting at the best time and the other at the second best time, the network with the best time earns US$16 million, and the other network earns only US$8 million.

In this particular game, both players have a **dominant strategy**, meaning each player's optimal decision is the same regardless of what the other player does.[2] Looking at ABC's choices as an example, suppose that FOX chooses "Best." ABC maximizes their payoff by also choosing "Best." If FOX instead goes with "Second best," ABC is still better off choosing "Best." Because the optimal choice for ABC is independent of FOX's choice, ABC has a dominant strategy. Verify for yourself that FOX also has a dominant strategy to choose "Best."[3]

If they play the game only once, and assuming they both follow their dominant strategy, the networks will both choose the "best" time. However, if we look at the totals for each cell of the payoff matrix, we see that the combined profit is greater (US$24 million vs. US$20 million) if they stagger the bowl offerings. The outcome of the game is a form of **prisoners' dilemma** in that both can be made better off, if a different set of choices is made. In this case, ABC and FOX have an incentive to cooperate rather than compete directly, if they can agree on some form of profit-sharing.

Historically, ABC and FOX have both had extended contracts to broadcast major bowl games; in such cases there is an opportunity for a **repeated game** between the players. Assuming that the payoffs in Figure 7.1 remain constant over time, ABC and FOX might

---

[2] This assumes that the game is competitive — no collusion occurs between the players.

[3] In the absence of a dominant strategy, there are multiple strategies a firm might employ. One typical approach is a **maximin strategy**, which means to "maximize the minimum gain" one expects to receive. Another common strategy is to maximize the expected value of the payoffs, choosing the strategy that gives the highest *average* payoff.

agree to take the second best slot in alternating years. If they form and stick to this agreement, both will earn US$24 million every two years versus the US$20 million each would receive if their media providers' dilemma extended over two years.

Suppose they form the agreement described above, with ABC taking the second best slot in Year 1 of the agreement, but in Year 2 FOX defects and also broadcasts its game in the best slot. By cheating on the agreement, FOX gains US$2 million in Year 2 (US$10 million vs. US$8 million), but incurs the wrath of ABC. If the game continues, ABC is unlikely to trust FOX again, and we would expect the outcome to revert to the media providers' dilemma for as long as the game is played. While FOX gained US$2 million in the short run by cheating, it will be worse off beginning in Year 3 (they will only earn US$10 million rather than US$16 million) than if it had honored the agreement.

If a game such as this is to be repeated into the foreseeable future, both players will be better off sticking to the agreement. But what if both networks have contracts with definite end dates and low probability of renewal? Suppose ABC and FOX both have four-year contracts to broadcast their respective bowl games. They enter the agreement described above, with ABC agreeing to take the second best slot in Years 1 and 3, and FOX in Years 2 and 4. When Year 4 rolls around, what incentive does FOX have to stick to the agreement? Unless ABC has some other mechanism with which to punish FOX for defection, FOX is US$2 million better off by cheating, especially if it thinks it can "kiss and make up" with ABC should such collusive opportunities present themselves in the future.

The benefits of programming cooperation can be even greater if staggering agreements also include non-sports broadcasts. Bowl games competing for the New Year's Day audience are all vying for the same set of viewers. If a media provider not showing a bowl game can offer up a holiday favorite such as *The Sound of Music* at the same time as the Orange Bowl, for example, both can appeal to large audiences (and the accompanying profits) with less risk of losing viewers to the competition.

7.5 Why Do Colleges Need the Media?

Just as college sports generate revenue for the media, the media helps college sports programs generate revenue for themselves. Colleges and the NCAA have become dependent on this revenue to maintain or increase current levels of spending on their sports programs. The benefits of media coverage, however, extend beyond the direct infusion of revenue. Colleges also benefit, or at least believe they do, from the exposure they receive during media-covered events.

Media revenue is the major source of revenue for the NCAA and its member institutions. The NCAA Men's Basketball Tournament alone contributes 90% of the NCAA's annual income, with US$712 million of the US$797 million projected for 2012–2013 coming from media contracts with Turner Broadcasting and CBS Sports ("Finances," n.d.). As shown in Figure 1.2, the majority of this income is ultimately distributed to member institutions, and as we saw in Table 6.2, Division I-FBS universities rely directly and indirectly on media revenue to support 19% of their budgets. This revenue supports expenditures on coaches, equipment, and transportation. Schools with greater revenue have more to spend on recruiting efforts, including facilities upgrades. Better recruiting attracts higher quality athletes, which often leads to more competitive success. Program success enhances the media attention, encouraging alumni and boosters to "support a winner" by increasing their giving. Despite the logic of this system, as we saw in the previous chapter, the evidence does not support the universities' belief that greater spending systematically improves winning or the overall financial position of universities.[4]

Even if the broadcast revenue distributed to member schools only fuels the arms race, some of the money retained by the NCAA is used for the benefit of student-athletes. In 1990–1991, after CBS and the NCAA signed a US$1 billion broadcast agreement for March Madness, the NCAA set up three funds to support student

---

[4]On the bright side for schools, however, Sperber (2000) reports that bad publicity from scandals does not adversely affect program donations.

athletes. The first fund expanded the Catastrophic-Injury Insurance Program to cover all NCAA athletes. The second established the Special Assistance Fund that is used to help student-athletes facing emergency expenses for things like education, medical care, and travel. The third fund, the Academic Enhancement Fund, was created to distribute money to member institutions to enhance academic programs for NCAA student-athletes (Copeland, 2006). In its 2011–2012 fiscal year, the NCAA allocated US$15.1 million to the Special Assistance Fund and US$24.6 million to the Academic Enhancement Fund. This accounted for about 4.9% of NCAA revenue that year. Another US$51 million went to the Student-Athlete Opportunity Fund ("Finances," n.d.).

Fast fact. *In 2012, the average cost for a 30-second ad slot for the March Madness title game was US$1.5 million. Slots for BCS bowl games sold for up to US$670,000 each for the four non-championship games and US$1.3 million for the national title contest. In contrast, World Series slots sold for US$450,000 (in 2011), NBA Finals slots for US$500,000, and Super Bowl slots for US$3.5 million.*

7.6 Bowl Game Revenue

Media coverage of bowl games is critical to generating the millions of dollars paid to the NCAA institutions and their conferences. Corporate sponsors of bowl games reap millions of dollars in benefits from having their logos appear during broadcasts. Research by Image Impact, a sponsorship measurement firm, estimated that Frito-Lay (the producer of Tostitos) received "an extra US$30 million worth of exposure during the Fiesta Bowl and other BCS game broadcasts" (Goetzi, 2006). Additionally, the stocks of publicly traded primary college football sponsors for 2011–2012 bowl games gained more than twice the S&P 500 over a one-year period (Ozanian, 2012). It is no wonder that companies like Frito-Lay, Allstate, AT&T, Discover, and Capital One are willing to pay millions of dollars to sponsor the bowls that generate the millions of dollars distributed to bowl participants.

Payouts to schools participating in bowl games for the 2013–2014 season ranged from US$325,000 to US$22 million, with twenty-six exceeding the US$1 million mark, and the four non-championship BCS games paying US$18 million each to the participating teams ("BCS explained," 2013). A portion of the BCS payouts stays with the teams that compete; the remainder is shared with the teams' respective conferences. The five automatic qualifier conferences (ACC, Big Ten, Big 12, Pac 12, and SEC) are all guaranteed the largest share of BCS money. Of the US$174.07 million in BCS distributions in 2011, US$145.2 million (83.4%) went to the automatic qualifier conferences, with the remaining money (just under US$29 million) going to the non-qualifier FBS conferences (US$24.72 million), FCS conferences (US$2.25 million) and independent schools such as Notre Dame (US$1.7 million), Army (US$100,000), and Navy (US$100,000) (Smith, 2011). A full listing of BCS payouts appears in Table 2.2. What is clear from the payout information is that the major conferences effectively use their power within the NCAA (a "cartel within the cartel") to reap "winner-take-all" returns from bowl participation.

The true picture is clouded by the fact that the listed payouts don't necessarily match what schools receive. In 2006–2007, for example, the US$17 million per team payouts for BCS games applied only to teams from the six major conferences. Notre Dame received only US$4.5 million and Boise State only US$9 million. Who gets the best deal? It isn't apparent from the payout numbers; one must look at how those payouts are distributed. Though Notre Dame only received US$4.5 million, as an independent it did not have to share its bowl revenue. Boise State, on the other hand, had to share its US$9 million with five non-major conferences (Conference USA, WAC, Mountain West, Sun Belt, and Mid-American), and itself kept only about US$3 million. The major conference participants in the BCS shared their US$17 million payouts according to conference formulas. After expenses for traveling to bowl games are deducted, conferences such as the Atlantic Coast and Big Ten share bowl revenue equally. The Big East, on the other hand, returns a larger share to BCS-participating schools, and lesser shares to those in minor or no bowl games. (O'Toole, 2006)

Payouts for other bowl games are also deceiving. In addition to revenue sharing obligations, officially listed payouts sometimes exceed what schools and their conferences actually receive. In the 2006 Texas Bowl, for example, Kansas State received the published payout of US$750,000, while Rutgers received only US$500,000. What makes these bowl revenue distribution figures more misleading is that they fail to account for ticket purchase requirements. Each school is required to buy a large block of tickets, and they may choose to give away some tickets to loyal supporters or simply be unable to resell them all. Bowl officials and conferences are free to negotiate payouts, so a team receiving a lesser payment may also be obligated to buy fewer tickets than the opposing school. (O'Toole, 2006)

As we saw in Chapter 6, revenue generated from the college football bowl system plays a unique role in athletic department budgets. A portion of bowl revenue, the annual split between conference members, is a regular fixture in budgets. The part earned from actually participating in a bowl game in a given year is spent almost exclusively on attending the event. In the 2010–2011 bowl season, for example, there were 34 bowl games played. Of the 68 teams playing in those games, at least 13 of the teams spent more to participate than their conference received in payment from the hosting bowl game. (Eichelberger, 2010)

To understand why colleges do not use this share of bowl money to improve facilities or otherwise enhance their programs, it is important to remember that communities host these bowls to stimulate the local economy. In fact, bowl games were first started to attract tourists to the warm winter destinations where they were played — Southern California, Arizona, Texas, and Florida. The goal was to draw visitors and the dollars that come with them. Participating schools are not only required to purchase a minimum number of tickets, they are expected to spend heavily on local accommodation, food, and tourist attractions for the players,

---

Box 7.1.   BYU and bowls.

The experience of Brigham Young University (BYU) football underscores the expectation that invited bowl teams and their fans will spend generously in the bowl's host city. In 1996, BYU finished the season 13-1 and ranked #5 nationally, yet failed to receive a Bowl Alliance invitation. In U.S. Senate hearings on the Bowl Alliance held in 1997, Utah Senator Bob Bennett explained that "BYU does not travel well. I'll be very blunt. There is a perception out there, and it may be true, that [BYU fans] do not drink and party the way the host city would prefer. Our football coach has been quoted as saying that BYU fans travel with a US$50 bill and the Ten Commandments in their pocket, and they leave without breaking either one". (Zimbalist, 1999, p. 106)

---

coaches, university personnel, and "friends of the program." Schools that fail to bring freely spending fans to bowl games are less likely to be invited to future bowls (see Box 7.1). This raises the question, if schools are expected to spend all of their bowl participation revenue at the event, why bother? If bowl revenue was the only consideration, schools might not care, but colleges believe that the exposure they receive still leaves them better off, even if all of the extra bowl money is spent attending the event.

7.7   Other Benefits from Media Exposure

While revenue from media contracts provides substantial budgetary support, it is not the only benefit of the college sports–media relationship. Exposure benefits universities with successful teams in ways that are quite tangible, but sometimes difficult to measure. As we saw in Chapter 6, athletic success may draw the attention of high school students in the midst of their college application and selection process. To the extent it actually exists, the boost in applications from the **Flutie effect** provides schools with the opportunity to enhance revenue through enrollment growth or greater selectivity.

> **Fast fact.** *In 1998, Valparaiso University in Indiana was a 13-seed in the NCAA Men's Basketball Tournament. It made a "Cinderella" run, eventually losing in the "Sweet 16." Shortly thereafter, materials from the admissions office began to play on that success and the media attention it gained. The brochure for the Valparaiso Law School (yes, the law school!) had a picture of a basketball on the front, and began with the words, "You've seen us in the NCAA tournament … ." If Valparaiso was correct in its assumption that prospective law students would be drawn in by an appearance in March Madness, imagine how prospective first-year undergraduate students would respond.*

Critics bemoan the commercialization of college sports; the loss of innocence and amateurism that makes college sports more pure; and the sense that the "student" part of "student-athlete" doesn't mean much. To battle those perceptions, during televised college sporting events, the NCAA runs public relations advertising to convince us that these concerns are minor, with mature undergraduates dressed in non-sports professional attire telling audiences that "There are over 400,000 NCAA student-athletes, and just about all of us will be going pro in something other than sports." It is the NCAA's way of telling us that student-athlete priorities are in order and that the high-profile cases of athlete misconduct and academic failure are the exception rather than the rule.

Why would the NCAA use the media in this way? Like any cartel or monopoly, the NCAA has reason to fear the government stepping in to regulate operations. In order to quell public calls for government intervention, the NCAA uses public relations advertising to extol the virtues of college sports and its athletes. While allocating resources toward public relations advertising may not maximize short run profits for the NCAA, in the long run, it may be cheaper than complying with tougher regulations or devoting additional resources to lobby those legislators willing to consider greater government oversight of college sports.

7.8   Media-driven (or at least supported) Changes in College Sports

Has the media tainted the "purity" of college sports? For economists, the bigger questions are: (1) How has media involvement affected college sports; (2) What is the economic rationale behind media-driven changes; and (3) What are the economic impacts of media-driven changes? Here we look at a few changes, first focusing on football, then basketball, that have occurred in college sports that are connected with media involvement.

7.8.1   *Scheduling*

Scheduling of major college football and basketball games is driven heavily by the demands of television coverage. Subject to the constraint that most college football games will occur on a Saturday, times are juggled to allow networks to show multiple games in a day. In addition, there are Thursday and Friday night games broadcast every week, and occasionally games on Sunday and Monday. Since 2006, for virtually every week of the college football season, ABC (including its affiliated stations ESPN, ESPN2, ESPNU, and ESPN360) broadcast at least one game each on Thursday and Friday, and multiple games each Saturday, including weekends (Thursday to Saturday) that included around 20 regular season games. The majority of the off-Saturday games, and the staggered schedules of Saturday games, were engineered by the NCAA primarily to provide media programming.

To the dismay of traditionalists, media programming demands have also resulted in the rescheduling of games with established histories of playing on a certain date. For example, the annual football game between the University of Oregon and Oregon State University, known locally as "the Civil War," was played on a Saturday for 79 years, often during the weekend after Thanksgiving. In 2006, in order to accommodate an FSN national telecast, the game was moved from Saturday, November 25, to the afternoon of Friday, November 24. Why did Oregon and Oregon State agree to the change? Both teams received an additional $250,000 from FSN, but as OSU's athletic director Bob De Carolis explained, "I'm not going to say the financial part didn't have anything to do with it, but that certainly wasn't the driving force. It was more about getting exposure on a national basis" (Beseda, 2006).

In response to the media providers' dilemma described above, bowl games are now distributed across a wider spectrum of dates and times. There were 35 scheduled games for the 2013–2014 bowl season, running from December 21, 2013, to January 6, 2014. Historically, on New Year's Day the schedules for the Rose, Fiesta, Orange, and Sugar Bowls (the four non-championship BCS games) would often overlap. Beginning in 2007, with the introduction of the separate championship game, those overlaps were eliminated; that year the four games were spread over prime time slots on January 1st, 2nd, and 3rd. The championship game was played on January 8th. In 2007, all except for the Rose Bowl (ABC) were broadcast by FOX. With ESPN now holding the rights to broadcast all BCS games, as well as a number of other bowl games, chances of schedule conflicts are minimal.

Critics of building schedules around media programming demands claim that travel to and participation in these games (particularly those on Thursdays) increases absenteeism and further distracts student-athletes from their studies. Economists might support that argument on the grounds that it inhibits human capital formation, diminishing productivity growth. In measured terms, however, consumer demand for additional broadcast games, and satisfaction of that demand by networks and the NCAA, appears to have an overall positive impact on economic welfare. Despite the objections, consumers remain willing to pay for the sports product (e.g., Thursday night games).

7.8.2   *Creation and expansion of the BCS*

For many years, college football bowl games operated independently, focused on generating economic activity for the host community. As explained earlier, teams accepting invitations to bowl games were required to purchase a block of tickets and spend most, if not all, of their bowl payout in the local economy, often providing lavish accommodations and entertainment for players, coaches, and other university officials. Some bowls had formal arrangements with conferences that agreed to furnish participants. Since 1947, for example, the Rose Bowl had always been played between the Pacific-10 and Big 10 conference champions. Other bowls, like the Sugar and Cotton, were hosted by a particular conference champion (Southeastern and Southwestern, respectively), with the opponents not confined to a particular conference. These bowls would issue invitations to prospective opponents that schools would accept, or decline in favor of a better bowl offer. The lesser-known bowls would have a variety of arrangements, some tying themselves to the second- or third-place team of a major conference, others simply offering invitations geared at creating an appealing contest.

For the media, the old bowl system created tremendous financial uncertainty. Rights fees were negotiated and broadcast schedules were set well in advance of knowing a given bowl's participants. Networks fortunate enough to have secured a bowl game with national championship implications or some other intriguing match-up did well. Less appealing games not only lost networks advertising revenue (from the projected lack of viewers), but dedicating three hours or more to a bowl game meant three less hours available for potentially more profitable sports or non-sports programming.

As we saw in Chapter 1, in an effort to create a more stable financial climate, in 1992 the Atlantic Coast (ACC), Big East, Big Eight (now the Big Twelve), Southeastern (SEC) and the Southwestern conferences, in conjunction with Notre Dame, formed the Bowl Coalition with the IBM (now Tostitos) Fiesta

Bowl, the Mobil (now AT&T) Cotton Bowl, the Federal Express (now Discover) Orange Bowl, and the USF&G (then Nokia, now Allstate) Sugar Bowl. The purpose was of course to ensure that these games would attract the maximum number of viewers, as all stood to gain from the greater revenue and exposure.

The problem with the new coalition was that bowl organizers were initially reluctant to give up historic conference ties. Affiliated conference champions were still required to host their respective bowls, and it failed to correct the situation where the top ranked teams vying for a national championship might never play each other. Uncertainty of match-ups remained, leaving advertisers hesitant to spend as freely as they would for a game certain to attract a large audience.

The system was revised when the Bowl Alliance began in 1995 between the ACC, Big East, Big 12 (the Big Eight plus four teams from the Southwest conference now merged), SEC, and Notre Dame, and the Orange, Sugar, and Fiesta Bowls. Conferences were no longer tied to a particular bowl game, so the alliance was free to create match-ups between the top-ranked teams, with the top game rotating amongst the three bowls. Each of the four conference champions plus Notre Dame (assuming it had a winning record) would be featured in these bowl games. Remaining slots could be filled either from within or outside the alliance.

One of the goals of the Bowl Alliance was to create a national championship game. Prior to creation of the BCS, the "mythical" national champion was determined by the sports writers' and coaches' polls. Each group would vote to determine national rankings, sometimes arriving at different conclusions. For example, in 1991 the University of Washington and the University of Miami both finished the season undefeated. Washington soundly defeated the University of Michigan in the Rose Bowl, while Miami trounced the University of Nebraska in the Orange Bowl. The result was a split national championship, with the writers selecting the Miami Hurricanes #1 and the coaches crowning the UW Huskies as national champions.

While the Bowl Alliance reduced the chances for a split national championship, the possibility would remain as long as the Pac-10 and Big 10 remained tied to the Rose Bowl. In 1997, they joined the Bowl Alliance and formed the BCS, creating a national title game that would rotate between the four bowls. The six conference champions would fill six of the eight BCS slots. Participants in the championship game were determined by the top two teams in the BCS rankings, as determined by the Associated Press (media) poll, the *USA Today*/ESPN coaches' poll, and the average of a computer ranking system. The computer rankings factor in strength of schedule (including both opponents and opponents' opponents), losses, and quality wins (bonus points for beating a team ranked 15th or above).

From 1997 through the 2005–2006 bowl season, the BCS remained largely intact. The rating system changed over the decade, with additions and deletions of various computer rating systems. The main controversy during the time, besides the circumstances of specific years, was that the BCS allowed few opportunities for non-BCS conference teams to participate. To improve access and generate additional revenue, another BCS game was added beginning with the 2006–2007 bowl season. The new fifth game is a national championship game separate from the four original bowls, but held on a rotating basis in the cities hosting the four bowls. For the 2013–2014 BCS season, for example, the Rose and Fiesta Bowls were held on January 1, the Sugar Bowl on January 2, the Orange Bowl on January 3, and the BCS Title Game was held on January 6 in Pasadena (host of the Rose Bowl a week earlier).

In June 2012, the NCAA approved a four-team playoff to begin in 2014 (the 2014–2015 bowl season) and run through the 2025 season. The initial plan called for a selection committee to determine the four teams, with semifinal games occurring around New Year's Day and rotating among existing major bowl sites. The championship game will be played on a Monday, about a week following the semifinal contests (Dinich, 2012). The first two semifinal games were awarded to the Sugar and Rose Bowls on January 1, 2015, with the National Championship game following on January 12, in Arlington, Texas. The other bowl games in the College Football Playoff Semifinal rotation include the Fiesta Bowl, Cotton Bowl, Orange Bowl, and Chick-fil-A Bowl.

Addition of a national championship game has not eliminated controversy, as we will see later in this chapter. It has increased the probability, however, that the top teams will have the opportunity to meet in a final game to determine a slightly less mythical national champion.

Fast fact. *In the new four-team playoff system, 10% of a team's revenue from a BCS bowl is contingent on team meeting an established academic progress rate (APR) threshold. Teams falling short will lose that share of revenue. Additionally, the 10% share is to be used to support academics. ("Agreement," 2012)*

7.8.3 *Bowl proliferation*

The first college football bowl game was the Rose Bowl, held in Pasadena on January 1, 1902. After a 13-year hiatus, the Rose Bowl returned in 1916, and would be the only bowl game until the 1920s, when the Fort Worth Classic (1921), San Diego East-West Christmas Classic (1921–1922), and Los Angeles Christmas Festival (1924) briefly joined bowl lore. It was not until the 1930s that new, permanent bowls would emerge with the Sugar (1935), Orange (1935), Sun (1936), and Cotton (1937).[5] These five major bowls (including the Rose Bowl) continued through World War II, but no new bowls were added during this time. After the war, however, there was a brief surge in the number of bowl offerings, but by the 1950s there were less than 10 in operation. The early 1960s saw the number of bowls again reach double-digits, but it wasn't until the late 1960s

---

[5] One other bowl, the Bacardi Bowl, also began in 1937 in Havana, Cuba. Although it only lasted one year, it appears to have been the first bowl named for its commercial sponsor.

that bowl numbers would permanently exceed that threshold. From there the number of bowls slowly drifted upward, reaching 18 in 1984, 19 in 1993, and 21 in 1997. The bowl lineup continued to grow to 28, where it settled for the period 2002–2006, until jumping to 32 for the 2006–2007 bowl season (Hickok, 2006). By 2010–2011, there were 35 bowl games.

Given the growth of the country, has the number of bowl games really increased that dramatically? In 1916, there were just over 100 million people in the United States and one bowl game. The number of bowls reached 15 in 1978, and the population was about 222 million. Since 1978 the number of bowls has more than doubled, but population has only increased about 41% (reaching 314 million in 2012). On a per capita basis, it would be fair to say that bowl games have proliferated.

While it is easy to see the expansion of the bowl lineup, it is unclear whether this has been driven by the media, educational institutions, or some other force. Division I conferences and their member universities have enjoyed the proliferation of bowls, as it has increased their exposure and access to bowl revenues. Still, other than the demonstrated willingness of fans to travel to bowl games, it does not appear that schools have contributed directly to the addition of bowl games.

A more difficult question to answer is whether the media is responsible for this proliferation of bowl games, or whether media has expanded in response to the growing number of games. ESPN began operations in September 1979, when there were only 15 bowl games. As of 2012–2013 there were 35, but a third of those have been added since the late 1990s, and it is unclear whether the creation of ESPN itself spawned significant growth or just went along for the ride. ESPN's expansion of media coverage of sports may well have stimulated the demand for more bowl games, and recently ESPN has become directly involved in adding bowls. The New Mexico Bowl, first played in December 2006, was financed by a US$2 million line of credit from ESPN. The BBVA Compass Bowl (initially the Papajohns.com Bowl), also launched in December 2006, is one of seven bowls owned by ESPN Regional Television

("About us," n.d.[b]). In contrast, CSTV and the FOX College Sports channels have emerged since the expansion of the bowl system, and it is likely that their creation is more of a *reaction* to the growing popularity of college sports, including bowl games.

While media coverage stimulates consumer demand for the sports product, and media providers have not objected to an expanding bowl lineup, there is another important set of characters in the bowl proliferation story — corporate sponsors. Local communities hosting bowl games in the early years chose simple names that reflected basic commodities that one might find in the host's region, and possibly even in a real bowl — Sugar or Oranges, for example. Today, all of the major bowls except for the Rose Bowl have a named sponsor, including the Tostitos Fiesta Bowl and Discover Orange Bowl. Other bowls make no attempt to connect to goods broadly associated with the host city, instead naming the bowl for the main corporate sponsor — the GoDaddy.com (internet services), Outback (steak restaurant), and Capital One (financial services) Bowls. Some bowls have dropped their traditional name in favor of the sponsoring company, such as when the Peach Bowl became the Chick-fil-A Peach Bowl, and eventually just the Chick-fil-A Bowl. (Hickok, 2006)

Regardless of who is responsible for the proliferation of bowl games, the media, corporate sponsors, and colleges and universities (and their fans) all perceive benefits of the system and continue to support it. But is this expansion really beneficial, and can we expect the number of bowls to continue to grow? The media benefits from the additional programming, schools like the exposure and revenue, and corporate sponsors enjoy having their name attached to widely publicized events. The problem is that with 70 teams now playing in bowl games, some teams considered fairly mediocre end up reaching a postseason contest. Of the 70 teams playing in the 2012–2013 bowl season, 12 had a 0.500 record (6-6; 6 wins is the minimum requirement for bowl eligibility), and 13 were 7-5 or 7-6 going into their bowl games. At some point bowl saturation may threaten overall interest, as fans question whether teams are worth watching or even deserve to be there.

Technological change may explain why media providers continue to place a premium on bowl games and other college and professional sporting events. With enhanced recording technology, and the ability to bypass commercials, as well as on-demand availability of programming, viewing non-sports programs in real time is less urgent. Watching favorite (non-sports) shows the next day instead of when they first air does not matter to most viewers. As a result, ad time during non-sports programming has less value relative to something demanded in real time. Sports programming, whose value depends heavily on uncertainty of outcome must be watched in real time or the viewer risks learning the outcome before having a chance to watch the contest. That unique attribute of the sports product helps ensure its long-term value to media providers. Additionally, the expanded number of channels (for all types of programming) means that each program attracts fewer viewers. Whatever is left standing in the battle for audiences, often times sports programming, attracts the higher ratings and the advertisers' dollars.

7.8.4   *Rule changes*

Networks, especially those centered on sports, try to maximize profits by increasing the number of contests shown. In order to fit games into traditional program timing blocks (ending at the top or bottom of an hour), there has been a push to shorten the length of games. Rather than shorten media timeouts and reduce the number of revenue-generating advertising slots, the emphasis has been on shortening the actual playing time.

In 2006, the NCAA implemented three rule changes expressly aimed at shortening the length of football games. The first, Rule 3-2-1-b limits the intermission between halves to 20 minutes. Teams may agree in advance to change the length of halftime, but the encouragement is definitely to shorten rather than lengthen (NCAA Football Rules Committee [NCAA FRC], 2006).

Two of the three rule changes affected the running of the clock during play. Rule 3-2-5 directed officials to start the game clock when the foot touches the ball on a free kick (kickoff), rather than when the ball is first touched by the receiving team (NCAA FRC, 2006). There is typically only a four or five second difference between when the ball is kicked and when it is received, so even high scoring games with a lot of kickoffs are unlikely to have much time shaved off the game clock.

The most significant rule change involving the clock was Rule 3-2-5-e, commonly referred to as the "change of possession" rule. When possession of the ball changed, the clock stopped as usual, but the referee then restarted the game clock with the "ready for play" signal. Previously, the game clock would not start until the team gaining possession began their first play of the new series by snapping the ball. Based on studies done at the Division I-A conference level, the NCAA anticipated that this rule change would shorten games by about five minutes, approximately 10-14 plays (NCAA FRC, 2006). Although broadcasts overall were shorter, there was actually an increase in the amount of commercial time. Ultimately the drop in the number of plays per game exceeded expectations and the resulting coach and fan ire led to removal of this rule.

More recent football rule changes have focused on safety issues. While not directly initiated by media providers, media attention to safety concerns helped provide impetus for change. Further, these changes stand to benefit the media if they keep the most talented athletes in the games and keep fans interested and watching. These rule changes deal both directly with on-field play, as well as handling of injured players. The NCAA banned horse-collar tackles and imposed tighter restrictions related to head contact, beginning in 2008. In 2009, conferences were given the power to review fouls and impose penalties for egregious fouls. In 2010, wedge blocking was further restricted, all hits to the opposing players neck and head were made illegal, and tighter rules were imposed for allowing concussed and other injured players to return to play. ("A primer on NCAA rules," 2010). Safety related rules were further enhanced in 2012, with movement of the kickoff (from 30- to 35-yard line, greater restrictions on blocking below the waist, and better defined procedures for when helmets come off during play. (Redding, 2011)

As we learned in Chapter 1, safety issues in the early 20th century threatened college football's existence. With increased awareness and attention to the physical toll of football, particularly with regard to head trauma (including repeated concussions), the NCAA is implementing new and tighter safety rules to allow the survival of one of the golden geese of intercollegiate athletics.

7.8.5 *Instant replay*

One rule implemented in 2006, criticized by some for lengthening and disrupting the momentum of college football games, is the addition of instant replay. Rule 12 allows, but does not require, schools and conferences to adopt the uniform instant replay review system established by the NCAA FRC. The replay system was implemented nationally after two years of study in the Big 10 Conference. The objective of instant replay, according to then NCAA Rules Committee Chairman Charles Broyles, is to "correct game-changing errors with minimal interruption to the game". ("One replay challenge approved," 2006)

While the replay system is intended as a safeguard against poor calls that would definitively alter the outcome of a game, there are strict limits imposed to prevent an unreasonable extension of game times. Coaches are allowed to challenge only one call per game, but only if they have a time-out remaining, and the team is charged a time-out if the call is not overturned by the replay official. A team is granted a second challenge, if their initial one is successful. The replay official also has the authority to stop play and initiate a review.

Is the implementation of instant replay a rule change driven by the media? This is difficult to determine. Out of a sense of fair play and desire to preserve the integrity of contests, the NCAA itself has sufficient incentive to implement procedures to improve officiating. Media providers want demand for the sports product to expand, and that could certainly be compromised by poor officiating. At the same time, controversy attracts viewers, so preserving some room for error also has value to broadcasters. As described above, television networks have no interest in extending game times, so there is no compelling case either way as to whether media providers should support instant replay.

Even if the media is not consciously promoting the use of instant replay, the strategies of networks and improvements in media coverage have undoubtedly played a role in creating the demand for video replay. Instant replay has long been a part of sports broadcasts, providing material for commentators to maintain audience interest by filling the time between plays. The numerous camera angles provided for most televised games allow the public to see officiating errors, and announcers are happy to discuss them on the air. Supporters of instant replay, including fans, coaches, and administrators, reason that if the technology allows us to correct errors and make the right call, we ought to use it for the betterment of the game.

Outrage over injustice is an understandable, even noble response (see Box 7.2). When our most vocal outrage is about college football, or any sporting event, one must question whether our priorities are as they should be. Sure the money, prestige, and principles of fair play are all important at some level, but in the end it is just a game … or is it?

Box 7.2. The ruling on the field stands … or does it?

The instant replay tool is designed to improve officiating so that the players on the football field, and not the referees, decide the outcome. Unfortunately, the system doesn't always work, as the University of Oklahoma found out in its game against the University of Oregon on September 16, 2006. The important lesson from the incident was not that referees make bad calls; that is a long-standing tradition in many sports. What the event demonstrated vividly is, how the drive for national prominence and lucrative BCS payoffs has raised the stakes and sharpened the reactions of alleged victims.

The visiting and then 15th ranked Sooners led the game 33-20 with a little over a minute remaining in the contest. The 18th ranked Ducks scored with 1:12 left in the 4th quarter to cut the score to 33-27. On the ensuing onsides kick, Oregon

(Continued)

Box 7.2.   (Continued)

---

was awarded the ball, but replays revealed that the Ducks' Brian Paysinger was guilty of "first touching," meaning that he (as a member of the kicking team) made contact with the ball before it had advanced 10 yards forward from the kickoff. Officials on the field missed it, and the replay booth did not have access to the footage that clearly demonstrated the violation. Rather than waiting for additional video replay evidence, as they were allowed to do, the head replay official ruled that there was not indisputable visual evidence that would warrant overturning the call. Some have speculated that the decision was rushed as the replay officials felt pressure to act quickly out of media concerns. As Oregonian sports columnist John Canzano reported, "A source in the replay booth on Saturday said that [Gordon] Riese [the head replay official] found himself crunched for time, pressured by television and the on-field referee for a rapid decision, and there was such a delay in getting the video feed to Riese that he never even got to properly review the play" (Canzano, 2006a). To make matters worse, Oklahoma player Allen Patrick came away from the pile with the football, but officials on the field ruled that Oregon player Patrick Chung had already had possession.

Two plays after the controversial onside kick, Oklahoma was flagged for pass interference. The pass, however, had been tipped, negating the possibility of pass interference. That call was also not overturned; on the next play Oregon scored what would prove to be the winning touchdown, making the score 34-33 in favor of the Ducks.

Further fueling the controversy was the fact that the officiating crew was from the Pac-10. Most nonconference games are officiated by a crew from the road team's conference, which in this case would have been the Big 12. Pac-10 policy required that Pac-10 officials be used for nonconference home games, and accepts officials from the competing conference for away games.

(Continued)

Box 7.2. (Continued)

Officiating mistakes combined with dramatic finishes are not unusual in sports. It is also not unusual for the losing head coach to express outrage at the events, as Oklahoma coach Bob Stoops did in this case. What makes this case particularly illustrative of the stakes involved were the subsequent reactions of Stoops and University of Oklahoma President David Boren. Boren formally and publicly requested that the Big 12 Conference Commissioner pursue having the game removed from the record books, and that the Pac-10 suspend the entire officiating crew for the remainder of the season. Additionally, Stoops and Boren both indicated that Oklahoma might cancel its scheduled 2008 game at the University of Washington (they did not), unless the conference changes its rules requiring a Pac-10 crew at home games. In addition to the official outrage expressed by Stoops, Boren, and other supporters of Oklahoma, replay official Gordon Riese received numerous threatening phone calls, including one from an Oklahoma fan who told Riese that he would fly to Portland to kill Riese and his wife (Canzano, 2006a). Riese received some form of harassment (hate mail, email, phone calls, and even mobs assembling on his lawn) every day for the first 82 days after the incident (Canzano, 2006b). In February 2007, Riese revealed that he had been diagnosed with depression, and that the Pac-10 informed him that he "was not wanted in the replay booth". (Hunt, 2007)

The game stands in the record books, but Pac-10 officials apologized to Oklahoma for the mistakes and the entire crew was suspended for one game. By winning the Big-12 championship, Oklahoma ended up securing a place in the Fiesta Bowl (receiving a US$17 million payout despite losing to Boise State University in overtime), so the financial damage was minimal compared to if Oklahoma had slipped into a non-BCS bowl (the next highest payout available was US$4.25 million). Meanwhile, the debate over instant replay continues.

7.8.6   *Expansion of march madness*

The history of the NCAA men's basketball tournament (also known by the NCAA's registered trademark name of "March Madness") began in 1939 with eight teams. Over the years, the number of teams, the coverage, and the dollars involved have all increased dramatically. Here are some of the key dates and events:

1946   The finals were televised for the first time. CBS broadcast the game in New York City to an estimated 500,000 viewers.

1951   The tournament was expanded to 16 teams.

1952   Regional telecasts of games occurred for the first time.

1953   The field expanded to 22 teams; the number of teams would vary between 22 and 25 through the 1974 tournament.

1954   LaSalle defeated Bradley in the first nationally televised championship game.

1963   "Sports Network" agreed to pay US$140,000 for the rights to broadcast the championship game nationally through 1968.

1969   NBC paid US$547,500 for the rights to televise the tournament finals. It was the first time net tournament income exceeded US$1 million.

1973   NBC paid US$1,165,755 for broadcast rights, surpassing the million-dollar mark for the first time. It was also the first time the championship game was broadcast in prime time, drawing an estimated 39 million viewers.

1975   The tournament field was expanded to 32 teams, and the term "Final Four" was used officially for the first time by the NCAA.

1979   The tournament bracket grew to 40 teams. The championship game between Michigan State (with Earvin "Magic" Johnson) and Indiana State (with Larry Bird) received a record rating of 24.1 (% of households with televisions viewing). To this day it is the highest rated college basketball game of all time.

1980   Eight more teams were added to the tournament field, bringing the total to 48 teams.

1981   "Final Four" becomes a registered trademark of the NCAA.

1982   A three-year, US$48 million television agreement between CBS and the NCAA began. It was the first year that the "selection show" appeared on live national television.

1983   The tournament was expanded to 52 teams, with four of the teams playing into a 48-team bracket.

1985   The tournament field expanded to 64 teams, eliminating the first-round byes that were necessary under the previous bracketing systems. The 23.2 rating of the championship game between Villanova and Georgetown is the second highest rated college basketball game of all time. CBS and the NCAA began their second three-year contract.

1988   The NCAA and CBS began their third three-year contract; CBS broadcast all regional semifinal games during prime time.

1991   The NCAA and CBS began a seven-year, US$1 billion contract.

1995   CBS and the NCAA extended their agreement through 2002, replacing the 1991 contract with one worth US$1.75 billion.

1996   The NCAA expanded coverage of the tournament to the Internet, creating the first web page for the Final Four. Preliminary rounds of the tournament were added to the NCAA's web page the following year.

1999   CBS and the NCAA signed a new 11-year, US$6 billion contract for tournament coverage through 2013. CBS is scheduled to pay the NCAA US$764 million in the final year of the contract. The agreement includes rights to not only television programming, but also to radio and Internet broadcasts.

2000   The tournament adds another team to the tournament, creating a "play in" round between the 64th and 65th seeds. The tournament nickname "Big Dance," is registered by the NCAA.

2001   The NCAA and Illinois High School Association are granted a trademark for the term "March Madness."

2002   CBS expands the tournament selection show to a full hour; ESPN airs its first broadcast of a first round game.

2005   CBS contracts with CSTV.com to provide Internet coverage of the first 58 tournament games. CBS buys CSTV in November for US$325 million. The NCAA purchases the rival NIT in August for US$56 million.

2006   The Ratings Percentage Index (RPI), used in seeding teams in the tournament, is released to the public for the first time.

2010   CBS Sports, Turner Broadcasting, and the NCAA sign a 14-year contract (2011–2024) for more than US$10.8 billion.

2011   Three more teams are added to the tournament, creating three more "play in" games, collectively dubbed the "First Four."

2013   Division I, II, and III championship games occur for the first time in the same city (Atlanta) over the same weekend.

Sources: ncaasports.com/basketball/mens/story/9033549; ncaasports.com/basket ball-men/2010-04-21/cbs-sports-turner-broadcasting-ncaa-reach-14-year-agreement.

It is unclear how much of the tournament expansion was driven by media pressure, but as the numbers suggest, both the NCAA and broadcasters (CBS, in particular) benefit from the relationship. Participating colleges and universities also have reason to support the expansion, as the additional attention they receive is seen as a positive tool for cultivating donations and applications for admission.

7.8.7 *Media timeouts*

Media (television and radio) timeouts are a way to ensure that networks have a sufficient number of advertising slots to sell. NCAA basketball games have 2 twenty-minute halves of play. Depending on the media coverage for the event and the local or national media agreement, there can be as few as zero or as many as four media timeouts each half. For national television coverage, for example, there are media timeouts roughly every four minutes of play, occurring at the first dead ball after the 16-, 12-, 8-, and 4-minute marks in each half. With restrictions, regular team timeouts can also be extended as media timeouts. (Bilik, 2007)

Why might media timeouts matter? The frequency of play stoppages can have a significant impact on how a coach manages a game or builds a team. Depending on the type of media coverage, teams can call five or six timeouts each game. Timeouts serve three main functions for a team: (1) Providing rest for players, (2) stopping the opponent's momentum, (3) stopping play to conserve time or reorganize in the waning moments of a game. With an additional four timeouts in each half of a televised basketball game, coaches are better able to conserve timeouts for the endgame. This may carry additional advantages for networks, as frequent timeouts at the end of a close game provide even greater opportunities to secure advertising revenue.

Frequency of play stoppages also impacts the use and possibly even the recruiting of players. Fitness becomes less important in a game where play is interrupted frequently, and a team attempting to "run its opponent into the ground" with an up-tempo style of play will find it more difficult to wear them down. While a slower game and frequent play stoppages would seem likely to deter fans, the continued and growing popularity of college basketball would suggest that this is not a problem.

7.9 Media-prevented (or at least discouraged) Changes in College Sports

Until a four-team playoff was introduced for the 2014 season, all of the divisions except for I-FBS had a playoff system for football. Though the media lacks the authority to stop implementation of a playoff system at the top level, there are at least three good reasons why for many years they discouraged such a change.

First, implementation of a playoff system threatened to dismantle or weaken the attraction of the bowl games. In 2012–2013, there were 35 bowl games played from December 15, 2012 to January 7, 2013, up from 28 games as recently as the 2005–2006 bowl season. All of these bowl games are important to network profitability. In 2003–2004, the Walt Disney Co. (broadcasting through ABC and various ESPN channels) held the television rights to 25 of the 28 bowl games, including the four BCS games. ABC reported to the Knight Commission on Intercollegiate Athletics that they had lost money on the BCS games that year. The commission's assessment was that ABC's claim was probably accurate in a narrow sense, but that overall the Walt Disney Co. likely turned a profit from the venture. The Knight Commission Report (Frank, 2004) indicated a number of factors that may not have been included in ABC's analysis:

1. Shoulder (ancillary) programming (pregame and postgame shows) revenue was likely not included in ABC's report. Not only do these programs generate advertising revenue, but production costs are relatively low, especially given that no rights fees must be paid.
2. Profits from network-owned affiliated stations are typically not included in the national network's income statements. As such, local advertising revenue that would accrue to the affiliate owner was probably not included in ABC's testimony before the commission.
3. The non-BCS bowls broadcast by ABC and ESPN generated positive net revenue for Disney. The commission concluded that the broadcast rights fees Disney paid many of the bowl games were "less-than-market value." This allowed Disney to reap profits and use the money to subsidize the BCS broadcasts.

Second, and perhaps less recognized, implementation of a playoff system threatens to weaken interest in the regular season. Under the old (pre-playoff) BCS structure, every game counted, at least for the contending teams. With a playoff system, once a team qualifies for the postseason, interest in regular season games would wane. Early season games could also diminish in importance, as there may be less concern about losing an early season match-up. To contend for the national championship in the old BCS system, teams with even one loss often found themselves on the outside looking in. If the playoff selection process, for example, is dominated by conference champions, early season inter-conference match-ups lose significance. Keeping the BCS in lieu of a playoff system means keeping the regular season more interesting for fans, and maintaining viewers each Saturday (and Thursday, Friday, and sometimes Sunday) in the fall. As University of Georgia coach Mark Richt claims, "I think college football has the most exciting regular season of any sport because there is not a playoff system. The whole season is a playoff system" ("Bowl games," n.d.). With only four teams, the new playoff structure may not diminish regular season interest too much, but it is something BCS organizers and the NCAA will watch closely.

A third reason for opposing a playoff system is that the BCS, like the system it replaced, is controversial. Seemingly as important as any other tradition in college football is the annual debate over "Who's number one?" The debates over specific teams, as well as the general controversy of bowls versus a playoff system provide volumes of material for sports talk shows and other non-event sports programming. The following examples illustrate clearly why the issue is so contentious among fans and sports experts in the media. In 2001, the University of Nebraska was ranked #2 by the BCS, but only #4 in both the coaches (USAT/ESPN) and sportswriters' (AP) polls. Nebraska was selected as the national title opponent of #1 University of Miami, despite Nebraska taking its first loss late in the season to the #3 ranked University of Colorado, the eventual Big 12 champion (but with two regular season losses). The University of Oregon, ranked #4 by the BCS, but #2 in the two main polls, and also with only one loss, was overlooked for the title game. Miami dominated Nebraska 37-14 in the 2002 Rose Bowl, easily winning the national championship. Meanwhile, in the

Tostitos Fiesta Bowl, Oregon dismantled Colorado 38-16. ("All-time results," n.d.)

In 2006, Big Ten rivals Ohio State and Michigan were undefeated and ranked #1 and #2 in the polls until their annual meeting in November. Ohio State defeated Michigan 42-39 in a game that some billed as the national championship game. Certainly, it left some fans hoping for an Ohio State-Michigan rematch in the BCS title game. Michigan's loss, however, dropped them just below the University of Florida, also with one loss (to Auburn, who finished 10-2) but with perhaps the toughest schedule of the one-loss teams. Ohio State and Florida squared off in the 2007 BCS championship game, but many fans were left unsatisfied with the selection process. Michigan fans were initially upset, but their claim was weakened by a decisive 32-18 loss to USC in the Rose Bowl. The University of Wisconsin (11-1) also had cause to be upset, not so much because they deserved a chance at the national title, but because as the third place team in the Big Ten, they were excluded from a US$17 million BCS game in favor of the US$4.25 million Capital One Bowl. The strongest objections came from fans of Boise State University, the undefeated team from the mid-major Western Athletic Conference that defeated a highly-regarded University of Oklahoma team in the Fiesta Bowl. The final twist came when heavily favored Ohio State, predicted by some to win in a rout, were instead blown out by Florida, 41-14. In the end, there was one team that went undefeated, another that won the BCS championship, a conference looking like it had been vastly overrated (the Big Ten), and many people calling for some type of a playoff system.

The BCS system is even more controversial when there are more than two undefeated teams. It creates a situation where teams can go undefeated in the regular season, win their bowl game, and despite no one beating them, still not receive a share of the national title or even the opportunity to play for it. In 2004, there were four undefeated teams at the end of the regular season (the Universities of Southern California, Oklahoma, Auburn, and Utah). #1 USC crushed #2 Oklahoma 55-19 for the title in the 2005 FedEx Orange

Bowl, while #3 Auburn and #6 Utah were left out of the BCS Championship game. Auburn defeated Virginia Tech University 16-13 in the Nokia Sugar Bowl, remaining undefeated, and made their claim for a share of the national championship. Utah soundly defeated the University of Pittsburgh 35-7 in the Tostitos Fiesta Bowl, also remaining undefeated, but the Utes did not press their case as legitimate co-champions (Utah's #6 BCS ranking, despite being undefeated, was aided by a relatively weak schedule).

Utah made a stronger case in 2008–2009, when it ended the season as the country's only undefeated team (national champion Florida had one loss during the regular season). Officially attributed to having played a weak schedule, Utah, then in the Mountain West Conference, was excluded from the national championship game. It was more likely that the BCS was concerned about ratings and maintaining the stature and power of the BCS conferences. Utah's exclusion from the championship game prompted Utah Senator Orrin Hatch in 2008 to declare that congressional hearings on the BCS would be held. In 2011, Utah's Attorney General initiated an antitrust lawsuit against the BCS, a lawsuit that could legally establish whether or not the BCS is a cartel or an illegal trust. Utah, meanwhile, in 2011 joined the Pac-12, one of the BCS conferences.

In 2010–2011, three teams (Auburn, Oregon, and TCU) finished the regular season undefeated. Auburn narrowly defeated Oregon in the National Championship game, while TCU edged out Wisconsin in the Rose Bowl to remain undefeated. The various polls and computer rankings that comprise the BCS had Auburn and Oregon ahead of TCU entering the bowl season, but with a four-team playoff system, TCU would have had its chance to compete for the national championship.

Finally, in 2011–2012, LSU finished the regular season as the only undefeated team. Alabama and Oklahoma State were ranked #2 and #3 behind LSU in the BCS, with Alabama ranking ahead in the polls and Oklahoma State sitting higher in the computer rankings. In the end, Alabama got the nod, setting up a rematch of the regular season and an all-SEC national title game.

Fast fact. *In November 2008, with the U.S. economy in deep recession and the country engaged in wars in Iraq and Afghanistan, then President-elect Barack Obama weighed in on the issue of a playoff in college football. In an interview on CBS's 60 Minutes, Obama told CBS reporter Steve Kroft, "This is important... I think any sensible person would say that if you've got a bunch of teams who play throughout the season, and many of them have one loss or two losses, there's no clear decisive winner that we should be creating a playoff system. Eight teams. That would be three rounds to determine a national champion. ... It would add three weeks to the season. You could trim back the regular season. I don't know any serious fan of college football who has disagreed with me on this ... . I'm gonna throw my weight around a little bit. I think it's the right thing to do".* ("Obama calls for NCAA playoffs," 2008)

In years where there are more than two legitimate contenders for the title, one would expect the non-championship bowl games to take on added significance in the eyes of viewers, as reflected by the ratings. In 2001, both the Rose and Fiesta Bowls drew close fan attention, especially from those already critical of the team selection process for the national championship game. In 2004, the Sugar Bowl drew closer scrutiny as fans and experts looked for a sense of Auburn's legitimacy as a claimant to the national title. Conversely, the 2009 Sugar Bowl that pitted undefeated Utah against Alabama earned one of the lowest ratings in BCS history and was rated lower than two other BCS bowls that year (Rose and Fiesta) that had less significance to the national championship debate. While the BCS may have been wrong to exclude Utah from the title game based on its on-field performance, it may have been onto something regarding Utah's ability to draw fans.

Such controversies stimulate debate and provide material for ancillary programming, but the important question for media providers, and their taste for the BCS, is how viewership is affected. Table 7.2 shows the Nielsen Media Research ratings for BCS

Table 7.2.   BCS bowl all-time TV ratings (1998–2013).

Ranking	Bowl	Year	Teams	Rating
1	Rose	2006	Texas – USC	21.7*#
2	Orange	2001	Florida State – Oklahoma	17.8*
3	Sugar	2000	Florida State – Virginia Tech	17.5*#
4	BCS Championship	2007	Florida – Ohio State	17.4*
5 (tie)	Fiesta	2003	Ohio State – Miami	17.2*#
5 (tie)	Fiesta	1999	Florida State – Tennessee	17.2*
7	BCS Championship	2010	Alabama – Texas	17.17*
8	BCS Championship	2009	Florida – Oklahoma	15.8*
9	BCS Championship	2011	Oregon – Auburn	15.29*
10	BCS Championship	2013	Alabama – Notre Dame	15.1*
11	Sugar	2004	LSU – Oklahoma	14.5*
12 (tie)	BCS Championship	2008	LSU – Ohio State	14.4*
12 (tie)	Rose	2004	Michigan – USC	14.4+
14	Rose	2000	Wisconsin – Stanford	14.1
15 (tie)	BCS Championship	2012	Alabama – LSU	14.0*
15 (tie)	Rose	2001	Washington – Purdue	14.0
17 (tie)	Rose	2002	Miami – Nebraska	13.9*

(*Continued*)

Table 7.2. (*Continued*)

Ranking	Bowl	Year	Teams	Rating
17 (tie)	Rose	2007	USC – Michigan	13.9
19	Orange	2005	USC – Oklahoma	13.7*
20	Rose	1999	Wisconsin – UCLA	13.3
21	Rose	2010	Ohio State – Oregon	13.18
22 (tie)	Sugar	2001	Miami – Florida	12.9
22 (tie)	Fiesta	2006	Ohio State – Notre Dame	12.9
24	Rose	2005	Texas – Michigan	12.4
25	Orange	2006	Penn State – Florida	12.3
26	Rose	2009	USC – Penn State	11.7
27	Sugar	1999	Ohio State – Texas A&M	11.5
28 (tie)	Fiesta	2002	Oregon – Colorado	11.3+
28 (tie)	Orange	2000	Michigan – Alabama	11.3
28 (tie)	Rose	2003	Oklahoma – Washington State	11.3
31	Rose	2011	Wisconsin – TCU	11.26+
32	Rose	2008	USC – Illinois	11.11
33	Fiesta	2001	Oregon State – Notre Dame	10.7
34	Fiesta	2009	Texas – Ohio State	10.4

(*Continued*)

Table 7.2. (*Continued*)

Ranking	Bowl	Year	Teams	Rating
35	Rose	2012	Oregon – Wisconsin	10.2
36 (tie)	Orange	2003	USC – Iowa	9.7
36 (tie)	Orange	2004	Miami – Florida State	9.7
38 (tie)	Fiesta	2000	Nebraska – Tennessee	9.5
38 (tie)	Sugar	2005	Auburn – Virginia Tech	9.5+
38 (tie)	Orange	2002	Florida – Maryland	9.5
41	Rose	2013	Stanford – Wisconsin	9.4
42	Sugar	2007	LSU – Notre Dame	9.3
43	Sugar	2003	Florida State – Georgia	9.2
44	Sugar	2002	LSU – Illinois	8.6
45	Sugar	2010	Cincinnati – Florida	8.5
46 (tie)	Fiesta	2012	Oklahoma State – Stanford	8.4
46 (tie)	Orange	1999	Florida – Syracuse	8.4
46 (tie)	Fiesta	2007	Boise State – Oklahoma	8.4
49	Fiesta	2010	Boise State – TCU	8.23
50	Sugar	2011	Ohio State – Arkansas	8.2
51	Sugar	2009	Utah – Alabama	7.8+

(*Continued*)

Table 7.2.   (*Continued*)

Ranking	Bowl	Year	Teams	Rating
52	Fiesta	2008	West Virginia – Oklahoma	7.7@
53 (tie)	Orange	2008	Kansas – Virginia Tech	7.4@
53 (tie)	Fiesta	2013	Oregon – Kansas State	7.4
53(tie)	Fiesta	2005	Utah – Pittsburgh	7.4
56 (tie)	Sugar	2008	Georgia – Hawaii	7.0@
56 (tie)	Orange	2007	Louisville – Wake Forest	7.0
58	Orange	2010	Iowa – Georgia Tech	6.8@
59	Orange	2011	Stanford – Virginia Tech	6.75
60	Sugar	2013	Louisville – Florida	6.2@
61	Fiesta	2011	Connecticut – Oklahoma	6.15
62 (tie)	Sugar	2012	Michigan – Virginia Tech	6.1
62 (tie)	Orange	2013	Florida State – Northern Illinois	6.1@
64	Orange	2009	Virginia Tech – Cincinnati	5.4@
65	Orange	2012	West Virginia – Clemson	4.5@

* — BCS National Championship Game.

+ — game involving "jilted" team, as described above.

\# — match-up of the only no-loss major conference teams.

@ — game with lower ratings than at least one non-BCS bowl that year.

Sources: "TV ratings" (n.d.); Barron (2007); Consoli (2007).

National Championship games and other selected BCS games. For comparative purposes, most non-BCS bowl games garner ratings from 0.8 to around 6.0. Ratings represent the percentage of households with a television watching the game. Nielsen Media Research estimates that there are 111.4 million "television households" in the United States, representing approximately 98% of US households and over 283 million people.

As Table 7.2 reveals, the highest rated BCS National Championship Game was the 2006 Rose Bowl between undisputed #1 USC and #2 Texas, attracting over 35 million viewers; it was also the highest rated college football game since 1987. The 2003 Fiesta Bowl, another uncontroversial championship game (between Ohio State and Miami), drew just over 29 million viewers. The controversial national title games of 2004 and 2005, however, averaged only 22.7 million viewers, and the 2005 Orange Bowl, the BCS title game between USC and Oklahoma, was the lowest rated BCS championship game since they began. The 2002 Rose Bowl between Miami and Nebraska was the second lowest rated BCS title game. The third lowest rated BCS title game was the all-SEC contest between LSU and Alabama. The poor showing was likely a combination of only one conference being represented and some controversy over Oklahoma's exclusion from the game. The 2004 Sugar Bowl, the controversial title game between LSU and Oklahoma (USC was left out despite a top ranking in both the Associated Press and *USA Today*/ESPN polls; all three teams had one loss) was the fifth lowest rated BCS national championship game.

Based on the ratings, while the debates over who belongs in the championship game generate a lot of activity in ancillary programming, it does not appear to benefit the media provider of the game itself.

The 2006–2007 bowl season was the first in which a stand-alone BCS championship game was played after the New Year's bowl games. It is unclear whether the teams involved in the BCS games were less appealing, or whether the addition of a later title game decreased interest in other BCS bowls, but the Fiesta, Orange, and Sugar bowls all finished in the bottom 10 (at that time) of all-time

BCS game ratings. The Rose Bowl has maintained its position as the strongest of the non-championship bowl games, but since the inception of the championship game, overall ratings for all non-championship games have dropped. As revealed in Table 7.2, the bottom ten of the BCS bowl game ratings is now comprised entirely of non-championship games played since the creation of the BCS Championship game. Is the drop solely due to the implementation of a championship game? It is unlikely, given the proliferation of programming substitutes that would dilute audiences across the spectrum, but it is something BCS officials should consider as they play with the structure of the college football postseason. Though controversies about who belongs in the title game appear to hurt ratings of the championship game, they can provide a boost to the other BCS games, particularly those involving the jilted team(s). For example, the 2004 Rose Bowl, the non-title game between USC and Michigan, was the highest rated BCS non-championship game, drawing almost equal ratings to that year's title game between LSU and Oklahoma. However, neither the 2002 Fiesta Bowl (Oregon v. Colorado) nor the 2005 Sugar Bowl (Auburn v. Virginia Tech) drew ratings that would make up for the shortfall in the title game.[6] In fact, the 2005 Rose Bowl pitting Texas v. Michigan drew more viewers than the Sugar Bowl, even though neither Texas nor Michigan could make a claim for the title. Given the likely boost to ancillary programming, but the negative impact on the ratings for the main event, it is unclear whether controversy over the BCS rankings serves media providers' interests. The four-team playoff system set to begin in 2014–2015 should provide something of a natural experiment. Whether that structure becomes permanent will depend heavily on its rating success.

While the media have some good reasons to support the BCS rather than a playoff system, they are not the only important

---

[6] It should be noted, however, that the 2002 bowl games were the first after the September 11, 2001, terrorist attacks on the United States. National enthusiasm for sports of all kinds was somewhat muted, and this may have been reflected in the lower ratings.

stakeholder in this decision. Despite the media's financial influence, the major conferences and their member schools (the "cartel within the cartel") have a vested interest in maintaining a system that offers lucrative payouts, provides national exposure, and allows half of the participating teams to end their season on a positive note. As long as the playoff system implemented for 2014–2015 maintains or enhances the financial position of the automatic qualifier conferences, it is likely to become a permanent fixture.

7.10   Wider Impacts of Media Coverage of College Sports

We have addressed the relationship between the media on college sports, as well as its financial impact on networks and athletic departments of colleges and universities. Media coverage of college sports also has important consequences beyond the ivy-covered buildings of academia, some of which are measurable, others of which are more qualitative, but no less significant.

7.10.1   *Lost productivity (March Madness)*

Every March, the NCAA men's basketball tournament (and to a lesser degree the women's tournament) turns ordinary folks into college basketball fans and illegal gamblers. Offices across the country become abuzz with talk of tournament brackets and betting pools, #1 seeds and "Cinderellas," all of it revolving around "March Madness." Break times and even work times find office workers checking scores online, or catching a glimpse of games on the closest television.

While the tournament is fun and exciting for these fans, it has been criticized because of the adverse effect it has on worker productivity. The outplacement firm Challenger, Gray, and Christmas, Inc. estimated that the 2013 NCAA men's basketball tournament would cost American companies US$134 million over just the first two days of the tournament. Their estimates were based on the following assumptions: (1) Three million workers spend one hour per day watching games online (rather than working), based on survey data, (2) workers earn an average hourly wage of US$22.38, based on Bureau of Labor Statistics figures. That works out to US$67.1 million per day, or US$134 million over two days.

Those numbers could be conservative, as survey data reveal that 66% of workers follow the tournament during work hours. Thirty percent of employees anticipated spending at least three hours per day watching March Madness. Based on a U.S. labor force nearing 136 million, approximately 40 million workers would spend three or more hours daily watching the tournament, far more than the 3 million assumed in the study Another 12% of survey respondents reported that they had called in sick in previous years so they could watch games at home. If 40 million workers spent just one hour per day watching games at work, the daily losses would approach US$900 million (Challenger, Gray & Christmas, Inc., 2013).

Fast fact. *In 2009, Challenger, Gray and Christmas suspended the study for a year, out of respect for the economic hardships many were facing, and the reasonable assumption that people already fearing job loss would not risk it by wasting time at work. As John Challenger explained, "In the current environment, any attempt to estimate the impact of March Madness on productivity would be counterproductive and inappropriate. The fact is that our whimsical examination of the intersection of sports and the workplace is often misinterpreted and taken too seriously in the best of times. Now that we are in the worst of times, there is no need to generate additional sources of anxiety and stress. We hope to continue this study of our national preoccupation with sports and how it may impact workplace productivity once the economy is on surer footing". ("No March Madness," 2009)*

How accurate are the Challenger, Gray and Christmas estimates? It is difficult to say, as there are strong reasons to believe they underestimate the productivity loss, and equally compelling arguments for why the estimates exaggerate the loss. Let us turn to those arguments now, first considering why the estimates may be too low.

1. The distraction of the tournament starts before the games begin. On the Sunday before the tournament starts (usually on a Thursday, not counting the play in game), the NCAA announces the 68-team field. As the brackets come out, the madness begins. As CEO John Challenger explains, "Beginning that Monday, college basketball fans across the country will begin organizing office pools and researching teams for their brackets. Even people who do not follow college basketball for the entire season can easily get wrapped up in the excitement of March Madness and trying to pick the winners". (Challenger, Gray & Christmas, Inc., 2006)

2. As suggested above, the hour per day estimate may be too low. Survey data suggest most extensive viewing, and users may visit websites far more often, via work computers or mobile technology, especially when games are provided online at no charge. There may also be considerable time spent consulting newspapers, sports magazines, and co-workers, none of which is factored into the Challenger figures.

3. March Madness brings out people who don't normally consider themselves to be fans, but who participate in the office pools. That may add to the numbers checking websites or otherwise distracted by the tournament.

While there is cause to suspect that the estimates are too low, there are also good reasons why the Challenger figures may overstate the loss of productivity.

1. While productivity losses may be heavy in the first week of the tournament, as March Madness gets past the opening rounds, fewer games occur during regular 9-5 work hours, and there are fewer games for workers to follow. Also, many brackets have long since gone into the recycle bin, as hopes of winning the office pool have been smashed for millions.

2. The estimates assume that the tournament is not merely a substitute for other office distractions, such as playing solitaire on the computer or conversing at the water cooler about other topics. Additionally, these "distractions" may actually enhance productivity over the work day if they provide workers a quick mental break that helps them refocus their attention.

3. Many workers lack regular access to a computer during the workday, although the explosion of Smart Phone use has expanded access. Many employees in both the manufacturing and service industries spend their day on their feet, not sitting in front of a computer where they could easily sneak onto a website for score updates.

4. Many employees that have access to a computer are salaried workers, meaning that they are paid to accomplish tasks rather than put in a certain number of hours. Many full-time salaried workers work more than 40 hours per week with no additional compensation, so as long as tasks are accomplished in a timely fashion, we would expect no productivity loss for these workers. As Challenger explains, "in the end, the work still gets done and businesses are no worse for wear" (Challenger, 2009). For the lucky few of us, who get to be sports economists or otherwise employed in the sports industry, checking scores and studying teams is part of the job.

While we can debate the magnitude, most would agree that there is some productivity loss due to March Madness. Whether it provides a net *utility* loss for society is another question, one that is even more difficult to answer. To some degree the lost output for firms and their owners is offset by the enjoyment fans get from participating in the madness. Still, for firms competing in tough markets, lost productivity can be a serious concern.

7.10.2   *Loss of amateurism and educational focus*

Expansion of media coverage and substantial growth in the dollars involved have caused some to decry the loss of amateurism in college sports. As the financial stakes rise, the opportunities and incentives for cheating (e.g., player payments) increase. Some have called outright for paying players and dispensing with the illusion of football and men's basketball as amateur sports. Many prefer college sports to their professional counterparts, believing that college players have purer motives, playing unselfishly and for the love of the game.

A greater concern is that the commercialization of college sports, as fueled by the media, further distracts players from being true *student*-athletes. The Football Bowl Association praises the bowl system for many reasons, including that "Coaches get to work with their players for an extra two to five weeks, which pays dividends for young players" ("FAQ," n.d.). While the extra time may benefit those with legitimate professional sports aspirations and potential, those whose time would be better spent on academics lose an additional two to five weeks of study time, often around the time of final exams. These effects extend beyond the players, as cheerleaders, band members, and other students involved take time from studies to prepare for the bowl event. How many are affected in a typical bowl season?

> The numbers don't lie. Truly, everybody wins at a college postseason bowl game. There are 28 communities and the thousands of citizens of those communities who win from having the game in their city. There are more than 7,000 student-athletes who take part in the game. But don't forget the more than 13,800 band members, the more than 100,000 additional performers who take part in the entertainment and other productions associated with the games, and the more than 1,280 cheerleaders who support their teams and fan bases. Most notably, there are more than 1.8 million fans who celebrate their teams, the games, the bowls and the traditions created every postseason. It's easy to spot the winners at a bowl game. Point in any direction. It's everyone. ("College bowl games," n.d.)

Despite the Football Bowl Association's claim that "everybody wins," there are costs imposed on the various participants. To the extent that the media has influenced proliferation of the bowl system, it bears some responsibility for the lost study time and the "beer and circus" path that some colleges and universities have gone down.

7.10.3   *Alcohol advertising and campus drinking*

The problems of underage drinking, particularly by college students, are well documented. Causes of underage drinking are numerous; one factor alleged to contribute is alcohol advertising on sports programs. According to the Center on Alcohol Marketing and Youth, in 2001, 93% of kids between 8 and 17 followed sports through television, radio, internet, and print media, with television being the most popular. That same year, alcohol companies spent US$811.2 million per year on television ads. Of that amount, almost US$53 million was spent on alcohol ads for college sports programs. (Center on Alcohol Marketing and Youth, n.d.)

Not surprisingly, the beer industry disputes any connection between its advertising and alcohol abuse amongst college students. According to John Kaestner, a vice president for consumer affairs for Anheuser-Busch, "Preventing underage drinking or reducing excessive drinking has nothing to do with restricting beer ads on televised college sports." Jeff Becker of the Beer Institute supports this claim, contending that "Young people themselves consistently rank advertising last when asked what influences them to drink". (Fatsis and Lawton, 2003)

Despite the claims of the beer industry, public efforts have been made to curb alcohol advertising. In 2004, Representative and former University of Nebraska football coach Tom Osborne (R–NE) co-sponsored House Resolution 575. The resolution was supported by a number of prominent current and former college coaches, including John Wooden (UCLA Basketball), Dean Smith (UNC Basketball), Joe Paterno (Penn State Football), and Jim Calhoun (Connecticut Basketball). It called on the NCAA and its member colleges and universities to "voluntarily end alcohol advertising on college sports broadcasts" (Center for Science in the Public Interest

[CSPI], 2004). In their letter supporting this resolution, these coaching legends wrote, "We share a common belief that alcohol and college sports do not belong together. Advertising alcoholic beverages during college sports telecasts undermines the best interests of higher education and compromises the efforts of colleges and others to combat epidemic levels of alcohol problems on many campuses today". (CSPI, 2004)

Since the Center for Science in the Public Interest launched its "Campaign for Alcohol-Free Sports TV," 247 colleges and universities and 2 conferences have signed "The College Commitment." Schools signing The College Commitment pledge to not accept alcohol advertising for locally produced sports programs, and to support policies against alcohol advertising at the conference, NCAA, and BCS levels (CSPI, n.d.). As mentioned earlier in this chapter, the new Big Ten Channel has already announced that they will not accept alcohol advertising for any program shown on the network.

Few would dispute that society would benefit from less underage and excessive drinking. The important question here is whether reduced alcohol advertising will significantly impact this drinking, or whether schools and media providers are turning their backs on easy money. Hopefully the anti-alcohol advertising efforts will reduce the extent to which the media relationship with college sports promotes underage drinking and the problems it creates, but if the beer industry is correct, the effects will be negligible.

7.10.4 *Increased costs for cable TV subscribers*

Significant growth in the value of sports programming rights contracts contributes to rising costs for cable TV subscribers, including many who place little or no value on watching sports. Through a process known as **bundling**, cable TV companies combine channels and sell them as a package, rather than individually. This means that sports fans only interested in ESPN programming are also buying access to shows such as *America's Top Model* and *Iron Chef*, while fans of those shows may be buying access to sports channels they will never watch. Understandably, non-sports fans are upset at seeing their cable bills rise because sports programming is now more costly. Cable companies worry that the rising cost of channel packages may price some consumers out of the market.

In response to this issue, some have called for **a la carte pricing** of cable channels, allowing cable subscribers to only purchase those stations they want to watch. Arizona Senator John McCain introduced a bill to Congress that would "encourage the wholesale and retail unbundling of programming by distributors and programmers." McCain, who claims bundling is "unfair and wrong," was motivated in part by his 74-year-old widowed neighbor having to pay ever increasing rates for sports channels she never watches. (White, 2013)

Bundling increases profits for cable companies. Since demand for a bundle exhibits much less variability than would the demand for individual channels, cable companies can price bundles closer to the average consumer's willingness to pay. Profits increase as firms are not forced to choose between pricing high and only drawing a few customers, or pricing low and attracting many consumers, but earning small margins on each buyer. Overall, consumers have much closer to the same willingness to pay, though what part of the bundle they really want to buy can vary dramatically.

To illustrate, suppose Balin is willing to pay US$80 per month for ESPNU, but only US$20 per month for the Cooking Channel. Zera, conversely, is willing to pay US$10 and US$80, respectively, for those same channels. If sold individually, our cable provider, Package TV would choose to sell ESPNU for either US$80 or US$10 per month (assume that the marginal cost of providing each channel is zero). Pricing at US$80 gives Package US$80 in profit, as only Balin buys the channel for US$80. At a price of US$10 both consumers buy ESPNU, but Package's profit is only US$20 per month. Following the same logic with the Cooking Channel, Package earns US$80 per month if it prices high, only US$40 if it prices low. By selling both channels at the high price (the best of the options available), Package earns US$160 per month.

Now suppose that Package bundles the two channels. Balin is willing to pay US$100 per month for the bundle, Zera US$90. If Package charges US$100, its profit is US$100 per month, as Balin is the only buyer. If instead Package charges US$90 per month, its profit is US$180. Package earns a higher profit through bundling (and selling at US$90 per month), but notice something else that results. With individual pricing, Balin and Zera end up with only one channel each. By purchasing the bundle, both buyers end up with both channels, and are better off in the sense that both place a positive value on the two channels.

While some of the profits from bundling result from a transfer of consumer surplus from buyers to sellers, the rest comes from efficiency gains through increased sales. Programming often has high fixed costs to produce but very low (sometimes zero) marginal costs, meaning the economies of scale are extensive. Expanded sales reduce the per unit costs and allow firms to charge lower prices, in some cases low enough to offset what consumers might pay for unused channels.[7]

Would a la carte pricing be better for consumers, and non-sports fans in particular? The reasoning is that by paying only for the channels a person wants, say 30 out of 100 channels in the current package, the customer would pay only US$30, instead of US$100. The problem with this is that efficiency losses from unbundling would likely raise costs and prices, reducing sales and profits for cable providers. While few would shed a tear over cable companies earning fewer profits, it is these profits that allow for and encourage investment in a greater quantity and quality of programming and distribution technology. In short, while a la carte pricing would restore consumer surplus to some buyers, consumer welfare overall might drop.

---

[7] For a more thorough explanation of bundling and how it can benefit both sellers and buyers, see Alex Tabarrok's (May 11, 2013) discussion on http://marginalrevolution.com/marginalrevolution/2013/05/bundling.html.

7.11   Chapter Summary

Earlier in this chapter, we asked whether the relationship between the NCAA and the media was normal productive economic exchange or an unhealthy co-dependence. The media clearly benefit from the college sports product, as evidenced both by the profits earned and by the creation and expansion of networks specializing in college sports. Whether the media has benefited college sports is less clear. Media coverage has increased the profile of college sports, expanding greatly the revenues for athletic departments and the exposure of top athletes. A number of coaches and athletic directors, and a handful of athletes, have reaped tremendous financial rewards, but it is unclear whether the majority have benefited. Universities earn millions for participating in bowl games, but then turn around and spend it to send the team, their families, and "friends of the program" to these events. The quest for money from bowl games and NCAA tournament appearances, leads universities to engage in an arms race for the best athletes and facilities.

7.12   Key Terms

A la carte pricing	Horizontal integration
Ancillary programming	Implicit cost
Brand proliferation	Maximin strategy
Bundling	Maximum Contract Offer
Dominant strategy	Media providers' dilemma
Economies of scale	Oligopoly
Economies of scope	Present value
Explicit cost	Prisoners' dilemma
Flutie effect	Shoulder programming
Future value	Winner's curse

7.13   Review Questions

1. How has media coverage changed over the past 30 years?
2. What is horizontal integration and why do firms pursue it?
3. What are some ways that media providers can achieve economies of scale and economies of scope?
4. What is the relationship between ancillary programming and shoulder programming? What are examples of each?
5. What are the main factors determining the maximum contract offer a media provider should be willing to make for broadcast rights?
6. How does the timing of expected revenues and costs affect the maximum contract offer? How does the interest rate affect it?
7. What is the media providers' dilemma?
8. BCS bowl payments for 2013–2014 were listed as US$18 million per team. Explain why none of the participating teams will actually claim that much as revenue for their athletic departments.
9. What are the various ways that colleges benefit from media exposure?
10. What are some ways that the media have influenced college sports?
11. What forces have driven the formation and expansion of the BCS?
12. Why were bowl games created? What economic consequence does that have for schools that play in them?
13. Why is ABC's claim that it lost money on the BCS in 2003–2004 probably inaccurate in the bigger picture?
14. Why would media providers oppose moving from the bowl system to a playoff in DI-FBS college football?
15. What are some of the broader social and economic impacts of media coverage of college sports?

7.14   Discussion Questions

1. How will the proliferation of college sports networks affect the contracts that universities and their conferences sign with these networks?

2. How will the movement of college sports programming into the Internet and mobile phone technology affect offerings by traditional media (radio, television, and print)?

3. Given what we learned about collusion and game theory in Chapter 2, how might we expect FOX and ABC to behave in bowl scheduling?

4. Do you believe that instant replay has enhanced the fan experience? The quality of contests? Fan demand for contests? Explain.

5. What are some externalities created by media coverage of college sports? Does the presence of these externalities suggest that the market is over- or under-providing coverage relative to what is socially optimal?

6. Suppose that NBC is contemplating a bid for the 2016 Party-Time Punch Bowl. If NBC expects to generate US$300 million in advertising revenue, US$50 million in ancillary programming revenue, and a US$20 million boost to its non-sports programming. NBC also expects production costs of US$200 million and it could earn US$140 million by broadcasting other programming in that time slot. What is the maximum contract offer NBC should be willing to make?

7. Suppose that the numbers in Question 6 are the annual figures NBC expects over a three-year contract for the Punch Bowl. If the current interest rate is 5% and the rights must be paid for up front, what is the maximum contract offer NBC will make? (Assume that the revenues and costs generated over the three years are incurred at the *beginning* of each year.) Now assume that the revenues and costs are incurred at the *end* of each year; what effect will that have on the maximum contract offer?

8. What controversies in college sports would you expect to stimulate fan demand, and which would you expect to reduce it? Explain.

9. Many NCAA basketball tournament betting pools are illegal, and some are NCAA violations. Why then does the NCAA not do more to discourage gambling on March Madness?

10. March Madness has gradually expanded from 8 teams in 1939 to 68 in 2011. Evaluate the costs and benefits of the NCAA further expanding the tournament.

11. If you were a media provider would you prefer the old BCS bowl system or the new College Football Playoff? How would the structure of the playoff system (e.g., the number of teams) affect your analysis?

7.15   Internet Assignment

1. Table 7.2 covers through the 2012–2013 bowl season. If you are reading this book after the January 2014 bowl games, visit the FOX Sports BCS Football website (http://bcsfootball.org) and update Table 7.2. Are the new data consistent with the earlier evidence that uncontroversial (in terms of participants) BCS National Championship games earn higher television ratings? If there was controversy over which teams belonged in the title game, did the games involving the excluded teams receive higher ratings than is typical for that bowl game?

7.16   References

2013–2014 College Football Bowl Game Schedule (n.d.). Retrieved from http://www.collegefootballpoll.com/bowl_games_bowl_schedule.html on June 22, 2013.

A Primer on NCAA Rules for Football Safety (October 20, 2010). Retrieved from http://ncaastudent.org/wps/wcm/connect/public/ncaa/resources/latest+news/2010+news+stories/october/a+primer+on+ncaa+rules+for+football+safety on June 23, 2013.

About Us (n.d.[a]). Retrieved from http://cstv.com/online on July 4, 2013.

About Us (n.d.[b]) Retrieved from http://www.bbvacompassbowl.com/about-us.php on June 22, 2013.

Agreement on BCS Playoff Structure Reached (November 12, 2012). *USA Today*. Retrieved from http://www.usatoday.com/story/sports/ncaaf/bowls/2012/11/12/bcs-playoff-presidents-meeting-college-football-denver/1700455/ on June 22, 2013.

All-time Results (n.d.). Retrieved from http://bcsfootball.org/bcsfb/results on January 31, 2007.

Barron, D. (2007, January 8). Florida-Ohio State turns in solid rating. Retrieved from http://blogs.chron.com/sportsmedia/2007/01/nfl_net_sets_super_replays_wil/html on January 31, 2007.

BCS, ESPN Reach Deal to Air Games From 2011–2014 (2008, November 18). *SPN.com* Retrieved from http://sports.espn.go.com/espn/wire?section=ncf&id=3710611 on July 4, 2013.

BCS Explained (April 9, 2013). Retrieved from http://collegefootballpoll.com/bcs_explained.html on June 2, 2013.

Beseda, J. (2006, June 3). Football's civil war moves to Friday. *The Oregonian*, p. D01.

Bilik, E. (2007). *2007 NCAA Men's and Women's Basketball Rules and Interpretations.* Indianapolis, IN: National Collegiate Athletic Association.

Bowl Games … Where Everybody Wins (n.d.). Retrieved from http://footballbowlassociation.com on December 5, 2006.

Canzano, J. (2006a, September 19). Football is just a game, until you're on the clock. *The Oregonian*, p. D01.

Canzano, J. (2006b, December 10). 82-day wait for reason to prevail. *The Oregonian*, p. D01.

CBS Officially Acquires CSTV: College Sports Television Networks (2006, January 5). Retrieved from http://cstv.com/genrel/010606.aaa.html on December 6, 2006.

Center For Science in The Public Interest (n.d.). Campaign for alcohol-free sports fact sheet. Retrieved from http://www.cspinet.org/booze/CAFST/QuickFacts.pdf on December 7, 2006.

Center For Science in The Public Interest (2004, May 14). College greats join call for end to alcohol ads on college sports broadcast. Retrieved from http://cspinet.org/new/200405141.html on December 7, 2006.

Center on Alcohol Marketing and Youth (n.d.). *Alcohol Advertising on Sports Television 2001–2003.* Retrieved from http://camy.org/factsheets/pdf/AlcoholAdvertisingSports-Television2001-2003.pdf on December 6, 2006.

Challenger, J. (2009, March 17). No March Madness workplace productivity loss: Recession is the big bracket buster. *U.S. News and World Report.* Retrieved from http://www.usnews.com/opinion/articles/2009/03/17/no-march-madness-workplace-productivity-loss-recession-is-the-big-bracket-buster on June 23, 2013.

Challenger, Gray & Christmas, Inc. (2006, February 28). *March Madness.* Retrieved from http://www.challengergray.com/marchmadness.aspx on December 4, 2006.

Challenger, Gray & Christmas, Inc. (2013, March 13). *Challenger March Madness Report*. Retrieved from http://www.challengergray.com/press/PressRelease.aspx?PressUid=262 on June 23, 2013.

College Bowl Games Are Where Everybody Wins ... (n.d.). Retrieved from http://footballbowlassociation.com on June 23, 2013.

Consoli, J. (2007, January 9). Fox's BCS Championship Game nets 28.7 mil. in prime. Retrieved from http://www.mediaweek.com/mw/news/recent_display.jsp?vnu_content_id=1003529854 on January 30, 2007.

Copeland, J. (2006, December 18). Defining The Future: Television Agreements Established Support Funds For Student-athletes. *The NCAA News*, p. 5.

CSTV Kicks Off First Full Season On The Air August 26 With 9 New Programs in 13 Days (2003, August 19). Retrieved from http://cstv.com/genre/052104aae.html on December 6, 2006.

Dinich, H. (2012, June 27). Playoff plan to run through 2025. Retrieved from http://espn.go.com/college-football/story/_/id/8099187/ncaa-presidents-approve-four-team-college-football-playoff-beginning-2014 on August 6, 2012.

Eichelberger, C. (2010, December 22). College Football Winners Still Lose As Bowl Costs Exceed Payouts. *Bloomberg*. Retrieved from http://www.bloomberg.com/news/2010-12-23/college-football-winners-still-lose-as-bowl-game-expenses-exceed-payout.html on June 22, 2013.

ESPN, Inc. Fact Sheet (n.d.). *ESPNMediaZone.com*. Retrieved from http://espnmediazone.com/espn-inc-fact-sheet/ on July 2, 2013.

ESPN Lands Rights To College Playoff for $470M per year through 2025 (2012, November 21). *CBSSports.com*. Retrieved from http://www.cbssports.com/collegefootball/story/21083692/espn-lands-rights-to-college-playoff-for-470m-per-year-through-2025 on July 4, 2013.

FAQ (n.d.). Retrieved from http://footballbowlassociation.com/faq.html on December 5, 2006.

Fatsis, S. and C. Lawton (2003, November 12). Beer Ads On TV, College Sports: Explosive Mix? *Wall Street Journal*, p. B1.

FCN to create the Big Ten Channel (2007, January 16). Retrieved from http://foxsports.com/other/story/5715770 on January 20, 2007.

Finances (n.d.). *NCAA.org*. Retrieved from http://www.ncaa.org/wps/wcm/connect/public/NCAA/Finances/index.html on June 22, 2013.

Frank, R. (2004). *Challenging the myth: A review of the links among college athletic success, student quality, and donations*. Knight Foundation

Commission on Intercollegiate Athletics. Retrieved from http://www.knightfdn.org/default.asp?story=publications/2004_frankreport/index.html on May 10, 2005.

Goetzi, D. (2006, June 28). Tostitos Stays on as Sponsor for Fiesta Bowl. *Media Daily News.* Retrieved from http://publications.mediapost. com/index.cfm?fuseaction=Articles.showArticle&art_aid=45065 on December 8, 2006.

Hickok, R. (2006, November 26). College bowl games. Retrieved from http://www.hickoksports.com/history/collbowl.shtml on December 12, 2006.

Hunt, J. (2007, February 6). Error cost an official his Pac-10 job. *The Oregonian,* p. C1.

Jacobson, G. (2006, March 16). March Madness means money. *The Dallas Morning News.* Retrieved from http://www.dallasnews.com/ sharedcontent/dws/spt/colleges/national/tournament/ncaamen/ stories/031606dnsponcaamoney.173e5d7f.html on December 2, 2006.

Marte, J. and S. Morgan (2013, March 25). 10 things NCAA Basketball Won't Tell You. *Market Watch (Wall Street Journal).* Retrieved from http://www.marketwatch.com/story/10-things-ncaa-basketball-wont-tell-you-2013-03-22?pagenumber=1 on June 22, 2013.

NCAA Football Rules Committee (2006, June 9). *2006 Football Rules Changes.* Retrieved from http://www1.ncaa.org/eprise/main/playingrules/ football/2005/6-9-2006RulesChanges.pdf on November 20, 2006.

No March Madness Workplace Productivity Loss: Recession Is the Big Bracket Buster (2009, March 17). *U.S. News & World Report.* Retrieved from http://www.usnews.com/opinion/articles/2009/03/17/no-march-madness-workplace-productivity-loss-recession-is-the-big-bracket-buster July 4, 2013.

Obama Calls for NCAA Playoffs (2008, November 17). *CBS News.* Retrieved from http://www.cbsnews.com/video/watch/?id=4608949n on July 4, 2013.

One Replay Challenge Approved (2006). *NCAA Football Rules* (Supplement). Retrieved from http://www1.ncaa.org/eprise/main/playingrules/ football/NCAANewsletter2006.pdf?ObjectID=40647&ViewMode=0 &PreviewState=0 on September 21, 2006.

O'Toole, T. (2006, December 6). $17M BCS Payouts Sound Great, But …: League, Bowl Rules Skew Cuts. *USA Today,* p. C1.

O'Toole, T. (2010, April 22). NCAA Reaches 14-Year Deal With CBS/ Turner for Men's Basketball Tournament, Which Expands to 68 Teams for Now. *USA Today*. Retrieved from http://content.usatoday.com/communities/campusrivalry/post/2010/04/ncaa-reaches-14-year-deal-with-cbsturner/1#.UBa9-aB4PRg on July 30, 2012.

Ozanian, M. (2012, December 6). College Bowl Sponsors Beat The Stock Market. *Forbes*. Retrieved from http://www.forbes.com/sites/mikeozanian/ 2012/12/06/college-bowl-sponsors-beat-the-stock-market/ on June 23, 2013.

Redding, R. (2011). *2011 and 2012 NCAA Football Rules And Interpretations*. Indianapolis, IN: National Collegiate Athletics Association.

Sperber, M. (2000). *Beer and circus: How Big-Time College Sports Is Crippling Undergraduate Education*. New York: Henry Holt.

Smith, M. (2011, January 24). TV Fee Boosts BCS Payout 22 Percent. *Sports Business Journal*. Retrieved from http://www.sportsbusinessdaily.com/Journal/Issues/2011/01/20110124/Colleges/BCS-payout.aspx?hl=One%20On%20One&sc=0 on June 9, 2013.

TV Ratings (n.d.). Retrieved from http://bcsfootball.org/bcsfb/tvratings on January 31, 2007.

White, C. (2013, May 9). McCain Introduces Bill For 'A La Carte' Cable TV. *Mashable.com*. Retrieved from http://mashable.com/2013/05/09/mccain-a-la-carte/ on July 12, 2013.

Zimbalist, A. (1999). *Unpaid Professionals: Commercialism and Conflict in Big-Time College Sports*. Princeton, NJ: Princeton University Press.

Chapter 8

Race and Gender Issues in Intercollegiate Sports

I would never in my wildest dreams thought there would be so many [Black coaches] in the [ACC]. But these days, schools look for the best person for the program. Presidents and chancellors look at is as, "Who can get us to the NCAA tournament ..."?

— Bob Wade, Former Head Maryland Men's Basketball Coach

52% of NCAA football players and 61% of NCAA men's basketball players are African-American, compared with 12.5% for the general U.S. population ... [t]he excess revenues generated by these ... athletes are spent on other programs (sports and academics) elsewhere on campus where the population is often predominately white.

— Daniel Rascher, Sports Economist

We're not anywhere close to where we need to be in football .... I'm encouraged that coaches of color are appearing as finalists for positions, but seven out of 119, that's just too darn low.

— Myles Brand, former NCAA President

8.1 Introduction

In Chapter 3, we focused on the labor market for college athletes. You learned that in traditional competitive labor markets, economists expect workers to be paid according to their marginal revenue product (MRP), their contribution to a firm's profitability. The NCAA's cartel position, however, allows some athletes to receive compensation that is far less than what they contribute to the team's bottom line, while a majority of athletes (particularly those in non-revenue generating sports) may receive compensation greater than their MRP.

In this chapter we examine another factor that influences athlete participation and compensation — racial and gender discrimination. We will examine the extent to which discrimination occurs and the economic motivations for and consequences of discrimination. Finally, we will look in-depth at Title IX, the highly controversial 1972 legislation intended to increase opportunities for female athletic participation and to promote gender equity in sports programs offered by educational institutions. We will follow Title IX along its legislative and legal journey, examine its costs and benefits, and clear up some commonly held misconceptions.

8.2   Does Discrimination Exist in College Sports?

Instances of discrimination occur in all aspects of life, so there is no reason to believe that college sports are immune. The question is whether or not discrimination is widespread and systemic, or whether it occurs only sporadically, in isolated cases. How we answer that question can help us determine the appropriate policy response. A widespread problem might call for a more sweeping policy action, while sporadic instances might be better handled through the courts. Before we worry about policy, we need to identify the relevant types of discrimination, and then determine the extent of the problem.

8.2.1   *Wage and occupational discrimination*

Labor economists distinguish between two main forms of discrimination, wage discrimination and occupational (or employment or access) discrimination. **Wage discrimination** occurs when workers from different demographic groups (race, gender, ethnic) earn different pay for the same job. Not all wage differentials are discriminatory; some are attributable to discrepancies in education, skills, or experience. Only when someone receives greater or less pay due to their gender, race, ethnicity, religion, age, or sexual orientation is it considered wage discrimination. **Occupational discrimination** refers to disparities in access to certain types of employment. If women, for example, are not allowed to coach football because of their gender, that is occupational discrimination. Alternatively, if a woman is passed over for a football coaching job in favor of a qualified male coach with more training and experience, that would not be considered occupational discrimination.[1] As we turn now to measuring the problem of discrimination, we look first at occupational discrimination.

The Racial and Gender Report Card (Lapchick, 2012), put out by the Institute for Diversity and Ethics in Sport at the University of Central Florida's DeVos School of Sport Business Management, presents data on both professional and college sports, issuing grades on progress toward racial diversity and gender balance. Specifically, the performance of the NCAA and its member schools is compared to Major League Baseball (MLB), Major League Soccer (MLS), the National Basketball Association (NBA), the National Football League (NFL), and the Women's National Basketball Association (WNBA).

Data are collected from and verified by the NCAA. The 2012 Report covers the 2010–2011 academic year. Though data from all NCAA divisions are included, in most categories grades are only issued for the Division I level. Grades are based on how well the racial and gender profiles in colleges and professional sports organizations compare to the general population. An "A" for race is earned if the racial profile of employees (measured as a percentage of total employees) matches the racial profile of the population. For the 2012 Report, an "A" required that at least 24% of employees (or student-athletes) were people of color. A "B" was earned for 12% representation, and a "C" for 9%.

---

[1] That does not mean, however, that it is not the product of some past discrimination, and that's where the matter gets sticky. Even if current employers are non-discriminatory in their hiring practices, the system may still be biased against applicants who, as a result of prior discrimination, were unable to acquire the necessary qualifications to compete in that labor market.

On the gender side of the *Report Card*, employing 40% women earned an "A," 32% received a "B," 27% a "C," and 22% for a "D." Anything below 22% received a failing grade. In the section of this chapter on Title IX, we will see that earning an "A" grade for gender in *The Racial and Gender Report Card* does not necessarily equate to compliance with the law.

The 2012 Report reveals, that college sports were at the bottom in terms of racial diversity (all professional sports leagues in the report card received A or A+ grades), but above average in terms of gender (both the NBA and WNBA scored better for gender). These grades reflect substantial improvement in representation by racial minorities from the 2004 Report, but little change in terms of gender balance in the various employment levels of intercollegiate sports.

The report card evaluates college sports from top to bottom, issuing grades for NCAA headquarters, conference commissioners, athletic directors, head coaches, assistant coaches, associate and assistant athletic directors, senior women's administrators, professional administration, and student-athletes. The NCAA is also graded on Diversity Initiatives — demonstrated efforts to improve inclusion of historically underrepresented groups. While the NCAA received an overall B for race and a B for gender, performance at the different levels in the NCAA hierarchy varies tremendously. Grades for each group appear in Table 8.1.

As Table 8.1 reveals, higher grades for racial and gender diversity tend to be earned at lower levels in the system. There are exceptions, but the NCAA and its members score well in hiring assistant and associate coaches and directors, but do poorly in the higher ranks of coaching and administration. On the gender side, this is consistent with the "glass ceiling"[2] commonly reported in non-sports corporations.

Turning now to wage discrimination, college basketball provides the most directly comparable evidence of gender discrimination in

---

[2]The "glass ceiling" refers to the circumstance where women's advancement beyond certain corporate management levels is limited. The ceiling (upper limit) is glass because it is often not readily discernible (i.e., transparent).

Table 8.1.   Grades for the NCAA from *The 2011 racial and gender report card.*

	Grade for race	Grade for gender
NCAA Headquarters	A–	A+
Division I Conference Commissioners	F	F
Diversity Initiatives	A+	A+
Division I Athletic Directors	C+	F
Division I Associate and Assistant Athletic Directors	B	C+
Senior Women's Administrators	B	A+
Division I Professional Administrators	B	B+
Head Coaches: all Division I Men's Teams	B	N/A
Head Coaches: all Division I Women's Teams	B	C
Head Coaches: Division I Football Teams	B	N/A
Head Coaches: Division I Men's Basketball Teams	A–	N/A
Head Coaches: Division I Women's Basketball Teams	B+	A+
Assistant Coaches — All Men's Teams (Division I)	A	N/A
Assistant Coaches — All Women's Teams (Division I)	A	B+
Student-athletes Opportunities	A+	A/A+

Source: Lapchick (2012).

the coaching ranks. In 2010, the median salary for the head coach of a Division I men's basketball team was US$329,300, almost double the median of US$171,600 for head coaches of women's teams ("Pay for women," 2012). This does not include additional compensation opportunities typically available only to men, including product endorsements, broadcasting, performance bonuses, and speaking engagements. Defenders of these pay differences argue that they are justified because men's basketball generates positive net revenue, while women's basketball does not. To the extent this is true (despite perceptions, few college sports programs, men's or women's, actually pay for themselves), coaches of men's teams would have greater MRPs than for women's teams, and the salary differentials could be justified by the productivity differences. However, part of the revenue differential between men's and women's programs results from greater institutional spending on publicity, facilities, equipment, and support staff for men's sports (Zimbalist, 1999, p. 86). Furthermore, even if the pay disparities are solely the result of market forces, most colleges and universities receive support from public funds and should have some accountability to the public interest. As Zimbalist (1999, p. 89) points out,

> ... the drive toward gender equity in intercollegiate athletics has caught the NCAA in its ultimate contradiction. When the NCAA wants to protect its members from payroll taxes, unrelated business income taxes, and antitrust review as well as to preserve their tax-exempt bonding status, it raises the lofty banner proclaiming college sports, above all else, to be an integral part of the larger educational enterprise. Yet when women's demand for equal access to educational resources becomes too strident, the NCAA and its member schools are quick to point out the inherent commercial nature of big-time college sports. As long as the struggle for gender equity endures, intercollegiate sports will be confronted with this deepening identity crisis.

In a study of over 3600 NCAA basketball coaches, sociologist Mikaela Dufur (2000) identified a number of explanations for occupational disparities between White male, female, and minority coaches. These include productivity, human capital, social and professional connections, family structure, and an institution's exposure to Title IX. Differential impacts of these factors across racial and gender lines suggest that discrimination is still a going concern. For example, coaching productivity was a necessary characteristic for female and minority coaches; strong productivity helped White males secure coaching positions, but low productivity did not adversely affect them.[3] In the area of human capital, White males had a significant advantage if they had professional playing experience. Women did not have the same access to such opportunities, and the stereotype of minority players was that they reached the professional level more because of natural ability than from hard work and intelligence. In the area of family rearing, having children appeared to benefit White male coaches, but negatively impacted minority women's coaching prospects.

8.2.2   Other forms of discrimination

There are other, more subtle forms of discrimination that may exist in college sports. In Chapter 4, we discussed how admission requirements such as those in Proposition 48 may be racially biased, particularly if they are based on standardized tests that put racial minorities at a disadvantage relative to White students. Given the already disadvantaged educational backgrounds of some minority student-athletes, racially biased admissions tests would increase the likelihood of minority players being unable to secure athletic eligibility. For some, this would close off the only avenue to economic advancement, whether that student has the potential for a professional sports career or merely needs the scholarship access to complete a college degree and earn a decent wage.

The media also discriminates, both on the basis of gender and race, in its presentation of college sports. On the gender side, as one would expect, coverage is heavily tilted toward coverage of men's sports. Some would say that this is evidence enough of gender discrimination, and that even if media providers are just broadcasting what the public "wants," the media is responsible for perpetuating

---

[3]According to Dufur (2000, p. 281), the issue of productivity is complex, as there are many ways it can be measured. Winning percentage, number of championships, tournament appearances, fundraising, recruiting, and graduation rates are all potential measures of success. Which measure is appropriate depends, in part, on the level of the institution. Prominent Division I schools emphasize athletic success; Division III schools are more likely to favor high graduation rates.

those gender-biased wants. Beyond the quantitative differences in coverage, there are two other important ways in which media coverage is gender-biased. First, studies suggest that presentation of women's sports often sexually objectifies the female athlete. Rather than present women's sports for fans to enjoy the contest or athleticism as they would with men's sports, some women's sports coverage becomes an exercise in sexual voyeurism. (Messner *et al.*, 2003)

Second, the language used to describe female athletes and their play exhibits gender bias. An analysis of the 1989 men's and women's NCAA basketball tournaments revealed some subtle but pervasive forms of discrimination (Messner *et al.*, 1993). This includes practices such as **gender marking**, identifying a sport by gender. References were made to "The Women's Final Four" and the "NCAA Women's National Championship Game," but the men's contests were simply "The Final Four" and the "NCAA National Championship Game." Additionally, commentators would often refer to women as "girls," "young ladies," and "women." Boys were referred to as "men" or "young men," but never as "boys." Team mascot names are sometimes preceded by "Lady" when women's teams play, with no corresponding qualifier for men's teams. Finally, and perhaps most illustrative of biased attitudes, commentators' analysis of men's and women's play differed in important ways. Men succeeded because of talent, instinct, and intelligence; they failed because of the abilities of their opponents. Women also succeeded for the reasons men did, but also because of luck, togetherness, and family. Women's failures were attributed to nervousness, lack of confidence, and lack of aggression, not because of the strength of the opposition.

Media discrimination along racial lines is revealed in how commentators comparatively describe the accomplishments of White and Black athletes. White players succeed because of intelligence and hard work; Blacks because of natural athleticism (Messner *et al.*, 1993). Regardless of the intentions of commentators, their choice of language perpetuates both racial and gender stereotypes.

Race and gender are not the only characteristics against which people discriminate. Discrimination against members of the Lesbian, Gay, Bisexual, Transgender (LGBT) population has occurred for many years, but only recently has it garnered significant attention, particularly with regard to sports.

Unlike race and gender, sexual orientation can be concealed. Because some people associate LGBT status more with behavior than with overt physical characteristics, there is controversy (on religious, if not scientific grounds) as to whether orientation is a choice versus an innate characteristic. This becomes a basis for justifying and perpetuating discriminatory attitudes and behavior, and complicates the implementation of relevant antidiscrimination policies.

Discrimination against student-athletes and coaches on the basis of sexual and gender orientation manifests itself in multiple ways. As in general society, name-calling, rumor spreading, and avoidance are common, as are physical threats and damage to property. More specific to athletics, coaches sometimes encourage athletes to change or at least conceal their sexual orientation. In extreme cases, gay and lesbian athletes are banned from teams, or receive unfavorable treatment in terms of coaching attention or playing time. ("LGBT people in sports," retrieved June 25, 2013)

Discrimination on the basis of sexual orientation is also used as a recruiting tactic. Particularly in women's sports, coaches

Fast fact. *Supported by the National Center for Lesbian Rights (NCLR) Sports Project, in 2007, Penn State University basketball player Jen Harris sued the University and Coach Rene Portland for discrimination. Following its own investigation, Penn State initially fined Portland US$10,000, required her to undergo diversity training, and established a "zero tolerance" of future violations of the university's antidiscrimination policy. Ultimately, the lawsuit was settled out of court and, facing accusations that she had engaged in negative recruiting on the basis of sexual orientation for over 20 years, Portland resigned. Harris transferred to and graduated from James Madison University, but an ankle injury ended her playing career and dream of playing in the WNBA. (Ryan, retrieved June 25, 2013; Lieber, 2006)* engage in negative recruiting by telling prospective athletes and their parents that the rival team (that is trying to recruit them) is "all a bunch of lesbians," or that our team promotes a "family atmosphere," which is sometimes code for "no lesbians allowed." ("Panel says things are better," 2012)

The "T" in LGBT has been the most problematic component, as it involves an element where the characteristic may in fact unfairly advantage or disadvantage the athlete. By definition, a transgender individual has a gender identity or expression that does not conform to typical masculine or feminine norms. A transgender individual, for example, might exhibit primarily the outward physical characteristics of a male, yet possess other characteristics and a gender identity that is female. Should the person be able to choose whether to participate in a men's sport or a women's sport? Male physical characteristics (e.g., strength) could give a transgender athlete a physical advantage against female competitors. Forcing participation in a men's sport might put the same athlete at a disadvantage. According to Helen Carroll of the National Center for Lesbian Rights, "No one's known how to address it … . There haven't been models out there. It's just beginning to come to the attention of athletic administrators that there are transgender students out there participating in competitive sports." (Ryan, retrieved June 25, 2013)

On September 7, 2011, the NCAA adopted a new transgender policy that allows transgender participation in sex-separated sports as long as any hormone therapy does not violate NCAA substance policies. More specifically, the policy states,

> A trans male (female to male) student-athlete who has received a medical exception for treatment with testosterone for gender transition may compete on a men's team but is no longer eligible to compete on a women's team without changing the team status to a mixed team. A mixed team is eligible only for men's championships.
>
> A trans female (male to female) student-athlete being treated with testosterone suppression medication for gender transition

may continue to compete on a men's team but may not compete on a women's team without changing it to a mixed team status until completing one calendar year of documented testosterone-suppression treatment. (Lawrence, 2012)

While discrimination of all kinds still exists, in the historical scheme of things it appears that LGBT discrimination is being addressed with less angst than when policies against racial and gender discrimination were implemented.

A final and unique form of discrimination that has drawn considerable attention in recent years comes in the form of mascots. A number of schools, when they formed athletic teams and looked for symbols to rally fans around, chose Native American based nicknames and imagery. Some names were generic (Arkansas State *Indians*; Bradley *Braves*), others were linked to specific tribes with historic, if not present, connections to the area (Florida State *Seminoles*; Illinois *Illini*). All have drawn criticism from within the Native American community. The complaint is that Native Americans are portrayed as primitive and savage, perpetuating long-standing stereotypes that hinder Native American acceptance and integration into the rest of American society. Defenders of these schools, including some within the Native American community, claim that their use of Native American mascots is done in a way that honors and respects those cultures.

In August 2005, the NCAA announced that it would prohibit the use of Native American mascots during postseason events. Effective February 1, 2006, team uniforms or other apparel worn during an NCAA tournament were not allowed to portray any nicknames or mascots considered "hostile or abusive." No mascot prohibition was extended to preseason or regular season contests, or to other college or university events.

Schools have responded to the mascot ban in a number of ways. Some have changed their nicknames and imagery; the St. John's *Redmen* became the *Red Storm*, and Marquette University changed from the *Warriors* to the *Golden Eagles*. Other schools, such as the University of North Dakota (*Fighting Sioux*) and Bradley, have appealed the ban. The NCAA and North Dakota are currently locked in a court battle over the issue. Florida State, Central Michigan (*Chippewas*), and Utah (*Utes*) received the support of local Native American tribes, and were allowed to retain their nicknames and logos.

Fast fact. In 2002, an intramural basketball team at the University of Northern Colorado adopted the nickname "The Fighting Whities," complete with a logo of a middle-aged White man. The team, comprised of Native Americans, Hispanics, and Whites, chose the mascot to protest nearby Eaton High School's refusal to change its nickname (the Fightin' Reds) and logo (a Native American caricature). The nickname "Fighting Whities" drew a mixture of support and criticism, and generated a fair amount of entrepreneurial activity. To make their point clearly understood, the team printed and sold t-shirts with their nickname and logo, and added the phrase "Fighting the use of Native American stereotypes."

Banning Native American mascots raises questions about other potentially offensive team symbols. Should Notre Dame be forced to change mascots if the Irish community objects? What about the Bethany College *Swedes* or Albion College *Britons*? If Native American caricatures are banned, what about the Florida Southern College *Moccasins* or the Massachusetts College of Liberal Arts *Mohawks*? In the interest of religious tolerance, should the NCAA ban the mascots of the Earlham College *Hustlin' Quakers* or the Ohio Wesleyan University *Battling Bishops*?

On a more serious note, the NCAA has effectively banned schools in Mississippi and South Carolina from hosting preset postseason contests (like March Madness) because both states fly the Confederate flag. In January 2007, the NCAA considered extending the restrictions, but the Minority Opportunities and Interests Committee decided against it. Their position was that, unlike mascots, colleges and universities could not control the states' placement of the "hostile and abusive" symbols. ("NCAA keeps policy," 2007)

Whether one views the mascot issue as a legitimate social concern or as political correctness run amok, there is no question about the economic implications for the schools involved. Fans spend hundreds of thousands of dollars (and more) on merchandise depicting their team's logo. The costs of designing new mascots and replacing old images can be extensive. On the other hand, schools failing to comply can lose significant revenues if they are unable to host or participate in postseason events. In the middle of all this are some alumni and boosters that donate millions to these universities. Some have tied their contributions to the continued used of Native American imagery, putting school officials in the uncomfortable position of either accepting the money but incurring the wrath of the NCAA, or turning down hefty sums to be in compliance.

Fast fact. The University of North Dakota's hockey team plays in the Ralph Engelstad Arena, known affectionately as "The Ralph." Engelstad financed the US$104 million arena under the condition that the Fighting Sioux name and imagery remain. The arena is under the ownership and control of an Engelstad trust until 2033, when the arena becomes university property.

One solution to the mascot dilemma is to have all schools adopt non-human mascots. Most schools would likely adopt animal mascots, but this is not without problems. In recent years, there has been increased scrutiny on the use of animal mascots, particularly when it involves acts of cruelty on live animals. Some schools that used to have live mascots now rely solely on costumed caricatures, such as Washington State University and "Butch T. Cougar." Others such as LSU (Tigers), Baylor University (Bears), and the University of Colorado ("Ralphie" the buffalo) continue to use live animals, particularly at home football games, drawing the ire of animal rights groups.

Animal rights supporters reject the use of animal mascots on multiple grounds. At a basic level, holding animals in captivity is itself seen as an act of cruelty. Even the best cared for animals are still deprived of the freedom to live in their natural habitats. Of greater concern is the manner in which some of these live animals are treated, particularly on game day. LSU, for example, has been criticized for their treatment of "Mike," their live Bengal tiger on game days. Mike has been agitated via cattle prod and cage pounding so that he will growl ferociously at the opposing team as they enter the field.

Even when schools treat live animal mascots well, or do not even use live mascots, there is still the potential for animal cruelty and abuse. Opposing coaches and supporters trying to motivate their teams have been known to maim or kill the live animal corresponding to their opponent's mascot. In 1992, for example, Mississippi State coach Jackie Sherrill had a bull castrated in front of his team prior to playing the Texas Longhorns. Sherrill claimed that it was done more to educate than to motivate his players, as none could tell him the difference between a bull and a steer (Schlabach, 2007). Regardless of Sherrill's motives, animal rights activities have some cause to fear that a gung-ho coach will go too far when trying to fire up his team.

While animal mascots are not strictly a discrimination issue, at least not in the traditional sense, it may constrain the alternatives for schools looking to change mascots, and create additional costs for those who already have animal mascots.

8.3 The Economic Explanation for Discrimination

Most people would agree that it is wrong to discriminate on the basis of race, gender, and orientation. Even if it were not illegal, many would object to discrimination on moral and ethical grounds. Most economists would agree with the moral and ethical arguments, and yet economists recognize that discrimination can sometimes be an economically rational behavior.

Discriminatory attitudes develop from many factors outside the normal purview of economic analysis. Broader social and psychological forces are at work forming racial and gender biases. Regardless of the source, discriminatory behaviors that result may still be economically rational, even if they result in monetary losses. Economist Gary Becker's (1971) **taste for discrimination** model identifies three different types of discrimination that we can apply to the sports industry: employer discrimination, employee discrimination, and consumer discrimination.

Employer discrimination occurs when employers (coaches, general managers, and/or owners) favor a certain race so much that they are willing to make material sacrifices (i.e., less revenue or profit) in order to have employees (players and coaches) of a particular racial profile (Becker, 1971, p. 39).[4] In professional sports, this means paying higher salaries for preferred-race players or coaches, or discriminating against non-preferred race players and coaches in the hiring process. In college sports, where the maximum "wage" for a player is limited to a full-ride scholarship, discrimination may take the form of offering scholarships disproportionately to preferred-race players.

Employee discrimination in sports (teammate or **player discrimination**) occurs when players refuse to play with members of a non-preferred race, or require additional compensation above the amount necessary to secure their services on a racially homogenous team (Becker, 1971, p. 55). Player discrimination was common in the United States until the last 25 years or so of the 20th century, especially around the moments when racial integration in sports was beginning, but cases of player discrimination based on race now appear to be mostly isolated events. The greater concern in the early 21st century has been discrimination on the basis of sexual or gender orientation, but even that has diminished rapidly as an issue.

Consumer discrimination (**fan discrimination**) occurs when fans are biased against a particular race and willing to pay more to see preferred race players than non-preferred race players (Becker, 1971, p. 75). As we developed in Chapter 3, economists expect firms to hire inputs so long as an input's marginal revenue product (MRP) exceeds the marginal cost of securing its services. Fan

---

[4]While this explanation of Becker's model focuses on race, the analytical framework also applies to discrimination on the basis of gender, religion, disability, and sexual orientation.

demand (both live and via media) generates the revenue for the sports product and, by extension, the demand for the inputs that produce it (what economists call **derived demand**). If fan discrimination is present, fans have a greater willingness to pay to see preferred race players, and the MRPs of those players will exceed those of non-preferred race players. Under those circumstances, discriminating against the non-preferred race may reap financial rewards for the team, making discrimination economically rational, even if it is morally reprehensible.

One alleged example of consumer discrimination in college football is **booster discrimination**, and it appears to be directed toward the coaching ranks. Historically, minorities have been poorly represented in the head coaching ranks, and some have attributed the lack of diversity to the influence of predominantly White boosters wanting same-race coaches. Boosters, as they have since the beginning of college sports, want their contributions to exert influence. Some boosters may believe that their influence is weakened if the coach is of a different race, and athletic directors don't want to risk alienating the big spending boosters. As University of Washington Coach Tyrone Willingham put it, "It's access to power. It's about asking, is my access to power diminished because of diversity?" (*New York Times*, January 28, 2007) While there is still progress to be made, this appears to be a waning issue. In 2011, nineteen of the head football coaches of FBS programs were minorities (earning the NCAA a "B" grade in that category, up from seven (earning an "F") less than a decade prior. (Lapchick, 2012)

Fast fact. Tyrone Willingham, who is Black, coached at Notre Dame for three years before being fired, and replaced by Charlie Weis, who is White. The reason for Willingham's termination was the team's failure to win big games, but Weis hasn't exactly flourished in high-profile contests. Comparing the two, Jon Wilner (2007) asked "So why hasn't Irish Coach, Charlie Weis been fired? Weis was fired from Notre Dame in November 2009, five years after he replaced Willingham.

In Becker's model, the degree of bias can be represented with a **discrimination coefficient** (Becker, 1971, p. 14). The coefficient can be thought of in a couple of different ways. *First*, it can represent how much extra it "costs" to hire employees of the non-preferred race. These costs represent the disutility resulting from having to interact with the non-preferred race. *Second*, the coefficient can represent how much extra employers are willing to pay for preferred race (or gender) employees over non-preferred race employees. Suppose, for example, Alex and Brandon both have an MRP of US$12 per hour, but Alex is White and Brandon is Black.[5] If a biased employer prefers White employees and has a discrimination coefficient of US$3 per hour, and the market wage is US$12 per hour, the employer will view the cost of employing Brandon as US$15 per hour. Alternatively, one can view the discrimination coefficient as how much more the employer is willing to pay to have a preferred race employee. If the employer is selling in a competitive market, the higher costs faced to satisfy racial bias will make it difficult to compete against firms unwilling to pay a **race premium** for preferred race employees.

As another example of how the discrimination coefficient can produce hiring decisions that are less than economically efficient, suppose that Brandon's MRP is US$14 per hour, US$2 per hour higher than Alex's. With a discrimination coefficient (US$3) greater than the difference in their MRPs (US$2), the employer will hire the less productive Alex, and pay more to get him! Brandon would have to be at least US$3 per hour more productive than Alex, or receive at least US$3 less per hour, in order for Brandon to be hired over Alex.

Becker (1971) argued that under competitive market conditions, discrimination by employers wouldn't last. Discriminating firms would pay wages to the preferred race that were too high, and not secure the most productive workers by excluding non-preferred

---

[5] The authors considered thoughtfully whether to use the term "African-Americans" or "Blacks." We opted for the latter for two main reasons: *First*, there are many NCAA athletes of color that are not American. *Second*, organizations that work to eliminate discrimination in college sports or promote the advancement of racial minorities tend to use "Black" in their names. We will only deviate from that convention when necessary to accurately represent quoted sources.

race employees. The economic losses incurred by discriminating would either drive firms out of the market or require them to stop discriminating to be economically viable. In the case of fan discrimination, however, discriminating against the non-preferred race may not only be economically viable, it may be the most profitable course of action.

As we have seen many times throughout this book, the structure and dynamics of college sports makes it somewhat different from professional sports and non-sports business operations. Do these differences suggest anything about whether college sports are more or less likely to discriminate? If college sports programs attempt to profit-maximize, then the decision to discriminate only makes sense if the fans demand a particular racial profile. Even then, discrimination may have adverse economic effects for a sports team. If satisfying racial bias comes at the expense of a less talented pool of athletes, the team may sacrifice competitive success. Fans may have a taste for a particular racial group, but they also have a taste for winning. Less success on the field or court may adversely affect ticket sales and profit (suggesting that the MRPs of the preferred race players fall below those of the non-preferred race players). An additional consideration is that almost every college and university receives some type of federal and state financial support, be it through a direct budgetary support or student financial aid. Colleges risk losing that government-based financial support if found guilty of discrimination.

If college sports are not driven by profit-maximization, does that increase or lessen the likelihood of discrimination? Absence of a profit motive, on the one hand, would free colleges from the economic pressures of fan discrimination. On the other hand, discrimination by coaches or management that is not supported by fans could not be punished effectively by the market. Based on the data from the race and gender report card, discrimination in the coaching and administrative ranks does not generate sufficient monetary costs to discourage its occurrence.

Even when the market punishes discrimination, it will often persist when it is motivated by non-economic considerations. As reflected in the race and gender report card, racial minorities are underrepresented in head coaching positions. In their study of NCAA Division I men's basketball programs, George Cunningham and Michael Sagas (2005) found evidence of occupational discrimination, and two explanations for it that do not bode well for improving diversity. The first explanation, **homologous reproduction**, is that those in power are most likely to hire someone with similar social and physical characteristics (particularly race and gender). The second, **self-categorization**, argues that out of a need to boost self-esteem by comparing themselves to others, those in power positions will hire like individuals. The two explanations are complementary and both suggest that White head coaches will hire more White assistant coaches relative to the pool of applicants, and that Black coaches are more likely to hire Black assistants. Given that new head coaches are drawn from the assistant ranks, and given the predominance of White head coaches, Cunningham and Sagas' findings suggest that these biases will only perpetuate the lack of diversity in the head coaching ranks.

Coaches are in a unique position in that in many cases they are both employers and employees. Especially in the college system, coaches decide whom they want to pursue with scholarship offers and, subject to the constraint of what admissions committees will allow, coaches decide which student-athletes to bring to the team. At the same time, coaches are employees and may themselves be victims or beneficiaries of employer discrimination. Those coaches that are hired as a result of employer discrimination on the part of the athletic director or upper administration may be expected to extend that preferential treatment in the recruitment of players. For reasons identified above, there is a tendency for head coaches to hire assistant coaches of their same race.

Coaches represent the athletic director and upper administration. In the language of economists, the coach is the **agent** and the administration hiring the coach is the **principal**. If coaches have and act on a taste for discrimination not shared by the athletic director and upper administration, then a **principal–agent problem** occurs. In general economic terms, the principal–agent problem occurs when the principal and the agent have conflicting interests, and the agent, acting on behalf of the principal, behaves in ways harmful to the principal. In a large corporation, the principal might be the stockholders wanting maximum share value or dividends, while the agents are the managers trying to maximize their salaries and budgets. If a coach is discriminatory and upper administrators and fans are not, we would expect less-than-optimal outcomes for the program, both financially and on the field of play.

8.4   Discrimination Remedies and Long Term Prospects

Legal remedies for discrimination already exist. The 1964 Civil Rights Act, along with subsequent amendments, make discrimination on the basis of race, gender, ethnic origin, etc. illegal and open for litigation by injured parties. **Title IX**, which we shall examine shortly, addresses the issue of gender equity at the player level. Racial inequity at the player level does not appear to be a widespread problem as previously blocked minorities are now overrepresented in some sports relative to the student population.

As the racial and gender report card reveals, under-representation of minorities and females occurs in the coaching ranks, but is most egregious at the level of athletic director and above. **Title VII** of the Civil Rights Act addresses treatment of employees, requiring equal treatment in terms of hiring, compensation, and workplace conditions. As with Title IX, private litigation is the usual means by which discrimination is remedied.

In 2009, the State of Oregon passed a law requiring all public universities in the state to interview a minority candidate for every head coaching vacancy. This is a version of the National Football League's "Rooney Rule," which requires NFL teams to interview qualified minority candidates for open head coaching positions. Oregon was the first and so far only state to pass such a law, although there are no penalties stipulated for noncompliance. The rule has drawn both praise and criticism. Supporters commend Oregon for the progressive move; critics claim that racial diversity can't (or shouldn't) be legislated and point to the problems of trying to find qualified minority candidates for certain coaching positions (i.e., historically White-dominated sports such as tennis and golf).

> **Fast fact.** *The NCAA itself has introduced a number of committees and initiatives intended to promote diversity. The NCAA Committee on Women's Athletics (CWA) works to ensure equity and fairness, and to "promote opportunities for female student-athletes, administrators, and coaches." The NCAA Minority Opportunities and Interests Committee (MOIC) seeks to promote the "education and welfare of minority student-athletes, as well as the enhancement of opportunities for ethnic minorities and women in coaching, athletics administration, officiating, and the NCAA governance structure." The CWA and MOIC work jointly to promote the above objectives, and to address LGBT and disability issues. The NCAA also offers a number of education, training, and professional development programs targeted at women and minorities, as well as financial grants to other organizations doing the same. (Lapchick, 2012, pp. 163–164)*

Although the members of the NCAA fail to achieve racial and gender diversity in the most prominent positions, there may be reason to believe that that will improve over time. Current imbalances are frequently the result of past imbalances, so as diversity improves at the lower levels, one might see this trickle up as more minority and female players move through college athletics and aspire to coaching and administrative positions. This isn't to say that the NCAA couldn't achieve greater diversity more quickly, but even in the absence of deliberate action, the change will come eventually.

8.5 What is Title IX?

> *The principle objective of Title IX is to avoid the use of federal money to support sexually discriminatory practices in education programs such as sexual harassment and employment discrimination, and to provide individual citizens effective protection against those practices.*
>
> — Civil Rights Division of the U.S. Department of Justice
> (2001b)

Title IX is the legislation that has probably generated the most controversy, in both legal courts and the court of public opinion, that college sports has seen over the past 35 years. Supporters point to the dramatic growth in women's sports as evidence of both its necessity and its success. Opponents decry the loss of participation opportunities for male athletes. The remainder of this chapter describes what Title IX is, what it is not, and evaluates the benefits and costs of this highly contentious legislation.

Title IX is part of the 1972 Education Amendments of the 1964 Civil Rights Act. The law prohibits any educational program or activity that is receiving federal funds from discriminating on the basis of gender. Forms of discrimination include exclusion from participation and denial of program benefits. The law covers schools ranging from the elementary to college levels, plus any other institution that offers educational programs and receives federal financial assistance, even if the institution's primary mission is not educational. Title IX applies to virtually every program an educational institution might offer. As it applies specifically to athletics, the law states that:

> No person shall on the basis of sex, be excluded from participation in, be denied the benefits of, be treated differently from another person, or otherwise be discriminated against in any interscholastic, intercollegiate, club or intramural athletics offered by a recipient [of federal financial assistance], and no recipient shall provide such athletics separately on such basis.[6]

Title IX requires that schools "effectively accommodate the interests and abilities of members of both sexes,"[7] which has meant providing equal opportunities for male and female athletes in the following three ways:

1. Proportionality in participation opportunities — the percentage of a gender group represented in the student population must

---

[6] 65 Fed. Reg. 52872 at § ___.450 (a) as cited in USDOJ (2001a, p. 93).
[7] 34 CFR §106.41 as cited in USDOE (2003, p. 15).

match the percentage of that gender group represented on athletic teams.

2. Proportionality in scholarship dollars — the percentage of a gender group represented in the student population must match the percentage of athletic scholarship dollars going to that gender group.

3. Equity in other program benefits — both gender groups must receive comparable benefits in terms of practice and competitive facilities, equipment, coaches, travel, recruiting, and scheduling of games and practices. This goes beyond simply providing facilities, equipment, etc. to both genders; it requires that the *quality* of those benefits be comparable.

The basic principle of Title IX is captured in the following analogy often used by its proponents. Suppose there is a community school with 100 students, where 50 are female and 50 are male. Now suppose that in the school, there are only 20 desks for female student use, but 50 available for male students. Alternatively, suppose that Apple donates computers to the school, but only male students (or only female students) are allowed to use them.

Most would agree that the inequities portrayed in our fictitious school should not be tolerated, and in fact both cases would clearly violate Title IX's provisions. Proponents of Title IX and gender parity in sports argue that athletics should be treated no differently than any other educational program.

8.6   How is Compliance Assessed?

The list above might suggest that assessing compliance is easy — schools that achieve proportionality in participation and scholarships, and equity in program benefits, are in compliance; those failing to meet any of those three standards are not. It was recognized early into Title IX's existence that compliance was difficult for any school to attain, and was especially difficult if the percentages of males and females interested in athletic participation did not already match their relative proportion to the student population. This gave rise to the **three-part test** implemented by the Department of Health, Education, and Welfare's 1979 *Intercollegiate Athletics Policy Interpretation*. This test judges an institution to be in compliance if it satisfies one of the following three provisions (as cited in U.S. Department of Education [USDOE], 1996):

1. The ratio of male to female athletes is "substantially proportionate" to the ratio of male to female undergraduates enrolled at the institution.
2. The institution has one sex underrepresented but can demonstrate a "history and continuing practice of program expansion" for the historically underrepresented sex.
3. The institution cannot satisfy either of the first two tests, but can demonstrate that "the interests and abilities of the members of that [underrepresented] sex have been fully and effectively accommodated by the present program."

8.7   What Does Title IX *Not* Require?

There are many misconceptions about what Title IX includes. Some of the misunderstanding has been sown by the opponents of Title IX; some has resulted from misreading or changes in the law. Specific misconceptions, followed by the correct interpretation, include:

1. *Title IX requires schools to cut participation opportunities.* Title IX does *not* require that any school eliminate teams or reduce the number of participants on teams. Reducing participation opportunities for one gender (typically males) is one option schools have, but it is up to each school to decide where and how to achieve proportionality. For reasons we'll examine later, Title IX has been blamed for cuts in men's programs, but the law does not mandate any reductions in programs for either gender. Still, some schools have chosen to comply by limiting men's sports. However, as Title IX scholars Linda Carpenter and Vivian

Acosta (2005, p. 159) explain, "Capping team roster size [for men] is legal, but doing so is not within the spirit of Title IX because it does not provide fuller access to opportunities long denied to females. The action is a sham and a shell game, but it is legal. It is a substitute for reevaluating bloated or expansive budgets for some favored men's teams, but it is legal."

2. *Title IX requires that there be an equal number of teams for each gender.* Title IX does *not* require that there be an equal number of teams for each gender, nor does it specify what sports must be offered. The law requires that men and women be provided opportunities proportional to their representation in the general student population. If 60% of students at an institution are male, then men are entitled to 60% of the slots on athletic teams.

3. *Title IX requires equal (or proportional) dollar expenditures for each gender.* Title IX does *not* require equal (or proportional) dollar expenditures (except for scholarships) so long as the benefits provided by expenditures are equitable. For example, if a school hires two head basketball coaches of comparable quality, one each for its men's and women's programs, but the coach of the men's team commands a higher salary (as determined by that labor market), the inequality in expenditure for coaches would not violate Title IX.[8] If, however, the two teams travel to face the same conference opponent and one team flies while the other is required to take a bus, the inequality of benefits provided could constitute a Title IX violation.[9]

4. *Title IX applies only to athletics.* Athletics is only a small part of Title IX. The law also applies to course offerings, counseling services, housing, health care, financial aid, employment

---

[8] Although it does not violate Title IX, it could be a violation of Title VII. For an interesting case that may violate both Titles VII and IX, see the story of Marianne Stanley in Zimbalist (1999, pp. 74–79).

[9] This assumes all else equal. If the team that rides the bus chooses the bus so that they can apply some of their budgetary allocation to travel to an extra competitive event (such as an out-of-state preseason tournament), this is allowed under Title IX.

assistance, and issues such as sexual harassment. Title IX may be best known for its impact on interscholastic and intercollegiate athletics, but its actual scope is far greater and its original intent was only marginally focused on athletics. (U.S. Department of Justice [USDOJ], 2001a)

8.8   History and Rationale

Prior to the passage of Title IX, collegiate women's sports were virtually nonexistent, especially in comparison to men's athletics. In 1971–1972, there were slightly fewer than 30,000 female athletes in NCAA institutions, representing only 15% of the total number of athletes (U.S. Department of Education [USDOE], 2003, p. 13). Facilities and equipment were generally substandard. Coaches, if they were provided, were poorly paid (if at all), and many lacked expertise in coaching the sport. Female athletes often had to buy their own uniforms and equipment, and pay for any travel expenses. Despite the lack of resources and recognition, participation in 1971–1972 was almost double that of 1966–1967, reflecting females' growing interest in intercollegiate sports. (USDOE, 2003, p. 13)

In the 1960s and early 1970s, female labor force participation increased dramatically, the women's civil rights movement was growing, and attention was turning to problems of sex bias and discrimination in schools. The significant gap in earnings between men and women was a central concern, and eliminating bias in schools was seen as critical to improving women's future employment prospects (USDOJ, 2001a, p. 16). In response to a number of class action suits filed against colleges and universities by women's advocacy groups, Congress formed a special House Subcommittee on Education that began hearings in 1970. In 1971, Subcommittee chair and Representative Edith Green (Oregon) introduced a bill similar to Title IX that would have made sex discrimination illegal under the Education Amendments of 1971 (USDOJ, 2001a, pp. 16–17). Representative Green's attempt failed, but the next year Senator Birch Bayh (Indiana) introduced the amendment that would become Title IX and be signed into law by President Nixon in June 1972. Senator Bayh's testimony highlighted the connection between education and employment opportunities for women:

> The field of education is just one of many areas where differential treatment [between men and women] has been documented but because education provides access to jobs and financial security, discrimination here is doubly destructive for women. Therefore a strong and comprehensive measure is needed to provide women with solid legal protection from the persistent, pernicious discrimination which is serving to perpetuate second-class citizenship for American women (118 Cong. Rec. 5806-07, as cited in USDOJ, 2001a, p. 17).

Although Title IX includes reference to athletics, its initial focus was on educational opportunities for women and girls in general. It would be a few years before it would gain the teeth to significantly impact intercollegiate athletics. The **Javits amendment** in 1974 directed the then Department of Health, Education, and Welfare to develop and implement Title IX regulations pertaining to intercollegiate athletics (USDOE, 2003, p. 15). The Javits amendment also declared that dollar expenditures need not be equal so long as there is equity in benefits received. (Carpenter and Acosta, 2005, p. 31)

The first federal regulations for enforcing Title IX were not implemented until 1975, and those regulations gave schools until 1978 to comply with the law. The 1975 regulations dealing with athletics required schools to "effectively accommodate the interests and abilities of members of both sexes" and required that men and women be provided athletic facilities and support services on an equal basis (34 CFR §106.41, as cited in USDOE, 2003, p. 15).

When 1978 arrived, the stated requirements of Title IX were far from being met. Although female participation at the high school and college levels had more than doubled from when Title IX was implemented, schools were a long way from achieving proportionality (Zimbalist, 1999, p. 58). Recognizing that the vast majority of institutions were not in compliance, nor were they likely to be any time soon thereafter, the Office of Civil Rights adopted the three-part test in 1979. The three-part test remains in effect today.

Supporters of Title IX suffered a setback when the Supreme Court effectively gutted the law in its 1984 decision in *Grove City College v. Bell*. The high court effectively ruled that Title IX didn't apply to college athletics by decreeing that only programs receiving federal financial assistance directly were covered. Following the *Grove City* decision, several colleges eliminated scholarships for female athletes and began dismantling women's teams. Lawsuits and complaints filed with the Office of Civil Rights were cancelled or dismissed (Carpenter and Acosta, 2005, p. 121). For Title IX proponents the good news from *Grove City* was that it affirmed that any federal funding, even funds received indirectly through federal financial aid to students, gives Title IX jurisdiction over an institution. (Carpenter and Acosta, 2005, p. 120)

In 1988, in response to the *Grove City* ruling, Congress overrode the veto of President Reagan and established clearly in the **Civil Rights Restoration Act of 1987** that Title IX applies to athletics. This certainly did not end the debate about the scope of Title IX, but it did mean that once again institutions would have to work toward proportionality in athletics.

The U.S. Supreme Court ruled unanimously in the 1992 case *Franklin v. Gwinnett County Public Schools* that successful Title IX plaintiffs could receive compensatory and punitive damages. This ruling was a watershed event in the history of Title IX, as prior to this time the only punishment schools faced was the threatened removal of federal financial aid. These federal funds were never taken away so there was no real cost to noncompliance (Carpenter and Acosta, 2005, p. 128). Prior to *Franklin*, schools would delay compliance in hopes that those filing complaints would give up or graduate, or that the law would change to make compliance easier.

Monetary damages serve an important economic function, as they provide schools with a financial incentive to comply. With the *Franklin* ruling, lawyers smelled blood in the water and were happy to take on contingency cases that could earn significant monetary damages. A number of lawsuits were filed after the

Franklin ruling and many schools soon discovered it was more cost effective to expand women's sports than to fight lawsuits. In addition to litigation costs and potential monetary damages, schools risked the negative publicity that often comes with a prolonged legal battle.

Among the lawsuits filed in the aftermath of *Franklin, Favia v. Indiana University of Pennsylvania* (1993) addressed a number of important questions. *First,* it established that fiscal constraints do not justify discrimination. The court opinion stated that "Title IX does not provide for any exception to its requirements simply because of a school's financial difficulties. In other words, a cash crunch is no excuse" (Favia v. Indiana University of Pennsylvania [IUP], 1993, p. 7). *Second,* the ruling established that the promise of future programs is not an acceptable substitute for actual compliance in the present. In the court's words, "You can't replace programs with promises" (Favia v. IUP, 1993, p. 9). *Third,* Indiana University had attempted to comply by cutting equal numbers of men's and women's teams, and leaving equal numbers of each remaining. However, the percentage of women participating in intercollegiate athletics, already well below the proportion of women at the university, fell even further. The court cited the low and falling percentages when ruling that IUP failed to meet the first two parts of the three-part test. The effect of this ruling was to deny the right to claim compliance through an equal number of teams (Favia v. IUP, 1993, p. 9). *Favia* established that even those with the best of intentions could be found in violation of Title IX. While the court sympathized with the financial problems of the university and recognized that equal cuts in the number of teams was done with good intention, it ordered reinstatement of the women's gymnastic and field hockey teams that had been eliminated (Favia v. IUP, 1993, p. 10).

In response to the numerous legal challenges that have emerged since the *Franklin* decision, congressional subcommittee hearings were held in 1995, and the Commission on Opportunities in Athletics was formed and conducted hearings in 2002 (Carpenter and Acosta, 2005, pp. 196–197). Both the 1995 and 2002 hearings resulted in affirmation of the three-part test. The Commission on

Opportunities in Athletics report was issued in February 2003. It offered 23 recommendations, 15 of which were approved unanimously (USDOE, 2003, p. 1). Most of the recommendations were affirmations of the need to effectively communicate and enforce Title IX requirements; some provided clarification. One of potential import to programs deciding how best to comply was Recommendation 5: "The Office for Civil Rights should make clear that cutting teams in order to demonstrate compliance with Title IX is a disfavored practice" (USDOE, 2003, p. 34). While this does not prohibit programs from cutting men's sports, it does affirm that the intent of Title IX is to expand opportunities for participation, not promote reverse discrimination.

8.9　The NCAA's "Relationship" with Title IX

As mentioned in Chapter 1 on the history of college sports, for many years the NCAA focused exclusively on men's sports. Women's sports existed, but were administered under different organizations.[10] In 1964, two women from the Division of Girls and Women in Sport (DGWS) visited the NCAA convention to inquire about the NCAA's plans to include women's intercollegiate sports. In March 1966, the NCAA responded that their jurisdiction was limited to male athletes and that regulations prohibited women from participating in NCAA championships. At the same time, the NCAA offered its support to the DGWS efforts. (Carpenter and Acosta, 2005, pp. 102–103)

The DGWS formed the Commission on Intercollegiate Athletics for Women (CIAW) that, in conjunction with the DGWS, would ultimately form the Association for Intercollegiate Athletics for Women (**AIAW**). Shortly after forming the CIAW, however, the NCAA changed its position and expressed an interest in controlling women's intercollegiate athletics (Carpenter and Acosta, 2005, pp. 103–104). The AIAW began operating in 1971, providing "41

---

[10] More accurately, women's sports were administered by a single organization that went through a series of name changes. For more on the history of these organizations, see Carpenter and Acosta (2005, pp. 93–109).

national championships in 19 sports to cover 6,000 teams in 960 member colleges and universities" in its lifetime (Carpenter and Acosta, 2005, pp. 106–107). It was aided and emboldened in its efforts by passage of Title IX.

The NCAA fought Title IX both before and following its passage. It initially lobbied against the inclusion of Title IX in the 1972 Education amendments. The NCAA then spent US$300,000 from 1972 to 1974 attempting to get the athletics component removed from Title IX (Zimbalist, 1999, p. 59). This included direct lobbying of the Department of Health, Education, and Welfare, and then supporting the 1974 **Tower amendment** (see Box 8.1).

Box. 8.1. Highlights of the Title IX timeline.

1964   Civil Rights Act passed.

1972   Educational amendments to the 1964 Civil Rights Act create Title IX.

1974   Tower amendment failed — would have removed revenue generating sports from Title IX jurisdiction.

1974   Javits amendment passed — inequality in expenditures does not constitute a Title IX violation so long as there is equity in benefits received.

1975   First regulations for Title IX compliance implemented; 1978 set as compliance deadline.

1978   First year for which compliance is required.

1979   Department of Health, Education, and Welfare issues Intercollegiate Athletics Policy Interpretation that implements three-part test for Title IX compliance.

1984   *Grove City College v. Bell* Supreme Court ruling strips Title IX of its jurisdiction over athletics. However, it also establishes that programs receiving only indirect federal funding (e.g., federal financial aid) are still subject to Title IX jurisdiction.

(Continued)

Box 8.1. (Continued)

1988   Civil Rights Restoration Act 1987 passed by congressional override of President Reagan's veto, establishes definitively that Title IX applies to athletics.

1992   *Franklin v. Gwinnett County Public School* ruling establishes that successful Title IX plaintiffs are eligible to receive both compensatory and punitive damages.

1992   NCAA completes first comprehensive assessment of female athletic participation.

1993   *Favia v. Indiana University of Pennsylvania* court ruling establishes that financial constraints are not a valid excuse to discriminate, future promises do not constitute present compliance, an equal number of men's and women's teams does not ensure compliance, and intent to discriminate is irrelevant to compliance.

1994   Equity in Athletics Disclosure Act (EADA) passed, requiring colleges and universities to report financial information on their men's and women's sports programs.

1995   House Subcommittee on Postsecondary Education holds hearings on the three-part test in response to flurry of lawsuits filed after *Franklin v. Gwinnett* decision. No change is made in the three-part test.

2002   National Wrestling Coaches Association (NWCA) files lawsuit against the Department of Education challenging the three-part test.

2002   Commission on Opportunities in Athletics is formed and hears testimony on Title IX.

2003   Commission issues its final report, *Open to All: Title IX at Thirty*. The report offers 23 recommendations, 15 approved unanimously by the committee.

2003   NWCA ("wrestlers case") dismissed; appeals follow later in the year.

(Continued)

Box 8.1.   (Continued)

2003   Gerald Reynolds, Assistant Secretary for OCR, issues the 2003 *Further Clarification of Intercollegiate Athletics Policy Guidance Regarding Title IX Compliance*. Title IX and the three-part test are reaffirmed.

2004   NWCA appeal is denied.

2005   Department of Education issues "Additional Clarification" that allows schools to survey female athletes to comply under part three.

2006   Eric Butler files Title IX case claiming the pregnancy exception to the eligibility clock should apply to both males and females. (See Box 8.2, at the end of Section 8.11)

2010   Department of Education rescinds "Additional Clarification."

2011   Department of Education clarifies that Title IX protections against sexual harassment and sexual violence apply to all students, including athletes.

2012   Title IX celebrates its 40th anniversary.

Unable to stop or effectively weaken Title IX, the NCAA tapped its significant resources in an effort to take control over women's sports. As successful as the AIAW was, it lacked the resources to compete with the NCAA, which in 1980 began offering its own women's championships that competed directly with AIAW events, and included television coverage and paid expenses for participants. The AIAW closed its doors in 1982. (Zimbalist, 1999, p. 60)

As far as gender equity and Title IX are concerned, we might ask, what difference does it make whether the AIAW or NCAA is controlling women's intercollegiate sports? The answer lies in the gender composition of the administrative structure. The AIAW was run primarily by women, the NCAA primarily by men (exclusively for many years). When the NCAA took control of women's sports, men held and maintained leadership roles (e.g., athletic directors) in sports programs. The effect of that is apparent when one examines the significant rise in the percentage of men coaching women's teams since the passage of Title IX (detailed in the next section). It would also help explain why few schools have achieved Title IX compliance under the first part of the three-part test, and why the progress of many schools has been slow.

8.10   What Has Title IX Achieved?

Without a doubt, Title IX has opened the doors of opportunity for generations of women and girls to compete, to achieve, and to pursue their American Dreams. This Administration is committed to building on those successes.

— Rod Paige, U.S. Secretary of Education

In order to evaluate the success or failure of Title IX, it is necessary to examine how things have changed since implementation. The evidence will show that while strides toward gender equity have been made, full compliance with Title IX has not yet been achieved.

In 1968, there were approximately 16,000 female college athletes (Carpenter and Acosta, 2005, pp. 171, 175). In 2012, there were 9,274 women's college *teams*, carrying about 200,000 female athletes (Carpenter and Acosta, 2012, pp. A, 1). In 1970, there was an average of 2.5 women's teams per school. By 1978, Title IX's first compliance date, the number had risen to 5.61 per school. In 2012, there were 8.73 women's intercollegiate NCAA teams per school. (Acosta and Carpenter, 2012, p. 1) The percentage of intercollegiate athletes that are women has risen to over 42%. (USDOE, n.d.)

The benefits to women of participating in sports are well documented. Fewer health problems (breast cancer, stroke, osteoporosis, depression), more healthy decisions (decreased smoking, drinking, illegal drug use), greater academic success (higher graduation rates), and better self-esteem are just a few of the positive outcomes attributed to female participation in athletics (Carpenter and Acosta, 2005, pp. 165–166). Given the individual and social costs of treating health problems, substance abuse, unwanted pregnancies, and other social ills, our investment in women's athletics appears to have been a good bargain for society.

While the gains cited above are substantial, full equity (as defined by the Title IX legislation) has not yet been achieved. The 42% participation figure cited above represents substantial improvement, but it should be noted that 57% of the college student population is female, meaning the overall gap is still more significant than might first appear (Women's Sports Foundation, 2013, p. 19). Scholarship and recruiting expenditures still heavily favor men's programs. In the NCAA, female athletes receive only 45.6% of the scholarship money, US$183 million less than men (Women's Sports Foundation, March 2013). In 2011, colleges and universities spent nearly than twice as much (US$136.8 million to US$69.7 million) recruiting male athletes as they did recruiting female athletes (USDOE, n.d.). These disparities are significant in and of themselves, but they are particularly problematic when one considers that scholarships and recruiting are the main instruments used to attract athletes. Opponents of Title IX claim that women are less interested in participating in college sports, but would that be the case if the same number of dollars were spent to attract them? Title IX opponents also claim that men's sports are more popular to fans than women's sports. While this is no doubt true in many cases, some differences in fan support may be artificially created. Evidence presented in the *Favia* case revealed that at halftime of each football and men's basketball game, IUP would raffle off a scholarship for a semester's tuition (*Favia v. IUP*, 1993, p. 5). No wonder football and men's basketball were popular for fans at IUP!

In some areas, the relative position of women has worsened. In 1972, more than 90% of the head coaches of women's college teams were women. By 2012, this percentage had slipped to just 42.9%. In contrast, from 2 to 3.5% of the head coaches for men's teams are women, a figure that has been stable since the inception of Title IX. (Carpenter and Acosta, 2012, p. 17)

The decline in the percentage of female head coaches for women's teams is not a violation of Title IX. As noted earlier, prohibitions on employment discrimination (including hiring and compensation) are covered under Title VII of the 1964 Civil Rights Act. Title IX specifies that both genders must receive the same benefit in terms of coaching services; it does not specify that the coach be of a certain gender. As the creation of new women's programs added head coaching positions, and as pay increased for new and existing head coaching positions, these jobs attracted men seeking to join or advance in the coaching ranks. Women who had coached prior to the implementation of Title IX were often physical education teachers forced to choose between teaching and coaching. Most chose teaching, in part because women's sports now fell under the supervision of male athletic directors (Carpenter and Acosta, 2005, p. 174).

There is another, somewhat curious explanation as to why the percentage of female head coaches has fallen. In her research, sociologist Mikaela Dufur (2000) found that schools exposed to or threatened by Title IX lawsuits were more likely to hire White male coaches for women's teams. At first glance, one might expect the opposite result, with schools hiring more female coaches to improve appearances. However, as Dufur (2000, p. 236) explains, "Athletic directors who have had to deal with Title IX may perceive female coaches as potential troublemakers, even if there is no evidence that these women have instigated Title IX investigations."

Though having a smaller percentage of women coaches may not be a violation of Title IX, it may help explain why female interest in sports isn't greater. For the same reasons cited earlier in the chapter as to why head coaches tend to hire same race and gender assistants, female athletes may identify more readily with female head coaches.

8.11   Criticisms of Title IX

Between 1993 and 1999 alone 53 men's golf teams, 39 men's track teams, 43 wrestling teams, and 16 baseball teams have been eliminated. The University of Miami's diving team, which has produced 15 Olympic athletes, is gone.

— Christine Stolba, fellow, Independent Women's Forum

The most common criticism of Title IX is that it has led to the reduction of opportunities for male participation in sports, either by cutting teams or limiting roster sizes. Overall, this criticism is not supported, as the number of male participants has increased over the past 40 years. While it is true that many programs, such as wrestling and gymnastics, have been cut since the passage of Title IX, the evidence suggests that factors unrelated to Title IX are to blame. As sports economist Andrew Zimbalist (2003, pp. 55–56) observes, most of the cuts in men's wrestling and gymnastics teams occurred during 1982–1992, a period where enforcement was lax and the 1984 *Grove City* Supreme Court decision effectively gutted Title IX. Furthermore, over the same period more than twice as many women's gymnastics teams (83) were eliminated than men's (39). If anything, the cuts that occurred while Title IX was at its weakest only serve to affirm that Title IX is not to blame for the demise of certain men's sports. As explained above, Title IX does not require cuts in any programs. Institutions choose how to comply, and some have chosen to move toward proportionality goals by removing opportunities for men rather than creating more opportunities for women. Many cuts in men's programs, however, have nothing to do with meeting Title IX requirements.

Opponents of Title IX sometimes claim that "revenue generating" sports like football subsidize women's sports. As we demonstrated in earlier chapters, few college sports programs generate positive net revenue themselves, let alone have the ability to subsidize other teams. Economists Michael Leeds *et al.* (2004, pp. 149–150) found that only nine Division I-A football programs provided subsidies for women's sports. They found that, on average, Division I-A football programs *drained* about US$184,000 per year from women's sports.

Football is the "sacred cow" often extolled as the "cash cow" for colleges and universities, and is frequently the target for legislative protection from those opposed to Title IX. The evidence of Leeds, Suris, and Durkin raises the controversial question: would it be so bad to cut football programs? Football rosters often carry five or more players for each position on the field. Many of these players never play in actual contests, yet put in countless hours of practice that could be spent in more academic pursuits. In addressing the important question of how athletic participation impacts academic performance, economists John Fizel and Timothy Smaby (2004, pp. 172–173) found that only in football was there a negative impact both in terms of grade point average and in taking a less challenging curriculum. Schools are allowed to offer 85 football scholarships, enough to fill 3 or 4 women's teams (or other men's teams) in various sports. Significant resources are expended by both the program and the participants, and many of these resources could be reallocated to more productive purposes.

One criticism that Title IX supporters accept, is that although Title IX has improved gender equity, its benefits have disproportionately favored White women. Many of the women's sports added in the wake of Title IX, such as gymnastics, lacrosse, and swimming, tend to attract a disproportionate number of White participants. While it is recognized that Black females tend to concentrate in well-established sports such as basketball and track and field, many believe that opportunity expansion should occur for all women, not just those of a certain racial group. How should this be accomplished? Some, such as Tina Sloan-Green, President of the Black Women in Sport Foundation, contend that "Within Title IX there needs to be some sort of initiative that provides an incentive for organizing bodies or colleges to include African–American women or recruit them in sports or to take on administrative roles" (Hammer, 2003). Others emphasize the need to create participation opportunities at earlier ages, so that there is interest in a wider variety of sports once college age is reached.

Ironically, Title IX has also been blamed for contributing to the United States' obesity epidemic. Critics claim that the law has driven up the cost of physical education programs, leading to cutbacks that have reduced activity levels of elementary and secondary students. In 1999, only 29% of U.S. high school students were enrolled in daily physical education courses, down from 42% in 1991. (Greenblatt, 2003)

Much of the Title IX debate centers on the general and nebulous issue of fairness. Some claim that the law effectively discriminates in favor of women, particularly when it appears that, for whatever reason, men have greater interest in sports than women at a given institution. Taking it one step further, some argue that "two wrongs don't make a right," so we should not discriminate against one group in an attempt to correct past discrimination against another (**reverse discrimination**). Title IX supporters would respond by saying that the law does not discriminate in favor of women; it merely requires colleges and universities to provide equal opportunity in sports, just as they would in the provision of other educational services. While the authors of this book would tend to side with Title IX supporters on that argument, there is at least one case, presented in Box 8.2, where the law may discriminate against men.

Box 8.2.   Reverse discrimination or the birth of a new policy?

When an NCAA athlete begins at a college or university, he or she has five years in which to complete four years of athletic eligibility. This five-year period is sometimes referred to as the "eligibility clock." The NCAA has policies that allow an extension of the eligibility clock, one such being the pregnancy exception. According to NCAA Bylaw 14.2.1.3, a school "may approve a one-year extension of the five-year period of eligibility for a female student for reasons of pregnancy."

Eric Butler's eligibility clock began in 2001, when he enrolled in DeVry University. Butler took the year off from athletics that year to help his wife following the birth of their daughter. Butler finally took the field in 2003, playing for Avila University of the NAIA, and as a walk-on at the University of Kansas in 2005. His eligibility expired after the 2005 season. Out of five seasons of eligibility, Butler was only able to play for two, and his request to the NCAA for an extension of eligibility was denied.

(Continued)

Box 8.2.   (Continued)

Butler filed a federal civil rights lawsuit in spring 2006, claiming that the NCAA violated Title IX because the extension for pregnancy is only granted to females. The NCAA indicated that this is the first time a male student athlete has challenged the pregnancy rule. (Whiteside, 2006)

The main point of contention is whether the rule applies only to the physical condition of pregnancy, or whether it includes child-rearing, something for which paternity leave might be appropriate. According to NCAA spokesman Erik Christianson, "The pregnancy exception is explicitly written for female students whose physical condition due to pregnancy prevents their participation in intercollegiate athletics, and therefore is not applicable in this case". (Whiteside, 2006)

In the end, Butler's petition to play was denied, but he was awarded financial aid covering most of the cost of attending Kansas for one year. Even if the court had sided with Butler, it is unlikely the decision would significantly impact Title IX. There may be a few players who would extend their eligibility clock with "pregnancy redshirting," but it is hard to imagine that college football players will start a baby boom for the purpose of playing one more year.

8.12 Proposed Reforms to Title IX

Supporters and opponents both agree that the goal of Title IX is not to eliminate participation opportunities, but to create them. Compliance has been difficult for most institutions; most have fallen short, and some have turned to cutting men's sports to move closer to proportionality. This has led some to propose changes that would ease the compliance burden; these include:

1. *Interest surveys.* Part three of the three-part test allows compliance by demonstrating that "interests and abilities have been fully and effectively accommodated." Surveys could potentially

measure whether interests are being met, but they would have to be constructed carefully. The danger for institutions wanting to use surveys for compliance is that expressed interests might overwhelm a school's ability to meet them. If an institution opts to use surveys, are they bound by the results, even if the results pose a seemingly impossible challenge? In *Cohen v. Brown University* (1997), the court ruled that surveys are not acceptable as a means of compliance. Brown argued that based on its survey of students it satisfied part three of the three-part test (interests and abilities accommodated). The court responded to Brown's assertion as follows:

> We view Brown's assertion that women are less interested than men in participating in intercollegiate athletics, as well as its conclusion that institutions should be required to accommodate the interests and abilities of its female students only to the extent that it accommodates the interests and abilities of its male students, with great suspicion. To assert that Title IX permits institutions to provide fewer athletic participation opportunities for women than for men, based upon the premise that women are less interested in sports than are men, is (among other things) to ignore the fact that Title IX was enacted in order to remedy discrimination that results from stereotyped notions of women's interests and abilities.
>
> Interest and ability rarely develop in a vacuum; they evolve as a function of opportunity and experience. The Policy Interpretation recognizes that women's lower rate of participation in athletics reflects women's historical lack of opportunities to participate in sports. (Cohen v. Brown, 1997)

In the eyes of the court, interest surveys merely reflect existing biases bred from past discrimination. To both gauge and build interest, court rulings suggest that programs for women should be built to levels comparable to men's sports. Only then can we judge whether there is comparable interest.

In 2005, the Department of Education weakened Title IX with its "Additional Clarification." It stated that schools only needed to survey female students about what additional sports they might have an interest and ability to play. Conducted by email, if survey results reveal a lack of interest or ability, the institution is not required to add any sports and is deemed in compliance with Title IX. In 2010, the Department of Education reversed its position and rescinded the "Additional Clarification," again making interest surveys a difficult route for institutions to achieve Title IX compliance. (Women's Sports Foundation, n.d.)

2. *Exclusion of football and other "revenue generating sports" from Title IX counts.* Institutions with large football programs often have the greatest difficulty complying with Title IX requirements. Some programs carry over 100 players, though not all on scholarship, and there is no equivalent female sport to offset the high number of males on the football roster. Volleyball, the women's sport that runs along with football in the fall season, accommodates about 20 players per season. Junior varsity teams for women's sports can help balance the numbers, but that requires sufficient interest for those teams. Excluding football teams from the count would improve proportionality, but would do nothing to create more opportunities for women.

There have been numerous efforts to exclude football and other "revenue generating sports" from Title IX jurisdiction. The failed 1974 Tower amendment would have exempted revenue generating sports from Title IX participation counts. Schools would have been allowed to remove a sport from compliance calculations by declaring it as "potentially revenue producing" (Carpenter and Acosta, 2005, pp. 122–123). In a 1987 case tried under state Title IX law in Washington, *Blair v. Washington State University*, the appellate court ruled that "The football program may not be excluded from the calculations of participation opportunities, scholarships, or distribution of nonrevenue funds". (Blair v. Washington State University, 1987)

In fact, critics contend, excluding football numbers would reduce the impetus for schools to expand women's athletic programs. While helping schools meet the letter of Title IX, it would not be consistent with the objective of increasing women's participation in sports.

Zimbalist (2003) rejects the exclusion of football because he sees too many resources directed that way, resources that could be used to expand women's programs or spare men's programs such as wrestling from budgetary elimination.

> ...DIA [Division I-A] football does not need 85 scholarships. Sixty would do fine. NFL teams have 45 roster, plus seven reserve, players. The average Division 1A team has 32 walk-ons plus 85 scholarship players. If football scholarships were cut to 60, the average college would save approximately US$750,000 annually, enough to finance more than two wrestling teams (whose average cost is US$330,000 per team). (p. 57)

In response to coaches' concerns about injuries depleting rosters, Zimbalist (2003, p. 57) notes that the injury rates in college football are so low that even tripling the average number of injuries in games and practice would mean that fewer than ten players per game would sit out injured. At 60 scholarships per team, teams would still have 50 players, not counting walk-ons.

3. *Count slots, not actual number of participants.* Some have suggested that compliance requirements should be satisfied if an institution provides a proportionate number of spaces on men's and women's athletic teams. The rationale is that even if schools provide opportunities, they should not be held accountable if athletes don't come forward to participate. Changing current requirements would effectively overturn precedents set by case law. **Cohen v. Brown University** (1997) established that simply providing slots was not sufficient. Adding spaces to existing teams would be an easy, low cost path to compliance, but in the court's opinion would not adequately meet the interests and abilities of athletes. This decision is consistent with what we saw in *Favia*, where the court ruled that having an equal number of teams does not satisfy proportionality requirements.

Court rulings have clearly established that it is the number and percentage of people served that matter, and that alternate methods susceptible to manipulation are not acceptable.

> **Fast fact.** *Cheerleading, marching bands, drill teams, and dance teams can be counted as intercollegiate sports if they can demonstrate to the Office of Civil Rights that they engage in a sufficient number of events at a high enough level of competition. A team's primary purpose must be to compete against other teams, not to provide ancillary entertainment for other sporting events such as football or basketball.*

8.13 An Economic Analysis of Title IX

Often in economics, we find that policies that strive to promote equity do so at the expense of efficiency. By revisiting marginal benefit–marginal cost analysis, in this section, we will examine whether attempts to comply with Title IX hinder or promote efficiency. For a more in-depth analysis, consult the appendix to this chapter.

Assessing efficiency in traditional markets is relatively easy — does the amount produced and sold at a given price match what society wants and is willing to pay for? College sports are different in that in most cases they do not generate sufficient revenue to cover their costs. We have already seen that the revenue generating sports at most institutions do not turn a profit. Even in the absence of Title IX requirements, few sports are likely to meet the strictest criteria for efficiency. Despite this, many would agree that the benefits of participation to athletes and society outweigh the costs (with the possible exception of the sometimes egregious behavior of high-profile-sport athletes).

In a private market sense, it is difficult to justify virtually any college sport. However, college sports generate both benefits and costs that extend beyond what we can measure directly in the market. It is long recognized that participants on sports teams develop teamwork, time management, and leadership skills, and that these skills carry forward into subsequent professional life and create significant positive externalities. The health and lifestyle benefits for women participating in sports have already been documented. Beyond the turnstiles, there are benefits to offering intercollegiate sports that are not measured by how much fans are willing to pay to see games.

It has also been long recognized that participation in college athletics, or at least what some see as the obsession with college sports, can carry significant costs. Emphasis on winning games versus educating the athlete, as reflected through rigorous training schedules and the provision of academic "short cuts," impose costs by diminishing the educational experience and the positive externalities they create. Scandals surrounding performance-enhancing substances, and the criminal exploits of high profile players and programs, undermine the positive effects college sports can have on society.

Identifying, understanding, and ultimately measuring the positive and negative externalities are critical to determining what resources society should allocate toward college sports. Externalities, combined with the costs and benefits faced by the direct participants are all important to determining whether society has achieved the efficient level of intercollegiate athletics.

Economists typically identify two types of efficiency: **productive efficiency** and **allocative efficiency**. Productive efficiency occurs when output is produced in the least-costly way possible. Allocative efficiency is achieved when the allocation of resources among different products maximizes the satisfaction of society. Allocative efficiency is achieved, when for each product the marginal benefit of the last unit produced equals the marginal cost (MB = MC). How much we value the last unit (MB) should never fall below the value of the resources used to produce the last unit (MC); otherwise those resources are better allocated to some other purpose. Productive efficiency is a necessary but not sufficient condition for allocative efficiency, as producing in a manner that does not minimize cost implies that more of that good could be produced without taking away resources from other goods, thus improving society's well-being. For purposes of this discussion, we will make the somewhat tenuous assumption that athletic departments minimize cost, allowing us to focus exclusively on the question of allocative efficiency. We will also assume that the marginal benefit and cost curves we're about to examine incorporate any positive or negative externalities created by the college sports product.

As it applies to college sports, the question is whether Title IX gives us the most desired allocation of resources possible. Figure 8.1 illustrates the views of those who criticize Title IX for its adverse effects on men's programs. Figures 8.1a and 8.1b depict hypothetical MB and MC curves for men's and women's sports participation opportunities. In each graph, Q_T represents the quantity of opportunities offered because of institutional responses to Title IX. Q_O represents the optimal amount of participation opportunities based on the marginal benefits and marginal costs of providing those opportunities for each gender.[11] Figure 8.1a represents circumstances where the marginal benefit (MB_{TM}) of additional male participation opportunities, beyond what the school provides (Q_{TM}), outweighs the marginal cost (MC_{TM}) of providing those opportunities, up to the point Q_{OM}. The value to society that is lost by providing only Q_{TM} opportunities, as opposed to Q_{OM}, is the **deadweight loss** (or **efficiency loss**) that we learned about in Chapter 3, and is represented by the shaded triangle. Conversely, in Figure 8.1b, the opportunities provided because of Title IX exceed the optimal quantity. The marginal benefit (MB_{TF}) of opportunities beyond Q_{OF} is outweighed by the marginal cost (MC_{TF}) of providing them. As in Figure 8.1a, there is an efficiency loss created, this time by an overallocation of resources to female participation opportunities.

---

[11] This treatment presumes nothing about the optimal quantity for men versus for women; it only compares the optimal quantity for each gender relative to the institutional choices made in light of Title IX requirements. This analysis is also hypothetical, recognizing that the actual benefits and costs will vary according to the specific circumstances, including the preferences of the relevant parties.

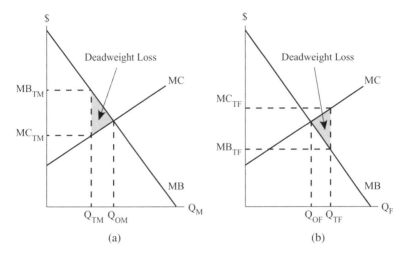

Figure 8.1. Efficiency argument against Title IX.

The views of Title IX supporters are represented in Figure 8.2. Figure 8.2, like 8.1a, depicts circumstances where the number of opportunities falls short of the optimal. In this case, the marginal benefit of providing additional opportunities for women would outweigh the marginal cost of providing them. The difference between Figures 8.2 and 8.1a is that there are no legal constraints discouraging the provision of more female opportunities. Why then don't institutions provide the spaces on athletic teams? Even though the marginal benefit outweighs the marginal cost, the school will incur most of the costs while the benefits will be widely dispersed among the participants and as positive externalities. In other words, the increased expenditures necessary to provide these opportunities would not generate sufficient revenue to support them. The marginal benefit curve from society's perspective (such as in Figure 8.2) won't be the same as the one faced by the college or university.

At this point, you may be wondering who bears the deadweight loss of an inefficient allocation? There can be many affected, but in the case of an underallocation of resources, those who suffer the deadweight loss are those excluded from participation and those who would have benefited (positive externalities) from their

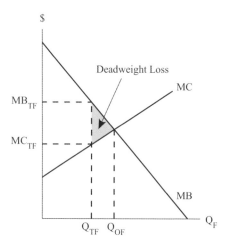

Figure 8.2.   Efficiency argument for Title IX.

participation. In the case of an overallocation, the institution incurs the direct monetary cost, but ultimately bearing the cost are tax-payers, tuition-paying students, potential beneficiaries in non-sports programs, and those in the underallocated segment that are denied participation opportunities.

Do supporters of Title IX believe that too many opportunities are provided to men, creating a situation similar to Figure 8.1b? The views on this issue are mixed. Title IX proponents generally have no interest in cutting back men's sports; their focus is on increasing opportunities for women. At the same time, when women are denied opportunities to play intercollegiate sports, Title IX supporters ask why sports like football need rosters that near or exceed 100 players.

Figure 8.1 represents a situation where institutional responses to Title IX produce an inefficient outcome. An important caveat here is that it is the institutional response, and not necessarily Title IX itself, that causes the misallocation of resources. Some schools decide to cut male programs to keep athletic department budgets within certain constraints, rather than expand athletic department budgets to provide more female opportunities without losing male opportunities. In all fairness, some institutions choose this path because of severe budget constraints, but others simply place a lower priority on expanding opportunities for women. However, if Figure 8.1 represents a situation where the school is in compliance under the first part of the three-part test, then there is no reallocation of participation slots that will be both efficient and in compliance with Title IX.

As we have seen, institutions have two basic budgetary options for complying with Title IX. The first is to leave the total athletics budget as it is, and reallocate funds within existing budget constraints. If the school is not already in compliance, this approach requires programs to curtail men's opportunities in favor of women's sports. This is not the only option for institutions, however. Expanding the budget for athletics would allow additions to women's sports without reducing men's participation opportunities. Scarcity forces choices, and Title IX constrains those choices, but Title IX does not dictate what those choices will be. A more in-depth analysis of that decision-making process appears in the appendix to this chapter.

8.14   Reductions in Men's Programs — How to Decide What to Cut

For schools that determine that men's programs shall be cut to comply with Title IX, how do they decide whether to scale back roster sizes or eliminate teams altogether? Some schools have opted to cut entire teams rather than scale back football rosters already carrying more players than can ever be accommodated in terms of playing time. Is this a rational economic decision or simply an unhealthy obsession with football? Wrestling programs have been hit particularly hard; why might it make sense to eliminate those opportunities rather than keep but simply scale back all programs?

Sports teams tend to have high fixed costs and except in the case of scholarships, relatively low marginal costs. Coaches' salaries, practice and game facilities, equipment, and travel costs are largely fixed. The cost of 25 extra uniforms for football players who will use existing facilities and may never travel with the team (because of travel roster limitations) is far less than the cost of providing a full team for, say, wrestling or gymnastics. While reducing the football roster and preserving wrestling would provide more opportunities for actual intercollegiate participation, it would also place more of a strain on the athletic department budget.

Football programs have an incentive to maximize roster size so that they can stockpile talent. Beyond simply protecting against inevitable injuries and academic ineligibility, Division I football teams try to improve their competitive position by hoarding talented players who would see regular playing time in rival programs.

The decline in programs such as wrestling and gymnastics has a cascading effect. As each program is eliminated, it becomes more difficult and costly for remaining teams at other schools to secure competition. The increased cost makes it harder to justify the sport's inclusion in the athletic department budget. Further, as the pool of competitors shrinks, athlete interest wanes. High school athletes are attracted to a college or university not only because of the teams for which they would play, but also by the teams against whom they would compete. The process of decline is mutually reinforcing; as colleges eliminate certain sports it reduces the incentive for high school students to pursue those sports. Declining interest at the high school level means that fewer athletes show interest in the sport at the intercollegiate level. Disinterest and cuts breed further disinterest and cuts, up and down the levels of competition.

Wrestling's downfall is football's boon. As the lower profile sports are eliminated, student-athletes seeking participation opportunities shift to other sports, even if their chances of seeing the field are slim. As a sport that can accommodate large numbers, football attracts many of these athletes. Football participation increases by default, but athletic directors point to the large numbers of students coming to the sport as evidence of its popularity, both in absolute terms and relative to other sports. This twist of logic further reinforces the decision to keep football rosters large, even if it means eliminating other men's sports.

8.15 What About Donations?

When cuts in a sports program appear imminent, prospective donors often step forward to offer financial support. Donors also offer to finance projects that expand or improve facilities for their favored sport. These donations are a way to save programs or enhance facilities, but not without constraint. If donor dollars are pouring in to buy equipment, facilities, or opportunities for men, there needs to be equivalent expenditures for women's programs if the institution is to be or remain in compliance with Title IX requirements. Suppose, for example, that someone donates funds to install lights at the baseball stadium. An institution could accept those donated funds for that purpose, so long as money is also found, for example, to install lights on the softball field.

8.16 Chapter Summary

In this chapter, we have seen that significant progress has been made improving opportunities for women and minorities in college sports, but that there is still room for improvement. Economic theory helps us understand that sometimes discrimination is rational, at other times costly. Policies to correct racial, gender, and orientation imbalances may not fit society's short-term interests, even if they may maximize society's well-being in the long run. We are also left with questions. To what extent are current preferences the result of past discrimination? Should we discriminate in the present to compensate for past discrimination? In industries regulated by private market forces, we expect discrimination to be punished and ultimately eliminated. In college sports, where market forces are at best distorted, can we rely on them to correct inequities? The overarching normative question society must address is, what is the fairest way to allocate the scarce resources available for college sports?

8.17   Key Terms

Access discrimination
Agent
AIAW
Allocative efficiency
Booster discrimination
Budget constraint
    (appendix)
Civil Rights Restoration
    Act
Cohen v. Brown University
Consumer discrimination
Deadweight loss
Derived demand
Discrimination coefficient
Efficiency loss
Employee discrimination
Employer discrimination
Fan discrimination
*Favia v. Indiana University of
    Pennsylvania*
*Franklin v. Gwinnett County
    Public Schools*
Gender marking

Grove City College v. Bell
Homologous reproduction
Indifference curve
Javits amendment
Indifference curve
    (appendix)
Marginal revenue product
Player discrimination
Principal
Principal–agent problem
Productive efficiency
Proportionality
Race and Gender Report
    Card
Race premium
Reverse discrimination
Self-categorization
Taste for discrimination
Three-part test
Title VII
Title IX
Tower amendment
Treatment discrimination

8.18   Review Questions

1. How do *wage discrimination* and *occupational discrimination* differ? How are they similar?
2. What is *The Racial and Gender Report Card*, how are the grades determined, and what areas receive the best and worst grades?
3. According to Andrew Zimbalist, how does the issue of gender equity reveal a major contradiction in the NCAA?
4. How does the media discriminate along racial and gender lines in its coverage of college sporting events?

5. Why are some Native American mascots allowed and others banned?

6. What are the three types of discrimination from Becker's *taste for discrimination* model that are relevant to college sports?

7. Why does the source of the discrimination matter in terms of the market's ability to eliminate it?

8. How can discrimination in the recruiting of college athletes be an example of the *principal–agent problem*? Is it necessarily a principal–agent problem? Explain.

9. What is Title IX, what are its requirements, and what is the three-part test?

10. State and refute the common misconceptions about Title IX.

11. Explain the significance of the Javits Amendment, the Tower Amendment, *Grove City College v. Bell*, Civil Rights Restoration Act of 1987, *Franklin v. Gwinnett County Public Schools, Favia v. Indiana University of Pennsylvania*, and *Cohen v. Brown University*, to the history and current status of Title IX.

12. What has Title IX accomplished? What negative impacts have resulted from responses to the legislation?

13. Identify the common criticisms of Title IX.

14. Why are interest surveys generally not an acceptable way to determine interest in athletic programs?

15. What are some ways that schools can comply with the letter of the Title IX law, but still violate its spirit?

16. Under what circumstances would the addition of participation opportunities for women not satisfy Title IX requirements?

17. Why do cuts in particular sports give rise to further cuts in that sport (at other institutions)?

18. Explain how donations may or may not be violations of Title IX.

8.19   Discussion Questions

1. Does the *Racial and Gender Report Card* discriminate by labeling coaching positions for all men's teams as "N/A" in terms of their grade for gender?

2. If media broadcasters were to refer to women in the same manner as men, do you think fans would start taking women's

sports more seriously? If so, would it be enough to noticeably increase fan demand?

3. When asked about the *Fighting Irish* mascot question, one NCAA official indicated that it was not a concern because no Irish had complained. Should these bans be based on whether someone vocalizes offense, or should there be a more objective standard?

4. Where does the "taste for discrimination" come from? Why might that question be important in terms of designing policies to discourage it?

5. Suppose that a university is looking at two quarterback recruits. Lucian, a non-preferred race player, is expected to have an MRP of US$200,000 per year. Brinley is of a preferred race, but is only expected to generate US$150,000 per year. Assuming the head coach decides who is offered the scholarship, what would the coach's discrimination coefficient have to be to make him indifferent between the two players? Is this a case of employer or consumer discrimination? Explain.

6. Has the involvement of the NCAA in women's sports advanced or hindered the objectives of Title IX? Explain.

7. Should we reform Title IX? If so, how. Explain your rationale?

8. Respond to the following statement: "Eliminating college football would solve the gender equity problem in college sports."

9. Suppose that Equity University is currently providing sports participation opportunities that are out of compliance with Title IX (60/40 male to female ratio despite a 50/50 ratio in the general student population), yet the quantity of participants relative to the optimal is represented by Figure 8.1a and Figure 8.2. Assuming Equity U. has made improvements in the past, what options are available that would keep them in compliance? Are these options necessarily efficient? Explain.

10. The number of college wrestling programs has been in decline in recent years. Some attribute it to Title IX, others to the "arms race" in the revenue generating sports. Based on what you've read in this book (and other places), what is your assessment?

11. Will women's sports ever be as popular as men's? Consider the question from the perspective of both of fans and prospective college athletes. Why is the answer to this question important from a Title IX perspective?

12. (Appendix) The presentation of budget lines assumes that the cost of providing opportunities is the same across sports and genders. What would be the effect on the budget line and efficient allocation if women's sports were only half the cost of men's sports for an equal number of participation slots? (Hint: Use Appendix Figure 8.1 and assume that the maximum number of men's slots doesn't change. Then construct an indifference map with curves tangent to both the old and new budget lines.)

13. (Appendix) As more and more women participate in intercollegiate sports and then go on to raise female children that play sports, what would happen to society's indifference curve for men's and women's sports?

8.20 Assignments/Internet Questions

1. Tune into one of the many ESPN stations, CSTV, or one of the FOX sports stations, and watch both a men's and women's team event. Listen to how the commentators refer to men v. women, and Whites v. non-Whites. Are there differences that support the claims of this chapter? Provide evidence for your conclusions. Also note, if possible, the races and genders of the commentators. If there is a mix, does it seem to affect whether their remarks exhibit racial or gender bias.

2. Using a search engine, type in terms like "NCAA mascot ban" and update the status of the North Dakota, Bradley, or similar cases.

3. Go to the Internet and find the most recent *Racial and Gender Report Card*. Have the requirements for the letter grades changed since the 2012 Report? Have there been any significant changes in the grades assigned?

8.21   References

Acosta, R. V. and L. J. Carpenter (2012). *Women in Intercollegiate Sport: A Longitudinal, National Study, Thirty Five Year Update, 1977–2012.* Unpublished manuscript. Retrieved from www.acostacarpenter.org, http://acostacarpenter.org/AcostaCarpenter2012.pdf on June 26, 2013.

Acosta, R. V. and L. J. Carpenter (2004). *Women in Intercollegiate Sport: A Longitudinal, National Study — Twenty Seven Year Update, 1977–2004.* Brooklyn, NY: Smith College's Project on Women and Social Change & Brooklyn College of the City University of New York. Retrieved from http://www.webpages.charter.net/womeninsport on August 9, 2006.

Baranko, J. (2011). Hear me roar: Should universities use live animals as mascots? *Marquette University Sports Law Review*, 21, 599–619.

Becker, G. S. (1971). *The Economics of Discrimination* (2nd ed.). Chicago: University of Chicago Press.

Blair v. Washington State University, 740 P. 2d 1385 (1987).

Carpenter, L. J. and R. V. Acosta (2005). *Title IX.* Champaign, IL: Human Kinetics.

Cohen v. Brown University, 991 F. 2d 888 (1st Cir. 1993); 101 F. 3d 155 (1st Cir. 1996), cert. denied 520 U.S. 1186 (1997).

Cunningham, G. B. and M. Sagas (2005). Access discrimination in intercollegiate athletics. *Journal of Sport & Social Issues*, 29(2), 148–163.

Dufur, M. J. (2000). Riding the coaching carousel: The effects of sex, race, and institutional environment on the occupational internal labor market mobility of collegiate managerial personnel (Doctoral Dissertation, Ohio State University, 2000). Ann Arbor, MI: Bell & Howell Information and Learning Company.

Favia v. Indiana University of Pennsylvania, 812 F. Supp. 578 (W.D. PA) (1992).

Fizel, J. and T. Smaby (2004). Participation in collegiate athletics and academic performance. In J. Fizel and R. Fort (Eds.), *Economics of College Sports* (pp. 163–173). Westport, CT: Praeger.

Greenblatt, A. (2003, January 31). Obesity epidemic. *CQ Researcher*, pp. 73–104.

Hammer, B. (2003, April 10). Reconsidering the status of Title IX. *Black Issues in Higher Education*, p. 20.

Lapchick, R. (2005). *The 2004 Racial and Gender Report Card: College Sports.* Orlando, FL: DeVos Sport Business Management Program, Institute for Diversity and Ethics in Sport.

Lawrence, M. (n.d.). Transgender Policy Approved. *Ncaa.org*. Retrieved from http://www.ncaa.org/wps/wcm/connect/public/NCAA/Resources/Latest+News/2011/September/Transgender+policy+approved?pageDesign=print+template on June 25, 2013.

Leeds, M. A., Y. Suris and J. Durkin (2004). College football and Title IX. In J. Fizel and R. Fort (Eds.), *Economics of College Sports* (pp. 137–151). Westport, CT: Praeger.

Lieber, J. (2006, May 11). Harris Stands Tall in Painful Battle With Penn State Coach. *USA Today*. Retrieved from http://usatoday30.usatoday.com/sports/college/womensbasketball/2006–05–11-jennifer-harris_x.htm?POE=SPOISVA on June 25, 2013.

Messner, M. A., M. C. Duncan and C. Cooky (2003). Silence, sports bras and wrestling porn. *Journal of Sport and Social Issues*, 27, 38–51.

Messner, M. A., M. C. Duncan and K. Jensen (1993). Separating the men from the girls: The gendered language of televised sports. *Gender and Society*, 7, 121–137.

NCAA Keeps Policy On Championships in States with Confederate Flags (2007, January 24). p. 10. Retrieved from http://chronicle.com/news/index.php?id=1563 on January 25, 2007.

Panel Says Things Are Better, But Not Perfect (2012, April 23). *Inside Higher Ed*. Retrieved from http://www.insidehighered.com/news/2012/04/23/panel-says-things-are-better-not-perfect-lgbt-athletes on June 25, 2013.

Pay For Women's Basketball Coaches Lags Far Behind That of Men's Coaches (2012, April 2). *New York Times*. Retrieved from http://www.nytimes.com/2012/04/03/sports/ncaabasketball/pay-for-womens-basketball-coaches-lags-far-behind-mens-coaches.html?pagewanted=all on June 27, 2013.

Ryan, M. (n.d.). Gay Athletes on campus: Progress and prejudice in college sports. *Realjock.com*. Retrieved from http://www.realjock.com/articleprint?id=1071 on June 25, 2013.

Schlabach, M. (2007, October 29). Richt's Motivational Gamble Pays Off for Georgia. *ESPN.com*. Retrieved from http://sports.espn.go.com/ncf/columns/story?columnist=schlabach_mark&id=3084918 on June 23, 2013.

U.S. Department of Education (2012, June 20). *Remarks of U.S. Secretary of Education Arne Duncan on the 40th Anniversary of Title IX*. Retrieved from http://www.ed.gov/news/speeches/remarks-us-secretary-education-arne-duncan-40th-anniversary-title-ix on June 26, 2013.

U.S. Department of Education, Office for Civil Rights (1996, January 16). *Clarification of Intercollegiate Athletics Policy Guidance: The Three-Part Test*. Retrieved from http://www.ed.gov/about/offices/list/ocr/docs/clarific.html#two on January 31, 2007.

U.S. Department of Education, Office Postsecondary Education (n.d.). *Equity in Athletics Data Analysis Cutting Tool*. Retrieved from http://ope.ed.gov/athletics/ on June 26, 2013.

U.S. Department of Education, Secretary's Commission on Opportunity in Athletics (2003, February 28). *Open to all: Title IX at Thirty*. Washington, DC: Author.

U.S. Department of Health, Education, and Welfare, Office for Civil Rights (1979, December 11). *Intercollegiate Athletics Policy Interpretation*, 44 Fed. Reg. 71413 *et seq.* (1979).

U.S. Department of Justice, Civil Rights Division (2001a, January 11). *Title IX Legal Manual*. Washington, DC: Author.

U.S. Department of Justice, Civil Rights Division (2001b, February 7). *Nondiscrimination on the Basis of Sex in Federally Assisted Programs*. Retrieved from http://www.usdoj.gov/crt/cor/Pubs/sexbrochure.htm on January 31, 2007.

Whiteside, K. (2006, August 24). Suit tests ban on leave for father-athletes. Retrieved from http://www.usatoday.com/sports/college/2006–08–24-titleix-lawsuit_x.htm on August 29, 2006.

Wilner, J. (2007, January 15). Why does Weis get a golden pass? *San Jose Mercury News*, p. 1D.

Women's Sports Foundation (2013, March 18). *Title IX Myths and Facts*. Retrieved from http://www.womenssportsfoundation.org/home/advocate/title-ix-and-issues/what-is-title-ix/title-ix-myths-and-facts on June 26, 2013.

Women's Sports Foundation, Sharp Center (2013, February). *Progress and Promise: Title IX at 40 Conference*. Retrieved from http://www.womenssportsfoundation.org/home/research/articles-and-reports/equity-issues/progress-and-promise-title-ix-at-40 on June 26, 2013.

Women's Sports Foundation (n.d.). *Title IX Legislative Chronology*. Retrieved from http://www.womenssportsfoundation.org/home/advocate/title-ix-and-issues/history-of-title-ix/history-of-title-ix on June 26, 2013.

Zimbalist, A. (1999). *Unpaid Professionals: Commercialism and Conflict in Big-Time College Sports*. Princeton, NJ: Princeton University Press.

Zimbalist, A. (2003). What to do about title IX. *Gender Issues*, 21(2), 55–59.

Appendix 8.1 Indifference Curve Analysis

Indifference curve analysis is another way to assess whether resource allocation is optimal. Budget constraints (lines) show us all of the feasible options, and indifference curves allow us to identify the combination of goods that will yield the most utility. Using the hypothetical institution Egalitarian University, we will develop and apply indifference curves and budget constraints to Title IX compliance decisions.

Egalitarian's athletic department is limited in what it can spend, requiring it to make decisions on the allocation between men's and women's programs and among the various sports (soccer, football, basketball, etc.). For purposes of analyzing Title IX, we will examine the decision of how to allocate spending between men's and women's athletics. With a given pool of money, also known as a **budget constraint**, every dollar that Egalitarian allocates toward women's sports cannot be allocated toward men's sports, and vice versa. Our simple budget constraint is illustrated in Appendix Figure 8.1.

What is Egalitarian University's athletics budget buying? In keeping with the focus of Title IX, we will assume that the athletic department is buying participation opportunities for male and female athletes. In Appendix Figure 8.1, the vertical and

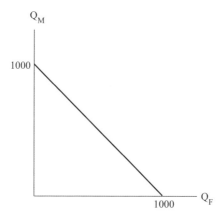

Appendix Figure 8.1. Egalitarian University's budget constraint.

horizontal intercept quantities of 1000 for men's and women's sports represent the maximum of each that could be provided if no opportunities were provided for the other sex.

The location of a budget line depends not only on how much money an athletic department has available to spend, but also on the prices of what they are buying. Appendix Figure 8.1, with a slope of −1, reflects a case where the price of providing opportunities for men equals the price of providing opportunities for women. In other words, if men's and women's sports face the same costs for coaches, equipment, facilities, travel, etc., then a given amount of money will buy the same number of participation opportunities for either gender. The slope of the budget line will differ if, for example, men's sports are more expensive to provide (perhaps the prevailing market wage for coaches of men's teams is higher than for women's teams). If the cost of providing opportunities for men is twice the cost of providing opportunities for women, the maximum number of men's sports participation opportunities will be only half the number for women (500 in Appendix Figure 8.1). Of course, Egalitarian can expand the maximum number of participation opportunities for both men and women if budgetary allocations to the athletic department are increased and prices remain unchanged.

What combination of men's and women's sports should Egalitarian provide? In order to comply with Title IX requirements, it should be proportionate to male and female ratios in the general student population. Faced with the budget line in Appendix Figure 8.1, if 55% of Egalitarian U. students are female, then the university should provide 550 spaces for women, and 450 slots for men. For the remainder of our discussion, we will assume that Egalitarian U. has an equal number of men and women in attendance.

If Egalitarian U. complies with Title IX requirements, is that allocation of budgetary resources efficient in the sense that it maximizes total utility? In order to answer that, we need to introduce *indifference curves*, a tool that will help us represent what combination of men's and women's sports society would most prefer.

Indifference curves represent different combinations of goods that give the same level of utility, or satisfaction. In this case, our bundle of goods consists of men's and women's sports participation opportunities. Indifference curves have a few important properties that must be identified:

1. Every point on a given indifference curve represents an equal level of utility, hence the label "indifference." If an indifference curve accurately represents our preferences, we do not care whether we are at one point or another on a given curve. If the participation combinations of 400 men and 200 women, and 200 men and 300 women both lay on the same indifference curve, we would say they are equally preferred (that is, they give equal satisfaction). Points not on a given indifference curve lay on another curve and represent different levels of utility, by definition.

2. Indifference curves can be constructed for cheeseburgers and milkshakes, or any bundle of goods we want, and we can construct budget constraints for those same bundles of goods. Indifference curves can be constructed for individuals or communities (societies).

3. Indifference curves rank bundles of goods based on a consumer's or society's preferences, and more is preferred to less. The goal is to reach the highest indifference curve possible, as that represents the maximum amount of utility that can be attained under a given budget constraint. Indifference curves in the northeastern part of the graph (up and to the right) are preferred to those in the southwestern region (closest to the origin). An indifference curve containing the combination 300 men and 400 women would lay above (i.e., yield greater utility) our hypothetical indifference curve that contains the combination of 200 men and 300 women.

4. Indifference curves are everywhere on the graph. Just as any point on a map represents a geographic space, any point on an indifference map represents a level of utility that could be attained if that combination of goods was produced.

5. Indifference curves are generally convex to the origin. This reflects a preference for variety. For example, in Appendix Figure 8.2,

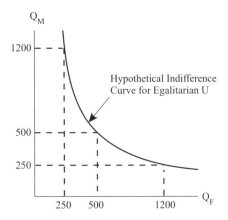

Appendix Figure 8.2. A hypothetical indifference curve
for Egalitarian University.

indifference curve IC_1 contains the combination of 500 men's and
500 women's participation opportunities. If we move up and to
the left along that indifference curve, we see that society is
increasingly less willing to give up opportunities for women to
gain more opportunities for men. Society would only be willing
to give up 250 spaces for women, if it created an additional 600
spaces for men. The same thing occurs if we move down and to
the right. Society is only willing to give up 250 spaces for men if
it gains an additional 300 spaces for women.

6. Indifference curves cannot intersect. The formal way economists
   say this is that preferences must be transitive. If we are indifferent between bundles A and B, and indifferent between bundles
   B and C, then logically we must also be indifferent between
   bundles A and C. As a counter example, suppose that A and B
   lay on indifference curve IC_1. If bundles B and C lay on indifference curve IC_2 that intersects IC_1 at point B, then bundles A and
   C will lay on different curves, meaning those bundles provide
   different levels of utility.[12]

---

[12]Strictly speaking, intransitivity of preferences can occur with social (v. individual) indifference curves. The classic illustration of this problem is Kenneth
Arrow's impossibility theorem (also known as the voting paradox). For our purposes, however, we will assume that the property of transitivity holds.

Finding the optimal mix — indifference curves and budget lines combined

A budget line tells us the maximum number of goods we can obtain. For purposes of our Title IX discussion, it tells us how many men's and women's sports opportunities can be created given an athletic department's budget and the cost of providing opportunities (which for now we assume to be equal for men's and women's sports). The budget constraint is a boundary that we cannot exceed without changing prices or the amount of money available.

Indifference curves reflect the utility we can attain from various combinations, and the goal is to reach the highest possible curve given the budget constraint. Graphically, this occurs when we have reached the indifference curve that is tangent to the budget line (see Appendix Figure 8.3). Any lower indifference curve, by definition, gives us less satisfaction and represents an inefficient allocation of resources. Higher indifference curves are not attainable unless the budget line can be shifted out.

Suppose that Appendix Figure 8.3 represents our fictitious Egalitarian U. Recall that indifference curves are everywhere on this graph, but let's look at three of particular interest. If Egalitarian U. initially provides 800 spaces for men and 200 for women, it will be at point I on indifference curve IC_1. From society's point of view,

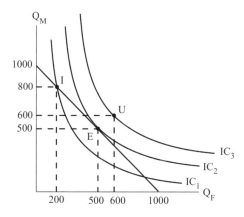

Appendix Figure 8.3. Efficient, inefficient, and unattainable allocation decisions.

point I ("inefficient") represents an inefficient allocation of resources (expressed as participation opportunities), because it is possible to reallocate the existing budget and reach a higher indifference curve. Point E ("efficient") on IC_2 (with 500 spaces each for men and women) represents the most efficient allocation for Egalitarian U., and assuming an equal number of males and females in the general student population, would also represent compliance with Title IX. Point U ("unattainable") on IC_3 would also satisfy the proportionality requirements of Title IX and provide even greater utility (with 600 spaces each for men and women), but point U is unattainable given the current budget.

Appendix Figure 8.3 presents a case supportive of Title IX. It is also something of a special case in that it represents the Title IX requirements aligning perfectly with society's preferences. Given the contentious nature of Title IX, that is probably not a safe assumption.

Appendix Figure 8.4 presents a case against Title IX, where compliance reduces society's total utility. Point E (700 men, 300 women) represents the most efficient allocation of participation opportunities, given the budget and society's preferences. Again assuming a gender-balanced student population, resource reallocation to comply with Title IX would move the institution to point P ("proportional" at 500/500), a point that balances participation

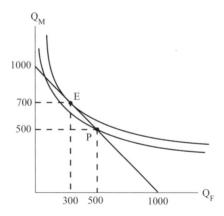

Appendix Figure 8.4.   Proportional allocations that are not efficient.

opportunities but provides less than the maximum attainable utility.

The case against Title IX made by Appendix Figure 8.4 assumes a fixed budget and a reallocation of participation opportunities from men to women. Compliance can also be achieved by expanding the budget to provide more opportunities for women without sacrificing opportunities for men. Suppose that Appendix Figures 8.4 and 8.5 depict the preferences and budget constraint facing another fictitious institution, Utils University. Even though it is maximizing utility, Utils finds itself out of compliance at E_1 and decides to increase the athletic department's budget to create 400 more opportunities for women. Assume that Utils also decides to leave men's sports capped at 700 until proportionality is reached. The decision to increase the budget shifts the budget line from B_1 to B_2, but the restriction that the budgetary increases apply only to women's sports means that B_2 does not extend all the way to the vertical axis (a discontinuity in the function is created). The dashed part of B_2 represents that part of the new budget line that would exist if not for the capping of men's opportunities at 700. Given Utils University's indifference map, and its self-imposed restrictions to achieve Title IX compliance, it would provide an equal

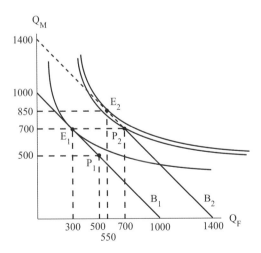

Appendix Figure 8.5. Expanding the budget to achieve IX compliance.

number of opportunities and achieve proportionality at point P_2. This point would not be efficient, however, if shifting some of the additional budget allocation to men's sports would increase total utility by moving us to the higher indifference curve containing point E_2.

Is it possible for Utils to move to E_2 and still be in compliance? Recall that compliance can be achieved, at least in the short run, by demonstrating a "history and continuing practice of program expansion" for the underrepresented sex. At E_2, Utils would increase the number of men's slots by 150, and the number of women's spaces by 250. They would also be closer to proportionality, moving from a 70/30 split to almost 60/40. Assuming that Utils has a history of increasing opportunities for women, moving from E_1 to E_2 would leave Utils in compliance under Part 2 of the three-part test. The upside for Utils is that it would achieve short-run compliance while maximizing utility. The downside is that future budgetary expansion or reallocation would be necessary for the university to continue making progress toward proportionality.

Limitations to the above analysis

The indifference curves presented in this discussion are intended to represent society's preferences. The question is, how do we know society's desires? Are they determined (ascertained?) primarily by the athletic department or the university as a whole? What about fans and boosters? What about those who dislike college sports and what it has become (commercialized)? The preferences of the athletes themselves would be part of the society's indifference map. All of those groups and many more form society's preferences for college sports in general, and for the distribution of men's and women's sports opportunities in particular. Some preferences are clearly expressed in the market; some sports generate more ticket sales and revenue than others. Colleges and universities want the positive publicity (and resultant surge in admission applications) that results from a winning sports program. However, as we've discussed before, college sports also create externalities. Homeowners around a football stadium experience negative externalities in the form of noise and game day traffic. Positive externalities are created when success of the local college team generates wider excitement in the community, and when student-athletes use their scholarship-funded educations to give back to society. It is difficult to measure the value of these externalities, but they affect the total value of college sports to society.

Social preference functions are an amalgamation of many individual functions. Clearly not everyone will agree on the optimal allocation or more desirable combination of sports opportunities. Further complicating the issue is how to measure the intensity of preferences. Direct participants in the athletic program tend to have stronger preferences for certain outcomes than do members of the general public. Within athletic programs intensity of preferences can vary. In our 50/50 split (500 men, 500 women), suppose that the utility that would be gained by the 501st male athlete exceeds that of the 500th female athlete (assume all athletes enter the program in order of the utility they expect to receive from participation). That would suggest that total satisfaction could be increased by reallocating that 500th female slot to the 501st male athlete.

Preference functions also change over time. Proponents of Title IX have long held that the allegedly low interest in female sports is the result of few opportunities. Legal rulings with regard to survey use support this position. As society as a whole becomes less discriminatory and more accepting of women in roles traditionally held by men, the notion of equal opportunity in sports becomes more acceptable. As the first generation of Title IX beneficiaries imparts the love of sports in their daughters, we would expect society's indifference map to shift toward preferring greater equality of opportunity.

What does experience tell us about society's preferences? The implementation of Title IX suggests two obvious things: (1) Pre-Title IX preferences of athletic departments were strongly skewed toward men's sports. (2) Part of society (and those representing them in the legislature) had a preference function favoring much greater equality of opportunity than was being provided in the early 1970s. Over 30 years later, the ongoing battles to reform and challenge Title IX, and the general lack of compliance under Part 1 of the three-part test, suggest that the preferences of those allocating the resources continue to favor men's sports.

Chapter 9

Reforming College Sports

This is like déjà vu all over again.

— Yogi Berra

A basic purpose of this Association is to maintain intercollegiate athletics as an integral part of the educational program and the athlete as an integral part of the student body and, by doing so, retain a clear line of demarcation between intercollegiate athletics and professional sports.

— NCAA Constitution, Article 1.3.1

"[T]he NCAA has become expert at resisting true reform and co-opting would-be, well-intentioned reform initiatives.... .

— Frank Splitt, Fellow at Northwestern University

Quis custodiet ipsos custodes? (Who guards the guardians?)

— Latin phrase

[T]he NCAA has been charged with the formidable — and perhaps impossible — task of simultaneously guarding the integrity of intercollegiate athletics while generating hundreds of millions of dollars in income for its member institutions.

— James Duderstadt, former President of University of Michigan

553

9.1   Introduction

In the previous eight chapters, you learned about the economics of college sports and the National Collegiate Athletic Association (NCAA). By now, you should understand why the NCAA was formed, how it evolved into a cartel, the kinds of cheating that occur within the cartel, why **monopsonistic rents** arise and how they are distributed, the tension between athletics and academics, how the labor market for coaches works, the financial structure of the athletic department and its relationship to the university, the role of the media, and matters of gender and race. This chapter describes a variety of potential reforms to the college sports landscape and their probable impact. These range from small-scale and relatively non-controversial changes to more substantial and contentious proposals. It highlights questions regarding fairness and equity and suggestions about what should, or ought to, be done. This chapter and the book, finishes by examining the likelihood of reform.

9.2   Sources of Reform Initiatives

Proposed changes usually originate from university administrators at NCAA member institutions, like the athletic director or the president. But other groups make proposals as well, including university faculty, trustees or alumni, national higher education associations like the American Council on Education or the American Association of University Professors, organizations that focus specifically on college sports like the Knight Commission, the Drake Group, the National College Players Association (NCPA) and the Coalition on Intercollegiate Athletics, sports economists such as Andrew Zimbalist, and even journalists who cover college sports. We will learn more about these groups as we examine specific reforms. As you will see, the groups advocating reform policies can have dramatically different, and often opposing, views on reform.

Reforms tend to be initiated by schools, unilaterally or multilaterally, or by the government. A **unilateral change** typically involves an individual university acting alone to change its sports program. Examples include Vanderbilt's decision to eliminate its athletics department and Rutgers' elimination of six sports. A **multilateral change** requires coordination among NCAA members and typically results from discussions among institutional representatives, often during the yearly NCAA convention or periodic meetings of specific NCAA committees or subcommittees we mentioned in Chapter 1. One example is the **Academic Progress Rate** (APR), an important reform that we introduced in Chapter 4 and will discuss in greater detail in Section 9.6.5. Because the NCAA is a quasi-government that provides public goods to its members, the process for enacting a specific reform is analogous to that of a bill working its way through Congress or a state legislature. After the bill is proposed a vote is taken, if the vote is approved the bill becomes law. If a reform is approved and adopted by the NCAA, it is documented in the NCAA bylaws and all member institutions are required to abide by it.

A government-initiated reform is one that is proposed and enacted by state or federal government. Perhaps the preeminent example of such a reform is Title IX (Chapter 8). Other notable examples include the Supreme Court decisions regarding pay for assistant coaches (Chapter 2) and control over television broadcasting (Chapter 1), and the **Student-Right-to-Know Act** of 1990, legislation sponsored by Senators Ted Kennedy and Bill Bradley (a former All-American basketball player at Princeton and, later, New York Knick) that forced the NCAA to make graduation rates public. There are also on-going discussions in Congress about making the NCAA exempt from antitrust prosecution and revoking its tax-exempt status.

Finally, regardless whether a change is made unilaterally, multilaterally, or by state or federal government, it must be enforced and evaluated. There is little point in making a change to the rules if no enforcement occurs. Similarly, it does not make sense to implement a reform that is ineffective.

9.3 Reform Options

In the next four sections, we describe 19 commonly mentioned proposals and some of the individuals and organizations advocating them. The proposals are organized as follows: student-athlete compensation reforms, financial structure reforms, and academic reforms. One additional reform, involving an antitrust exemption for the NCAA, is discussed separately.

Once you finish this section, you will understand the main objectives of each proposal as well as the variety of organizations involved. After you read each proposed reform, take a few minutes and try to answer the following questions:

- Who would benefit from the reform?
- Who would be harmed?
- How likely is it that the reform will occur in the near future?
- Would it create any perverse incentives?
- Can the reform be circumvented (remember the little Dutch boy)?
- How would you evaluate the effectiveness of the reform?
- Do you support or oppose the reform? Why?

9.4   Student-Athlete Compensation Reforms

9.4.1   *Pay the players*

We begin with the most obvious and controversial proposal — paying student-athletes. Economists consider the labor market for college athletes to be a monopsony because the NCAA prevents schools from engaging in price competition with one another. As discussed in Chapter 3, this is unlike other labor markets where firms compete with one another to hire accountants, software engineers or restaurant chefs. You now know that some college athletes generate revenues, their marginal revenue product (MRP), well in excess of the maximum value of their athletics scholarship. In professional sports leagues, total player compensation equals 50–60% of total team revenues. At Ohio State, one of the top football programs, scholarship expenses as a percentage of football revenue are less than 4%.[1] Economist Dan Rascher (2003), appearing before the

---

[1] In 2011–2012, total football revenue at Ohio State was US$58.1 million and football scholarship expense was US$3.4 million.

California State Senate Select Committee on the Entertainment Industry, indicated that across DI, athletes' grants-in-aid consume only 4–12% of basketball and football revenues. Because of this monopsonistic exploitation, one commonly mentioned reform is to pay the players.

The simplest way to implement such a reform is to have the NCAA rescind all prohibitions on "pay for play" and transfers between schools. This would allow the colleges and universities to compete with one another on the basis of wages and salaries for players as they already do for coaches and athletics department staff. For the best athletes this would mean a significant financial gain since the payment they received would begin to approach their MRP. As an example, let's return to Jennifer, the All-American soccer player at the University of Southern California (from Chapter 3). Under this proposed reform, if Jennifer was getting a full-ride scholarship worth US$25,000 but was generating US$100,000 in MRP, USC must increase her compensation or risk losing her to another school. If USC does not offer more the US$25,000, there is nothing to prevent Notre Dame, or North Carolina (two schools with excellent women's soccer programs), or anybody else, from offering Jennifer any amount between US$25,000 and US$100,000. As you know from Chapter 3, in a competitive labor market workers tend to earn an amount close to their MRP.

A player like Jennifer would be free to move from school to school every year to find the best offer, or she could sign a "multi-year" contract and agree to play for 2, 3, or 4 years. Not only would this system eliminate monopsonistic exploitation, it would allow those athletes who fail to turn pro to earn money while they are still in school. From Jennifer's perspective, this would be fairer than the current system in which hundreds of athletes exhaust their athletics eligibility each year and leave school with no professional prospects, an empty bank account, and often with no degree. Ironically, this kind of reform would "turn back the clock" because it would create a kind of competitive market process that existed in college sports prior to the consolidation of the NCAA's power in the early 1950s. The fact that such a system existed previously, even if imperfectly, suggests it remains feasible today.

It is important to understand that this reform would not benefit all student-athletes equally. As indicated earlier, many athletes in the "non-revenue" sports receive scholarships valued in excess of the MRP they generate. The star shooting guard on the Duke basketball team could be paid several hundred thousand dollars because his talents generate significant revenues for the university. The third-string guard who sits at the end of bench and rarely plays except during "garbage time" is unlikely to get a penny more than his current scholarship (assuming he already gets one).

What about Jennifer? In reality, her MRP is not US$100,000, and it may not be US$25,000; it may even be US$0 because soccer is a non-revenue sport. Not only would this reform not increase her compensation, but there is also a chance that she would lose her scholarship completely. Remember that it is claimed that football and basketball subsidize all the other sports. If a competitive labor market for basketball and football players reduces the funds available for subsidization, it could cause universities to reduce scholarships or even eliminate non-revenue sports, like women's soccer or men's golf. Some money-losing DI universities may move to Division II or III where the financial commitment for sports is far less.

As we discussed in Chapter 8, any system which puts women's sports in peril is almost certain to be interpreted as non-compliant with Title IX, and challenged in a court of law. Even a more equitable proposal to provide student-athletes with additional compensation that is not explicitly linked to MRP (see Box 9.1), will be unlikely to survive if it results in unequal opportunities across genders.

Box 9.1.   Pay for play in Nebraska.

Nebraska State Senator, Ernie Chambers introduced legislation in 2003, which proposed that football players at the University of Nebraska-Lincoln and men's basketball athletes

(Continued)

Box 9.1. (Continued)

be given a stipend of US$200–US$500 each month in addition to their scholarship. Nebraska Legislative Bill 688 stated that NCAA restrictions on compensation for student-athletes were "unduly restrictive and unreasonable." Any Nebraska player "may be granted a stipend, the amount of which shall be determined by the university." The bill, which allows players in other sports to be compensated as well, was signed into law by Nebraska's Governor in April 2003. However, it will only take effect when at least four other states with schools in the Big 12 Conference pass similar laws.[2]

Most reform-minded groups, even those who are the harshest critics of the NCAA, do not support paying players. The Knight Commission, the Drake Group, and the Coalition on Intercollegiate Athletics are all prominent reform-minded organizations that adamantly oppose "pay for play."[3] Also, while economists are frequent supporters of proposals to pay players, there are exceptions. Andrew Zimbalist (1999, p. 205) argues that paying players is "neither feasible nor desirable" and that a true unrestricted labor market "would create too many invidious distinctions, administrative headaches, and tax burdens."

You should also be aware of the recommendations made by the National College Players Association (NCPA, formerly the Collegiate Athletes Coalition). The Association was formed by members of the football team at UCLA in 2001. To the best of our knowledge, it is the only reform-minded organization that consists only of current and former student-athletes. In addition, the NCPA is affiliated with a prominent labor

---

[2] Nebraska legislative Bill 688. Legislature of Nebraska, Ninety-Eighth Legislature, First Session (http://srvwww.unicam.state.ne.us/unicamAllDrafting.html). See also, Skidmore (2004).

[3] For a list of the schools belonging to COIA see http://www.neuro.uoregon.edu/~tublitz/COIA/Members.html.

union, the United Steelworkers of America. Because it recognizes that the NCAA extracts monopsonistic rents at the expense of student-athletes, one of the Coalition's goals is to increase the amount of monthly stipends. ("Mission & goals," n.d.)

The stipend is the "living expenses" portion of the overall scholarship package and is often used for rent, food, transportation, utilities and miscellaneous personal expenses. Using the example of a UCLA football player living in west Los Angeles, the Coalition estimates that the current monthly stipend of US$820 falls below his estimated expenses of US$1,000. This means that the player must generate roughly US$2,250 during the academic year to cover all his expenses. Until recently, NCAA rules left few options for players in this situation. They were not allowed to work during the academic year, even if the job was off-campus. They also could not apply for other sources of financial aid. This left employment during summers and approved school breaks as the only way to earn enough to keep afloat. In 1997, with a push from its Student-Athlete Advisory Committee, the NCAA passed legislation that allowed part-time work during the academic year, but earnings were limited to enough to cover "incidental expenses." Each school was responsible for calculating the appropriate amount based on living costs in their area, with amounts varying from US$1,200 to US$2,500. Because of the difficulties of monitoring income from off-campus employment, most student-athletes were steered to on-campus jobs. However, for many students this reform did not really address the problem. For many, the demands of training and competing were already the equivalent of a part-time job, forcing them to choose between studying and working a regular on-campus job. For students with families to support, an annual limit of US$2,500 was simply not nearly enough.

In 2003–2004, with prodding by the Student-Athlete Advisory Committee and reform groups such as the CAC, two other reforms were instituted. *First*, student-athletes could supplement their athletic scholarship with other scholarships, as long as the total amount did not exceed the full cost of attendance (tuition, books, room and board, and incidental expenses). The NCAA estimated that this would be US$2,000 to US$4,000 more than the maximum amount of a full athletic scholarship, but it was again up to each school to determine the appropriate amount. *Second*, the upper limit on earnings during the academic year was removed. To avoid large payments by boosters for sham work, three restrictions were imposed. The student can only be paid for work actually performed, the wage rate cannot exceed the going rate for similar employment in that area, and the student's value to the employer cannot be based on publicity or fame resulting from athletic ability.

The NCPA wants NCAA universities to simply increase the value of the grant-in-aid so that it covers all living expenses. Since a university or the NCAA is unlikely to voluntarily propose such a change, the NCPA recommends government intervention and encourages student-athletes to contact their state legislative or Congressional representative. The NCPA's goal might also be achieved through the courts. In February 2006, four former players filed a class-action lawsuit in the United States District Court, Central District of California, The lawsuit, *White et al. v. NCAA* sought the equivalent of "back pay" for the out-of-pocket expenses not covered by a grant-in-aid. If the court had ruled in favor of the four players, as well as the estimated 98 other plaintiffs, the NCAA could have been forced to pay US$100 million (Wolverton, 2006c). Instead, a settlement reached in August 2008, required the NCAA to establish a US$10 million Former Student-Athlete Fund, to assist former student-athletes with educational and job-search expenses. It also added flexibility to the NCAA's Special Assistance and Academic Enhancement fund. (Elfman, 2008)

In 2011, the NCAA approved additional support for student-athletes. Specifically, the new rules allow student-athletes receiving full athletic scholarships to receive "additional athletics aid up to the full cost of attendance or US$2,000, whichever is less" (Hosick, 2011). The legislation does not require schools to offer this additional aid or stipend, but conferences are encouraged to adopt a common standard. Slated to be effective starting with the 2013–2014 academic year, these rules have drawn criticism from Division I members concerned about costs, competitive balance, and Title IX implications. This has slowed the implementation as the NCAA continues work on logistics of the policy. (Hosick, 2012)

In response to the NCAA measure, in 2011, *Sports Illustrated* conducted a feasibility study of providing equal stipends to all student-athletes (we first mentioned this study in Chapter 3, Box 3.4). The main challenge in conducting this study is the variability in accounting practices of athletic departments, so *SI* was cautious in its estimates. It developed a financial model under which paying student-athletes is feasible, but not without sacrifice (no big surprise to economists).

In football, rosters would be limited to 90 players, with only 63 scholarships for football (versus the current limit of 85). All four schools examined would have to cut men's teams, with Oregon cutting two, Mississippi cutting three, San Jose State four, and Louisville seven. This would require the NCAA to eliminate the minimum number of teams currently required for Division I status (16 for DI-FBS, 14 for DI-FCS and DI-no football). Title IX requirements would effectively prevent the elimination of women's sports for Mississippi and Oregon, but not Louisville and San Jose State, who at the time of the study met the first part of Title IX's three-part test.

While the *SI* study determined that stipends for all student-athletes at the four schools would be feasible, it recognized that how much each institution could afford would vary considerably. Based on the *SI* assumptions and calculations, Louisville could afford to pay each student-athlete US$32,333 per year (not counting regular scholarships), while San Jose State student-athletes would receive a more modest US$11,172 per year. The study cautioned that the potential for such discrepancies, and the fact that there are institutions worse off than San Jose State (the least profitable school in the study, recording on over US$3 million deficit in 2009–2010), could cause some schools to drop football or leave Division I altogether. (Dohrmann, 2011)

Fast fact. *In 2009, former Arizona State and Nebraska football player, Sam Keller, along with former UCLA basketball player Ed O'Bannon, became lead plaintiffs in a class-action lawsuit known as In re NCAA Student Athlete Names & Likenesses Litigation. The suit, which is being brought against the NCAA, EA Sports, and Collegiate Licensing Company, seeks compensation for college athletes, past and current, for use of their images (as avatars) in video games. The plaintiffs claim that EA (Electronic Arts Inc.) and the NCAA conspiring to deny payments to former college athletes, in violation of antitrust law. The plaintiffs also claim that the defendants violated the former athletes' rights to publicity. In 2011, the judge dismissed the antitrust claim against EA, but the rights to publicity claim had not been settled. As of June 2013, the case had not been resolved.*

9.4.2 *Allow student-athletes to transfer without losing eligibility*

Recall our story in Chapter 4 about Joe Cool, the hypothetical prep football player who is recruited by Oregon State. Joe is excited about playing for the Beavers because the head coach is Dennis Erickson, a well-known coach with experience in both college and the NFL. Unfortunately for Joe, after his first season as a Beaver, Coach Erickson leaves Oregon State to take a more lucrative coaching opportunity elsewhere. Joe decides to transfer to Utah, but in accordance with NCAA rules, he cannot play in his first year at Utah and loses a year of eligibility. Why are coaches, or other athletic department personnel, allowed to move from job to job with no penalty while players lose a year of eligibility?

Prior to the cartelization of the NCAA in the early 1950s, it was common for universities to "pirate" players from other institutions. The reason some elite players were willing to switch schools was simple; they played for the team that offered them the most money. The incentive to pirate players did not diminish when the NCAA prohibited price competition, in fact, it intensified. Schools no longer had to offer more money, just the chance to play for a winning team and be seen on national television, among other non-monetary inducements. Rather than impose penalties on schools that encourage athletes to transfer, the NCAA chose to punish the students by not allowing them to play during their first year and taking away one year of eligibility. How does this benefit the student-athletes? Why not let them transfer as freely as non-athletes as long as they maintain academic eligibility?

One possible compromise position would be to allow student-athletes a one-time opportunity to transfer if the head coach leaves the program. This would allow the players to find a better fit if the incoming coach, for example, has a personality or style of play that clashes with the student-athlete's interests and abilities. The obvious danger is that departing coaches would try to take their best players with them, but a prohibition on student-athlete transfers to their old coach's new school would eliminate that problem.

9.4.3   *Create minor league affiliates of the NBA and NFL*

If you are a sufficiently talented high school baseball or ice hockey player, you may be lucky enough to be drafted by a professional sports team. The team will assign you to one of its minor league affiliates and you will begin a difficult but exciting journey that one day may put you in the "big leagues." But what about your high school peers who have dreams of playing professional basketball or football? They will embark on a different path. They must attend a university in order to prepare themselves for a professional career because those sports do not have an established minor league system (the exception being the handful of prep basketball players like Kobe Bryant and LeBron James, who skipped college entirely).

Why are there minor league teams for baseball and ice hockey but not for basketball and football? The answer, as usual, is money. University teams already serve as *de facto* minor league teams to the National Baseball Association (NBA) and National Football League (NFL) even though neither league pays any player development costs (the costs of training players while in college). Andrew Zimbalist (1999, p. 197) estimated that each Major League Baseball (MLB) team spends about US$9 million on player development at their minor league affiliates, a sum that each NBA and NFL teams could match if they wanted to. But why should they? Why would the Los Angeles Lakers or Miami Dolphins offer to pay when universities like UCLA and the University of Miami already do so? Why not continue to free-ride?

How would a minor league system work? A couple of options come to mind. The NBA and NFL owners could decide which universities each franchise will be affiliated with. The allocation of universities to franchises could be based on geography; for example, the Miami Dolphins might be assigned all schools in Florida other than Florida and Florida State, which could be assigned to Tampa Bay and Jacksonville respectively. Alternately, and more realistically, since NFL franchises based outside of Florida are probably interested in an alliance with Florida football schools, the NFL could hold a lottery to assign universities to franchises. It would be each franchise's responsibility to provide the funding to run the football program at each school. Not only would this solve the financial difficulties that plague so many DI schools, it would also allow the athletes to receive a salary just like minor leaguers in baseball and ice hockey.

Another option is that the NFL teams could each contribute an equal amount of money to collectively support a select group of football programs in the United States. Once an athlete's eligibility expires, or the athlete decides to leave school early, the NFL could conduct a draft to allocate talent across franchises just as it does today.

Fast fact. In April 2007, a new football league was scheduled to begin. The All American Football League (AAFL) was to consist of six teams located in the southern United States. The AAFL's Chairman was former NCAA President Cedric Dempsey, and former President Myles Brand had endorsed the league. The league adopted college rules of play and games were to be played in university facilities. An interesting twist is that players would have had to graduate from college to be able to play. This requirement was intended to create an incentive for players to complete their degree. After suspending the league's launch multiple times, the last time in February 2010, as of spring 2011, the league appeared to be defunct.

The proposal to establish working relationships between colleges and franchises extends beyond financial questions. As we just indicated, it would allow athletes to be paid to play and it would allow the leagues — in consultation with the athletic department and the university — to determine the educational requirements for athletes. In its purest form, athletes would attend the institution only to improve their skills and performance, not to get an education, but the precise requirements would be left to the leagues and the universities. In all probability, the basketball and football teams would become separate for-profit entities with only loose ties to the university.

Variations of these kinds of proposals are attracting more attention. A former president of the University of Michigan, James Duderstadt, has written extensively about intercollegiate athletics reforms. Duderstadt (2000) supports the bifurcation of sports into commercial and non-commercial realms; he suggests, for example:

> Those universities currently conducting Division I-A programs would be faced with a decision. They could retain big-time football programs by owning and operating franchises in this new professional league, using school facilities, emblems, and mascots. If so, they would have to operate these franchises as true commercial enterprises, much as the owners of professional NFL teams. Although the primary functions of these junior professional teams would be to develop young football players for the NFL, to entertain the public, and perhaps to turn a profit, universities could also commit to providing players with educational benefits, provided they met admissions standards.
>
> If universities did not desire affiliation with this professional league, they could retain football but only as an amateur university activity, with true students as participants and teaching staff as coaches. There would be no athletics scholarships, no redshirting, no freshman eligibility or spring practice, no commercial endorsements or media patronizing, and no drafting of players until their eligibility was completed or they decided to turn pro (p. 279).

A 2006 article in the *Tucson Weekly* (Downing, 2006) made a similar proposal: the establishment of "the men's basketball and football teams as separate corporations" at the University of Arizona. It proposed that:

> The University would grant a license to those corporations to use the University name for the teams. The fee for the license would be a percentage of the revenues the corporations generate from ticket sales, broadcasting rights, advertising, etc. The University would use part of the license-fee income to support the nonrevenue sports it decides to retain, such as gymnastics and soccer. This is a solution which would enable the sports fans to continue to enjoy the games and enable the University to focus on its academic mission.

Fast fact. *The men's soccer team at Brigham Young University (BYU) does not compete in the Mountain West conference with most of the other BYU sports. Instead, it is a member of the United Soccer Premier Development League, which supports Major Soccer League (MLS) franchises like the Los Angeles Galaxy, Kansas City Wizards, and DC. United. Economist Brian Goff asked why the NCAA would allow BYU to do this since it seems to contradict Bylaw 3.2.4.5 (which says that the rules apply to all varsity sports). It turns out that the United Soccer Premier Development League is not a professional league but the most advanced amateur soccer league in the United States (Goff, 2006; "New BYU PDL club," 2003). The soccer team is therefore considered an amateur, non-collegiate, team. Interestingly, the team broke away from the NCAA after the association refused to allow BYU to join DI soccer because an additional men's sport would have put the university in non-compliance with Title IX.*

There is no question that this change would make college sports even more commercialized and professionalized than it is today. But some reformers are willing to allow basketball and football to go their own way, if it means that a "firewall" is established to keep commercialization from "infecting everybody else" (that is, all other sports) (Price, 2004). Also, it seems unlikely that the NFL and NBA would be willing to support all current DI football and basketball programs, or that all those institutions would agree to an affiliation. It would probably be restricted to the Bowl Championship Series (BCS) automatic qualifier schools and conferences, and perhaps a few more. The Knight Commission, which supports the establishment of minor leagues for the NBA and NFL, but prefers they have no relationship with NCAA schools, estimates that 40 to 60 institutions might commercialize their basketball and football programs. Murray Sperber, whose "beer and circus" story appeared in Chapter 6, thinks about 60 DI institutions would professionalize their basketball and football teams while the rest would migrate to DII and DIII.[4]

Fast fact. *The NBA's Development League, better known as the D League, began in 2001. The NBA's Commissioner, David Stern, has referred to it as a "true minor league system," but that is a misnomer. In reality, it is a parallel minor league operating alongside NCAA schools. Rather than siphoning players from the NCAA, the team rosters consist primarily of players who have already attended college. In 2013, 132 NBA players had D League experience. In the 2012–2013 season, the league has 17 teams in Austin, Bakersfield, Boise, Canton, Des Moines, Erie, Fort Wayne, Frisco (TX), Hidalgo (TX), Los Angeles, Newark (DE), Portland (ME), Reno, Santa Cruz, Sioux Falls, Springfield (MA), and Tulsa. Most D League teams are affiliated with a single NBA team, usually franchises that are in close geographic proximity.*

---

[4]Rascher (2003, Appendix K.3) mentions "[m]any sports enterprises, such as Summer and Winter Olympics, golf, tennis, track and field, figure skating, rugby union in England [and] rugby in Australia, went from amateur status to professional status-and flourished after the transition."

Now let us consider reforms focusing on the financial operations of athletic departments.

9.5 Financial Structure Reforms

9.5.1 *Standardize the financial disclosure process among all athletic departments*

In Chapter 6, you learned that one of the main reasons why it is difficult to understand athletic department budgets is the lack of a common accounting standard like GAAP that applies to corporations. Reform is unlikely to occur as long as those outside of athletic departments are unaware of the true financial situation. In addition, choosing the appropriate reform requires accurate and complete information. Ironically, current federal requirements for financial disclosure under the Equity in Athletics Disclosure Act (EADA) encourage schools to disclose financial information for the sake of disclosure; compliance does not require transparency or a simplified and easy to understand set of measurements (such as the athletic department's debt burden). An NCAA subcommittee on fiscal responsibility has discussed this possibility but no tangible proposal has yet appeared.

9.5.2 *Reduce football scholarships*

NCAA regulations currently allow a maximum of 85 athletics scholarships to be allocated to the football team (football is a head count sport). Reducing the number of scholarships, as groups like the Knight Commission argue, would generate significant direct savings and might result in additional savings in uniform and equipment, travel, coaching staff, and other areas. These savings could be used to support non-revenue sports, or be redirected to the university's general fund if the athletics department budget is reduced.

Why cut back on football scholarships rather than scholarships in other sports? Simple; football is both the most expensive sport to support as well as the sport with the largest roster. Assigning one scholarship for each offensive and defense position would require 22 scholarships in total. Taking into consideration the "depth chart," and the need for substitutes, suggests doubling the number of scholarships from 22 to 44. Adding 11 more players who specialize in special team activities, plus a kicker and a punter, increases the total to 57. In the NFL, there are 53 players on the active roster (plus the reserves).

A precedent for cutting scholarships does exist. At one time, a football team was allowed a maximum of 105 scholarships, according to NCAA rules. This was later reduced to 95 in 1988 and subsequently to the present 85 in 1994. Not surprisingly, football coaches oppose any further reductions and argue that a maximum limit of approximately 60 scholarships would exclude many student-athletes, especially injured players and red-shirts.

How would a significant reduction in football scholarships affect competitive balance? Would this take away some of the advantage currently enjoyed by programs with large budgets, which would no longer be able to stockpile as many talented athletes? Research by Katherine Baird (2004) suggests that reductions in football scholarships do not increase competitive balance. Ohio State, which spends roughly US$35 million annually on football, will still have a more competitive team than Troy State, which spends US$4.9 million. Ohio State's budget allows them to have superior facilities and a better coaching staff, both of which contribute to winning. In addition, the best athletes are attracted to the best programs, in part because it increases their chances for a professional career after graduation. The 20 or so students that Ohio State would no longer be able to offer athletic scholarships are not likely to be the players who make the difference between winning and losing.

Fast fact. *Missouri State University (now Emeritus) Economics Professor Tom Wyrick proposed elimination of all football scholarships at MSU. He estimated the yearly savings at US$500,000.*

9.5.3 *Restrict sources of outside income for coaches*

As you learned elsewhere in this book, commercial endorsements are a lucrative source of outside income for college coaches but they may constitute a potential conflict of interest. Reform-minded organizations like the Knight Commission suggest bringing coaches' salaries in line with the salary structure for faculty and administrators. Although the base salary of basketball and football coaches typically exceeds those of even the highest paid professor, it is the additional compensation coaches receive that propels their compensation into the one million dollar plus range. Reform organizations advocate restrictions on additional earnings, especially from corporations that have advertising and endorsement contracts with the athletic department and its staff.

9.5.4 *Reorganize the athletics department*

Reorganizing the athletics department as a separate administrative unit and merging its operations into general university operations would reduce its autonomy. Top university administrators would gain control over athletics revenues and expenditures, which might mitigate the arms race mentality and persistent financial losses. It could also reduce the *independence* or discretion of the athletic department to act in ways that may conflict with the mission of the university. This might lead to a reduction in NCAA violations and improved academic performance by student-athletes.

Could it be there be any benefit to having an independent athletic department? An analogy is the relationship between the Federal Reserve System (the Fed) and Congress. You may remember from your macroeconomics or money and banking classes that the Fed does not rely on Congressional appropriations. The Fed generates its own income from interest earned on government securities and payments for services provided to banks and other financial institutions. The Fed has freedom to act with less political interference. This independence is generally thought to be beneficial for our country because it prevents monetary policy from becoming politicized (for example, it prevents Congress from manipulating the money supply and interest rates to serve its own interests).

While many valid arguments exist for maintaining the Fed's independence from the legislative and executive branches, the same logic does not apply to college sports. In theory, less independence on the part of the athletic department, not more, will curtail excesses like stratospheric salaries for coaches and Taj Mahal athletics facilities. Having said that, there are at least two reasons why such a result may not occur. As Chapter 6 explained, the president of the university, ancillary administrators and trustees, may all adopt the "sports as savior" perspective and be more than willing to funnel seemingly unlimited resources to the athletic department. In other words, the fact that the president is in control does not prevent her from either acquiescing to the actions of the athletic director or being fully supportive. In that case, little will change.

We are also skeptical of what are called "presidentially-led institutional reforms." These are situations in which the president of the university more or less single-handedly implements reforms to ensure the university avoids the arms race trap. Our skepticism is two-fold. First, in any large organization, be it business, politics, or academics, it is difficult for an individual to be effective in changing the behavior of the collective. In many situations this "institutional inertia" is desirable because it prevents "institutional hijacking" by a small group of people. But it also stifles change and reinforces the status quo.

Second, organizations consist of myriad interest groups, some of whom may favor reform and others who oppose it. Without the support of the board of trustees, faculty, alumni, and other "stakeholders," little of significance will occur. Given that the Athletic Director, or football and basketball coach, often wield power equal to or greater than the president, reforms can be blocked or watered down. Also, even in situations in which the president appears to have "tamed" the athletic department and aligned interest groups, like the situation at Vanderbilt, it remains an open question whether the institution has decided to withdraw from the arms race. In his book *Unpaid Professionals*, Andrew Zimbalist (1999, p. 191) recounts the story of the president of Michigan State University attempting to prevent the football coach from serving simultaneously as the athletics director. The president's decision was overturned by the university's Board of Trustees, which then granted the coach a ten-year appointment as athletic director. Other university presidents have alluded to similar problems (e.g., Duderstadt, 2000, pp. 102–103).

> **Fast fact.** *In 2003, Vanderbilt University took an unprecedented step in college sports: it dissolved its athletic department and subsumed all athletics functions in other administrative operations. The decision was based on two considerations: the need to make athletics less "isolationist" — get student-athletes more involved in campus activities like student government — and to try to control athletics expenditures. (Powers, 2006)*

9.5.5 Remove the NCAA's nonprofit status and eliminate tax deductions on contributions to college sports

Organizations engaged in charitable or humanitarian activities typically qualify for a tax-exempt status. United States Internal Revenue Code Section 501.c.3 states that a tax-exempt status only applies if the institution is "… organized and operated exclusively for religious, charitable, scientific, … public safety, literary, or educational purposes, or to foster national or international amateur sports competition (but only if no part of its activities involve the provision of athletic facilities or equipment), or for the prevention of cruelty to children or animals …" . (Internal Revenue Service, 2006, § 4.76.2.8)

Qualifying charitable, humanitarian and religious organizations that come to mind are the Red Cross, Habitat for Humanity, and the Salvation Army. Others, like the United Negro College Fund or Children's Scholarship Fund, focus on educational objectives. But what about the NCAA; why is it tax-exempt? The NCAA is considered a tax-exempt organization because, according to the Association, it is "organized and operated exclusively for educational purposes."

Most of the NCAA's yearly revenue comes from contracts with television broadcasters, especially the US\$10.8 billion, 14-year, contract with CBS for the broadcast rights to the men's basketball tournament. Is March Madness an educational activity, a commercial activity, or some combination of both? If it is the former, then money generated by the tournament is tax exempt. If the latter, it is subject to taxation. The NCAA continues to claim that it is not a big business, not because of a lack of revenue (it is hard to disguise over a half-billion dollars in annual income), but due to the fact that any suggestion that its activities are business-oriented, more commercial than educational, could result in a large chunk of that income becoming taxable.

The NCAA's claim that it qualifies for tax exempt status continues to draw attention from the Internal Revenue Service and Congress. An article in the *Chronicle of Higher Education* (Wolverton, 2006a) indicated that "lawmakers are concerned that big-time sports programs are evolving into commercial entertainment businesses that are only marginally connected to the tax-exempt purposes of higher education." The federal government is specifically interested in unrelated business income — income received through *regular* commercial activities *unrelated* to education. Income received by the NCAA and its member institutions from broadcasting rights and corporate advertising and sponsorships occurs on a regular basis (see Box 9.2). That income certainly appears to be commercial. The litmus test is whether the income is *integral* to the educational mission of the university. Are million-dollar coach's salaries, swanky luxury suites at arenas and stadiums, and lavish training facilities part of the educational process? How does the arms race increase academic opportunities for students? What does participation in a postseason game, like the BCS have to do with education, when football teams playing in bowl games receive \$12 million but have graduation rates barely in the double digits?

Providing definitive answers to these questions is necessary before Congress and the Internal Revenue Service (IRS) can issue guidelines as to what constitutes unrelated business income. How that classification will be defined is crucial in determining the NCAA's tax liability. For the moment, as one researcher noted, "current statutory provisions and regulations provide a somewhat ambiguous framework for analyzing commercial activities to determine their relatedness ... to the educational purpose of a college or university ... the current provisions have evolved to create a loophole for educational institutions to escape taxation on revenues from wholly commercial activities" (Guruli, 2005, pp. 68–69).[5]

If the NCAA's tax-exempt status is removed or reduced, the impact could be cataclysmic. Such a loss would reverberate at all levels of NCAA activity and among all member institutions. How the NCAA and the universities would respond is difficult to predict. Let us consider a couple possible scenarios. *First*, if the NCAA were considered by the IRS to be more of a commercial entity than an educational one, it would increase the likelihood of antitrust investigations. Such an investigation might, and we must stress "might," force universities to pay their players. Just as the Supreme Court decided against the NCAA's TV contract, the courts might rule in favor of students objecting to the agreement among NCAA members to limit their compensation. However, if this sequence of events occurred, it would introduce the types of problems we discussed in Section 9.4.1; could players be paid without *either* cutting non-revenue sports or violating Title IX? *Second*, would a rescission of the exemption change sports fans' perception of college sports? Put simply, would it shift the demand schedule for college sports? And in what direction?

A related issue is how direct contributions to university athletic departments would be considered in light of any changes to the NCAA's tax status. As we saw in Chapters 5 and 6, contributions from boosters and others are most often used to help supplement the salaries received by coaches and fund new facilities construction.

---

[5] See also Golden (2006).

Box 9.2.   Congress questions the NCAA's tax exemption.

In October, 2006, Congress, led by Congressman William Thomas (R-CA), Chairman of the House Committee on Ways and Means, asked NCAA President Myles Brand thirteen questions concerning the NCAA's educational mission and its finances. Many of the questions revolved around one issue: why should the NCAA continue to be granted a federal tax exemption on its income? University of Illinois College of Law Professor John D. Colombo provides a thorough and insightful discussion of the issue that can be found at http://illinoislawreview.org/wp-content/ilr-content/articles/2010/1/Colombo.pdf.

They also qualify the donor for exclusive privileges such as club seats or luxury suites, access to private entertainment facilities, and other benefits. The IRS has investigated these contributions to determine if they are tax deductible. Fortunately for the NCAA schools, the IRS ruled in 1999 that boosters were allowed to deduct 80% of the cost of a luxury box. Thus far, while such contributions continue to be almost entirely tax-exempt, they continue to be scrutinized by the IRS. Any unfavorable reinterpretation would create significant repercussions and make it more difficult for athletic departments to raise money for, among other things, facilities construction and athletic department salaries. This, of course, would impact the arms race.

9.6   Academic Reforms

9.6.1   *Increase enforcement by the NCAA*

The NCAA has no shortage of rules, many of which are intended to protect the status of student-athletes as students first, and athletes second. However, these rules are meaningless without an effective system to uncover serious violations and impose sanctions that will deter future violations. As we first saw in Chapter 2, the NCAA devotes few resources to policing and often imposes only probation and minor penalties.

Sports economist Andrew Zimbalist is perhaps the most vociferous critic about the lack of enforcement by the NCAA. Zimbalist (1999, p. 201) argues that "[s]pending under US\$2 million a year to enforce over a thousand pages of rules and regulations at 964 member institutions is a joke." He suggests the NCAA increase its commitment to enforcing the rules by a factor of three or four. Along with an increase in the resources devoted to catching violations, he supports harsher punishments, including more frequent use of the "death penalty" for recidivists.

9.6.2 *Make academic eligibility requirements tougher and/or increase academic accountability*

The Drake Group, a collection of mainly current and former faculty members, is one of the most vocal advocates for greater academic accountability. It wants to see universities make publicly available a list of the courses and majors taken by student-athletes, the names of the professors who teach those classes, the percentage of athletes in each class, and GPAs of those students. This type of public disclosure can increase pressure from groups outside of the athletic department to ensure that student-athletes are receiving an actual education, not just accumulating credits. This proposal to divulge academic progress is controversial because it requires an exception to Family Educational Rights and Privacy Act (FERPA). Other organizations, notably the Coalition on Intercollegiate Athletics, support increased information gathering and disclosure, and monitoring of student-athletes' academic performance by university administrators and the faculty, but only if the anonymity of students is protected and the disclosure adheres to FERPA provisions. The Coalition on Intercollegiate Athletics also suggests that universities scrutinize those courses taught by coaches to ensure that are no conflicts of interest or bogus "underwater basket weaving" or "rocks for jocks" classes, so that no classes like Georgia assistant coach Jim Harrick Jr.'s "Coaching Principles and Strategies of Basketball" are offered (we recounted that story in Section 4.7).

9.6.3   *Reinstate four-year scholarships*

One commonly mentioned recommendation is that scholarships be offered to student-athletes for more than one year. This would increase the likelihood that a student-athlete would graduate, especially in the case of a severe injury that makes playing impossible. It would also give athletes more freedom to make academic decisions (e.g., choice of major) without fear of reprisal by a coach who controls their scholarship from year to year. This recommendation involves a bit of *déjà vu*; until 1973, it was standard for universities to offer multi-year scholarships to their athletes. But the fact that the NCAA changed this policy, as we argued in Chapter 4, is potential evidence of both the NCAA's disinterest in athletes' academic performance as well as the existence of a **cartel within the cartel**.

As discussed in Chapter 2, in October 2011, the NCAA approved allowing schools to extend multi-year scholarships. Athletic programs are not required to offer scholarships beyond one year, but they now have the flexibility to provide that option (Hosick, 2011). The Drake Group began advocating for multi-year scholarships in 2004, picketing in front of a San Antonio hotel with basketball coaches were staying during that year's Final Four (Drake, 2013). As of 2013, according to the *Chronicle of Higher Education*, "nearly two-thirds of the 56 most powerful Division I public universities now offer multiyear awards." However, they also note that in most cases multiyear scholarships are awarded to only a small number of athletes at these institutions (Wolverton and Newman, 2013).

9.6.4   *Make freshmen ineligible to play*

Many reformers, including the Coalition on Intercollegiate Athletics, the Drake Group, and the Knight Commission, want freshmen to be ineligible. Prior to 1968, freshmen eligibility in sports other than football and basketball was up to the discretion of the universities. Ivy League schools tended to restrict freshmen and the Big Ten Conference limited freshmen participation to students making adequate academic progress. Other schools and conferences were more lenient. Arguments against freshmen eligibility were, and remain, based on the belief that incoming student-athletes need a year to adapt to the rigors of college, and learn to balance the demands between class, study, and practice time before allowing them to suit up and to travel. In 1972, the NCAA enacted a rule that made freshmen in all sports eligible. If the NCAA was serious about ensuring that student-athletes succeed in the classroom, why not prohibit or limit their athletics participation in their first year to give them a chance to adapt to college?

9.6.5 *Strengthen institutional incentives to increase graduation rates*

Chapter 4 discussed student-athlete graduation rates. You learned that graduation rates for student-athletes are not significantly different from students who are not involved in intercollegiate athletics. Yet when the total population of student-athletes is broken down into specific population sub-samples, some notable differences emerge. In particular, graduation rates for athletes who participate in the primary revenue sports — basketball and football — have lower graduation rates than both other athletes and the overall student population. There are also differences in graduation rates by race, especially among Black athletes, who are typically heavily represented on the basketball and football team.

As we did in Chapter 4, we stress that graduation rates must be interpreted with caution, especially if one is advocating specific policies in response to that information. Also, any policies designed to improve graduation rates should be applicable to all students, athletes and no-athletes alike. Nevertheless, concern about graduation rates, especially among basketball and football players irrespective of race, has produced numerous reform proposals. The

NCAA's most recent policy change to increase graduation rates is based on the Academic Progress Rate.

The APR is a measurement of a team's academic performance. It went into effect in fall 2005 and applies to the more than 6,000 teams at the 347 DI institutions. The method used to calculate the APR is described in Box 9.3. The policy initially established a cut-off point at 925 (out of a maximum of 1,000); this meant that any team with an APR below 925 was subject to a variety of penalties. Why was 925 the magic number? According to the Association, an APR of 925 is the equivalent of a 50% graduation rate over a five-year period. This means that another way to interpret the APR is that it wants the graduation rate for all athletes in all sports at all schools to be 50% or better. Since the initial benchmark of 925, the NCAA reduced the standard to 900. For 2012–2013, and 2013–2014, a team had to earn a four-year average of 900 of above. Beginning with the 2014–2015 season, teams must earn a four-year average APR of 930 or above.

Box 9.3.   Calculating the APR.

The APR is determined by two factors: first, whether a student-athlete achieves the minimum GPA and second, if the student stays in school. A student is "awarded" one point if she meets either criterion. Total points are calculated for each team and compared to the total points possible for the academic term or year. Let X represent total points achieved and Y total points possible; X/Y is the APR for the team, the percentage of points earned compared to the amount possible. If the APR is less than 930 (93%), then the team is subject to penalties (the APR calculation, and cut-off threshold, is slightly different for the handful of DI schools on the quarter term calendar).

Let us use the women's soccer team at the University of Southern California as an example. Since there are 20 players

(Continued)

Box 9.3.   (Continued)

on the roster, each semester the team can earn a maximum of 40 points (or 80 points per academic year). This term two players fail to meet the minimum GPA requirement and are academically ineligible to play. However, they remain in school to try to boost their grades and return to the team. This means the team earned 38 out of 40 possible points for an APR of 950 (95%) which exceeds the cutoff of 930. USC will not be penalized. Suppose next semester the same two players again have low grades and decide to leave school (these players are called "0 for 2s"). Now the USC women's soccer team has a score of 36 out of 40, which results in an APR of 900 and falls below the cutoff.

One of the interesting consequences of the APR is that since it uses a percentage, teams with smaller rosters are more likely to be penalized. Take a look at Table 9.1: How many "small roster" sports like cross-country, golf, or wrestling are on the list? If the golf team has 10 players and one player is in academic trouble and leaves school, the team's APR is 900. Compare that to the football team with a roster of 100. It would take 10 players in academic difficulty (and not enrolled) to produce an APR of 900. For that reason, in 2011, the NCAA modified the APR requirements for 2012–2013 and beyond, requiring teams to earn a minimum four-year average. This helps to mitigate the volatility effects of small rosters.

Note that the point system gives schools credit for athletes who have low grades but remain in school. The system also does not penalize students who transfer provided they were academically eligible. It also does not penalize early entry as long as the student was academically eligible. The 40/60/80 rule (see Chapter 4) remains in place.

More information about the APR can be found on the NCAA's website (www.ncaa.org). Select "Research" from "About Us" and then click on "Academic Progress Rate (APR)."

Table 9.1.   Division I teams failing to meet APR requirements in 2011–2012 and level of penalties (in parentheses).

Institution	Team(s)
Alabama A&M University	men's golf (1)
Alabama State University	baseball (1), football (2), men's basketball (2), softball (1), women's volleyball (1)
Alcorn State University	men's basketball (1)
Charleston Southern University	men's track, indoor (1) and outdoor (1)
Chicago State University	women's volleyball (3)
Florida A&M University	men's basketball (1), men's track, indoor (1) and outdoor (1), women's volleyball (2)
Florida International University	men's basketball (1)
Grambling State University	men's basketball (3)
Mississippi Valley State University	baseball (1), men's basketball (2)
Norfolk State University	men's track, indoor (1) and outdoor (1), women's track, indoor (1) and outdoor (1), women's volleyball (1)
North Carolina A&T State University	men's track, indoor (1) and outdoor (1)
Savannah State University	football (1), men's basketball (1)
Southern University, Baton Rouge	men's track, indoor (2) and outdoor (2)
Towson University	men's basketball (1)
University of Arkansas, Pine Bluff	men's basketball (2), men's golf (1)
University of Louisiana at Monroe	men's basketball (3)
University of New Orleans	men's basketball (3), women's basketball (1)

Source: http://fs.ncaa.org/Docs/newmedia/public/rates/index.html.

Notes: Penalty levels are cumulative; every school at Level Two has also been at Level One; Level Three schools have incurred Level One and two penalties. Some of the penalties listed above were under review and/or appeal at the time of publication.

Originally, there were two categories of penalties for the APR, contemporaneous and historical. The **contemporaneous penalties** represented, as the NCAA put it, "a real-time snapshot of a team's academic performance." For every student-athlete who was on a team with an APR below 925 and who left school before graduation, the team lost that scholarship, usually during the next academic year. Unlike contemporaneous penalties, which were designed to be a kind of "wake-up call" for universities, the second category of penalties, called **historically-based penalties**, were punitive in nature and designed to inflict substantial punishment on teams that were repeat offenders, especially teams with significantly lower graduation rates than teams at peer institutions, and lower rates for athletes at their own institution than non-athletes. These included the loss of scholarships, restrictions on recruiting, prohibitions on participation in the postseason (and access to the revenue generated in championships), and reductions in conference distributions.

As part of the 2011 APR policy revision mentioned earlier, there are now three levels of penalties the NCAA can impose for teams with an APR below 930. Level One penalties, imposed when a team first fails to meet the standard, limits team practices to 16 hours per week. This represents a reduction of four hours, which much be replaced with academic activities. Level Two penalties (for second infractions) result in a loss of contests for the team, in addition to the Level One practice reductions. Level Three, for third and subsequent violations, may result in a variety of penalties as determined by the Committee on Academic Performance. These may include the suspension of coaches, reductions in financial aid, and restrictions on NCAA membership. Note that ineligibility for postseason play is not one of the stated penalties, even though teams failing to meet the 930 APR are ineligible. The NCAA's rationale is that "Just as teams must win in competition to be eligible for championships, they now must also achieve in the classroom". (Frequently Asked Questions, n.d.)

As discussed in Chapter 7, with the new BCS playoff system, 10% of a team's bowl revenue will also be tied to their APR. This will provide additional financial incentive for schools to pay attention to the "student" side of their student-athletes. This reform was initially recommended by the Knight Commission in its 2010 *Restoring the Balance* Report, and then regularly until the policy's adoption in 2012. (Knight Commission, 2012)

In addition to the APR policy, the NCAA instituted another significant change as part of a package of academic reforms. The **Graduation Success Rate** (GSR) is a calculation different from the one used by the Federal Government. It was developed in response to college and university presidents who wanted graduation data that more accurately reflect the mobility among students in today's higher education climate. The NCAA believes the GSR is an improved measure since it accounts for student-athletes who transfer. As Chapter 4 indicated, the *omission* of transfers can increase or decrease a school's graduation rate. And the same problem can occur when transfers are *included*. For example, Duke University's graduation rate was probably harmed when basketball player Michael Dunleavy Jr., a good student on track to graduate, turned pro. But had Dunleavy been an academic liability when he transferred, his departure would have improved Duke's graduation rate. In 2011, the NCAA decided to focus on a "single penalty structure," simplifying the system by using only the APR standards addressed earlier and not a specific GSR requirement.

The APR and GSR reforms have been praised by some members of the athletics community. For example, University of Washington athletic director Todd Turner said "[t]his is the first time that I'm aware of that the NCAA has assigned any kind of competitive penalty to the lack of academic progress or academic success on the part of students. It will change the culture" (Crystal, 2005). There are already news reports of "success stories" — athletes, coaches, and athletic department staff working together to improve academic performance.[6] Perhaps more important, the graduation

---

[6] See, for example, Wolverton (2006b).

Table 9.2. Graduation rates for entering classes of 2002–2005 by sport at DI institutions.

Men	Graduation success rate (%)	Federal rate (%)	Women	Graduation success rate (%)	Federal rate (%)
Baseball	73	48	Basketball	84	64
Basketball	68	47	Bowling	74	55
XC/track	76	61	XC/track	84	71
Fencing	88	76	Crew	93	82
Football (FBS)	68	57	Fencing	93	79
Golf	82	66	Field hockey	94	80
Gymnastics	89	87	Golf	90	73
Ice hockey	83	63	Gymnastics	93	83
Lacrosse	86	72	Ice hockey	91	77
Rifle	78	64	Lacrosse	94	81
Skiing	87	71	Rifle	78	N/A
Soccer	79	59	Skiing	93	70
Swimming	85	71	Soccer	89	72
Tennis	86	65	Softball	86	69
Volleyball	76	66	Swimming	92	78
Water polo	82	74	Tennis	90	72
Wrestling	74	57	Volleyball	89	70
			Water polo	90	78

Source: NCAA Research Staff (2012).

rate revision has resulted in a substantial historically-adjusted increase in the rate across almost all sports (see Table 9.2), a result that Myles Brand describes as "really spectacular" (Lederman, 2005). Using the new calculation also raises the ex-post graduation rates for two academically-suspect sports, men's basketball and football (see Table 9.3).

Fast fact. *In 2013, ten men's basketball teams were banned from the NCAA tournament (and other postseason tournaments) for poor academic performance. Most notable of these was the University of Connecticut, a perennial presence in March Madness. By earning an APR score of 947 for 2012–2013, UConn restored its postseason eligibility for 2014. ("APR: Ten Teams Lose Postseason", 2012; Doyle, 2013)*

Table 9.3. Graduation rates for entering classes of 2002–2005 for men's basketball and football at selected DI institutions.

Institution	Men's basketball		Football	
	Graduation success rate (%)	Federal rate (%)	Graduation success rate (%)	Federal rate (%)
Boston College	88	43	94	90
Duke University	100	54	92	80
Gonzaga University	90	75	—	—
Indiana U. Bloomington	43	23	70	54
Michigan State University	89	62	64	46
North Carolina State University	73	46	62	52
University of California Los Angeles	70	54	62	51
University of Connecticut	11	0	69	56
University of Florida	17	6	75	49
University of Illinois Champaign	100	69	75	56
University of Iowa	89	44	82	66
University of Kentucky	78	54	65	54
University of Louisville	75	33	63	47
University of Memphis	50	31	74	69

(*Continued*)

Table 9.3.   (Continued).

Institution	Men's basketball		Football	
	Graduation success rate (%)	Federal rate (%)	Graduation success rate (%)	Federal rate (%)
University of Nebraska Lincoln	60	29	68	53
University of Nevada Las Vegas	92	86	67	68
University of North Carolina Chapel Hill	91	71	75	57
University of Oklahoma	71	45	47	38
University of Texas Austin	71	33	58	58
University of Washington	78	75	74	67
University of Wisconsin Madison	40	33	65	51
University of Michigan	64	58	69	59
Villanova University	100	83	83	84
Wake Forest University	100	64	86	78
Washington State University	78	60	53	50

Source: NCAA Research (2012).

The APR has its share of detractors. A study at the Institute for Diversity and Ethics in Sport (Lapchick, 2005) suggests that a gap in academic performance still exists between White and Black athletes. For example, Bachman (2005) notes that at Oregon State University the average GPA for Black football players had declined from 2.57 to 1.9. Lapchick also mentions, that 23 of the 56 DI-A football teams that went to a 2005 or 2006 bowl game had APR numbers below the cut-off, a problem that has since been addressed with the new APR standards.

There are also arguments that, like many prior NCAA regulatory changes, the APR is merely "window dressing" designed to fool its member institutions, journalists, legislators, and the general public into thinking that it is serious about making substantive changes. There are two specific criticisms of the APR rules.

First, athletic directors and coaches may simply "teach to the test," that is, find ways to meet the new requirements without actually conforming to the intent of the reform. The intent of the APR is to force athletic departments to improve the academic performance of their athletes or face penalties. Imagine that you are the head men's basketball coach at Towson University. Your APR in 2011–2012 was 871, down slightly from the year before. If nothing is done to boost the rate, your school will lose contests and may be prohibited from playing in a postseason tournament. How can you raise your player's graduation rates quickly and substantially? Is it possible to increase the APR for the football team to comply with the rules change without improving your athletes' education?

A second argument that challenges the integrity of the APR is based on the enforcement activities conducted by the NCAA. For the 2011–2012 academic year, 35 teams across 17 DI schools failed to meet the APR standard and received at least a Level One penalty (the schools and sports are listed in Table 9.1). How many FBS automatic qualifier football teams are listed (for a list of BCS conferences and schools, visit http://www.bcsfootball.org)? How many men's basketball teams from the major conferences like the Big East are included? Does it seem odd to you that the big-time schools, the schools with the largest budgets and the largest investment in sports, the BCS schools, are mostly absent from the list?

9.6.6   *Reduce the length of the season and hours of practice*

Some sports, like baseball and softball, have many games per season even though a majority of the games are confined to one semester. Basketball and hockey seasons are not only lengthy, but often span more than one academic term. For example, consider the 2012–2013 schedule for the Duke University men's basketball team. Their season spanned five months, from their home opener on Saturday, October 27, 2012, until it ended with an 85–63 NCAA tournament loss to Louisville in Indianapolis on Sunday, March 31, 2013. Even sports confined to one semester with a relatively short season, such as football, require significant practice time in and out of season (football has added games over time; prior to 2002, most schools played 11 regular season games and even earlier, only 10. Twelve games is now the standard and some play 13).

NCAA Bylaw 17.1.6.1 restricts athletics participation to no more than 4 hours per day and 20 hours per week. But this rule, known as the **4 and 20 Rule**, only applies to practice sessions supervised by the coaching staff. "Unofficial" voluntary practice sessions where no coach is present, such as weight training, studying the playbook or watching film are commonplace. A student-athlete is not required to attend these sessions but most athletes consider them to be equally important since non-participation may result in the loss of playing time, or lessen a player's status with teammate or coaches. As one BYU football player put it, "[t]he only thing I have to say about the voluntary part is, it's voluntary whether the coaches put you on the field in the fall" (Johnston, 2003).

The argument for reducing the length of the season and practice time is based on opportunity cost: every hour spent playing, practicing, training, traveling, or sitting in team meetings is an hour that could be spent in class, in the library, in the computer lab, studying at home, or participating in a tutoring session — time required to gain an education and a degree. As groups like Coalition on Intercollegiate Athletics emphasize, "[m]issed class days are a matter of academic integrity ... when athletes miss more than a minimal number of classes instructional goals are undermined" (Coalition on Intercollegiate Athletics, 2005). While one might argue that the same statement applies to all students, keep in mind that athletes have far less discretion in determining which classes to attend. On the other side of coin, fewer games means less revenue for the athletic department. A single home football game at a BCS automatic qualifier conference school can generate US$5–US$6 million just in ticket revenues. Are schools willing to forego that potential revenue?

9.6.7 *Reduce the number of games played on weekdays*

In some sports, notably men's and women's basketball, more and more games are being played on "school nights" (Sunday through Thursday evenings). This is partly due to the number of games per season, which makes it difficult to restrict games to Friday and Saturday evenings, and Saturday and Sunday afternoons. But if this is the cause, then a reduction in season length, as discussed in the previous section, could solve the problem.

As we saw in Chapter 7, the other explanation for the proliferation of weeknight games is television. As you know, television contracts are the single most important source of revenue for the NCAA and its member institutions. This creates a significant conflict of interest. If television networks like ESPN chose to broadcast basketball games only on the weekend, they would encounter the fundamental economic problem of *scarcity*; there are far more games to broadcast than number of broadcasting slots available. To make matters worse, there are only a limited number of "prime" slots available (a 7:00 p.m. broadcast is more valuable than one at 4:30 a.m.).

ESPN and other sports broadcasters have found a solution to this problem; they can broadcast games on Monday through Thursday, if they can convince the universities to adopt schedules that allow for weekday or weeknight games. This seems like a "win–win" situation. ESPN can fill up its Monday–Thursday programming with DI basketball games, games that will produce decent Nielsen ratings and advertising revenue. The NCAA and its member institutions get broadcasting revenue and regional or national television exposure.

But how do the athletes benefit from this scheduling? Returning to our example of the Blue Devils, 15 (47%) of their preseason and regular season games in 2012–2013 took place on a Tuesday, Wednesday or Thursday, and seven were away games. By the time a home evening game ends, a Duke basketball player is headed back to his residence at midnight or later for a few precious hours of sleep before his Principles of Macroeconomics class at 8:00 the next morning with Professor Tedious (recall that because of practices, most student-athletes have to schedule classes between 8:00 a.m. and 2:00 p.m.). Away games are even worse since they may result in an athlete missing the majority, or all, of the next day's classes. But, of course, remember that every game cut from the season is a game that does not generate revenue for the university.

9.6.8 *Encourage members of the coaching staff to earn advanced degrees*

A report by The National Institute for Sports Reform (National Institute for Sports Reform) noted that "[a] major influence in the academic development and career aspirations of college athletes is their day-to-day interaction with their coaches. With such influence, it is important that coaches are effective in their roles as educators and teachers" (Gerdy *et al.*, n.d., p. 1). The effectiveness of coaches in helping their athletes earn an education may be assessed in a number of ways. As discussed in Chapter 5, the performance of a coach is measured, at least in theory, by any number of criteria, including graduation rates, the types of majors and classes athletes are enrolled in, and the number of academic-related violations that occur.

How prepared is a coach to emphasize the importance of education to his athletes? One approach is to see what advanced degrees a coach has attained. Almost every full-time faculty member teaching at a university in the United States holds a Master's degree or a Ph.D., and it is increasingly common to encounter part-time instructors and adjuncts with those credentials as well. According to the National Institute for Sports Reform Report (Gerdy *et al.*, n.d.), roughly 30% of DI men's, and 34% of women's basketball coaches have at least a Master's degree. The authors of the report consider this to be an "alarmingly low percentage" that should be addressed through policies designed to encourage greater attainment if coaches are considered to have a vital role as "teachers and educators." One suggestion is to include a financial incentive to earn an advanced degree in the coach's contract. (Gerdy, 2006a, p. 217)

9.6.9   *Abolish all athletics scholarships*

In his book *Air Ball, American Education's Failed Experiment with Elite Athletics*, John Gerdy (2006a, p. 151) advocates eliminating all athletic scholarships and replacing them with need-based financial support. Gerdy, who is affiliated with National Institute for Sports Reform, argues that this would dramatically de-emphasize the importance of college sports on campuses across the United States and increase the emphasis on academics. He acknowledges that this change could have a disproportionate impact on Black athletes, but he asks, what is ultimately the main reason for student-athletes, Black or otherwise, to be on campus — to get an education or to play sports? (Gerdy, 2006a, p. 157)

Under such an approach, financial aid would be based on academic merit or financial need, not on athletic prowess. This would reduce the now common practice of recruiting the academically suspect and disinterested solely on the basis of their athletic talent. As we addressed at length in Chapter 4, hundreds, perhaps thousands, of young men and women are attending American universities only to play ball. They have neither the interest nor the aptitude to get an education. Furthermore, those students who attempt to learn often find themselves directed into easy classes and majors by their coach or other athletic department personnel. If this change was put in place, "the student would continue to receive his or her financial aid regardless of what transpires on the athletics field. As a result, the student would be less beholden to the athletics department's competitive and business motives and freer to explore the wide diversity of experiences college offers … [and] it would fundamentally change the relationships among the athlete, the coach, and the institution". (Gerdy, 2006b)

A precedent for this reform is well-known. To begin with, as we mentioned in Chapter 1, a NCAA subcommittee made a similar proposal in 1952 as part of the Sanity Code. While the proposal was largely unsuccessful — adopted only by the Ivy Leagues and very briefly by the Big Ten Conference — the prohibition on athletics scholarships is a defining characteristic of Division III institutions like football powerhouse Mount Union College in Alliance, Ohio.

According to the NCAA, "Division III athletics features student-athletes who receive no financial aid related to their athletic ability and athletic departments are staffed and funded like any other department in the university." Currently, approximately 170,000 men and women (almost as many as those participating in DI) play at over 400 DIII institutions. It is rare for a DIII athlete to go on to a professional sports career. For the majority, being at a DIII school allows them to continue to engage in a sport while focusing primarily on getting an education and a degree.

Despite the fact that a template already exists for this kind of reform, it is unlikely that individual schools will seriously consider it unless they are forced to. Since sports are almost never eliminated for reasons other than money, it is difficult to envision a set of circumstances in which a DI school would choose to drop down to DIII unless it faced severe financial exigencies. One such example is Centenary College of Louisiana, which in 2009, for financial reasons announced its move from DI to DIII ("Centenary board OKs switch," 2009). At the time, it was the smallest member of Division I.[7] The University of New Orleans also considered such a move in 2009, in response to declining attendance and revenue following Hurricane Katrina, but the school ultimately decided to stay at DI. What is more common, as indicated in Chapter 6, are the "wannabe" schools like Portland State moving up the divisional ladder.

---

[7] In 2010–2011, Centenary's final season for DI men's basketball, they won just one game and lost 29. This is not the worst record in the history of DI. In 2004–2005, the Longwood University men's basketball team went 1–30 while in transition from DII to DI.

9.6.10 *Eliminate intercollegiate sports*

The proposal to eliminate intercollegiate sports entirely has advocates such as Bruce Svare (2004) who, in his book *Reforming Sports Before the Clock Runs Out*, argues for the adoption of sports programs similar to those established in Europe and Australia. In those nations, sports teams are run as independent clubs that have no academic ties other than the fact that some of the players may happen to be students. The teams are funded privately through membership dues and other contributions, and their membership may span the gamut from young children to retired folks — through families participating in recreational sports — to young men and women training for a professional career or a chance to participate in the Olympic Games. If Svare's divestiture proposal seems odd to you, it really is not. These organizations already exist in the United States. Golf clubs, swimming and tennis clubs and academies, elite/travel teams and adult amateur leagues all represent the kind of sports organizations that Svare is referring to.

The most attractive aspect of Svare's proposal is that it cuts the Gordian knot of college athletics, the seemingly intractable entanglement of commerce and profit with amateurism and academics. Nevertheless, there is an obstacle to his proposal that may be insurmountable: culture. Simply put, Australians and Europeans think about academics and sports in a completely different way that your average North American does. Outside of the United States (and to some extent in Canada) sport is peripheral to education. Even in elementary and middle school, let alone secondary and postsecondary institutions, educational establishments are not expected to devote resources to, and create opportunities to play, sports. Yet can you imagine the University of Nebraska without a football team? Or Duke without a basketball team? Can you imagine the reaction if you recommended eliminating those sports at those two universities? Svare's divestiture proposal is interesting and has a precedent in the United States; but what is the probability it will occur?

9.7 Exempt the NCAA from Antitrust Prosecution

Given our discussion and analysis throughout the book of the NCAA as a cartel, it might seem odd that some individuals want to make the NCAA immune to antitrust prosecution. The primary federal antitrust legislation is the **Sherman Act**, enacted in 1890. It has been refined and augmented by subsequent legislation like the Clayton and FTC Acts (both enacted in 1914). The intent of antitrust legislation is to prevent firms and industries from engaging in business practice that reduce competition, like price fixing, group boycotts, and restrictions on output. Since the NCAA exercises monopoly power in both the input and output market, what possible benefit could there be in allowing the NCAA and its member institutions to be exempt from prosecution?[8]

Some reformers suggest it would allow the NCAA to "control sports telecasts and sports spending" (Price, 2004, p. 257). If protected from the Sherman Act and ancillary laws, the NCAA could take control of the current postseason bowl system to create a true DI football playoff. This could open up the playoff to more DI schools, not just the current members of the BCS. In addition, the members of the NCAA could agree to impose spending limits on DI athletic departments (including coaches' salaries). This would slow the arms race and create increased parity across institutions (Ohio State would not be allowed to have an athletics budget of $116 million while Northwestern, another Big 10 school, has only $61 million). The NCAA could also step in to prevent schools from cutting non-revenue men's sports when their intent is to redistribute money from non-revenue to revenue sports, rather than supporting sports for women (Price, 2004). An exemption would allow the NCAA to regain control over television broadcasts, power it lost after the 1984 Supreme Court decision.

Reform of the BCS is one of the goals of those who espouse an antitrust exemption. As you learned in Chapter 2, only a small

---

[8] For an excellent summary of the NCAA and antitrust law, see Rascher and Schwarz (2000).

portion of the proceeds generated by the bowl games trickles down to the DI-FBS (formerly DI-A) schools that are not in BCS automatic qualifying conferences. For example, the first five years of the BCS generated about US$450 million for the 64 BCS automatic qualifier schools, while the remaining 54 DI-A schools got about US$17 million (from testimony by Scott Cowen as found in "Competition in college athletic conferences," 2003, p. 37). The BCS automatic qualifier conferences act as a cartel within the NCAA cartel, and the NCAA is currently powerless to stop it. BCS critics argue that excluding almost half of the 125 DI-FBS schools from participating in the BCS is discriminatory and inconsistent with NCAA rules. Except for those non-automatic qualifier football teams, *any* NCAA school in *any* sport in *any* division is eligible for postseason competition. The BCS arbitrarily denies many schools access to the postseason championship and shunts them to less illustrious (and far less lucrative) bowl games like the Holiday, Liberty, or Sun Bowls. As former football pro quarterback Steve Young (a graduate of Brigham Young University and a member of the Football Hall of Fame) testified "it must be clear to even the casual observer that the BCS [automatic qualifiers] represents a powerful combination of a small number of schools which have created a powerful barrier to entry, whose purpose is to exclude all non-members of that elite group from any meaningful participation in postseason play". ("Competition in college athletic conferences," 2003, p. 63)

Because DI-FBS schools like Tulane and BYU are excluded from the BCS, it limits their ability to recruit athletes and hire and retain coaches. How would you like to play football at a DI-FBS school that can never play in the Rose, Orange, Fiesta, or Sugar Bowls? The inability to capture a larger share of BCS generated revenue also makes it harder for the "shunned" institutions to participate in the arms race.

On the other side of the coin, economists point out that an antitrust exemption will not curtail the NCAA's monopsony power, rather it will enhance it. In addition, increased control over television broadcasts is likely to increase the value of the contracts if the NCAA, as we would predict, reduces the quantity of games broadcast to increase the value of broadcasting contracts. This would mean more money for the NCAA, but how would this benefit those of us who enjoy watching college sports on television? Recall the Supreme Court's ruling during the 1984 case (Chapter 2).

Other organizations, like the Knight Commission, are somewhat ambivalent about eliminating the exemption but tend to believe that it would cause more harm than good. It is not clear whether an antitrust exemption, and the concomitant increase in the NCAA's power, will allow it to actually rein in the big-time programs. It is one thing for the NCAA to say that it wants to reduce the arms race, or impose other substantive changes, but implementation is a completely different matter. Even with an exemption, they may lack sufficient power to control the elite programs. There is a distinct possibility, because of the cartel within the cartel phenomenon, and the NCAA's weakness as the cartel manager, that the problems of collegiate sports would multiply rather than diminish.

As we discuss further below, government intervention is perhaps the NCAA's single greatest fear. In September 2003, the House of Representatives Committee on the Judiciary (which has oversight for antitrust) held hearings regarding antitrust aspects of the BCS. The committee met to address the concerns mentioned above about the BCS, and the ranking member of the committee, John Conyers Jr. from Michigan, reminded the NCAA's representative at the hearings, President Brand, that "this friendly hearing is just to let you know that we're watching." ("Competition in college athletic conferences," 2003, p. 11). You know by now that the NCAA is not keen on having Congress looking over its shoulder.

9.8 How Likely is Reform?

We cannot estimate the probability of any of the aforementioned reforms being enacted without also knowing who the reformers are and what their commitment to reform is. Individuals and organizations that advocate reform can be distinguished based on two dimensions: how much reform they advocate and who they

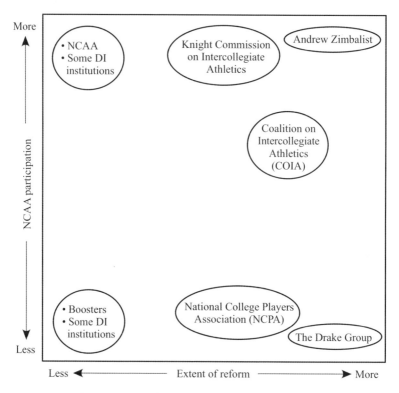

Figure 9.1.   The two dimensions of reform.

believe should be in charge of implementing reform. We can think of these two dimensions forming the grid illustrated in Figure 9.1. Moving from the left to the right indicates a greater amount of reform; moving from bottom to top indicates a greater interest in having the NCAA lead the reform process.

Figure 9.1 helps us understand where reform organizations are "located" and how they differ from one another. Those reformers located in the upper left corner acknowledge there are problems but tend to think that the NCAA is doing a satisfactory job. Any changes or reforms require only fine-tuning, and the NCAA should be in charge of making those changes. Not surprisingly, this view is offered by those who have a vested interest in the current system — namely the NCAA administration and some of big time sports programs. It should not be surprising that the individuals and institutions that benefit from the current structure do not have an incentive to rock the boat.

The second and third groupings of organizations are highly critical of problems in college sports like low graduation rates, academic and recruiting violations, excessive commercialization and a perceived lack of control by the NCAA. However, they differ in their opinion of who should be responsible for reform. Organizations located toward the upper right corner, such as the Knight Commission and the Coalition on Intercollegiate Athletics, and individuals like Andrew Zimbalist, think that the NCAA should be in charge of reform. They favor the NCAA leading the reform efforts in consultation with university presidents, trustees, alumni, and other stakeholders, to restore educational and financial integrity (namely better academic performance by student-athletes and a de-escalation of the arms race). Their proposed reforms are generally substantive and attempts to get off of the treadmill of reforms that have little or no effect. They also suggest that their approach has the support of the general public. For example, a 2005 survey conducted by the Knight Commission indicates that about 90% of Americans surveyed support NCAA-led reforms such as the APR. (Knight Commission, 2005)

Located toward the lower right corner are those organizations that are less sanguine about any joint effort involving the NCAA. To organizations like the Drake Group and the NCPA, either universities must act unilaterally — which is doubtful unless a financial crisis occurs — or else intervention by the government is required. Virtually all of the proposals suggested by The Drake Group, for example, need-based financial aid and freshman ineligibility, overlap with those proposed by the Coalition on Intercollegiate Athletics and individuals like Zimbalist. The most important difference is that The Drake Group emphasizes the need for government intervention, preferably by Congress, starting with a modification to FERPA to allow public disclosure of student-athletes' academic performance.

The Drake Group's position places it at odds not only with the NCAA, but also other reform groups like the Knight Commission who are willing to use the NCAA legislative process to achieve the desired results. The Drake Group believes that organizations like the Knight Commission, while well-intentioned, are — to use an expression from regulatory economics — **captured** by the NCAA and thus unable to implement any meaningful reform. The Knight Commission, perhaps the best known of the reform advocacy groups, strongly disagrees with this characterization. Regardless of whether government intervention is warranted, or even likely, the Drake Group recognizes that since the NCAA fears the federal government far more than any other potential participant in the reform process, the threat of intervention is the most likely route to success.

Any calls for government intervention should be tempered by some understanding of public choice theory. Shaw (n.d.) provides the following definition:

> Public choice takes the same principles that economists use to analyze people's actions in the marketplace and applies them to people's actions in collective decision making. Economists who study behavior in the private marketplace assume that people are motivated mainly by self-interest. Although most people base some of their actions on their concern for others, the dominant motive in people's actions in the marketplace — whether they are employers, employees, or consumers — is a concern for themselves. Public choice economists make the same assumption — that although people acting in the political marketplace have some concern for others, their main motive, whether they are voters, politicians, lobbyists, or bureaucrats, is self-interest.

In a nutshell, public choice theory suggests that just because Congress *could* act in the public interest and force the NCAA to change its policies does not mean that Congress *will* force the NCAA to change its policies. This is because of the behavior of special interest groups. You may have learned in other economics

classes that barriers to foreign trade, like tariffs and quotas on for-
eign-produced steel, cause more economic harm to a country than
good. Price controls on domestic agricultural products are another
example where the economic costs greatly exceed the benefits.
Why does Congress allow trade barriers and price controls to exist?
The answer is that domestic steel producers and farmers have significant political influence; they can offer votes and campaign contributions to members of Congress provided they get something in
return, trade barriers and price controls.

You may be beginning to wonder: What does all this have to
with college sports? The NCAA operates a Government Relations
Office in Washington D.C. to keep track of Congressional and other
governmental activities. Periodic reports are issued and information is disseminated to NCAA schools to allow them to keep
abreast of possible government interest into concerns relevant to
collegiate sports, like the regulation of sports agents, gambling,
and Title IX.[9] But information collection and dissemination is only
a small part of the story. The office's primary purpose is to lobby
Congress to ensure that governmental intervention is prevented or
limited in impact. Like any other special interest group, the NCAA
is not always successful in achieving its desired outcomes. For
example, it lobbied strenuously — to no avail — against Title IX.
But the implication is that a call for government intervention, like
that from the Drake Group, could be successfully thwarted by the
NCAA's political action.

Are there any organizations or individuals who would be
located in the bottom left corner of the Figure 9.1? Probably. This
corner of the grid is the true *status quo* position — no reforms are
necessary and no one needs to be in charge. Our guess is that this
is where many of the big-time sports schools are located, including
their boosters. They are the ones that benefit the most from the current system, why on earth would they want to change it?

---

[9]See, e.g., http://www1.ncaa.org/membership/governance/assoc-wide/execu-
tive_committee/docs/2003/Agenda/supp4.htm.

There is another reform scenario that is outside the dimensions of the grid. That would be if the cartel falls apart because the big-time sports programs secede from the NCAA and form a new association. This is usually how cartels fragment, a subset of members break out of the cartel and strike out on their own. But Zimbalist (1999, p. 206) argues this is risky because fans may no longer consider athletes true amateurs and consequently lose interest in sports. Also, the secessionists may expose themselves to workman's compensation claims, antitrust challenges, and the potential loss of their tax-exempt status.

Also not visible in the grid are situations in which some schools "hit the wall" because of a financial crisis. Adverse financial conditions will cause sports to be cut and schools will drop from DI-FBS to DI-FCS, or move to DI-No Football. Some might even transfer to DII or DIII, and join Western Oregon University and Linfield College, where the NCAA requires fewer sports and athletics department budgets are in the US$1–2 million range.

As we indicated in Section 6.6.2, between 2001 and 2003, the average DI-A school reduced the total number of sports from 19 to 16 and DI-AA and DI-AAA institutions went from 19 to 15, and 16 to 14, respectively. As examples, Iowa State slashed baseball and men's swimming and diving, UCLA cut men's swimming and gymnastics, and East Tennessee State eliminated the football program. At San Jose State, in April 2004, the Faculty Senate "recommended withdrawing from Division I-A and the Western Athletic Conference" and cutting the athletics budget by one half (Bartindale, 2004). Florida A&M has dropped men's tennis and golf and men's and women's swimming and diving because of budget difficulties (Johnson, 2005). Rutgers cut six sports for a savings of $1.2 million (adversely impacting 153 athletes and 10 coaches). Maryland eliminated seven sports in 2012, in an effort to stop mounting budget deficits (Giannotto, 2012). Questions have been raised about the sustainability of athletics spending at the University of Minnesota, a member of the Big Ten Conference (Moore, 2002). State universities in particular may feel the wrath of legislatures as the politicians apply fiscal discipline when university administrators do not. But, perhaps Gladwell's (2000) **tipping point** analogy is applicable. As more and more schools resort to desperate measures to extricate themselves from the arms race, perhaps a sea change in attitudes towards big-time sports programs will emerge.[10]

> *Fast fact. Spelman College, an historically black liberal arts women's college in Atlanta, announced in November 2012 that was eliminating all intercollegiate sports at the end of the 2012–2013 academic year. The former DIII institution's President, Beverly Daniel Tatum, decided that the US$1 million previously spent on intercollegiate athletics would be redirected to a campus-wide fitness and wellness program. (Grasgreen, 2012)*

Should we be optimistic or pessimistic about reform? Gerdy, among others, is an optimist. His primary proposal is the elimination of all athletic scholarships, which he argues would dramatically change the college sports landscape, a change for the better. Gerdy (2006a) claims:

> The elimination of the athletic scholarship will provide American higher education with the much needed opportunity to recalibrate every aspect of its relationship with athletics … .
>
> Even if there were a negative impact on [athletics] revenues and public interest in college athletics, it would be a small price to pay to remake college athletics in a way that would allow athletes to be genuine students, coaches to be true educators, and the athletics department to supplement, rather than undermine, academic values … .

---

[10]Synonyms for "tipping point" identified by Gladwell include "the moment of critical mass, the threshold, the boiling point" (Gladwell, 2000, p. 12). Phrases like "the straw that broke the camel's back" would also apply. It describes a situation where things can be going along smoothly until the buildup of forces becomes too much for the status quo to handle, resulting in rapid (and often unexpected) change in a system.

> Such changes would increase college athletics' public appeal,
> as many who have lost interest … may regain respect for and
> interest in college sports (pp. 186–187).

Yet pessimists point out that in over a century of collegiate
sports very few substantive reforms have occurred. Many of the
problems mentioned in the Carnegie Foundation Report in 1929
still plague college sports. Given that the NCAA celebrated its
100th anniversary not long ago, it seems reasonable to ask: How
successful is the NCAA in implementing reform? One possible
answer is "not very." That should not come as a surprise; why
implement reforms that weaken the cartel and threaten its profitability? This suggests that the treadmill will continue to turn. As the
French say: *plus ça change, plus c'est la même chose* — the more things
change, the more they stay the same.

9.9   Chapter Summary

If you have come this far, you deserve congratulations. You read
nine chapters consisting of over 500 pages of text, tables, graphs,
quotes, footnotes, fast facts, and assorted brilliant insights by the
authors. Now it is the time for you to close the book and put it
away. *Or is it?*

You learned about the activities of the NCAA that are claimed
to be in the best interests of student-athletes, as well as those
actions which appear to be inconsistent with that claim. You discovered the core ideas that we believe are most important in understanding the world of college sports. And you considered the many
questions, some we attempted to answer but others we left for your
own consideration. Ultimately, we are hopeful that you now
believe that there is some value in looking at college sports through
the prism of economics.

Now it is time to put your understanding into further action.
Your first opportunity is to turn to the next and final chapter,
and apply that knowledge to the well-publicized and controversial
cases of Penn State, Miami, Oregon, and Cal Tech. Engage in

serious discussion about the important issues raised in Chapter 10. Beyond that, turn on the television and watch a game or other sports programming. Go to a campus sporting event, buy a ticket, and watch a game in person. Get on the web and surf for the latest in college sports news. Go to the library and read *Sports Illustrated*, *ESPN The Magazine*, or the sports section of *USA Today* or another newspaper. Get together with some of your friends for pizza and talk about this season's best teams and players, the BCS and March Madness. But don't forget the economics and the themes developed in this book!

The college sports world is not static, and we need to consider any changes using the framework of the central themes presented in the Introduction. Do we see new evidence of cartel behavior or the arms race? Does the media appear to have a growing influence over college sports? Do we observe instances of "cat and mouse" behavior between athletic departments and the NCAA? Are strides being made to resolve racial or gender inequities? And finally, when the NCAA periodically announces a new set of policy changes, are those substantive changes, or more of the same?

9.10   Key Terms

4 and 20 Rule	Multilateral reform
Academic Progress Rate	Opportunity cost
Capture	Public Choice theory
Cartel within the cartel	Sherman Act
Contemporaneous penalty	Special interest group
Graduation Success Rate	Student Right to Know Act
Group boycotts	Tipping point
Historical penalty	Treadmill of reform
Illusion of control	Unilateral reform
Marginal revenue product	Unrelated business income
Monopsonistic rents	

9.11   Review Questions

1. What is the difference between a unilateral and a multilateral change?
2. What are the three categories of reform?
3. Why would economists tend to support paying players?
4. Which student-athletes would support paying players? Which ones would oppose?
5. What are the pros and cons of allowing transfer student-athletes to compete during their first year at the new school?
6. What incentive do the NBA and NFL have to create a minor league system? Why don't they currently push for it?
7. What is the purpose of reforming financial disclosure rules?
8. What is the difference between contemporaneous and historically-based penalties? Why would the NCAA use both?
9. How does the Graduation Success Rate differ from the federal government's calculation of graduation rates?
10. What are the penalties for failing to meet APR standards?
11. What are the criticisms of the APR?
12. What is the "4 and 20 Rule?"
13. What is the Sherman Act? What is its relevance to college sports?

9.12   Discussion Questions

1. Pick three of the proposed reforms and answer the questions posed in Section 9.3.
2. Are there any club sports on your campus? Do you know why these sports are offered at the club level and not as intercollegiate activity?
3. Should historically-based academic penalties be directed towards the coaches or the institutions?
4. In your opinion, what is the most significant problem in intercollegiate sports today? How would you fix it?
5. In what ways can coaches get around the NCAA's 4 and 20 Rule?
6. If the NCAA were to increase enforcement of existing rules, would it be better to hire more investigators, increase penalties for violations, or some combination of the two? Explain.

7. Are there any "rocks for jocks" classes on your campus? Who teaches these courses? Are they predominantly male or female? Do they tend to be younger or older faculty? Do they come from particular academic departments? Conversely, are there professors who appear to be biased against athletes?

8. If you were trying to limit the amount of time athletes spend on their sport, would it be more effect to reduce the season length and hours of practice, or reduce the number of weekday games? Explain.

9. What would be the effect of an NCAA rule requiring all new coaches to earn advanced degrees (Master's degree or above)? Consider not only the effect on educational standards, but also the impact on the market for coaches.

10. If the NCAA abolished all athletic scholarships, how would that affect the allocation of athletic talent across colleges and universities? Are there ways that schools might try to get around the prohibition?

11. How would the elimination of intercollegiate sports affect colleges and universities in the U.S.? How would the impacts differ from Division I down to Division III? Would it improve higher education in the U.S.?

12. How would the different reform options discussed in this chapter fit in the reform spectrum pictured in Figure 9.1?

13. In response to the assertion that the NCAA has "captured" the regulatory process, an NCAA official might argue that the NCAA should play a large role because they have an intimate knowledge of college sports. Do you agree or disagree with that claim? Discuss.

14. Are intercollegiate sports close to the "tipping point?" Why or why not?

9.13 Internet Questions

1. Visit the web sites listed under the "Organizations Advocating Reform" section on the list of Internet sites at the end of the book. Select any one organization and, using the information

provided on the web site, determine which of the 19 proposed reforms are supported by that organization.

2. Visit the NCAA website and update the status of the APR and GSR reforms.

3. Visit the NCAA homepage and type "APR data for NCAA schools" into the website search engine. Select your college or university, or one of your choosing, and print out the "Academic Progress Rate Public Report." Given the APR cutoff, determine which sports meet the NCAA standard.

9.14 References

APR: Ten Teams Lose Postseason (2012, June 20). *ESPN.com*. Retrieved from http://espn.go.com/mens-college-basketball/story/_/id/8077431/connecticut-huskies-9-others-sit-postseason-apr on June 30, 2013.

Bachman, R. (2005, October 1). Black players fall as OSU rises. *The Oregonian*, p. A01.

Baird, K. (2004). Dominance in college football and the role of scholarship restrictions. *Journal of Sport Management*, 8, 217–235.

Bartindale, B. (2004, April 23). 110 and Done? Board Vote Jeopardizes SJSU Football. Retrieved from http://www.thetraveleronline.com/media/paper688/news/2004/04/23/Sports/110-And.Done.Board.Vote.Jeopardizes.Sjsu.Football-669312.shtml on August 28, 2006.

Centenary Board OKs Switch to Division III (2009, July 22). *CBSsports.com*. Retrieved from http://www.cbssports.com/collegebasketball/story/11972499 on July 12, 2013.

Coalition on Intercollegiate Athletics (2005). *Academic Integrity in Intercollegiate Athletics: Principles, Rules, and Best Practices*. Retrieved from http://www.neuro.uoregon.edu/~tublitz/COIA/AID.html on February 4, 2007.

Competition in College Athletic Conferences and Antitrust Aspects of the Bowl Championship Series: Hearings before the House Committee on the Judiciary, 108th Cong., 1st Sess. (2003). Testimony of Scott Cowen and and Steve Young. Retrieved from http://commdocs.house.gov/committees/judiciary/hju89198.000/hju89198_0.HTM on August 15, 2006.

Crystal, L. M. (Executive Producer) (2005, March 14). *The News Hour With Jim Lehrer [Television broadcast]*. New York and Washington, DC: Public

Broadcasting Service. Retrieved from http://www.pbs.org/news-hour/bb/sports/jan-june05/ncaa_3-14.html on April 14, 2014.

Downing, R. (2006, May 4). When It Comes To College Athletics, Schools Need To Stop Playing Games. *Tucson Weekly*. Retrieved from http://www.tucsonweekly.com/tucson/downing/Content?oid=1083992 on July 12, 2013.

Dohrmann, G. (2011, November 7). Pay for play. *Sports Illustrated*. Retrieved from http://sportsillustrated.cnn.com/vault/article/magazine/MAG1191778/index.htm on July 12, 2013. http://sportsillustrated.cnn.com/vault/article/magazine/MAG1191778/index.htm

Doyle, Paul. (2013, June 11). UConn Men Earn 947 APR Score; Eligible for Postseason in 2014. *The Courant*. Retrieved from http://articles.courant.com/2013-06-11/sports/hc-apr-scores-0612-20130611_1_ncaa-tournament-basketball-team-program on June 30, 2013.

Drake Group (2013, January 14). Drake Group Scholarship Proposal Adopted By NCAA. *Thedrakegroup.org*. Retrieved from http://thedrakegroup.org/2013/01/14/hello-world/ on June 30, 2013.

Duderstadt, J. J. (2000). *Intercollegiate Athletics and the American University*. Ann Arbor, MI: University of Michigan Press.

Elfman, L. (2008, August 8). NCAA To Provide Former Student-athletes With Benefits. *Diverse Issues in Higher Education*. Retrieved from http://diverseeducation.com/article/11535/# on June 29, 2013.

Frequently Asked Questions About Academic Progress Rate (n.d.). *ncaa.org*. Retrieved from http://www.ncaa.org/about/resources/research/frequently-asked-questions-about-academic-progress-rate-apr on April 4, 2014.

Gerdy, J. (2006a). *Air Ball, American Education's Failed Experiment With Elite Athletics*. Jackson, MS: University of Mississippi Press.

Gerdy, J. (2006b, May 12). For True Reform, Athletics Scholarships Must Go. *Chronicle of Higher Education*, p. B6.

Gerdy, J., D. Ridpath, E. Staurowsky, and B. Svare (n.d.). *2004 NCAA Division I Men's and Women's Basketball Coaches' Academic Degree Attainment Survey*. National Institute for Sports Reform. Retrieved from http://www.nisr.org/documents/2004coachesstudy.pdf on January 31, 2007.

Giannotto, M. (2012, July 2). Maryland Cuts Seven Sports On 'Sad Day' in College Park. *Washington Post*. Retrieved from http://articles.washingtonpost.com/2012-07-02/sports/35486395_1_athletic-programs-track-program-athletic-director-kevin-anderson on June 30, 2013.

Gladwell, M. (2000). *The Tipping Point: How Little Things Can Make a Big Difference.* Boston: Back Bay Books.

Goff, B. (2006, January 18). BYU Goes Pro (sort of). *The Sports Economist.* Retrieved from http://thesporteconomist.com/archive/2006_01_01__arch_file.htm on December 12, 2006.

Golden, D. (2006, December 27). Tax Breaks For Skyboxes. *Wall Street Journal*, p. B1.

Grasgreen, A. (2012, November 1). Beyond Sports. *Inside Higher Ed.* Retrieved from http://www.insidehighered.com/news/2012/11/01/spelman-eliminates-athletics-favor-campus-wide-wellness-initiative on June 30, 2013.

Guruli, E. (2005, Spring). Commerciality of college sports: Should the IRS intervene? *Sports Lawyers Journal*, 12(43), 43–69.

Hosick, M. B. (2011, October 27). *DI Board Adopts Improvements In Academic Standards and Student-athlete Support.* Retrieved from http://www.ncaa.org/wps/wcm/connect/public/NCAA/Resources/Latest+News/2011/October/DI+Board+of+Directors+adopt+changes+to+academic+and+student-athlete+welfare on June 29, 2013.

Hosick, M. B. (2012, January 14). *DI Board Reaffirms Expense Allowance, Multi-year Scholarships.* Retrieved from http://www.ncaa.org/wps/wcm/connect/public/NCAA/Resources/Latest+News/2012/January/DI+Board+reaffirms+expense+allowance,+multi-year+scholarships on June 29, 2013.

Internal Revenue Service (2006). *Internal Revenue Manual.* Retrieved from http://www.irs.gov/irm/ on December 15, 2006.

Johnson, T. (2005, August 1). FAMU Cuts Four Sports. *IMDiversity.com.* Retrieved from http://www.imdiversity.com/Jobs/articles/bcwire_famu_0805.asp on December 8, 2006.

Johnston, J. T. (2003). Show them the money: the threat of NCAA athlete unionization in response to the commercialization of college sports. *Seton Hall Journal of Sports Law*, 13(203), 203–238.

Knight Commission on Intercollegiate Athletics (2005, December). Public Opinion Poll. *Knightcommission.org.* Retrieved from http://www.knightcommission.org/images/pdfs/polldecember2005.pdf on June 30, 2013.

Knight Commission on Intercollegiate Athletics (2012, November 13). Knight Commission's Recommendation to Include Academic Performance As a Part of Football Revenue Distribution Process Takes Hold. *Knightcommission.org.* Retrieved from http://www.knight

commission.org/recent-news/783-november-13-2012-bcs-includes-academic-performance-as-a-part-of-revenue-distribution-process on June 30, 2013.

Lapchick, R. (2005). *Keeping Score When it Counts: Assessing the Graduation Rates of Bowl Bound Teams*. Orlando, FL: University of Central Florida, Institute for Ethics and Diversity in Sport.

Lederman, D. (2005, December 20). A New Way to Keep Score. *Inside Higher Ed*. Retrieved from http://www.insidehighered.com/news/2005/12/20/grad on August 18, 2006.

Mission & Goals (n.d.). National College Players Association. Retrieved from http://www.ncpanow.org/more?id=0004 on July 14, 2013.

Moore, R. (2002, April 30). Sports, Money, and The "Arms Race" at the University of Minnesota. *Kiosk*. Retrieved from http://www1.umn.edu/urelate/kiosk/0502kiosk/sports.html on January 31, 2007.

NCAA Research Staff (2012, October). Trends in Graduation-Success Rates and Federal Graduation Rates at NCAA Division I Institutions. *NCAA Research*. Retrieved from http://www.ncaa.org/wps/wcm/connect/public/ncaa/pdfs/2012/D1GsrFgrTrendsPdf on June 30, 2013.

New BYU PDL Club Featured on Front Page of New York Times: Successful BYU Club Team First to Join the PDL (2003, March 7). United Soccer Leagues. Retrieved from http://pdl.uslsoccer.com/home/54133.html on December 12, 2006.

Powers, E. (2006, July 10). Life After the A.D. (Athletics Director). *Inside Higher Ed*. Retrieved from http://insidehighered.com/news/2006/07/10/Vanderbilt on August 12, 2006.

Price, T. (2004, March 19). Reforming Big-time College Sports. *CQ Researcher*, 14, 249–271.

Rascher, D. A. and D. Schwarz (2000). "Amateurism" in Big-time College Sports. *Antitrust*, 14(2), 51–73.

Rascher, D. A. (2003, April 9). Oral Testimony Regarding California State Senate Bill 193, *Student Athletes' Bill of Rights*, to the California State Senate Subcommittee on Entertainment.

Shaw, J. (n.d.). *Public Choice Theory*. Library of Economics and Liberty. Retrieved from http://www.econlib.org/library/enc/PublicChoiceTheory.html on January 9, 2007.

Skidmore, G. (2004). Recent Development: Payment for College Football Players in Nebraska. *Harvard Journal on Legislation*, 41, 319–335.

Svare, B. B. (2004). *Reforming Sports Before the Clock Runs Out*. Delmar, NY: Bordalice Publishing, Inc.

Wolverton, B. (2006a, March 10). House Committee is Looking Into Whether Some College Sports Revenue Should Be Taxed. *Chronicle of Higher Education*, p. A35.

Wolverton, B. (2006b, March 10). Making the Grade: How One Tutor Helped a Star Athlete Hit the Books and Regain His Academic Eligibility. *Chronicle of Higher Education*, p. A36.

Wolverton, B. (2006c, March 10). Three Former Football and Men's Basketball Players Have Accused the National Collegiate Athletic Association of Creating a Hardship for Big-time College Athletes by Unfairly Capping the Amount of Athletics Aid Any Student May Receive. *Chronicle of Higher Education*, p. A35.

Wolverton, B. and J. Newman (2013, April 19). Few Athletes Benefit From Move to Multiyear Scholarships. *Chronicle of Higher Education*. Retrieved from http://chronicle.com/article/Few-Athletes-Benefit-From-Move/138643/ on July 12, 2013.

Zimbalist, A. (1999). *Unpaid professionals: Commercialism and Conflict in big-time college sports*. Princeton, NJ: Princeton University Press.

Chapter 10

Four Case Studies

10.1 Introduction

Up to this point we have provided a foundation of institutional and theoretical information, as well as some practical examples, to help you better understand the world of intercollegiate athletics. In this concluding chapter, we apply that knowledge to four cases that have occurred since the first edition of the book, including what is sure to be remembered as one of the most infamous cases in college football history — Penn State University's cover-up of charges of child molestation against former assistant coach Gerald ("Jerry") Sandusky. We also look at the cases of the University of Miami (Florida), the University of Oregon, and the California Institute of Technology (Caltech). In these cases, we'll see a range of activities, violations, and responses that will highlight many of the principles we have discussed over the first nine chapters.

10.2 University of Miami

In June 2013, the NCAA Committee on Infractions convened to hear testimony regarding a series of violations by the University of Miami. The committee's report will appear late in 2013, after the NCAA has made a determination what, if any, penalties will be applied to the university.

The alleged violations are centered on illegal payments made to Miami football players, coaches, and recruits by booster Nevin Shapiro. In 2010, Shapiro was convicted of securities fraud and money laundering for running a US$930 million Ponzi (pyramid) scheme. He was sentenced to 20 years in federal prison in June 2011. It was Shapiro's own disclosures to the NCAA in February 2011, prior to his sentencing, that first brought the alleged violations to light. Shapiro stated that for almost a decade (2002–2010), he contributed US$2 million or more to the Miami sports program. While some of this total was donated to the Miami athletic department, Shapiro also provided Miami football players and prospective recruits with cash, meals, prostitutes, bounties for big hits on the field, Miami Heat basketball tickets, televisions, travel, jewelry, clothing, lodging, and many other payments or gifts — reputedly including payment for an abortion by a player's girlfriend. Shapiro plied players with food, drink and entertainment at his homes in Miami, aboard his yacht, at restaurants and numerous strip clubs. Journalist Charles Robinson (Robinson, August 16, 2011) substantiates many of these payments — all violation of the bylaws — in an extensive investigation conducted by *Yahoo! Sports.* To compound matters, Shapiro was also a part-owner of the sport agency Axcess Sports & Entertainment. While Shapiro himself was not a sports agent, his involvement with such an organization (including making payments to Miami players his agency hoped to represent when they turned pro) should have made him persona non grata at the university. Shapiro also gambled on sports, including betting on Miami football games at least 23 times, bets he placed after he culled information from players and coaches.

Shapiro's fessing up may just be a bad case of sour grapes by a popular and important booster who was shunned by the university once he was convicted. But just as some of the most important campaigns against organized crime have come from "insiders" and "whistleblowers" cooperating with law enforcement, Shapiro might believe since he had nothing left to lose, he might as well try to redeem himself by helping to shine a light on a dirty program.

The university acknowledged that violations were committed; it admits that approximately US$170,000 was directed to around 72 recruits, players and coaches. But its argues that no further action by the NCAA is necessary because the university self-imposed penalties and "took itself out of postseason play in each of the past two football seasons [2011 and 2012] and multiple players served suspensions". ("University of Miami starts NCAA hearings," 2013)[1]

While "boosters gone wild" is hardly front page news in the world of college sports, this case is significant for several reasons: we highlight two of them. First, the violations are alleged to have occurred over an extended period of time, from 2002 to 2010. If this is true, it suggests not only "lack of institutional control" (a common catch-all infraction applied by the NCAA), but the possibility that individuals within the university administration and athletic department were long aware of Shapiro's illegal payments but chose to ignore them. Shapiro alleges the university "didn't want to know what he was doing ... [and] looked the other way because it was desperate to retain a booster who had donated hundreds of thousands of dollars to the program," including $250,000 for a players' lounge (Robinson, August 16, 2011).[2] Can the university plausibly claim it had no knowledge of the actions of Shapiro, a booster who flew on team charters and had on-the-field access during football games? Such willful misconduct by athletics department officials, if proven, especially in a program that has a history of prior NCAA violations, raises the possibility that the death penalty may be applied.

Second, in a manner akin to "man bites dog," the university has filed complaints against the NCAA. One complaint, made in March 2013, arose because of actions by NCAA investigator Ameen

---

[1] In a statement on February 19, 2013, Miami President Donna Shalala said "[t]he University of Miami deeply regrets and takes full responsibility for those NCAA violations that are based on fact and are corroborated by multiple individuals and/or documentation. We have already self-imposed a bowl ban for an unprecedented two-year period, forfeited the opportunity to participate in an ACC championship game, and withheld student-athletes from competition". ("Statement from UM President," 2013)

[2] *Sports Illustrated* (Mandel, 2011) points out that the Athletic Director at Miami from 1993–2008 was Paul Dee. Dee later joined the NCAA and was the chairman of the infractions committee that investigated USC. During that investigation, Dee rebuked Pete Carroll and the SC athletics department administration for claiming that they were unaware that Reggie Bush was receiving improper benefits. Dee died in May 2012.

Najjar. As Thamel and Wolff (2013) note, "[b]ecause the NCAA lacks subpoena power, Najjar contracted with Shapiro's lawyer in the bankruptcy case, Maria Elena Perez, to pose questions to … the booster's former associates who had not been cooperating with the NCAA." Recall that virtually all of what the NCAA considers violations are breaches of NCAA rules, not violations of state or federal civil or criminal code. Therefore, when it conducts an investigation, the NCAA cannot compel people to provide information necessary to the investigation. In the Miami case, Najjar believed that at least three people had vital information: one of Shapiro's former bodyguards, a former Miami assistant equipment manager, and Shapiro's partner in Axcess Sports & Entertainment. In September 2011, when Ms. Perez proposed that Shapiro's bankruptcy proceeding provided a way to acquire this testimony, Najjar agreed. Concerned that payment for such information might be a breach of NCAA internal policies, Najjar informed the NCAA's legal department of his intentions. He also notified his immediate superiors, Vice President of Enforcement Julie Roe Lach, and Managing Director of Enforcement Tom Hosty. The legal department responded with a memo that advised him not to undertake such an action. For reasons open to speculation, Najjar, an experienced compliance officer, ignored the memo. Najjar was either fired or left the association of his own accord in early to mid-2012. But the damage was already done; when top NCAA administrators, including President Emmert, were made aware of Najjar's action, the law firm Cadwalader, Wickersham & Taft LLP was retained by the NCAA in January 2013 to conduct an extensive external review of the episode. When the dust settled, Najjar's supervisor, enforcement chief Julie Roe Lach, was fired (or, depending on your perspective, thrown under the bus as a scapegoat) and, according to the *New York Times* (Eder, 2013), "[o]ther enforcement agents involved in the investigation are no longer employed by the NCAA." Lach's boss, Tom Hosty, remains with the organization. The Cadwalader report (Wainstein, 2013) is very clear that while the NCAA did not violate its own bylaws, or civil or criminal law, its internal system of checks and balances during compliance investigations failed. When the University of Miami got wind of what occurred, it immediately filed a request that the entire NCAA investigation be dropped. The NCAA rejected that request, and the university subsequently issued a complaint against the Association, a complaint that has garnered considerable publicity.

The second complaint was filed against now-retired NCAA compliance officer Richard Johanningmeier by a Hurricanes football player alleging the official coerced the player into making statements to support the NCAA's case against the university. The Florida state attorney's office declined to pursue this complaint.

Sports Illustrated journalists Pete Thamel and Alexander Wolff (2013) suggest that Miami's complaints were triggered by more than just one embarrassing episode for the NCAA. They suggest the Miami case is the latest in a series of gaffes by the NCAA's compliance division, mistakes caused by disarray within the organization itself, notably considerable turnover in staff, few experienced investigators, and President Emmert's push to resolve every case within one year's time (the USC/Reggie Bush case took four years). Emmert denies the NCAA is in serious trouble, stating that "he does not believe the NCAA's enforcement process is broken. But he said the long-term effect of this policy failure and subsequent internal review could be a new model for how NCAA Enforcement and the Committee on Infractions conduct business. He said he is initiating the process of seeking feedback from NCAA member schools about the best way for that vital, controversial arm of the association to operate". (Forde and Robinson, 2013)

The university has cooperated with the investigation but, at the same time, has adopted a combative stance toward the NCAA. Is it unwise to provoke the organization that holds regulatory oversight over it, or is the university behaving opportunistically in response to perceived institutional weaknesses within the NCAA's compliance division (the illusion of control)? By the time you read this, the NCAA will have issued its final report and the punishments it imposes on Miami, if any, will be public knowledge. But, what are the long-term repercussions? And how does the dynamic between the NCAA and its member institutions, the enforcer and the enforced, change?

10.3   University of Oregon

Beginning in 1995, with the appointment of Mike Bellotti as head coach, the University of Oregon football program has been elevated into the top ranks of college football. Their success continued under coaches Chip Kelly and Mark Helfrich. As of 2013, it ranked in the top ten for appearances in BCS bowl games, including a 2011 appearance in the BCS National Championship game. However, as the football program moved into the big time, the pressure to continue winning may have led to questionable recruiting practices.

On February 28, 2011, the NCAA was notified by a confidential source of possible violations in Oregon's football program. The story became public just three days later, when Charles Robinson, an investigative reporter for *Yahoo! Sports*, published an article about payments by UO to two companies that provided scouting services (Robinson, March 3, 2011). In 2010, Complete Scouting Services, run by Willie Lyles, was paid US$25,000 and Baron Flenory's New Level Athletics was paid US$3,745:

> Lyles is a former athletic trainer who recently was serving as a mentor to highly touted Ducks running back recruit Lache Seastrunk. Meanwhile, Flenory runs the Badger Sports Elite 7-on-7 football camps which have featured several celebrated Ducks signees including running back DeAnthony Thomas, defensive back Cliff Harris, defensive back Dior Mathis and wideout Tacoi Sumler. Flenory had a personal training relationship with recent Ducks signee Anthony Wallace.
>
> If Lyles and Flenory aided in or were involved in any way in the recruitment of student athletes to Oregon, they would be classified as boosters by the NCAA, and any payment to them from the school would be considered a violation of Bylaw 13. Bylaw 13 prohibits boosters from directing a recruit to a school. (Robinson, March 3, 2011).

Recruiting service companies typically provide written reports and highlight videos on top high school athletes to college recruiters and fans. They also hold camps for the top prospects to be evaluated and showcase their talents, although they are not allowed by NCAA rules to operate evaluation or conditioning camps on college campuses. One of the largest firms is *Rivals.com*, which was acquired in 2007 by Yahoo! for a reported US$100 million. The Rivals staff ranks about 3,000 high school football players each year from one star to five stars. In 2013, they also held 17 evaluation camps, with 15 for specific regions in the US and two that were nationwide. The company claims that "[i]t's safe to say that all major Division One programs subscribe." Diehard fans also pay an average of US$100 per year for detailed reports and videos (Burke, 2013). At the other end of scale are companies run by one individual, such as Lyle's Texas-based Complete Scouting Services, which rely on their in-depth knowledge about programs in a particular region.

The NCAA is concerned that a school could get a competitive advantage in the recruiting process by buying inside information and access to specific recruits.

> The NCAA has developed specific rules regarding scouting services to preserve competitive equity. A school may purchase one annual subscription to an NCAA-certified service as long as the service is available to all schools for the same public fee, provides information about prospective student-athletes four times a year, reflects geographically broad coverage, provides individual analysis for each prospective student-athlete, gives access to samples and supplies video of regularly scheduled high school or two-year college contests. ("Division I football recruiting," 2013)

UO's payments raised suspicions for multiple reasons. The US$25,000 paid to Lyles was significantly higher than the US$5000 or less that would be typical for the type of services that Lyles was contracted to provide (Schad and Schlabach, 2011). In addition, Lyles had close relationships with several players from Texas that committed to playing for Oregon, notably LaMichael James and

Lache Seastrunk. While the payment to Flenory's New Level Athletics was much smaller, Oregon was the only school to purchase a recruiting report from the company. Flenory also had a personal training relationship with Anthony Wallace, who had recently signed with Oregon. After Robinson's article appeared, Flenory explained that the NCAA had recently adopted rules prohibiting companies that operated training camps on college campuses from also selling recruiting reports. Because his primary business was running camps, he had simply chosen to stop selling recruiting packages. Oregon was his company's first and only client, in part because of his relationship with head coach Chip Kelly, who was an assistant coach at New Hampshire when Flenory played football there. In any case, Mr. Flenory's relationship with Oregon was not found to be in violation of any NCAA rules and the investigation focused on Mr. Lyles.

In addition to UO's relationship with Willie Lyles, three non-coaching staff members were found to have placed or received approximately 730 recruiting-related telephone calls with student-athletes, parents, and high school coaches that were not allowed by NCAA rules. They calls were claimed to be related to logistics for arranging visits by the student to campus or a UO coach to the prospects home. The operations staff falsely believed that these calls were not of an official recruiting nature.

The following is a chronology of events related to Lyle's activities and the NCAA inquiry ("Timeline," n.d.):

May 2004	Oregon is deemed by the NCAA to have committed a major infraction in the recruiting of a junior college football player in January 2003. The school is placed on probation for two years. Another major violation within five years would make Oregon a repeat offender and subject to severe penalties.
February 2007	Chip Kelly hired as the UO offensive coordinator by head coach Mike Bellotti.
December 2007	Lyles' first contact with UO. He sends game film of LaMichael James to UO and other schools and has conversations with Chip Kelly and others.

January 2008	Darron Thomas and LaMichael James, both from Texas, officially sign with UO.
Spring 2008	Lyles begins mentoring Lache Seastrunk, who played on a 7-on-7 team Lyles coached.
2008–2009	Lyles is employed by Elite Scouting Services, which is paid a total of US$16,500 for recruiting services provided over two seasons (Schad and Schlabach, 2011).
December 2008	Chip Kelly meets with Lyles in Texas.
March 2009	Chip Kelly is officially named head football coach at UO following Mike Bellotti's move to the position of Athletic Director.
May 2009	While accompanied by at least one UO coach, Lyles has impermissible contact with a high school student. Lyles also accompanies a UO coach for a visit to a Texas high school. The two UO coaches involved were Chip Kelly and assistant coach Gary Campbell.
October 2009	UO hosts three high school players selected by Lyles at a game against USC. One later signed with UO. UO sends a thank you note to Lyles for arranging the visit.
December 2009	Lyles starts his own company, Complete Scouting Services. After discussions with Chip Kelly, UO agrees to be his first client. Lyles is provided with a pregame access pass for the game against Oregon State and access to the area where recruits are seated.
January 2010	Lyle leaves Elite Scouting Services and UO does not renew its contract with Elite. Lyles attends the US Army All-American Bowl with Lache Seastrunk, whom he mentors. Chip Kelly leaves a handwritten letter at Seastrunk's hotel. The UO assistant director of football operations and assistant athletic director for compliance advise Lyles on changing guardianship for Seastrunk from his mother, who opposes her son attending UO, to his grandmother, who would sign the letter of intent for UO.
February 2010	Dontae Williams and Seastrunk sign letters of intent with UO. Both have been advised by Lyles, and

	Seastrunk's grandmother signs his letter. Lyles' Complete Scouting Services bills UO for a "2011 National Package" for recruiting services.
March 2010	UO pays Lyles US$25,000.
January 2011	UO requests the quarterly scouting reports required by NCAA rules, which Lyles has not been submitting. Lyles sends two emails to UO about two players.
February 2011	Kelly and Josh Gibson, assistant director of football operations, urgently request the required quarterly scouting reports. Lyles sends a spreadsheet with information on players in Texas and Louisiana and later sends outdated and largely useless recruiting material. Dontae Williams leaves UO without playing in any games. The NCAA is notified of possible violations by a confidential source.
March 2011	*Yahoo! Sports* publishes its article with more details than were provided to the NCAA. The NCAA requests detailed recruiting records from UO. UO hires the Overland Park, Kansas, law firm Bond, Schoeneck & King, led by Michael "The Cleaner" Glazier, to conduct an internal investigation. The NCAA conducts its own interviews independent of UO, including Texas high school coaches and students advised by Lyles. A former Texas A&M coach alleges, Lyles wanted $80,000 to deliver a commitment from a highly recruited player.
March 2011– August 2011	The NCAA conducts 42 interviews, including two with Lyles.
June 2011	UO releases phone records and the outdated recruiting reports submitted by Lyles. The records include hundreds of calls and text messages between Lyles and Chip Kelly and Gary Campbell, UO's running back coach.
August 2011	Seastrunk leaves UO and eventually transfers to Baylor in Texas near his hometown.
September 2011	UO receives a notice of inquiry from the NCAA.

September 2011– January 2012	The NCAA conducts 24 additional interviews and grants immunity to five people.
December 2011	The NCAA provides a first draft of its findings to UO.
February 2012	UO's internal investigation concludes that violations occurred from 2008 to 2011 and begins negotiations to resolve differences with the NCAA's conclusions and reach a summary disposition (similar to a plea bargain).
March 2012	UO and the NCAA agree to attempt a summary disposition.
July 2012	The NCAA notifies UO that are "meaningful disagreements" between the two parties.
October 2012	The UO President and the Athletic Director agree that the violations were major in nature.
November 2012	The NCAA notifies UO that the summary disposition has failed and the case would be decided by the NCAA's Committee on Infractions.
January 2013	Chip Kelly is hired by the NFL Philadelphia Eagles.
February 2013	The NCAA vice president of enforcement, Julie Roe Lach is fired in the wake of the scandal related to the Miami investigation. Other enforcement officers also leave.
April 2013	UO releases a report which agrees which major violations occurred from 2008 to 2011 and proposes to impose penalties, including a two-year probation and a loss of one football scholarship per year for three years. It leaves the decision on repeat violations to the NCAA Committee on Infractions.
June 2013	The NCAA reports that UO committed major violations and that Chip Kelly failed to monitor the football program. The school is not deemed to be a repeat offender, sparing it from harsher sanctions. The penalties include a public reprimand and censure, three years of probation, a loss of one scholarship (from 85 to 84) for three years, a reduction in official recruiting visits from 56 to 37 for three years, a reduction

in evaluation days, and a ban on subscriptions to recruiting services during probation. Chip Kelly was given an 18-month show-cause order and Josh Gibson, the UO assistant director of football operations who accompanied Kelly to the NFL, was given a 12-month show-cause order.

A show-cause order means that any penalties will apply to another NCAA member institution which hires that individual unless the school appears before the Committee on Infractions to "show cause" why it should not be penalized. A coach cannot leave the penalties behind by simply moving to a different school. If a coach in this circumstance is fired, it can be very difficult to find another college coaching position. Fortunately for Kelly and Gibson, they were already employed by the NFL and thus unlikely to be seeking jobs at the college level during the life of the order.

The investigations by the NCAA and the UO concluded that Willie Lyles had indeed become a representative of the football program, making contact with recruits on behalf of the university. Lyles provided:

> … valuable information that would not typically be included in the recruiting/scouting services written reports. Specifically, because the recruiting service provider developed relationships and familiarity with prospective student-athletes early in their recruitment, he was able to inform Oregon coaches of information such as the identity of key individuals who were integral to the prospective student-athletes recruitment (e.g., an uncle, a grandmother, a nonscholastic seven-on-seven coach, etc.), and those prospective student-athletes who were unlikely to be interested in being recruited by Oregon. ("University of Oregon Public Infractions Report," 2013, pp. 4–5)

The latter was seen as a significant advantage by the university's recruiters. They were able to use their limited resources to pursue interested candidates and not waste time on those who were not likely to choose UO.

The NCAA had been increasingly concerned about athletic departments using middlemen in the recruiting process and wanted to use the Oregon case to clearly state those concerns. An attorney who specializes in NCAA enforcement issues speculated that this was the reason the Committee on Infractions did not accept the negotiated summary disposition and elected to hold its own hearing (Goe, 2012). If true, were the sanctions they imposed a sufficiently strong message, or were both the Committee and the NCAA enforcement staff distracted by the ongoing controversy over the bungled investigation into the University of Miami case?

10.4 Penn State University

For many years, Penn State University football and its renowned coach, Joe Paterno, were held up as shining examples of class and integrity. "JoePa," as he was affectionately known by the Penn State faithful, was a beloved and iconic figure and, prior to the scandal, the winningest coach in NCAA Division I football history. As egregious as the Sandusky scandal was in its own right, as the details will show, the sense of shock and dismay was perhaps magnified by the fact that it happened on the watch of such a legendary figure in such a revered program. It also served to illuminate how the culture of football at Division I-FBS programs can lead to pernicious, horrific behavior.

10.4.1 *Timeline*

In one of the most publicized scandals ever surrounding college football, Pennsylvania State University (Penn State), was found by an independent investigation to have both enabled and covered up multiple cases of child sexual abuse committed by former assistant football coach Jerry Sandusky. What follows is a timeline of significant events in the case, as identified and reported by the Special Investigative Council (discussed below, Freeh Report, 2012, pp. 19–30, timeline edited for brevity).

1969	Jerry Sandusky joins the Penn State football coaching staff.
February 1998	Head Football Coach Joe Paterno informs Sandusky that he [Sandusky] will not be the next head football coach. Athletic Director Tim Curley and Sandusky begin discussions about other possible roles for Sandusky within Penn State.
May 3, 1998	Sandusky assaults Victim 6 in the Lasch Football Building (on the Penn State campus) shower.[3]
May 4–30, 1998	Victim 6's mother reports to university police that Sandusky showered with her 11-year old son in the Lasch Building. The police launch an investigation.
	Senior Vice President Finance and Business Gary Schultz is informed of the investigation, which he then reports to Curley and Penn State President Graham Spanier. Schultz's confidential notes from May 4, 1998, state: "Behavior — at best inappropriate @ worst sexual improprieties," "At min — Poor Judgment," "Is this the opening of pandora's box?" and "Other children?"
	University Police Department Chief Harmon informs Schultz via email that: "We're going to hold off on making any crime log entry. At this point in time, I can justify that decision because of the lack of clear evidence of a crime."
	Curley reports to Schultz and Spanier that he has "touched base with" Paterno. Curley later emails Schultz: "Anything new in this department? Coach is anxious to know where it stands."
	Spanier fails to notify the Board of Trustees at their May 15 meeting of the ongoing investigation.
June 1998	District Attorney decides not to charge Sandusky.
	Sandusky is interviewed in Lasch Building by a University police detective and a Department of Public Welfare caseworker. Sandusky admits to

---

[3] The Freeh Report identifies victims in the Sandusky case according to the Grand Jury designations.

hugging Victim 6 in the shower but claims that was nothing "sexual about it." When advised by the detective not to shower with any child. Sandusky stated that he "wouldn't."

Harmon reports to Schultz that officers "met discreetly"with Sandusky and "his account of the matter was essentially the same as the child's." Sandusky also disclosed that "he had done this with other children in the past. Sandusky was advised that there was no criminal behavior established and that the matter was closed as an investigation."

Schultz emails Curley and Spanier to report "I think the matter has been appropriately investigated and I hope it is now behind us."

January 1999	Curley informs Spanier and Schulz that Sandusky intends to coach one more year and then move to an outreach program.
May–August 1999	Sandusky negotiates and phases into retirement from coaching, but works "to maintain a long-term relationship with the University." One of Sandusky's proposals is to run a middle school youth football camp and identify other ways he could "continue to work with young people through Penn State."[4] As part of the transition, Sandusky receives a one-time payment of US\$168,000, free lifetime use of the East Area Locker Room facilities, and is granted "emeritus" status, a rank that carries special privileges at the university and which is normally only awarded to those of a higher academic rank than Sandusky had attained at the University.
December 1999	Sandusky brings Victim 4 to the Alamo Bowl in Texas and assaults Victim 4 at the team hotel.

[4]Including the Second Mile program, a nonprofit organization for underprivileged and at-risk youth, founded by Sandusky in 1977, headquartered in Pennsylvania, and referred to later in the timeline.

November 2000   Sandusky assaults Victim 8 in Lasch Building
                       shower. The assault is observed by a janitor who,
                       fearing that "they'll get rid of all of us," decides not
                       to report. Second janitor believes that "the
                       University will close ranks to protect the football
                       program."

February 9–12, 2001   Sandusky assaults Victim 2 in Lasch Building
                       shower. The assault is observed by Assistant
                       Football Coach Mike McQueary (he was also a
                       former Penn State quarterback who played for
                       Paterno), who reports it to Joe Paterno the next
                       day (February 10). Paterno tells McQueary, "you
                       did what you had to do. It's my job now to figure
                       out what we want to do." Paterno waits until
                       February 11 to report to Curley and Schultz so as
                       not to "interfere with their weekends." Schultz
                       consults with Wendell Courtney, University
                       outside counsel, regarding "reporting of suspected
                       child abuse."

                       On February 12, Spanier, Schultz and Curley
                       meet. Schultz and Curley discuss the 1998 incident;
                       Curley agrees to meet with Paterno and Sandusky.
                       Schultz's notes about the Curley–Sandusky
                       meeting state, "Unless he confesses to having a
                       problem, [Curley] will indicate we need to have
                       DPW [Dept. of Public Welfare] review the matter
                       as an independent agency concerned with child
                       welfare." Schultz verifies with Chief Harmon that
                       the 1998 incident report is in police files.

February 25–26, 2001   Meeting between Spanier, Schultz and Curley
                       results in an action plan described by the following
                       notes from Schultz: "3) Tell chair* of Board of
                       Second Mile 2) Report to Dept. of Welfare. 1) Tell JS
                       [Sandusky] to avoid bringing children alone into
                       Lasch Bldg *who's the chair??" A later email
                       confirms the plan.

February 27–28, 2001   After consulting with Paterno, Curley decides to
                       offer Sandusky "professional help." If Sandusky

cooperates, Curley will help him inform Second Mile. If not, Curley indicates DPW and Second Mile will be informed anyway. Sandusky is to be instructed that his guests are not permitted to use Penn State athletic facilities. Curley emails this plan to Spanier and Schulz.

Spanier informs Curley and Schulz that "This approach is acceptable to me." He goes on further to say that "The only downside for us is if the message isn't 'heard' and acted upon, and we then become vulnerable for not having reported it. But that can be assessed down the road. The approach you outline is humane and a reasonable way to proceed." Schulz agrees, writing to Spanier and Curley, "this is a more humane and upfront way to handle this," adding, "we can play it by ear" about reporting the assault to DPW.

March 5, 2001	Curley and Sandusky meet. According to Curley's Grand Jury testimony in 2011, Sandusky was told the incident would be reported to Second Mile, and was directed to stop bringing children to the athletic facilities. According to Sandusky's legal counsel, Curley did not accuse Sandusky of sexual abuse.
March 16, 2001	Spanier fails to report Sandusky incident at the Board of Trustees meeting.
March 19, 2001	Curley meets and "shared the information" with Second Mile executive director, who determines, this is a "non-incident" and takes no further action.
August 2001	Sandusky assaults Victim 5 in Lasch Building shower.
September 21, 2001	Board of Trustees approves a land sale to Second Mile that had been led by Sandusky. Neither Spanier nor Schultz report about any Sandusky incidents.
2001–2010	No reported events.
January 7, 2010	Pennsylvania Attorney General subpoenas Penn State personnel records and correspondence related to Sandusky.

December 28, 2010– January 11, 2011	Grand Jury subpoenas for Schultz, Paterno and Curley lead to a series of meetings and email exchanges between those individuals and Penn State General Counsel Cynthia Baldwin, Spanier, and Courtney.
January 12, 2011	Schultz, Paterno and Curley testify before the Grand Jury.
March 31, 2011	*Patriot-News* publishes an article on the Sandusky investigation. This followed a September 2010 contact between the *Patriot-News* and Spanier.
April 1, 2011	Trustee contacts Spanier to ask if he will brief the Board on the investigation. Spanier responds, "Grand Jury matters are by law secret, and I'm not sure what one is permitted to say, if anything. I'll need to ask Cynthia [Baldwin] if it would be permissible for her to brief the Board on the matter."
April 13, 2011	Trustee contacts Spanier again, writing: "despite grand jury secrecy, when high ranking people at the university are appearing before a grand jury, the university should communicate something about this to its Board of Trustees." Spanier downplays the matter, responding, "I'm not sure it is entirely our place to speak about this when we are only on the periphery of this." Spanier asks Baldwin to contact the Trustee, telling her in a separate email that "[the Trustee] desires near total transparency. He will be uncomfortable and feel put off until he gets a report." Spanier appears before the Grand Jury.
April 17, 2011– September 9, 2011	Various meetings occur between Spanier, Baldwin, Board Chair Steve Garban and the Board of Trustees. At one Board meeting, Spanier and Baldwin report on the investigation but downplay the significance and the Board asks few questions. At two subsequent meetings, no update is provided and the Board asks no questions about the Sandusky matter.

October 27–28, 2011	Baldwin notified of upcoming Grand Jury indictment. Baldwin, Spanier and Curley meet. Baldwin, Spanier and Garban meet and draft a press statement stating their "unconditional support" for Schultz and Curley.
October 29, 2011	Sandusky attends a Penn State football game at Beaver Stadium, sitting in the Nittany Lion Club.
November 4, 2011	Sandusky criminal charges filed in Centre County. Schultz and Curley criminal charges filed in Dauphin County. Courtney emails a newspaper story on the Sandusky charges to Schulz, to which he replies, "I was never aware that 'Penn State police investigated inappropriate touching in a shower' in 1998."
November 5, 2011	Sandusky arrested.

Grand Jury presentment indicates there was no "attempt [by Penn State officials] to investigate, to identify Victim 2 or to protect that child or any others from similar conduct, except as related to preventing its reoccurrence on University property."

Trustee asks Spanier if Board will be briefed; Baldwin advises Spanier to tell the Trustee that he [Spanier] is "briefing the chair and the Board will be briefed next week." Spanier statement to the press conveys "unconditional support" for Schulz and Curley, but about the child victims only says, "Protecting children requires the utmost vigilance." Spanier informs Baldwin that the briefing to the Board "will be nothing more than what we said publicly." The Board meets via conference call.

An independent review is suggested by a senior administrator, to which Baldwin replies, "If we do this, we will never get rid of this group in some shape or form. The Board will then think that they should have such a group." Spanier agrees with Baldwin.

November 6, 2011	Board of Trustees meet and put Curley on administrative leave; Schulz retires. Spanier altered the press release, stating that Curley and Schulz changed their employment status voluntarily. Members of the Board disagreed with the change in tone of the release, but Spanier claimed his edits were only "grammatical."
November 7, 2011	Charges against Sandusky, Schulz and Curley are announced by the Pennsylvania Attorney General and Pennsylvania State Police Commissioner at a press conference. In response to the previous day's [altered] press release, one Trustee writes to other Board members, "Unfortunately the statement that was issued last night, in my opinion, did not reflect the sense of the Board."
November 8, 2011	Via conference call the Board opts to issue another press release, this time expressing their "outrage" at the "horrifying details" of the Grand Jury's presentment. They announce that a task force will be formed to review the issues related to the criminal charges.
November 9, 2011	Board of Trustees meets and removes Spanier as President. Rodney Erickson named Interim President (made permanent on November 17, 2011). Joe Paterno removed as Head Football Coach. Board Vice Chair contacts Paterno to notify him of removal as head coach. The Board holds a press conference to announce its actions. Penn State students demonstrate in protest of Paterno's removal.
November 21, 2011	Freeh Sporkin & Sullivan, LLP is named Special Investigative Counsel by the Special Investigative Task Force on behalf of the Penn State Board of Trustees. (Freeh Sporkin & Sullivan LLP, 2012, p. 8)
January 22, 2012	Joe Paterno dies of lung cancer.
June 22, 2012	Jerry Sandusky found guilty of 45 of the 48 counts. ("Jury convicts Jerry Sandusky," 2012)

July 12, 2012   Special Investigative Counsel issues its report (the Freeh Report discussed below).

10.4.2 *The Freeh Report*

The Penn State Board of Trustees, on November 21, 2011, contracted with the law firm Freeh Sporkin & Sullivan, LLP, to serve as Special Investigative Council and "perform an independent, full and complete investigation of:

- The alleged failure of Pennsylvania State University personnel to respond to, and report to the appropriate authorities, the sexual abuse of children by former University football coach Gerald A. Sandusky ("McCarthy, 2013");
- The circumstances under which such abuse could occur in University facilities or under the auspices of University programs for youth" (Freeh Sporkin & Sullivan LLP, 2012, p. 8).

Additionally, the board asked the Special Investigative Council to recommend remedial actions to improve prevention of and response to future incidents.

The final report of the Special Investigative Council, now known as the "Freeh Report," was released on July 12, 2012. The entire report, including findings, recommendations and exhibits (including copies of email correspondence between key parties in the case and the results of interviews of 430 individuals), came to 267 pages. The following are excerpts from the three pages of findings reported in the Executive Summary of the Freeh Report:

> The most saddening finding by the Special Investigative Counsel is the total and consistent disregard by the most senior leaders at Penn State for the safety and welfare of Sandusky's child victims ... there was no "attempt to investigate, to identify Victim 2, or to protect that child or any others from similar conduct except as related to preventing its reoccurrence on University property."

Four of the most powerful people at The Pennsylvania State University — President Graham B. Spanier, Senior Vice President — Finance and Business Gary C. Schultz, Athletic Director Timothy M. Curley and Head Football Coach Joseph V. Paterno — failed to protect against a child sexual predator harming children for over a decade. These men concealed Sandusky's activities from the Board of Trustees, the University community and authorities. They exhibited a striking lack of empathy for Sandusky's victims ...

These individuals, unchecked by the Board of Trustees that did not perform its oversight duties, empowered Sandusky to attract potential victims to the campus and football events by allowing him to have continue, unrestricted and unsupervised access to the University's facilities and affiliation with the University's prominent football program. Indeed, that continued access provided Sandusky with the very currency that enabled him to attract his victims. Some coaches, administrators and football program staff members ignored the red flags of Sandusky's behaviors and no on warned the public about him. (Freeh Sporkin & Sullivan LLP, 2012, pp. 14–15)

The Freeh Report goes on to cite President Spanier's failure to execute this duties by failing to report to the Board of Trustees, and the Board's failure to "inquire reasonably" and "demand detailed information from Spanier". (Freeh Sporkin & Sullivan LLP, 2012, p. 15)

The findings also address the responses by Spanier, Schultz, Curley, and Paterno as to their failure to take action in response to McQueary's report of the assault on Victim 2 on February 9, 2001. Their responses ranged from ignorance of any sexual abuse to uncertainty as to how to handle the situation properly. In response to these claims, the Special Investigative Council found:

that it is more reasonable to conclude that, in order to avoid the consequences of bad publicity, the most powerful leaders at the University — Spanier, Schultz, Paterno and Curley — repeatedly concealed critical facts relating to Sandusky's child abuse from the authorities, the University's Board of Trustees, the Penn State community, and the public at large. (Freeh Sporkin & Sullivan LLP, 2012, p. 16)

While the report attributes the "avoidance of the consequences of bad publicity" as the primary reason, they also identified the following causes for the parties' "failure to protect child victims and report to authorities:"

- A striking lack of empathy for child abuse victims by the most senior leaders of the University.
- A failure by the Board to exercise its oversight functions in 1998 and 2001 ....
- A failure by the Board to make reasonable inquiry in 2011 ....
- A President who discouraged discussion and dissent.
- A lack of awareness of child abuse issues, the Clery Act, and whistleblower policies and protections.[5]
- A decision by Spanier, Schultz, Paterno and Curley to allow Sandusky to retire in 1999, not as a suspected child predator, but as a valued member of the Penn State football legacy, with future "visibility" at Penn State and ways "to continue to work with young people through Penn State," essentially granting him license to bring boys to campus facilities for "grooming" as targets for his assaults. Sandusky retained unlimited access to University facilities until November 2011.
- A football program that did not fully participate in, or opted out, of some University programs, including Clery Act compliance ....
- A culture of reverence for the football program that is ingrained at all levels of the campus community. (Freeh Sporkin & Sullivan LLP, 2012, pp. 16–17)

10.4.3 *NCAA sanctions*

The most severe sanctions for Penn State were imposed by the NCAA. In the Consent Decree signed on July 23, 2012, by PSU President Rodney Erickson and NCAA President Mark Emmert,

---

[5]The Clery Act requires schools to publish an annual report on campus crime statistics security policies and procedures, and basic rights for victims of sexual assault.

Penn State agreed to accept a set of both punitive and corrective sanctions.[6] The Consent Decree prefacing the specific sanctions included the following remarks, and addressed the question of whether the NCAA was the appropriate institution to level such penalties.

> The NCAA concludes that this evidence presents an unprecedented failure of institutional integrity leading to a culture in which a football program was held in higher esteem than the values of the institution, the values of the NCAA, the values of higher education, and most disturbingly the values of human decency. The sexual abuse of children on a university campus by a former university official — and even the active concealment of that abuse — while despicable, ordinarily would not be actionable by the NCAA. Yet, in this instance, it was the fear of or deference to the omnipotent football program that enable a sexual predator to attract and abuse his victims. Indeed, the reverence for Penn State football permeated every level of the University community. That imbalance of power and its result are antithetical to the model of intercollegiate athletics embedded in higher education. Indeed, the culture exhibited at Penn State is an extraordinary affront to the values all members of the Association have pledged to uphold and calls for extraordinary action. ("Binding Consent Decree," 2012, p. 4)

The following punitive sanctions were imposed. The NCAA also reserved the right to conduct further investigations and impose additional penalties related to individuals involved in the case.

1. *$60 million fine.* Penn State was directed to pay a minimum of $12 million per year for five years, beginning in 2012, until the fine was paid. The amount was based on the approximate average of one year's gross football revenue. Proceeds were directed to an endowment for child sex abuse

---

[6] For more details, the "Binding Consent Decree" (2012) can be found at the NCAA website, NCAA.org.

prevention and victim assistance programs. Requirements stipulated that the money could not be used to fund programs at Penn State, and that funding the fine could not come from cuts to current Penn State athletic teams.

2. *Four-year postseason ban.* From 2012–13 through 2015–16, Penn State football was banned from postseason play, including participation in conference championship games, bowl games, or any other postseason competition.

3. *Four-year reduction of grants-in-aid.* From 2013–14 through 2016–17, Penn State football was limited to 15 initial grants-in-aid (as opposed to the usual 25 allowed). Penn State was further restricted to a total of 65 scholarship players per year for the years 2014–15 through 2017–18, meaning Penn State football effectively lost 80 scholarships over a four-year period.

4. *Five years of probation.* As occurs with most major violation cases, the NCAA imposed a probationary period that required additional monitoring and threatened additional sanctions for further violations or failure to comply with other sanctions.

5. *Vacation of wins from 1998 to 2011.* Prior to the scandal and subsequent sanctions, Joe Paterno was recognized as the winningest coach in Division I college football history. The sanctions removed 111 wins from his record, lowering his official lifetime win total to 298.

6. *Waiver of transfer rules and scholarship retention.* In the interest of minimizing the harm to then current Penn State football players, the NCAA opted to allow any player an immediate transfer, without loss of eligibility. In total, nine players transferred and a number of top recruits decommitted and played for different schools (Tierney, 2012). Additionally, student-athletes who wanted to remain at Penn State but leave the football program, would maintain their grant-in-aid as long as they satisfied the appropriate academic requirements.

The Special Investigative Council that prepared the Freeh Report offered 119 recommendations for corrective action; the binding consent decree between Penn State and the NCAA called for adoption of all of them. Most of the remedial recommendations involve creating institutional structures to improve oversight of programs involving children; to educate and train university personnel to recognize and act upon improper behavior; and to create a culture at Penn State that lessens the reverence for football and its pernicious effects, and that instead encourages integrity and accountability.

A central component of the corrective sanctions was the creation and implementation of an "Athletics Integrity Agreement" ("AIA") with the NCAA and Big Ten Conference. The AIA required Penn State to adopt all of the Freeh Report, Chapter 10, Section 5.0 recommendations. In addition, Penn State was required to add the following: Compliance Officer for Athletics; Compliance Council; Disclosure Program; Internal Accountability and Certifications; External Compliance Review/Certification Profess; Athletics Code of Conduct; and Training and Education. This combination of programs was created to enhance compliance, provide mechanisms for and encourage the reporting of legal and ethical violations (actual or suspected), and rebuild the overall integrity of the program and both its internal and external accountability processes.

The severity of the Penn State case had some calling for the death penalty for Penn State football. According to the Consent Decree, the NCAA considered that option, but concluded that the death penalty was not the most effective way to change the culture that resulted in this tragedy. Additionally, the NCAA recognized that no student-athletes were responsible for these events, and therefore attempted to craft sanctions that would minimize the costs to Penn State student-athletes. The NCAA also acknowledged that Penn State University,

> has never before had NCAA major violations, [has] accepted these penalties and corrective actions, has removed all of the individual offenders identified by FSS [Freeh Sporkin & Sullivan,

LLP] from their past senior leadership roles, has itself commissioned the FSS investigation and provided unprecedented access and openness, in some instances, even agreed to waive attorney-client privilege, and already has implemented many corrective actions. Acknowledging these and other factors, the NCAA does not deem the so-called "death penalty" to be appropriate. ("Binding Consent Decree," 2012, p. 4)

Upon hearing the sanctions that were imposed, some analysts pondered whether Penn State wouldn't have been better off (or at least no worse off) with the death penalty.

10.4.4   *Conference level sanctions*

As a member of the Big Ten, Penn State was also subject to conference level disciplinary action. In addition to affirming the probation and postseason ineligibility sanctions imposed by the NCAA, the Big Ten added censure — formally condemning Penn State for its conduct. The Big Ten also opted to fine Penn State its share of bowl revenue for the period of postseason ineligibility. Estimated to total approximately US$13 million over the four-year period, the Big Ten pledged to donate the money to charities in Big Ten communities that work to protect children. ("Big Ten Council," 2012)

10.4.5   *Reaction to the sanctions*

As one might expect, reactions to the sanctions were mixed. Many outside Pennsylvania and the Penn State Community felt that the sanctions were appropriate or not severe enough. Supporters of Penn State believed the penalties were too harsh, particularly given that the individuals identified as most responsible for the events had already been removed from the University. We won't cover the range of reactions in more detail here; countless stories can be found on the internet and other media sources. What we will emphasize here are the legal challenges that have been issued.

In January 2013, on behalf of the Commonwealth of Pennsylvania, Governor Tom Corbett filed an antitrust suit against the NCAA in an effort to have the sanctions reversed. In filing the suit, Corbett claimed that "The NCAA and [president] Mark Emmert seized upon the opportunity for publicity for their own benefit.... These sanctions are an attack on past, present and future students of Penn State, the citizens of our commonwealth and our economy." Interestingly, back in July 2012, Governor Corbett had said, "Part of the corrective process is to accept the serious penalties imposed today by the NCAA on Penn State and its football program". (Kercheval, January 2, 2013)

US Middle District Judge, Yvette Kane dismissed the suit, claiming that imposing the sanctions did not constitute an antitrust violation. As Kane explained:

> The fact that Penn State will offer fewer scholarships over a period of four years does not plausibly support [the plaintiffs] allegation that the reduction of scholarships at Penn State will result in a market-wide anticompetitive effect, such that the 'nation's top scholastic football players' would be unable to obtain a scholarship in the nationwide market for Division I football players. (Kercheval, June 6, 2013)

In July 2013, Governor Corbett announced that he would not appeal the dismissal. (Smeltz, 2013)

Two other state officials, State Senator Jake Corman and State Treasurer Rob McCord, also filed a lawsuit in January 2013. The object of this suit is to keep the payments of the US$60 million fine within Pennsylvania borders, serving sexual abuse awareness programs within the state. Corman based his case, in part, on the Institution of Higher Education Monetary Penalty Endowment Act, a Pennsylvania State law enacted February 20, 2013, in direct response to the fine imposed in the Consent Decree. This "Endowment Act" would effectively require that "monetary penalties" imposed on Pennsylvania public colleges and universities by "governing bodies" (i.e., the NCAA) would be paid into an endowment fund that would be used for programs within the state.

This case was not resolved as of July 2013. The NCAA has challenged the lawsuit both on the basis of the constitutionality of the new Endowment Act, and on Corman's legal standing to bring forward such a suit.

A third lawsuit was filed in May 2013, by members of the Paterno family and "several members of the Penn State Board of Trustees, faculty and former players and coaches." The suit, which seeks the overturning of the sanctions and both compensatory and punitive damages against the NCAA, is based on the belief that Emmert and the NCAA forced Penn State to accept the Freeh Report and sign the Consent Decree (Kercheval, May 29, 2013). In the statement accompanying the announcement of the suit, the plaintiffs' attorney, Wick Sollers, states:

> This case is further proof that the NCAA has lost all sense of its mission. If there was ever a situation that demanded meticulous review and a careful adherence to NCAA rules and guidelines, this was it. Instead, the NCAA placed a premium on speed over accuracy and precipitous action over due process.
>
> An illegally imposed penalty that is based on false assumptions and secret discussions is a disservice to the victims and everyone else who cares about the truth of the Sandusky scandal.... This matter will never be resolved until the full facts are reviewed in a lawful and transparent manner (as quoted in Kercheval, May 29, 2013).

This lawsuit had not been resolved when this book went to press, but some analysts questioned its chances for success, as none of the plaintiffs had the legal standing to challenge the sanctions.

10.4.6   *Impact of the sanctions*

At the time this edition was published, the one-year anniversary of the Freeh Report had just passed. The full impact had not yet been felt, but Penn State appeared to be handling the situation better than one might expect. According to PSU Board Chairman Keith Masser, efforts had been made up to complete 115 of the 119 recommendations, and the University had been given strong performance reviews on progress up to that point (Masser, 2013).

In July 2013, the Board of Trustees authorized financial settlements for Sandusky's victims, though specific details were not announced at that time ("PSU authorizes," 2013). A few days later, it was reported that total settlements had reached approximately US$60 million, covering 25 of the 31 outstanding claims. ("Penn State payout," 2013)

Financially, by the end of 2012, Penn State had paid more than US$41.1 million in NCAA fines and legal and consulting fees. In April 2013, they took their first hit from the Big Ten Conference's US$13 million sanction, losing out on the US$3.25 million they would have earned from their share of 2012 conference bowl revenue. These figures represent the direct financial impact of the sanctions; other financial impacts are discussed later. ("McCarthy," 2013)

Despite the aforementioned loss of players, the football team had a respectable 2012 record of 8-4 (6-2 in the Big Ten) under new coach Bill O'Brien. Football attendance dropped 4.6%, but this was the fifth consecutive year of falling attendance, so its connection to the Sandusky scandal is unclear. ("McCarthy," 2013)

10.4.7 *Other fallout*

In addition to the direct financial costs of the sanctions, and the inevitable settlement payments to victims, a significant financial concern to Penn State was the loss of sponsors. By the end of 2012, *Advertising Age* had estimated that "Penn State lost more than $1 million in sponsorship/advertising dollars from the likes of General Motors, Cars.com and Sherwin Williams." In addition, Penn State lost US$700,000 in licensing royalties from merchandise sales. The lost sponsorship and royalty revenue, along with the aforementioned fines and fees, put the total cost to Penn State at US$46 million through early 2013. ("McCarthy," 2013)

General Motors' Chevrolet pulled its sponsorship of football, but continued to sponsor other Penn State sports. As of the 2012–2013 season, Chevrolet has not reinstated its sponsorship. *Cars.com* removed its television ads from ESPN broadcasts of Penn State football in 2011, but restored them in 2012 and 2013. Sherwin Williams removed its logo from the Penn State banner (used as a backdrop for football press conferences), but didn't drop its sponsorship of football or other Penn State athletic programs. State Farm insurance pulled its radio advertisements during Penn State football games in 2011 and 2012, but was considering their reinstatement for the 2013 season. ("McCarthy," 2013)

Despite the scandal, some sponsors stayed with Penn State. Nike, Pepsi, and Highpoint maintained their connections with Penn State athletics, though Nike removed Joe Paterno's name from one of its child-care centers at its headquarters in Beaverton, Oregon. These companies kept a low profile ("went dark") with their partnerships in 2012, but did not sever their relationships with Penn State. ("McCarthy," 2013)

Fast fact. *The Penn State Athletics website (http://www.gopsus-ports.com) has a page dedicated to its "Corporate Partners." A glance at that page on July 18, 2013, found the following statement: "Penn State Athletics would like to thank its Corporate Partners for their support." No corporate partners were named on the page.*

The Sandusky scandal also resulted in the downgrading of Penn State's long-term credit rating from Aa1 to Aa2, by Moody's Investor Service. This was based on the estimated financial impact of the costs to Penn State in resolving the scandal, including the known cost of fines, but also the uncertain costs of resolving the various legal claims of the victims. As the Moody's press release explained, "the total number of claims and the ultimate full cost to the university is unknown and may not be known for years, but could be significant". ("Moody's downgrades," 2012)

What is the significance of a rating downgrade? An institution's rating affects the ease at which it can secure loans, whether through a bond issue or direct lending from a financial firm. Lower ratings indicate a greater risk of default, meaning that lenders will be less likely to issue credit to Penn State, or they will require a higher rate of interest to compensate for the increased risk. As of October 2012, Penn State carried $893 million in outstanding rated debt, meaning that even small increases in interest rates could increase Penn State's debt repayment costs substantially ("Moody's downgrades," 2012). Despite the downgrade, Penn State's rating remains relatively strong, reflecting Moody's assessment that the institution is still on solid financial footing.

If there is a financial bright spot for Penn State, it is that alumni and other donors appeared to rally around the institution. In the 2011–2012 fiscal year, Penn State received US$208 million in donations, the second-highest total in the school's history. Membership in the Penn State Alumni Association also grew by 2.4% over the same period. Overall enrollment was steady from 2011 to 2012, so the scandal did not appear to drive off prospective students to any measurable degree. ("McCarthy," 2013)

Mike McQueary was placed on administrative leave in November 2011, and fired in July 2012. McQueary filed a whistleblower and defamation lawsuit against Penn State in October 2012, "seeking US$4 million in lost future earnings plus unspecified damages for legal fees and the distress, anguish and humiliation caused by his role in the Sandusky case" (Pearson, 2012). The suit claims McQueary was dismissed because he cooperated with state prosecutors, which could violate Pennsylvania's Whistleblower Law. Penn State claims McQueary's contract was simply not renewed by new Head Football Coach Bill O'Brien, a common practice when a head coaching change occurs ("Mike McQueary," 2013). The case was still pending when this book went to press, but the outcome may have serious ramifications on the actions of future potential whistleblowers.

In November 2012, Spanier, Schultz, and Curley were all charged with "perjury, obstruction of justice and endangering children in an alleged cover-up of sexual abuse of children by assistant football coach Jerry Sandusky" ("Ex-Penn State president charged,"

2012). At the time this book went to press, all three denied the allegations and were awaiting a July 29, 2013 preliminary hearing. Officially, as of July 2013, Spanier was on faculty leave, and Curley and Schultz had retired. Paterno died of lung cancer in January 2012. ("PSU authorizes," 2013)

Perhaps the most symbolic action taken as a result of the scandal was the removal of the Joe Paterno statue from the Penn State campus one month after Sandusky's conviction. The statue itself was a testament to the power and legacy of Joe Paterno at Penn State, as well as to the culture of football at the University; its removal reflected the egregiousness of the events leading to its removal. In any case, the statue was divisive. Students wanting to protect the statue camped out it; at the same time "a plane flew overhead towing a banner that read, 'Take down the statue, or we will'". ("Joe Paterno statue," 2012)

In his statement explaining the decision to remove the statue, Penn State President Rodney Erickson offered the following:

> With the release of Judge Freeh's Report of the Special Investigative Counsel, we as a community had had to confront a failure of leadership at many levels. The statue of Joe Paterno outside Beaver Stadium has become a lightning rod of controversy and national debate, including the role of big time sports in university life....
>
> I now believe that, contrary to its original intention, Coach Paterno's statue has become a source of division and an obstacle to healing in our University and beyond. For that reason, I have decided that it is in the best interest of our university and public safety to remove the statue and store it in a secure location. I believe that, were it to remain, the statue will be a recurring wound to the multitude of individuals across the nation and beyond who have been the victims of child abuse. ("Joe Paterno statue," 2012)

The statue was not the only tribute to Paterno on the Penn State campus. The Joe Paterno Library, for which the Paterno family donated US$4 million to help fund construction, kept its name. As Erickson explained, the Paterno Library symbolizes the substantial and lasting contributions to the academic life and education excellence that the Paterno family has made to Penn State University. The library remains a tribute to Joe and Sue Paterno's commitment to Penn State's student body and academic success, and it highlights the positive impacts Coach Paterno had on the University. ("Joe Paterno statue," 2012)

It is uncertain what Joe Paterno's lasting legacy will be. For many years he was a coach loved by the Penn State community and respected by even his fiercest opponents. Will history remember a coach who otherwise appeared to maintain the highest standards of integrity, or the coach who allowed a child predator to operate largely unchecked on campus?

The more important question is, will the events of the Sandusky scandal fundamentally change the culture of college football, at Penn State and around the country, in ways that will prevent similar tragedies from happening in the future?

10.5   California Institute of Technology

Caltech, located in Pasadena, CA, is one of the most prestigious universities in the world. Contributing to its academic reputation are the 31 Caltech alumni and faculty who won the Nobel Prize, including economist Vernon Smith. Notable alumni include astronauts Frank Borman, C. Gordon Fullerton, and Harrison Schmitt; Gordon Moore, cofounder of Intel (and father of Moore's Law); Simon Ramo and Dean Wooldridge, cofounders of TRW (a past employer of one of your authors); Donald Knuth, inventor of TeX; film director Frank Capra; William Shockley, coinventor of the transistor; and food science writer Harold McGee. Physicists Richard Feynman and Murray Gell-Mann and chemist Linus Pauling taught at Caltech. Its faculty and alumni often work on NASA projects through the university-operated Jet Propulsion Laboratory, which successfully landed and deployed the Mars exploration vehicle Curiosity in 2012.

The university has roughly 1,000 undergrads and 1,200 graduate students. About 13% of undergraduate applicants are admitted. Of those men and women, 97% were in the top ten academic standing in high school and 98% tested in the 700–800 range on the mathematics portion of the SAT. The undergraduate graduation rate is 87%. But Caltech students are not all eggheads, geeks, and nerds; the university offers 9 men's sports and 8 women's sports, and competes as a NCAA DIII school in the Southern California Intercollegiate Athletic Conference.

> **Fast fact.** *Caltech is better known in intercollegiate sports for its classic Rose Bowl pranks. In 1961, Caltech students switched the instruction sheets given to University of Washington fans for holding up cards during halftime. Thirty million television viewers saw the image of a beaver, Caltech's mascot, instead of a husky, and "CALTECH." For the 1984 Rose Bowl, the scoreboard was altered to read "Caltech 38, MIT 6."*

Caltech's 2011–2012 women's basketball roster listed nine players, none taller than five foot eight. In the online players bios, the players described their ideal future job: two wanted to be astronauts, one a manufacturer of artificial organs, another a Major League Baseball (MLB) sabremetrician, three said some form of engineering, one envisaged employment as a biotech consultant, and one said she was undecided. Note that none of them said they planned on playing in the Women's National Basketball Association (WNBA). Their record in 2011–2012 was 0-25 and included a 100-26 loss to MIT, a 107-34 loss to Alverno, and a 140-83 loss to Arizona Christian. The 2012 baseball roster consisted of 15 players including one woman, outfielder Kayla McCue. The team's 0-33 record included being swept 23-5 and 23-1, and 19-0 and 12-1, during doubleheaders against La Verne and Pomona-Pitzer respectively. The team batting average was 0.211 and the ERA was 12.27. They scored 77 runs compared to their opponents' 441. To the best of our knowledge, no Caltech player has ever made it to the major leagues ... or the minors either. Perhaps the most notable event in Caltech's athletics history was the defeat of Bard College by the men's basketball team in 2007, the team's first victory in 207 previous contests (this event became the subject of the documentary *Quantum Hoops*).

No institution is above NCAA suspicion and it should come as no surprise that eventually this athletic powerhouse would run afoul of the NCAA bylaws. On July 12, 2012, the NCAA issued a public report finding numerous rules violations at Caltech ("California Institute of Technology," 2012). The violations were considered major since they concerned the use of 30 ineligible players during games. The punishment included three years probation, one year of ineligibility for postseason competition for 12 sports, vacating all wins in games in which ineligible athletes participated, a US$5,000 fine, and a one-year ban on all off-campus athletic recruiting.

Of the 30 players declared ineligible, nine were disallowed because they were not in good academic standing and three were not in good academic standing and not enrolled full time. These 12 cases represented unequivocal violations of the NCAA bylaws. The remaining 18 were either not registered for classes, or registered only part-time, at the time they engaged in intercollegiate competition. But the reason they were not registered full-time was due to the fact that they were "shopping for classes." Contrary to what you might think, this academic "browsing" is encouraged by the institution and is part of its campus and academic culture. Caltech, which operates on ten-week terms, allows *all* students to attend class for up to three weeks before officially registering. The NCAA report itself noted that this is "a unique institutional policy." Not wrong or harmful, just unique.

What is striking about the NCAA's decision concerning these 18 student-athletes is that it seems like a double standard. The NCAA often rules that a violation occurred because a student-athlete was treated *more* favorably than a non-athlete student at the same institution. A common example would be impermissible benefits; if an athlete gets a car, or cash from an overzealous booster, how likely is it that a Chemistry or Economics student got a similar gift? Yet in the Caltech case, these 18 students were behaving *exactly* like their peers, taking advantage of the opportunity to sit in classes before deciding to enroll.

One aspect of the NCAA bylaws that we have not discussed before is that, with occasional exceptions, they are "one size fits all" rules. All NCAA schools have to abide by them even if, as the Caltech decision suggests, there are unique circumstances underlying the apparent violation. It may be argued that, since more than 1,000 schools are active members of the NCAA, that it would be too cumbersome to tailor the rules to every school. Fair enough. But this does not answer the question why the NCAA, after investigating the circumstances of the Caltech violations, chose not to allow any leeway in *interpreting* the rules.

10.6   References

Big Ten Council of Presidents and Chancellors Statement On Penn State (2012, July 23). *Bigten.org*. Retrieved from http://www.bigten.org/genrel/072312aaa.html on July 17, 2013.

Binding Consent Decree Imposed By the National Collegiate Athletic Association and Accepted By the Pennsylvania State University (2012, July 23). *NCAA.org*. Retrieved from http://s3.amazonaws.com/ncaa/files/20120723/21207236PDF.pdf on July 16, 2013.

Burke, M. (2013, May 28). Yahoo's *Rivals.com* Makes a Play To Become the Dominant College Football Recruiting Site On the Web. *Forbes.com*. Retrieved from http://www.forbes.com/sites/monteburke/2013/05/28/yahoos-rivals-com-makes-a-play-to-become-the-dominant-college-football-recruiting-site-on-the-web/ on July 15, 2013.

California Institute of Technology Public Infractions Report (2012, July 12). NCAA Committee on Infractions. Retrieved from http://www.ncaa.org/wps/wcm/connect/public/ncaa/pdfs/2012/caltech+summary+disposition on August 14, 2012.

Division I Football Recruiting (2012, November 6). *NCAA.org*. Retrieved from http://www.ncaa.org/wps/wcm/connect/public/NCAA/Resources/Behind+the+Blue+Disk/Division+I+Football+Recruiting on July 17, 2013.

Eder, S. (2013, February 18). Top Enforcement Officer of NCAA Is Ousted. The *New York Times*. Retrieved from http://www.nytimes.com/2013/02/19/sports/ncaa-ousts-julie-roe-lach-as-vice-president-of-enforcement. html?_r=0&pagewanted=print on July 17, 2013.

Ex-Penn State President Charged In Sandusky Case (2012, November 2). *USA Today*. Retrieved from http://www.usatoday.com/story/news/nation/2012/11/01/penn-state-president-graham-spanier-charges-jerry-sandusky/1674037/ on July 18, 2013.

Forde, P. and C. Robinson (2013, February 18). NCAA Fires VP of Enforcement, Pledges Change After 'Debacle' In Miami Probe. *Yahoo!Sports.com*. Retrieved from http://sports.yahoo.com/news/ncaaf--ncaa-firing-vp-of-enforcement-171556026.html on July 17, 2013.

Freeh Sporkin & Sullivan, LLP. (2012, July 12). Report of the Special Investigative Counsel Regarding the Actions of the Pennsylvania State University Related To the Child Sex abuse Committed By Gerald A. Sandusky. *Progress.psu.edu*. Retrieved from http://progress.psu. edu/the-freeh-report on July 16, 2013.

Goe, K. (2012, December 21). UO Athletic Director Rob Mullens Says a Summary Disposition Was Scuttled By the NCAA's Committee On Infractions. *The Oregonian*. Retrieved from http://www.oregonlive. com/ducks/index.ssf/2012/12/uo_athletic_0director_rob_mull. html on July 16, 2013.

Joe Paterno Statue Removed From Penn State Campus, President Says It Became Divisive, But Library Stays (2012, July 23). *Huffington Post*. Retrieved from http://www.huffingtonpost.com/2012/07/23/joe-paterno-statue-penn-state_n_1694899.html on July 18, 2013.

Jury Convicts Jerry Sandusky (2012, June 22). *ESPN.com*. Retrieved from http://espn.go.com/espn/print?id=8087028&type=story# on July 16, 2013.

Kercheval, B. (2013, May 29). As expected, Paterno Family Files Suit Against the NCAA. *NBCsports.com*. Retrieved from http://college-footballtalk.nbcsports.com/2013/05/29/as-expected-paterno-family-files-suit-against-the-ncaa/ on July 18, 2013.

Kercheval, B. (2013, June 6). AP: Judge Throws Out Tom Corbett's Lawsuit Against NCAA. *NBCsports.com*. Retrieved from http://college footballtalk.nbcsports.com/2013/06/06/ap-judge-throws-out-tom-corbetts-lawsuit-against-ncaa/ on July 18, 2013.

Mandel, S. (2011, August 16). Credibility of NCAA Enforcement Will Be Tested By Miami Allegations. *Sports Illustrated.com*. Retrieved from http://sportsillustrated.cnn.com/2011/writers/stewart_mandel/08/16/miami.hurricanes.allegations.reaction/index.html#ixzz2ZKyGKmUl on July 17, 2013.

Masser, K. (2013, July 15). A Year After the Freeh Report, PSU Has Made Significant Changes. *Philly.com*. Retrieved from http://articles.philly.com/2013-07-15/news/40571542_1_freeh-report-governance-child-abuse on July 16, 2013.

McCarthy, M. (2013, March 25). Sandusky sex-abuse Scandal Has Cost Penn State $46 million. *Advertising Age*. Retrieved from http://adage.com/article/news/cost-penn-state-scandal-46-million/240488/ on July 18, 2013.

Mike McQueary Wants Penn State Firing Decision Date (2013, May 26). *USAToday.com*. Retrieved from http://m.usatoday.com/article/news/2361469 on July 20, 2013.

Moody's Downgrades Pennsylvania State University's Long-term Rating to Aa2 from Aa1, Affecting $893 Million of Outstanding Rated Debt (2012, October 26). *Moodys.com*. Retrieved from http://www.moodys.com/research/Moodys-downgrades-Pennsylvania-State-Universitys-long-term-rating-to-Aa2--PR_258616 on July 18, 2013.

Pearson, S. (2012, October 3). Penn State Sued By Former Coach McQueary Over Firing. *Bloomberg.com*. Retrieved from http://mobile.bloomberg.com/news/2012-10-02/penn-state-sued-by-ex-assistant-football-coach-mcqueary.html on July 20, 2013.

Penn State Payouts Reach $60 Million (2013, July 19). *Oregonian*, p. A2.

PSU Authorizes Sandusky Settlements (2013, July 12, updated July 15). *ESPN.com*. Retrieved from http://espn.go.com/college-football/story/_/id/9473998/penn-state-university-board-authorizes-settlements-several-jerry-sandusky-victims on July 16, 2013.

Robinson, C. (2011, March 3). Documents: Oregon Paid Pair With Ties To Recruits. *Yahoo! Sports*. Retrieved from http://sports.yahoo.com/ncaa/football/news?slug=cr-oregon030311 on July 14, 2013.

Robinson, C (2011, August 16). Renegade Miami Football Booster Spells Out Illicit Benefits To Players. *Yahoo! Sports*. Retrieved from http://sports.yahoo.com/investigations/news?slug=cr-renegade_miami_booster_details_illicit_benefits_081611 on July 15, 2013.

Remarks of Louis Freeh in Conjunction with Announcement of Publication of Report Regarding the Pennsylvania State University (2012, July 12). *Progress.psu.edu*. Retrieved from http://progress.psu.edu/the-freeh-report on July 16, 2013.

Schad, J. and M. Schlabach (2011, March 4). Sources: Man Who Helps Ducks Probed. *ESPN.com*. Retrieved from http://sports.espn.go.com/ncf/news/story?id=6179423 on July 16, 2013.

Statement from UM President Donna Shalala On NCAA Internal Investigation (2013, February 18). Retrieved from http://www.miami.edu/index.php/ncaa_investigation/statements_and_releases/#17 on July 17, 2013.

Smeltz, A. (2013, July 9). Gov. Tom Corbett Won't Appeal of His Antitrust Lawsuit Against NCAA. *Triblive.com*. Retrieved from http://triblive.com/state/pennsylvania/4327675-74/state-ncaa-antitrust#axzz2ZPh7Qajm on July 18, 2013.

Tierney, M. (2012, August 2, updated subsequently). Penn State Football: How Many Players Have Transferred or Decommitted? *Bleacher Report*. Retrieved from http://bleacherreport.com/articles/1282837-2012-penn-st-football-players-who-have-transferred on July 17, 2013.

Thamel, P. and A. Wolff the Institution Has Lost Control (2013, June 17). *Sports Illustrated*. Retrieved from http://sportsillustrated.cnn.com/vault/article/magazine/MAG1207801/index.htm on July 14, 2013.

Timeline: Oregon Ducks, Willie Lyles and the NCAA Investigation (n.d.). *The Oregonian*. Retrieved from http://projects.oregonlive.com/ducks/timeline on July 17, 2013.

University Of Miami Starts NCAA Hearings As Nevin Shapiro Makes New Allegations (2013, June 13). *HuffingtonPost.com*. Retrieved from http://www.huffingtonpost.com/2013/06/13/miami-ncaa-hearings-nevin-shapiro-new-allegations_n_3432143.html on July 14, 2013.

University of Oregon Public Infractions Report (2013, June 26). NCAA Committee on Infractions. Retrieved from http://www.ncaa.org/wps/wcm/connect/public/ncaa/pdfs/2013/university+of+oregon+public+infractions+report on July 14, 2013.

Wainstein, K. L. (2013, February 17). Report On the NCAA's Engagement of a Source's Counsel and Use of the Bankruptcy Process In Its University of Miami Investigation. Retrieved from http://www.ncaa.org/wps/wcm/connect/public/ncaa/pdfs/2013/1302171 on July 17, 2013.

Selected Bibliography

The following readings are not referenced in the book but are additional valuable, and interesting, perspectives on universities and college sports. If you come across other articles or books that should be added to this list, please send your suggestions to the authors (rgrant@linfield.edu, leadlej@wou.edu, or zygmonz@wou.edu).

Bok, D. (2003). *Universities in the Marketplace: The Commercialization of Higher Education*. Princeton, NJ: Princeton University Press.

Byers, W. (2005). *Unsportsmanlike Conduct: Exploiting College Athletes*. Ann Arbor, MI: University of Michigan Press.

Clotfelter, C. T. (2011). *Big Time Sports in American Universities*. New York: Cambridge University Press.

Crowley, J. N. (2006). *In the Arena: The NCAA's first century*. NCAA: Indianapolis, IN: National Collegiate Athletic Association.

Fort, R. (2008). Research on intercollegiate sports: a working bibliography 2008. *Journal of Intercollegiate Sport* 1 (147–169).

Gerdy, J. (2002). *Sports: The All-American Addiction*. Jackson, MS: University of Mississippi Press.

Guttmann, A. (1988). *A Whole New Ball Game: An Interpretation of American sports*. Chapel Hill, NC: University of North Carolina Press.

Joravsky, B. (1995). *Hoop Dreams: A True Story of Hardship and Triumph*. Kansas City, MO: Andrews and McMeel.

Knight Foundation Commission on Intercollegiate Athletics (2001). A Call to Action: Reconnecting College Sports and Higher Education. Miami, FL: John S. and James L. Knight Foundation. Retrieved from http://knightcommission.org/images/pdfs/2001_knight_report.pdf on June 12, 2014.

O'Connor, I. (2005). *The Jump: Sebastian Telfair and The high Stakes Business of High School Ball*. New York: Rodale Press.

Oriard, M. (2009). *Bowled Over: Big-Time College Football from the Sixties to The BCS Era*. Chapel Hill, NC: University of North Carolina Press.

Ridpath, B. D. (2012). *Tainted Glory: Marshall University, the NCAA, and One man's Fight for Justice.* Bloomington, IN: iUniverse.

Shulman, J. L. and W. G. Bowen (2001). *The Game of Life: College Sports and Educational Values.* Princeton, NJ: Princeton University Press.

Smith, R. A. (2010). *Pay for Play: A History of Big-Time College Athletic Reform.* Urbana-Champaign: University of Illinois Press.

Sperber, M. (1998). *Onward to Victory: The Crises that Shaped College Sports.* New York: Henry Holt.

St. John, W. (2004). *Rammer Jammer Yellow Hammer: A Road Trip into the Heart of Fan Mania.* New York: Three Rivers Press.

Suggs, W. (2005). *A Place on the Team: The Triumph and Tragedy of Title IX.* Princeton, NJ: Princeton University Press.

Telander, R. (1996). *The Hundred Yard Lie: The Corruption of College Football and What We Can Do to Stop It.* Urbana, IL: University of Illinois Press.

Yaeger, D. (1991). *Undue Process: The NCAA's Injustice for All.* Champaign, IL: Sagamore Publishing.

Selected Web Sites

Intercollegiate Athletics Organizations

National Collegiate Athletic Association: http://ncca.org
National Association of Intercollegiate Athletics: http://naia.org
Bowl Championship Series: http://www.bcsfootball.org/bcsfootball/

Media

Chronicle of Higher Education: http://chronicle.com/athletics/
    (subscription required)
College Athletics Clips: http://www.collegeathleticsclips.com/
    (subscription required)
ESPN: http://sports.espn.go.com/ncaa/espnu/index
The NCAA News: http://www.ncaa.org
National Public Radio: http://www.npr.org/ (search by "college
    sports")
Sports Business News: http://www.sportsbusinessnews.com/
Sports Business Journal: http://www.sportsbusinessjournal.com/
    (subscription required)
Sports Illustrated: http://sportsillustrated.cnn.com/
USA Today: http://www.usatoday.com/sports/front.htm

Organizations Advocating Reform

The Black Coaches Association: http://www.bcasports.org
Center for the Study of Sport in Society: http://www.sportinsoci-
    ety.org
Coalition on Intercollegiate Athletics: http://www.neuro.uoregon.
    edu/~tublitz/COIA/index.html

The Drake Group: www.thedrakegroup.org

Knight Commission on Intercollegiate Athletics: http://www.knightfdn.org/athletics/index.html

National Association of Academic Advisors for Athletes (N4A): http://www.nfoura.org/index.php

National College Players Association: http://www.ncpanow.org

Women's Sports Foundation: http://www.womensspportsfoundation.org

Academic Journals Specializing in Sports

International Journal of Sports Finance: http:///www.fitinfotech.com/IJSF/IJSF.tpl

Journal of Sports Economics: http://jse.sagepub.com/

Journal of Sport Management: http://www.humankinetics.com/JSM/journalAbout.cfm

Blogs

The Business of Sports: http://www.jsonline.com/blog/?id=92

College basketball: http://www.yocohoops.com/

The NCAA: http://www.doubleazone.com/

The Sports Economist: http://www.thesportseconomist.com/

Sports Law: http://sports-law.blogspot.com/

Women's Hoops: http://www.womenshoops.blogspot.com/

Women's Sports: http://ijo.typepad.com/keeping_score/

Miscellaneous

Rod Fort's (Washington State University) up-to-date bibliography of academic articles on college sports at: http://www.rodney-fort.com/ SportsBibliography/BibliogFrame.htm (click "sports economics bibliography" scroll down and then click "college sports")

John Vrooman's (Vanderbilt University) list of sports sites: http://www.vanderbilt.edu/Econ/faculty/Vrooman/sports.htm

Glossary

40/60/80 Rule — Bylaw 14.4.3.2 requires a student-athlete, in order to remain eligible, to have completed 40% of her degree requirements by the end of her second (sophomore) year, 60% by the end of her third (junior) year, and 80% by the end of her fourth (senior) year.

4 and 20 Rule — Bylaw 17.1.6.1 limits the number of hours a student-athlete may participate in athletics during the playing season to a maximum of 4 hours per day and 20 hours per week.

Academic Progress Rate (APR) — A measurement of a team's academic performance; each player on a team can contribute up to two points per semester: one point if she remains academically eligible and one point if she remains enrolled in classes. The maximum APR each semester for a team is 1000. Generally, a team must have an APR of 930 or higher to avoid being penalized by the NCAA.

Access discrimination — Denying someone access to employment or other opportunities based on their race (or gender).

Admission requirement — Benchmarks established by the NCAA that must be met by prospective student-athletes in order to be eligible to play intercollegiate sports. Students not meeting these requirements are typically ineligible to play as a freshman or as a transfer. Freshman requirements are listed in Bylaw 14.3.

Agent — According to Bylaw 12.2, an agent is "[a]ny person who represents an individual in the marketing of his or her athletics ability" and expects to represent the student-athlete in "future professional sports negotiations." If a student-athlete agrees to be represented by an agent she will lose her remaining eligibility.

Agreement — Refers to specific restrictions on inputs and/or outputs established by a cartel and applied to cartel members.

Allocative efficiency — When the distribution of resources among different products maximizes social satisfaction.

Amateur Athletic Union (AAU) — An organization established in 1888 to promote amateur sports. The AAU sponsors approximately 30 sports and championships for young men and women under the age of 18.

Ancillary programming — Television broadcasts and other media presentations designed to increase the demand for sporting events.

Association for Intercollegiate Athletics for Women (AIAW) — An organization established in 1971, similar to the NCAA, that governed women's collegiate sports. It suspended operations in 1983.

Autocorrelated errors — In regression analysis, a condition that the occurs with time series data when the value of the error term at one period of time is correlated with the value of the error term in previous periods, which can result in incorrect conclusions on the statistical significance of the independent variables.

Booster discrimination — A type of consumer discrimination in which boosters are more willing to donate money to an athletics program if it hires employees (e.g., a head coach) of a specific race (or gender).

Bowl Championship Series (BCS) — A coalition of conference and bowl committees formed in 1998 to determine a national champion in DI football.

Bilateral monopoly — A market structure in which there is a monopoly buyer (monopsony) and a monopoly seller.

Brand proliferation — When a firm expands its product differentiation in an attempt to capture every potential consumer.

Capture — When a regulatory agency acts in the best interests of the industry, it is supposed to regulate rather than in the best interests of the public.

Cartel — A more formal and comprehensive type of collusion, with agreements on specific ways to reduce competition and eliminate cheating by strict enforcement.

Cartel within the cartel — A type of cheating in a cartel in which a subset of cartel participants form an alliance in an attempt to make themselves better off at the expense of the remaining members of the cartel; also referred to as "intra-cartel cheating."

Civil Rights Restoration Act — Congressional legislation passed in 1987 which overturned *Grove City v. Bell* decision. It specified that any educational institution that received any federal funds, in any amount, must comply fully with all parts of the Civil Rights Act and amendments made thereto, especially Title IX.

Cohen *vs*. Brown — Brown University used a survey of students to demonstrate that it accommodated the interest and abilities of the underrepresented sex, thereby complying with the three-part test for Title IX. A US District Court ruled that surveys could not be used for this purpose, and in 1997 the US Supreme Court declined to hear Brown's appeal.

College Football Association (CFA) — An alliance of 64 DI schools formed in 1977 to challenge the NCAA's Television Plan. The CFA alliance sought to increase television appearance and revenues, as well as negotiate broadcasting contracts independently. The alliance later filed an antitrust lawsuit against the NCAA which resulted in the *NCAA v. Board of Regents of the University of Oklahoma*.

Cheating — When a firm that is colluding with other firms violates an explicit or implicit agreement, often by lowering its price below the agreed level.

Collusion — When two or more firms agree to engage in anticompetitive behavior that is harmful to consumers or rival firms. Price-fixing is a common example.

Competitive balance — Any set of rules established by a sports league designed to maximize the probability that any team in the league has an equal chance of winning the league championship.

Competitive labor market — A labor market in which there are many buyers and sellers.

Consumer discrimination — When consumers (e.g., fans at a sporting event) are biased against persons of a specific race (or gender) and are willing to pay more to see employees (e.g., players) from a favored race (or gender).

Consumer surplus — The difference between what an individual is willing to pay for a good or service and the price she actually pays (typically represented by the equilibrium market price).

Contemporaneous penalty — One of two categories of penalties applied by the NCAA, when a team does not meet the minimum academic progress rate. Designed to be a "real-time" punishment, it is usually applied soon after a team has failed to meet the APR benchmarks.

Deadweight loss — The reduction of consumer and/or producer surplus when a distortion in a market results in fewer voluntary exchanges between buyers and sellers.

Death penalty — The most severe penalty that may be imposed by the NCAA; it requires a team to cease operations for a specified period of time (usually a minimum of one season) during which the team may not recruit, practice or compete.

Demand — The willingness and ability of an individual to purchase a good or service for a price in a market.

Dependent variable — In a mathematical model, the variable which depends on the value of independent variables, usually denoted by the letter Y.

Derived demand — Demand for an intermediate good created by the demand for a final good; for example, the demand for college football games creates a demand for the inputs necessary to produce a football game, notably football players.

Diminishing marginal productivity — When the additional contribution to total output by a variable input begins to decline; graphically, it is illustrated by the portion of the marginal product schedule that has a negative slope.

Discrimination coefficient — In Gary Becker's 1971 model of discrimination, it represents the disutility or cost of having to interact with individual of a disfavored race (or gender), or the additional cost employers are willing to pay the favored individuals.

Dominant strategy — A concept from game theory which refers to a strategy or choice by an individual which represents the best possible outcome for that individual regardless of the strategy or choice of her opponent(s).

Early entry — When a student-athlete leaves her institution to turn pro before her eligibility has elapsed.

Economic rent — The difference between a resource owner's opportunity cost and the payment received by that resource owner.

Economies of scale — When long-run average cost decreases as a firm's output increases.

Economies of scope — When a firm can reduce it production costs (and/or increase its revenues, by using its inputs to produce a wider variety of outputs. For example, a cattle rancher producing beef decides to use the skins of the cattle to produce leather.

Efficiency loss — See deadweight loss.

Elasticity of demand — The amount by which the quantity demanded of a product changes (in %) when price changes (in %).

Elasticity of supply — The amount by which the quantity supplied of a product changes (in %) when price changes (in %).

Eligibility — When a student-athlete is in compliance with the NCAA's rules on academics and amateurism; a student-athlete must become initially eligible when she enters a college or university as well as remain eligible.

Employee discrimination — Discrimination when employees refuse to work with a co-worker of a certain race (or gender) or require higher wages in order to work with that person.

Employer discrimination — Discrimination when employers favor a person of a certain race (or gender) even though that person exhibits lower productivity than a person from the less favored race (or gender). Engaging in such discrimination means the employer is willing to accept a monetary penalty (less revenue or profit) because they hired the favored employee.

Entry — When a new firm enters an existing market and begins competing against incumbent firms.

Equilibrium — A situation in a market when there is no incentive to change.

Equivalency sport — A sport in which the NCAA determines the maximum amount of money that may be offered in team scholarships but allows each scholarship to be divided across multiple student-athletes. All sports other than head count sports are equivalency sports.

Explicit cost — A cost that is easy to estimate or observe.

Externality — A situation in which an individual action creates costs (a negative externality) or benefits (a positive externality) that affect other people as well.

Extra benefits — Also known as impermissible benefits, it represents something that a student-athlete receives than is not commonly available to student non-athletes.

Family Education Rights and Privacy Act (FERPA) — U.S. federal law established in 1974. According to the U.S. Department of Education, "it protects the privacy of student education records ... [p]arents or eligible students have the right to inspect and review the student's education records maintained by the school ... [p]arents or eligible students have the right to request that a school correct records which they believe to be inaccurate or misleading [and] ... schools must have written permission from the parent or eligible student in order to release any information from a student's education record."

Fan discrimination — See consumer discrimination.

Favia v. Indiana University of Pennsylvania — In 1991, Indiana University of Pennsylvania eliminated two men's and two women's sports because of budget difficulties. In response to a lawsuit filed by one of the women's' teams, a Pennsylvania state Circuit Court decided in 1993 that the university's actions violated Title IX. Part of the ruling stated that financial difficulties cannot be used as a justification for non-compliance with Title IX.

Federal Graduation Rate (FGR) — A measurement expressed as a percentage of students who graduate within six years of matriculating.

Fixed cost — A cost of production that does not vary with the quantity produced and it cannot be changed in the short-run.

Flutie effect — The belief that success in sports will lead to increased undergraduate applications.

Football Bowl Subdivision (FBS) — The highest tier of Division I football, formerly referred to as DI-A. As of 2012, it consists of the 11 conferences and 120 teams eligible for bowl games and the national championship.

Football Championship Subdivision (FCS) — The second tier of Division I football, formerly referred to as DI-AA. As of 2014, it consists of the 13 conferences and 142 teams eligible, and has a 20 team postseason championship tournament for bowl games.

Franklin v. Gwinnett County Public Schools — A 1992 Supreme Court decision that originated as a lawsuit concerning sexual harassment at a Georgia high school. The court's decision established a precedent under which plaintiffs in Title IX case could receive compensatory and punitive damages from the defendant.

Free riding — When an individual attempts to benefit without incurring any costs.

Future value — The value today of an asset at a specific point in the future based on assumptions about the asset's rate of appreciating and the length of time between today and the specific point in the future.

Gains to trade — The combined consumer and producer surplus generated in a market. In a competitive market gains to trade will be maximized.

Game theory — A sub-discipline of mathematics, and widely used in the social sciences, that analyzes interactive decision making.

Gender marking — Language usage that may create or reinforce potentially discriminatory stereotypes.

Generally Accepted Accounting Principles — A standardized set of rules used in the accounting profession when reporting financial information.

Golden parachute — A type of contractually guaranteed severance payment made to an employee when that employee is fired or laid off.

Graduation rate — A measurement expressed as a percentage of students who graduate within a specified period of time.

Graduation success rate (GSR) — A graduation rate developed by the NCAA to "more accurately reflect the mobility among all college students today. The rate measures graduation rates at Division I institutions and includes student-athletes transferring into the institutions. In that regard, it differs from the methodology of the rate mandated by the federal government, which does not count incoming transfer student-athletes at all and counts student-athletes who transfer out as not having graduated, regardless of whether they actually did. The graduation success rate also allows institutions to exclude from the computation student-athletes who leave their institutions before graduation, so long as they would have been academically eligible to compete had they remained."

Grant-in-aid — The name officially used by the NCAA for athletics scholarships that provide financial aid.

Group boycotts — According to the Federal Trade Commission, "an agreement among competitors not to do business with targeted individuals or businesses [which may be] may be an illegal ... especially if the group of competitors working together has market power.

Grove City College v. Bell — A lawsuit that led to the 1984 Supreme Court ruling that Title IX did not apply to intercollegiate sports; overturned in 1987 with the Civil Rights Restoration Act.

Ham sandwich violation — A type of secondary violation that is so trivial and inadvertent that the individuals committing the infraction are unaware that their actions contravene the Bylaws.

Head count sport — A sport in which the NCAA determines the maximum amount of team scholarships that may be offered in team scholarships and requires each scholarship to be allocated in its entirety to a student-athlete. The head count sports are: men's and women's basketball, FBS football, and women's gymnastics, tennis, and volleyball.

Heteroskedasticity — In regression analysis, the condition that the amount of variance in the error term depends on the value of one of the independent variables, which can result in incorrect conclusions on the statistical significance of the independent variables.

Historically-based penalty — One of two categories of penalties applied by the NCAA, when a team does not meet the minimum Academic Progress rate. It is usually applied soon after a team has failed to meet the APR benchmarks repeatedly over time.

Home rule — Refers to the period of time (roughly 1905–1951) in which the NCAA had no effective mechanism for punishing member institutions that broke the rules. This meant that each member institution was free to implement (or not implement) polices to prevent rules violations.

Horizontal integration — When two or more firms in the same industry merge their operations. Because this leads to increased concentration in that industry such a merger typically required the permission of the federal government.

IAAUS — Intercollegiate Athletic Association of the United States, the name from 1906 to 1910 of the current NCAA.

Illusion of control — The tendency for the NCAA to promulgate rules and regulations to promote the appearance that very little malfeasance is occurring by NCAA member institutions.

Implicit cost — A cost that does not have a price that is easy to estimate or observe; one example is time.

Incentive compatibility — When the objectives of individuals engaged in a contract or transaction overlap an moral hazard or adverse selection problems are minimized.

Independent variable — In a mathematical model, one of the variables which determines the value of the dependent variable, usually denoted by the letter X.

Indifference curve — A graphical representation of all combinations of various bundles of two or more goods or services that yield the same level of utility for a consumer.

Intercollegiate Football Association (IFA) — A student-led organization established in 1976 to standardize the rules of collegiate football and create a Thanksgiving Day championship game.

Javits amendment — Congressional legislation in 1974 that instructed the cognizant federal agency to develop and implement Title IX regulations for intercollegiate athletics.

Labor union — An organization that acts to monopolize the supply of labor in a particular profession. Unions typically form to bargain for better working conditions and supra-competitive wages and salaries.

Law of unintended consequences — When a specific action generates an outcome that was neither expected nor desired.

Level I violation — The most serious violation of NCAA rules; this includes "any violation that provides or is intended to provide a significant or extensive recruiting, competitive or other advantage, or significant or extensive impermissible benefit." Prior to 2012, this would have been referred to as a major violation.

Level II violation — "A violation that provides or is intended to provide a minimal to significant recruiting, competitive or other advantage; or includes a minimal to significant impermissible benefit; or involves a pattern of systemic violations in a particular area."

Level III violation — "A violation that is isolated or limited in nature; provides no more than a minimal recruiting, competitive or other advantage." Prior to 2012, this would have been referred to as a secondary violation.

Level IV violation — An action of an inadvertent or isolated nature that does not result in competitive advantage.

Little Dutch boy — The tendency for schools to react to increased oversight and regulation by the NCAA by seeking loopholes and new ways to circumvent the Bylaws; the NCAA typically reacts by promulgating even bylaws.

Logrolling — Vote trading between individuals, or "if you vote for the legislation I want, then I will vote for the legislation you want."

Major violation — One of two categories of violations used by the NCAA prior to 2012; it represents "a violation that provides or is intended to provide a significant or extensive recruiting, competitive or other advantage, or significant or extensive impermissible benefit." Currently referred to as a Level I violation.

Marginal cost — The change in total cost, when an additional unit of output is produced.

Marginal cost of labor — The change in the total labor cost, when an additional unit of labor is hired.

Marginal revenue — The change in total revenue received by a firm, when an additional unit of output is sold.

Marginal revenue product (MRP) — The monetary value created by an individual employee for his/her employer in a specific period of time. It is calculated by multiplying an individual worker's productivity by the price of the final output.

Maximin strategy — In game theory, a strategy which maximizes the minimum possible gain, or making the best (maximum) of what you assume will be a bad (minimum) situation.

Monopoly — A market structure in which there is only one seller.

Monopsonistic rent — an economic rent that occurs when a monopoly buyer of inputs is able to pay those inputs a price equal to the input's reservation wage but less than the equilibrium price.

Monopsony — a market structure in which there is only one buyer.

Moral hazard — A situation in which an individual does not bear all of the costs of her actions.

Morrill Act — Law passed in 1862, granting federal land to states to establish colleges for the education of the working class in agriculture and the mechanical arts.

Multicollinearity — In regression analysis, the condition that two or more of the independent variables are highly correlated with each other, making it difficult to estimate the effect of changing one of those variables while holding the others constant.

Multilateral reform — Changes to the NCAA bylaws resulting from coordinated action among NCAA member institutions, usually during the annual NCAA convention or periodic meeting of specific NCAA committees or subcommittees.

Nash equilibrium — In game theory, a situation where if player #1 chooses strategy A then player #2's best choice is strategy B, and if player #2 chooses strategy B then player #1's best choice is strategy A, which means that neither player has any reason to change their current strategy based on what the other person is doing.

National Association of Intercollegiate Athletics (NAIA) — After the NCAA, the second most prominent governing body for intercollegiate sports in the United States. Formed in 1937, it oversees over 300 member institutions and 60,000 college athletes.

National Collegiate Athletic Association (NCAA) — The primary governing body for intercollegiate sports in the United States, it began with the formation of the IAAUS in 1906 with the name of the association changing to NCAA in 1910. As described in Bylaw 1.3.1, the Association "is to maintain intercollegiate athletics as an integral part of the educational program and the athlete as an integral part of the student body and … retain a clear line of demarcation between intercollegiate athletics and professional sports."

Non-excludable — One of two characteristics that define a public good; when a good or service is provided to one person, other individuals cannot be prevented from consumption the good or service as well.

Non-price competition — Forms of competition between firms that are not based on price; some examples include product quality, product guarantees and warranties, store location, and product marketing.

Non-qualifier — A prospective student-athlete who does not meet the NCAA's rules on initial eligibility.

Non-rival — One of two characteristics that define a public good; it represents a situation in which an individual consumption of a good or service does not reduce the availability of that product for others. Sometimes referred to as non-diminishability.

Occupational discrimination — When individuals of a specific race (or gender) are either denied access to, or underrepresented, in specific occupations.

Old boy networks — The idea that individuals make gain employment because of "who they know" rather than any innate talent or productivity. In certain case, it may represent a type of occupational discrimination.

Oligopoly — A market structure which is dominated by a few large firms who have a large market share.

Opportunity cost — What is given up when a person makes a choice.

Optimal policing — The level of deterrence and apprehension where the marginal costs are equal to the marginal benefits.

Ordinary least squares — A form of regression analysis which estimates the best-fitting line for a sample of observations by minimizing the sum of squared distances from the line to each data point

Partial qualifier — A prospective student-athlete who does not meet all of the initial eligibility requirements (high school diploma, minimum GPA, minimum SAT/ACT). This student could be awarded a scholarship but was not eligible to play in her first year. This classification was eliminated by the NCAA in 1989 with Proposition 42.

Perfectly elastic — When the quantity demanded or supplied (in percentage terms) increases or decreases even though there is no corresponding change in price. Graphically, it is represented by a horizontal demand or supply schedule.

Player discrimination — See employee discrimination.

Present value — The discounted value of a sum or money or an asset today that is to be received in the future.

Price ceiling — A price control that establishes the legal price below the equilibrium price; by law, a product with a price ceiling can only be sold at that price or below it.

Price control — A government imposed legal price in a market; the price can be set above the equilibrium market price or below it.

Price fixing — When firms in the same market agree to set the price of their product at a specific price that is above the equilibrium price in an attempt to earn additional profit.

Principal — See principal–agent problem.

Principal–agent problem — A situation in which two individuals engage in a contract or transaction. One individual, the principal wants a specific task or activity to be performed by the second individual, her agent. If incentive incompatibility exists, the agent may be in a position to take advantage of principal.

Prisoners' Dilemma — A form of a strategic game in which each player's dominant strategy is to not cooperate. The resulting Nash equilibrium represents a set of payoffs that are lower than those that would occur if both players chose to cooperate.

Producer surplus — The difference between the minimum price an individual is willing to accept for a good or service she can supply and the price she actually receives (typically represented by the equilibrium market price).

Productive efficiency — When the maximum amount of an output is produced from a specific amount of inputs or, when a specific amount of outputs are produced with the minimum amount of inputs.

Proportionality — One of the basic principles embodied in Title IX; it must be achieved in both opportunities to participate (the percentage of student-athletes of a specific gender must be proportional to the total number of students of that gender); and in scholarship dollars (the percentage of student-athletes of a specific gender receiving grants-in-aid funds must be proportional to the total number of students of that gender).

Proposition 16 — Enacted in 1992 and implemented in 1996, it amended Proposition 48 and required student-athletes to have a high school diploma, a 2.00 GPA in 13 academic core courses, and a score of 820 or higher on the SAT (68 or above on the ACT). It also established a sliding scale between the college entrance exam score and GPA. A student-athlete with a 2.00 GPA was eligible if she had 1010 SAT score (or ACT score of 86); or a 2.50 GPA with a 820 SAT. It also restored scholarships to partial qualifiers.

Proposition 42 — A 1989 NCAA rules that prohibited scholarships from being awarded to partial qualifiers.

Proposition 48 — Enacted in 1983 and introduced in the 1986–1987 academic year, an initial eligibility rule requiring student-athletes to have a high school diploma, a 2.00 GPA in 11 academic core courses, and a score of 700 or higher on the SAT (15 or above on the ACT). A student who graduated but met only one of the other two criteria could be admitted as a partial qualifier.

Proposition 68 — Introduced in 1997, this rule denied freshman eligibility for partial qualifiers but granted them four years of eligibility once they became qualifiers.

Public Choice theory — A sub-discipline of economics that applies economic concepts to the decision-making of individuals in political institutions.

Public good — A good or a service that is both non-excludable and non-rival; it is often, though not exclusively, provided by government. A classic example of a public good is a lighthouse.

Qualifier — A prospective student-athlete who meets the NCAA's rules on initial eligibility.

Quantity demanded — The amount that consumers purchase at a specific price.

Race and Gender Report Card — A report issued annually by the Institute for Diversity and Ethics in Sport at the University of Central Florida; the report issues grades on progress toward racial diversity and gender balance in professional and intercollegiate sports organizations.

Race premium — The additional amount an employer is willing to pay to an employee from a favored racial or gender grouping only because of that person's race or gender.

Rank-order tournament — A contest in which prizes are not awarded in proportion to a competitors finish (the person finishing 10th gets a prize 1/10th that of the first place finisher), but skewed disproportionately in favor of the top finishers.

Ratcheting — A situation in a labor market in which an increase in one person's salary causes an increase in the salaries of others.

Regression analysis — The estimation of the effect of a set of independent variables on a dependent variable based on a sample of observations.

Repeated game — A game of strategy that is played more than once between opponents.

Reservation wage — The minimum amount a person has to be paid in order for them to agree to perform a specific task.

Reverse discrimination — When discrimination is applied to individuals of a certain race (or gender) in order to make up past discrimination against others.

Risk aversion — When an individual is only willing to accept a payment of a specified value rather than accept a bet or lottery payoff with an equivalent expected value. More generally, when people attempt to protect themselves from potentially harmful outcomes.

Rule 1.6 — A rule on eligibility introduced by the NCAA in 1964; the rule required that a student-athlete have sufficiently high GPA and entrance exam test scores to predict that they would earn at least a 1.6 GPA or higher in their first year of college. Rescinded in 1973.

Rule 2.0 — In 1986, the NCAA enacted Proposition 48, which included the requirement of a minimum high school GPA of 2.0 in

11 core courses and a minimum 700 score on the SAT to qualify for play in Division I athletics as a freshman. Students with a higher GPA can qualify with a lower SAT score (a sliding scale). Effective August 2016, the minimum GPA for 16 core courses is 2.3, with those between 2.0 and 2.3 allowed to have an athletic scholarship and practice with their team but not participate in games.

Sanity Code — "Sanity clause? Everybody knows there ain't no sanity clause."

Secondary violation — One of two categories of violations used by the NCAA prior to 2012; "a violation that is isolated or limited in nature; provides no more than a minimal recruiting, competitive or other advantage." Now referred to as a Level III violation.

Self-categorization — When an employer hires someone with similar characteristics, including race or gender, to boost their own self-esteem.

Self-reporting — NCAA Bylaw 2.8.1 requires each member institution "to identify and report to the Association instances in which compliance has not been achieved."

Sherman Act — Implemented in 1890, the primary federal legislation that prohibits anticompetitive behavior by firms.

Shoulder programming — A type of ancillary programming that occurs immediate before or after a televised sproting event; typical examples are "pre-game" and "post-game" shows.

Simultaneous equations — In regression analysis, the condition that occurs when the values of two or more variables are determined by a system of equations rather than a single equation, which results when the Y variable depends on the X variable and the X variable depends on the Y variable.

Soft budget constraint — A concept originated by economist Janos Kornal to explain certain inefficiencies in centrally planned economies like the former USSR. As applied to college athletics, it refers to situations in which the athletic department spends more than its allocated budget because it knows that it will not be penalized by the university's administration. This is an example of the principal–agent problem.

Special admits — Students who are admitted to a college or university without meeting that institution's admission criteria.

Special interest group — A community willing to invest resources with an interest in advancing a specific agenda.

Statistically significant — In regression analysis, when the hypothesis that an independent variable has no effect on a dependent variable can be rejected with a high degree of confidence for a given sample of observations.

Student Right to Know Act — A law passed by Congress in 1990 that required colleges and universities eligible for federal student financial aid to report graduation rates to current and prospective students. The report includes graduation rates for student-athletes by race/ethnicity and gender and by sport.

Sunk cost — A cost incurred that cannot be recovered.

Superstar — A worker whose compensation is disproportionally large when her productivity is compared to the productivity of similar workers.

Supply — The willingness and ability of an individual to produce a good or service for a price in a market.

Taste for discrimination — An economic model developed by Gary Becker in 1971 suggests that individuals will discount the cost of a decision if it involves other people of a race or gender whom the decision-maker favors. The opposite is true as well: individuals will increase the cost of a decision if it involves other people of a race or gender whom the decision-maker disfavors (is biased against).

Television Plan — NCAA policy implemented in 1951 restricting the number of football games that could be televised nationally. The plan was unpopular with many NCAA member institutions and later led to the creation of the CFA.

Three-part test — Criteria adopted in 1979 for compliance with Title IX based on (1) the ratio of male to female athletes, (2) a history of program expansion for the underrepresented sex and (3) failure of first two tests but full accommodation of the interests and abilities of the underrepresented sex.

Tipping point — A phase coined by the author Malcolm Gladwell in his book of the same name; the process in which an idea or other phenomenon reaches a critical mass and cannot be prevented from further expansion.

Tit-for-tat — A strategy used in a repeated game in which a player alternates between cooperating with her opponent and punishing her opponent when her opponent does not cooperate; the strategy is designed to induce cooperation by the other player.

Title VII — A part of the Civil Rights Act of 1964, it prohibits discrimination in employment on the basis of race, color, religion, sex and national origin.

Title IX — A part of the Education Amendments of 1972 to the Civil Rights Act, it prohibits discrimination on the basis of sex for participation in any education program or activity receiving federal financial assistance. While commonly recognized for its impact on high school and college athletics, sports were not explicitly mentioned in the law.

Tower Amendment — Legislation introduced by United States Senator John Tower in 1974 exempting revenue-producing sports, such as men's football and basketball, from compliance with Title IX. The legislation was not passed by the Senate.

Treadmill of reform — The idea that repeated attempts at reform occur over time and these reform efforts are both duplicative and ineffective.

Unilateral reform — A situation in which change a single institution, usually a university, changes its intercollegiate sports policies and practices. An example would be the elimination of one of its sport teams.

Unrelated business income — Gross income derived from trade or business that is not substantially related to the purpose of an organization. For universities, the issue is whether revenue from sports is related to its mission to educate students.

Wage discrimination — When a person of a specific race or gender is paid less for their job than a person with equal productivity but from a different racial or gender group.

Willingness to pay — The maximum amount an individual will voluntarily pay for a product.

Winner's curse — A situation that usually, though not exclusively, occurs in auctions whereby a person pays more for an object than their willingness-to-pay.

Winner-take-all labor market — A labor market in which a small percentage of those employed earn a disproportionate amount of the total earnings in the market and individual earnings are determined by relative not absolute performance. Also known as the economics of superstars.

X-outlier — In regression analysis, an observation for which the value of one or more of the independent variables is different from the values for the other observations.

Y-outlier — In regression analysis, an observation for which the value of the dependent variable is different from the value predicted by the estimated line.

Zero-sum game — In game theory, a situation when the gain to one player is equal to the loss for the other player, so adding the gains and losses for all players results in zero net gain.

Name Index

Subject Index